NEW PROBLEMS IN

READING AND WRITING

New Problems in Reading & Writing

PERSONAL EXPERIENCE · CHARACTERIZATION OF A PERSON · CHARACTERIZATION OF A TYPE · DEFINITION · DESCRIPTION OF A PROCESS · COMPARISON AND CONTRAST · EXAMPLES AND ILLUSTRATIONS · ANTECEDENTS AND CONSEQUENCES · ASSUMPTIONS · ANALYSIS · CLASSIFICATION · HISTORICAL NARRATIVE · VARIETIES OF EXPOSITORY ORGANIZATION

compiled and edited by

Henry W. Sams *and* Waldo F. McNeir

UNIVERSITY OF CHICAGO   LOUISIANA STATE UNIVERSITY

PRENTICE-HALL, INC.   *New York · 1953*

PRENTICE-HALL SERIES IN ENGLISH COMPOSITION

Thomas Clark Pollock, Editor

First printing..............April, 1953
Second printing..........October, 1953

L. C. Cat. Card No.: 53-5993

~~~ Contents

III. CHARACTERIZATION OF A TYPE

SUCCESS IN AMERICA

IV. DEFINITION

THE MEANING OF "COLLEGE" AND "UNIVERSITY"

V. DESCRIPTION OF A PROCESS

A SCIENTIST AT WORK

VI. COMPARISON AND CONTRAST

AN AUTHOR AND HIS CRITICS

VII. EXAMPLES AND ILLUSTRATIONS

SOME DIFFICULTIES OF COMMUNICATION

VIII. ANTECEDENTS AND CONSEQUENCES

THE TROUBLED CAREER OF WALTER MITTY

IX. ASSUMPTIONS

THE CASE AGAINST THE COMICS

X. ANALYSIS

CHOOSING A VOCATION

XI. CLASSIFICATION

THE IDEA OF PROGRESS

❧ Preface

OUR AIMS IN THIS REVISED EDITION of *Problems in Reading and Writing* have been chiefly three. We have tried to simplify the book so as to bring it within general reach, to lighten its tone somewhat without sacrificing its essential seriousness, and to include a greater variety of short selections, especially in the earlier assignments. Users of the book have been generous with suggestions, and in these aims we have followed some of them.

Although most of the reading material is new, the idea behind the book remains unchanged. It is our belief that a good way to improve students' composition work is to give them readings that focus their attention, not on ideas and on subject matter alone, but also on structure, organization, and form. Several pieces of writing all dealing with the same topic and all illustrating a similar structural pattern will go further toward giving students the ability to shape their own ideas than several pieces of writing all dealing with the same general theme, or even the same topic, but illustrating divergent, if not disparate, structural patterns. The bringing together of readings that are homogeneous in the double sense of subject matter and form remains, therefore, the leading principle of the book.

As in the first edition, each individual reading represents one of the primary forms of discourse—narration, exposition, argument—and, more particularly, illustrates a structural pattern of organization—definition, comparison and contrast, analysis, and so forth. The subject material of the various assignments is adapted to the structures they illustrate. For example, the topic *The Meaning of "College" and "University"* suggests definition, and the topic *Choosing a Vocation* invites development by analysis of the factors which enter into this important process. It is not to be expected, however, that the only possible method of developing the topic is the one illustrated in the readings and recommended for student use by the Writing and Study Aids. Teachers will quite rightly want to make occasional departures from the pattern of the book and encourage the use of some other method of development than the one associated with a given assignment; in fact, some topics suggested for themes in the Writing and Study Aids are capable of treatment in a number of ways.

The assignments are arranged in order of difficulty, giving students a chance to progress from the simple to the complex in the techniques of writing represented. Thus, Characterization of a Person is studied before Classification, and Examples and Illustrations before Assumptions. Following the advice of teachers who have used the book, we have made a few important shifts. Personal Experience—*Autobiography* is now the first assignment, because this kind of writing is relatively simple and because many teachers like to begin the course by having students write one or more autobiographical papers. Historical Narrative—*John Brown at Harper's Ferry* now stands near the end, not because this kind of writing is unfamiliar but because this assignment makes certain demands, particularly in close reading, that students can meet more successfully if they come to it late in the course.

The editorial apparatus accompanying each assignment is primarily intended to help the student solve some of the problems he faces in reading and writing. It is also intended to lighten the burden of the teacher in the sense that it suggests one way, but by no means the only way, of approaching the class discussions of the topic and the writing assignments growing out of them.

Accompanying each assignment are an Introduction, Guide Questions, Vocabulary lists, Writing and Study Aids, and Readings for Further Study. The Introduction to each topic aims to orient the student by describing the nature of the problem. Attention is called to the pattern of organization to be observed in the readings, and, in general, an approach is indicated for a critical understanding of each selection in relation to the problem as a whole. The Guide Questions following each selection are of two kinds: questions of fact, requiring close reading of the text; and questions of rhetoric, requiring interpretation and evaluation of ideas, attitudes, special devices, organization, and style. Both kinds are intended to aid the student in his preparation for class discussion. The Vocabulary lists may be used to sharpen the sensitivity of the class to word values and levels of diction in a specific context, or they may be made the basis of more ambitious exercises in etymology and semantics.

The Writing and Study Aids are the culmination of each unit of work. Having studied the problem posed by the general topic, having analyzed the organizational methods and the structural pattern of the readings, the student is now in a position to develop his own ideas on the subject. A brief review of the readings and a suggestion of how the student may handle the writing assignment are given under "Pattern of Organization Suggested by the General Topic." This is followed by "Assignments," ideas for "Short themes" and "Long themes" that the teacher will add to or subtract from as he sees fit. We have found that for ordinary purposes the short theme topics will suffice, but this should not be taken to mean that an occasional longer essay is not worthwhile. Especially useful, we believe, is a preliminary paper, a class theme, perhaps, dealing with a single aspect of the general problem. Such an assignment will keep the students practicing and yield valuable samples of their work for criticism. The "Readings for Further Study," which appear as part of the Writing and Study Aids, are not exhaustive bibliographies. They list a few important sources in which the student, if so inclined or directed, may pursue the topic.

We are indebted to many interested people for ideas which have gone into this revision. The English staff of the College of the University of Chicago and the teachers of composition at Louisiana State University have made valuable contributions, but we alone are to blame for any shortcomings. And we want to express special gratitude to Carol and Corinne: see "To My Wife, Without Whose Help . . . ," AAUP *Bulletin*, Vol. 38 (Spring, 1952), 71-73.

HENRY W. SAMS
WALDO F. McNEIR

NEW PROBLEMS IN
READING AND WRITING

I. PERSONAL EXPERIENCE

✺ Autobiography

THOSE WHO WRITE THEIR OWN PERSONAL HISTORIES HAVE AN ADVANTAGE OVER other historians in that they are their own best authorities. The writers of autobiography have an unchallengeable superiority over other researchers in their own particular fields. They are able, therefore, to choose from a more inclusive selection of facts than other historians, and to provide a more intimate interpretation of these facts.

But, like all historians, they must select, and they must interpret. Even so well understood a matter as a person's own life presents him with problems of choice, explanation, and emphasis in writing about it. The most interesting and valuable autobiographies do not all give accounts of exciting or extraordinary lives; as much depends on the telling as on what is told. The readings for this assignment consist of several documents of personal history; they are recollections of childhood and youth. As you read them, notice that the problems of choice, explanation, and emphasis receive due consideration.

Jean-Jacques Rousseau's *Confessions,* which was written about 1766, is the first great modern autobiography. Edmund Wilson says that after Rousseau, "the simple record of one's feelings and impressions became an end and a form in itself; you assumed that a thing was interesting, not by virtue of its absolute importance, but because it had happened to you, and you assumed that the things that happened inside you were more important than the things you actually did." In "My Beginnings," Rousseau reveals the circumstantial self-interest that is essential to successful autobiography; here he is concerned with establishing his earliest personal context. Cornelia Otis Skinner's "Report Card" shows that childhood can be both ludicrous and touching; it also shows that the ability to laugh at oneself

I

never does any harm when the time comes to "tell all." Floyd Dell's "Egotism" and Agnes Repplier's "Sin" are incisively told incidents of school life that carry conviction because of their natural handling of early conflicts—mental and moral. Lincoln Steffens' account of his "miserable, merry" Christmas combines the emotional storms of childhood with a picture of affectionate home life. The poignancy of growing up is tenderly but not sentimentally treated by Thomas Sancton in "The Silver Horn." He deals vividly and evocatively with subjects of perennial importance to youth: the bewilderments and joys of being young, human dignity, nature, first love, and self-discovery. What you read here will undoubtedly suggest many other things—persons, places, events—as appropriate to your own autobiography.

Jean-Jacques Rousseau

MY BEGINNINGS

I WAS BORN IN GENEVA, in 1712, son of Isaac Rousseau and Susanne Bernard, citizens. My father's share of a moderate competency, which was divided among fifteen children, being very trivial, his business of a watchmaker (in which he was indeed expert) was his only dependence. My mother's circumstances were more affluent; she was the daughter of a Monsieur Bernard, minister, and possessed both modesty and beauty; indeed, my father found some difficulty in obtaining her hand.

The affection they entertained for each other was almost as early as their existence; at eight or nine years old they walked together every evening on the banks of the Treille, and before they were ten could not support the idea of separation. A natural sympathy of soul confirmed those sentiments which habit at first produced. Born with minds susceptible of exquisite sensibility and tenderness, each only awaited the encounter of a kindred disposition;—rather, perhaps, should I say, the happy moment awaited them, when each surrendered a willing heart. The obstacles that opposed served only to give a degree of vivacity to their affection; and the young lover, not being able to obtain his mistress, was overwhelmed with sorrow. She advised him

From *The Confessions of Jean-Jacques Rousseau,* translated from the French.

to travel that he might forget her. He consented; he traveled, but returned more passionate than ever, and found her equally constant, equally tender. After this proof of mutual affection, what could they resolve?—to dedicate their future lives to love! The resolution was ratified with a vow, on which Heaven shed its benediction.

My mother's brother, Gabriel Bernard, fell in love with one of my father's sisters; she had no objection to the match, but made the marriage of his sister with her brother an indispensable preliminary. Love soon removed every obstacle, and the two weddings were celebrated on the same day; thus my uncle became the husband of my aunt, and their children were doubly my cousins-german. Before a year was expired both had the happiness to become fathers but were soon afterwards obliged to submit to a separation.

My uncle Bernard, who was an engineer, went to serve in the Empire and Hungary under Prince Eugene, and distinguished himself both at the siege and battle of Belgrade. My father, after the birth of my only brother, set off, on recommendation, for Constantinople, and was appointed watchmaker to the Seraglio. During his absence, the beauty, wit, and accomplishments of my mother attracted a number of admirers, among whom Monsieur de La Closure, Resident of France, was the most assiduous in his attentions. His passion must have been extremely violent, since after a period of thirty years I have seen him affected whenever we spoke of her. My mother had a defense more powerful even than her virtue: she tenderly loved my father, and conjured him to return; he sacrificed all, and did so. I was the unfortunate fruit of this return, being born ten months after, in a very weakly and infirm state; my birth cost my mother her life, and was the first of my misfortunes.

I am ignorant how my father supported her loss at that time, but I know he was ever after inconsolable. In me he still thought he saw her, but could never forget I had been the innocent cause of his misfortune; nor did he ever embrace me but his sighs, the convulsive pressure of his arms, witnessed that a bitter regret mingled with his caresses, though, as may be supposed, they were not on this account less tender. When he said to me, "Jean-Jacques, let us talk of your mother," my usual reply was, "Yes, father, but then you know we shall cry," and immediately the tears started from his eyes. "Ah!" exclaimed he, with agitation, "give her back to me; at least console me for her loss; fill up the void she has left in my soul. Could I love thee thus wert thou only *my* son?" Forty years after this loss he expired in the arms of a second wife, but the name of the first still vibrated on his lips—still was her image engraved on his heart.

Such were the authors of my being. Of all the gifts it had pleased Heaven to bestow on them, a feeling heart was the only one that descended to me; this had been the source of their felicity—it was the foundation of all my misfortunes.

I came into the world with so few signs of life that they entertained but little hope of preserving me. I brought with me the seeds of a disorder that has gathered strength with years, and from which I am now relieved at intervals, only to suffer a different, though more intolerable, evil. I owed my preservation to one of my father's sisters, an amiable and virtuous girl, who took the most tender care of me; she is yet living, nursing, at the age of fourscore, a husband younger than herself, but worn out with excessive drinking. Dear aunt! I freely forgive your having preserved my life, and lament that it is not in my power to bestow on the decline of your days the tender solicitude and care you lavished on the first dawn of mine. My nurse, Jacqueline, is likewise living, and in good health—the hands that opened my eyes to the light of this world may close them at my death.

I suffered before I thought; it is the common lot of humanity. I experienced more than my proportion of it. I have no knowledge of what passed prior to my fifth or sixth year. I recollect nothing of learning to read; I only remember what effect the first considerable exercise of it produced on my mind; from that moment I date an uninterrupted knowledge of myself. Every night, after supper, my father and I read some part of a collection of romances which had been my mother's. My father's design was only to improve me in reading, and he thought these entertaining works were calculated to give me a fondness for it; but we soon found ourselves so interested in the adventures they contained, that we alternately read whole nights together, and could not bear to give over until at the conclusion of a volume. Sometimes, in the morning, on hearing the swallows at our window, my father, quite ashamed of this weakness, would cry, "Come, let us go to bed; I am more a child than thou art."

I soon acquired, by this dangerous custom, not only an extreme facility in reading and comprehension, but, for my age, a too intimate acquaintance with the passions. An infinity of sensations were familiar to me, without possessing any precise idea of the objects to which they related—I had conceived nothing—I had felt the whole. This confused succession of emotions which crowded upon my mind did not retard the future efforts of my reason, though they added an extravagant, romantic notion of human life, which experience and reflection have never been able wholly to eradicate. . . .

My brother, who was seven years older than myself, was brought up to my father's profession. The extraordinary affection they lavished on me caused him to be somewhat neglected; this was certainly a fault which cannot be justified. His education and morals suffered by this neglect, and he acquired the habits of a libertine before he arrived at an age to be really one. He was placed under another master, but his escapades were as numerous as when he lived at home. Though I saw him so seldom that it could hardly be said we were acquainted, I loved him tenderly, and I believe he had as strong an affection for me as a scapegrace is capable of. One day, I remember, when my father was correcting him severely, I threw myself between them, embracing my brother, whom I covered with my body, receiving the strokes designed for him. I persisted so obstinately in my protection, that, either softened by my cries and tears, or fearing to hurt me most, his anger subsided, and he pardoned his fault. In the end, my brother's conduct became so bad that he suddenly disappeared, and we learned some time after that he was in Germany; but he never wrote to us, and from that day we heard no news of him. Thus I became an only son.

If this poor lad was ill reared, it was quite different with his brother, for the children of a king could not be treated with more attention and tenderness than were bestowed on my infancy, being the darling of the family, and, what is rather uncommon, though treated as a beloved, never a spoiled child. I was never permitted, while under the paternal roof, to play in the street with other children; I never had any occasion to contradict or indulge those fantastical humors which are usually attributed to nature, but are in reality the effects of education. I had the faults common to my age; I was talkative, a glutton, and sometimes a liar; I made no scruple of stealing sweetmeats, fruits, or, indeed, any kind of eatables; but I never took delight in ill-doing, in mischievous waste, in accusing others, or tormenting harmless animals. I recollect, indeed, that one day, while Madame Clot, a neighbor of ours, was gone to church, I made water in her kettle; the remembrance even now makes me smile, for Madame Clot (though, if you please, a good sort of creature) was one of the most grumbling old

women I ever knew. Thus have I given a brief but faithful history
of my childish transgressions.

How could I become cruel or vicious, when I had before my eyes
only examples of mildness, and was surrounded by some of the best
people in the world? My father, my aunt, my nurse, my relations, our
friends, our neighbors, all I had any connection with, did not obey me,
it is true, but loved me tenderly, and I returned their affection. I
found so little to excite my desires, and those I had were so seldom
contradicted, that I was hardly sensible of possessing any, and can
solemnly aver I was an absolute stranger to caprice until after I had
experienced the authority of a master. Those hours that were not employed in reading or writing with my father, or walking with my governess, I spent with my aunt; and whether seeing her embroider or
hearing her sing, whether sitting or standing by her side, I was ever
happy. Her tenderness and unaffected gaiety, the charms of her countenance, have left such indelible impressions on my mind, that her manner, look, and attitude are still before my eyes; I recollect her little
caressing questions; I could describe her clothes, her headdress, nor
have the two curls of black hair which hung on her temples, according to the mode of that time, escaped from my memory.

Though my taste, or rather passion, for music did not show itself
until a considerable time after, I am fully persuaded it is to her I
am indebted for it. She knew a great number of songs, which she sang
with great sweetness and melody. The serenity and cheerfulness which
were conspicuous in this lovely girl banished melancholy, and made all
around her happy. The charms of her voice had such an effect on me
that not only several of her songs have ever since remained in my
memory, but, now when I have lost it, some I have not thought of
from my infancy, as I grow old return upon my mind with a charm
altogether inexpressible. Would any one believe that an old dotard
like me, worn out with care and infirmity, should sometimes surprise
himself weeping like a child, and in a voice querulous and broken by
age, muttering out one of those airs which were the favorites of my
infancy? . . .

Such were my affections on entering this life. Thus began to form
and demonstrate itself a heart at once haughty and tender, a character
timid, yet invincible, which, fluctuating between weakness and courage,
ease and virtue, has ever set me in contradiction to myself, causing
abstinence and enjoyment, pleasure and prudence, equally to shun me.

GUIDE QUESTIONS

1. What does the factual and detailed account of the romance and marriage of Rousseau's parents contribute to our impression of Rousseau himself?
2. Explain why you agree or disagree with Rousseau's idea of the effect which his early reading had on him. Relate this idea to the alleged effect on modern children of comics, movies, radio, and television.
3. Comment on the influence, as you see it, of Rousseau's brother and of his aunt on his "beginnings."
4. Given a childhood such as Rousseau describes, why does he say, "I suffered before I thought"? What do you think of the statements that follow: "[suffering] is the common lot of humanity. I experienced more than my proportion of it"? Is there an element of self-pity in this? Defend your view.
5. What impression do you get from his "brief but faithful history of my childish transgressions"? Might these be given in more detail in a modern autobiography, and, if so, why?
6. Discuss Rousseau's final estimate of himself as a child. What dominant impression does he wish to leave? Which parts of this account of himself would you say contribute most to this impression?

VOCABULARY

Give the derivations and definitions of the following words:

affluent, susceptible, exquisite, vivacity, benediction, cousin-german, assiduous, convulsive, amiable, solicitude, facility, eradicate, libertine, scapegrace, persist, fantastical, humors, scruple, transgression, aver, caprice, indelible, serenity, dotard, querulous, invincible, fluctuating, abstinence, shun.

Cornelia Otis Skinner

REPORT CARD

ALTHOUGH SCHOOL FROM A SOCIAL VIEWPOINT was going much better for me, from a scholastic one, it was going much worse. Out of a class

From *Family Circle* by Cornelia Otis Skinner. Copyright 1948 by Cornelia Skinner Blodget. Reprinted by permission of Houghton Mifflin Company.

not remarkable for brilliance, I was by far the poorest student. My monthly record showed a noteworthy consistency in the steady failure in all subjects with the exception of English and something called "Sloyd," which was a highly educational way of saying carpentry work.

Days on which I bore home my report card, I walked with leaden feet. I dreaded that "scene" with Mother and hoped some dire but more welcome fate would overcome me before I reached the house. An automobile might run over me or I might be kidnaped by gypsies or, if I prayed hard enough, a compassionate God might whip up an earthquake. Once, when my marks had reached an all-time low, feeling that life was no longer worth facing, I stretched myself out on the grass of a vacant lot, placed under my head my school bag, and on my chest the card, securing it against the breeze by a piece of brick, and tried to bring about an untimely end by holding my breath. Whoever in childhood despondency has been driven to similar desperate measures will recall how far from simple is this form of self-annihilation, even if one says, "I *will* this time," and takes a deep breath first. After a series of unsuccessful explosions and gasps, I began imagining Mother when she came across my pitiful corpse, and the picture of her anguished remorse was so acute that I scrambled to my feet, grabbed up my bag, and tore home to hurtle myself onto Mother's chest and assure her I was all right. Mother, who had not been in any particular doubts on that score, said obviously I was, but was my report? I produced the wretched thing and it in turn produced the inevitable scene. "Really and truly, Cornelia, when I was your age . . ." it invariably began, and ended in making me feel the vilest cretin ever born to dazzling parents. At the finish of the session we'd both be in tears.

For Mother, with her gentle manner, her golden voice, and her Bellini Madonna face, could take the heart out of me as neatly as an apple cutter tunnels out the core of a Jonathan. She wanted perfection from me.

GUIDE QUESTIONS

1. How do the choice of words, sentence structure, and tone of this selection indicate the writer's humorous intention?

2. What similar emotional experiences or "tragedies" of your own childhood do you now see in an amusing light?
3. Tell why you approve or disapprove of Mrs. Skinner's attitude concerning the grades her daughter made in school.

VOCABULARY

Give the derivations and definitions of the following words:

Sloyd, dire, compassionate, despondency, annihilation, anguished, remorse, acute, hurtle, cretin.

Floyd Dell

EGOTISM

IT WAS, I THINK, when I was ten years old, that I laid public claim to my birthplace, and was officially rebuked for my presumption in doing so.

I had had pointed out to me, as the house in which I was born, the great brown-painted frame building now known as Blair's Boarding-House. I was not quite pleased with it as a birthplace. Perhaps I felt that I should have been born in a log-cabin, like Lincoln. There was only one log-cabin in Barry, and I went to look at it several times and stared curiously at the old Irishwoman who lived there.

Blair's Boarding-House was on my way to and from school. And one morning not long before I left Barry, I wrote my name all along the side of the house in large letters with a piece of chalk.

And that afternoon it happened that the principal of the school, a tall, rubber-heeled man who liked to catch somebody doing something wrong and make an example of him, visited the room. The writing exercise was going on. I had finished it long since, and sat dreaming— perhaps of future greatness. And as I dreamed, I unconsciously wrote on my tablet, "Floyd Dell" and the date of my birth.

The principal was softly making the rounds of the room. I had not

From *Homecoming.* Copyright 1933 by Floyd Dell, and reprinted by permission of Rinehart and Company, Inc., publishers.

seen him enter, and was not aware of his presence until I saw the tall shape leaning over my shoulder, looking at my tablet. I was proud of my handwriting, and I pushed the writing exercise over for the principal to see. But the principal kept looking at my name on the tablet.

"Are you Floyd Dell?" he asked.

"Yes, sir."

"Did you write your name on the side of Blair's Boarding-House?" The question came like an earthquake. I had forgotten all about that.

"Yes, sir," I said faintly.

"What did you do that for?" the principal asked sternly.

At that moment I became conscious of the tell-tale words written on the paper in front of me. I blushed all over. These words seemed to me a naked revelation of all my secret thoughts. I wanted to destroy the paper, but I could not make a movement.

"I don't know," I said dully.

"You don't know?" repeated my torturer. "You must be very proud of your name." He took up the tablet on which the name was written, and read what else was written there.

I shrank in my clothes, while the principal read it over carefully to himself. Then he turned to me.

"I want you," he said bitingly, "to show the room what you have been doing instead of writing your lesson. Write that on the board three times."

My teacher flushed angrily, and made a protesting gesture.

Like one under sentence of death, pale, but rigid to conceal my trembling, I walked slowly to the blackboard, faced the whole room with its hundred staring eyes, and summoned the pride not to care what they thought. Then I turned to the blackboard and wrote the offending words slowly in large defiant letters.

Then I broke the chalk between my fingers, let it drop to the floor, and walked back to my seat.

There was a hush all over the room. Nobody knew what it all meant. My bearing was so little that of a culprit that it did not seem that they were intended to laugh at my discomfiture. The principal was embarrassed.

"That," he said, "is what is known as egotism," and went out.

The teacher hastily called the arithmetic class, and herself erased from the blackboard the words I had written. I left the room, took my cap, and hurried to Blair's Boarding-House, trembling with rage and shame. Ignoring the people about, I commenced to rub out my name with my handkerchief, my cap, my coat-sleeve, my bare hands. The letters seemed to have grown gigantic, overtopping my height. A crowd began to gather. I stopped suddenly, and ran home.

That night I tossed in bed in sleepless torment. But a kindly rain came and washed the offending letters from the wall. They were not there to reproach me with my egotism when I went to school the next day.

GUIDE QUESTIONS

1. What would be the effect on the incident in the classroom if it were told as straight narrative, without the use of dialogue?
2. What is suggested by the statement, "The principal was embarrassed"?
3. Point out specific details concerning the boy's original act, his feelings during the incident in the classroom, and his actions and emotions afterward that make this a realistic treatment of child psychology.
4. What embarrassing moments of your own, in which you either were or were not at fault, does Floyd Dell's experience suggest to you?

VOCABULARY

Give the derivations and definitions of the following words:

egotism, presumption, tell-tale, defiant, culprit, discomfiture.

Agnes Repplier

SIN

I WAS TWELVE YEARS OLD, and very happy in my convent school. I did not particularly mind studying my lessons, and I sometimes persuaded

From "Small Tragedies," by Agnes Repplier in *The Atlantic Monthly,* June, 1938. Reprinted by arrangement with the Fidelity-Philadelphia Trust Company, Broad and Walnut Streets, Philadelphia 9, Pennsylvania.

the less experienced nuns to accept a retentive memory as a substitute for intelligent understanding, with which it has nothing to do. I "got along" with other children, and I enjoyed my friends; and of such simple things is the life of a child composed.

Then came a disturbing letter from my mother, a letter which threatened the heart of my content. It was sensible and reasonable, and it said very plainly and very kindly that I had better not make an especial friend of Lilly Milton; "not an exclusive friend," wrote my mother, "not one whom you would expect to see intimately after you leave school."

I knew what all that meant. I was as innocent as a kitten; but divorces were not common in those conservative years, and Mrs. Milton had as many to her credit as if she were living—a highly esteemed and popular lady—today. I regretted my mother's tendency to confuse issues with unimportant details (a mistake which grown-up people often made), and I felt sure that if she knew Lilly—who was also as innocent as a kitten, and was blessed with the sweetest temper that God ever gave a little girl—she would be delighted that I had such an excellent friend. So I went on happily enough until ten days later, when Madame Rayburn, a nun for whom I cherished a very warm affection, was talking to me upon a familiar theme—the diverse ways in which I might improve my classwork and my general behavior. The subject did not interest me deeply,—repetition had staled its vivacity,— until my companion said the one thing that had plainly been uppermost in her mind: "And Agnes, how did you come to tell Lilly Milton that your mother did not want you to go with her? I never thought you could have been so deliberately unkind."

This brought me to my feet with a bound. "Tell Lilly!" I cried. "You could not have believed such a thing. It was Madame Bouron who told her."

A silence followed this revelation. The convent discipline was as strict for the nuns as for the pupils, and it was not their custom to criticize their superiors. Madame Bouron was mistress general, ranking next to the august head, and of infinitely more importance to us. She was a cold, severe, sardonic woman, and the general dislike felt for her had shaped itself into a cult. I had accepted this cult in simple good faith, having no personal grudge until she did this dreadful thing; and I may add that it was the eminently unwise custom of reading all the letters written to or by pupils which stood responsible for the trouble. The order of nuns was a French one, and the habit of surveillance, which did not seem amiss in France, was ill-adapted to America. I had never before wasted a thought upon it. My weekly home letter and the less frequent but more communicative epistles from my mother might have been read in the market place for all I cared, until this miserable episode proved that a bad usage may be trusted to produce, sooner or later, bad results.

It was with visible reluctance that Madame Rayburn said after a long pause: "That alters the case. If Madame Bouron told Lilly, she must have had some good reason for doing so."

"There was no good reason," I protested. "There couldn't have been. But it doesn't matter. I told Lilly it wasn't so, and she believed me."

Madame Rayburn stared at me aghast. "You told Lilly it was not so?" she repeated.

I nodded. "I could not find out for two days what was the matter," I explained; "but I got it out of her at last, and I told her that my mother had never written a line to me about her. And she believed me."

"But my dear child," said the nun, "you have told a very grievous lie. What is more, you have borne false witness against your neighbor. When you said to Lilly that your mother had not written that letter, you made her believe that Madame Bouron had lied to her."

"She didn't mind believing that," I observed cheerfully, "and there was nothing else that I could say to make her feel all right."

"But a lie is a lie," protested the nun. "You will have to tell Lilly the truth."

I said nothing, but my silence was not the silence of acquiescence. Madame Rayburn must have recognized this fact, for she took another line of attack. When she spoke next, it was in a low voice and very earnestly. "Listen to me," she said. "Friday is the first of May. You are going to confession on Thursday. You will tell Father O'Harra the whole story just as you have told it to me, and whatever he bids you do, you must do it. Remember that if you go to confession and do not tell this you will commit the very great sin of sacrilege; and if you do not obey your confessor you will commit the sin of open disobedience to the Church."

I was more than a little frightened. It seemed to me that for the first time in my life I was confronted by grown-up iniquities to which I had been a stranger. The thought sobered me for two days. On the

third I went to confession, and when I had finished my customary
offenses—which, as they seldom varied, were probably as familiar to
the priest as they were to me—I told my serious tale. The silence with
which it was received bore witness to its seriousness. No question was
asked me; I had been too explicit to render questions needful. But after
two minutes (which seemed like two hours) of thinking my confessor
said: "A lie is a lie. It must be retracted. Tomorrow you will do one of
two things: You will tell your friend the truth, or you will tell Madame
Bouron the whole story just as you told it to me. Do you understand?"

"Yes," I said in a faint little voice, no louder than a sigh.

"And you will do as I bid you?"

"Yes," I breathed again.

"Then I will give you absolution, and you may go to Communion.
But remember, no later than tomorrow. Believe me, it will get no easier
by delay."

Of that I felt tolerably sure, and it was with the courage of despera-
tion that I knocked the next morning at the door of Madame Bouron's
office. She gave me a glance of wonderment (I had never before paid
her a voluntary call), and without pause or preamble I told my tale,
told it with such bald uncompromising verity that it sounded worse
than ever. She listened at first in amazement, then in anger. "So Lilly
thinks I lied to her," she said at last.

"Yes," I answered.

"And suppose I send for her now and undeceive her."

"You can't do that," I said. "I should tell her again my mother did
not write the letter, and she would believe me."

"If you told another such lie, you would be sent from the school."

"If I were sent home, Lilly would believe me. She would believe me
all the more."

The anger died out of Madame Bouron's eyes, and a look of be-
wilderment came into them. I am disposed to think that, despite her
wide experience as nun and teacher, she had never before encountered
an *idée fixe,* and found out that the pyramids are flexible compared
to it. "You know," she said uncertainly, "that sooner or later you will
have to do as your mother desires."

I made no answer. The "sooner or later" did not interest me at all.
I was living now.

There was another long pause. When Madame Bouron spoke again it was in a grave and low voice. "I wish I had said nothing about your mother's letter," she said. "I thought I could settle matters quickly that way, but I was mistaken, and I must take the consequences of my error. You may go now. I will not speak to Lilly, or to anyone else about this affair."

I did not go. I sat stunned, and asking myself if she knew all that her silence would imply. Children seldom give adults much credit for intelligence. "But," I began feebly—

"But me no buts," she interrupted, rising to her feet. "I know what you are going to say; but I have not been the head of a school for years without bearing more than one injustice."

Now when I heard these words sadly spoken something broke up inside of me. It did not break gently, like the dissolving of a cloud; it broke like the bursting of a dam. Sobs shook my lean little body as though they would have torn it apart. Tears blinded me. With difficulty I gasped out three words. "You are good," I said.

Madame Bouron propelled me gently to the door, which I could not see because of my tears. "I wish I could say as much for you," she answered, "but I cannot. You have been very bad. You have been false to your mother, to whom you owe respect and obedience; you have been false to me; and you have been false to God. But you have been true to your friend."

She put me out of the door, but I stood in the corridor facing the clock. I was still shaken by sobs, but my heart was light as a bird. And, believe it or not, the supreme reason for my happiness was—not that my difficulties were over, though I was glad of that; and not that Lilly was safe from hurt, though I was glad of that; but that Madame Bouron, whom I had thought bad, had proved herself to be, according to the standards of childhood, as good as gold. My joy was like the joy of the blessed saints in Paradise.

GUIDE QUESTIONS

1. Three passages of dialogue are used in this narrative. Why is the longest of the three passages used to relate the interview with Madame Bouron? Which of the three passages could be translated into indirect discourse with the least loss in dramatic effectiveness?

2. Discuss the various methods, direct or indirect, by which the other

persons in the story are characterized: Lilly Milton, Agnes's mother, Madame Rayburn, Father O'Harra, Madame Bouron. Which of these seems to you the most vivid?

3. Comment on the way Agnes behaved in the situation and on the way Madame Bouron behaved. What would you have done if you had been in either's place? Analyze their feelings about the situation as a whole, and toward each other. Do you agree or disagree with Agnes's final opinion of Madame Bouron?

4. Analyze Agnes's problem as one of conflicting loyalties: to her mother, to her friend Lilly Milton, to Madame Bouron, to God.

5. Aside from the special aspects of the convent school setting, show that similar problems could arise in non-Catholic circumstances. Would there be any essential difference in their solution? Discuss.

VOCABULARY

Give the derivations and definitions of the following words:

retentive, cherished, diverse, august, sardonic, cult, eminently, surveillance, amiss, usage, reluctance, aghast, grievous, acquiescence, sacrilege, iniquity, explicit, render, retract, absolution, tolerably, preamble, uncompromising, verity, disposed, propelled.

Lincoln Steffens

A MISERABLE, MERRY CHRISTMAS

WHAT INTERESTED ME in our new neighborhood was not the school, nor the room I was to have in the house all to myself, but the stable which was built back of the house. My father let me direct the making of a stall, a little smaller than the other stalls, for my pony, and I prayed and hoped and my sister Lou believed that that meant that I would get the pony, perhaps for Christmas. I pointed out to her that there were three other stalls and no horses at all. This I said in order that she should answer it. She could not. My father, sounded, said that some day we might have horses and a cow; meanwhile a stable added to the value of a house. "Some day" is a pain to a boy who lives in and knows only "now." My good little sisters, to comfort me, remarked that Christmas was coming, but Christmas was always coming and grown-ups were always talking about it, asking you what you wanted and then giving you what they wanted you to have. Though everybody knew what I wanted, I told them all again. My mother knew that I told God, too, every night. I wanted a pony, and to make sure that they understood, I declared that I wanted nothing else.

"Nothing but a pony?" my father asked.

"Nothing," I said.

"Not even a pair of high boots?"

That was hard. I did want boots, but I stuck to the pony. "No, not even boots."

"Nor candy? There ought to be something to fill your stocking with, and Santa Claus can't put a pony into a stocking."

That was true, and he couldn't lead a pony down the chimney either. But no. "All I want is a pony," I said. "If I can't have a pony, give me nothing, nothing."

Now I had been looking myself for the pony I wanted, going to sales stables, inquiring of horsemen, and I had seen several that would do. My father let me "try" them. I chose several, but my father always found some fault with them. I was in despair. When Christmas was at hand I had given up all hope of a pony, and on Christmas Eve I hung up my stocking along with my sisters', of whom, by the way, I now had three. I haven't mentioned them or their coming because, you understand, they were girls, and girls, young girls, counted for nothing in my manly life. They did not mind me either; they were so happy that Christmas Eve that I caught some of their merriment. I speculated on what I'd get; I hung up the biggest stocking I had, and we all went reluctantly to bed to wait till morning. Not to sleep; not right away. We were told that we must not only sleep promptly, we must not wake up till seven-thirty the next morning—or if we did, we must not go to the fireplace for our Christmas. Impossible.

We did sleep that night, but we woke up at six A.M. We lay in our beds and debated through the open doors whether to obey till, say, half-past six. Then we bolted. I don't know who started it, but there was a rush. We all disobeyed; we raced to disobey and get first to the fireplace in the front room downstairs. And there they were, the gifts, all sorts of wonderful things, mixed-up piles of presents; only, as I disentangled the mess, I saw that my stocking was empty; it hung limp; not a thing in it; and under and around it—nothing. My sisters had knelt down, each by her pile of gifts; they were squealing with delight, till they looked up and saw me standing there in my night-gown with nothing. They left their piles to come to me and look with me at my empty place. Nothing. They felt my stocking: nothing.

I don't remember whether I cried at that moment, but my sisters did. They ran with me back to my bed, and there we all cried till I became indignant. That helped some. I got up, dressed, and driving my sisters away, I went alone out into the yard, down to the stable, and there, all by myself, I wept. My mother came out to me by and by; she found me in my pony stall, sobbing on the floor, and she tried to comfort me. But I heard my father outside; he had come part way with her, and she was having some sort of angry quarrel with him. She tried to comfort me; besought me to come to breakfast. I could not; I wanted no comfort and no breakfast. She left me and went on into the house with sharp words for my father.

I don't know what kind of a breakfast the family had. My sisters said it was "awful." They were ashamed to enjoy their own toys. They came to me, and I was rude. I ran away from them. I went around to the front of the house, sat down on the steps, and, the crying over, I ached. I was wronged, I was hurt—I can feel now what I felt then, and I am sure that if one could see the wounds upon our hearts, there would be found still upon mine a scar from that terrible Christmas morning. And my father, the practical joker, he must have been hurt, too, a little. I saw him looking out of the window. He was watching me or something for an hour or two, drawing back the curtain ever so little lest I catch him, but I saw his face, and I think I can see now the anxiety upon it, the worried impatience.

After—I don't know how long—surely an hour or two—I was brought to the climax of my agony by the sight of a man riding a pony down the street, a pony and a brand-new saddle; the most beautiful saddle I ever saw, and it was a boy's saddle; the man's feet were not in the stirrups; his legs were too long. The outfit was perfect; it was the realization of all my dreams, the answer to all my prayers. A fine new bridle, with a light curb bit. And the pony! As he drew near, I saw that the pony was really a small horse, what we called an Indian pony, a bay, with black mane and tail, and one white foot and a white star on his forehead. For such a horse as that I would have given, I could have forgiven, anything.

But the man, a disheveled fellow with a blackened eye and a fresh-cut face, came along, reading the numbers on the houses, and, as my hopes—my impossible hopes—rose, he looked at our door and passed by, he and the pony, and the saddle and the bridle. Too much. I fell upon the steps, and having wept before, I broke now into such a flood of tears that I was a floating wreck when I heard a voice.

"Say, kid," it said, "do you know a boy named Lennie Steffens?"

I looked up. It was the man on the pony, back again, at our horse block.

"Yes," I spluttered through my tears. "That's me."

"Well," he said, "then this is your horse. I've been looking all over for you and your house. Why don't you put your number where it can be seen?"

"Get down," I said, running out to him.

He went on saying something about "ought to have got here at seven o'clock; told me to bring the nag here and tie him to your post and leave him for you. But, hell, I got into a drunk—and a fight—and a hospital, and—"

"Get down," I said.

He got down, and he boosted me up to the saddle. He offered to fit the stirrups to me, but I didn't want him to. I wanted to ride.

"What's the matter with you?" he said, angrily. "What you crying for? Don't you like the horse? He's a dandy, this horse. I know him of old. He's fine at cattle; he'll drive 'em alone."

I hardly heard, I could scarcely wait, but he persisted. He adjusted the stirrups, and then, finally, off I rode, slowly, at a walk, so happy, so thrilled, that I did not know what I was doing. I did not look back at the house or the man, I rode off up the street, taking note of everything—of the reins, of the pony's long mane, of the carved leather saddle. I had never seen anything so beautiful. And mine! I was going to ride up past Miss Kay's house. But I noticed on the horn of the saddle some stains like rain-drops, so I turned and trotted home, not to the house but to the stable. There was the family, father, mother, sisters, all working for me, all happy. They had been putting in place the tools of my new business: blankets, currycomb, brush, pitchfork—everything, and there was hay in the loft.

"What did you come back so soon for?" somebody asked. "Why didn't you go on riding?"

I pointed to the stains. "I wasn't going to get my new saddle rained on," I said. And my father laughed. "It isn't raining," he said. "Those are not rain-drops."

"They are tears," my mother gasped, and she gave my father a look which sent him off to the house. Worse still, my mother offered to wipe away the tears still running out of my eyes. I gave her such a look as she had given him, and she went off after my father, drying her own tears. My sisters remained and we all unsaddled the pony, put on his halter, led him to his stall, tied and fed him. It began really to rain; so all the rest of that memorable day we curried and combed that pony. The girls plaited his mane, forelock, and tail, while I pitch-forked hay to him and curried and brushed, curried and brushed. For a change we brought him out to drink; we led him up and down, blanketed like a race-horse; we took turns at that. But the best, the most inexhaustible fun, was to clean him. When we went reluctantly to our midday Christmas dinner, we all smelt of horse, and my sisters had to wash their faces and hands. I was asked to, but I wouldn't, till my mother bade me look in the mirror. Then I washed up—quick. My face was caked with the muddy lines of tears that had coursed over my cheeks to my mouth. Having washed away that shame, I ate my dinner, and as I ate I grew hungrier and hungrier. It was my first meal that day, and as I filled up on the turkey and the stuffing, the cranberries and the pies, the fruit and the nuts—as I swelled, I could laugh. My mother said I still choked and sobbed now and then, but I laughed, too; I saw and enjoyed my sisters' presents till—I had to go out and attend to my pony, who was there, really and truly there, the promise, the beginning, of a happy double life. And—I went and looked to make sure—there was the saddle, too, and the bridle.

But that Christmas, which my father had planned so carefully, was it the best or the worst I ever knew? He often asked me that; I never could answer as a boy. I think now that it was both. It covered the whole distance from broken-hearted misery to bursting happiness—too fast. A grown-up could hardly have stood it.

GUIDE QUESTIONS

1. By what particular devices does Steffens maintain a single point of view, that of the small boy he was at this time?
2. Was Steffens' father to blame for the miserable part of his Christmas?
3. How does Steffens indicate his attitude toward his sisters at the time of which he writes?
4. What is the shortest sentence of the reading? What is the longest? What reasons could Steffens have had for these sentence lengths?
5. The reading contains three short passages of dialogue. How would the effect of the whole be changed if these passages were omitted or replaced by direct narration?

VOCABULARY

Give the derivations and definitions of the following words:

sounded, reluctantly, bolted, disentangled, besought, lest, disheveled, persisted.

Thomas Sancton

THE SILVER HORN

THE SCENE IS A BOY SCOUT SUMMER CAMP, thickly grown with pines and cypress. There is a row of green clapboard cabins, with clean floors and neat double-decker bunks; there is an open field and a flag hanging still in the heavy air; and at the field's edge the land drops down a little to the dark water of a bayou. I spent five summers here, from the time I was twelve until I entered college. I did my first real living and my first real thinking in this camp.

And I think of it now. Like some reader of a long novel who turns back through the pages to find a forgotten part of the plot, and who comes with a flash of recognition across old scenes and dialogues, and

"The Silver Horn," by Thomas Sancton, from *Harper's Magazine*, February, 1944. Reprinted by permission of the author.

characters who have gone out of the narrative but whose personalities
and substance once filled pages and pages, I have gone turning back
through the pages of my life. When was it and where was it—I have
been asking—that I first began to believe what I now believe about
the Southern world I left not many years ago, about Negroes, about
democracy, about America, about life and death, about men and all
their curious fates? This search has been long and turning. Often it has
led me back to the years of my early teens and to the summers I spent
in the camp.

I was born to the sidewalks and asphalt of the largest city and the
widest street in the South. In New Orleans, broad Canal Street was
never empty of speeding automobiles and streetcars, even late at night,
and of people walking by, their footsteps echoing on the sidewalk. But
here on the bayou another world existed. In the morning it was the
strange, thin call of a bugle that broke into our sleep. Almost before
we were awake we could smell the wet exercise field and the forest.
Birds popped from tree to tree, plump and colorful, bluejays, mocking-
birds, cardinals, flickers—Audubon had painted in these woods. Rabbits ran into the bushes. Snakes we had no fear of, long thick blue
racers and speckled king snakes, slid through the weeds at our
approach.

Standing in the wet grass, still yawning and sleepy, we took the
morning exercises. Night chill was in the air, but behind our backs
the sun was rising, and its warmth crept onto our shoulders. After the
exercises we raced along a wagon road to the swimming pool, and as
we ran up, shouting and excited, two or three startled frogs made
tremendous leaps and plumped beneath the glassy surface of the water.
After the swim we dried our skinny sunburned bodies and ran to the
mess hall.

Most of us in the camp were poor boys, or boys who were almost
poor. It was not a welfare camp, but the fees were low, less than a
dollar a day for a camper. As a consequence it was filled with boys from
modest New Orleans neighborhoods and also from the tough ones.
There was always a smattering of the democratic rich: the son of the
traction company president came every summer. So did his cousin from
Texas, a wild, hard towhead with plenty of money and the soul of a
true picaroon. He fascinated and dominated the rest of us. He was the
first colorful outlaw I ever knew. But most of the well-to-do families
sent their boys to camps in the Maine woods or the North Carolina

mountains. Our camp was only forty miles from the city. Department store clerks, streetcar motormen, little grocers could afford the fees.

We had no saddle horses, no golf course, and only a weed-grown tennis court which no one used. For diversion we fell back on nature. In the morning we performed a work detail, cutting a patch of weeds or hauling dirt in wheelbarrows to mend a road. After this we were free to swim, to paddle on the bayou in slender little Louisiana boats called pirogues, to fish for the boisterous black bass and yellow perch and fat blue catfish, and to work for our Boy Scout medals and merit badges, tracking through the grassy cut-over pine lands, cooking dough and bacon on sweet-gum spits, bandaging one another with first-aid splints.

These little medals and bits of colored ribbon meant a great deal to us. We wrote home enthusiastic letters about our progress, describing in detail how we had passed the tests, forwarding the comments of some eighteen-year-old camp officer as though it really mattered. Our parents, most of whom did not have very big events happening in their own lives, were just as eager and simple-hearted about these things, and one or two of the fathers were foolishly ambitious to have their sons win the highest number of merit badges in the area.

Little things that happened during these years seemed of great importance. I remember that in my first year at camp I wore an ill-fitting Boy Scout hat. One of the councillors, a boy five years my senior who seemed to me to belong already to the grown-up world of brilliance and authority, began, in a pleasant way, to tease me about the hat. Every morning for a week he led us to the abandoned logging road and clocked us as we walked and trotted a measured mile. My hat was anchored down by a heavy chin strap; it flopped and sailed about my head as I ran to the finish line. The boy began to laugh at me. He waved his arms and called out, "Come on, you rookie!" The other kids took it up and Rookie became my first nickname. I loved it. I tingled when someone called it out. I painted it on my belt, carved it in my packing case, inked it into my hatband, and began to sign it to my letters home. Years later when we were grown I knew this camp officer again. The gap between our ages had vanished and in real life now he seemed to me a rather colorless young lawyer. He did not remember about the hat.

At mealtime we ate ravenously in the mess hall. There were steaming platters of pork and beans and cabbage and stew. As we walked to the long clapboard building with our hair freshly combed and water glistening on our faces, which we washed at the flowing pipe of a big artesian well, we existed in a transport of driving hunger. In the steamy fragrance of the mess hall we set up a clatter of knives and forks and china and afterward we went to our cabins and flopped on the bunks in a state of drowsy satisfaction. Somehow, fat never formed on our skinny frames. We ran too much. We paddled in the boats. We swam. We cut firewood and played softball after supper. When there was nothing else to do we climbed in the rafters of our cabins, trying to invent complicated monkey swings that no one else could do. Every year some campers broke their arms.

II

A giant Negro named Joe did the camp's heavy work. He cut and trimmed the big trees, dug the deep post holes, mixed the cement, cleaned out the underbrush. His strength was a never-ending fascination for the rest of us. Joe was a light-eyed Negro, with a tan cast of skin and a huge bald dome of a head. One of his grandparents must certainly have been a white man. He lived half a mile down the bayou with his large and hazily defined family, in an old "plantation house."

Actually it was not, and never had been, a pretentious place, and I do not know what kind of plantation could have been there. The ground round it was alternately sandy and swampy and there are no plantations where pine trees grow. Pines mean sandy land. In slave days the Negroes had boiled Southern history down to a couplet:

> Cain't make a living on sandy lan'—
> Ruther be a nigger den a po' white man.

Joe's place stood on a cleared bend in the bayou. The weatherboards and shingles were green with age. The house rested on high slender pillars and there were patches of bright red brick where the covering mortar had fallen away. The yard was shaded by two enormous water oaks, hung with gray Spanish moss, and an iron kettle stood beneath the trees where women did the washing. At the bank of the bayou five or six towering cypress trees leaned heavily toward the water, for the slow currents of a century had washed their roots completely bare of soil. To get a new anchorage on the land the trees had sent out a forest of gnarled roots and stubby knees along the shoreline. The house seemed beautiful and somber in these surroundings as we paddled past it on our expeditions down the bayou to the lake.

Obviously a white man had built this place long ago, and if he had not been a plantation owner, he had at least been a man of substance. Perhaps this had been the summer home for some wealthy old New Orleans Frenchman in years gone by. Sometimes the camp officers spoke of Joe as "caretaker" on the place. But that was hardly possible. He and his family inhabited every room; chickens roamed freely, and washing hung on lines stretched across the wide porch. It was clear to us that the Negro giant was no caretaker here. He possessed this place, to have and to hold. How he got it and why we never asked him; and his presence there did not seem a very curious thing to us. Already a dark, subjective understanding of Louisiana's history was in our blood and bones.

Joe smoked strong cigarettes and chewed tobacco. His teeth were rotted stumps. We delighted in bringing him supplies of smokes from the nearby town on Saturdays to win his quick and genuine appreciation. There were two or three measures of a Cajun French ditty he used to sing, dancing and stomping the ground, waving his hat and swaying his heavy shoulders with real grace. The words and the stomping finished together, with two hard accents. He would do this every time in exchange for a gift. Yet he did it in such a way that we knew always that this was nothing more than a grown-up man doing monkey-shines for children. He enjoyed making us laugh. There was nothing servile about it.

He got to be one of the people I liked best of all—not only in the camp but in my whole circumscribed world. I liked Joe very simply because he was a nice man. He recognized me every year when I returned to the camp, and after the second or third year I could tell that he considered me a real friend and was glad to have me back. We talked together often, equally and easily, and when I was sixteen and seventeen and by then a councillor in the camp, Joe would do me the honor of becoming quite serious with me and of placing our whole friendship on a mature plane. I do not remember many of the things we talked about, but I do remember that a conversation with him was a reassurance and a satisfaction; that it was always good to find him walking on the road and to fall in with him.

I saw a brief notice in the paper, some years after I had stopped going to the camp, that Joe had died of blood poisoning in the New

Orleans Charity Hospital. I thought of those stumps of teeth, and of the many years they had been seeping infection into his system. I thought also of the tall trees I had seen him fell, and that now Joe too had come toppling to the earth. And, though I felt a quiet sorrow, I felt no anguish. Life grew rank and lush along the bayou. His old house was teeming with the spawn of his years. The sun would beat upon the water forever, the trout would break the surface, the rushes would grow thick and green. Joe had done his share of hauling and of digging. Now he could lie down in the warm and sun-drenched earth and sleep.

III

During those summers in camp a love grew up in me for the rhythms of nature, for tropical rains that came sweeping through the pines and oaks, for the fiery midday sun, for long evenings, and the deep black nights. Great campfires were lit beside the bayou and a rushing column of luminous smoke and sparks ascended to the cypress trees. Fire gleamed in the water where bass were sleeping in the stumps. Campers wandered toward the meeting place, their flashlights swinging in the woods. We sat about the fire, singing, beating deep rumbling tom-toms made of hollowed oak logs, performing an ageless repertoire of skits and mimicry. And after these sessions one leader took the Protestant boys and another the Catholics and, standing in the open fields, in our separate groups, we prayed aloud.

My heart had strayed already from the formal, repetitious praying. A towering pine tree at the field's edge made a silhouette in the starry sky. I knew the constellations, the Giant, the Dipper, the Bear. I looked for the two inseparable stars, Misar and Alcar, horse and rider, and sensed the fact that Arabs named these stars a thousand years before me, and even in my boy's ignorance I felt aware of man's long and varied time upon the earth. I knew this night-filled wilderness had stretched beneath these stars for endless ages before Frenchmen had come in boats to build New Orleans. I thought of the Indians who had fished and hunted here, whose bones and broken pottery we sometimes found in grassy mounds. I felt worshipful of the earth, the pine tree, the night itself.

Sometimes we packed provisions and tents and mosquito bars and paddled down the bayou to the lake, ten miles away. The lake was a great inland finger of the Gulf of Mexico, twenty miles long, ten wide. Twenty miles below us, in prehistoric times, the mouth of the Mississippi river had built up new land, and these watery prairies had pinched off the small inland gulf and made a lake of it, but it connected still through a series of passes with the Mexican Gulf. The lake teemed with croakers, catfish, shrimp, and big blue-clawed crabs. At the northern end, where we camped, a network of tributary bayous emptied into the lake. For the last mile or so of their crooked lengths, where the brackish water of the lake crept into the slow-moving bayous, fish and small life were abundant, bass fed in the rushes, and muskrats built their cities of the plains.

There was a relatively high, sandy point near the mouth of the bayou, where we camped. The sun went down red into the lake and left a long, clear twilight. A few stars came out. A salty wind blew in from the Mexican Gulf; it came out of the south every night. The breeze swept over the rushes and made small waves break on the sandy, grassy shore. There was a red beacon light on weather-beaten piles out in the lake and its long reflection shimmered in the water. We sprayed our mosquito netting with citronella and built up a driftwood fire and lay down on canvas bedrolls spread upon the thin, tough grass and sand. The trade wind blew through our tents throughout the night. We listened to the waves. We could smell the vast salt marshes far below us. A yellow moon came out of the gulf. Far down the lake we could see the lights of a railroad bridge. We felt the beauty of this wilderness like a hunger.

After two days of fishing and swimming in the lake, our shoulders and faces darker from the sun, we paddled back up the winding bayou.

IV

One summer when I was sixteen a party of us, paddling upstream to buy some candy at a crossroads store, came upon three young girls who were bathing in a sandy cove. There were four of us in the long pirogue, all of an age. For a long moment we were speechless. At last we said hello, and they answered in warm gay voices. We drifted the boat into the cove and began to speak to them. Two of the girls were sisters. The three of them had come to visit a relative who kept a fine summer lodge in the woods across the bayou from the camp. One of

the sisters was fifteen and the others were seventeen. They were aglow
with fresh and slender beauty, and their bathing suits were bright
flags of color. Their impact upon us was overwhelming. We grew
silly, tongue-tied, said foolish things we did not mean to say, shoved
one another about in the boat, and finally overturned it. The loreleis
laughed musical little laughs. They seemed unbearably beautiful. We
had no idea what to do about it.

The girls had been at the lodge for a week. They missed their
beaux in New Orleans, they missed the dating and the dancing and
the music. It was a gay town in the summertime. The older girls
looked upon us as children; but still—they must have reflected—we
were not such children at that. The younger sister, a slender child
with thick brown hair and heavily crimsoned lips, sat on the bank and
regarded us with a happy open face.

At last we took courage and asked if we could call on them that
night.

"Oh, yes!" they cried eagerly. Life at that moment was dazzling.

Making this rendezvous was an impulsive thing to do, for it was
midweek and we should have to steal away after taps and walk down
a path without flashlights through a snake-infested lowland and—because the boats were counted and chained at nightfall—swim across
the bayou, holding our clothes above our heads.

We crept from our cabins at ten o'clock that night and met in the
pine woods. One of us intoned a counting-out rhyme; the loser had to
walk first down the path through the snake hole. He cut a long gum
sapling and rattled it down the path ahead of us. We walked bunched
tightly together, tense with fear, giggling at our own unbelievable
audacity, trembling in our eagerness. At the bayou's edge we slipped
out of our shorts and shirts and sneakers and, holding them above
our heads with one hand, we felt our way round the knees and along
the sunken roots of a cypress tree, and pushed off into the bayou and
began to swim.

The moon had not yet risen. We had only the silhouettes of trees
to guide us. We swam closely together, cautioning one another to
silence, bursting into convulsive squeals as water lilies brushed against
our bodies or when a fish broke the surface near us. We swam upstream from the camp, past two bends, and waded from the water
in the cove where we had met the girls. Now we were laughing with
relief and excitement, and popping one another on the backsides. We

scraped the glistening water from our bodies, dressed, and combed our wet hair and hurried off down the wagon path into the woods. Long ago the cove had been a landing stage for small schooners which came to load pine firewood for New Orleans.

The girls were waiting for us, dressed in bright print cotton dresses and wearing hair ribbons. The soft light gave age and mystery to their youthful shoulders, to their slender bodies; and, like nameless night-blooming vines in the woods about us, they bore a splendid fragrance all their own, a fragrance of youth and cleanliness and fresh cosmetics. They were playing a phonograph on the wide porch of the lodge. This was the summer of Maurice Chevalier's great success in American movies. The little sister sang his song, rolling her eyes, turning out her soft pink lip:

> If ze night-ting gail
> cood zing lak you . . .

And she sang another:

> . . . you make me feel so grand
> I want to hand the world to you.
> You seem to understand
> Each foolish little dream I'm dreaming, scheme
> I'm scheming . . .

I was so in love with her I could hardly catch my breath. I was in love with the other sister too, and with their friend. All of the boys were in love with all of the girls; the girls—so they said—had crushes on each of us. Our hearts were afire.

We walked hand in hand down the wagon trail to the cove and built a bonfire. We stretched out on blankets, laughing, singing. We sang the songs that people always sing by rivers and campfires, "There's a Long, Long Trail A-winding," "The Sweetheart of Sigma Chi," all the rest. We kissed the girls and they held fast to us. Before this night we had been only boys, holding hands with girls in movies, not quite sure why we pursued them and acted silly. Now, lying beneath the open sky, for the first time we understood the poignance and the beauty of the human heritage.

Every night for two weeks we came to see them. And when they told us good-by the last kiss was as much a discovery as the first, and we knew that love was a thing that could never grow old. After they

had gone we would steal from our cabins to sit on the back porch of
the camp hospital, on a hill, where we could see the bayou and the
cove and the woods where we had found them; and we sat there
talking late into the night, like daemon lovers in the ballads of old.
I never passed the cove again, even years later when I would paddle
down the bayou fishing, without remembering our meetings with a
suddenly racing heart. First love is unforgettable.

V

I had no lessons to do in those summer months of camp life. There
was plenty of time to think. I was living a communal life with other
boys. Among us were embryonic bullies, scoundrels, cheats, promoters,
Babbitts, Christers, and stuffed shirts; and there were also the boys
of good heart, the unselfish, the humorous, the courageous, boys who
were the salt of the earth, but who, often in their later lives, would
be misled and preyed upon and set against one another by the sharp
ones. One and all we lived together, ate together, slept together. Our
personalities clashed, fermented, or formed amalgams. Sitting together
at night in the lamplit cabins, with darkness and towering woods
closing in upon us, we had our first grave talks about religion, about
death, about sex. The future stretching before us was wide and fathom-
less. And all about us, in the grass, in the underbrush, in towering
summer skies, we beheld the face of nature and the earth's wide
harmonies as they had never been revealed in our city lives. At night
we could stretch out upon the field, observe the stars, and grasp for
the first time the fact that some were vastly deeper in space than
others. In our star-study courses we heard phrases like "light years."
It began to seep into the consciousness of many of us that a hundred
years or the life of an individual had little meaning in the total
universe; and from this point some of us began our first gropings
after moral philosophy, gropings for a belief that could give the total
universe a meaning in our own lives.

There was a bugler in our camp who was the first consummate
expert, in any field, that I had known. He had no other talent but
his music. He was a good-natured, chubby, curly-headed Italian boy,
rather lazy, and when he was not back in the woods practicing his
cornet he walked round with a dreamy look, as though our own
handicrafts could not possibly be of interest to him.

Paolo had a silver trumpet and he preferred it to the bugle. He wanted to be a great musician. He would take his horn and music back into a pine clearing a quarter of a mile from the camp and all day long we could hear him practicing the runs. He blew the trumpet with a clear, sweet tone. We had supreme confidence as we stood at attention on the parade grounds and the flag came down the creaking flagpole pulley in the late afternoon sunlight, and Paolo stood alone, with everyone watching, and bugled. We were proud of him when visitors came. He had that ability of experts to create a sense of possessiveness in others.

It was at bedtime that Paolo gathered up into his clear, thin music all the ineffable hungering of our awakening lives. At ten o'clock he climbed a high ladder to a life-guard platform we had nailed into the branches of a tall cypress tree beside the bayou. Paolo lived for this moment and, with the whole camp silent and listening below him in the darkness, he blew taps with a soft and ghostly beauty all his own. Somehow the music spoke for us, uttered the thing we knew but had no words for, set up a wailing in the pine trees of the brevity and splendor of human life. Lying in our bunks in the darkness of the cabin, some of us fell into sleep; but some lay in silence thinking longer, alive to the night, and I was of these.

One night some ten years later I entered a smoke-filled tavern in another city where Paolo was playing in a band. By this time he had made a small reputation as a boy with a hot trumpet. I watched his now older face as he tore through the hot routines. He was tired. The silver horn made noise but, though I knew little about it, I could see that he was not a great jazz musician.

I did not go to see him any more. I wanted to remember Paolo before he had lost something, before any of us had lost it, a kind of innocence. I wanted to remember him in the land of our first discoveries, when he had climbed into a cypress tree to blow his horn, and there was a kind of Gothic night-drench in our lives.

GUIDE QUESTIONS

1. How is the theme or controlling idea of the essay implied in the first paragraph? How are the principal topics of the essay announced in the second paragraph, and what have they to do with the theme?

2. Why does Sancton emphasize the facts that he was a city boy and a poor boy?

3. What is suggested by the statement, "He did not remember about the hat"? How are this statement and the incident it concludes related to the theme which Sancton develops in the rest of the essay?

4. The first section creates the impression that the essay as a whole will consist chiefly of (a) descriptions of the physical appearance of the camp, (b) exposition of the pleasures of being a Boy Scout, (c) incidents that happened at the camp told for their own sake, (d) reflections on youth and a boy's formulation of his philosophy. Only one of these is correct. Which one? What difference would it make in the final effect of the essay if any of the other three were correct?

5. Consider section II. Why is a whole section devoted to the Negro, Joe? Why does Sancton say "there was nothing servile" about Joe's relations with the boys? Explain: "Already a dark, subjective understanding of Louisiana's history was in our blood and bones." What does the last paragraph of this section contribute to the developing theme of the essay?

6. Section III begins by saying, "a love grew up in me for the rhythms of nature," but the first part of it mentions religious services. What is the connection?

7. Look up the word *poignant*. Then explain fully why the statement, "First love is unforgettable," in view of the events leading up to it here, can be called poignant.

8. How does the story of Paolo in section V serve to draw the parts together and make clear Sancton's purpose throughout the essay? State this purpose.

9. The writer ends by saying that in the boyhood he recalls "there was a kind of Gothic night-drench in our lives." What does he mean?

10. Notice the many details that appeal to one or more of the senses of sight, hearing, taste, touch, and smell. What quality do these details give to Sancton's writing? Pick out particular details that seem to you especially vivid.

11. With what experiences that you have had, whether or not like those related by Sancton, do you associate your own "first real living" and "first real thinking"?

VOCABULARY

Give the derivations and definitions of the following words:

picaroon, pirogue, pretentious, subjective, Cajun, servile, circumscribed, luminous, mimicry, brackish, lorelei, intoned, audacity, embryonic, amalgam.

WRITING AND STUDY AIDS

PATTERN OF ORGANIZATION SUGGESTED BY THE GENERAL TOPIC:

In autobiographical writing, one of the principal difficulties lies in establishing and maintaining a suitable level of detail. Not even the most commonplace life, or the first fifteen or twenty years of one, can be written down complete in a thousand words; or if it is, the result is dull. Since you can not hope to record everything that has happened to you, select from your recollections a few experiences that you recall with special clarity. These experiences should have some variety of interest and implication. For example, prowess in athletics can be illustrated by one anecdote; a second to the same effect would be superfluous. Another difficulty in writing autobiography arises from the necessity of seeing yourself as you were at some time in the past. Even though you may be writing about the recent past, bear in mind that you are trying to recreate what you thought and felt then, not what you think and feel now. It is important to maintain a single, consistent point of view, that of the person you were at the time of the events you are relating.

After you have made a selection of manageable materials, and after you have decided who and what you were at that period of your life, develop each experience completely and carefully, giving it a specific setting in place and time, and giving each character introduced an individual personality. In a short theme, one experience will probably be all you can handle; in a long theme, several experiences—but not too many—may be effectively presented.

The readings you have studied offer models and suggestions for the kind of self-revelation you might undertake. Autobiography can be written in different ways. It may consist of an account of one's family background, of direct self-analysis, of incidents illustrating the strains or the pleasures of being a child, of people and places and self-discoveries that have contributed to your personal development. If an experience has some special significance in your private way of regarding life, by all means tell what the significance is. Any autobiographical paper will have more value, both for you and for your reader, if you avoid fictional embroidery and adhere strictly to the truth.

ASSIGNMENTS:

Short themes:

1. Choosing one's parents
2. In praise of grandmothers/grandfathers/aunts/uncles
3. Are brothers and sisters necessary?
4. My first day at school
5. I learned the hard way
6. On finding reading a pleasure
7. Innocence/Disillusionment
8. I was born unlucky
9. Small fry
10. That Christmas
11. Scouting
12. Pets
13. A city kid's childhood
14. On getting acquainted with new places
15. Where are they now?

Long themes:

1. Getting started in college
2. A personal inventory
3. "Where I come from. . . ."
4. Heredity and/or environment
5. Reminiscences of a pleasant childhood
6. The happiest days of my life
7. Beginnings of personal philosophy
8. People and places
9. Me

READINGS FOR FURTHER STUDY:

Augustine, Saint (Aurelius Augustinus). *Confessions.*

Austin, Mary. *Earth Horizon.* Boston: Houghton Mifflin Company, 1932.

Canby, Henry Seidel. *American Memoir.* Boston: Houghton Mifflin Company, 1947.

Cellini, Benvenuto. *Autobiography.*

Chase, Mary Ellen. *A Goodly Heritage.* New York: Henry Holt and Company, 1932.

Clemens, Samuel L. (Mark Twain). *Autobiography.* New York: Harper and Brothers, 1929. Stormfield edition, Vol. 1, 93-129.

Dell, Floyd. *Homecoming*. New York: Farrar and Rinehart, Inc., 1933. Pages 3-180.

Franklin, Benjamin. *Autobiography*. Edited by A. H. Smyth. New York: The Macmillan Company, 1905.

Rousseau, Jean-Jacques. *Confessions*. New York: Alfred A. Knopf, 1923. Pages 13-105.

Scudder, Vida Dutton. *On Journey*. New York: E. P. Dutton and Company, 1937. Pages 15-96.

Skinner, Cornelia Otis. *Family Circle*. Boston: Houghton Mifflin Company, 1948.

Steffens, Lincoln. *Autobiography*. New York: Harcourt, Brace and Company, 1931. Pages 3-166.

Wagenknecht, Edward, editor. *When I Was a Child*. New York: E. P. Dutton and Company, 1946.

White, William Allen. *Autobiography*. New York: The Macmillan Company, 1946.

Interesting People

THE NOVELIST JOHN GALSWORTHY ONCE SAID THAT THE BEST POSSIBLE PLOT was a human being, implying that no other element in a work of fiction is as important as the people in it. Modern critics of the short story, by stressing character as the most essential single ingredient in that art form, seem to agree with him. In other types of writing, too, in biography and its allies —character sketch, interview, feature article—frequently in the essay, and even in historical writing, the portrayal of human personality becomes a prime objective. Many kinds of written discourse with which you are familiar derive part of their forcefulness and appeal from what may be called "human interest," a general term of broad applicability.

The fact is that we are insatiably curious about our fellow men. Certain psychologists would explain this by affirming that the second most interesting topic in the world to any person is some other person—the most interesting being himself. Whether or not we accept this view, it is undeniable that many of our judgments and opinions on a wide variety of matters are formed on the basis of our knowledge or supposed knowledge of the behavior of the human animal, a creature of endless diversity. Fortunately, since an understanding of individual character is highly useful to us, nothing comes more naturally to us than the study of it.

In the readings for this assignment you will find a number of persons— dead or alive—who are worth attention. Not only are they interesting in themselves, but also interesting are the methods by which they are portrayed. Lytton Strachey, in his portrait of "John Aubrey," who was himself an early characterizer of persons, displays the sense of detail and the historical imagination that have made him one of the most discerning of modern biographers. Virginia Woolf's first impression of an unknown traveling companion, whom she calls "Mrs. Brown," shows what anyone can do in this direction if he exercises his natural interest in people with a little ingenuity and insight. Inherently more intimate than these sketches is A. A. Milne's description of his mother, a model of affectionate yet dispassionate reminiscence. Max Miller's "Slats" is a realistic picture of a boyhood playmate that may remind you of your own younger days; it is in short story form and is made vivid by action and dialogue. Finally, Irwin Edman's candid account of one of his college teachers, who happened to be one of America's foremost philosophers, should suggest to you that teachers as a class offer excellent material for the study of character. As you read these selections, try to determine just what it is that makes each of these persons memorable; again, you should observe that varied methods of presentation may result in successful characterization.

Lytton Strachey

JOHN AUBREY

IF ONE WERE ASKED to choose a date for the beginning of the modern world, probably July 15, 1662, would be the best to fix upon. For on that day the Royal Society was founded, and the place of Science in civilization became a definite and recognized thing. The sun had risen above the horizon; and yet, before that, there had been streaks of light in the sky. The great age of Newton was preceded by a curious twilight period—a period of gestation and preparation, confused, and only dimly conscious of the end towards which it was moving. It might be called, perhaps, the age of Hobbes, whose half-mediaeval, half-modern mind was the dominating influence over intellects which came to maturity in the middle years of the century. Another even more typical, though less eminent, representative of this embryonic generation was John Aubrey (1626-1697). Aubrey was among those chosen by the first President and Council to be the first Fellows of the Royal Society; and he was extremely proud of the distinction. But in reality the scientific movement which gave the Royal Society its significance did not mean very much to him. His mind moved in a circle of ideas which was rapidly becoming obsolete, and which, so long as our civilization lasts, can never come into existence again.

His life was not a fortunate one. Born a country gentleman, with estates in Brecknockshire, Herefordshire, and Wiltshire, and educated at Trinity College, Oxford, his happy studies at the University were interrupted by the Civil Wars, and his considerable possessions were dissipated in a long series of unsuccessful lawsuits. In 1666, he tells us, "all my businesses and affairs ran kim kam; nothing took effect"; and the words are applicable to the whole of his life. It was not only luck that was against him; he was by nature an amiable muddler; in love and in literature, no less than in business, it was always the same —"nothing took effect." Neither Madam Jane Codrington, nor "that incomparable good conditioned gentlewoman, Mistress M. Wiseman, with whom at first sight I was in love," would smile upon him; and though "domina Katherina Ryves," with a dowry of £2,000, was kinder, just as she was about to marry him she died. He sought distraction abroad, but without success. "In 1664, in August," he noted, "had a terrible fit of the spleen, and piles, at Orleans." Yet worse was to follow: "In an ill hour," he began to make his addresses to Joan Sumner, whose cruelty was more than negative. She had him arrested in Chancery Lane, and for three years pursued him with lawsuits. His ruin followed; all his broad lands vanished; even Easton Piers, the house of his birth, with its terraced gardens, its "jedeau," its grotto and "volant Mercury," had to be sold; even his books went at last. By 1670 poor Aubrey had lost everything. But then, unexpectedly, happiness descended upon him. Free at last from the struggles of love and law and the tedious responsibilities of property, he found himself in a "sweet *otium*." "I had never quiet, nor anything of happiness till divested of all," he wrote. "I was in as much affliction as a mortal could be, and never quiet till all was gone, and I wholly cast myself on God's providence."

God's providence, in Aubrey's case, took the form of a circle of kindly friends, who were ready enough to give him food and shelter in town and country, in return for the benefit of his "most ingenious conversation." He would spend the winter in London—often with Sir William Petty or Sir Christopher Wren,—and then, with the spring, he would ride off on a round of visits—to Lord Thanet's in Kent, to the Longs in Wiltshire, to Edmund Wylde in Shropshire—until the autumn came, and he would turn his horse's head back to London. Grumpy Anthony Wood might write him down "a shiftless person, roving and maggoty-headed, and sometimes little better than crazed"; but his boon companions thought otherwise. They relished to the full the extraordinary quantity and the delightful variety of his information, and could never tire of his engaging manner of presenting it. "My head," he said himself, "was always working; never idle, and even travelling did glean some observations, of which I have a collection in folio of 2 quires of paper and a dust basket, some whereof are to be valued."

His inquiries were indeed indefatigable; he was learned in natural history, geology, Gothic architecture, mineralogy, painting, heraldry; he collected statistics, he was a profound astrologer, and a learned geometrician; he wrote a treatise on education; even the mysteries of cookery did not elude him, and he compiled "a collection of approved receipts." Before he died he had written sufficient to fill several volumes; but, characteristically enough, he brought only one book to the point of publication: his *Miscellanies,* in which he briefly discussed such fascinating subjects as "Apparitions, Impulses, Knockings, Blows Invisible, Prophecies, Marvels, Magic, Transportation in the Air, Visions in a Bevel or Glass, Converse with Angels and Spirits, Corpse-Candles in Wales, Glances of Love and Envy, and Second-Sighted Persons in Scotland." It is in this book, in the chapter on Apparitions, that the sentence occurs which so much delighted Mr. Jonathan Oldbuck of Monkbarns: "*Anno* 1670, not far from Cirencester, was an apparition; being demanded, whether a good spirit, or a bad? returned no answer, but disappeared with a curious perfume and most melodious twang."

Certainly the learned Ray was right when he said of his friend that he was "a little inclinable to credit strange relations." Yet it would be an error to dismiss Aubrey as a mere superstitious trifler; he was something more interesting than that. His insatiable passion for singular odds and ends had a meaning in it; he was groping towards a scientific ordering of phenomena; but the twilight of his age was too confusing, and he could rarely distinguish between a fact and a fantasy. He was clever enough to understand the Newtonian system, but he was not clever enough to understand that a horoscope was an absurdity; and so, in his crowded curiosity-shop of a brain, astronomy and astrology both found a place, and were given equal values. When fortune favoured him, however, he could make real additions to knowledge. He was the first English archaeologist, and his most remarkable achievement was the discovery of the hitherto unknown Druidical temple of Avebury. Encouraged by Charles II, he made a careful survey of the great stone circle, writing a dissertation upon it and upon Stonehenge, and refuting the theory of Inigo Jones, who, in order to prove that the latter was Roman, had given an entirely factitious account of it. As he rode over the Wiltshire downs, hawking with Colonel Long, he had ample opportunities for these antiquarian investigations. "Our sport," he wrote, "was very good, and in a romantic country, for the prospects are noble and vast, the downs stocked with numerous flocks of sheep, the turf rich and fragrant with thyme and burnet; nor are the nut-brown shepherdesses without their graces. But the flight of the falcons was but a parenthesis to the Colonel's facetious discourse, who was *tam Marti quam Mercurio,* and the Muses did accompany him with his hawks and spaniels."

The country was charming; but London too was full of pleasures, and the winter nights passed swiftly with wine and talk. For the company was excellent. There was Robert Hooke "that invented the pendulum-watches, so much more useful than the other watches," and a calculating machine, and hundreds of other contrivances—"he believes not fewer than a thousand"—and who declared he had forestalled Mr. Newton; and there was Dr. Tonge, who had first taught children to write by means of copper-plates, and left behind him "two tomes in folio of alchemy"; and Francis Potter, the first to practise the transfusion of blood, who, at 10 o'clock in the morning of December 10, 1625, as he was going upstairs, had discovered "the mystery of the Beast"; and John Pell, the inventor of the division-sign in arithmetic, who "has said to me that he did believe that he solved some questions *non sine divino auxilio."* And then the gentle gossip went back to earlier days—to old Mr. Oughtred, Sir Christopher's master, who "taught all free," and was an astrologer, though he confessed "that he was not satisfied how it came about that one might foretell by the stars, but so it was," and whose "wife was a penurious woman, and would not allow him to burn candle after supper, by which means many a good notion is lost, and many a problem unsolved"; and so back to a still more remote and bizarre past—to Dr. John Dee, of Queen Elizabeth's time, "who wore a gown like an artist's gown, with hanging sleeves and a slit," made plates of gold "by projection," and "used to distill eggshells."

Aubrey lived on into old age—vague, precise, idle, and busy to the last. His state of life, he felt, was not quite satisfactory. He was happy; but he would have been happier still in some other world. He regretted the monasteries. He wished "the reformers had been more moderate on that point." It was "fit there should be receptacles and provision for contemplative men"; and "what a pleasure 'twould have been to have travelled from monastery to monastery!" As it was, he did the next best thing—he travelled from country house to country house. In the summer of 1697, when he was over seventy, as he was riding through Oxford on his way to Lady Long's, he was seized with sudden illness, and his journeying was ended for ever.

In the great mass of papers that he left behind him it was hardly to be supposed that there could be anything of permanent value. Most of the antique science was already out of date at his death. But it so happened that Aubrey's appetite for knowledge had carried him into a field of inquiry which, little explored in his own day, attracts the greatest interest in ours. He was an assiduous biographer. Partly to help the ungrateful Anthony Wood in the compilation of his *Athenae Oxonienses,* but chiefly for his own delight, Aubrey was in the habit of jotting down on scraps of paper every piece of information he could acquire concerning both his own contemporaries and the English worthies of previous generations. He was accurate, he had an unfailing eye for what was interesting, and he possessed—it was almost inevitable in those days—a natural gift of style. The result is that his *Short Lives* (which have been admirably edited for the Clarendon Press by Mr. Andrew Clark) are not only an authority of the highest importance upon seventeenth-century England, but one of the most readable of books. A biography should either be as long as Boswell's or as short as Aubrey's. The method of enormous and elaborate accretion which produced the *Life of Johnson* is excellent, no doubt; but, failing that, let us have no half-measures; let us have the pure essentials—a vivid image, on a page or two, without explanations, transitions, commentaries, or padding. This is what Aubrey gives us; this, and one thing more—a sense of the pleasing, anxious being who, with his odd old alchemy, has transmuted a few handfuls of orts and relics into golden life.

GUIDE QUESTIONS

1. To what extent does Strachey give the "facts" of Aubrey's life, such as dates? Would more of these be a hindrance or a help?
2. Why does Strachey mention so many of Aubrey's friends? What connection can you see between this feature of the account and Aubrey's manner of life after he had lost all his worldly possessions?
3. Notice the way in which Aubrey is allowed to characterize himself through frequent quotations from his own writings. What is the advantage of this technique?
4. Why, if Aubrey was a learned man in so many fields of knowledge, does Strachey indicate that his learning was largely useless?
5. Is Strachey's attitude toward his subject (a) condescending, (b) indulgent, (c) contemptuous, or (d) admiring? Defend your choice.
6. In what way is the theme or controlling idea of Strachey's essay clearly established in the first paragraph?
7. Observe carefully Strachey's remarks in his last paragraph on the problem of this assignment—the characterization of a person. Tell why you agree or disagree with what he says about the art of biography.
8. Read the account of John Aubrey in the *Dictionary of National Biography*. What qualities does Strachey's essay have that the other lacks?

VOCABULARY

Give the derivations and definitions of the following words:

gestation, embryonic, volant, divest, insatiable, fantasy, horoscope, Druid, factitious, facetious, penurious, bizarre, assiduous, accretion, ort.

Virginia Woolf

MRS. BROWN

MY FIRST ASSERTION is one that I think you will grant—that everyone is a judge of character. Indeed it would be impossible to live for a year without disaster unless one practiced character-reading and had some skill in the art. Our marriages, our friendships depend on it; our business largely depends on it; every day questions arise which can only be solved by its help. . . . But it is the art of the young. In middle age and in old age the art is practiced mostly for its uses, and friendships and other adventures and experiments in the art of reading character are seldom made. But novelists differ from the rest of the world because they do not cease to be interested in character when they have learned enough about it for practical purposes. They go a step further, they feel that there is something permanently interesting in character in itself. When all the practical business of life has been discharged, there is something about people which continues to seem to them of overwhelming importance, in spite of the fact that it has no bearing whatever upon their happiness, comfort, or income. The study of character becomes to them an absorbing pursuit; to impart character an obsession. And this I find very difficult to explain: what novelists mean when they talk about character, what the impulse is that urges them so powerfully every now and then to embody their view in writing.

So, if you will allow me, instead of analysing and abstracting, I will tell you a simple story which, however pointless, has the merit of being true, of a journey from Richmond to Waterloo, in the hope that I may show you what I mean by character in itself; that you may realize the different aspects it can wear; and the hideous perils that beset you directly you try to describe it in words.

One night some weeks ago, then, I was late for the train and jumped into the first carriage I came to. As I sat down I had the strange and uncomfortable feeling that I was interrupting a conversation between two people who were already sitting there. They were both elderly, the woman over sixty, the man well over forty. They were sitting opposite each other, and the man, who had been leaning over and talking emphatically to judge by his attitude and the flush on his face, sat back and became silent. I had disturbed him, and he was annoyed. The elderly lady, however, whom I will call Mrs. Brown, seemed rather relieved. She was one of those clean, threadbare old ladies whose extreme tidiness—everything buttoned, fastened, tied together, mended and brushed up—suggests more extreme poverty than rags and dirt. There was something pinched about her—a look of suffering, of apprehension, and, in addition, she was extremely small. Her feet, in their clean little boots, scarcely touched the floor. I felt that she had nobody to support her; that she had to make up her mind for herself; that, having been deserted, or left a widow, years ago, she had led an anxious, harried life, bringing up an only son, perhaps, who, as likely as not, was by this time beginning to go to the bad. All this shot through my mind as I sat down, being uncomfortable, like most people, at travelling with fellow passengers unless I have somehow or other accounted for them. Then I looked at the man. He was no relation of Mrs. Brown's I felt sure; he was of a bigger, burlier, less refined type. He was a man of business I imagined, very likely a respectable corn-chandler from the North, dressed in good blue serge with a pocket-knife and a silk handkerchief, and a stout leather bag. Obviously, however, he had an unpleasant business to settle with Mrs. Brown; a secret, perhaps sinister business, which they did not intend to discuss in my presence.

"Yes, the Crofts have had very bad luck with their servants," Mr. Smith (as I will call him) said in a considering way, going back to some earlier topic, with a view to keeping up appearances.

"Ah, poor people," said Mrs. Brown, a trifle condescendingly. "My grandmother had a maid who came when she was fifteen and stayed till she was eighty" (this was said with a kind of hurt and aggressive pride to impress us both perhaps).

"One doesn't often come across that sort of thing nowadays," said Mr. Smith in conciliatory tones.

Then they were silent.

"It's odd they don't start a golf club there—I should have thought one of the young fellows would," said Mr. Smith, for the silence obviously made him uneasy.

Mrs. Brown hardly took the trouble to answer.

"What changes they're making in this part of the world," said Mr. Smith, looking out of the window, and looking furtively at me as he did so.

It was plain, from Mrs. Brown's silence, from the uneasy affability with which Mr. Smith spoke, that he had some power over her which he was exerting disagreeably. It might have been her son's downfall, or some painful episode in her past life, or her daughter's. Perhaps she was going to London to sign some document to make over some property. Obviously against her will she was in Mr. Smith's hands. I was beginning to feel a great deal of pity for her, when she said, suddenly and inconsequently:

"Can you tell me if an oak-tree dies when the leaves have been eaten for two years in succession by caterpillars?"

She spoke quite brightly, and rather precisely, in a cultured, inquisitive voice.

Mr. Smith was startled, but relieved to have a safe topic of conversation given him. He told her a great deal very quickly about plagues of insects. He told her that he had a brother who kept a fruit farm in Kent. He told her what fruit farmers do every year in Kent, and so on, and so on. While he talked a very odd thing happened. Mrs. Brown took out her little white handkerchief and began to dab her eyes. She was crying. But she went on listening quite composedly to what he was saying, and he went on talking, a little louder, a little angrily, as if he had seen her cry often before; as if it were a painful habit. At last it got on his nerves. He stopped abruptly, looked out of the window, then leaned towards her as he had been doing when I got in, and said in a bullying, menacing way, as if he would not stand any more nonsense:

"So about that matter we were discussing. It'll be all right? George will be there on Tuesday?"

"We shan't be late," said Mrs. Brown, gathering herself together with superb dignity.

Mr. Smith said nothing. He got up, buttoned his coat, reached his bag down, and jumped out of the train before it had stopped at Clapham Junction. He had got what he wanted, but he was ashamed of himself; he was glad to get out of the old lady's sight.

Mrs. Brown and I were left alone together. She sat in her corner opposite, very clean, very small, rather queer, and suffering intensely. The impression she made was overwhelming. It came pouring out like a draught, like a smell of burning. What was it composed of— that overwhelming and peculiar impression? Myriads of irrelevant and incongruous ideas crowd into one's head on such occasions; one sees the person, one sees Mrs. Brown, in the centre of all sorts of different scenes. I thought of her in a seaside house, among queer ornaments: sea-urchins, models of ships in glass cases. Her husband's medals were on the mantel-piece. She popped in and out of the room, perched on the edges of chairs, picking meals out of saucers, indulging in long, silent stares. The caterpillars and the oak-trees seemed to imply all that. And then, into this fantastic and secluded life, in broke Mr. Smith. I saw him blowing in, so to speak, on a windy day. He banged, he slammed. His dripping umbrella made a pool in the hall. They sat closeted together.

And then Mrs. Brown faced the dreadful revelation. She took her heroic decision. Early, before dawn, she packed her bag and carried it herself to the station. She would not let Smith touch it. She was wounded in her pride, unmoored from her anchorage; she came of gentlefolks who kept servants—but details could wait. The important thing was to realize her character, to steep oneself in her atmosphere. I had no time to explain why I felt it somewhat tragic, heroic, yet with a dash of the flighty and fantastic, before the train stopped, and I watched her disappear, carrying her bag, into the vast blazing station. She looked very small, very tenacious; at once very frail and very heroic. And I have never seen her again, and I shall never know what became of her.

The story ends without any point to it. But I have not told you this anecdote to illustrate either my own ingenuity or the pleasure of travelling from Richmond to Waterloo. What I want you to see in it is this. Here is a character imposing itself upon another person. Here is Mrs. Brown making someone begin almost automatically to write a novel about her. I believe that all novels begin with an old lady in the corner opposite. I believe that all novels, that is to say, deal with character, and that it is to express character—not to preach doctrines, sing songs, or celebrate the glories of the British Empire, that the form of the novels, so clumsy, verbose, and undramatic, so rich, elastic, and alive, has been evolved. To express character, I have said; but you will at once reflect that the very widest interpretation can be put upon those words. For example, old Mrs. Brown's character will strike you very differently according to the age and country in which you happen to be born. It would be easy enough to write three different versions of that incident in the train, an English, a French, and a Russian. The English writer would make the old lady into a "character"; he would bring out her oddities and mannerisms; her buttons and wrinkles; her ribbons and warts. Her personality would dominate the book. A French writer would rub out all that; he would sacrifice the individual Mrs. Brown to give a more general view of human nature; to make a more abstract, proportioned, and harmonious whole. The Russian would pierce through the flesh; would reveal the soul—the soul alone, wandering out into the Waterloo Road, asking of life some tremendous question which would sound on and on in our ears after the book was finished. And then besides age and country there is the writer's temperament to be considered. You see one thing in character, and I another. You say it means this, and I that. And when it comes to writing each makes a further selection on principles of his own. Thus Mrs. Brown can be treated in an infinite variety of ways, according to the age, country, and temperament of the writer.

GUIDE QUESTIONS

1. Comment on the statements that "everyone is a judge of character," but that character-judging "is the art of the young."
2. How can you account for the fact that novelists never cease to be interested in the youthful art of character-judging?
3. Analyze the order or arrangement of the details and impressions concerning Mrs. Brown and Mr. Smith which Mrs. Woolf says "shot through my mind as I sat down." Why do the details proceed from the general to the particular? How long do you estimate that it took the author to form an impression of "all this"?
4. Relate to your own experience while traveling the author's statement that she was "uncomfortable, like most people, at traveling with fellow passengers unless I have somehow or other accounted for them."
5. Invent another interpretation of Mrs. Brown's background, character, and present situation.
6. Mrs. Woolf says the story is "pointless" and "ends without any point at all." Clearly this is not to be taken literally. What is her particular point in telling the story? What other, larger point does it have?
7. Which version of the incident in the train do you think would be most interesting—the English, French, or Russian? Discuss.

VOCABULARY

Give the derivations and definitions of the following words:

obsession, embody, abstracting, apprehension, harried, chandler, furtively, affability, tenacious, verbose.

A. A. Milne

MY MOTHER

MY MOTHER CAME, as novelists say, of "good yeoman stock," or, more simply, was a farmer's daughter. At least, I think she was, but I am as uncertain of the farmer as of the stone-mason. When my father met her, she was keeping a School for Young Ladies. This piece of family history, which we picked up as children, never seemed authentic; for it was part of our creed that Papa knew everything, and Mama knew nothing. She didn't even know that *mensā* meant "by, with or from a table" until we told her, and our daily triumphs over Euclid aroused an enthusiasm unrelated, only too obviously, to the proportions of the victory. This, which we were learning, was Knowledge; this was what was taught in schools. Mama teaching! How funny.

But I see now that it is what clever women teach in girls' schools which is funny. My mother's girls were taught to be good wives to hard-working men, and there was never anybody so good as she at that. She could do everything better than the people whom so reluctantly she came to employ: cook better than the cook, dust better than the parlourmaid, make a bed better than the housemaid, mend better than the sewingmaid, wash clothes better than the laundress, bandage better than the matron. She was simple, she was unemotional, she was common-sensible. Nothing upset her. At one of those inevitable end-of-term entertainments Father would be twittering like a sparrow with nervousness, wondering if the claret-cup would go round, and whether he would remember Tommy Tucker's parents, whom last term he had mistaken for Peter Piper's; and Mother would be completely calm, knowing that if there weren't enough claret-cup, it was all they were going to get, and that if she mistook Mrs. Tucker for Mrs. Piper, as she always did, it wouldn't matter, as she would probably call them both Mrs. Hogbin. She was a great believer in the name of Hogbin, and often offered it to Father as a solution of the difficulties which a bad memory brought him. Somewhere, at some time, I suppose, she had met a Mr. Hogbin, and was always expecting to hear of him again; or of some of his family; or of the village, Hogbin, from which he derived. We nearly traced him once: "a man with a funny moustache who used to come about the gas." But on going into the matter we discovered that this man's name was Pedder, and he was clean-shaven. "Well, I know I used to call *him* Mr. Hogbin," insisted Mother, to show that there was a good deal to be said for her side of the argument. There always was. Once, at dinner, when Father was telling us proudly, as if partly responsible for it, that Light travelled at the rate of 150,000 miles a second, our awed silence was broken by Mother's simple announcement from the other end of the dinner-table: "I don't believe it." What the answer to that is I don't know, nor did Father ever discover it.

They had musical evenings at Mother's school, and that nice, shy Mr. Milne, the new master at the boys' school, was a great addition to the parties, for not only was he religious-minded (which meant something in those days) but he played accompaniments on the flute. And when he had got over his shyness, he talked a lot of nonsense which made the ladies laugh, and you felt somehow that you could trust him. And he was brave. Because one Sunday the Headmaster had preached a sermon to the boys, in which he told them that they were all going straight to Hell, or anyhow the boys who hadn't attended in class last week, and he described Hell in words which would terrify anybody who knew that he was going there. And that nice little Mr. Milne got permission to preach to the boys on the next Sunday, and he told them that there was no such place as Hell, and no such thing as Everlasting Fire, but that they would all be very silly if they didn't work now, when work was made easy for them, because it would mean that they would have to work much harder later on, when it wouldn't be so interesting. And then he had offered the Headmaster his resignation, but the Headmaster wouldn't hear of it, and said that he was sorry, and that perhaps there wasn't Everlasting Fire after all. So that nice Mr. Milne would be there next Thursday as usual, with his flute.

He was there, and when he said good-night to Mother, he left a note in her hand, asking her to marry him. For he was still very shy.

It was only after my mother's death that I knew she had said "No," and had gone on saying "No" for more than a year to Father's insistent wooing. How hard to realize that one's father, that elderly Olympian, may also have endured the agonies and ecstasies of love, as we have endured them! How hard to believe that one's mother, one's own mother, could have inspired those agonies and ecstasies, and have failed to respond to them, because she too had suffered them on another man's behalf! Father and Mother—who knew nothing of these things!

At the last she accepted him; at the last, perhaps, fell in love with him. Did she? I don't know. I don't think I ever really knew her. When I was a child I neither experienced, nor felt the need of, that mother-love of which one reads so much. I learnt no prayers at my mother's knee, as so many children seem to have done. It was Papa who told us about God, and we who told the governess. No doubt Mama felt that Papa was so good at it that she oughtn't to interfere. She may also have felt that Papa was so good at playing with a child, and amusing a child, and making a child love him, that she oughtn't to interfere there either. Certainly as a child I gave my heart to my father. If he were there, all was well; if he were away, I asked Mama when he was coming back. Later on, when I formed the opinion that, even if Father knew everything, he knew most of it wrong, it was with my mother that I was happier. She didn't argue; she didn't drive the moral home. She was simple; she was wise; she was affectionate. She was restfully aloof. . . .

GUIDE QUESTIONS

1. Milne's style in this selection has been described as "breathless." What does this mean?
2. Milne, in most of his writings, is thought by many critics to be a sentimentalist. To what extent is this vignette of his mother sentimental?
3. Comment on the anecdote intended to show that Milne's father "was brave." Why is this anecdote introduced into a sketch of his mother?
4. What is the basic connection between the first paragraph and the last two sentences of the selection?

VOCABULARY

Give the derivations and definitions of the following words:

authentic, creed, insistent, aloof.

Max Miller

SLATS

HE WAS MUCH TALLER than we were, and our lives centered around him. We called him Slats. He knew so much about freight cars, log-booms, skid-roads and the river that he could have been on earth before.

His exact age I do not remember, nor do I remember my own age at the time, either. But he must have been somewhat older than the rest of us because he always was talking about going to get a sawmill job next summer.

We perhaps were not afraid of him in the true sense of the word, but we always preferred to agree with him in whatever he wanted to do. Nobody his own age or size seemed to be around. There were not many of us in the river neighborhood, anyway, and he either had to play with us or go with the older fellows who already were working. He seemed to be just in between somehow.

The river carried the melted snows of the Cascade Mountains down into Puget Sound. The sawmills were all around the mouth of the river, and their burners at night lit up the sky as though houses were afire. Each mill had its own distinct whistle. The whistles would start blowing at six in the morning. They would wait an hour while the wives of the millmen cooked breakfast, then blow again at seven. The next time they blew was at noon, then at one, then again at five and six.

He could distinguish the different whistles, although there must have been a dozen of them. He would say: "There goes Swanson's," or "There goes the Medley-Clark's." He was the first to make us realize that all the whistles were not just something which made a noise.

The millmen on their way to work in the morning would pass the board fence on the north side of our house. The board fence was so high that only the hats of the men could be seen from the back yard. The hats, faded and covered with sawdust, would bob along the top of the fence almost as though they were cats running along there. On the homeward journey at night the hats usually were followed by a bundle of kindling. The men carried this kindling home by fastening the bundle to a stick slung over the shoulder. Both the hats and the bundles bobbed up and down in jagged discord, but from the back yard the men may as well not have been there at all.

At the beginning, then, sawmills were to me but a manner of going back and forth. As a career for the men of the neighborhood, the mills were quite inevitable. Slats showed us, though, how more could be obtained from them than planer-ends. Each noon his job was to carry his father's lunch to the nearest mill on the river, and whenever we liked we could go along.

Slats started us all hunting for buckskin strips with which to make whips. He showed us how the buckskin could be found beneath the mill, and we made long whips of it by tying the strips together.

"When I'm foreman," he said, "I'll let you have all the buckskin you want. I won't chase you away like they do now."

"You'll never be foreman in a pig's eye," Harold answered. He should not have said this. It made Slats mad. He squeezed his hand around the back of Harold's neck.

"Take that back," Slats ordered, and he squeezed his hand until Harold had to take back what he had said.

"I take it back. I take it back."

But Slats was not contented. He kept his hand there and squeezed again. "Now you say, 'I'm a dirty liar.' Say it."

"I'm a dirty liar."

None of us had known till then how really strong Slats' fingers could be. He himself apparently had not known either, for he began to use the trick on the least excuse. Sometimes he did not have an excuse, so would make one up.

He knew how strict my parents were on making me attend Sunday school. One time about four of us were out in the woods walking down an old skid-road. I forget whether we were on our way to the lake for a swim, or were out hunting chipmunks with our sling-shots. But we were walking along when his fingers closed upon my neck. I had not done anything to him, nor had I said anything. But his fingers were there, anyway, and they began to hurt.

"Tell us what you say when you say your prayers."

"Aw cut it out, Slats, gee."

"Go on. Tell us what you say."

His fingers could have been a big pair of pliers, they hurt so much. I did not know how I could stand it if he squeezed any harder, but he did squeeze harder.

"Then if you won't tell us that, tell us what they do on Market Street."

Market Street was a small block boarded off with a wall as high as the wall around the baseball park. The women who lived inside of it all wore short dresses of green and red and blue. Boys were not allowed through the gate, but we knew how it looked inside because every time we went by there on our way uptown we would peek through the cracks. We always did this as a matter of course. But Slats was the only one of us who ever had gone through the gate. This was when he first had the paper route.

"Come on," he demanded. "Tell us what they do on Market Street."

I knew that God would put me in hell forever if I used the word. But his fingers, when I thought they could not possibly squeeze tighter, did squeeze tighter.

"Come on," he said. "What do they do?"

"They—they—"

"Come on, say it."

So I gurgled the word. He laughed, and released his fingers. I was some time getting back to my feet, for my neck seemed broken.

The firs and cedars, when first I remember, were everywhere and were high. But now in the hills around they were being cut down day by day, even as we watched. Miles of stumps were now the same as miles of tombstones, marking the spot where each tree had met its death. The corpses, barked and scarred, would be brought back to the mills of the town, and we would watch the daily procession. Our grandstand was the river bank.

One game was to count the flat-cars bearing the logs, and another game was to try to catch rides on the log-booms being towed along the river. Slats was so good at riding slippery logs that we asked him why he did not want to be a logger instead of a mill foreman.

He answered that loggers live in camps too far away and never get into town each Saturday night the same as millmen do. He said he was going to get a suit of long pants with his first money next summer, and that he was going to do the lights like the other fellows he knew.

"You ain't big enough to wear long pants." This came from Harold, who should have known better. Slats began to lift his hand, and Harold climbed to his feet to start to run. But Slats caught Harold by the ankle, holding him. We were seated on the bank between the railroad and the river. We heard the whistle for the afternoon passenger train. It always whistled before reaching the trestle about a mile away.

"I mightn't be big enough to wear long pants," Slats said. "But I'm big enough to make you take yours off." He gripped Harold's neck. "Take'm off."

"Wait'll the train passes."

"Take'm off."

"Ow. God. Jesus."

"Take'm off."

Harold began to obey, although he stalled through the pain as long as he could. I could see that he was hoping to outlast Slats' grip until the train passed. Slats apparently suspected this, too, for his knuckles grew whiter.

"Take'm off."

"Aw, go ahead," Andy put in. "If they've seen it before it won't make no difference. If they ain't, they won't know what it is." This had been our stock phrase if ever a train should pass at a distance while we were swimming naked. But we were all a lot closer to the train now, and the phrase did not carry quite as much conviction.

Slats turned to Andy. "Who told you to butt in?"

"Nobody."

"Well, you take yours off too." He grabbed Andy's neck by the other hand. Slats stood back of them, a hand on each neck. Harold and Andy tried to squirm away, but there was no use. Slats' hands were even stronger than we had thought they were. Slowly the two pairs of pants dropped like hobbles around the two pairs of feet, the train rushed by, and the two pairs of pants were permitted to come up again. Harold and Andy sat down on the river grass to rub their necks. But before I could move away, Slats next turned to me.

"And what've you got to say about it?" His fingers already were on my neck. They were not squeezing yet.

"Nothing," I answered quickly.

"I think you're thinking something, though. I think you're thinking that you wish I was dead."

His mind reading amazed me, and his fingers began drawing together. "No, I ain't thinking that at all. I ain't thinking nothing like that. I'm just thinking—"

"Well, what are you just thinking?" His thumb began burrowing inward as though to reach his forefinger on the other side.

"I'm just thinking how swell you'll look uptown in long pants. That's what I'm thinking."

"You sure?"

"Yes. Sure."

"Well, long pants ain't all I'm going to have. I'm going to have a stickpin and gloves. I'm sick of being around with just you kids all my life." He tightened his fingers. "What you got to say to that?"

"Nothing. Ow."

"Can't you say more'n 'Ow'?"

"Yes."

"Well, say it then. Say what Harold said. Say, 'God. Jesus. Ow!' "

"Gahjeesusow."

"There, now. That's better." He released his fingers. "We'll make a man of you yet, won't we, guys?"

"Yes," they chorused through their bruises.

Late that school year the street car company extended its tracks to our neighborhood. The tracks, lined on each side with a dirt road, stopped in front of Mr. Gustavson's grocery store, on the corner. A turntable had been built there for swinging the car around so it could go back uptown again. As soon as the passengers were all out, the motorman and conductor would push the car around, and they did not mind if we helped. Slats said he could push it around all by himself, and one day he did.

The conductor and the motorman, after the car was turned around, usually had a few minutes to wait before going uptown again. They either would go into the grocery store to talk with Mr. Gustavson, or they would sit on the bench in front. But even while they were sitting there, and with nobody in the car at all, the car would begin to rumble on its own accord as though somebody had pushed a switch. Neither the motorman nor the conductor ever seemed to be surprised at this, but the miracle was something which only Slats dared try to explain. "It's stored-up energy," he said. If ever we asked for more particulars, he would answer: "Aw, wait'll you grow up."

After all the passengers were in, and the motorman started the car, we often hooked rides on the outside steps. We would crouch there beneath the glass of the closed door hoping the conductor would not see us. The car would go too fast for us to jump off, and we would have to stay there till the next corner-stop. Slats once rode for three blocks this way, a record. And once he jumped off when the conductor, suspecting that somebody was riding on the outside, folded the doors open without warning. Although the car was going fast, Slats was not hurt.

"There," he said, after walking back to us, "when you can do that you're all right."

We believed him, but when Andy and I had a similar crisis a few evenings later, we failed his faith in us most miserably. The conductor, while the car was in the middle of the block, folded the doors open and found us there. This was the time to jump, but our nerve would not permit it. The conductor dragged us inside to the back platform.

"I'm taking you two to the police station," he said. The passengers in the car turned around to stare at us. They were neighbors. We knew them by name, and they knew who we were. There was nothing we could do except stand there while they stared and smiled, and Andy and I were sure we would be sent to the reform school now.

But the next stop the conductor said: "I'm going to give you one more chance. I'm going to let you off this time, but if I catch you again it's the police station sure for both of you."

We walked back to Slats and he called us a couple of babies. But we did not try to hook any more rides for a long while, and meanwhile school closed, and Slats left us to work in a sawmill.

"I ain't ever going back to school," he announced on the last day, while walking home with Harold and me. "My old man says I don't have to."

"You'll be back," Harold told him. "You'll be back as soon as the Hooky Cop starts around."

"Say, if the Hooky Cop ever starts after me, you know what I'll do to him. I'll do this—" And before either Harold or I knew what was happening, Slats grabbed the back of our necks with those same two hands again, and he banged our heads together. He laughed: "That's to remember me by."

We did not see him much after that, for he went to work at seven and came home at six. I did not even see his hat go by the top of our board fence, as he took another street to the mill. But he must have earned all the money he said he was going to earn because he began going with that older crowd which went uptown each Saturday night. In fact, a Saturday night was the first time we really saw him again.

Andy and I had decided once more to go in for stealing street car rides. I don't know why, but the thought just came to us one evening after we had grown tired of trying to kill bats beneath the corner arc-light. We had tied a short string to a fishpole, and at one end of the string was a tiny bit of paper to resemble a moth. A bat would dart around as though after the imitation moth, and we would try to strike the bat to the ground.

"Hell," Andy said, "this ain't no fun no more. They're too wise."

The street car just then was starting up again from the corner-stop, and we ran and caught onto the outside platform. But we were there hardly a second before the door was folded open by the conductor, the same conductor, and he dragged us inside the same as he had before.

"And now," he said, "you two *are* going to the police station. How do you like that?"

We had nothing to say. The car had more passengers than usual, this being Saturday night. And they all stared around at us again. But on the back platform with the conductor was Slats. Lots of the young fellows did not like to go inside and take seats, as seats were for sissies. So they stood up in back with the conductor. About four other millmen were back there with Slats, and this was one reason we did not recognize him right away. Another reason was that he was an entirely different person now.

His box coat was pressed harder than any of the others', and he gave me special reason to notice his square-toed shoes. I felt a foot pressing down on my own foot. I looked down, saw the polish on the shoe, then followed it up to Slats' face. He had his Indian-head stick-pin. And, sure enough, he had his gloves, too. He permitted me to examine his clothes all I liked, and although I was not in the mood to examine clothes at that moment, they appeared so unusual that I could not help staring at them, anyway. I caught Andy staring at him, too.

"What are you going to do with these two kids?" Slats asked the conductor.

"I'm going to take them to the police station."

"Naw," Slats said. "Let'm have a ride for a ways." He reached his gloved hand into his trouser's pocket and brought out a handful of nickels, dimes and quarters. He displayed the money to the conductor. "Take a couple nickels out o' that."

The conductor did. Slats returned the rest of the money to his pocket. He had not called us by name, nor had he indicated in the slightest that he ever had seen us before. But after another couple of corner-stops, he said: "You two youngsters might as well get off now unless you aim to go to Market Street."

This made all the men on the platform laugh, and they were still laughing when we got off the car.

A week or so after this was when the neighborhood heard of the accident. We heard of it first around noon. We heard at first that Slats had been killed, but this was not true. We heard next that he was bleeding to death, but this was not true, either. We went to his house, but nobody was inside of it. Everybody there had gone to the hospital. Not until the afternoon paper came around did we learn what had really happened. A small story about him was on the second page, but his full name, Gerald C. Shoemaker, appeared so strange in print that we hardly could believe he and Slats were the same person.

In a few days he was brought back to his own house to save hospital board. My parents said it would be all right if I went to see him now. "But you mustn't stay too long, remember."

Slats was propped up in the bed of his room. His face was not hurt at all, but his two arms were outside the quilt. They were bundled up to the elbow. On the dresser were his Indian-head stickpin and his gloves.

"Hello, kid," he said.

"Hello." The room was so filled with the smell of medicine that I felt uncomfortable. I stared at the bandages, then tried to stare some other place. But his eyes followed me, and when they saw me looking at the gloves again, Slats said: "Oh, I see what you came for. Well, you can have them." He called to his mother: "Hey, Ma, give the kid the gloves."

The mother came into the room.

Slats continued: "Yes, and one more thing, Ma. It's up to you from now on to squeeze his neck every so often for me."

The mother tried to laugh, but did not get along so well doing it. I tried to laugh, too, but Slats changed the subject.

"Anyhow," he went on, "I'm going to grow two more in the spring."

GUIDE QUESTIONS

1. Where did the events of the story take place? How much does its vividness depend on details of the physical background or geographical setting?

2. When, approximately, did the events of the story take place? What details give an indication of the time setting?

3. What would be the effect on the story if the geographical setting and the time setting were different? Would this make it necessary to change the character of Slats, and if so, how?

4. Notice that Miller characterizes Slats through action—by what he says, and by what he does. What are the advantages of this method?

5. Does the dialogue sound like the real talk of small boys, or not? Discuss.

6. Throughout most of the story it is clear that the reader's sympathy is directed away from Slats. Tell why you think the reader's sympathy begins to be directed towards Slats (a) in the fully-developed incident of the stolen street car ride, (b) with the pitiful turn at the end, (c) nearer the beginning, or (d) nowhere in the story.

7. If any experiences of your own childhood involve a young bully like Slats, compare them with this account, explaining the resemblances and differences.

VOCABULARY

Give the derivations and definitions of the following words:

inevitable, conviction, stickpin, chorused.

Irwin Edman

JOHN DEWEY

A FIGURE WIDELY KNOWN outside purely academic circles was and is John Dewey. In 1915 his name was already, if not a household, cer-

From *Philosopher's Holiday*, by Irwin Edman. Reprinted by permission of the Viking Press, Inc., New York.

tainly a schoolroom word. His *How We Think* was used in all the
normal schools of the country, and even fashionable ladies dipped into
his far from easy books. I had read almost all of Dewey I could get
hold of by the time I was a senior, but it was not until my first year as
a graduate student that I heard, or, I believe, saw him. His familiar
figure and speech, seeming at first that of a Vermont farmer, the casual
gait, the keen but often absent eyes, seem so familiar now that I can
scarcely believe I did not know them before.

I admit the first lecture was quite a shock, a shock of dullness and
confusion, if that can be said. It was at any rate a disappointment. I
had not found Dewey's prose easy, but I had learned that its difficulty
lay for the most part in its intellectual honesty, which led him to qualify
an idea in one sentence half a page long. In part also it lay in the fact
that this profoundly original philosopher was struggling to find a vocabulary to say what had never been said in philosophy before, to find
a diction that would express with exactness the reality of change and
novelty, philosophical words having been used for centuries to express
the absolute and the fixed. Once one had got used to the long sentences,
with their string of qualifying clauses, to the sobriety, to the lack of
image and of colour, one sensed the liberating force of this philosophy.
Here was not an answer but a quest for light in the living movement
of human experience; in the very precariousness of experience there
lay open to the perplexed human creature the possibilities that peril itself provocatively suggested. I had found here, as have so many of my
generation, a philosophy that, instead of laying down a diagram of an
ideal universe that had nothing to do with the one of actual human
doings and sufferings, opened a vision of conscious control of life, of
a democracy operating through creative intelligence in the liberation of
human capacities and natural goods. In *How We Think* I had learned
that thinking itself was simply a discipline of the animal habit of trial
and error, and of the possible human habit of imagination and foresight. In *Democracy and Education* I had gathered that it was not
in the forms of democratic government that true democracy lay, but
in the substance of intelligent co-operation, largely dependent on education. Dewey was not easy, but once one had mastered his syntax, a
vision of a liberal and liberated commonwealth was one's reward, and
a philosophy that was not only a vision but a challenge.

I was naturally prepared, therefore, to expect something of intellectual excitement from the lectures in "Psychological Ethics." Intellectual excitement was the last term to describe what I experienced that September afternoon. The course came, in the first place, directly after lunch. It was well attended; there were even some fashionably dressed society ladies, for Dewey had become a vogue. But this famous philosopher who had written so much on "Interest in Education," as the essence of the educational process, could not, save by a radical distortion of the term, be said at first hearing to sound interesting. He had none of the usual tricks or gifts of the effective lecturer. He sat at his desk, fumbling with a few crumpled yellow sheets and looking abstractedly out of the window. He spoke very slowly in a Vermont drawl. He looked both very kindly and very abstracted. He hardly seemed aware of the presence of a class. He took little pains to underline a phrase, or emphasize a point, or, so at first it seemed to me, to make any. Occasionally he would apparently realize that people in the back of the room might not hear his quiet voice; he would then accent the next word, as likely as not a preposition or a conjunction. He seemed to be saying whatever came into his head next, and at one o'clock on an autumn afternoon to at least one undergraduate what came next did not always have or seem to have a very clear connexion with what had just gone before. The end of the hour finally came and he simply stopped; it seemed to me he might have stopped anywhere.

But I soon found that it was my mind that had wandered, not John Dewey's. I began very soon to do what I had seldom done in college courses—to take notes. It was then a remarkable discovery to make on looking over my notes to find that what had seemed so casual, so rambling, so unexciting, was of an extraordinary coherence, texture, and brilliance. I had been listening not to the semi-theatrical repetition of a discourse many times made—a fairly accurate description of many academic lectures—I had been listening to a man actually *thinking* in the presence of a class. As one became accustomed to Dewey's technique, it was this last aspect of his teaching that was most impressive— and educative. To attend a lecture of John Dewey was to participate in the actual business of thought. Those pauses were delays in creative thinking, when the next step was really being considered, and for the glib dramatics of the teacher-actor was substituted the enterprise, careful and candid, of the genuine thinker. Those hours came to seem the most arresting educational experiences, almost, I have ever had. One had to be scrupulously attentive and one learned to be so. Not every day or in every teacher does one overhear the palpable processes of thought.

One came to enjoy and appreciate the homely metaphor, "the fork in the road," the child and his first attempts to speak, the New England town meeting, instead of the classical images one had been accustomed to from more obviously eloquent lips. Moreover, if one listened attentively one discovered apophthegm and epigram delivered as casually and sleepily as if they were clichés. I remember one instance. It had been rather a long lecture designed to show that the crucial tests of the morals of a group came in what that group regarded as violations of its conventions. The bell rang. Professor Dewey began to crumple up his notes. "And so," he said, "I think sometimes one can tell more about the morals of our society from the inmates of its jails than from the inmates of its universities." The student next to me who had been semi-dozing stirred in half-alarmed surprise.

I learned later in a seminar to see Dewey's greatest gifts as a teacher, that of initiating inquiry rather than that of disseminating a doctrine. The subject matter of the seminar was innocent enough and removed from the immediacies of current controversy. It was a year's course, meeting every Tuesday afternoon, on "The Logic of John Stuart Mill." The seminar remains in my memory, it must be added, not simply for John Dewey or John Stuart Mill. It consisted, looking back on it and indeed as it appeared then, of a very remarkable group. It included two now well-known professors of philosophy, Brand Blanshard of Swarthmore College and Sterling Lamprecht of Amherst, Paul Blanshard, later to become Commissioner of Accounts under Mayor La Guardia, and Albert C. Barnes, the inventor and manufacturer of Argyrol and collector of French paintings, even then a grey-haired man who used to come up from Philadelphia every week with his secretary expressly to study philosophy with his friend John Dewey.

I do not suppose Professor Dewey said more than five percent of the words actually uttered in that seminar. For the latter consisted largely of papers presented by various members of the group. But one remembered what he said. The subject matter was obviously close to him, for had not Mill been one of the great nineteenth-century leaders of the empirical school of thought; had he not been, in his way, a pragmatist and, like Dewey himself, a liberal? But one noticed particularly Dewey's gift for pointing to the exact difficulty or the exact limitations of a man or a paper; his capacity for sympathetically seeing what a student was driving at, even when he did not quite succeed in saying it, and Dewey's candid expression of his own position or his own prejudices.

One instance of Dewey's frankness comes to my mind. There was among the group a young lady who had come from England where she had studied philosophy with Bertrand Russell at Cambridge. She listened patiently for weeks to Dewey's varied insistence that the truth of an idea was tested by its use. One day she burst out toward the close of the seminar in the sharp, clipped speech of the educated Englishwoman: "But, Professor, I have been taught to believe that true means true; that false means false, that good means good and bad means bad; I don't understand all this talk about more or less true, more or less good. Could you explain more exactly?"

Professor Dewey looked at her mildly for a moment and said: "Let me tell you a parable. Once upon a time in Philadelphia there was a paranoiac. He thought he was dead. Nobody could convince him he was alive. Finally, one of the doctors thought of an ingenious idea. He pricked the patient's finger. 'Now,' he said, 'are you dead?' 'Sure,' said the paranoiac, 'that proves that dead men bleed. . . .' Now I'll say true or false if you want me to, but I'll mean better or worse."

There are all kinds of talents that go to make up a great teacher. Among those not commonly noted in the textbooks are simplicity and candour. These qualities in Dewey even an undergraduate could recognize and understand.

GUIDE QUESTIONS

1. What opinion had Edman formed of Dewey as a philosopher before he came to know Dewey as a teacher?
2. How does Edman emphasize his first shock of disappointment in Dewey's class? What is the over-all first impression produced by the description of Dewey's methods in the classroom?
3. "I had been listening to a man actually *thinking* in the presence of a class." Why does Edman consider this the "most impressive—and educative" thing about Dewey's teaching?
4. Edman says that Dewey's finest quality as a teacher was "that of initiating inquiry." What does this mean?
5. Try to summarize in a couple of sentences Dewey's weaknesses and strong points as a teacher. How does Edman's final estimate compare with your own ideal of a teacher?

6. Read an article on John Dewey in a good encyclopedia. What does Edman's account have that the other lacks?

VOCABULARY

Give the derivations and definitions of the following words:

casual, sobriety, precariousness, perplexed, provocatively, syntax, distortion, abstracted, glib, arresting, scrupulously, palpable, apophthegm, epigram, cliché, disseminating, empirical, pragmatist, paranoiac, ingenious, candour.

WRITING AND STUDY AIDS

PATTERN OF ORGANIZATION SUGGESTED BY THE GENERAL TOPIC:

No single method of organization guarantees a successful characterization of a person. The problem presented by this assignment has varied aspects. The readings you have studied solve it in different ways, but each achieves a measure of success; that is, each of them is a credible portrait of someone who is made worthy of our attention. This can be done by emphasizing an individual's relation to the historical environment that produced him, by putting your imagination to work on a person whom you may have seen only once or with whom your contact may have been entirely casual, by frankly discussing in a highly personal manner someone you know intimately, by using dramatic action and dialogue, or by analyzing the calibre of a mind that has made an impression on your own.

These are the methods used in the readings. Of course there are other methods. For example, you can characterize a person by relating significant and revealing anecdotes about him, or by giving your considered estimate of his personality in straight exposition. In a short theme it would probably be advisable to adopt one method and stick to it. In a long theme, however, you may be able to combine several methods effectively. In any event, be sure which pattern of organization or combination of patterns you are using in your composition, for only by planning what you want to do can you make the person you are characterizing credible and worthy of attention.

ASSIGNMENTS:

Short themes:

1. He reminds me of John Aubrey
2. As I see "Mrs. Brown"

3. On the train/bus/plane
4. A character sketch of father/mother/brother/sister/uncle/aunt
5. There's always one in every class/neighborhood/family
6. A childhood playmate
7. An extraordinary individual
8. My best friend
9. First impressions are always wrong
10. Traits of a teacher I know

Long themes:

1. I want you to meet ———
2. The person who influenced me most in high school
3. The man/girl I want to marry
4. Portrait of a roommate
5. The person I admire/dislike most
6. A characterization of George Washington/Thomas Jefferson/Abraham Lincoln/Franklin D. Roosevelt

READINGS FOR FURTHER STUDY:

Aubrey, John. *Brief Lives*. Edited by Andrew Clark. Oxford: Clarendon Press, 1898. 2 vols. Especially Raleigh, Bacon, Milton, Hobbes.
Bradford, Gamaliel. *Saints and Sinners*. Boston: Houghton Mifflin Company, 1932. And other biographical sketches by the same author.
Eastman, Max. *Heroes I Have Known: Twelve Who Lived Great Lives*. New York: Simon and Schuster, 1942.
Garnett, Richard. "John Aubrey," *Dictionary of National Biography*. Vol. 2, 244-45.
Hook, Sidney. *John Dewey, an Intellectual Portrait*. New York: John Day Company, 1939.
MacLaurin, C. *Post Mortems of Mere Mortals*. Garden City, N. Y.: Doubleday, Doran and Co., 1935.
"The Most Unforgettable Character I've Met," regular feature in *The Reader's Digest*.
Strachey, Lytton. *Eminent Victorians: Cardinal Manning, Dr. Arnold, Florence Nightingale, General Gordon*. New York: The Modern Library, 1933.
Van Loon, Hendrik Willem. *Van Loon's Lives*. New York: Simon and Schuster, 1943.

≈ Success in America

THE SUCCESS STORY HAS BEEN A FAVORITE FROM THE DAYS OF STALWART Horatio Alger to the feature article in this month's *Reader's Digest* called "My Most Unforgettable Character." In the typical success story, as formerly written, the hero ascended from rags to riches by hard work and thrift. In the end he was rewarded with an excellent job, a beautiful wife (who just happened to be the boss's daughter), a fine home, and social prominence. Generally, however, the hero was characterized only vaguely; since his virtue was proved by success, there was no need to analyze it. The rule was this: if a man is good, he will be rich; if he is rich, he must be good.

Such a forthright equation of wealth with virtue is no longer likely to win wide acceptance. It becomes a challenging question, then, to determine what kind of man it is to whom our society actually yields the greatest rewards, the highest success and happiness. Moreover, what kind of success do Americans value most—social recognition, money, power, public popularity? Some thought-provoking answers to every side of this problem are suggested in the readings for this assignment.

In *The American Credo* George Jean Nathan and H. L. Mencken deliver some shrewd jibes at the aspirations of the social climber. They believe that the desire for social advancement characterizes Americans of all classes. Sinclair Lewis, in the selection from *Babbitt*, deals with an embodiment of this type of person in the struggles of his socially ambitious hero, in whom, however, the desire for social success has its basis in a more material desire to "get ahead" in business. These authors are clearly satirizing what they consider a false scale of values. The three sketches by John Dos Passos

66

present three individuals who achieved fame in widely separated fields—finance, entertainment, and applied science. Did their fame bring them success? Dos Passos' answer, in each case, is strongly implied. The last reading tells of an athlete who won a place for himself in major league baseball. For him there were special difficulties. The story is an old one now. But certainly it is a story of success, a success so thorough that one forgets how hard a battle Jackie Robinson had to fight, and takes for granted both him and the many other Negro stars who have followed after him.

A focal point for all the readings, from the standpoint of the expository method used, will be found in the characterizations of various types of people striving for success as they see it. What standards of success are held up to view, and what types of people are characterized? These are the questions which should be asked and answered as you read.

George Jean Nathan and *H. L. Mencken*

WHAT ALL AMERICANS MOST DESIRE

BUT WHAT, THEN, IS THE CHARACTER that actually marks the American —that is, in chief? If he is not the exalted monopolist of liberty that he thinks he is nor the noble altruist and idealist he slaps upon the chest when he is full of rhetoric, nor the degraded dollar-chaser of European legend, then what is he? We offer an answer in all humility, for the problem is complex and there is but little illumination of it in the literature; nevertheless, we offer it in the firm conviction, born of twenty years' incessant meditation, that it is substantially correct. It is, in brief, this: that the thing which sets off the American from all other men, and gives a peculiar colour not only to the pattern of his daily life but also to the play of his inner ideas, is what, for want of a more exact term, may be called social aspiration. That is to say, his dominant passion is a passion to lift himself by at least a step or two in the society that he is a part of—a passion to improve his position, to break down some shadowy barrier of caste, to achieve the countenance of what, for all his talk of equality, he recognizes and accepts as his betters. The American is a pusher. His eyes are ever fixed upon some round of the ladder that is just beyond his reach, and all his secret ambitions, all his extraordinary energies, group themselves about the yearning to grasp it. Here we have an explanation of the curious restlessness that educated foreigners, as opposed to mere immigrants, always make a note of in the country; it is half aspiration and half impatience, with overtones of dread and timorousness. The American is violently eager to get on, and thoroughly convinced that his merits entitle him to try and to succeed, but by the same token he is sickeningly fearful of slipping back, and out of the second fact, as we shall see, spring some of his most characteristic traits. He is a man vexed, at one and the same time, by delusions of grandeur and an inferiority complex; he is both egotistical and subservient, assertive and politic, blatant and shy. Most of the errors about him are made by seeing one side of him and being blind to the other.

Such a thing as a secure position is practically unknown among us. There is no American who cannot hope to lift himself another notch or two, if he is good; there is absolutely no hard and fast impediment to his progress. But neither is there any American who doesn't have to keep on fighting for whatever position he has; no wall of caste is there to protect him if he slips. One observes every day the movement of individuals, families, whole groups, in both directions. All of our cities are full of brummagem aristocrats—aristocrats, at all events, in the view of their neighbors—whose grandfathers, or even fathers, were day labourers; and working for them, supported by them, heavily patronized by them, are clerks whose grandfathers were lords of the soil. The older societies of Europe, as every one knows, protect their caste lines a great deal more resolutely. It is as impossible for a wealthy pork packer or company promoter to enter the *noblesse* of Austria, even today, as it would be for him to enter the boudoir of a queen; he is barred out absolutely and even his grandchildren are under the ban. And in precisely the same way it is as impossible for a count of the old Holy Roman Empire to lose caste as it would be for the Dalai Lama; he may sink to unutterable depths within his order, but he cannot get himself out of it, nor can he lose the peculiar advantages that go with membership; he is still a *Graf,* and, as such, above the herd. Once, in a Madrid café, the two of us encountered a Spanish marquis who wore celluloid cuffs, suffered from pediculosis and had been drunk for sixteen years. Yet he remained a marquis in good standing, and all lesser Spaniards, including Socialists, envied him and deferred to him; none would have dreamed of slapping him on the back. Knowing that he was quite as safe within his ancient order as a dog among the *canidæ,* he gave no thought to appearances. But in the same way he knew that he had reached his limit—that no conceivable effort could lift him higher. He was a grandee of Spain and that was all; above glimmered royalty and the hierarchy of the saints, and both royalty and the hierarchy of the saints were as much beyond him as grandeeism was beyond the polite and well-educated head-waiter who laved him with ice-water when he had *mania-a-potu.*

No American is ever so securely lodged. There is always something just ahead of him, beckoning him and tantalizing him, and there is always something just behind him, menacing him and causing him to sweat. Even when he attains to what may seem to be security, that security is very fragile. The English soap-boiler, brewer, shyster attorney or stock-jobber, once he has got into the House of Lords, is reasonably safe, and his children after him; the possession of a peerage connotes a definite rank, and it is as permanent as anything can be in this world. But in America there is no such harbour; the ship is eternally at sea. Money vanishes, official dignity is forgotten, caste lines are as full of gaps as an ill-kept hedge. The grandfather of the Vanderbilts was a bounder; the last of the Washingtons is a petty employé in the Library of Congress.

It is this constant possibility of rising, this constant risk of falling, that gives a barbaric picturesqueness to the panorama of what is called fashionable society in America. The chief character of that society is to be found in its shameless self-assertion, its almost obscene display of its importance and of the shadowy privileges and acceptances on which that importance is based. It is assertive for the simple reason that, immediately it ceased to be assertive, it would cease to exist. Structurally, it is composed in every town of a nucleus of those who have laboriously arrived and a chaotic mass of those who are straining every effort to get on. The effort must be made against great odds. Those who have arrived are eager to keep down the competition of newcomers; on their exclusiveness, as the phrase is, rests the whole of their social advantage. Thus the candidate from below, before horning in at last, must put up with an infinity of rebuff and humiliation; he must sacrifice his self-respect today in order to gain the hope of destroying the self-respect of other aspirants tomorrow. The result is

that the whole edifice is based upon fears and abasements, and that
every device which promises to protect the individual against them
is seized upon eagerly. Fashionable society in America therefore has
no room for intelligence; within its fold an original idea is dangerous; it carries regimentation, in dress, in social customs and in political
and even religious doctrines, to the last degree. In the American
cities the fashionable man or woman must not only maintain the
decorum seen among civilized folks everywhere; he or she must also
be interested in precisely the right sports, theatrical shows and opera
singers, show the right political credulities and indignations, and
have some sort of connection with the right church. Nearly always,
because of the apeing of English custom that prevails everywhere in
America, it must be the so-called Protestant Episcopal Church, a sort
of outhouse of the Church of England, with ecclesiastics who imitate
the English sacerdotal manner much as small boys imitate the manner of eminent baseball players. Every fashionable Protestant Episcopal congregation in the land is full of ex-Baptists and ex-Methodists
who have shed Calvinism, total immersion and the hallelujah hymns
on their way up the ladder.

This social aspiration, of course, is most vividly violent and idiotic
on its higher and more gaudy levels, but it is scarcely less earnest
below. Every American, however obscure, has formulated within his
secret recesses some concept of advancement, however meagre; if he
doesn't aspire to be what is called fashionable, then he at least aspires
to lift himself in some less gorgeous way. There is not a social organization in this land of innumerable associations that hasn't its waiting
list of candidates who are eager to get in, but have not yet demonstrated their fitness for the honour. One can scarcely go low enough
to find that pressure absent. Even the tin-pot fraternal orders, which
are constantly cadging for members and seem to accept any one not
a downright felon, are exclusive in their fantastic way, and no doubt
there are hundreds of thousands of proud American freemen, the
heirs of Washington and Jefferson, their liberty safeguarded by a million guns, who pine in secret because they are ineligible to membership in the Masons, the Odd Fellows or even the Knights of Pythias.
On the distaff side, the thing is too obvious to need exposition. The
patriotic societies among women are all machines for the resuscitation
of lost superiorities. The plutocracy has shouldered out the old gentry
from actual social leadership—that gentry, indeed, presents a pro-

digious clinical picture of the insecurity of social rank in America—but there remains at least the possibility of insisting upon a dignity which plutocrats cannot boast and may not even buy. Thus the county judge's wife in Smithville or the Methodist pastor's daughter in Jonestown consoles herself for the lack of an opera box with the thought (constantly asserted by badge and resolution) that she had a nobler grandfather, or, at all events, a decenter one, than the Astors, the Vanderbilts and the Goulds.

"More than any other people," said Wendell Phillips one blue day, "we Americans are afraid of one another." The saying seems harsh. It goes counter to the national delusion of uncompromising courage and limitless truculence. It wars upon the national vanity. But all the same there is truth in it. Here, more than anywhere else on earth, the status of an individual is determined by the general consent of the general body of his fellows; here, as we have seen, there are no artificial barriers to protect him against their disapproval, or even against their envy. And here, more than anywhere else, the general consent of that general body of men is coloured by the ideas and prejudices of the inferior majority; here, there is the nearest approach to genuine democracy, the most direct and accurate response to mob emotions. Facing that infinitely powerful but inevitably ignorant and cruel corpus of opinion, the individual must needs adopt caution and fall into timorousness. The desire within him may be bold and forthright, but its satisfaction demands discretion, prudence, a politic and ingratiating habit. The walls are not to be stormed; they must be wooed to a sort of Jerichoan fall. Success thus takes the form of a series of waves of protective colouration; failure is a succession of unmaskings. The aspirant must first learn to imitate exactly the aspect and behaviour of the group he seeks to penetrate. There follows notice. There follows toleration. There follows acceptance.

GUIDE QUESTIONS

1. What do Nathan and Mencken believe to be the "dominant passion" of most Americans?
2. To what extent would this same "dominant passion" apply to farmers, lawyers, baseball players, postal clerks, undertakers, and plumbers?
3. Interpret: "[The American] is a man vexed, at one and the same time, by delusions of grandeur and an inferiority complex."

4. What point do the authors intend to make in their sketch of the Spanish marquis? Show the relationship of this sketch to the selection as a whole.
5. "Fashionable society in America therefore has no room for intelligence..." Attack or defend this statement, first deciding whether you consider yourself a member of "fashionable society."
6. What is the authors' attitude toward "fashionable" religion? Is this attitude consistent with the general tone of the whole selection?
7. Comment on the authors' interpretation of the typical American desire to join fraternal organizations, patriotic societies, and other associations. Show that the organization of the selection as a whole would be incomplete without some treatment of this subject.
8. How are the general characteristics of Americans stated? Are their habits of mind and act summed up in a way that is consistent with your own experience? Discuss.
9. What is meant by the "protective colouration" that the authors say is necessary for social acceptance?
10. Which of the following seems the most accurate description of the authors' general attitude toward the standards of success in America: (*a*) scornful and sneering, (*b*) serious and sensible, (*c*) smiling but disapproving, (*d*) frivolous and flippant? Explain your choice.

VOCABULARY

Give the derivations and definitions of the following words:

timorousness, subservient, blatant, pediculosis, hierarchy, abasement, decorum, sacerdotal, cadging, truculence, politic, ingratiating.

Sinclair Lewis

DINNER WITH THE BABBITTS

I

FAME DID NOT BRING the social advancement which the Babbitts deserved. They were not asked to join the Tonawanda Country Club nor invited to the dances at the Union. Himself, Babbitt fretted, he didn't "care a fat hoot for all these highrollers, but the wife would like to be Among Those Present." He nervously awaited his university class-dinner and an evening of furious intimacy with such social leaders as Charles McKelvey the millionaire contractor, Max Kruger the banker, Irving Tate the tool-manufacturer, and Adelbert Dobson the fashionable interior decorator. Theoretically he was their friend, as he had been in college, and when he encountered them they still called him "Georgie," but he didn't seem to encounter them often, and they never invited him to dinner (with champagne and a butler) at their houses on Royal Ridge.

All the week before the class-dinner he thought of them. "No reason why we shouldn't become real chummy now!"

II

Like all true American diversions and spiritual outpourings, the dinner of the men of the Class of 1896 was thoroughly organized. The dinner-committee hammered like a sales-corporation. Once a week they sent out reminders:

TICKLER NO. 3

Old man, are you going to be with us at the livest Friendship Feed the alumni of the good old U have ever known? The alumnae of '08 turned out 60% strong. Are we boys going to be beaten by a bunch of skirts? Come on, fellows, let's work up some real genuine enthusiasm and all boost together for the snappiest dinner yet! Elegant eats, short ginger-talks, and memories shared together of the brightest, gladdest days of life.

The dinner was held in a private room at the Union Club. The club was a dingy building, three pretentious old dwellings knocked together, and the entrance-hall resembled a potato cellar, yet the Babbitt who was free of the magnificence of the Athletic Club entered with embarrassment. He nodded to the doorman, an ancient proud Negro with brass buttons and a blue tail-coat, and paraded through the hall, trying to look like a member.

Sixty men had come to the dinner. They made islands and eddies in the hall; they packed the elevator and the corners of the private dining-room. They tried to be intimate and enthusiastic. They appeared to one another exactly as they had in college—as raw youngsters whose present mustaches, baldnesses, paunches, and wrinkles were but jovial disguises put on for the evening. "You haven't changed a particle!" they marveled. The men whom they could not recall they addressed, "Well, well, great to see you again, old man. What are you— Still doing the same thing?"

Some one was always starting a cheer or a college song, and it was always thinning into silence. Despite their resolution to be democratic they divided into two sets: the men with dress-clothes and the men without. Babbitt (extremely in dress-clothes) went from one group to the other. Though he was, almost frankly, out for social conquest, he sought Paul Riesling first. He found him alone, neat and silent.

Paul sighed, "I'm no good at this handshaking and 'well, look who's here' bunk."

"Rats now, Paulibus, loosen up and be a mixer! Finest bunch of boys on earth! Say, you seem kind of glum. What's matter?"

"Oh, the usual. Run-in with Zilla."

"Come on! Let's wade in and forget our troubles."

He kept Paul beside him, but worked toward the spot where Charles McKelvey stood warming his admirers like a furnace.

McKelvey had been the hero of the Class of '96; not only football captain and hammer-thrower but debater, and passable in what the State University considered scholarship. He had gone on, had captured the construction-company once owned by the Dodsworths, best-known pioneer family of Zenith. He built state capitols, skyscrapers, railway terminals. He was a heavy-shouldered, big-chested man, but not sluggish. There was a quiet humor in his eyes, a syrup-smooth quickness in his speech, which intimidated politicians and warned reporters; and in his presence the most intelligent scientist or the most sensitive artist felt thin-blooded, unworldly, and a little shabby. He was, particularly when he was influencing legislatures or hiring labor-spies, very easy and lovable and gorgeous. He was baronial; he was a peer in the rapidly crystallizing American aristocracy, inferior only to the haughty Old Families. (In Zenith, an Old Family is one which came to town before 1840.) His power was the greater because he was not hindered by scruples, by either the vice or the virtue of the older Puritan tradition.

McKelvey was being placidly merry now with the great, the manufacturers and bankers, the land-owners and lawyers and surgeons who had chauffeurs and went to Europe. Babbitt squeezed among them. He liked McKelvey's smile as much as the social advancement to be had from his favor. If in Paul's company he felt ponderous and protective, with McKelvey he felt slight and adoring.

He heard McKelvey say to Max Kruger, the banker, "Yes, we'll put up Sir Gerald Doak." Babbitt's democratic love for titles became a rich relish. "You know, he's one of the biggest iron-men in England, Max. Horribly well-off.... Why, hello, old Georgie! Say, Max, George Babbitt is getting fatter than I am!"

The chairman shouted, "Take your seats, fellows!"

"Shall we make a move, Charley?" Babbitt said casually to Mc-Kelvey.

"Right. Hello, Paul! How's the old fiddler? Planning to sit anywhere special, George? Come on, let's grab some seats. Come on, Max. Georgie, I read about your speeches in the campaign. Bully work!"

After that, Babbitt would have followed him through fire. He was enormously busy during the dinner, now bumblingly cheering Paul, now approaching McKelvey with "Hear you're going to build some piers in Brooklyn," now noting how enviously the failures of the class, sitting by themselves in a weedy group, looked up to him in his association with the nobility, now warming himself in the Society Talk of McKelvey and Max Kruger. They spoke of a "jungle dance" for which Mona Dodsworth had decorated her house with thousands of orchids They spoke, with an excellent imitation of casualness, of a dinner in Washington at which McKelvey had met a Senator, a Balkan princess, and an English major-general. McKelvey called the princess "Jenny," and let it be known that he had danced with her.

Babbitt was thrilled, but not so weighted with awe as to be silent. If he was not invited by them to dinner, he was yet accustomed to talking with bank-presidents, congressmen, and clubwomen who entertained poets. He was bright and referential with McKelvey:

"Say, Charley, juh remember in Junior year how we chartered a sea-going hack and chased down to Riverdale, to the big show Madame Brown used to put on? Remember how you beat up that hick constable that tried to run us in, and we pinched the pants-pressing sign and took and hung it on Prof. Morrison's door? Oh, gosh, those were the days!"

Those, McKelvey agreed, were the days.

Babbitt had reached "It isn't the books you study in college but the friendships you make that counts" when the men at the head of the table broke into song. He attacked McKelvey:

"It's a shame, uh, shame to drift apart because our, uh, business activities lie in different fields. I've enjoyed talking over the good old days. You and Mrs. McKelvey must come to dinner some night."

Vaguely, "Yes, indeed—"

"Like to talk to you about the growth of real estate out beyond your Grantsville warehouse. I might be able to tip you off to a thing or two, possibly."

"Splendid! We must have dinner together, Georgie. Just let me know. And it will be a great pleasure to have your wife and you at the house," said McKelvey, much less vaguely.

Then the chairman's voice, that prodigious voice which once had roused them to cheer defiance at rooters from Ohio or Michigan or Indiana, whooped. "Come on, you wombats! All together in the long yell!" Babbitt felt that life would never be sweeter than now, when he joined with Paul Riesling and the newly recovered hero, McKelvey, in:

> Baaaaaattle-ax
> Get an ax,
> Bal-ax,
> Get-nax,
> Who, who? The U.!
> Hooroo!

III

The Babbitts invited the McKelveys to dinner, in early December, and the McKelveys not only accepted but, after changing the date once or twice, actually came.

The Babbitts somewhat thoroughly discussed the details of the dinner, from the purchase of a bottle of champagne to the number of salted almonds to be placed before each person. Especially did they mention the matter of the other guests. To the last Babbitt held out for giving Paul Riesling the benefit of being with the McKelveys. "Good old Charley would like Paul and Verg Gunch better than some highfalutin' Willy boy," he insisted, but Mrs. Babbitt interrupted his observations with, "Yes—perhaps—I think I'll try to get some Lynnhaven oysters," and when she was quite ready she invited Dr.

J. T. Angus, the oculist, and a dismally respectable lawyer named Maxwell, with their glittering wives.

Neither Angus nor Maxwell belonged to the Elks or to the Athletic Club; neither of them had ever called Babbitt "brother" or asked his opinions on carburetors. The only "human people" whom she invited, Babbitt raged, were the Littlefields; and Howard Littlefield at times became so statistical that Babbitt longed for the refreshment of Gunch's, "Well, old lemon-pie-face, what's the good word?"

Immediately after lunch Mrs. Babbitt began to set the table for the seven-thirty dinner to the McKelveys, and Babbitt was, by order, home at four. But they didn't find anything for him to do, and three times Mrs. Babbitt scolded, "Do please try to keep out of the way!" He stood in the door of the garage, his lips drooping, and wished that Littlefield or Sam Doppelbrau or somebody would come along and talk to him. He saw Ted sneaking about the corner of the house.

"What's the matter, old man?" said Babbitt.

"Is that you, thin, owld one? Gee, Ma certainly is on the warpath! I told her Rone and I would jus' soon not be let in on the fiesta to-night, and she bit me. She says I got to take a bath, too. But, say, the Babbitt men will be some lookers to-night! Little Theodore in a dress-suit!"

"The Babbitt men!" Babbitt liked the sound of it. He put his arm about the boy's shoulder. He wished that Paul Riesling had a daughter, so that Ted might marry her. "Yes, your mother is kind of rouncing round, all right," he said, and they laughed together, and sighed together, and dutifully went in to dress.

The McKelveys were less than fifteen minutes late.

Babbitt hoped that the Doppelbraus would see the McKelveys' limousine, and their uniformed chauffeur, waiting in front.

The dinner was well cooked and incredibly plentiful, and Mrs. Babbitt had brought out her grandmother's silver candlesticks. Babbitt worked hard. He was good. He told none of the jokes he wanted to tell. He listened to the others. He started Maxwell off with a re-sounding, "Let's hear about your trip to the Yellowstone." He was laudatory, extremely laudatory. He found opportunities to remark that Dr. Angus was a benefactor of humanity, Maxwell and Howard Littlefield profound scholars, Charles McKelvey an inspiration to ambitious youth, and Mrs. McKelvey an adornment to the social circles of Zenith, Washington, New York, Paris, and numbers of other places.

But he could not stir them. It was a dinner without a soul. For no reason that was clear to Babbitt, heaviness was over them and they spoke laboriously and unwillingly.

He concentrated on Lucille McKelvey, carefully not looking at her blanched lovely shoulder and the tawny silken band which supported her frock.

"I suppose you'll be going to Europe pretty soon again, won't you?" he invited.

"I'd like awfully to run over to Rome for a few weeks."

"I suppose you see a lot of pictures and music and curios and everything there."

"No, what I really go for is: there's a little *trattoria* on the Via della Scrofa where you get the best *fetuccine* in the world."

"Oh, I— Yes. That must be nice to try that. Yes."

At a quarter to ten McKelvey discovered with profound regret that his wife had a headache. He said blithely, as Babbitt helped him with his coat, "We must have lunch together some time, and talk over the old days."

When the others had labored out, at half-past ten, Babbitt turned to his wife, pleading, "Charley said he had a corking good time and we must lunch—said they wanted to have us up to the house for dinner before long."

She achieved, "Oh, it's just been one of those quiet evenings that are often so much more enjoyable than noisy parties where everybody talks at once and doesn't really settle down to—nice quiet enjoyment."

But from his cot on the sleeping-porch he heard her weeping, slowly, without hope.

IV

For a month they watched the social columns, and waited for a return dinner-invitation.

As the hosts of Sir Gerald Doak, the McKelveys were headlined all the week after the Babbitts' dinner. Zenith ardently received Sir Gerald (who had come to America to buy coal). The newspapers interviewed him on prohibition, Ireland, unemployment, naval aviation, the rate of exchange, tea-drinking *versus* whisky-drinking, the psychology of American women, and daily life as lived by English county families. Sir Gerald seemed to have heard of all those topics. The McKelveys gave him a Singhalese dinner, and Miss Elnora Pearl

Bates, society editor of the *Advocate-Times,* rose to her highest lark-note. Babbitt read aloud at breakfast-table:

'Twixt the original and Oriental decorations, the strange and delicious food, and the personalities both of the distinguished guests, the charming hostess and the noted host, never has Zenith seen a more recherche affair than the Ceylon dinner-dance given last evening by Mr. and Mrs. Charles McKelvey to Sir Gerald Doak. Methought as we—fortunate one!—were privileged to view that fairy and foreign scene, nothing at Monte Carlo or the choicest ambassadorial sets of foreign capitals could be more lovely. It is not for nothing that Zenith is in matters social rapidly becoming known as the choosiest inland city in the country.

Though he is too modest to admit it, Lord Doak gives a cachet to our smart quartier such as it has not received since the ever-memorable visit of the Earl of Sittingbourne. Not only is he of the British peerage, but he is also, on dit, a leader of the British metal industries. As he comes from Nottingham, a favorite haunt of Robin Hood, though now, we are informed by Lord Doak, a live modern city of 275,573 inhabitants, and important lace as well as other industries, we like to think that perhaps through his veins runs some of the blood, both virile red and bonny blue, of that earlier lord o' the good greenwood, the roguish Robin.

The lovely Mrs. McKelvey never was more fascinating than last evening in her black net gown relieved by dainty bands of silver and at her exquisite waist a glowing cluster of Aaron Ward roses.

Babbitt said bravely, "I hope they don't invite us to meet this Lord Doak guy. Darn sight rather just have a nice quiet little dinner with Charley and the Missus."

At the Zenith Athletic Club they discussed it amply. "I s'pose we'll have to call McKelvey 'Lord Chaz' from now on," said Sidney Finkelstein.

"It beats all get-out," meditated that man of data, Howard Littlefield, "how hard it is for some people to get things straight. Here they call this fellow 'Lord Doak' when it ought to be 'Sir Gerald.'"

Babbitt marvelled, "Is that a fact! Well, well! 'Sir Gerald,' eh? That's what you call um, eh? Well, sir, I'm glad to know that."

Later he informed his salesmen, "It's funnier 'n a goat the way some folks that, just because they happen to lay up a big wad, go entertaining famous foreigners, don't have any more idea 'n a rabbit how to address 'em so's to make 'em feel at home!"

That evening, as he was driving home, he passed McKelvey's

limousine and saw Sir Gerald, a large, ruddy, pop-eyed, Teutonic Englishman whose dribble of yellow mustache gave him an aspect sad and doubtful. Babbitt drove on slowly, oppressed by futility. He had a sudden, unexplained, and horrible conviction that the McKelveys were laughing at him.

He betrayed his depression by the violence with which he informed his wife, "Folks that really tend to business haven't got the time to waste on a bunch like the McKelveys. This society stuff is like any other hobby; if you devote yourself to it, you get on. But I like to have a chance to visit with you and the children instead of all this idiotic chasing round."

They did not speak of the McKelveys again.

V

It was a shame, at this worried time, to have to think about the Overbrooks.

Ed Overbrook was a classmate of Babbitt who had been a failure. He had a large family and a feeble insurance business out in the suburb of Dorchester. He was gray and thin and unimportant. He had always been gray and thin and unimportant. He was the person whom, in any group, you forgot to introduce, then introduced with extra enthusiasm. He had admired Babbitt's good-fellowship in college, had admired ever since his power in real estate, his beautiful house and wonderful clothes. It pleased Babbitt, though it bothered him with a sense of responsibility. At the class-dinner he had seen poor Overbrook, in a shiny blue serge business-suit, being diffident in a corner with three other failures. He had gone over and been cordial: "Why hello, young Ed! I hear you're writing all the insurance in Dorchester now. Bully work!"

They recalled the good old days when Overbrook used to write poetry. Overbrook embarrassed him by blurting, "Say, Georgie, I hate to think of how we been drifting apart. I wish you and Mrs. Babbitt would come to dinner some night."

Babbitt boomed, "Fine! Sure! Just let me know. And the wife and I want to have you at the house." He forgot it, but unfortunately Ed Overbrook did not. Repeatedly he telephoned to Babbitt, inviting him to dinner. "Might as well go and get it over," Babbitt groaned to his wife. "But don't it simply amaze you the way the poor fish doesn't

know the first thing about social etiquette? Think of him 'phoning
me, instead of his wife sitting down and writing us a regular bid!
Well, I guess we're stuck for it. That's the trouble with all this class-
brother hooptedoodle."

He accepted Overbrook's next plaintive invitation, for an evening
two weeks off. A dinner two weeks off, even a family dinner, never
seems so appalling, till the two weeks have astoundingly disappeared
and one comes dismayed to the ambushed hour. They had to change
the date, because of their own dinner to the McKelveys, but at last
they gloomily drove out to the Overbrooks' house in Dorchester.

It was miserable from the beginning. The Overbrooks had dinner at
six-thirty, while the Babbitts never dined before seven. Babbitt permitted himself to be ten minutes late. "Let's make it as short as
possible. I think we'll duck out quick. I'll say I have to be at the
office extra early to-morrow," he planned.

The Overbrook house was depressing. It was the second story of a
wooden two-family dwelling; a place of baby-carriages, old hats
hung in the hall, cabbage-smell, and a Family Bible on the parlor
table. Ed Overbrook and his wife were as awkward and threadbare as
usual, and the other guests were two dreadful families whose names
Babbitt never caught and never desired to catch. But he was touched,
and disconcerted, by the tactless way in which Overbrook praised him:
"We're mighty proud to have old George here to-night! Of course
you've all read about his speeches and oratory in the papers—and
the boy's good-looking, too, eh?—but what I always think of is back
in college, and what a great old mixer he was, and one of the best
swimmers in the class."

Babbitt tried to be jovial; he worked at it; but he could find nothing
to interest him in Overbrook's timorousness, the blankness of the
other guests, or the drained stupidity of Mrs. Overbrook, with her
spectacles, drab skin, and tight-drawn hair. He told his best Irish story,
but it sank like soggy cake. Most bleary moment of all was when
Mrs. Overbrook, peering out of her fog of nursing eight children
and cooking and scrubbing, tried to be conversational.

"I suppose you go to Chicago and New York right along, Mr.
Babbitt," she prodded.

"Well, I get to Chicago fairly often."

"It must be awfully interesting. I suppose you take in all the
theaters."

"Well, to tell the truth, Mrs. Overbrook, thing that hits me best is a great big beefsteak at a Dutch restaurant in the Loop!"

They had nothing more to say. Babbitt was sorry, but there was no hope; the dinner was a failure. At ten, rousing out of the stupor of meaningless talk, he said as cheerily as he could, " 'Fraid we got to be starting, Ed. I've got a fellow coming to see me early to-morrow." As Overbrook helped him with his coat, Babbitt said, "Nice to rub up on the old days! We must have lunch together, P. D. Q."

Mrs. Babbitt sighed, on their drive home, "It was pretty terrible. But how Mr. Overbrook does admire you!"

"Yep. Poor cuss! Seems to think I'm a little tin archangel, and the best-looking man in Zenith."

"Well, you're certainly not that but— Oh, Georgie, you don't suppose we have to invite them to dinner at our house now, do we?"

"Ouch! Gaw, I hope not!"

"See here, now, George! You didn't say anything about it to Mr. Overbrook, did you?"

"No! Gee! No! Honest, I didn't! Just made a bluff about having him to lunch some time."

"Well....Oh, dear....I don't want to hurt their feelings. But I don't see how I could stand another evening like this one. And suppose somebody like Dr. and Mrs. Angus came in when we had the Overbrooks there, and thought they were friends of ours!"

For a week they worried, "We really ought to invite Ed and his wife, poor devils!" But as they never saw the Overbrooks, they forgot them, and after a month or two they said, "That really was the best way, just to let it slide. It wouldn't be kind to *them* to have them here. They'd feel so out of place and hard-up in our home."

They did not speak of the Overbrooks again.

GUIDE QUESTIONS

1. What did George Babbitt expect to gain from the class dinner?
2. Why was he eager to promote his friendship with McKelvey?
3. What did the McKelveys' acceptance of the invitation signify to the Babbitts? What did it signify to the McKelveys?
4. How was this situation paralleled in the dinner the Overbrooks gave for the Babbitts?

5. What does this reveal concerning American social life?
6. Sinclair Lewis is best known as a recorder of the average American scene. To what extent, in your opinion, does he give here an accurate picture of the ambitions of the average American?
7. What was George Babbitt's idea of success? How does it compare with your own?

VOCABULARY

Give the derivations and definitions of the following words:

pretentious, intimidate, placidly, laudatory, plaintive, disconcert.

John Dos Passos

THREE KINDS OF SUCCESS

THE HOUSE OF MORGAN

I commit my soul into the hands of my savior, wrote John Pierpont Morgan in his will, *in full confidence that having redeemed it and washed it in His most precious blood, He will present it faultless before my heavenly father, and I intreat my children to maintain and defend at all hazard and at any cost of personal sacrifice the blessed doctrine of complete atonement for sin through the blood of Jesus Christ once offered and through that alone,*

and into the hands of the House of Morgan represented by his son, he committed,

when he died in Rome in 1913,

the control of the Morgan interests in New York, Paris and London, four national banks, three trust companies, three life insurance companies, ten railroad systems, three street railway companies, an express company, the International Mercantile Marine,

power,

on the cantilever principle, through interlocking directorates

From *U. S. A.* by John Dos Passos, Modern Library edition. Reprinted by permission of the author.

over eighteen other railroads, U.S. Steel, General Electric, American Tel and Tel, five major industries;

the interwoven cables of the Morgan Stillman Baker combination held credit up like a suspension bridge, thirteen percent of the banking resources of the world.

The first Morgan to make a pool was Joseph Morgan, a hotelkeeper in Hartford Connecticut who organized stagecoach lines and bought up Ætna Life Insurance stock in a time of panic caused by one of the big New York fires in the 1830's;

his son Junius followed in his footsteps, first in the drygoods business, and then as partner to George Peabody, a Massachusetts banker who built up an enormous underwriting and mercantile business in London and became a friend of Queen Victoria;

Junius married the daughter of John Pierpont, a Boston preacher, poet, eccentric, and abolitionist; and their eldest son,

John Pierpont Morgan

arrived in New York to make his fortune

after being trained in England, going to school at Vevey, proving himself a crack mathematician at the University of Göttingen,

a lanky morose young man of twenty,

just in time for the panic of '57.

(war and panics on the stock exchange, bankruptcies, warloans, good growing weather for the House of Morgan.)

When the guns started booming at Fort Sumter, young Morgan turned some money over reselling condemned muskets to the U.S. army and began to make himself felt in the gold room in downtown New York; there was more in trading in gold than in trading in muskets; so much for the Civil War.

During the Franco-Prussian war Junius Morgan floated a huge bond issue for the French government at Tours.

At the same time young Morgan was fighting Jay Cooke and the German-Jew bankers in Frankfort over the funding of the American war debt (he never did like the Germans or the Jews).

The panic of '75 ruined Jay Cooke and made J. Pierpont Morgan the boss croupier of Wall Street; he united with the Philadelphia Drexels and built the Drexel building where for thirty years he sat in his glassedin office, redfaced and insolent, writing at his desk, smoking great black cigars, or, if important issues were involved, playing solitaire in his inner office; he was famous for his few words, Yes or No, and for his way of suddenly blowing up in a visitor's face and for that special gesture of the arm that meant, *What do I get out of it?*

In '77 Junius Morgan retired; J. Pierpont got himself made a member of the board of directors of the New York Central railroad and launched the first *Corsair*. He liked yachting and to have pretty actresses call him Commodore.

He founded the Lying-in Hospital on Stuyvesant Square, and was fond of going into St. George's church and singing a hymn all alone in the afternoon quiet.

In the panic of '93
at no inconsiderable profit to himself
Morgan saved the U.S. Treasury; gold was draining out, the country was ruined, the farmers were howling for a silver standard, Grover Cleveland and his cabinet were walking up and down in the blue room at the White House without being able to come to a decision, in Congress they were making speeches while the gold reserves melted in the Subtreasuries; poor people were starving, Coxey's army was marching to Washington; for a long time Grover Cleveland couldn't bring himself to call in the representative of the Wall Street moneymasters; Morgan sat in his suite at the Arlington smoking cigars and quietly playing solitaire until at last the president sent for him;

he had a plan all ready for stopping the gold hemorrhage.

After that what Morgan said went; when Carnegie sold out he built the Steel Trust.

J. Pierpont Morgan was a bullnecked irascible man with small black magpie's eyes and a growth on his nose; he let his partners work themselves to death over the detailed routine of banking, and sat in his back office smoking black cigars; when there was something to be decided he said Yes or No or just turned his back and went back to his solitaire.

Every Christmas his librarian read him Dickens' *A Christmas Carol* from the original manuscript.

He was fond of canarybirds and pekinese dogs and liked to take pretty actresses yachting. Each *Corsair* was a finer vessel than the last.

When he dined with King Edward he sat at His Majesty's right; he ate with the Kaiser tête-à-tête; he liked talking to cardinals or the pope, and never missed a conference of Episcopal bishops;

Rome was his favorite city.

He liked choice cookery and old wines and pretty women and yachting, and going over his collections, now and then picking up a jewelled snuffbox and staring at it with his magpie's eyes.

He made a collection of the autographs of the rulers of France, owned glass cases full of Babylonian tablets, seals, signets, statuettes, busts,

Gallo-Roman bronzes,

Merovingian jewels, miniatures, watches, tapestries, porcelains, cuneiform inscriptions, paintings by all the old masters, Dutch, Italian, Flemish, Spanish,

manuscripts of the gospels and the Apocalypse,

a collection of the works of Jean-Jacques Rousseau,

and the letters of Pliny the Younger.

His collectors bought anything that was expensive or rare or had the glint of empire on it, and he had it brought to him and stared hard at it with his magpie's eyes. Then it was put in a glass case.

The last year of his life he went up the Nile on a dahabiyeh and spent a long time staring at the great columns of the Temple of Karnak.

The panic of 1907 and the death of Harriman, his great opponent in railroad financing, in 1909, had left him the undisputed ruler of Wall Street, most powerful private citizen in the world;

an old man tired of the purple, suffering from gout, he had deigned to go to Washington to answer the questions of the Pujo Committee during the Money Trust Investigation: Yes, I did what seemed to me to be for the best interests of the country.

So admirably was his empire built that his death in 1913 hardly caused a ripple in the exchanges of the world: the purple descended to his son, J. P. Morgan,

who had been trained at Groton and Harvard and by associating with the British ruling class

to be a more constitutional monarch: *J. P. Morgan suggests...*

By 1917 the Allies had borrowed one billion, nine-hundred million dollars through the House of Morgan: we went overseas for democracy and the flag;

and by the end of the Peace Conference the phrase *J. P. Morgan suggests* had compulsion over a power of seventyfour billion dollars.

J. P. Morgan is a silent man, not given to public utterances, but during the great steel strike, he wrote Gary: *Heartfelt congratulations on your stand for the open shop, with which I am, as you know, absolutely in accord. I believe American principles of liberty are deeply involved, and must win if we stand firm.*

(Wars and panics on the stock exchange,
machinegunfire and arson,
bankruptcies, warloans,
starvation, lice, cholera and typhus:
good growing weather for the House of Morgan.)

§

ADAGIO DANCER

The nineteenyearold son of a veterinary in Castellaneta in the south of Italy was shipped off to America like a lot of other unmanageable young Italians when his parents gave up trying to handle him, to sink or swim and maybe send a few lire home by international postal moneyorder. The family was through with him. But Rodolfo Guglielmi wanted to make good.

He got a job as assistant gardener in Central Park but that kind of work was the last thing he wanted to do; he wanted to make good in the brightlights; money burned his pockets.

He hung around cabarets doing odd jobs, sweeping out for the waiters, washing cars; he was lazy handsome wellbuilt slender goodtempered and vain; he was a born tangodancer.

Lovehungry women thought he was a darling. He began to get engagements dancing the tango in ballrooms and cabarets; he teamed up with a girl named Jean Acker on a vaudeville tour and took the name of Rudolph Valentino.

Stranded on the Coast he headed for Hollywood, worked for a long time as an extra for five dollars a day; directors began to notice he photographed well.

He got his chance in *The Four Horsemen*
and became the gigolo of every woman's dreams.

Valentino spent his life in the colorless glare of klieg lights, in stucco
villas obstructed with bricabrac oriental rugs tigerskins, in the bridal-
suites of hotels, in silk bathrobes in private cars.

He was always getting into limousines or getting out of limousines,
or patting the necks of fine horses.

Wherever he went the sirens of the motorcyclecops screeched ahead
of him
flashlights flared,

the streets were jumbled with hysterical faces, waving hands, crazy
eyes; they stuck out their autographbooks, yanked his buttons off,
cut a tail off his admirablytailored dress suit; they stole his hat and
pulled at his necktie; his valets removed young women from under
his bed; all night in nightclubs and cabarets actresses leching for
stardom made sheepseyes at him under their mascaraed lashes.

He wanted to make good under the glare of the milliondollar
searchlights
of El Dorado:
the Sheik, the Son of the Sheik;
personal appearances.

He married his old vaudeville partner, divorced her, married the
adopted daughter of a millionaire, went into lawsuits with the
producers who were debasing the art of the screen, spent a million
dollars on one European trip;

he wanted to make good in the brightlights.

When the Chicago *Tribune* called him a pink powderpuff
and everybody started wagging their heads over a slavebracelet he
wore that he said his wife had given him and his taste for mushy
verse of which he published a small volume called *Daydreams* and the
whispers grew about the testimony in his divorce case that he and
his first wife had never slept together,

it broke his heart.

He tried to challenge the Chicago *Tribune* to a duel;
he wanted to make good
in heman twofisted broncobusting pokerplaying stockjuggling
America. (He was a fair boxer and had a good seat on a horse. he

loved the desert like the sheik and was tanned from the sun of Palm Springs.) He broke down in his suite in the Hotel Ambassador in New York: gastric ulcer.

When the doctors cut into his elegantlymolded body they found that peritonitis had begun; the abdominal cavity contained a large amount of fluid and food particles; the viscera were coated with a greenish-grey film; a round hole a centimeter in diameter was seen in the anterior wall of the stomach; the tissue of the stomach for one and onehalf centimeters immediately surrounding the perforation was necrotic. The appendix was inflamed and twisted against the small intestine.

When he came to from the ether the first thing he said was, "Well, did I behave like a pink powderpuff?"

His expensivelymassaged actor's body fought peritonitis for six days.

The switchboard at the hospital was swamped with calls, all the corridors were piled with flowers, crowds filled the street outside, filmstars who claimed they were his betrothed entrained for New York.

Late in the afternoon a limousine drew up at the hospital door (where the grimyfingered newspapermen and photographers stood around bored tired hoteyed smoking too many cigarettes making trips to the nearest speak exchanging wisecracks and deep dope waiting for him to die in time to make the evening papers) *and a woman, who said she was a maid employed by a dancer who was Valentino's first wife, alighted. She delivered to an attendant an envelope addressed to the filmstar and inscribed From Jean, and a package. The package contained a white counterpane with lace ruffles and the word Rudy embroidered in the four corners. This was accompanied by a pillowcover to match over a blue silk scented cushion.*

Rudolph Valentino was only thirtyone when he died.

His managers planned to make a big thing of his highlypublicized funeral but the people in the streets were too crazy.

While he lay in state in a casket covered with a cloth of gold, tens of thousands of men, women, and children packed the streets outside. Hundreds were trampled, had their feet hurt by policehorses. In the muggy rain the cops lost control. Jammed masses stampeded under the clubs and the rearing hoofs of the horses. The funeral chapel was gutted, men and women fought over a flower, a piece of wallpaper, a piece of the broken plateglass window. Showwindows were burst in. Parked cars were overturned and smashed. When finally the mounted police after repeated charges beat the crowd off Broadway, where traffic was tied up for two hours, they picked up twentyeight separate shoes, a truckload of umbrellas, papers, hats, tornoff sleeves. All the ambulances in that part of the city were busy carting off women who'd fainted, girls who'd been stepped on. Epileptics threw fits. Cops collected little groups of abandoned children.

The fascisti sent a guard of honor and the antifascists drove them off. More rioting, cracked skulls, trampled feet. When the public was barred from the undertaking parlors hundreds of women groggy with headlines got in to view the poor body

claiming to be exdancingpartners, old playmates, relatives from the old country, filmstars; every few minutes a girl fainted in front of the bier and was revived by the newspapermen who put down her name and address and claim to notice in the public prints. Frank E. Campbell's undertakers and pallbearers, dignified wearers of black broadcloth and tackersup of crape, were on the verge of a nervous breakdown. Even the boss had his fill of publicity that time.

It was two days before the cops could clear the streets enough to let the flowerpieces from Hollywood be brought in and described in the evening papers.

The church service was more of a success. The policecommissioner barred the public for four blocks round.

Many notables attended.

America's Sweetheart sobbing bitterly in a small black straw with a black band and a black bow behind, in black georgette over black with a white lace collar and white lace cuffs followed the coffin that was

covered by a blanket of pink roses

sent by a filmstar who appeared at the funeral heavily veiled and swooned and had to be taken back to her suite at the Hotel Ambassador after she had shown the reporters a message allegedly written by one of the doctors alleging that Rudolph Valentino had spoken of her at the end

as his bridetobe.

A young woman committed suicide in London.

Relatives arriving from Europe were met by police reserves and Italian flags draped with crape. Exchamp Jim Jeffries said, "Well, he made good." The champion himself allowed himself to be quoted that the boy was fond of boxing and a great admirer of the champion.

The funeral train left for Hollywood.

In Chicago a few more people were hurt trying to see the coffin, but only made the inside pages.

The funeral train arrived in Hollywood on page 23 of the New York *Times*.

§

THE ELECTRICAL WIZARD

Edison was born in Milan, Ohio, in eighteen fortyseven;

Milan was a little town on the Huron River that for a while was the wheatshipping port for the whole Western Reserve; the railroads took away the carrying trade, the Edison family went up to Port Huron in Michigan to grow up with the country;

his father was a shinglemaker who puttered round with various small speculations; he dealt in grain and feed and lumber and built a wooden tower a hundred feet high; tourists and excursionists paid a quarter each to go up the tower and look at the view over Lake Huron and the St. Clair River and Sam Edison became a solid and respected citizen of Port Huron.

Thomas Edison only went to school for three months because the teacher thought he wasn't right bright. His mother taught him what she knew at home and read eighteenth century writers with him, Gibbon and Hume and Newton, and let him rig up a laboratory in the cellar.

Whenever he read about anything he went down cellar and tried it out.

When he was twelve he needed money to buy books and chemicals; he got a concession as newsbutcher on the daily train from Detroit to Port Huron. In Detroit there was a public library and he read it.

He rigged up a laboratory on the train and whenever he read about anything he tried it out. He rigged up a printing press and printed a

paper called *The Herald,* when the Civil War broke out he organized
a newsservice and cashed in on the big battles. Then he dropped a
stick of phosphorus and set the car on fire and was thrown off the
train.

By that time he had considerable fame in the country as the boy
editor of the first newspaper to be published on a moving train. The
London *Times* wrote him up.

He learned telegraphy and got a job as night operator at Stratford
Junction in Canada, but one day he let a freighttrain get past a
switch and had to move on.

(During the Civil War a man that knew telegraphy could get a
job anywhere.)

Edison traveled round the country taking jobs and dropping them
and moving on, reading all the books he could lay his hands on,
whenever he read about a scientific experiment he tried it out, whenever he could get near an engine he'd tinker with it, whenever they
left him alone in a telegraph office he'd do tricks with the wires. That
often lost him the job and he had to move on.

He was a tramp operator through the whole Middle West: Detroit,
Cincinnati, Indianapolis, Louisville, New Orleans, always broke, his
clothes stained with chemicals, always trying tricks with the telegraph.

He worked for the Western Union in Boston.

In Boston he doped out the model of his first patent, an automatic
voterecorder for use in Congress, but they didn't want an automatic
voterecorder in Congress, so Edison had the trip to Washington and
made some debts and that was all he got out of that; he worked out a
stockticker and burglar alarms and burned all the skin off his face
with nitric acid.

But New York was already the big market for stocks and ideas and
gold and greenbacks.

(This part is written by Horatio Alger:)

When Edison got to New York he was stony broke and had debts
in Boston and Rochester. This was when gold was at a premium and
Jay Gould was trying to corner the gold market. Wall Street was
crazy. A man named Law had rigged up an electric indicator (Calla-
han's invention) that indicated the price of gold in brokers' offices.
Edison, looking for a job, broke and with no place to go, had been

hanging round the central office passing the time of day with the operators when the general transmitter stopped with a crash in the middle of a rush day of nervous trading; everybody in the office lost his head. Edison stepped up and fixed the machine and landed a job at $300 a month.

In sixtynine the year of Black Friday he started an electrical engineering firm with a man named Pope.

From then on he was on his own, he invented a stock ticker and it sold. He had a machineshop and a laboratory; whenever he thought of a device he tried it out. He made forty thousand dollars out of the Universal Stock Ticker.

He rented a shop in Newark and worked on an automatic telegraph and on devices for sending two and four messages at the same time over the same wire.

In Newark he tinkered with Sholes on the first typewriter, and invented the mimeograph, the carbon rheostat, the microtasimeter and first made paraffin paper.

Something he called etheric force worried him, he puzzled a lot about etheric force but it was Marconi who cashed in on the Hertzian waves. Radio was to smash the ancient universe. Radio was to kill the old Euclidian God, but Edison was never a man to worry about philosophical concepts;

he worked all day and all night tinkering with cogwheels and bits of copperwire and chemicals in bottles, whenever he thought of a device he tried it out. He made things work. He wasn't a mathematician. I can hire mathematicians but mathematicians can't hire me, he said.

In eighteen seventysix he moved to Menlo Park where he invented the carbon transmitter that made the telephone a commercial proposition, that made the microphone possible

he worked all day and all night and produced
    the phonograph
        the incandescent electric lamp

and systems of generation, distribution, regulation and measurement of electric current, sockets, switches, insulators, manholes. Edison worked out the first systems of electric light using the direct current

and small unit lamps and the multiple arc that were installed in
London Paris New York and Sunbury Pa.,

the threewire system,

the magnetic ore separator,

an electric railway.

He kept them busy at the Patent Office filing patents and caveats.

To find a filament for his electric lamp that would work, that would
be a sound commercial proposition he tried all kinds of paper and
cloth, thread, fishline, fibre, celluloid, boxwood, cocoanut-shells, spruce,
hickory, bay, mapleshavings, rosewood, punk, cork, flax, bamboo and
the hair out of a redheaded Scotchman's beard;

whenever he got a hunch he tried it out.

In eighteen eightyseven he moved to the huge laboratories at West
Orange.

He invented rockcrushers and the fluoroscope and the reeled film
for movie cameras and the alkaline storage battery and the long
kiln for burning out portland cement and the kinetophone that was
the first talking movie and the poured cement house that is to furnish
cheap artistic identical sanitary homes for workers in the electrical age.

Thomas A. Edison at eightytwo worked sixteen hours a day;

he never worried about mathematics or the social system or generalized philosophical concepts;

in collaboration with Henry Ford and Harvey Firestone who never
worried about mathematics or the social system or generalized philosophical concepts;

he worked sixteen hours a day trying to find a substitute for rubber;
whenever he read about anything he tried it out; whenever he got a
hunch he went to the laboratory and tried it out.

GUIDE QUESTIONS

1. Dos Passos' special devices are (*a*) broken paragraphs, (*b*) telescoped
   words, (*c*) conspicuous placing for emphasis, and (*d*) unconventional
   punctuation. What effects does he achieve by their use? Which of
   these devices do you find most effective? Least effective?
2. What details concerning the education, early career, and personal
   habits of J. Pierpont Morgan are used to characterize him? What
   impression are these details intended to produce?

3. Analyze the motives and attitudes of J. Pierpont Morgan in connection with his famous art collection.
4. Interpret the phrase, "good growing weather for the House of Morgan."
5. Compare the rise of Rudolph Valentino with that of some contemporary celebrity of stage, screen, radio, or television.
6. What personal qualities of Valentino are emphasized?
7. Do you regard this as a typical success story? Explain.
8. What traits in Edison's character might be considered eccentric or unconventional? Were these traits a help or a hindrance to him?
9. Comment on the statement, "I can hire mathematicians but mathematicians can't hire me."
10. How would you account for Edison's achievements?
11. What was the Morgans' idea of success? Valentino's? Edison's? How do these ideas of success compare with your own?

VOCABULARY

Give the derivations and definitions of the following words:

cantilever, abolitionist, morose, croupier, irascible, viscera, necrotic, tinker, rheostat, caveat.

from *Time*

ROOKIE OF THE YEAR

IT WAS ONLY A MONTH since Speedster Enos Slaughter of the St. Louis Cardinals, galloping into first base, had spiked First Baseman Jackie Robinson. Jackie, the first avowed Negro in the history of big-league baseball, looked at his ripped stocking and bleeding leg. It might have

From *Time*, September 22, 1947. Courtesy of *Time*, copyright Time Inc., 1947.

been an accident, but Jackie didn't think so. Neither did a lot of others who saw the play. Jackie set his teeth, and said nothing. He didn't dare to.

Last week the Brooklyn Dodgers faced the Cards again, and this time the pennant—and the Dodgers' none-too-healthy 4½-game lead—was at stake. The Cards, somewhat housebroken descendants of the rough-&-tumble Gashouse Gang, were fighting back, late and hard. In the second inning, Jackie Robinson was spiked again—this time by trigger-tempered Catcher Joe Garagiola.

Next inning, at the plate, there was a face-to-face exchange of hot words between Robinson and Garagiola—the kind of rough passage that fans appreciatively call a "rhubarb." Umpire "Beans" Reardon hastily stepped between the two and broke it up. That was the end of it: no fisticuffs on the field, no rioting in the stands. But it was a sign, and an important one, that Jackie had established himself as a big leaguer. He had earned what comes free to every other player: the right to squawk.

That change of attitude showed, as nothing else could, the progress of Jackie Roosevelt* Robinson in the toughest first season any ballplayer has ever faced. He had made good as a major leaguer, and proved himself as a man. Last week *The Sporting News,* baseball's trade paper, crowned him the rookie of the year. *The Sporting News* explained, carefully and a little grandiloquently, that it had made the choice solely on the basis of "stark baseball values." Wrote Editor J. G. Taylor Spink:

"Robinson was rated and examined solely as a freshman player in the big leagues—on the basis of his hitting, his running, his defensive play, his team value. The sociological experiment that Robinson represented, the trail-blazing he did, the barriers he broke down did not enter into the decision."

The "sociological experiment" may not have been foremost in Taylor Spink's mind, but it was never out of Jackie's. He, his teammates and the National League had broken baseball's 60-year color line. Only two years had passed since Rogers Hornsby declared, and baseball know-it-alls everywhere had nodded in assent: "Ballplayers on the road live close together . . . it won't work."

Wobbling Rabbit. The man who had made it work is a well-muscled, pigeon-toed, 28-year-old rookie from Pasadena, Calif., who, along with

* After Theodore, not Franklin.

Glenn Davis and Babe Didrikson Zaharias, is one of the great all-round athletes of his day.

He looks awkward, but isn't. He stops and starts as though turned off & on with a toggle switch. He seems to hit a baseball on the dead run. Once in motion, he wobbles along, elbows flying, hips swaying, shoulders rocking—creating the illusion that he will fly to pieces with every stride. But once he gains momentum, his shoulders come to order and his feet skim along like flying fish. He is not only jack-rabbit fast, but about one thought and two steps ahead of every base-runner in the business. He beats out bunts, stretches singles into doubles. Once Jackie made second on a base-on-balls; he saw that the catcher had lost the ball, so he just kept on going.

He has stolen 26 bases this season, more than any other National Leaguer. He dances and prances off base, keeping the enemy's infield upset and off balance, and worrying the pitcher. The boys call it "showboat baseball." He is not, in his first year, the greatest baserunner since Ty Cobb, but he is mighty good. Cobb made a practice of coming in with spikes aimed at anyone brave enough to get in his way. It wouldn't have been politic for Jackie to do it that way very often. Robinson's base running, which resembles more the trickiness of "Pepper" Martin, is a combination of surprise, timing and speed. Says Jackie: "Daring...that's half my game."

Turnstile Sociology. Jackie's daring on the baselines has been matched by shrewd Branch Rickey's daring on the color line. Rickey gave Robinson his chance. As boss of the Brooklyn Dodgers, Rickey is a mixture of Phineas T. Barnum and Billy Sunday, who is prone to talk piously of the larger and higher implications of what he is doing. There were large implications, of course, in signing Jackie Robinson, but the influence on the box office was a lot easier to figure. Jackie Robinson has pulled about $150,000 in extra admissions this season.

Wherever the Dodgers have played, Negroes have turned out in force to see their hero. In Chicago, where Negro fans sported Jackie Robinson buttons, Jackie's fans came early and brought their lunch. In Jim Crowish St. Louis, where Negroes must sit in the right-field pavilion, the Robinson rooting section was more noticeable. Their adulation embarrassed Robbie: it made it harder for him to act like just another ballplayer. Rickey had promised to treat Jackie "just like any other rookie," and he certainly did on the payroll. Though he may have to pay Jackie more next season, so far Rickey has paid the crowd-pulling rookie-of-the-year only $5,000. Under league rules that is the least that the poorest rookie can be paid.

This week, as the Dodgers raced toward the finish seven games ahead, it was at least arguable that Jackie Robinson had furnished the margin of victory. The Dodgers are certainly not a one-man ball club. They have a bull-necked power-house of a catcher named Bruce Edwards, 24, whose special talents are steadiness and hustle. In Pee Wee Reese and Eddie Stanky, both short of height but long on skill, they have the best keystone combination in the league. The Dodgers also have a special affection for 34-year-old relief pitcher Hugh Casey, who has come onto the hill to save game after game, and is held in higher esteem by his team mates than strong-arm Ralph Branca, the Dodgers' only 20-game winner. And of course there is Dixie Walker, the "Peepul's Cherce," who at 36 still hits when it will do the most good—with men on base. In a locker-room gab-fest a few weeks ago, the Dodgers agreed among themselves that Jackie Robinson was the team's third most valuable player—behind Edwards and Reese.

No Drink, No Smoke. Branch Rickey, the smartest man in baseball, had looked hard and waited long to find a Negro who would be his race's best foot forward, as well as a stout prop for a winning ball team. Rickey and his men scouted Robinson until they knew everything about him but what he dreamed at night. Jackie scored well on all counts. He did not smoke (his mother had asthma and cigaret fumes bothered her); he drank a quart of milk a day and didn't touch liquor; he rarely swore; he had a service record (as Army lieutenant in the 27th Cavalry) and two years of college (at U.C.L.A.). He had intelligence, patience and willingness. He was aware of the handicaps his race encounters, but he showed it not by truculence or bitterness, and not by servility, but by a reserve that no white man really ever penetrated. Most important of all Robinson's qualifications, he was a natural athlete. Says Rickey: "That's what I was betting on."

Pepper Street Gangman. It ran in the family. His older brother, Mack, was second in the 200-meter run at the Berlin Olympics in 1936. Jackie was a broad-jumper who once set a Southern California junior college record of 25 ft. 6½ in.

The Robinson family—four boys and a girl—grew up on Pepper Street in the poor section of well-to-do Pasadena. They never knew their father (mother still doesn't talk about him). To support the kids, mother Robinson took in washing & ironing. Jackie, the youngest, was a charter member of the Pepper Street Gang, half a dozen Negroes and three or four American-Japanese who liked to break street lamps and watch the changing colors of the shattered bulbs. "It was awful pretty," recalls Jackie.

He played softball on the corner lot with the gang, occasionally earned pocket money by sneaking onto neighboring golf courses to retrieve lost balls. He could outrun the gang—and the cops—every time. But a stern talk from Ma Robinson put him out of business. She was, and is, a fervent Methodist who can be volubly graphic on the subject of hell. (A few weeks ago, when the Dodgers were not doing so well, Jackie wrote to his ma: "Quit praying just for me alone, Ma, and pray for the whole team.")

Ma Robinson regarded it as sinful for twelve-year-old Jackie to be playing baseball at Brookside Park on Sundays while the pews at Preacher Scott's church were half empty. "The devil is sending the people to watch you play," said Mama, "and he's also sending you to play." Jackie won her over by taking her to a few games. She kept quiet until he began playing football, a game which disturbed both her religious and maternal instincts. One Saturday three Glendale High School players piled on Jackie and cracked two of his ribs. She still remembers that day: "I seen them throwing water on my boy and I wanted to rush down there and help him. But he got up and walked off the field and I sat down. After that, I always worry about my baby."

Man in Motion. But Jackie could take care of himself. At U.C.L.A. he was one of the slickest halfbacks who ever put on cleats. His ball-carrying average: a remarkable twelve yards a try. Jackie was used mostly as the man-in-motion on offense, because of his skill at faking and feinting. He won All-America honorable mention. U.C.L.A.'s heavy-duty ball-carrier was another Negro, talented Kenny Washington, who made the All-America first team. He and Jackie had no particular love for each other, but both deny persistent campus rumors that they once had a knock-down, drag-out fight in a dark alley. "T'ain't so," says Jackie, "I'm not dumb enough to have a fight with Kenny. He's too big."

Jackie has never tried boxing, but Branch Rickey is convinced that Jackie would be sensational at it—or at any other sport he tried. In basketball, Jackie was the leading scorer of the Pacific Coast Conference for two years. He did not play tennis much, but the first time he played in the Negro National Tournament, he got to the semifinals. Baseball was the game he had played longest and liked least.

Two years ago, after 31 months in the Army, Jackie signed up as a shortstop for the barnstorming Kansas City Monarchs. It was a Negro club featuring old and reliable Pitcher "Satchel" Paige, who would have been a big leaguer once, had the big leagues been willing to admit Negroes sooner. The grubby life with the Monarchs was a shock to college-bred Jackie. The Monarchs traveled around in an old bus, often for two or three days at a time (the league stretches from Kansas City to Newark) without a bath, a bed, or a hot meal, and then crawled out long enough to play a game. The smart ones got aboard the bus early, rolled up their uniforms for a pillow, and slept in the aisle. "After two months of it, I was for quitting," says Jackie. "No future." He didn't know it, but all the time Branch Rickey was getting reports of Jackie's playing, and of his .340 batting average.

When Rickey hired Jackie away from the Monarchs there were loud and angry outcries, and not all of them were in a Southern accent. Some of the ugliest comments were spoken in ripe, raucous Brooklynese. Even some owners in the low-paying Negro leagues protested against "raiding" their men. There had been Negroes in big-league ball before, but they had been careful to identify themselves as Indians or "Cubans." The late Minor League President Bill Bramham cried: "Father Divine will have to look to his laurels, for we can expect Rickey Temple to be in the course of construction in Harlem soon." Rickey, ignoring the uproar, treated Jackie "white," giving him a year's seasoning in the minors. The four other Negroes who followed Robinson to the big leagues this season (and were generally failures) had no such break.

Jackie faced hostility, suspicion, curiosity and every newspaper camera within miles when he reported to the International League's Montreal club for training.

Jackie spoke to his teammates only when spoken to, and his replies were brief and polite. He had long ago made it a rule to "let them make the first move." Soon after the season opened, the Montreal players were with him. It took longer to win over some of the fans, and the other players in the League.

Black Cat, Good Luck. He was booed in Baltimore. In Syracuse one day, the rival team let out a black cat from their dugout as Jackie walked up to bat. Jackie got mad and hit a triple with the bases loaded.

By the time the season ended, his doctor told him that he was on the verge of a nervous breakdown, but nobody would have guessed it by looking at his record. Second Baseman Robinson led the International League in batting (with a .349 average) and in fielding (with a .985 average). Montreal won the pennant, and the fans, after one game, chaired Jackie and carried him around the field. Jackie Robinson was ready for the Dodgers.

Do's & Don'ts. Montreal had been won over, but that cut no ice in Flatbush. Branch Rickey, who knows his fellow citizens, set out to soften them up. He organized a group of Brooklyn's leading Negro citizens, including one judge, into a formal "how-to-handle-Robinson committee." In every other city in the National League, Rickey set up similar committees. The Brooklyn committee drew up a list of do's and don'ts a yard long; Jackie's deportment in public & private was to be supervised as thoroughly as Princess Elizabeth's.

He could not, like other ballplayers, endorse breakfast foods (or any other product, for that matter) at the usual $1,000 per endorsement. He could sign his name to no magazine or newspaper articles. When he got what he considered a bad decision from the umpire, he was not to object. When another player insulted him, he was to grin and bear it. He had to leave the ballpark after games by a secret exit. It was as important to avoid adulation as it was to avoid brickbats; there were to be no Jackie Robinson Days at Ebbets Field. He was not to accept any social invitations, from whites or blacks, and he was to stay away from night spots.

Jackie Robinson had already learned, by a lifetime's practice, the lesson another Robinson—soft-shoe dancing Bojangles *—once laid down while acting as the unofficial Mayor of Harlem. Bojangles' formula: "Do the best you can with what you've got ... and get along with the white folks." Jackie had no desire to be a martyr for his race; he was just a young fellow anxious to make a living as a ballplayer. Though he barely knew Joe Louis, he sought him out for advice. He got an earful which boiled down to three words: "Don't get cocky."

Jackie lives a long way from Harlem's high life, in a five-room, second-floor flat on Brooklyn's McDonough Street, in a Negro neighborhood. His name is not on the door, and he knows few of his neighbors. How he feels about them shows through the guarded brevity of

* No kin.

his speech, which sometimes carries a suggestion of dryness. Says he: "I don't want to bother with too many people who want to be my relatives."

Jackie's idea of a fine way to spend a night off is to go to bed early. He averages ten hours' sleep. He likes neither music nor dancing. "You know," he says, "colored people do not like music and dancing any better than white people ... the white people just think they do." At home, he carefully takes his vitamin pills, spends a lot of time baby-sitting with his nine-month-old son, and according to his wife (whom he met at U.C.L.A.), always has his face buried in a paper. Like most ballplayers, he soaks up every word in every newspaper in town that concerns him and his team. His reader reaction: "Some reporters write nice things about me and mean them, and others write nice things and don't mean them. I can always tell."

So that Jackie would have company when the Dodgers were on the road, Rickey persuaded a Negro newsman, Wendell Smith, to travel with the club. In two cities, Jackie said, he had hotel trouble; he was not welcome at the Chase, where the Brooklyn club stays in St. Louis, or at Philadelphia's Benjamin Franklin. ("They fooled me," said Jackie. "I thought it would be St. Louis and Cincinnati.")

No Help at First. Branch Rickey's do's & don'ts, strangely enough, did not include any instructions on how to play baseball. Although Jackie had played second base or shortstop all his life, he was handed a first-baseman's mitt and sent out to sink or swim at a new position —first base. Being right-handed was no help: first base is a left-hander's position. It is easier for a left-hander to throw from first to any other base, and easier to pick a man off the bag. Only a few great first basemen (among them the Cubs' Frank Chance and the Giants' George Kelly) were right-handed. But Robinson, with a tricky "scissors" pivot, manages to get rid of the ball as quickly as any southpaw first baseman in the league.

His biggest difficulty is trying to forget that he is a shortstop. Fielding ground balls, he scoops them up as if he had a quick throw to make. And because he does not crouch down to block the ball, a lot of grounders dribble between his legs. He also can't seem to break his habit of catching put-out throws two-handed. The Cardinals' Stan Musial, for example, gets a far longer reach by taking throws single-handed.

A right-handed hitter, Jackie has a habit of swinging too soon and his motion is half chop, half lunge. As a result, he fouls off a lot of balls to the left. But his batting average at week's end was a solid .301. The wise boys who judge a hitter by his Runs Batted In totals are apt to take too fast a look at Jackie's R.B.I. and grumble that Jackie can't hit in a tight spot. But as the club's No. 2 hitter in the line-up, Jackie's job is either to push along the lead-off man by a sacrifice, or to get on base himself. Jackie's R.B.I. total (44) is higher than most No. 2 hitters'—including Philadelphia's Harry Walker, who is baseball's current batting king with an average of .362.

Actually, Jackie at bat is most dangerous when the odds are against him. When the count gets to two strikes, as he explains it: "Then I begin to crowd the plate a little." Says Branch Rickey: "He is the best batter in the game with two strikes on him." Pitchers capitalize on his hasty swing by feeding him slow stuff. "I just can't hit those nuthin' pitches," Jackie complains. Because he is the best bunter in the game, the Dodgers "cut him loose" at the plate (*i.e.,* let him decide for himself whether to take, hit or bunt). He and Pete Reiser are also the only Dodgers good enough to be "cut loose" on the bases, allowed to steal without waiting for a signal.

Timing & Tricks. By now, Robbie has carefully catalogued pitchers' weaknesses. He has, for example, discovered that when Boston's Si Johnson crooks his neck in a certain way, Si has stopped worrying about the base-runner and is about to pitch. This discovery gives Jackie a split-second head start on his way to second.

A similar mixture of timing and careful study enabled him to steal home last month against the New York Giants. (It was the second time this year he had pulled off the most spectacular base-running trick of them all.) Standing on third, Jackie carefully watched Pitcher Joe Beggs' windup. Robinson ran in with the pitch as far as he dared, then slammed on the brakes and began to count: "One-two-three-four. ..." He ticked off how long it took Beggs to get the ball across the plate. Satisfied that he could have made it in that time, Jackie scurried back to third base and took a deep breath. Next pitch, as Beggs involved himself in another slow-motion windup, Robinson was off like an express, rushing for the plate. The pitcher froze like a man with a high-voltage electric wire in his hand. Jackie went home standing up.

Who taught him to do things like that? Says Branch Rickey: "Primarily God."

The Other Cheek. It is impossible to measure how much better, or how much worse, Jackie's first season might have been had his handicaps been fewer. It was not just that he was playing an unfamiliar position, or that at 28 he was pretty old for a rookie. He also had to turn the other cheek to abuses and insults. First he had to overcome the attitude of his fellow Dodgers, which ranged from mere wait-&-see stand-offishness to Southern-bred hostility.

And the rough stuff from rival teams began early and has never stopped. The first time the Dodgers played St. Louis, the Cards grumbled about playing on the same field with a Negro. They changed their minds—under pressure. Philadelphia was worse, because there the opposition had the open support of Phillies Manager Ben Chapman. He bawled insults at Robinson from the dugout. Chapman's second-division Phillies, notoriously the crudest bench-jockeys in baseball, chimed in. Says Rookie Robbie: "I'd get mad. But I'd never let them know it." The Phillies management finally called down Chapman. He had his picture taken with Robinson to prove to everyone that the ugly reports weren't true.

It was Robinson's own Dodger mates who first came round. One or two of his fellow Dodgers began to say "Hello" to him in the locker room. Jackie wrote to his high-school baseball coach: "It isn't too tough on me. I have played with white boys all my life. But they hadn't played with a Negro before, and it sure was rough on some of them." Soon he was invited to play cards on trips, but though he didn't like the deuces-wild type of poker the boys played, he joined in a few games of hearts.

As Branch Rickey had foreseen, if Jackie played good baseball, the rest took care of itself. Some of the southerners on the squad shared the attitude of an Atlanta newsman who, when asked what he thought of Jackie Robinson, replied "He's good, damn him." But they were ready to back any player, black or white, who might help bring them the bonus (about $6,000 for winners, $4,000 for losers) that each gets for playing in a World Series.

After Slaughter did his spiking job a month ago, a group of Brooklyn players came to Jackie and said: "If they give you the works, give it back to them—and the team will be behind you 100%." That was the day Jack Roosevelt Robinson won his long, patient battle.

GUIDE QUESTIONS

1. How can you account for the fact that Robinson established himself as a big leaguer in a seemingly trivial incident in which he won "the right to squawk"?

2. Why was the editor of the *Sporting News,* in naming Robinson the rookie of the year, careful to explain that sociological considerations had not influenced his choice?

3. Why were "baseball know-it-alls" convinced that a Negro ballplayer could never succeed?

4. Explain why, in your opinion, Robinson's home environment was or was not typical.

5. What was the necessity for the "how-to-handle Robinson committees"? What do you think of the "do's and don'ts" prescribed?

6. Comment on the advice given by Bojangles Robinson and Joe Louis.

7. What is shown by his remark after having "hotel trouble" in St. Louis and Philadelphia?

8. Analyze the statement: "As Branch Rickey had foreseen, if Jackie played good baseball, the rest took care of itself."

9. In your opinion, did the acceptance of him by his team mates really mean that Robinson had "won his long, patient battle"?

10. How would you define the success that Robinson achieved?

11. In what sense could this story be regarded as a refutation of Nathan, Mencken, Lewis, and Dos Passos?

12. This story is written in an easily recognizable style which is often referred to as "Timestyle." What are the characteristics of this style?

VOCABULARY

Give the derivations and definitions of the following words:

avowed, grandiloquent, politic, adulation, truculence, servility, voluble, raucous, brevity.

WRITING AND STUDY AIDS

PATTERN OF ORGANIZATION SUGGESTED BY THE GENERAL TOPIC:

A character sketch of a type is distinguished from a character sketch of a person in that its emphasis lies on similarities rather than differences. It is often possible, when called upon to explain one's view of a subject, to make the explanation clearer by selecting types whose general characteristics illustrate a principle, a conviction, an attitude, or a way of life. Thus, Nathan and Mencken deal with "the average American," and Sinclair Lewis calls this "average American" George F. Babbitt. In the readings which you have studied, characterizations of various types of people serve to illustrate various standards of success and differing conceptions of it.

When you write on this topic, think in terms of character types who may be used to vivify your own views concerning success in America—the meaning of it, the ways to achieve it, and the good and bad aspects of certain kinds of success.

ASSIGNMENTS:

Short themes:
1. Babbitts I have known
2. How to win friends and influence people
3. Dinner with the McKelveys
4. George F. Babbitt on success
5. "All that I am, I owe to . . ."
6. The most successful person I know
7. How to get ahead in college

Long themes:
1. The successful life
2. The tycoon and his circle
3. A practical code of ethics for college students
4. The booster in Utopia
5. The role of religion in success
6. What I want most in life
7. The rise of ——: a success story
8. A man who failed

READINGS FOR FURTHER STUDY:

Beard, Charles A., and Mary Beard. *The Rise of American Civilization.* New York: The Macmillan Company, 1933. 2 vols. Vol. 2, 181-91.

Chase, Stuart. "The Luxury of Integrity," *The Nemesis of American Business.* New York: The Macmillan Company, 1931. Chap. 2, 27-50.

Franklin, Benjamin. "The Way to Wealth," *Benjamin Franklin, Representative Selections.* Edited by Frank Luther Mott and Chester E. Jorgenson. New York: American Book Company, 1936. Pages 280-89.

Wecter, Dixon. "Poor Richard: The Boy Who Made Good," and "Gods from the Machine: Edison, Ford, Lindbergh," *The Hero in America.* New York: Charles Scribner's Sons, 1941. Chap. 4, 50-80, and Chap. 16, 415-44.

✒ The Meaning of "College" and "University"

THERE ARE TWO KINDS OF DEFINITIONS: LITERAL AND EXTENDED. THE FIRST kind comes out of a dictionary. The other is used in writing as a method of exposition or argument. An extended definition is usually an attempt to explain, to interpret, to determine the precise significance of a term or idea whose meaning is not generally agreed upon, or which means different things to different people. In the course of such an attempt to mark limits and set boundaries—in short, to explain a meaning—other expository methods, such as comparison and contrast, examples and illustrations, and analysis, may be used as auxiliary devices. Later on you will study these other devices and use them for their own sake, but in the readings for this assignment you will find them subsidiary or secondary to the method of definition. From the standpoint of utility, definition ranks high as a pattern of organization. From the standpoint of difficulty, however, it ranks lower than some other patterns to come later.

Among the terms which need careful definition, and which even those who see eye-to-eye may define differently, are "college" and "university." The reason for the diversity of opinion concerning the proper meaning of these two words is that they involve complex ideas. Before we can hope to define a college or a university in any meaningful way, we must examine our views as to the nature and purpose of education—what it should consist of, and what it should do for a person; and our views on these matters will inevitably influence our definition.

In the first two readings "college" and "university" are defined in terms of their place in the educational hierarchy. These are almost literal definitions, and they will give you the bare bones of the two terms. But what do a college and a university really *mean?* What ideas and ideals do they stand for; what are their aims; what conceptions of their duties have played a part in history? These questions require a different kind of answer, in the form of extended definitions. Woodrow Wilson says, in "What Is College For?" that its function is to train the leaders of the future. Ernest DeWitt Burton says, in "The Business of a College," that its function is to develop personalities. Both these views of the purpose of higher education, and the definitions of "college" arising from them, have certain historic associations that will become clear from Sir Walter Moberly's "Changing Conceptions of the University's Task," which analyzes and traces the Christian-Hellenic idea and the Liberal idea of what a university is meant to do. This last reading, therefore, illustrates the method of historical definition. As you read, use each writer's definitions to shape and refine your own opinions.

John Dale Russell

THE AMERICAN COLLEGE

A COLLEGE AS DEFINED by the National Conference Committee on Standards of Colleges and Secondary Schools in 1918, is an institution requiring for admission graduation from a standard secondary school, and offering a four-year curriculum leading to the first degree in arts and sciences, of such character as to qualify for admission to a graduate school of recognized standing. Good's *Dictionary of Education* defines a college as "(1) An institution of higher education, usually offering only a curriculum in the liberal arts and sciences, and empowered to confer degrees; (2) a major division of a university (usually the division of arts and sciences), especially one that requires for admission no study beyond the completion of secondary education." Dr. Good notes that "in the United States, there is some confusion in the use of the terms *university* and *college;* some institutions of higher learning

From *American Universities and Colleges,* 1948 edition. Reprinted by permission of the American Council on Education.

that are in reality colleges of liberal arts have been incorporated as *universities* and use the term in their name; some institutions incorporated as colleges are in reality *universities* containing graduate professional schools in addition to colleges of arts and sciences."

The American college, as distinguished from the professional school, is known by various titles such as the college of liberal arts, the college of arts and sciences, the college of literature, science, and the arts, and is usually called the "arts college" or simply "the college." The college may be the core or central unit around which the university is organized, or it may be a separate corporate entity, completely independent of direct connection with a university. The latter type of institution is particularly abundant in the United States: examples are Amherst College, Carleton College, and Mills College. The college provides its students with the broad intellectual foundation which will equip them either for immediate entrance into adult life and citizenship or for further specialized study at the graduate level. Its aim is usually to develop "the habit of mind, eager to know what the truth is, persistent in attempts to find it, and loyal to its implications when conviction is acquired that it has been found."

GUIDE QUESTIONS

1. How does the definition of a college by the National Conference Committee differ from the one in Good's *Dictionary of Education?*
2. Do you know of any college that calls itself a university?
3. Which of the two types of colleges are you enrolled in? How would you define it?
4. Why do you think the separate, independent college is "particularly abundant in the United States"? Give other examples of this type.

VOCABULARY

Give the derivations and definitions of the following words:

curriculum, corporate, entity, implication.

Donald H. Daugherty

THE AMERICAN UNIVERSITY

THE UNIVERSITY IN THE UNITED STATES may be defined as an educational institution comprising an undergraduate college of liberal arts and sciences, professional schools, and a graduate college or school which provides programs for study and research beyond the levels of the baccalaureate [B.A., etc.] and first professional [M.A., etc.] degrees. The word "university," however, is also employed in a much broader sense and is not infrequently used to describe almost any type of educational institution which offers instruction beyond the level of the secondary schools. In one of the noteworthy critical essays on American higher education, Abraham Flexner asserts that our universities "are secondary schools and colleges for boys and girls; graduate and professional schools for advanced students; 'service' stations for the general public."

Among the more than two hundred chartered American "universities" may be found evening schools of business and law; normal schools [teachers' colleges]; colleges of liberal arts offering only the bachelor's degree; colleges offering only the bachelor's degree but with programs outside the liberal arts, as in business administration, pharmacy, music; and colleges offering advanced studies only as far as the master's degree, as well as those institutions which maintain graduate and professional schools and award the doctorate. In educational circles the term "university" is often used with particular reference to the graduate school. Membership in the Association of American Universities, for example, is restricted to selected "institutions of the North American continent engaged in giving advanced or graduate instruction." The presence of an undergraduate college of liberal arts is usually taken for granted.

It should be observed, on the other hand, that many institutions not called universities in title conduct graduate studies and confer advanced degrees. This is illustrated by the following institutions, all of which

From *American Universities and Colleges,* 1948 edition. Reprinted by permission of the American Council on Education.

confer the doctorate in one or more fields: Claremont Graduate School, Bryn Mawr College, Carnegie Institute of Technology, Union Theological Seminary, Dropsie College for Hebrew and Cognate Learning (offering graduate studies only), and Colorado School of Mines.

GUIDE QUESTIONS

1. What part of Russell's definition of a college is repeated in Daugherty's definition of a university?
2. In what sense have our universities, as Flexner asserts, become " 'service' stations for the general public"? Do you approve or disapprove of this development?
3. Do you know other examples of institutions not called universities that confer advanced degrees?
4. Which is "worse," a college that calls itself a university or a real university that does not call itself one?

VOCABULARY

Give the derivations and definitions of the following words:

comprising, baccalaureate, doctorate, confer, cognate.

Woodrow Wilson

WHAT IS COLLEGE FOR?

WHAT SHOULD A LAD GO to college for,—for work, for the realization of a definite aim, for discipline and a severe training of his faculties, or for relaxation, for the release and exercise of his social powers, for the broadening effects of life in a sort of miniature world in which study is only one among many interests? That is not the only alternative suggested by recent discussions. They also suggest a sharp alternative with regard to the character of the study the college student should

"What Is College For?" appeared originally in *Scribner's,* November, 1909, and is reprinted by permission of Mrs. Woodrow Wilson.

undertake. Should he seek at college a general discipline of his faculties, a general awakening to the issues and interests of the modern world, or should he, rather, seek specially and definitely to prepare himself for the work he expects to do after he leaves college, for his support and advancement in the world? The two alternatives are very different. The one asks whether the lad does not get as good a preparation for modern life by being manager of a football team with a complicated programme of intercollegiate games and trips away from home as by becoming proficient in mathematics or in history and mastering the abstract tasks of the mind; the other asks whether he is not better prepared by being given the special skill and training of a particular calling or profession, an immediate drill in the work he is to do after he graduates, than by being made a master of his own mind in the more general fields of knowledge to which his subsequent calling will be related, in all probability, only as every undertaking is related to the general thought and experience of the world.

"Learning" is not involved. No one ever dreamed of imparting learning to undergraduates. It cannot be done in four years. To become a man of learning is the enterprise of a lifetime. The issue does not rise to that high ground. The question is merely this: do we wish college to be, first of all and chiefly, a place of mental discipline or only a school of general experience; and, if we wish it to be a place of mental discipline, of what sort do we wish the discipline to be,—a general awakening and release of the faculties, or a preliminary initiation into the drill of a particular vocation?

These are questions which go to the root of the matter. They admit of no simple and confident answer. Their roots spring out of life and all its varied sources. To reply to them, therefore, involves an examination of modern life and an assessment of the part an educated man ought to play in it,—an analysis which no man may attempt with perfect self-confidence. The life of our day is a very complex thing which no man can pretend to comprehend in its entirety.

But some things are obvious enough concerning it. There is an uncommon challenge to effort in the modern world, and all the achievements to which it challenges are uncommonly difficult. Individuals are yoked together in modern enterprise by a harness which is both new and inelastic. The man who understands only some single process, some single piece of work which he has been set to do, will never do anything else, and is apt to be deprived at almost any moment of the opportunity to do even that, because processes change, industry undergoes instant revolutions. New inventions, fresh discoveries, alterations in the markets of the world throw accustomed methods and the men who are accustomed to them out of date and use without pause or pity. The man of special skill may be changed into an unskilled laborer overnight. Moreover, it is a day in which no enterprise stands alone or independent, but is related to every other and feels changes in all parts of the globe. The men with mere skill, with mere technical knowledge, will be mere servants perpetually, and may at any time become useless servants, their skill gone out of use and fashion. The particular thing they do may become unnecessary or may be so changed that they cannot comprehend or adjust themselves to the change.

These, then, are the things the modern world must have in its trained men, and I do not know where else it is to get them if not from its educated men and the occasional self-developed genius of an exceptional man here and there. It needs, at the top, not a few, but many men with the power to organize and guide. The college is meant to stimulate in a considerable number of men what would be stimulated in only a few if we were to depend entirely upon nature and circumstance. Below the ranks of generalship and guidance, the modern world needs for the execution of its varied and difficult business a very much larger number of men with great capacity and readiness for the rapid and concentrated exertion of a whole series of faculties: planning faculties as well as technical skill, the ability to handle men as well as to handle tools and correct processes, faculties of adjustment and adaptation as well as of precise execution—men of resource as well as knowledge. These are the athletes, the athletes of faculty, of which our generation most stands in need. All through its ranks, besides, it needs masterful men who can acquire a working knowledge of many things readily, quickly, intelligently, and with exactness,—things they had not foreseen or prepared themselves for beforehand, and for which they could not have prepared themselves beforehand. Quick apprehension, quick comprehension, quick action are what modern life puts a premium upon,—a readiness to turn this way or that and not lose force or momentum.

To me, then, the question seems to be, Shall the lad who goes to college go there for the purpose of getting ready to be a servant merely, a servant who will be nobody and who may become useless, or shall he go there for the purpose of getting ready to be a master adventurer in the field of modern opportunity?

We must expect hewers of wood and drawers of water to come out of the colleges in their due proportion, of course, but I take it for granted that even the least gifted of them did not go to college with the ambition to be nothing more. And yet one has hardly made the statement before he begins to doubt whether he can safely take anything for granted. Part of the very question we are discussing is the ambition with which young men now go to college. It is a day when a college course has become fashionable,—but not for the purpose of learning, not for the purpose of obtaining a definite preparation for anything,—no such purpose could become *fashionable*. The clientage of our colleges has greatly changed since the time when most of the young men who resorted to them did so with a view to entering one or other of the learned professions. Young men who expect to go into business of one kind or another now outnumber among our undergraduates those who expect to make some sort of learning the basis of their work throughout life; and I dare say that they generally go to college without having made any very definite analysis of their aim and purpose in going. Their parents seem to have made as little.

The enormous increase of wealth in the country in recent years, too, has had its effect upon the colleges,—not in the way that might have been expected,—not, as yet, by changing the standard of life to any very noticeable extent or introducing luxury and extravagance and vicious indulgence. College undergraduates have usually the freshness of youth about them, out of which there springs a wholesome simplicity, and it is not easy to spoil them or to destroy their natural democracy. They make a life of their own and insist upon the maintenance of its standards. But the increase of wealth has brought into the colleges, in rapidly augmenting numbers, the sons of very rich men, and lads who expect to inherit wealth are not as easily stimulated to effort, are not as apt to form definite and serious purposes, as are those who know that they must whet their wits for the struggle of life.

There was a time when the mere possession of wealth conferred distinction; and when wealth confers distinction it is apt to breed a sort of consciousness of opportunity and responsibility in those who possess it and incline them to seek serious achievement. But that time is long past in America. Wealth is common. And, by the same token, the position of the lad who is to inherit it is a peculiarly disadvantageous one, if the standard of success is to rise above mediocrity. Wealth removes the necessity for effort, and yet effort is necessary for the attainment of distinction, and very great effort at that, in the modern world, as I have already pointed out. It would look as if the ordinary lad with expectations were foredoomed to obscurity; for the ordinary lad will not exert himself unless he must.

We live in an age in which no achievement is to be cheaply had. All the cheap achievements, open to amateurs, are exhausted and have become commonplace. Adventure, for example, is no longer extraordinary: which is another way of saying that it is commonplace. Any amateur may seek and find adventure; but it has been sought and had in all its kinds. Restless men, idle men, chivalrous men, men drawn on by mere curiosity and men drawn on by love of the knowledge that lies outside books and laboratories, have crossed the whole face of the habitable globe in search of it, ferreting it out in corners even, following its bypaths and beating its coverts, and it is nowhere any longer a novelty or distinction to have discovered and enjoyed it. The whole round of pleasure, moreover, has been exhausted time out of mind, and most of it discredited as not pleasure after all, but just an expensive counterfeit; so that many rich people have been driven to devote themselves to expense regardless of pleasure. No new pleasure, I am credibly informed, has been invented within the memory of man. For every genuine thrill and satisfaction, therefore, we are apparently, in this sophisticated world, shut in to work, to modifying and quickening the life of the age. If college be one of the highways to life and achievement, it must be one of the highways to work.

The man who comes out of college into the modern world must, therefore, have got out of it, if he has not wasted four vitally significant years of his life, a quickening and a training which will make him in some degree a master among men. If he has got less, college was not worth his while. To have made it worth his while he must have got such a preparation and development of his faculties as will give him movement as well as mere mechanical efficiency in affairs complex, difficult, and subject to change. The word efficiency has in our day the power to think at the centre of it, the power of independent movement and initiative. It is not merely the suitability to be a good tool, it is the power to wield tools, and among the tools are men and circumstances and changing processes of industry, changing phases of life itself. There should be technical schools a great many and the technical schools of America should be among the best in the world. The men they train are indispensable. The modern world needs more tools than managers, more workmen than master workmen. But even the technical schools must have some thought of mastery and adaptability in their processes; and the colleges, which are not technical schools, should think of that chiefly. We must distinguish what the college is for, without disparaging any other school, of any other kind. It is for the training of the men who are to rise above the ranks.

That is what a college is for. What it does, what it requires of its undergraduates and of its teachers, should be adjusted to that conception. The very statement of the object, which must be plain to all who make any distinction at all between a college and a technical school, makes it evident that the college must subject its men to a general intellectual training which will be narrowed to no one point of view, to no one vocation or calling. It must release and quicken as many faculties of the mind as possible,—and not only release and quicken them but discipline and strengthen them also by putting them to the test of systematic labor. Work, definite, exacting, long continued, but not narrow or petty or merely rule of thumb, must be its law of life for those who would pass its gates and go out with its authentication. By a general training I do not mean vague spaces of study, miscellaneous fields of reading, a varied smattering of a score of subjects and the thorough digestion of none. The field of modern knowledge is extremely wide and varied. After a certain number of really fundamental subjects have been studied in the schools, the college undergraduate must be offered a choice of the route he will travel in carrying his studies further. He cannot be shown the whole body of knowledge within a single curriculum. There is no longer any single highway of learning. The roads that traverse its vast and crowded spaces are not even parallel, and four years is too short a time in which to search them all out. But there is a general programme still possible by which the college student can be made acquainted with the field of modern learning by sample, by which he can be subjected to the several kinds of mental discipline,—in philosophy, in some one of the great sciences, in some one of the great languages which carry the thought of the world, in history and in politics, which is its framework,—which will give him valid naturalization as a citizen of the world of thought, the world of educated men,—and no smatterer

merely, able barely to spell its constitution out, but a man who ha
really comprehended and made use of its chief intellectual processe
and is ready to lay his mind alongside its tasks with some confidenc
that he can master them and can understand why and how they ar
to be performed. This is the general training which should be cha
acteristic of the college, and the men who undergo it ought to be mad
to undergo it with deep seriousness and diligent labor; not as sof
amateurs with whom learning and its thorough tasks are side interest
merely, but as those who approach life with the intention of becom
ing professionals in its fields of achievement.

GUIDE QUESTIONS

1. A college and a university are defined by Russell and Daugherty, re
   spectively, in terms of their distinctive physical structure or organiz
   tion. In what terms, or with reference to which of its characteristic
   does Wilson define a college?
2. What alternative purposes of a college does Wilson eliminate at th
   outset? How does he indicate, in each case, which are to be eliminated
3. Why is special training in special skills of no permanent value i
   Wilson's opinion?
4. In the paragraph beginning "These, then, are the things the moder
   world must have in its trained men," in what sense is the wor
   athletes used? Why is it used twice?
5. Why does Wilson fear the effects of national wealth on the colleges
   Trace the points he makes in this part of the essay. What has "a
   venture" got to do with it?
6. Explain the use of the terms "a master among men," "men who a
   to rise above the ranks," "professionals in . . . achievement."
7. How would you define the ideal underlying Wilson's definition?
8. Why are some of the sentences in the essay very long, and others ve
   short? Pick out examples of each kind and comment on (a) their r
   lation to the rest of the sentences in the paragraph, and (b) their effec

VOCABULARY

Give the derivations and definitions of the following words:

*faculties, resource, clientage, resorted, vicious, augmenting, whet, mediocrit
foredoomed, chivalrous, ferreting, coverts, quickening, phase, authentic
tion, traverse, diligent.*

Ernest DeWitt Burton

THE BUSINESS OF A COLLEGE

VERY LIVING INSTITUTION NEEDS constant re-examination and restudy to etermine whether its growth is in the right direction. Like a living lant, you can cut and prune it too much. You can pull it up by the oots and start it over again too often. Yet like the plant it yields its est results to diligent farming.

The American college is very much alive today. Its right to live has een challenged, and that challenge calls for answer at a suitable time, ut I shall not attempt that answer now. Instead, I shall assume that has been made, that you agree with me, that there is still a place or the college, and that we are interested in its future and in seeing) it that that future is the best possible. In short, I take it for granted, n the one hand, that the college is to remain, but, on the other hand, iat it is not to be stagnant and unchangeable, that it is alive, and is oing to remain alive, and therefore to develop. The question that I m interested in is, How ought it to develop?

The first answer that I make to this question is the negative one iat it is not the business of the college to become a research institute. esearch is not its primary business. The research institute and the raduate school of research are primarily concerned with things, things oncrete and things abstract, with stars and planets, with molecules id microbes, with light and heat and force, with the forces that made ie world and the forces that are making human society and history. he college is primarily concerned with personalities and their de- elopment.

Research, in the stricter sense of the word at least, is concerned with ddition to the sum of hitherto possessed human knowledge. By it we iscover a new star or planet, a new element or plant, a new fact of istory, a new law of social progress, a new language or a new prin- ple in accordance with which languages are developed. This is not

From *Education in a Democratic World.* Chicago: The University of Chicago Press, 27, Chapter 5. Reprinted by permission of the publisher.

the task of the college student, if for no other reason, for this sufficien
one that, with rare and negligible exceptions, discoveries that add t
the sum of human knowledge can be made only by those who alread
have a large stock of the acquired knowledge of the world.

Let me illustrate this by a striking example. Roy Chapman Andrew
relates how on a scientific expedition into northern Asia his party di
covered, one morning before breakfast, certain fragments of bone, anc
in a rapid examination after breakfast, other impressions of bone
outlined in the rock. On the basis of these seemingly trifling di
coveries, Mr. Andrews says that they "added that morning an entirel
new geological era to the knowledge of the continental structure c
Central Asia, opened up a paleontological vista dazzling in its bri
liancy, and proved that which the expedition was organized to prov
or disprove—that Asia was the Mother of the life of Europe an
America." What did these few pieces of broken bones mean to th
workmen who accompanied that expedition? What would they hav
meant to an American college boy? What would they have meant t
us here? The tremendous conclusion which Mr. Andrews and h
fellow-investigators drew from them they drew only because the
added these trifling facts to an already acquired body of scientif
knowledge.

Yet I must not leave the impression that I think there is no plac
for research in the college. On the contrary, it is my belief that :
an attitude of mind it is essential to the well-being of the colleg
The college student cannot be expected to make additions to the su
of already possessed human knowledge, but he can be daily addin
to the sum of his own knowledge. And he ought to do this, not l
the unquestioning acceptance of the dogmatic assertions of textboo
or teacher, but by a process of discovery entirely analogous to that l
which the more advanced investigator makes his additions to his ow
and to human knowledge. The day has gone by when the college ca
be regarded as a place for the authoritative impartation and the doci
acceptance of traditionally transmitted facts or dogmas.

In the first place, this method is against nature, and involves a r
versal of the process that every child adopts unconsciously. Ever
normal boy and girl is born with eyes that see and ears that hear, ar
all children begin before they are out of the cradle to accumula
facts, not out of a book, but by observation. Almost as early does t
child begin to put facts together, and to deduce conclusions. He

not adding to the sum of human knowledge, but he is constantly adding to his own fund of knowledge, and the method of the two processes is essentially the same. To project into the midst of this normal experience of the child a process of so-called education in which he is practically required to cease observing for himself, and to learn only from the printed page or the spoken word, is to do violence to nature herself.

Of course as soon as he can talk, the child seeks information from people also. He instinctively attempts to draw from the store of accumulated knowledge so far as this is accessible in parents or teachers. But unless he is forced to it by an unnatural process, he does not abandon his former method of acquisition, but only adds to it a new one. He is still an active investigator, skeptical until he has settled his doubt by experience, or had the investigative spirit crushed out of him by a perverse method of education.

Moreover, if he is to go on to higher study or to active life, he must again take up the method of research. No textbook was ever written, no lecture was ever delivered, that will furnish to the college student rules by which to deal with the situations which he will actually meet in post-collegiate life. He must face these in a spirit of inquiry and interpretation. In other words, he must go back to the methods of the cradle. When, therefore, the college, in bringing the student, as it must, into contact with books and teachers and the accumulated stores of the world's knowledge, attempts to confine education within the limits of acquisition from these sources, and to discourage and to repress the instinct of research, it is destroying something which is not only native to the youth, but which, if he is to succeed in after life, he must laboriously recover.

The college must therefore, in my judgment, be characterized by the spirit of research. The pupil, though he is for the most part only learning for himself what other people already know, adding, in other words, to the sum of his knowledge rather than to the sum of the world's knowledge, should do this in the same spirit as that which animates the chemist or the astronomer.

But there is another sense in which the college, I believe, should be permeated by the spirit of research. I am thinking now of the faculty. It is obvious that no teacher can stimulate in his students a spirit of research which he does not himself possess. If to him the word of the textbook is the "court of last resort," if he has himself no eyes to see facts or powers of mind to set them in relation to one another, he will not be likely to cultivate this spirit in his pupils. He may, in most cases, be unable to carry his researches to such a point that he will make additions to the sum of human knowledge, but there are always areas to him unknown, into which he may be making excursions. He ought to be animated by the spirit of research, sympathetic with it in his students, ready to learn from them, never suppressing the spirit of inquisitiveness by his own dogmatism, but always encouraging it and guiding it.

There is, moreover, one field in which college professors as a group, if not singly and as individuals, can well hope to add not only to their own knowledge but to that of the world. I am thinking of the problem of college education itself, and of what I believe at least to be the fact, that we have neither in this country nor elsewhere arrived as yet at the ultimate truth respecting the best method of doing our educational work in this field. Every college faculty should, in my judgment, be a formally or informally organized seminar on college education, always working at the question of how their work can be more successfully accomplished. The most valuable results of such study may not be the things that are discovered, but the maintenance on the part of the faculty of the spirit of inquiry, which will inevitably affect their teaching and permeate the atmosphere in which the student does his work.

Nevertheless, I come back to say that the primary task of the college is not research, and that the attempt to improve the college by forcing back into it the point of view and methods of the research institute or even of the graduate school is fraught with grave danger. The institute of research deals with things—things concrete and things abstract, with facts and principles and truths. The college deals primarily with personalities.

My second negative assertion about the college is that it is not a trade school. By trade school I mean one of those necessary institutions in which youths are taught the rules and methods of accomplishing certain standardized processes: schools for blacksmiths, schools for barbers, schools for bookkeepers, schools for teachers even, if the purpose of the school be to impart the rules for teaching by the standardized methods of conducting schools. The characteristic mark of what I am calling the trade school is not the field within which it operates, but the way it operates, namely, not by teaching the pupil to think his way through his problem, but to acquire and to practice, without originality, the standardized methods of the trade, be it blacksmithing, or hair-cutting, or bookkeeping, or school-teaching.

What, then, is the business of a college? If it is not to conduct research that adds to the sum of human knowledge, if it is not to produce the practicers of trades, what is its central task? . . . The central business of a college is, I believe, to develop, not ideas in the abstract, nor the human tools of the trades, but personalities capable of full participation in life and of significant contribution to life. One argument only I advance for this opinion, viz., that personalities of this type are the world's greatest need, and that the college rightly administered is capable of producing them—not, indeed, of finishing their training, but of starting them in the right direction. The process of education will necessarily be lifelong.

But if this is the central business of the college, what are the specific things that it ought to do for all its students? Three things, as I see it. First, a college ought to enable all its students to place themselves in the world, to recognize where they are. It ought to help each student to acquire such knowledge of the physical universe, of the history of the race, of the structure of society, and of the nature of the individual, that, taking his stand at the center of his own being, he may have a sense of where he is. I pity profoundly the man to whom all past history is a blank, who, looking back, sees an impenetrable wall at the moment to which his own memory extends. He lacks a fundamental condition of the highest enjoyment of life and of any large service to the world. The college ought to save him from such isolation, and enable him to find himself.

The second thing that a college ought to do for its students is to teach them to think; not to follow precepts, not to practice an art according to fixed methods, nor to play a game according to the rules of the game, but to observe facts, to set them in relation to one another, to view them dispassionately, and to draw conclusions from them. The impulse to do this is, as I said a few minutes ago, inborn; but it needs encouragement, development, practice, intensification. The thinker, dispassionate but acute, is one of the world's greatest needs.

The third thing that is necessary to the achievement of the business of the college is the development of character. If once we thought that an education that consisted in the acquisition of facts was all that was needed to make democracy safe for itself and the world, we have surely been thoroughly disillusioned. Breadth of knowledge, power to think, are indispensable prerequisites to large participation in life or large contributions to life. But apart from high moral character they are not only inadequate but positively dangerous. And because this is so, no institution that undertakes to give these former things can escape the obligation to concern itself for the latter also. It is my conviction on this point, indeed, that largely influenced me in the choice of that rather vague word "personality." I recently read an address in which, if I followed the writer's thought correctly, he summed up the duty of the college as teaching the student to think. I feel obliged, on the other hand, to maintain the old-fashioned doctrine, if it is old-fashioned, that any definition of the function of the college in purely intellectual terms, however broad and inclusive, or however rigid and exacting, is fatally false by defect. Unless to whatever it does for the student by enlarging his horizon and by sharpening his power of intellect it also does its best to see that he acquires sound principles and right habits of action, it has failed at a point where failure is fatally serious.

In naming these things as the chief function of a college, I do not wish to be understood as denying that a college education may also have occupational value, or even as affirming that occupational preparation must be purely incidental and indirect. I rather believe that when we have studied out our problem of college education a little further we shall discover ways in which much of what we do in the college course, if not all of it, will have a double value: on the one hand, adding to the student's knowledge and cultivating the power of discovery and the spirit of research, and on the other hand, by means of these things, directly preparing him for his future occupation.

So far as I know, however, this problem of the discovery of cultural values in occupational subjects and occupational values in cultural subjects has as yet been very imperfectly solved. This is a matter that calls for the spirit and practice of research on the part of college faculties and other students of education. While it remains unsolved, or very imperfectly solved, we must, I suspect, content ourselves with saying that every college course ought to contain a large element of what we commonly call the cultural effect of education, broadening of horizon, sharpening of perception, training to think and to appreciate, and it ought also in the majority of cases, at least, materially to contribute to the student's preparation for his occupation.

But be that as it may, I come back with emphasis to my assertion that the central and constant function of the college is the development of personalities. And if this be true, there follow from it certain corollaries that I think have an immediate practical significance.

When I spoke of the college as developing a certain type of personality, I used the word "develop" with intention; for, in fact, it cannot create them. Nor can it develop them out of every type of individual. It follows, then, that the college must select its students, and winnow out those that cannot or will not respond to its influence.

This is much more important than was formerly the case. The number of applicants for admission to college has so enormously increased, and the cost of education has also so greatly increased, that the colleges are compelled to consider whom they will admit. And this, in turn, means that the conditions of admission and retention must be carefully reconsidered. Obviously, ability to pay the tuition fee is not a sufficient criterion. Nor do I believe that a marking system taken by itself furnishes an adequate test. We must find tests at once more delicate and more exact.

This brings me to my second corollary, viz., that the college must deal with its students as individuals. Mass education is ill-adapted to produce the highest type of personalities. It is better than none, but it is far from being good enough. The touch of the *individual* teacher is the most potent educational force. If it be said that our colleges have not a staff adequate to supply such individualized guidance, I answer that if we are to do our work we shall have to find them. Better a few students well educated than many inadequately trained.

We have passed through three periods in reference to the rigidity of our curriculum: that of the wholly prescribed curriculum, all students taking the same studies; that of free electives, each student following his own more or less ignorant impulse; that of majors and minors, and more or less rigidly formulated sequences. For the college student I believe our next experiment must be that of a sympathetically guided individualism.

My third corollary is that if the college accepts the responsibility of developing personalities, it must make a comprehensive study of all the forces that make for such personality, including not only the curriculum in the specific sense, but every phase and element of college life—athletics, companionship, classroom discipline, voluntary reading, moral and religious influence—and must concern itself constantly with all of these things. And this, in turn, brings me back again to the necessity that college faculties shall be conducting research in the field of college education.

But, after all, the main thing that I want to say and to emphasize is that the business of the college is to develop personalities that are equipped to participate fully in life and to make large contribution to life. If we recognize this to be the business of the college, everything else will in time take care of itself.

GUIDE QUESTIONS

1. What is the advantage of defining the business of a college negatively at first, by saying what it is *not?*
2. What is the point of the anecdote about Roy Chapman Andrews?
3. In what sense is every child engaged in research? What definition of *research* does Burton assume in developing this point?
4. What is the difference between *research* and the "spirit of research"?
5. In eliminating the two things which he says are not the business of a college, why does Burton devote so much space to the first and so little to the second?
6. Why are the three specific things that Burton believes a college ought to do for its students taken up in the order in which he mentions them rather than in some other order?
7. What subjects would give a student "knowledge of the physical universe, of the history of the race, of the structure of society, and of the nature of the individual"? Why would these give a student "a sense of where he is"?
8. Discuss the ways in which most colleges have gone beyond Burton in the "occupational value" of the education they offer.
9. Explain the logical connection between Burton's three "corollaries" and his definition of a college's function. Why are these taken up in the order in which he mentions them rather than in some other order?
10. Where does Burton state affirmatively for the first time what he considers the primary business of a college? Why does he state it at that particular place? How many times does he restate the idea as he goes along? Comment on the places where these restatements occur.

11. Compare and contrast Wilson's definition with Burton's. Are they in substantial agreement, could their differences be compromised, or do they express irreconcilable views?

VOCABULARY

Give the derivations and definitions of the following words:

stagnant, paleontology, vista, dogmatic, analogous, impartation, docile, deduce, acquisition, skeptical, perverse, permeated, seminar, dispassionate, disillusioned, corollary, winnow, retention, criterion.

Sir Walter Moberly

CHANGING CONCEPTIONS OF THE UNIVERSITY'S TASK

I. CHRISTIAN-HELLENIC

For the greater part of the nineteenth century Oxford and Cambridge exemplified a highly distinctive type of university, based on Christian and Graeco-Roman traditions. In various respects this type has become inadequate to the modern world. But it represents the most characteristic English contribution to "the idea of the university," and it is of the first importance to understand and appreciate it. Its classical statement occurs in Newman's *Idea of a University* and is inimitable. But, in substance, it is by no means peculiar to Newman, and there is nothing about it that is specifically Catholic. He is drawing on his recollections of Oxford and is painting its characteristic excellences. What he depicts, is Jowett's ideal of Oxford quite as much as it is his own.

On this view the chief duty of the university is to produce good citizens. It should train an elite who are to be the future leaders in affairs and in the learned professions. Thus it differs from a seminary, a technical college, or a research institute. For neither training in the

From *The Crisis in the University,* 1949. Reprinted by permission of SCM Press, Ltd.

technique of particular callings, whether ecclesiastical or secular, nor the advancement of knowledge is its primary function, though it may contribute to each. The training it gives is an initiation of select young people into their cultural inheritance. In Matthew Arnold's words it seeks to familiarize them with "the best that has been thought and said in the world" and so to bind together the generations through their sharing in a common intellectual estate.

Such education has the following characteristics. First, it is "liberal" as opposed to "servile." That is, it aims at mental development for its own sake and not for any ulterior end. It seeks, not to make the student an effective tool to serve someone else's purpose or to give him power to make tools of others to serve his own purpose, but to train him to recognize, to respect and to delight in, what is intrinsically true, good and beautiful. It does so simply because this is a want of man's nature and in its satisfaction he fulfils himself. It encourages the student to master the Greek language, not because "it not infrequently leads to positions of considerable emolument," nor even because familiarity with Thucydides may make him a more capable statesman in after-life, but in order that he may appreciate and enjoy Homer or Plato for their own sake. By exposing young men to the acknowledged masterpieces of human thought and knowledge, it evokes a culture which is valuable for what it is rather than for what it does, and which is inseparable from mental health in all who are capable of it, since without it they would be less than fully human. Thus refinement rather than effectiveness is its direct aim; and yet, in a large view, it is just the people who have achieved refinement who are also the most effective and excel in practical judgment and knowledge of life. "A cultivated intellect, because it is good in itself, brings with it a power and a grace to every work and occupation which it undertakes."

Secondly, this education is general as opposed to specialized. "The man who has been trained to think on one subject only will never be a good judge even in that one"; while if he ventures to express opinions outside his own narrow field, he will be like a schoolboy or a ploughman presuming to judge a prime minister. The student needs to gain a synoptic view, like a man who possesses a map of the country or one who gets up on to high ground to see the panorama. Henceforward he will have some catholicity of outlook and sense of proportion; however intensively he studies any particular subject he will see it in its relation to the whole scheme. . . . But he does not necessarily acquire this sense through having a very wide curriculum. That in itself may be a snare. The dilettante is no better than the narrow specialist; a smattering in a dozen branches of study is not enlargement but shallowness. True enlargement is got rather from the fact that the student is a member of a community in which the whole range of knowledge is being studied and is in intimate association with those whose specialty differs from his own. Thus "he apprehends the great outlines of knowledge, the principles on which it rests, the scale of its parts, its lights and its shades, its great points and its little, as he otherwise cannot apprehend them." In this way he avoids provincialism.

Thirdly, this education is systematic. There must be no stuffing with knowledge, no passive reception of scraps, no "unmeaning profusion of subjects." What is important is, not the amassing of facts but their grasp, not cramming but mental digestion. Hence a habit of method must be formed. The student must learn to start from fixed points, to make good his ground as he goes, to distinguish clearly what he knows from what he does not know, to relate what he learns to what he knows already. Further he is being made acquainted with a world of intellectual order and not of intellectual anarchy and with a hierarchy of intellectual values in which some are fundamental and others subsidiary. He is introduced to laws and principles which are objective and independent of fashion or individual caprice. "Universities," says Whewell, "so far as they are schools of *general* cultivation, represent the permanent, not the fluctuating elements of human knowledge . . . They have to transmit the civilization of past generations to future ones, not to share and show forth all the changing fashions of intellectual caprice and subtlety." Or, to adapt an aphorism of Burke's, one object of a university education is to make the student independent of his own private stock of reason which, in the nature of the case, is small and to make available to him "the general bank and capital of nations and of ages."

So much for the traditional aims of our older universities, but what of the methods by which they have sought to achieve them? These are based on the fundamental principle that the university, as a community of teachers and learners, is to be regarded as a family. Or, in words whose felicity has caused them to become a familiar possession, "a university is . . . an Alma Mater, knowing her children one by one, not a foundry, or a mint, or a treadmill." In accordance with this principle, the bulk of the teaching has been tutorial . . . and has in-

volved the direct impact of person on person. The student is required
to answer questions, to write compositions or essays, or to engage in
disputations. He is to be, not only a passive recipient of instruction,
but an active co-operator in the process. His mental enlargement en-
tails "the mind's energetic and simultaneous action upon and towards
and among those new ideas which are rushing in upon it."

In conformity with the family analogy, the relation between staff
and students is regarded as being paternal on the one side and filial
on the other. The student is under authority. He is subjected to rules
and regulations, not many or burdensome but inescapable. He lives in
a world of definite duties requiring of him some degree of self-
restraint and self-regulation; and this is part of his preparation for life.
On the other side the teacher's is, to some extent, a pastoral office. He
has a responsibility towards his pupils as human beings which extends
far beyond his formal obligations as an instructor.

But the most potent educational influence of Oxford and Cambridge
has been found outside lecture room or laboratory and even outside
the private hour with the tutor. It arises, indirectly, from the character
of the community life. No passage in Newman is better remembered
or more frequently quoted than that in which he depicts and extols
the influence of students on one another and asserts that, if he had to
choose between one system in which students lived a corporate life
but received no formal teaching and were submitted to no examination and another in which they were rigorously examined but lived
no corporate life, he would unhesitatingly prefer the former. . . .

Of course it is not simply by being communities that Oxford and
Cambridge have exercised their educative influence. It is because they
are communities which possess an extremely distinctive and inspiring,
historic tradition. Their "atmosphere" is the result of many centuries of
corporate life. To wander among green lawns and stately buildings
of crumbling grey stone or mellow red brick—such as the garden front
of St. John's College, Oxford or the street front of St. John's College,
Cambridge—to dine in Hall with its walls lined with the portraits of
great men and its tables loaded with old silver, and to take part in the
time-honoured ritual of university ceremonies—all these have made the
undergraduate feel himself the citizen of no mean city and the inheritor
of an illustrious tradition. They have conduced to expansion and ele-
vation of mind and to that "energy of the soul" in which Aristotle
found the essence of true well-being.

In this tradition one of the most pervasive and characteristic ingredients has been religion. For far the greater part of their history, Oxford and Cambridge have deliberately set themselves to be "places of religious and useful learning." The two universities and their colleges were originally religious foundations and manifold traces of this origin still persist. Every college has its chapel, in which in term time there are daily and weekly services. . . . The Christianity which the ordinary undergraduate drank in was extremely diluted. Yet, such as it was, the atmosphere of the place was impregnated with it. Anyone going from Oxford or Cambridge to a modern and thoroughly secularized university must at once be conscious of the difference. Till quite lately the ancient universities have in this respect been in tune with the temper of our national life. Less than a hundred years ago it was possible for Newman to appeal confidently to the self-evident fact that belief in God was "the secret assumption, too axiomatic to be distinctly professed, of all our writers." Only too obviously that situation has changed. But, until comparatively recent times, the work and recreation and common life of Oxford and Cambridge, however little directly religious, have been carried on within the setting of an ultimate Christian commitment.

At their best the older English universities have admittedly had success in turning out men fit to exercise responsibility, and this is no easy task. Some years ago one who carried large responsibilities in connection with appointments in the public service said, "I can get any number of men with 'First Classes,' but what I want and find it hard to get, is 'round' men." To produce "round" men, in his sense of the word, is exactly what the older universities, through their traditional mental discipline, based on classics and mathematics, set themselves to do. What they have cultivated and valued most highly is neither technical expertness nor prodigious learning but, as Newman puts it, the quality of judgment or the power to grapple with any subject and to seize the strong point in it. This, he says, is "the education which gives a man a clear, conscious view of his own opinions and judgments, a truth in developing them, an eloquence in expressing them, and a force in urging them. It teaches him to see things as they are, to go right to the point, to disentangle a skein of thought, to detect what is sophistical, and to discard what is irrelevant. It prepares him to fill any post with credit, and to master any subject with facility. It shows him how to accommodate himself to others, how to throw himself into

their state of mind, how to bring before them his own, how to come
to an understanding with them, how to bear with them." In the same
vein the authors of the recent Harvard Report on *General Education
in a Free Society* define "the abilities to be sought above all others in
a general education," as being "to think effectively, to communicate
thought, to make relevant judgments, to discriminate among values."
In so doing, they echo Newman and imply that the qualities at which
Oxford and Cambridge aimed in the middle of the nineteenth century
are still of major importance in the middle of the twentieth. The fine
flower of such training has been seen in men such as Balfour and
Baldwin, Asquith and Milner, Curzon and Lang; and perhaps most
of all in Gladstone, of whom it was truly said in a recent broadcast
that he "habitually lived from day to day in communion with the
highest peaks of the human spirit" and, from that, derived much of his
strength. Naturally the average product fell far behind such outstanding figures. But this is the type which Oxford and Cambridge en-
deavoured to foster and, with the better of their alumni, did in some
measure achieve.

2. LIBERAL

Even in Oxford and Cambridge the traditional ideal has been
largely displaced by a newer one. In the other universities of this
country, as in Scotland, Germany and the United States, the triumph
of the new ideal has been complete. It has been reached by giving a
still stronger emphasis to some features in the Christian-Hellenic
conception and by the total omission of others. Its own most salient
traits are the following.

First, investigation matters more than instruction. The advancement rather than the communication—or, as some critics unkindly put
it, the embalmment—of knowledge is the primary business of the
university. The former is essential, the latter only incidental. It has
been well said that Socrates, Plato and Aristotle were resorted to, not
because they had made teaching their business, but because they were
believed to have made philosophy their business. It is indeed a reproach to the British universities that, till comparatively recently, the
great figures in our intellectual history have worked outside and not
within them. This is true among philosophers of Hume, Bentham,
Mill and Spencer; among historians of Gibbon, Hallam, Grote and

Macaulay; and among scientists of Dalton, Davy, Faraday and Darwin. In Germany, on the other hand, Kant and Hegel, Niebuhr, Ranke and Mommsen, Jhering and Savigny, Liebig, Helmholtz and Virchow were all university professors; and so they incurred less danger of a certain amateurishness, wastefulness and freakishness, which is liable to come from isolation. Moreover the quality of the education itself is greatly heightened by its linkage with the great masters. From such a man, "if he have also in any measure the special gifts of a teacher, all will come forth with a life and love, a power, fullness and freshness, which you will look for in vain from the man whose main business is to communicate, and not to possess something worth communicating."

Secondly, learning for learning's sake is the proper business of the university. This is a worthy, satisfying, and wholly self-justifying activity. As President Eliot of Harvard put it at the outset of his forty years' reign, the dominating idea should be "the enthusiastic study of subjects for the love of them and without any ulterior motive." The savant's is a high calling. Like the poet,

> He lives detachèd days
> He serveth not for praise
> > For gold
> He is not sold.

Alike in Germany and in Scotland this is recognized and he receives something of the esteem which the Indian villagers felt for Kipling's *Lama*. Here is implied an austere ideal of knowledge and a new type of scholar. In one of his books E. F. Benson, writing of Cambridge as it was sixty years ago, draws a vivid contrast between Walter Headlam and the ordinary college tutor. The ordinary classical tutor was widely read and an accomplished writer of elegant compositions; but his knowledge, though more extensive, was essentially of the same order as that of the better among his pupils. But "Walter Headlam's knowledge of Greek began where theirs left off." Now such mastery involves concentration and specialization. "A man who is not capable of, so to speak, putting on blinkers, and of working himself up into the idea that the fate of his soul depends on whether, shall we say, his conjecture about this particular passage in a manuscript is correct—then that man had better keep away from scholarship."

Thirdly, the function of the university as a community of science and learning is quite distinct from that of Church or State or of commerce and industry, and it should never be subservient to them. It has its own business which it understands better than any outsider can do. Its proper task is to promote neither money-making, nor good citizenship nor holiness, but simply sound learning. So, Dr. Doerne argues, the duty of the university is not to make but to interpret history, not to produce leaders of Germany but to be the guardians of pure knowledge in a time of fanaticism. So far as training goes, it is the training of the graduate rather than of the undergraduate that is the university's primary concern. A master and his disciples were the nucleus out of which the earliest universities grew. So Socrates trained Plato and Plato trained Aristotle; the training of Alcibiades or Critias for public life was, by comparison, incidental and secondary. In terms of American organization, the "college" is only a kind of junior department; the "university" proper consists of its graduate schools. On this view Oxford and Cambridge in the nineteenth century contrasted unfavourably with the German universities, since a hundred years ago they trained graduates hardly at all, and fifty years ago only to a small extent. They might indeed be regarded as finishing schools rather than universities, and Paulsen's irony is thinly veiled when he writes of them, "The general aim is to give a gentleman that broader and deeper culture with which custom demands that he should be equipped." Things are very different now. Even apart from the genuine researcher, the engineer or works manager who had come anywhere near Rutherford in Cambridge, the civil servant or business man who had come near Tout in Manchester, was often raised to a higher plane of intellectual life. As Paulsen wrote of the German situation at an earlier day, "Though only a limited number of students succeed in doing original scientific work, yet the majority have at some time or other been seized with the impulse to seek after the truth. This longing remains in the souls of many, they become permanently interested in science and scientific life. Even in their callings they regard themselves as parts of the academic world; the teacher in the gymnasium, the clergyman, the physician, the judge, all seek to keep in touch with science, and not a few succeed not merely in following the standard of science as sympathisers and sharers in its glories, but in serving under it, here and there, as active co-workers."

Fourthly, the academic thinker must have a completely open field and he should approach it with a mind free from antecedent bias or presupposition. For him all questions are open, all assumptions tentative, all conclusions provisional. There is no fixed framework of thought within which he must operate, no authoritative premises which must be the starting point of his reasoning and which it would be impious to question. He may and must follow the argument whithersoever it leads. . . . Each science is autonomous. In particular it must be free from all religious supervision. Neither the historian nor the physicist need look nervously over his shoulder to see what the theologian has to say of his hypothesis. The Darwinian theory, or any suggested modification of it, must be discussed on the basis of the scientific evidence and judged by biological canons. The discussion must not be cramped or bedevilled by any pressure to accommodate it to the Book of Genesis. . . . In the words of President Eliot, "The worthy fruit of academic culture is an open mind, trained to careful thinking, instructed in the methods of philosophic investigation, acquainted in a general way with the accumulated thought of past generations, and penetrated with humility."

Fifthly, the university must cultivate detachment. It must keep itself clear of matters of current practical controversy in fields, such as the political or the religious, which excite passion. The heat and turbidity and partisanship which these engender are incompatible with the objectivity and serenity inherent in a scientific attitude. A university is a "thought-organization" not a "will-organization," and its aim is understanding rather than action. It is a society for the pursuit of knowledge and not for the promotion of this cause or the prevention of that abuse. The only fanaticism permissible is "the fanaticism of veracity."

No doubt this emphasis is due to long experience of the distorting influence of the *odium theologicum* on the one hand and of "reasons of state" on the other. The moral has been drawn in two, slightly different, ways. Some modern universities have played for safety by excluding altogether from their purview the fields in which controversies are most liable to arise. Others, without such drastic self-mutilation, have insisted that their treatment, e.g., of religious or political issues, must be in quite a different temper and perspective from that of those engaged in the hurly-burly. This difference is very clearly expressed by Matthew Arnold in his essay on "The Function of Criticism at the Present Time." There he deprecates the tendency of the young and ardent to see everything in inseparable connection with politics and practical life, and he asserts the value of criticism which is disinterested in the sense that the critic has no axe to grind, however altruistic. True criticism, he says, requires a free play of mind. . . . The disinterestedness and free play of mind which Arnold here requires of the critic are precisely the characteristics which, on the Liberal conception, should mark contributions from the universities to the discussion of major issues.

This view is expressed very clearly by Paulsen writing at the turn of the century and by Dr. Flexner thirty years later. "The scholars," says Paulsen, "cannot and should not engage in politics." This is because some of the qualities required in the thinker are the opposite of those which the practical politician should possess. The latter must be a man of resolute will and even a certain one-sidedness, who having chosen one path, follows it without *arrière pensée*. The thinker must look at a question from all sides and must constantly return to his starting point to make sure that no error has crept into the argument though, in action, this would produce some indecisiveness. Dr. Flexner makes the same point. It is for the university to apply "free, resourceful, unhampered intelligence to the comprehension of problems," but it must preserve its "irresponsibility." By this of course he does not mean that the university is irresponsible absolutely; any theoretical advance in the field of the social sciences is likely to have practical repercussions. But immediate short-term applications are not its business: to concern itself with these would deflect it from its proper work. The professor "has no practical responsibility for the trouble he makes . . . But he must go on thinking."

Sixthly, the university should be highly selective and even fastidious in regard both to the subjects it treats and the methods it employs. It should abhor mediocrity: its business is with an intellectual aristocracy. Energy can too easily and insidiously be dissipated in a multiplicity of interests. The university should therefore look critically at all new claimants for the provision of professional training. (Here Dr. Flexner's devastating criticism of the lengths to which some American universities have allowed the "service-station" conception of their function to carry them is much in point.) The criterion to be employed is not the social importance of the proposed faculty or subject but its inherent and intellectual value. It is only the "learned professions" or those that have intellectual content in their own right with which the universities should concern themselves. So also they should eschew all that is half-baked or concerned with the shop-window. The public opinion to which the professor is rightly sensitive is that of his peers,

> Like Verdi when, at his worst opera's end . . .
> He looks through all the roaring and the wreaths
> Where sits Rossini patient in his stall.

Seventhly, in the university there should be plenty of elbow-room. It should not be rigidly organized or regimented. Members of its staff should have the greatest possible freedom of choice in regard to what they are to teach, and how, and when. A great deal of wastage can and should be tolerated, so long as a congenial atmosphere is provided for a Mommsen or a Rutherford.

Finally, the liberty, initiative and adult status of the student are strongly emphasized. . . . The extreme example of this is the "elective system" as it has flourished in the United States. This represents a violent reaction against the rigid curricula of earlier days. It is based on the principle that at all points the decision what to study and how hard to study should be made by, and not for, the student himself. His menu is to be "à la carte"; or, as Professor Morison says of President Eliot, "he wished every man's curriculum to be tailor-made." The curriculum is to be fitted to the student and not the student to the curriculum. It matters little what you study, provided you are interested. So it is for the university to offer the widest possible variety of choice. At one time in Harvard, "the Bachelor's degree could be earned by passing eighteen courses, no two of which need be related." Similarly it is the student's own affair whether he works or idles. No official pressure should be put on him; that is appropriate only at the schoolboy stage. The university is not a kindergarten. Admittedly such liberty may, and in some cases will, be abused, but that is part of the price of freedom. Again, if the student is to be regarded as an adult, his morals are his own affair. They are outside the cognizance and jurisdiction of the university. It is a part of his education that he should himself bear this responsibility. At the student stage it is true, as never before or after, that "the student belongs to himself, he is responsible to nobody and for nobody but himself." As Dr. Flexner has it, "one wonders, not whether character and manners are unimportant, but whether, like cleanliness or clear speech, they may not now more or less be taken for granted." Accordingly the traditional, pastoral function and obligations of the staff are repudiated. The professor has an objective responsibility for his subject but not a parental responsibility for his students. Such an office as that of a "moral tutor" is misconceived.

The original source of this "Liberal" conception was the French Enlightenment; and, through such a man as Jefferson, this had some direct influence on the American universities. In Great Britain the change was somewhat delayed through antipathy to the French Revolution. Here, as in America during most of the nineteenth century, the operative influence was the achievement and prestige of the German universities. This is seen in Sir William Hamilton's slashing *Edinburgh Review* attacks on Oxford in the early thirties and a generation later, in two almost simultaneous publications, Mark Pattison's *Suggestions for Academical Reorganization* and Matthew Arnold's *Schools and Universities on the Continent.* A generation later again it found a persuasive missionary in Lord Haldane. Even to-day this is probably "the idea of the university" to which most academic people would subscribe. It is true that, under the surface, it is in process of being eaten away by newer forces, and it is no longer even the avowed creed of many of the younger men. Here, as in so many other fields, the twilight of liberalism seems to have set in. But a spirited note of recall to its ideals is sounded in such books as Flexner's *Universities: American, English, German,* and the various writings of the author who styles himself "Bruce Truscot."

GUIDE QUESTIONS

1. "The chief duty of the university is to produce good citizens. It should train an elite who are to be the future leaders of affairs and in the learned professions." How does this definition compare with Wilson's? With Burton's? With your own idea?
2. In the third paragraph, in what sense is the word "servile" used?
3. Compare the special characteristics of higher education according to the Christian-Hellenic conception with those given it by Wilson and Burton.
4. To what extent does the "community life" of an American university or college resemble that of Oxford and Cambridge?
5. Which of these elements in the community life of a university do you

consider the greatest educational influence: (a) students living together, (b) traditions of the school, (c) religion?

6. It is generally admitted that American universities in the nineteenth century were less successful than English universities in turning out men of the calibre of those mentioned by Moberly as "the fine flower of such training." What reasons can you give for this?

7. Consider the "salient traits" of a university according to the Liberal conception. Which features of the Christian-Hellenic conception do you find omitted, and which more strongly emphasized? What are the new features in the Liberal idea of a university? Tell why you approve or disapprove of each of the traits discussed.

8. Try rearranging the order in which the "salient traits" are given. Can you make a more effective arrangement of them?

9. Sum up the points that you consider flaws in both the Christian-Hellenic and the Liberal conception of what a university should be.

10. Among the "newer forces" which have undermined both of these traditional conceptions of a university are technology and democracy. Discuss some of the changes in the definition of a modern American university that these two influences have made necessary.

11. Compare the style of Wilson, Burton, and Moberly. Which writer's style is clearest? Most compact? Most allusive? Most rhetorical? Which one, in your judgment, writes most forcefully?

VOCABULARY

Give the derivations and definitions of the following words:

inimitable, secular, ulterior, emolument, synoptic, panorama, catholicity, dilettante, provincialism, hierarchy, caprice, aphorism, felicity, recipient, pastoral, extol, skein, sophistical, salient, savant, austere, fanaticism, bias, premise, impious, autonomous, canon, turbidity, engender, incompatible, veracity, purview, deprecate, altruistic, fastidious, abhor, insidiously, eschew, cognizance, repudiate, Enlightenment, antipathy.

WRITING AND STUDY AIDS

PATTERN OF ORGANIZATION SUGGESTED BY THE GENERAL TOPIC:

Definitions proceed from the general to the specific, from broad to narrow, by way of a series of identifications and differentiations. For example, a *college* may be identified as *an institution of higher education;* and it may be differentiated by saying that *it is not a research institute,* or *it is not a trade school.* The process of definition may be further advanced by saying that *it is for the training of the men who are to rise above the ranks,* or *it is primarily concerned with personalities and their development.* Similarly, a *university* may be defined by saying that *it confers higher degrees,* or *it is not a college,* or by tracing the historical changes in prevailing conceptions of the university's task.

Definitions of *college* and *university* may thus be expressed in terms of their physical organization, in terms of what they are not, in terms of their purpose in relation to society, or in terms of the history of important ideas concerning them. All these methods of definition are illustrated in the readings.

Your aim in this assignment should be to arrive at some clear idea of the meaning of the two terms. You will not be able to define them in an absolute sense. They must be defined in relation to other ideas you have concerning education, ideas that arise from your personal philosophy. It would be especially useful to define them in relation to concrete situations and events. The specific limitations you put upon their meaning should fix their relation to your general beliefs concerning the purpose of education and to your interpretation of that purpose. Since the terms to be defined are very large, you will not be able to deal with them as wholes in a short theme, but will want to consider their various parts. For example, you may observe your course of study, your teachers, extracurricular activities, or some other special aspect of the life you are now leading. In a long theme, on the other hand, it may be possible to deal with some of the broader conceptions involved in the meanings of *college* and *university.*

ASSIGNMENTS:

Short themes:

1. How to tell the difference between a college and a university
2. One thing that a college is not
3. Advantages of the independent college/the college that is part of a university
4. A college is/is not a country club/kindergarten/prison/political arena /football factory/reform school/lunatic asylum
5. College and military life
6. The kind of teachers a college needs
7. When I enter the university ———
8. "Athletes of faculty"

9. Can everyone be educated?
10. College as an adventure/challenge/opportunity/escape
11. Handicaps of the rich boy/poor boy in college
12. "All work and no play . . ."
13. The spirit of research
14. The most important thing in college

Long themes:

1. The "service station" idea of a university
2. The Christian-Hellenic idea of a university
3. The Liberal idea of a university
4. Education for democracy/life/business/service/a profession/leadership
5. What is an educated man/woman?
6. The function of a college/university
7. "To become a man of learning is the enterprise of a lifetime"

READINGS FOR FURTHER STUDY:

Burton, Ernest De Witt. "The Business of a University," *Education in a Democratic World*. Chicago: University of Chicago Press, 1927. Pages 69-83.

Butler, Nicholas Murray. "The American College and the American University," *The Meaning of Education*. New York: The Macmillan Company, 1904. Pages 125-47.

Flexner, Abraham. "The Idea of a Modern University," *Universities: American, English, German*. New York: Oxford University Press, 1930. Pages 3-36.

Hale, William Harlan. "Over My Shoulder to Alma Mater," *Scribner's*, Vol. 90 (Oct., 1931), 373-78.

Hutchins, Robert M. "The Higher Learning," *No Friendly Voice*. Chicago: University of Chicago Press, 1936. Pages 24-32.

Lowell, A. Lawrence. "Universities, Graduate Schools, and Colleges"; "Universities and Colleges." *At War with Academic Traditions in America*. Cambridge, Mass.: Harvard University Press, 1934. Pages 207-20; 221-28.

V. DESCRIPTION OF A PROCESS

~~ A Scientist at Work

ANY SCIENTIFIC EXPERIMENT IS ESSENTIALLY A PROCESS, A STEP-BY-STEP procedure in which certain operations are performed in an orderly way. All processes, whether simple or complex, are governed by elementary laws of logic. A stranger on the campus following a student's directions on how to get to the Union Building, a motorist changing a tire on the highway, a biologist demonstrating the dissection of a specimen to a class in the laboratory—all are engaged in carrying out processes which are both physical and mental. Certain general rules may be established which apply to all processes. To begin with, there must be some conception of the nature of the problem to be solved. As each step is taken, its result is checked to see whether it is leading in what seems to be the right direction. This information, as it accumulates, is used to formulate what is called a hypothesis, or a tentative theory provisionally adopted to explain the facts that have been observed and to serve as a guide in pushing the investigation further. In this way, the process continues from point to point, each step being verified as a plausible outgrowth of the preceding one, with new hypotheses being formulated when necessary, until the desired result is reached or until a conclusion can safely be drawn. What has just been outlined indicates the part played by both deduction and induction in all scientific thinking, and scientific thinking is no different from the ordinary thinking directed to the solution of everyday problems. The biologist describing the dissection will be more fully aware of the principles behind his procedures than the stranger following a student's directions, or the motorist changing a tire; but the reasoning and the actions of all three are governed by the same logic.

In the readings for this assignment the classic researches of McCollum in biochemistry, of Douglass in astronomy, and of Jung in psychology are used to illustrate the methods of scientific investigation. McCollum's work is described in "The Discovery of Vitamins A and B." We take vitamins so much for granted nowadays that the state of knowledge, or of ignorance, from which McCollum started is difficult to reconstruct; but the preliminary groping of other men, which is also described, will enable you to see the imaginativeness and ingenuity of his epoch-making experiments. "Tree Rings and Sunspots," an account of Douglass's work, shows that the by-products of research are sometimes as interesting as the products. Douglass is an astronomer whose special field is meteorology, his main concern the possibility of long-range weather forecasting by the analysis of sunspot cycles. That was why he began to study the relation between sunspots and tree rings, thus calling to his aid the science of botany. His dramatic contribution to Southwestern archaeology by dating the Indian pueblos of New Mexico and Arizona was purely incidental. In "The Association Method" you will read about a test developed by a Swiss psychologist. Jung's association test was originally designed to reveal emotional disturbances, and it is widely used with mental patients; its "detective" use, of which an experimental example is given, has broad implications for criminology. The processes of thought and activity by which these scientists carried out their work are worth analysis. As you read, try to trace the mental steps and the physical steps in their experiments.

Bernard Jaffe

THE DISCOVERY OF VITAMINS A AND B

IN 1897, A DISEASE CALLED BERI-BERI, known in the East as *kak-ke* for nearly two thousand years, was ravaging the population of the Dutch East Indies. Beri-beri was a peculiar disease. In its victims the nerves of motion and sensation were gravely affected. General weakness, mental depression, dropsy, and anemia accompanied a creeping paralysis, which usually originated in the legs and spread upward till it reached the heart and ended in death. The Dutch government appointed a committee to study the cause of beri-beri and to seek a cure. Among the men sent to fight the disease was Christian Eijkman.

From *Outposts of Science*, by Bernard Jaffe. Copyright, 1935, by Bernard Jaffe. Reprinted by permission of Simon and Schuster, Publishers.

These were the halcyon days of that vigorous newcomer bacteriology, and Eijkman, as might have been expected, began searching for a causative germ. Scientists might still be searching for the microbe had not this Dutch doctor followed through a chance observation. A number of hens around his laboratory had developed paralysis which looked very much like that of beri-beri. This did not surprise Eijkman. Animals were subject to human diseases, and he thought these hens had caught beri-beri from human patients. Yet while he hunted for the bacterial cause, he watched the hens more closely. How did they contract this sickness?

Eijkman noticed that those hens which were allowed to run around in the sun and scrape up their meals from garden and dunghill never came down with polyneuritis (beri-beri in fowl). The chickens which had sickened had been fed indoors on the remains of rice given to the inmates of the prisons of Java. He made an investigation of prison food. The only unusual feature he found was that the rice, the chief item of food given to the prisoners, had in some cases been milled with modern machinery to remove its outer yellowish cover. This process prevented spoilage of the rice, and incidentally turned out a white polished product. The polishings were discarded as unfit to eat. It occurred to Eijkman to compare the incidence of beri-beri in the various prisons with the kind of rice fed to their inmates. He discovered some striking facts. One hundred and fifty thousand prisoners had been fed almost exclusively on white rice. One out of every 39 of these men had developed beri-beri. Of the 35,000 who had been fed on partially milled rice, one out of 400 came down with the nerve ailment; while of the 100,000 prisoners who had received rations of unpolished rice, only one out of 10,725 had ever suffered the ravages of this disease. The incidence of beri-beri among the polished-rice eaters was almost three hundred times as great as among the unpolished-rice eaters.

The next step was clear. Eijkman fed a group of chickens exclusively on white rice. They all developed polyneuritis and died. He fed another group of fowl unpolished rice. Not a single one of them contracted the disease. Then he gathered up the polishings from rice and fed them to other polyneuritic chickens, and in a short time the birds recovered. He had accurately traced the cause of polyneuritis to a faulty diet. For the first time in history, he had produced a food deficiency disease experimentally, and had actually cured it. It was a fine piece of work and resulted in some immediate remedial measures. Eijkman was later recalled to Holland to a professorship at the University of Utrecht.

In his interpretation of the results, however, Eijkman had really erred. True, he had advised the eating of the whole rice grain, but he could not interpret the results. He did not know why the outer covering of the rice was essential to health. His work was not considered significant at the time and the controversy over the cause of beri-beri did not subside. Besides, his was a more or less obscure piece of research of which most of the world heard little. Millions continued to succumb to this paralyzing disease. During the Russo-Japanese War fully one-sixth of the Japanese forces, fed principally on rice, were put out of active service by this malady. All over the world rice-eating peoples kept paying heavy toll to beri-beri.

Thirteen years after Eijkman's pioneer experiments, Casimir Funk, a young investigator from Warsaw who secured a fellowship at the Lister Institute in London, unearthed the classic investigation of the Holland professor. Reasoning that rice polishings contained some chemical constituent essential to health, Funk attempted to extract this life-giving compound, using pigeons as test animals. After innumerable solutions, precipitations and filtrations, he obtained one-fiftieth of an ounce of a white powder. A few milligrams of his product, when fed to pigeons gravely ill with polyneuritis, strengthened their legs, straightened out their drooping necks, and transformed them again to normal birds.

Since it was essential to life (*vita*) and contained the amino group of chemical elements, Funk christened this anti-beri-beri compound *vitamine*. Funk was entirely mistaken in his belief that he had isolated the pure vitamine. The name he had chosen was a misnomer, since the true compound does not contain the amino group. Yet such are the quirks of scientific glory that his term persisted, although slightly abbreviated in 1920 by the dropping of the "e." Funk was prophetic when he made the suggestion that in time other diseases would be traced to deficiencies of vitamins—certain essential chemicals present in foodstuffs in extremely small amounts.

At that time science was busily engaged in measuring the calorific value of all sorts of foods and estimating the fuel requirements of man, woman, child, and beast, not only asleep but also at work or play, but no attention was paid to the chemical composition of the diet. Respira-

tion calorimeters, bomb calorimeters, chair, bed, and portable calorimeters were invented and brought into action in elaborate and often
fantastic attempts to evaluate the advantages of meat, vegetable, nut,
and mixed diets. In the meantime chemistry had advanced far enough
to place in the hands of investigators the purified chemical components
of many foods. The idea occurred to a number of research workers to
feed test animals on chemically pure components of foodstuffs, and in
this way attempt to arrive at an ideal diet for each species. The living
organism was, after all, something more than an iron furnace stoked
with coal or oil to produce so many calories of heat. It seemed reasonable to suppose that perhaps only certain components of foods were
essential to physiological well-being regardless of their calorific values.
Was it not possible that an animal fed to satiety on certain foods might
yet starve to death?

Already in 1881, Lunin, working at Basle, Switzerland, had tried this
method with six mice. When fed on a milk diet they thrived, but
when he substituted for the milk a mixture of the purified components
of whole milk, that is, milk protein (casein), milk fat, milk sugar
(lactose), the various mineral salts found in milk, and water, the animals died within a month. Lunin concluded, "Substances other than
casein, fat, milk sugar, salts, and water are indispensable to health."

A decade later Lunin's teacher asked: "Are there really other substances in milk besides fats, proteins, and carbohydrates necessary to
the vital process? Had Lunin used a faulty technique?" And he added,
"It would be useful to continue these researches." Pekelharing at the
University of Utrecht accepted the suggestion in 1905. When he found
that his own white mice fed exclusively on the purified casein and
other constituents of milk refused to grow, and died young, he declared
emphatically, "There is a still unknown substance in milk which even
in very small quantities is of paramount importance to nourishment."
There seemed no other conclusion to be drawn from his painstaking
experiments. In the following year Frederick G. Hopkins, of the University of London, ignorant of the work of Lunin, Pekelharing, and
even Eijkman, took two batches of eight young male rats each, and
fed one group on purified casein, starch, cane sugar, lard, and mineral
salts. The rats ate greedily but refused to grow. The other batch received the same diet plus 3 cc. (about a small teaspoonful) of fresh
milk daily. These rats grew normally. Then he took away the milk

from the second group and gave it to the rats that had refused to grow. At once they continued to grow as normal rats. The second group, now deprived of milk, began to lose weight.

When his curves showed the remarkable growth effect of even small doses of raw milk, Hopkins, in 1912, reiterated the statement that "No animal can live upon a mixture of pure proteins, fats, and carbohydrates, and even when the necessary inorganic material is carefully supplied, the animal still cannot flourish." For this piece of research Hopkins shared the 1929 Nobel award in medicine with Eijkman, the Dutch scientist who had to wait thirty-two years for this recognition.

In June of the same year that Hopkins started on his classic study, Elmer Verner McCollum had just completed some work in organic chemistry at Yale. A tuition scholarship enabled him to continue with postgraduate studies, . . . and he spent another year under Lafayette B. Mendel working in physiological chemistry and experimental physiology, and waiting for an attractive opening. Simultaneously three different agricultural experiment stations called him. Mendel, a rare inspirational teacher and a sound counsellor of men, set McCollum on the road to the University of Wisconsin where at its Agricultural Experiment Station a unique experiment in animal nutrition was getting under way.

It was still the old question. Did it make any difference what the food was, provided its chemical composition and energy values were the same? Stephen M. Babcock planned an experiment to test the various theories then in vogue. He himself felt that calorific value was not the whole story. "Why not feed 'em coal or hot water?" he would ask. Besides, it was more than an academic question. Farmers around the University were constantly asking embarrassing questions about the *kind* of feed to give their cattle. On May 1, 1907, the experiment was started.

Four groups of young heifers were fed different rations. One received wheat, another corn, a third oats, and the last group was given a mixture of all three. By careful chemical analysis and accurate weighings, it was made certain that all animals received similar chemicals capable of supplying equivalent amounts of energy. All the sixteen animals were given all the salt they demanded, and were exercised in outside enclosures free from vegetation. The intake of these heifers was not the only mixture subjected to accurate testing. The feces and urine of the beasts were also quantitatively determined, and it was the largest part of McCollum's first job after reaching Madison to analyze the contents of the pails brought in from the experimental field.

Every morning the men would meet to talk over the progress of their work. Of course McCollum was interested, but somehow he looked askance at this attack on a problem that to him demanded a more easily controlled procedure. It was a well worthwhile investigation, and probably would yield interesting results, but it did not reach the heart of the great problem of nutrition. "Research men who were using small animals, on the other hand, were on the right track," thought McCollum. He was going to try Hopkins' technique with one important change. Nothing was to enter into the diet of his animals which could not be identified as a pure chemical whose composition was accurately known. Instead of corn, a complex substance of indefinite composition, he was going to use starch $C_6H_{10}O_5$, and similarly for milk he would substitute chemically purified milk protein (casein), chemically pure milk sugar, or lactose, and so forth.

A few months after arriving in Wisconsin, he started a rat colony for his experiments. Rats are excellent experimental animals, with a life span of three years. Their pregnancy period is three weeks; the female produces her first litter at three months; at fourteen months she has usually had six litters. It would not be very expensive to handle a large colony.

While Babcock's heifers were frolicking, McCollum found time even with his teaching program to work with his rat colony. This was housed in his office in cages built by himself out of empty boxes in which chemicals had been shipped. He could work hard. He was thorough, a good interpreter of events, a good theorizer. Ambition took hold of him at the start, and he was confident enough to believe he was on the right road. He regarded those experiments at Yale undertaken to determine the relative efficiency of flesh eaters and meat abstainers as superficial. The device of determining men's endurance by means of arm-stretching and knee-bending tests to prove that flesh abstainers showed from three to six times the endurance of the others was to him not a very deep inquiry into so fundamental a problem. McCollum was dealing with accurately controlled experiments, not with pseudo-scientific sideshows. The live rat in its cage was his unfailing test tube; his foods were pure chemicals, and his results could be accurately described

nd repeated by any student. That was his program from which he
efused to swerve.

In 1911, while McCollum was busy with his rats, Research Bulletin
No. 17 of the Wisconsin Agricultural Experiment Station appeared,
iving the final results of the heifer experiment. It was a strange an-
ouncement. Every animal had received the same quantities of starch,
ugar, protein, salt, and mineral matter as well as water, and yet they
ad reacted differently. Only the corn-fed heifers grew sleek and vigor-
us and gave birth to healthy young. The wheat-fed cattle were weak,
uzzy-haired, sluggish, and never carried their calves to birth alive.
he oat-fed animals as well as the heifers fed on a mixture of wheat,
orn, and oats, were not normal. Some of their young were born pre-
aaturely, and were sickly or died within a short time. Evidently the
ource of the food components *did* make a tremendous difference, but
his did not explain why corn maintained the animals whereas oats
id not. At this time McCollum had not heard of Eijkman, nor had
unk yet discovered that elusive vitamin. The answer to the puzzle of
aimal nutrition seemed to be still as far off as ever.

McCollum was giving his rats the right amount of inorganic calcium
hosphate, pure edestin from hemp seed, and pure zein from maize
two proteins), wheat starch and corn starch, milk sugar, cane sugar,
ad glucose, and enough fats to complete their energy requirements.
et the weight curves showed they could not maintain themselves
ormally, and they died prematurely. At first he thought something
as lacking to make the diet palatable. "Palatability of the ration is
aportant to the diet," he wrote at that time. That was a mistake, but
e did not know it; and so he added appetizing flavors to prevent fail-
re of appetite, and kept changing the combination of the various
omponents of his diets. Many continued to die but some of the rats
tually gained weight and lived at least until they were ready to be
iloroformed. McCollum believed that he had actually carried out the
st successful growth experiments with nothing but *highly purified*
odstuffs.

In the meantime, Thomas B. Osborne, of the Connecticut Agri-
iltural Experiment Station, and Lafayette B. Mendel had been work-
g on the relative nutritive value and physiological importance of the
fferent pure proteins. Different proteins contain different amino acids.
aey were trying to determine which amino acids had to be present

in the proteins used as foods—experiments which ended in a classi⟨
contribution. They, too, had been using some highly purified food
stuffs for their white rats, but failed to get McCollum's rising growt⟨
curves. When, however, they added to their rat diet "protein-free milk,"
a yellow powder obtained by removing the fat and casein and the⟨
evaporating the milk to dryness, they secured growth. Mendel a⟨
tributed the growth of his rats to the nice adjustment of inorgan⟨
materials in his "protein-free milk." This was another mistake.

The paper of Osborne and Mendel appeared in 1911. McCollur
studied it carefully. That "protein-free milk" bothered him. It was n⟨
altogether protein-free. It contained 0.7% of nitrogen, and might pr⟨
sumably contain in minute amounts other substances which coul⟨
account for the normal growth of the rats. This paper gave his wor⟨
fresh impetus, and McCollum continued to search for a pathwa⟨
through this dietary maze. The following year he was getting mor⟨
perplexing results. Rats fed on his standard diet to which some butt⟨
fat had been added grew normally; rats which had received lard instea⟨
of the butter fat were far below normal. The growth curves showe⟨
this singular phenomenon quite clearly.

In 1914 the *Journal of Biological Chemistry* published a paper fro⟨
McCollum's laboratory which opened up a new era in nutritional i⟨
vestigations. This paper entitled *Isolation of the Substance in Butt⟨
Fat which Exerts a Stimulating Influence on Growth* contained
curve which cleared up a number of errors, and led to the discove⟨
of a vitamin. For eighty days Rat No. 141 grew on a ration of pu⟨
casein, starch, lactose, agar agar, salt mixture, and lard. Then a sha⟨
decline in weight set in. An extract of butter was added to the diet ⟨
a very small amount. A definite increase in weight promptly resulte⟨
The rat gained fifty grams in the next thirty-five days. McCollum the⟨
used the extract of egg yolk instead of butter, and the curve ke⟨
moving upward. When, however, the extract of olive oil was subs⟨
tuted, growth stopped. McCollum drew his conclusion. Fats and oi⟨
differing slightly in chemical composition, were of different growth-pr⟨
moting potency, because associated with their ether extracts was son⟨
"yet unidentified dietary factor—fat-soluble (vitamin) A." (This u⟨
of an algebraic term to designate a vitamin gained wide acceptance⟨
McCollum had identified that "accessory food factor" which Pek⟨
haring and Hopkins had suspected to be present in milk.

Mendel repeated the experiments and confirmed the results of M⟨

Collum. But Mendel could not understand why his own "protein-free milk" gave the rising growth curves. Furthermore, he was unable to decide whether the deficiency of the purely artificial diet he used before he could get a rising growth curve was to be "attributed to improper proportions of its constituents or to the lack of some essential element." McCollum, too, was puzzled. His butter-fat and egg-yolk extracts worked with some diets, but not with others. Funk bobbed up and insisted that the potent factor in McCollum's butter fat was his own anti-beri-beri vitamin. It seemed one great comedy of errors.

McCollum went back to his rats. The heifer experiment was over and he had more time. Now McCollum set up a working hypothesis. He assumed that the only unknown factor contained in his diet must be associated with certain fats and oils. In 1914 he introduced a new biological method for the analysis of foodstuffs. The procedure and results were as follows:

1. The wheat kernel alone was fed to the rat.
    Result: The animal refused to grow and died prematurely.
2. Wheat kernel plus a purified protein was fed to the rat.
    Result: Again no growth and an early death.
3. Wheat kernel plus a salt mixture constituted the new ration.
    Result: Very little growth was obtained.
4. Wheat kernel plus butter-fat extract was now fed to the rat.
    Result: The magic butter fat *refused* to add weight to the animal.

This indicated a second dietary factor absent in wheat and necessary for growth. McCollum carried through a second series of experiments:

1. Wheat, a purified protein, and salt constituted the new diet of the rat.
    Result: Good growth for a time, but the animal had either no young at all, or small litters which died very early.
2. Wheat, a purified protein, and butter fat were now used.
    Result: No growth could be obtained and the rat's life was short.
3. Wheat, salt, and butter fat were given to a new batch of rats.
    Result: The animals showed a fair growth, but gave few young, and died prematurely.
4. Wheat, protein, salt, and butter fat were now tried.

Result: Good growth, normal litters, and a healthy life span fo: his animal.

These results indicated that wheat was deficient in salts, vitamin A and some protein. It seemed also to point to the need in an adequate diet of proteins, carbohydrate, salts, and vitamin A. With this hy pothesis, McCollum continued his biological analysis of cereal grains selecting rice in his next experiments. More months of labor. He ob tained growth with the use of unpolished rice, but polished rice coul: not be supplemented with salts, butter fat (vitamin A), and a purifie: protein to induce growth in his animals.

McCollum now made a change. Milk sugar or lactose was added a a fourth supplement to the protein, butter fat, and salt. Again his rat grew normally. That was a fortunate trial. Evidently besides that poten substance in butter fat, another unknown factor distributed in lactos (and soluble in water) was also needed. Then followed a painstakin effort to determine the purity of the milk sugar he was using. He foun it was not pure, after all. There was something in the water from whic the sugar had been crystallized that could actually cure polyneurit: in pigeons just as rice polishings could. This he had proved to his ow satisfaction. This new factor he called water-soluble B since, unlik vitamin A, it was soluble in water but not in fat. Vitamin B was alt: gether different from the potent substance in butter fat. It was identic: with Funk's vitamin which cured beri-beri.

McCollum's announcement of the discovery of "water-soluble vit: min B," the antineuritic vitamin which prevented polyneuritis, cleare up a number of difficulties. Both fat-soluble vitamin A and wate soluble vitamin B were necessary for normal growth. That was wh his rats would not grow when given butter fat but no lactose or mil sugar. His milk sugar had contained vitamin B as an impurity. Th: was also why Osborne and Mendel had obtained growth with the "protein-free milk," which contained vitamin B. That was why Hoj kins, too, was able to show a rising growth curve when his rats we: given very small portions of whole milk. The vitamin problem w: now clear-cut. There were certain chemicals which in infinitesim: quantities were necessary for well-being. McCollum had identified tw of them. Perhaps there were more.

The whole vitamin question was thrown open for general discussic and research.

GUIDE QUESTIONS

1. Why, after Eijkman had completed his investigation of prison diet, did he go back to experiments with chickens?
2. Why is it one of "the quirks of scientific glory" that Funk's term *vitamine* (minus the *e*) is still used?
3. What long-standing question was the heifer experiment at the University of Wisconsin supposed to throw light on? Why was this "a unique experiment in animal nutrition"?
4. Why are rats superior to heifers as experimental animals?
5. Describe McCollum's steps in his discovery of vitamin A. In his discovery of vitamin B.
6. Why was much of McCollum's research carried on by trial-and-error methods? To what extent are such methods characteristic of any research?
7. Describe the investigations of Eijkman, Funk, Pekelharing, Hopkins, and Osborne and Mendel as preliminaries to McCollum's discoveries. Which of these scientists made the most significant contribution to McCollum's work?
8. By reference to a table of vitamins in a scientific encyclopedia, find out how many vitamins are now known. McCollum also discovered vitamin D, in 1922. Who discovered the others, and when?

VOCABULARY

Give the derivations and definitions of the following words:

dropsy, halcyon, precipitation, filtration, misnomer, quirk, calorific, calorimeter, satiety, reiterate, askance, superficial, phenomenon, era, potent, infinitesimal.

J. H. Rush

TREE RINGS AND SUNSPOTS

THE MUSEUM OF THE UNIVERSITY OF ARIZONA at Tucson houses a unique exhibit. Down one side and up the other of a long display case runs a

Reprinted with permission from *Scientific American*, Volume 186, Number 1, January, 1952.

continuous strip photograph. It is a series of pictures of tree cross-sections showing their rings, and every ring is precisely dated with the year it grew. The rings are a continuous record of the annual growth of trees for nearly 2,000 years, from A.D. 11 to the present.

This remarkable exhibit goes back to a day in 1901 when Andrew E. Douglass, then first assistant at the Lowell Observatory in Arizona, was riding through the Arizona pine forest on a buckboard. Astronomer Douglass fell to thinking of the sunspot cycle, of its possible relation to weather and of the great age of the stately trees around him. It occurred to him that in this arid region, where plant growth depends crucially upon rainfall, the sunspot cycle might be reflected systematically in the growth rings of the trees. [In general, an increase in sunspots is thought to be accompanied by an increase in rainfall, and *vice versa*.] If so, then cross-sections of old trees might provide an index to solar variations for several centuries past. This idea led Douglass to undertake in 1904 what has become a classic investigation, involving elements of astronomy, meteorology, botany, and archaeology.

He began by analyzing cross-sections from 19 selected ponderosa pine trees near Flagstaff. The average age of the trees was 348 years, according to counts of their rings. When Douglass measured the width of the rings, he was able to identify certain sequences, or cycles, of wide and narrow rings. Furthermore, he was elated to find that these sequences matched in different trees; that is, the ring grown in a particular year in one tree could be matched with a ring grown the same year in another tree of the group, so that a period of time could be cross-identified or cross-dated in the two trees. Douglass compared these ring sequences with rainfall records at Flagstaff, and he found that the relative thicknesses of the annual rings faithfully reflected variations in the moisture supply from year to year. A broad white ring of wood laid on in a wet growing season might be followed by a hardly perceptible growth layer in a year of drought. The absolute widths of rings varied widely from tree to tree, and even at various locations in the same tree, but the relative widths of rings in any consecutive short sequence followed the rainfall curve. After analyzing the Flagstaff trees, Douglass got some specimens from Prescott, 70 miles away, and he was able to cross-identify these with the group at Flagstaff. Thus he established the feasibility of constructing a climatic record from tree rings.

In 1906 Douglass was appointed professor of physics and astronomy at the University of Arizona, and he continued his tree-ring studies with improved techniques and facilities there. By 1915 he had analyzed and cross-identified hemlock sections from Vermont, Douglas fir from Oregon, pine and spruce from Britain, Norway, Sweden and Germany. Most of the tree-ring sequences correlated well with sunspot cycles. In these groups of trees the remarkable fact was that the correlation of tree growth with sunspots was strong even though rainfall usually showed no such correlation. Apparently in these areas of abundant moisture, where the annual growth of trees was not so sensitive to variations in rainfall, tree growth still followed the rhythm of the sunspot cycle.

Douglass' task was tedious, slow and riddled with pitfalls. It was fortunate, as he realized later, that he had begun his work on the great ponderosa pines. Not many species of trees, he discovered, put on their annual growth in clear, continuous rings that can be counted and cross-identified consistently. Some trees, such as the ironwood of the Southwest, are wholly impossible to analyze because of the lack of a regular ring structure. Some others, such as the oak, yield good rings, but old specimens are hard to find. After much exploration Douglass came to the conclusion that the conifers were most suitable for his purposes. They are distributed over great regions and endure widely varied climates, and their rings are exceptionally clear and prominent. Most of his work has been done with the yellow (ponderosa) pine, Scotch pine, hemlock, Douglas fir, and sequoia.

The location of a tree also has a bearing on its suitability. Trees that grow in river valleys, basins or coastal regions where soil water is abundant cannot be accurately dated or cross-identified because their rings are too nearly uniform. The Coast redwood, which might otherwise have been a most useful tree for chronological purposes, was regretfully abandoned by Douglass for this reason. He had to get his specimens from hillside slopes or porous soils, where tree growth depends mainly on the water immediately available from rain and snow. Here the thickness of the growth rings faithfully reflects the variations in precipitation from year to year. Douglass found that an Arizona pine growing on a southerly slope sometimes even has thicker rings on the north side than on the south, evidently because the north side of the tree holds snow longer and intercepts more of the water flowing down the slope.

An uneven growing season can create another pitfall for the analyst. When a tree begins growing in the spring, it lays down a fresh layer of soft white sapwood upon the previous year's growth. Ordinarily this layer continues to thicken throughout the summer, and in the fall, when the growth slows down, it is capped by wood that is hard, compact and reddish brown in color. This brown layer normally marks the end of a growing season and the boundary of an annual ring. But a drought that interrupts the growing season may bring the growth of the sapwood to an unseasonable halt and cause the tree to lay down a hard brown layer in late spring or summer. Then later rains may produce another layer in the fall. The result is a double ring that may look like two years' growth. This was very troublesome to Douglass at first, but he learned that the outer boundary of the brown ring marking the end of the season is always sharp and clear-cut, whereas the edge of the midseason brown ring is fuzzy.

Other anomalies are occasionally found. A tree may put on two clearly defined rings in one year for no apparent reason, or fire injury may cause the insertion of a false brown ring. Sometimes a tree that grows in too dry a locality may miss a growing season entirely, so that the next ring it puts on covers an interval of two years with little or no clue to the omission. Usually at least the suspicion of a ring appears somewhere on the circumference, but Douglass remarks that occasionally he has "traced a missing ring entirely around a tree without finding it." In most such cases Douglass can deduce the existence of the missing ring by cross-matching with other trees.

To avoid having to handle full cross-sections of large, heavy trees, Douglass developed a technique of sawing out a pie-shaped triangular strip from the end of a log or top of a stump. To obtain specimens from living trees or from logs in old ruins he uses a tubular borer that cuts out a thin cylindrical core through the ring structure. The triangular strips or borings are glued to wood backings, planed and shaved smooth and oiled to bring out the rings in full detail.

Once the specimens have been prepared, the real work of analysis begins. Douglass first measured ring widths with a steel rule, but these readings were good only to about one-tenth millimeter. He now uses a special plotting micrometer. This instrument consists of a reading microscope which travels on a screw and is coupled to a revolving drum in such a way that the travel of the microscope across an individual ring (i.e., the ring's width) is recorded much magnified as a vertical line on the recording paper on the drum. In establishing cross-identifications the thin rings corresponding to drought years are most significant. They stand out in readily discernible patterns. For this reason it has been found that a most useful device for quickly establishing cross-identifications is a "skeleton plot," which records only the conspicuously thin rings.

Douglass had set out on his study of tree rings primarily to extend the record of sunspot activity back to earlier times. It had long been known that the number of spots on the sun grew and waned in a more or less regular cycle, averaging about 11 years from peak to peak. Regular, reliable records of sunspot activity went back less than 100 years. Douglass found that the tree-ring cycles correlated well with the known sunspot maxima and minima during this period. He also found clear evidence of an 11-year cycle appearing at intervals during most of the 500-year period covered by his tree records. The cycle seemed to break down at times, however, and in the period from about 1650 to 1720 it disappeared entirely.

Douglass turned to the ancient sequoia groves of California. He began in 1915 to collect sequoia specimens for detailed laboratory study. Expeditions to Kings River Canyon, General Grant Grove, Calaveras and other localities yielded a fine collection of sections, many of them over 2,000 years old and several over 3,000. Throughout most of this period they clearly showed the 11-year solar cycle. But again the cycle unaccountably disappeared in the late 17th century.

Not until 1922 was the puzzle resolved. In that year Douglass received a remarkable letter from E. W. Maunder, a meteorologist at the Royal Observatory in Greenwich, England. Maunder, who had long been concerned with the problems of sunspots and solar variation, had looked into the available records and compiled all the known sunspot observations for several centuries back. Knowing nothing of Douglass' difficulty, he wrote to let Douglass know that according to these records there was very little sunspot activity between 1645 and 1715.

The anomalous failure of the 11-year cycle in Douglass' trees during that period was explained! Thus after 18 years of work he could at last feel confident that he had established a reliable correspondence between tree growth and the sunspot cycle.

Meanwhile Douglass' study of tree rings had led him into a fascinating excursion in archaeology. It began as a result of his search for old specimens. The yellow pine that he was working with in the Southwest was an admirable wood for his purpose, but the living trees did not go back far enough; the oldest was a mere juvenile of 640 years. If the living specimens were too young, why not look among the dead— ancient pine logs or timbers that had somehow been preserved? If such remnants of long-dead trees could be found, their rings might be cross-identified with those of contemporary trees over an overlapping period; still earlier specimens in turn might be cross-identified with them, and so on indefinitely.

In 1916 Douglass had obtained from the American Museum of Natural History several sections of pine logs from prehistoric pueblo ruins near Aztec, N. M., and from Pueblo Bonito, grandest of the ancient pueblos, 50 miles south of Aztec. In 1919 Douglass made a trip to the Aztec ruin and obtained 50 more specimens from house beams with his tubular borer. By 1920 he had developed from this prehistoric material a continuous chronology of about 200 years. He demonstrated that the trees for the Aztec beams had been cut about 50 years later than those from Pueblo Bonito.

Douglass started, therefore, with a "floating" chronology of a 200-year period of unknown date before A.D. 1300. Soon afterward Neil M. Judd, director of a National Geographic Society expedition that had gone to Pueblo Bonito, sent Douglass 160 more specimens, and these expanded the floating chronology to about 350 years. But Douglass still had to find the missing links that would close the gap between these fragments of early pueblo history and his 600-year-old living trees.

In an effort to find log specimens that would close the time gap, the National Geographic Society in 1923 sent an expedition to some of the most likely Southwestern sites. They visited first the Hopi Villages in Arizona. Some of these settlements have been continuously inhabited since before the Spaniards came. But the specimens found there, though useful, did not bridge the gap, and the expedition went on from one to another of those old places of the romantically conglomerate names: to the Black Mesa, to Chinle, Zuni, Chaco Canyon and the Rio Grande Valley of New Mexico, to the enigmatic cliff dwellings at Mesa Verde, to Wupatki, Canyon de Chelly, Citadel and Solomon. Altogether the expedition brought a hundred new beam specimens to Douglass' laboratory at Tucson.

The work of analyzing and cross-dating proceeded slowly, for Douglass now had many other duties as professor of astronomy and director of the Steward Observatory. But by 1927 the pattern of the pueblo chronology began to take definite shape. Pueblo Bonito, the grandest enigma of them all, was cross-dated with four other ruins besides Aztec. Further, a new "floating" chronology appeared, linking Mesa Verde with several other ruins, but not connected with the chronology of the Pueblo Bonito group. A year later, by means of one good specimen from the great cliff houses of Betátakin which spanned a gap of 40 years, Douglass joined the chronology of the Mesa Verde group to the floating Pueblo Bonito chronology.

That same year, 1928, the National Geographic Society sent a second woodhunting expedition back to the ancient Hopi town of Oraibi. They collected more than 200 specimens, and these linked up with Douglass' modern pine sequence in the 14th century and extended back to A.D. 1260. In October Douglass dated his first prehistoric ruin. By cross-dating with this extended record he was able to say that the building of the pueblo called Kawaika in Arizona began in the year 1357.

The floating chronology of the Pueblo Bonito group had now grown to a span of 585 years. Twenty-six large ruins had been cross-dated by means of nearly 500 wood or charcoal specimens from their ancient timbers. But an obstinate gap of unknown duration still lay between this fragment of prehistory and the modern sequence. The modern sequence had been traced back with certainty to 1300. For the preceding 40 years, from 1260 to 1300, Douglass had the single specimen from Betátakin. But no good specimens overlapping the Betátakin period had been found.

Analysis of the Betátakin specimen provided a clue to the reason for the absence of timbers from this period. From 1276 to 1299 one thin ring after another told a terrible story of sustained and unprecedented drought. The effect of such a period upon the pueblo peoples, living always on the edge of disaster, is not hard to imagine. Many villages had to be abandoned, and in the rest further construction of houses was delayed many years.

Before undertaking more field work the National Geographic Society archaeologists studied the pueblo pottery as a means of narrowing the search. Pueblo pottery, they knew, had developed in a distinct sequence, from a black-on-white ware made by the earliest Pueblo Bonito people through several kinds of polychrome to a beautiful cream-colored pottery developed at the Kawaika settlement, whose date was known. The pottery study made it clear that the gap between the floating Pueblo Bonito chronology and the continuous modern sequence was not great, and that it lay in the period of transition from a polychrome pottery to cream. As the result of this study a certain ruin at the little town of Show Low, Arizona, was chosen for the next, and last, expedition.

In 1929 Douglass went with the archaeologists to this site, prepared to make on-the-spot analyses of any material they should find. From several specimens of wood and charcoal they soon succeeded in extending the floating chronology forward a few years into what appeared to be a time of extreme drought. Then the charred end of a timber was uncovered in a dirt pit. It was carefully sawed off and taken to Douglass. He studied it by lamplight that evening with increasing interest and assurance. Finally he remarked: "Well, this looks mighty good. And now I'm going to bed!"

Thus in one climactic evening the gap was closed and the dates of nearly 40 prehistoric communities were fixed. Southwestern archaeology took its place as the most precisely dated archaeology without written records in the world.

Since that eventful year Douglass has used the same techniques to push the tree-ring calendar of the pueblo region back to A.D. 11. The value of this continuous 1,900-year record is very great. Because in this region the growth response of trees is directly correlated with rainfall, the record gives a rather good picture of the long-run rainfall trends during the period it covers.

Douglass also obtained much older records from a few petrified trees in which the ring structure happened to be preserved. From Yellowstone Park he got 38 specimens of a petrified sequoia of the Tertiary Period, some 50 million years ago. He was able to measure and analyze in them more than 11,000 rings. These very ancient rings gave indications that an 11-year sunspot cycle existed as long ago as 50 million years. Similar results have been obtained on specimens of Pleistocene cypress from a peat bog in Germany.

Although his excursion into archaeology was rewarding and intensely interesting, Douglass remained an astronomer, and his prime interest in developing the tree-ring chronology was to extend the sunspot record beyond the history of direct observations. Satisfied that the tree rings truly reflected solar variations, he undertook to analyze these variations in detail.

Douglass distinguishes carefully between indefinitely sustained periodicities, which may be called true cycles, and periodicities that appear only transiently and sporadically, which he calls "cyclics." He had concluded from preliminary studies that the periodic variations in solar activity were cyclics and not persistent cycles; the 11-year sunspot "cycle," for example, was not continuous but disappeared from the record at various periods. To plot the cyclics in a form that would make it possible to analyze them quickly and efficiently Douglass developed a remarkable instrument called the cyclograph. With this instrument he examined the periodicities of sunspot numbers, rainfall, tree growth and the annual clay deposits of glaciers known as varves.

All these phenomena exhibit cyclics of one kind or another, with periods ranging from 5 to 23 years. They are not random statistical effects—they are too persistent for that. But they interrupt and succeed one another unpredictably, and sometimes, particularly in the tree records, two or more may persist simultaneously. Douglass has long recognized the complexity of his task, and has ventured few generalizations. He notes several intimations of order, however. In the records of sunspot numbers, in recent trees, in historically ancient buried trees, and in petrified trees of the Tertiary Period, cyclics with periods of about 8, 10, 11.5, and 14 years appear consistently. The 11.5 year cyclic is of course the familiar sunspot "cycle." This cycle has appeared rather regularly since about 1830, but before that date, according to the available records of direct observations, other periodicities were dominant at various times, and for a half-century in the late 1600s, as we have seen, no cyclic maxima were observed at all.

One of the complications, for example, is the so-called "Hellman cycle." Douglass found in trees from northern Europe what he took to be a two-crested sunspot cycle, one crest occurring at sunspot maximum and the next near sunspot minimum. Yet this double-crested cycle tended toward a period of more nearly 12 years than 11, which seemed puzzling. Then the German investigator G. Hellman and others showed that the two-crested cyclic is independent of the sunspot period, although it is stronger when one of its peaks coincides with a sunspot maximum. This cyclic was found in German rainfall records and is common in the Arizona trees since about 1800. Douglass believes that it is fundamentally related to the sunspot periodicity and is preparing a hypothesis attributing both to a common origin.

Douglas emphasizes that he is still far from his goal of predicting climatic cycles [for long-range weather forecasting]. But he finds some evidence that the pattern of cyclic variations and successions repeats itself about every 275 years. The 11.5-year cyclic, in particular, recurs throughout the sequoia records at some such interval, and persists about a hundred years after each recurrence. This latter point can be checked in the next few decades by direct observation, for the 11.5-year cyclic should now be in process of replacement by some other periodicity.

In all his long, tedious research Douglass has been animated by a dual motive. Intellectual curiosity, the natural wonder of man at the world about him, made him a scientist. But his years of living in the arid Southwest, feeling intimately the rhythm of rain and drought, channeled his interest and gave it a practical bent. He once commented on a Hopi Bean Dance he attended at Oraibi: "As I sat watching the dance, I realized that I was one of three terms in a human series: First, the Indians of a neighboring village, who believe that rain is actually controlled by proper magic performed by their powerful priests; then those dancers before me, who were praying to the more powerful spirits that rule the rain; and, lastly, I myself, who was there to study the rainfall history in pine timbers and learn of the great natural laws which govern the coming of rain. We were all doing exactly the same thing according to our lights."

GUIDE QUESTIONS

1. Why was it necessary for Douglass to compare the specimens from Prescott with those that he had already analyzed from Flagstaff before he could establish "the feasibility of constructing a climatic record from tree rings"?

2. How many "pitfalls" in the work of analyzing the growth rings in trees are mentioned? Why are these "pitfalls" emphasized by detailed statement of their nature?

3. Explain the connection between Maunder's letter and Douglass's work.

4. How did Douglass derive his "floating" chronologies? How were these used in dating the pueblos?

5. What is suggested about the nature of scientific research in general by the fact that the American Museum of Natural History and the National Geographic Society actively cooperated with Douglass in his work on the pueblos?

6. What is the connection between "cyclics" and the fact that Douglass "has ventured few generalizations"?

7. We are told that Douglass's research "has become a classic investigation, involving elements of astronomy, meteorology, botany, and archaeology." Comment on the part played by each of these four sciences.

Which of these elements in Douglass's work do you find most interesting? Which do you think will be most important in carrying further the work he has done?

VOCABULARY

Give the derivations and definitions of the following words:

feasibility, correlate, conifer, chronological, anomaly, millimeter, micrometer, pueblo, conglomerate, enigma, polychrome, transiently, sporadically, intimation, hypothesis.

Henry E. Garrett

THE ASSOCIATION METHOD

USED AS A MEANS OF DIAGNOSING EMOTIONAL DIFFICULTIES or complexes, the association test method was first employed by the Swiss psychiatrist Carl Jung. Jung's method was to present to his subject or patient a set of words (usually 100), to each of which the patient was instructed to give as quickly as possible the first word or association which occurred to him. The stimulus words were selected to cover a wide range of situations, including many which would presumably have emotional value for the subject. These so-called "critical words" were mixed in with many different or innocuous words. By way of illustration Table I gives a selection of twenty-five critical words from Jung's list. The theory underlying the association method is that extreme timidity, embarrassment, useless fears, anxieties, worries, and the like which occur in nervous or neurotic persons, and to a lesser degree in normal persons, center around forgotten and little-understood emotional episodes in the person's life.

Those words in the list which revive these occurrences, or "tap" complexes, should therefore provoke highly personal or emotional associations accompanied, say, by laughter or blushing. Lengthened reaction time, repetition of the stimulus word, silly or farfetched answers, or

From *Great Experiments in Psychology,* by Henry E. Garrett. Copyright, 1951, by Appleton-Century-Crofts, Inc. Reprinted by permission of the publisher.

TABLE I

A Selection of Twenty-five Critical Words from Jung's List of 100 Association Words

dead	old
to dance	to beat
sick	to wash
angry	to fear
to swim	brother
pity	false
to die	anxiety
to pray	to kiss
money	bride
despise	pure
unjust	contented
to marry	woman
ridicule	

an entire lack of response are interpreted as an attempt to avoid unpleasant associations connected with the stimulus word. Such reactions are called "complex indicators." A complex, as the psychoanalyst uses the term, denotes a group or constellation of ideas centered around some particular episode or theme which possesses emotional significance to the subject. An individual much excited or disturbed over religious matters is said to have a "religious complex"; other persons are described as having sex complexes, or inferiority complexes, the latter term being used to cover feelings of inadequacy of various kinds.

On the principle of psychic determinism, every reaction is explicable in terms of its antecedents, since all of these are inevitably linked up with the response. So it is argued that any word tied up in the subject's experience with an original emotional upset will, if followed up through free association, finally lead back to the source of his difficulty. To illustrate, a highly emotional or lengthened response to the word *ridicule* might enable the psychologist to discover by further questioning that the examinee's "touchiness" regarding ridicule grew out of his having a peculiarly shaped nose or a speech impediment. This defect had led others to tease and torment him so that feelings of inadequacy and the misery arising therefrom had interfered with his normal life. In Table I the words *kiss, bride, pray, ridicule, anxiety,* for instance, might conceivably lead to reactions which would be considered complex indicators.

The validity of a complex indicator as a revealer of emotional stress has been studied in several ways. Checking one indicator against another is perhaps the best procedure; and this method has revealed considerable agreements among certain responses. Repetition of the stimulus word and misunderstanding of the stimulus word are among the best indicators; long reaction time and irrelevant responses are also good but somewhat less valuable than the first two. Two indicators occurring together are more "diagnostic" than a single one. The emotionally toned or critical words differ from one investigation to another for different subjects, but they are usually concerned with love, anger, injustice, ridicule, pity, danger, and death.

The association method in one form or another has been much used by clinical psychologists. Perhaps the chief objection to association tests as indicators of troublesome and unconventional thoughts is that they may easily prove too much. Nearly every person has frequently been worried about religious matters or sex adjustments, or has felt inferior, and if sufficiently prodded, can probably reveal several "complexes." This is particularly true of the sex life, since present-day society curbs and limits freedom of expression in such matters.

Extensive use of free association has been made by Kent and Rosanoff in their comparison of the responses given by the normal and the insane. These investigators drew up a list of 100 words, some having probable emotional value (i.e., covering the usual worries and anxieties), and some being presumably indifferent such as *table, chair, stove*. This list was administered to 1,000 normal and 247 insane adults, the responses to each word being carefully tabulated. Probably the most striking result obtained from this mass of material was the large percentage of "individual" responses given by the insane as compared with the normal. If a person gives a response not duplicated by anyone else in the group, it is considered to be an "individual" response. The normal group gave about 7 per cent individual responses, the insane group 27 per cent. A number of individual responses is considered by the authors to be indicative of eccentric thinking or other peculiarity; while a number of "common" responses (those given by others) indicates normality in the sense of conformity to the standards of the group. Each response, together with the frequency of its occurrence, has been tabulated for each of the 100 words in the list. From these tables one can determine how commonplace or how exceptional his associations are.

Frequency tables have also been prepared giving the responses of 1,000 school children, ages 9-12, to 100 stimulus words—90 of these taken from the Kent-Rosanoff list. In general, children's responses are more concrete than those of adults. They tend to be in terms of use, or to tell something about the idea expressed by the stimulus word. To the stimulus word "table," for example, 36 per cent of the children answer "eat," while only 5 per cent of adults say "eat," 30 per cent answering "chair." To the stimulus word "man," children reply "work," adults, "woman"; to "soft," the children say "pillow," the adults "hard." *Coordinate* responses (man—woman, table—chair) and *opposites* (dark —light, deep—shallow) are given more often by adults than by children. These differences probably reflect the adult's larger vocabulary, and the tendency for adults to think in abstract terms to a greater degree than children.

The word association test has proved useful in mental hospitals as a research tool and as an aid in diagnosis. In their studies of clinical tests, Rapaport and his associates have employed a set of 60 stimulus words—called the Orbison List after its author. This list includes words relating to home and family as well as words having unpleasantly aggressive and sexual connotations. Twenty of the words are classified as "traumatic," that is, as being likely to arouse emotional disturbances. The test is administered first as a free-association test and later the list is read to the patient who is asked to reproduce his original answers.

Responses are studied and classified in various ways and are examined for indicators of emotional disturbance. In the analysis of (1) schizophrenics and depressives, (2) neurotics, and (3) normals, increasing maladjustment is evident as we go from the normals to the psychotics. The neurotics fall in between the two, being nearer to the normals than to the psychotics.

From the experimental point of view, the "detective" use of the free association test is one of the most direct applications of it. As its name implies, this method is intended to discover the "real" culprit from among several persons suspected of a "crime." In the psychological laboratory, the "crime" is usually a stunt of some kind through which one person out of several possible candidates is put. It is so arranged that neither the experimenter nor the class knows who is the "guilty" person. The object of the association test is to select this guilty individual from among the several suspects by means of his telltale associations. Usually these responses will be abnormally long or emotionally tinged (accompanied by laughter or embarrassment), or they will bear directly upon the stunt, thus giving the culprit away.

Jung has employed the word-reaction method in the following experiment, which may be used as an illustration. The supervisor of a hospital reported to him the theft of a pocketbook from one of the nurses in her charge. The purse contained a fifty-franc note, one twenty-franc piece, some centimes, a small silver watch-chain, a stencil, and a receipt from Dosenbach's Shoe Shop in Zurich. The purse had been taken from a clothes-closet in which it had been placed by the nurse. Owing to various circumstances which need not be described in detail, suspicion narrowed down to three nurses, all of whom were asked to submit to the association test. The critical words were the name of the robbed nurse, *cupboard, door, open, key, yesterday, banknote, gold, seventy, fifty, twenty, money, watch, pocketbook, chain, silver, to hide, fur, dark reddish leather* (color of the purse), *centimes, stencil, receipt, Dosenbach.* Other words not bearing directly upon the theft but having emotional value were *theft, to take, to steal, suspicion, blame, court, police, to lie, to bear, to discover, to arrest, innocent.* These critical words were distributed among twice as many indifferent words, the total constituting the final test.

To each of the three nurses the test was then given, the response and the time of reaction (in fifths of a second) being taken for each word. The median reaction times of the three nurses, whom we shall designate A, B, and C, to the indifferent and the critical words are given in the following table:

Reaction Time (Fifths of a Second) of A, B, and C to the Indifferent and Critical Words

	A	B	C
Indifferent words	10	11	12
Critical words	16	13	15
Difference	6	2	3

Although A's "normal" reaction time—as shown by her responses to the indifferent words—is the shortest of all, she is considerably slower than either B or C in replying to the critical words. This, of course, is mild though surely not conclusive evidence against A. Jung next computed the number of "imperfect reproductions" given by each nurse. An imperfect reproduction or reaction is one which is haltingly or stumblingly given, with repetition or evident emotional upset. Such responses may grow out of an association of strong feeling-tone aroused by the critical word which is carried over to several succeeding responses. The subject, so to speak, becomes "rattled," and gets more flustered as the experiment goes on. The result of this tabulation showed that A gave 65 per cent imperfect reactions, B 56 per cent, and C 30 per cent. The actual responses were distributed as follows:

Number of Imperfect Reactions Given to Indifferent and
Critical Words by A, B, and C

	A	B	C
Indifferent words	10	12	11
Critical words	19	9	12
Difference	9	3	1

A has an excess of 9 responses to the critical words, B has minus 3, and C has an excess of only 1. By this test, then, suspicion again points to A. Still another check was made in terms of the percentage excess for each subject of "complex indicators" given in response to the critical words, over and above those given in response to the presumably indifferent stimuli. A's excess is 100 per cent, B's 0, and C's 50 per cent. On the basis of these statistical results and upon careful study of the character of the responses, Jung decided that the greatest suspicion fell on A. Confession by A later on confirmed this judgment.

Perhaps it need not be pointed out that neither free association nor any of the other so-called "lie-detector" methods such as blood-pressure changes can pick out a guilty person with certainty. The habitual liar, for instance, is undisturbed in telling untruths, while a deluded or fanatical person may convince himself that he is sincere. Nor can these methods distinguish between one who is guilty and one who is not guilty but possesses guilty knowledge. They do yield valuable clues in many cases, however, and are often useful in leading to confession.

GUIDE QUESTIONS

1. What is the theory underlying the association method?
2. In what way is the "principle of psychic determinism" a basic assumption of the association method?

3. What are some of the "complex indicators," and how are these used?
4. Discuss the idea that "individual responses" in an association test are characteristic of the insane.
5. Plan a "detective" use of an association test for the class, using the method of the psychological laboratory as it is described.
6. Describe and discuss Jung's methods in the case of A, B, and C.
7. Which of the several applications of the association method do you think should prove most useful to science? Why?

VOCABULARY

Give the derivations and definitions of the following words:

innocuous, neurotic, psychic, determinism, explicable, antecedent, schizophrenic, psychotic, deluded.

WRITING AND STUDY AIDS

PATTERN OF ORGANIZATION SUGGESTED BY THE GENERAL TOPIC:

A simple essay of the "how to do this-or-that" type and a complex account of a scientific experiment present the same pattern of organization. They differ in degree rather than kind. Each is the description of a process. The first requirement of this kind of writing is that the reader should be able to follow it, step by step. In giving directions or instructions in a "how to do this-or-that" theme, you must plan carefully so that the reader can do without confusion what you would have him do. You must tell him to think in certain ways, and you must tell him to do certain things. Your direction of his thoughts will be governed by the necessities of logic; that is, you must keep the expected result before him, and you must make it clear that each step in the process moves closer to that result. Your direction of what your reader does will be subject to restrictions of time, for you cannot expect him to do two things at once. The motions which he must perform in order to complete the process successfully will have to be listed for him in chronological order.

These same features, with few modifications, are illustrated in the accounts you have studied of the methods employed by McCollum, Douglass, and Jung. The principal difference lies in the fact that their experiments have already been carried out, and are, therefore, described as completed processes. In each case, however, it was necessary to show clearly the steps they took, the reasoning behind their procedures, and the way in which the steps and the reasoning led to acceptable conclusions.

The problem of this assignment, then, whether you are giving directions for a simple process or describing a scientific experiment, is to make each step in your account so clear as a logical part of the whole that the reader can follow you easily and naturally to an understandable conclusion. In a short theme you can do better with a description of one part of a process, if it is a complicated one. In a long theme you can undertake to describe a process as a whole, or go into detail in discussing scientific method.

ASSIGNMENTS:

Short themes:

1. How to rumba/do the back stroke/park parallel/study/relax/get off to a good start
2. How to serve in tennis/kick a football/throw a curve ball/come in for a three-point landing/dribble a basketball/jump a horse
3. How to be a backseat driver/kibitzer/Monday morning quarterback/grandstand umpire
4. How to build a bird house/make a kite/bake a cake/set the dinner table/make a bed with hospital corners
5. How I practice my hobby
6. The usefulness of the work done by McCollum/Douglass/Jung
7. The relation between tree rings, sunspots, and weather
8. Why we need vitamins
9. The association method and crime detection

Long themes:

1. A description of the work of McCollum/Douglass/Jung
2. A criticism of the scientific methods of McCollum/Douglass/Jung
3. Preliminary knowledge necessary in the work of McCollum/Douglass/Jung
4. Some relations between chemistry and biology/astronomy and meteorology/physics and mathematics/psychology and sociology/archaeology and history
5. A great scientific experiment
6. Directions for a scientific experiment

READINGS FOR FURTHER STUDY:

Berman, Louis. *Food and Character*. Boston: Houghton Mifflin Company, 1932.

Brooks, C. E. P. *Climate Through the Ages*. London: Ernest Benn, 1926.

Climate and Man. Yearbook of Agriculture. Washington, D. C.: Department of Agriculture, 1941.

De Kruif, Paul. *Hunger Fighters*. New York: Harcourt, Brace, and Company, 1928.

Douglass, Andrew E. *Climatic Cycles and Tree Growth*. Washington, D. C.: Carnegie Institution, 1919-1928.

Garrett, Henry E. *Great Experiments in Psychology*, 3rd edition. New York: Appleton-Century-Crofts, Inc., 1951.

Hull, C. L., and L. S. Lugoff. "Complex Signs in Diagnostic Free Association," *Journal of Experimental Psychology*, Vol. 4 (1921), 111-136.

Jaffee, Bernard. *Outposts of Science*. New York: Simon and Schuster, 1935.

Jung, Carl G. "The Association Method," *American Journal of Psychology*, Vol. 21 (1910), 219-269.

✥ An Author and His Critics

THE RELATION BETWEEN AN AUTHOR AND HIS CRITICS IS AN INTERESTING one, and the more important the author is, the more interesting is this relation. Ernest Hemingway is one of the most important living American authors. On this the critics are in general agreement, but they have not always thought so, and they have not always liked what Hemingway wrote. Hemingway, on the other hand, has always liked what he wrote, and for twenty-five years he has kept on writing as he pleased.

In the 1920's he wrote some sharply focused, hard-hitting short stories that showed talent. He also wrote two novels, *The Sun Also Rises* and *A Farewell to Arms,* dealing with the violence and disillusionment of modern times. It was these stories and novels that established his reputation and made him a symbol of the Lost Generation, those expatriate Americans of the post-World-War-I decade. In the 1930's Hemingway seemed to lose his grip. *Death in the Afternoon,* a long book primarily about bullfighting, was disliked by nearly everybody; the short stories in *Winner Take Nothing,* although done with his old brilliant economy of language and detail, presented little that he had not done before; *Green Hills of Africa,* a book about big game hunting, was not considered very good; and *To Have and Have Not,* a loosely constructed novel about a Key West fisherman who gets mixed up with Cuban revolutionaries, seemed to most critics an inferior performance. But Hemingway was not through. To this same period belong three or four of his best short stories. And in 1940 he published *For Whom the Bell Tolls,* a robust novel about an American guerrilla in the Spanish Civil War that became his most popular book and redeemed him in the opinion of most critics. Yet ten years later he produced *Across the River and Into the Trees,* a novel about an American

Colonel loving and dying in Venice that was almost without exception condemned as the poorest thing he had ever written. Recently Hemingway has made another come-back. His *The Old Man and the Sea,* a short novel published in 1952, has been acclaimed by some reputable critics as a minor classic. What Hemingway will do in the future no one can tell, but it is safe to say that he will remain an important and controversial figure. His career thus far has been full of contrasts.

The readings for this assignment consist of some selections from Hemingway's work to give you an idea of what it is like, and some selections from the critics to show you what they have thought about it. You will read two of Hemingway's short stories, a passage from *Death in the Afternoon,* and the conclusion of *For Whom the Bell Tolls.* The critics and their opinions, both *yea* and *nay,* are representative ones. What you should do first is try to form an evaluation for yourself of Hemingway's work; if possible, read one or two additional stories or novels by him. Then compare what he has done with what the critics say about what he has done, looking at the critics in the light of your own evaluation. In this way several different kinds of worth-while comparisons and contrasts will arise.

Ernest Hemingway

INDIAN CAMP

AT THE LAKE SHORE there was another rowboat drawn up. The two Indians stood waiting.

Nick and his father got in the stern of the boat and the Indians shoved it off and one of them got in to row. Uncle George sat in the stern of the camp rowboat. The young Indian shoved the camp boat off and got in to row Uncle George.

The two boats started off in the dark. Nick heard the oar-locks of the other boat quite a way ahead of them in the mist. The Indians rowed with quick choppy strokes. Nick lay back with his father's arm around him. It was cold on the water. The Indian who was rowing them was working very hard, but the other boat moved further ahead in the mist all the time.

"Where are we going, Dad?" Nick asked.

Reprinted from *In Our Time,* by Ernest Hemingway, copyright 1925 by Charles Scribner's Sons. Used by permission of Charles Scribner's Sons, publishers.

"Over to the Indian camp. There is an Indian lady very sick."

"Oh," said Nick.

Across the bay they found the other boat beached. Uncle George was smoking a cigar in the dark. The young Indian pulled the boat way up the beach. Uncle George gave both the Indians cigars.

They walked up from the beach through a meadow that was soaking wet with dew, following the young Indian who carried a lantern. Then they went into the woods and followed a trail that led to the logging road that ran back into the hills. It was much lighter on the logging road as the timber was cut away on both sides. The young Indian stopped and blew out his lantern and they all walked on along the road.

They came around a bend and a dog came out barking. Ahead were the lights of the shanties where the Indian bark-peelers lived. More dogs rushed out at them. The two Indians sent them back to the shanties. In the shanty nearest the road here was a light in the window. An old woman stood in the doorway holding a lamp.

Inside on a wooden bunk lay a young Indian woman. She had been trying to have her baby for two days. All the old women in the camp had been helping her. The men had moved off up the road to sit in the dark and smoke out of range of the noise she made. She screamed just as Nick and the two Indians followed his father and Uncle George into the shanty. She lay in the lower bunk, very big under a quilt. Her head was turned to one side. In the upper bunk was her husband. He had cut his foot very badly with an axe three days before. He was smoking a pipe. The room smelled very bad.

Nick's father ordered some water to be put on the stove, and while it was heating he spoke to Nick.

"This lady is going to have a baby, Nick," he said.

"I know," said Nick.

"You don't know," said his father. "Listen to me. What she is going through is called being in labor. The baby wants to be born and she wants it to be born. All her muscles are trying to get the baby born. That is what is happening when she screams."

"I see," Nick said.

Just then the woman cried out.

"Oh, Daddy, can't you give her something to make her stop screaming?" asked Nick.

"No. I haven't any anaesthetic," his father said. "But her screams are not important. I don't hear them because they are not important."

The husband in the upper bunk rolled over against the wall.

The woman in the kitchen motioned to the doctor that the water was hot. Nick's father went into the kitchen and poured about half of the water out of the big kettle into a basin. Into the water left in the kettle he put several things he unwrapped from a handkerchief.

"Those must boil," he said, and began to scrub his hands in the basin of hot water with a cake of soap he had brought from the camp. Nick watched his father's hands scrubbing each other with the soap. While his father washed his hands very carefully and thoroughly, he talked.

"You see, Nick, babies are supposed to be born head first but sometimes they're not. When they're not they make a lot of trouble for everybody. Maybe I'll have to operate on this lady. We'll know in a little while."

When he was satisfied with his hands he went in and went to work.

"Pull back that quilt, will you, George?" he said. "I'd rather not touch it."

Later when he started to operate Uncle George and three Indian men held the woman still. She bit Uncle George on the arm and Uncle George said, "Damn squaw bitch!" and the young Indian who had rowed Uncle George over laughed at him. Nick held the basin for his father. It all took a long time.

His father picked the baby up and slapped it to make it breathe and handed it to the old woman.

"See, it's a boy, Nick," he said. "How do you like being an interne?"

Nick said, "All right." He was looking away so as not to see what his father was doing.

"There. That gets it," said his father and put something into the basin.

Nick didn't look at it.

"Now," his father said, "there's some stitches to put in. You can watch this or not, Nick, just as you like. I'm going to sew up the incision I made."

Nick did not watch. His curiosity had been gone for a long time.

His father finished and stood up. Uncle George and the three Indian men stood up. Nick put the basin out in the kitchen.

Uncle George looked at his arm. The young Indian smiled reminiscently.

"I'll put some peroxide on that, George," the doctor said.

He bent over the Indian woman. She was quiet now and her eyes were closed. She looked very pale. She did not know what had become of the baby or anything.

"I'll be back in the morning," the doctor said, standing up. "The nurse should be here from St. Ignace by noon and she'll bring everything we need."

He was feeling exalted and talkative as football players are in the dressing room after a game.

"That's one for the medical journal, George," he said. "Doing a Caesarian with a jack-knife and sewing it up with nine-foot, tapered gut leaders."

Uncle George was standing against the wall, looking at his arm.

"Oh, you're a great man, all right," he said.

"Ought to have a look at the proud father. They're usually the worst sufferers in these little affairs," the doctor said. "I must say he took it all pretty quietly."

He pulled back the blanket from the Indian's head. His hand came away wet. He mounted on the edge of the lower bunk with the lamp in one hand and looked in. The Indian lay with his face toward the wall. His throat had been cut from ear to ear. The blood had flowed down into a pool where his body sagged the bunk. His head rested on his left arm. The open razor lay, edge up, in the blankets.

"Take Nick out of the shanty, George," the doctor said.

There was no need of that. Nick, standing in the door of the kitchen, had a good view of the upper bunk when his father, the lamp in one hand, tipped the Indian's head back.

It was just beginning to be daylight when they walked along the logging road back toward the lake.

"I'm terribly sorry I brought you along, Nickie," said his father, all his post-operative exhilaration gone. "It was an awful mess to put you through."

"Do ladies always have such a hard time having babies?" Nick asked.

"No, that was very, very exceptional."

"Why did he kill himself, Daddy?"

"I don't know, Nick. He couldn't stand things, I guess."

"Do many men kill themselves, Daddy?"

"Not very many, Nick."

"Do many women?"

"Hardly ever."

"Don't they ever?"

"Oh, yes. They do sometimes."

"Daddy?"

"Yes."

"Where did Uncle George go?"

"He'll turn up all right."

"Is dying hard, Daddy?"

"No, I think it's pretty easy, Nick. It all depends."

They were seated in the boat, Nick in the stern, his father rowing. The sun was coming up over the hill. A bass jumped, making a circle in the water. Nick trailed his hand in the water. It felt warm in the sharp chill of the morning.

In the early morning on the lake sitting in the stern of the boat with his father rowing, he felt quite sure that he would never die.

GUIDE QUESTIONS

1. How old do you think Nick is?
2. Make a guess as to the geographical setting of the story. What details give you clues on this point?
3. Why did the Indian commit suicide?
4. Discuss the relations between Nick and his father. Compare their reactions to what happens.
5. Hemingway's style in this story might be characterized in several ways; it is tight-lipped, terse, flat, monosyllabic, etc. What else is it?
6. In your view, what is the main idea Hemingway is trying to get across? How is the last sentence related to this main idea—or does it convey the main idea? If so, how?

VOCABULARY

Give the derivations and definitions of the following words:

reminiscently, exalted, Caesarian, leader (angling term), *exhilaration.*

Ernest Hemingway

WHY IT DOESN'T MATTER ABOUT THE HORSES

THE QUESTION OF WHY the death of the horse in the bull ring is not moving, not moving to some people that is, is complicated; but the fundamental reason may be that the death of the horse tends to be comic while that of the bull is tragic. In the tragedy of the bullfight the horse is the comic character. This may be shocking, but it is true. Therefore the worse the horses are, provided they are high enough off the ground and solid enough so that the picador can perform his mission with the spiked pole, or vara, the more they are a comic element. You should be horrified and disgusted at these parodies of horses and what happens to them, but there is no way to be sure that you will be unless you make up your mind to be, no matter what your feelings. They are so unlike horses; in some ways they are like birds, any of the awkward birds such as the adjutants or the wide-billed storks, and when, lifted by the thrust of the bull's neck and shoulder muscles their legs hang, big hoofs dangling, neck drooping, the worn-out body lifted on the horn, they are not comic; but I swear they are not tragic. The tragedy is all centered in the bull and in the man. The tragic climax of the horse's career has occurred off stage at an earlier time; when he was bought by the horse contractor for use in the bull ring. The end in the ring, somehow, seems not unfitting to the structure of the animal and when the canvases are stretched over the horses, the long legs, and necks, the strange-shaped heads and the canvas covering the body to make a sort of wing, they are more like birds than ever. They look a little as a dead pelican does. A live pelican is an interesting, amusing, and sympathetic bird, though if you handle him he will give you lice; but a dead pelican looks very silly.

This is not being written as an apology for bullfights, but to try to present the bullfight integrally, and to do this a number of things must be admitted which an apologist, making a case, would slide over or avoid. The comic that happens to these horses is not their death then; death is not comic, and gives a temporary dignity to the most comic characters, although this dignity passes once death has occurred; but the strange and burlesque visceral accidents which occur. There is certainly nothing comic by our standards in seeing an animal emptied of its visceral content, but if this animal instead of doing something tragic, that is, dignified, gallops in a stiff old-maidish fashion around a ring trailing the opposite of clouds of glory it is as comic when what it is trailing is real as when the Fratellinis give a burlesque of it in which the viscera are represented by rolls of bandages, sausages and other things. If one is comic the other is; the humor comes from the same principle. I have seen it, people running, horse emptying, one dignity after another being destroyed in the spattering, and trailing of its innermost values, in a complete burlesque of tragedy. I have seen these, call them disembowellings, that is the worst word, when, due to their timing, they were very funny. This is the sort of thing you should not admit, but it is because such things have not been admitted that the bullfight has never been explained. . . .

I believe that the tragedy of the bullfight is so well ordered and so strongly disciplined by ritual that a person feeling the whole tragedy cannot separate the minor comic-tragedy of the horse so as to feel it emotionally. If they sense the meaning and end of the whole thing even when they know nothing about it; feel that this thing they do not understand is going on, the business of the horse is nothing more than an incident. If they get no feeling of the whole tragedy naturally they will react emotionally to the most picturesque incident. Naturally, too, if they are humanitarians or animalarians (what a word!) they will get no feeling of the tragedy but only a reaction on humanitarian or animalarian grounds, and the most obviously abused thing is the horse. If they sincerely identify themselves with animals they will suffer terribly, more so perhaps than the horse; since a man who has been wounded knows that the pain of a wound does not commence until about half an hour after it has been received and there is no proportional relation in pain to the horrible aspect of the wound; the pain of an abdominal wound does not come at the time but later with the gas pains and the beginnings of peritonitis; a pulled ligament or a broken bone, though, hurts at once and terribly; but these things are not known or they are ignored by the person who has identified himself with the animal and he will suffer genuinely and terribly, seeing only this aspect of the bullfight, while, when a horse pulls up lame in a steeplechase, he will not suffer at all and consider it merely regrettable. . . .

GUIDE QUESTIONS

1. Does Hemingway succeed in making the death of the horse in a bullfight seem comic? Why, or why not?
2. What is the purpose of the paragraph about "humanitarians or animalarians"?
3. Compare Hemingway's style in this selection with his style in "Indian Camp."

VOCABULARY

Give the derivations and definitions of the following words:

parody, integrally, visceral, ritual.

Ernest Hemingway

A CLEAN, WELL-LIGHTED PLACE

IT WAS LATE and every one had left the cafe except an old man who sat in the shadow the leaves of the tree made against the electric light. In the day time the street was dusty, but at night the dew settled the dust and the old man liked to sit late because he was deaf and now at night it was quiet and he felt the difference. The two waiters inside the cafe knew that the old man was a little drunk, and while he was a good client they knew that if he became too drunk he would leave without paying, so they kept watch on him.

"Last week he tried to commit suicide," one waiter said.

"Why?"

"He was in despair."

Reprinted from *Winner Take Nothing,* by Ernest Hemingway, copyright 1933 by Charles Scribner's Sons. Used by permission of Charles Scribner's Sons, publishers.

"What about?"

"Nothing."

"How do you know it was nothing?"

"He has plenty of money."

They sat together at a table that was close against the wall near the door of the cafe and looked at the terrace where the tables were all empty except where the old man sat in the shadow of the leaves of the tree that moved slightly in the wind. A girl and a soldier went by in the street. The street light shone on the brass number on his collar. The girl wore no head covering and hurried beside him.

"The guard will pick him up," one waiter said.

"What does it matter if he gets what he's after?"

"He had better get off the street now. The guard will get him. They went by five minutes ago."

The old man sitting in the shadow rapped on his saucer with his glass. The younger waiter went over to him.

"What do you want?"

The old man looked at him. "Another brandy," he said.

"You'll be drunk," the waiter said. The old man looked at him. The waiter went away.

"He'll stay all night," he said to his colleague. "I'm sleepy now. I never get into bed before three o'clock. He should have killed himself last week."

The waiter took the brandy bottle and another saucer from the counter inside the cafe and marched out to the old man's table. He put down the saucer and poured the glass full of brandy.

"You should have killed yourself last week," he said to the deaf man. The old man motioned with his finger. "A little more," he said. The waiter poured on into the glass so that the brandy slopped over and ran down the stem into the top saucer of the pile. "Thank you," the old man said. The waiter took the bottle back inside the cafe. He sat down at the table with his colleague again.

"He's drunk now," he said.

"He's drunk every night."

"What did he want to kill himself for?"

"How should I know."

"How did he do it?"

"He hung himself with a rope."

"Who cut him down?"

"His niece."

"Why did they do it?"

"Fear for his soul."

"How much money has he got?"

"He's got plenty."

"He must be eighty years old."

"Anyway I should say he was eighty."

"I wish he would go home. I never get to bed before three o'clock. What kind of hour is that to go to bed?"

"He stays up because he likes it."

"He's lonely. I'm not lonely. I have a wife waiting in bed for me."

"He had a wife once too."

"A wife would be no good to him now."

"You can't tell. He might be better with a wife."

"His niece looks after him."

"I know. You said she cut him down."

"I wouldn't want to be that old. An old man is a nasty thing."

"Not always. This old man is clean. He drinks without spilling. Even now, drunk. Look at him."

"I don't want to look at him. I wish he would go home. He has no regard for those who must work."

The old man looked from his glass across the square, then over at the waiters.

"Another brandy," he said, pointing to his glass. The waiter who was in a hurry came over.

"Finished," he said, speaking with that omission of syntax stupid people employ when talking to drunken people or foreigners. "No more tonight. Close now."

"Another," said the old man.

"No. Finished." The waiter wiped the edge of the table with a towel and shook his head.

The old man stood up, slowly counted the saucers, took a leather coin purse from his pocket and paid for the drinks, leaving half a peseta tip.

The waiter watched him go down the street, a very old man walking unsteadily but with dignity.

"Why didn't you let him stay and drink?" the unhurried waiter asked. They were putting up the shutters. "It is not half past two."

"I want to go home to bed."

"What is an hour?"

"More to me than to him."

"An hour is the same."

"You talk like an old man yourself. He can buy a bottle and drink at home."

"It's not the same."

"No, it is not," agreed the waiter with a wife. He did not wish to be unjust. He was only in a hurry.

"And you? You have no fear of going home before your usual hour?"

"Are you trying to insult me?"

"No, hombre, only to make a joke."

"No," the waiter who was in a hurry said, rising from pulling down the metal shutters. "I have confidence. I am all confidence."

"You have youth, confidence, and a job," the older waiter said. "You have everything."

"And what do you lack?"

"Everything but work."

"You have everything I have."

"No. I have never had confidence and I am not young."

"Come on. Stop talking nonsense and lock up."

"I am of those who like to stay late at the cafe," the older waiter said. "With all those who do not want to go to bed. With all those who need a light for the night."

"I want to go home and into bed."

"We are of two different kinds," the older waiter said. He was now dressed to go home. "It is not only a question of youth and confidence although those things are very beautiful. Each night I am reluctant to close up because there may be some one who needs the cafe."

"Hombre, there are bodegas open all night long."

"You do not understand. This is a clean and pleasant cafe. It is well lighted. The light is very good and also, now, there are shadows of the leaves."

"Good night," said the younger waiter.

"Good night," the other said. Turning off the electric light he continued the conversation with himself. It is the light of course but it is necessary that the place be clean and pleasant. You do not want music. Certainly you do not want music. Nor can you stand before a

bar with dignity although that is all that is provided for these hours
What did he fear? It was not fear or dread. It was a nothing that h
knew too well. It was all a nothing and a man was nothing too. I
was only that and light was all it needed and a certain cleanness an
order. Some lived in it and never felt it but he knew it all was nad
y pues nada y nada y pues nada. Our nada who art in nada, nada b
thy name thy kingdom nada thy will be nada in nada as it is in nada
Give us this nada our daily nada and nada us our nada as we nad
our nadas and nada us not into nada but deliver us from nada; pue
nada. Hail nothing full of nothing, nothing is with thee. He smile
and stood before a bar with a shining steam pressure coffee machine

"What's yours?" asked the barman.

"Nada."

"Otro loco mas," said the barman and turned away.

"A little cup," said the waiter.

The barman poured it for him.

"The light is very bright and pleasant but the bar is unpolished,
the waiter said.

The barman looked at him but did not answer. It was too late a
night for conversation.

"You want another copita?" the barman asked.

"No, thank you," said the waiter and went out. He disliked bar
and bodegas. A clean, well-lighted cafe was a very different thing
Now, without thinking further, he would go home to his room. H
would lie in the bed and finally, with daylight, he would go to sleep
After all, he said to himself, it is probably only insomnia. Many mus
have it.

GUIDE QUESTIONS

1. How many conflicts are there between the characters in the story
   Which one of these conflicts is most important?
2. Explain why the internal conflict of the old waiter who does not war
   to go home is the largest conflict of all.
3. How does Hemingway in this story make nothing mean a great deal
   How do we know, from the start, that this story is about "nothing"
4. The story is written in the baldest possible diction. Explain how th
   style is appropriate to the "nothing" that the story is about.
5. Mark Schorer says: "As the diction is of the sparsest, so the rhythm

of the sentences are either short and blunt, truncated like the characters' experience, or loose, running on to no organized syntactical end."
Explain what this means, and find sentences to compare and contrast
in illustration of it.

6. How does Hemingway convey, early in the story, before we find Spanish
   words, "peseta" and "hombre" and "bodega," the feeling that the scene
   is in Spain, that this is a Spanish cafe?

7. What is gained by having the old waiter lapse almost completely into
   Spanish in his negation of prayer? What is the effect of the repetitions
   of "nada"?

8. To quote Mark Schorer again: "The verbal economy of Hemingway's
   style expresses directly his preference for mute suffering in the face of a
   blankly intolerable universe." What does this mean?

VOCABULARY

Give the derivations and definitions of the following words:

colleague, syntax, reluctant, insomnia.

Ernest Hemingway

THE END OF ROBERT JORDAN

ROBERT JORDAN WAS on the big gray he had first seen in the snow of the
morning of the day before and he felt that it was much horse between
his legs and under his hands. He was wearing rope-soled shoes and
the stirrups were a little too short; his submachine gun was slung over
his shoulder, his pockets were full of clips and he was sitting reloading
the one used clip, the reins under one arm, tight, watching Pilar
mount into a strange sort of seat on top of the duffle lashed onto the
saddle of the buckskin.

"Cut that stuff loose for God's sake," Primitivo said. "Thou wilt
fall and the horse cannot carry it."

"Shut up," said Pilar. "We go to make a life with this."

"Canst ride like that, woman?" Pablo asked her from the *guardia-civil* saddle on the great bay horse.

"Like any milk peddler," Pilar told him. "How do you go, old one?"

"Straight down. Across the road. Up the far slope and into the timber where it narrows."

"Across the road?" Agustín wheeled beside him, kicking his soft-heeled, canvas shoes against the stiff, unresponding belly of one of the horses Pablo had recruited in the night.

"Yes, man. It is the only way," Pablo said. He handed him one of the lead ropes. Primitivo and the gypsy had the others.

"Thou canst come at the end if thou will, *Inglés*," Pablo said. "We cross high enough to be out of range of that *máquina*. But we will go separately and riding much and then be together where it narrows above."

"Good," said Robert Jordan.

They rode down through the timber toward the edge of the road. Robert Jordan rode just behind Maria. He could not ride beside her for the timber. He caressed the gray once with his thigh muscles, and then held him steady as they dropped down fast and sliding through the pines, telling the gray with his thighs as they dropped down what the spurs would have told him if they had been on level ground.

"Thou," he said to Maria, "go second as they cross the road. First is not so bad though it seems bad. Second is good. It is later that they are always watching for."

"But thou—"

"I will go suddenly. There will be no problem. It is the places in line that are bad."

He was watching the round, bristly head of Pablo, sunk in his shoulders as he rode, his automatic rifle slung over his shoulder. He was watching Pilar, her head bare, her shoulders broad, her knees higher than her thighs as her heels hooked into the bundles. She looked back at him once and shook her head.

"Pass the Pilar before you cross the road," Robert Jordan said to Maria.

Then he was looking through the thinning trees and he saw the oiled dark of the road below and beyond it the green slope of the hillside. We are above the culvert, he saw, and just below the height where the road drops down straight toward the bridge in that long sweep. We are around eight hundred yards above the bridge. That is not out of range for the Fiat in that little tank if they have come up to the bridge.

"Maria," he said. "Pass the Pilar before we reach the road and ride wide up that slope."

She looked back at him but did not say anything. He did not look at her except to see that she had understood.

"*Comprendes?*" he asked her.

She nodded.

"Move up," he said.

She shook her head.

"Move up!"

"Nay," she told him, turning around and shaking her head. "I go in the order that I am to go."

Just then Pablo dug both his spurs into the big bay and he plunged down the last pine-needled slope and crossed the road in a pounding, sparking of shod hooves. The others came behind him and Robert Jordan saw them crossing the road and slamming on up the green slope and heard the machine gun hammer at the bridge. Then he heard a noise come sweeeish-crack-boom! The boom was a sharp crack that widened in the cracking and on the hillside he saw a small fountain of earth rise with a plume of gray smoke. Sweeeish-crack-boom! It came again, the swishing like the noise of a rocket and there was another up-pulsing of dirt and smoke farther up the hillside.

Ahead of him the gypsy was stopped beside the road in the shelter of the last trees. He looked ahead at the slope and then he looked back toward Robert Jordan.

"Go ahead, Rafael," Robert Jordan said. "Gallop, man!"

The gypsy was holding the lead rope with the pack-horse pulling his head taut behind him.

"Drop the pack-horse and gallop!" Robert Jordan said.

He saw the gypsy's hand extended behind him, rising higher and higher, seeming to take forever as his heels kicked into the horse he was riding and the rope came taut, then dropped, and he was across the road and Robert Jordan was knee-ing against a frightened pack-horse that bumped into him as the gypsy crossed the hard, dark road and he heard his horse's hooves clumping as he galloped up the slope.

Wheeeeeeish-ca-rack! The flat trajectory of the shell came and he saw the gypsy jink like a running boar as the earth spouted the little black and gray geyser ahead of him. He watched him galloping, slow and reaching now, up the long green slope and the gun threw behind him and ahead of him and he was under the fold of the hill with the others.

I can't take the damned pack-horse, Robert Jordan thought. Though I wish I could keep the son of a bitch on my off side. I'd like to have him between me and that 47 mm. they're throwing with. By God, I'll try to get him up there anyway.

He rode up to the pack-horse, caught hold of the hackamore, and then, holding the rope, the horse trotting behind him, rode fifty yards up through the trees. At the edge of the trees he looked down the road past the truck to the bridge. He could see men out on the bridge and behind it looked like a traffic jam on the road. Robert Jordan looked around, saw what he wanted finally and reached up and broke a dead limb from a pine tree. He dropped the hackamore, edged the pack-horse up to the slope that slanted down to the road and then hit him hard across the rump with the tree branch. "Go on, you son of a bitch," he said, and threw the dead branch after him as the pack-horse crossed the road and started across the slope. The branch hit him and the horse broke from a run into a gallop.

Robert Jordan rode thirty yards farther up the road; beyond that the bank was too steep. The gun was firing now with the rocket whish and the cracking, dirt-spouting boom. "Come on, you big gray fascist bastard," Robert Jordan said to the horse and put him down the slope in a sliding plunge. Then he was out in the open, over the road that was so hard under the hooves he felt the pound of it come up all the way to his shoulders, his neck and his teeth, onto the smooth of the slope, the hooves finding it, cutting it, pounding it, reaching, throwing, going, and he looked down across the slope to where the bridge showed now at a new angle he had never seen. It crossed in profile now without foreshortening and in the center was the broken place and behind it on the road was the little tank and behind the little tank was a big tank with a gun that flashed now yellow-bright as a mirror and the screech as the air ripped apart seemed almost over the gray neck that stretched ahead of him, and he turned his head as the dirt fountained up the hillside. The pack-horse was ahead of him swinging too far to the right and slowing down and Robert Jordan, galloping, his head turned a little toward the bridge, saw the line of trucks halted behind the turn that showed now clearly as he was gaining height, and he saw the bright yellow flash that signalled the instant whish and boom, and the shell fell short, but he heard the metal sailing from where the dirt rose.

He saw them all ahead in the edge of the timber watching him and he said, *"Arre caballo!* Go on, horse!" and felt his big horse's chest surging with the steepening of the slope and saw the gray neck stretching and the gray ears ahead and he reached and patted the wet gray neck, and he looked back at the bridge and saw the bright flash from the heavy, squat, mud-colored tank there on the road and then he did not hear any whish but only a banging acrid smelling clang like a boiler being ripped apart and he was under the gray horse and the gray horse was kicking and he was trying to pull out from under the weight.

He could move all right. He could move toward the right. But his left leg stayed perfectly flat under the horse as he moved to the right. It was as though there was a new joint in it; not the hip joint but another one that went sideways like a hinge. Then he knew what it was all right and just then the gray horse knee-ed himself up and Robert Jordan's right leg, that had kicked the stirrup loose just as it should, slipped clear over the saddle and came down beside him and he felt with his two hands of his thigh bone where the left leg lay flat against the ground and his hands both felt the sharp bone and where it pressed against the skin.

The gray horse was standing almost over him and he could see his ribs heaving. The grass was green where he sat and there were meadow flowers in it and he looked down the slope across to the road and the bridge and the gorge and the road and saw the tank and waited for the next flash. It came almost at once with again no whish and in the burst of it, with the smell of the high explosive, the dirt clods scattering and the steel whirring off, he saw the big gray horse sit quietly down beside him as though it were a horse in a circus. And then, looking at the horse sitting there, he heard the sound the horse was making.

Then Primitivo and Agustín had him under the arm-pits and were dragging him up the last of the slope and the new joint in his leg let it swing any way the ground swung it. Once a shell whished close over them and they dropped him and fell flat, but the dirt scattered over them and the metal sang off and they picked him up again. And then they had him up to the shelter of the long draw in the timber where the horses were, and Maria, Pilar and Pablo were standing over him.

Maria was kneeling by him and saying, "Roberto, what hast thou?"

He said, sweating heavily, "The left leg is broken, *guapa."*

"We will bind it up," Pilar said. "Thou canst ride that." She pointed to one of the horses that was packed. "Cut off the load."

Robert Jordan saw Pablo shake his head and he nodded at him.

"Get along," he said. Then he said, "Listen, Pablo. Come here."

The sweat-streaked, bristly face bent down by him and Robert Jordan smelt the full smell of Pablo.

"Let us speak," he said to Pilar and Maria. "I have to speak to Pablo."

"Does it hurt much?" Pablo asked. He was bending close over Robert Jordan.

"No. I think the nerve is crushed. Listen. Get along. I am mucked, see? I will talk to the girl for a moment. When I say to take her, take her. She will want to stay. I will only speak to her for a moment."

"Clearly, there is not much time," Pablo said.

"Clearly."

"I think you would do better in the Republic," Robert Jordan said.

"Nay, I am for Gredos."

"Use thy head."

"Talk to her now," Pablo said. "There is little time. I am sorry thou hast this, *Inglés."*

"Since I have it—" Robert Jordan said. "Let us not speak of it. But use thy head. Thou hast much head. Use it."

"Why would I not?" said Pablo. "Talk now fast, *Inglés.* There is no time."

Pablo went over to the nearest tree and watched down the slope, across the slope and up the road across the gorge. Pablo was looking at the gray horse on the slope with true regret on his face and Pilar and Maria were with Robert Jordan where he sat against the tree trunk.

"Slit the trouser, will thee?" he said to Pilar. Maria crouched by him and did not speak. The sun was on her hair and her face was twisted as a child's contorts before it cries. But she was not crying.

Pilar took her knife and slit his trouser leg down below the left-hand pocket. Robert Jordan spread the cloth with his hands and looked at the stretch of his thigh. Ten inches below the hip joint there was a pointed, purple swelling like a sharp-peaked little tent and as he touched it with his fingers he could feel the snapped-off thigh bone tight against the skin. His leg was lying at an odd angle. He looked up at Pilar. Her face had the same expression as Maria's.

"*Anda,*" he said to her. "Go."

She went away with her head down without saying anything nor looking back and Robert Jordan could see her shoulders shaking.

"*Guapa,*" he said to Maria and took hold of her two hands. "Listen. We will not be going to Madrid—"

Then she started to cry.

"No, *guapa,* don't," he said. "Listen. We will not go to Madrid now but I go always with thee wherever thou goest. Understand?"

She said nothing and pushed her head against his cheek with her arms around him.

"Listen to this well, rabbit," he said. He knew there was a great hurry and he was sweating very much, but this had to be said and understood. "Thou wilt go now, rabbit. But I go with thee. As long as there is one of us there is both of us. Do you understand?"

"Nay, I stay with thee."

"Nay, rabbit. What I do now I do alone. I could not do it well with thee. If thou goest then I go, too. Do you not see how it is? Whichever one there is, is both."

"I will stay with thee."

"Nay, rabbit. Listen. That people cannot do together. Each one must do it alone. But if thou goest then I go with thee. It is in that way that I go too. Thou wilt go now, I know. For thou art good and kind. Thou wilt go now for us both."

"But it is easier if I stay with thee," she said. "It is better for me."

"Yes. Therefore go for a favor. Do it for me since it is what thou canst do."

"But you don't understand, Roberto. What about me? It is worse for me to go."

"Surely," he said. "It is harder for thee. But I am thee also now."

She said nothing.

He looked at her and he was sweating heavily and he spoke now, trying harder to do something than he had ever tried in all his life.

"Now you will go for us both," he said. "You must not be selfish, rabbit. You must do your duty now."

She shook her head.

"You are me now," he said. "Surely thou must feel it, rabbit."

"Rabbit, listen," he said. "Truly thus I go too. I swear it to thee."

She said nothing.

"Now you see it," he said. "Now I see it is clear. Now thou wilt go. Good. Now you are going. Now you have said you will go."

She had said nothing.

"Now I thank thee for it. Now you are going well and fast and far and we both go in thee. Now put thy hand here. Now put thy head down. Nay, put it down. That is right. Now I put my hand there. Good. Thou art so good. Now do not think more. Now art thou doing what thou should. Now thou art obeying. Not me but us both. The me in thee. Now you go for us both. Truly. We both go in thee now. This I have promised thee. Thou art very good to go and very kind."

He jerked his head at Pablo, who was half-looking at him from the tree and Pablo started over. He motioned with his thumb to Pilar.

"We will go to Madrid another time, rabbit," he said. "Truly. Now stand up and go and we both go. Stand up. See?"

"No," she said and held him tight around the neck.

He spoke now still calmly and reasonably but with great authority. "Stand up," he said. "Thou art me too now. Thou art all there will be of me. Stand up."

She stood up slowly, crying, and with her head down. Then she dropped quickly beside him and then stood up again, slowly and tiredly, as he said, "Stand up, *guapa.*"

Pilar was holding her by the arm and she was standing there.

"*Vamonos,*" Pilar said. "Dost lack anything, *Inglés?*" She looked at him and shook her head.

"No," he said and went on talking to Maria.

"There is no good-by, *guapa,* because we are not apart. That it should be good in the Gredos. Go now. Go good. Nay," he spoke now still calmly and reasonably as Pilar walked the girl along. "Do not turn around. Put thy foot in. Yes. Thy foot in. Help her up," he said to Pilar. "Get her in the saddle. Swing up now."

He turned his head, sweating, and looked down the slope, then back toward where the girl was in the saddle with Pilar by her and Pablo just behind. "Now go," he said. "Go."

She started to look around. "Don't look around," Robert Jordan said. "Go." And Pablo hit the horse across the crupper with a hobbling strap and it looked as though Maria tried to slip from the saddle but Pilar and Pablo were riding close up against her and Pilar was holding her and the three horses were going up the draw.

"Roberto," Maria turned and shouted. "Let me stay! Let me stay!"

"I am with thee," Robert Jordan shouted. "I am with thee now. We are both there. Go!" Then they were out of sight around the corner of the draw and he was soaking wet with sweat and looking at nothing.

Agustín was standing by him.

"Do you want me to shoot thee, *Inglés?*" he asked, leaning down close. "*Quieres?* It is nothing."

"*No hace falta,*" Robert Jordan said. "Get along. I am very well here."

"*Me cago en la leche que me han dado!*" Agustín said. He was crying so he could not see Robert Jordan clearly. "*Salud, Inglés.*"

"*Salud,* old one," Robert Jordan said. He was looking down the slope now. "Look well after the cropped head, wilt thou?"

"There is no problem," Agustín said. "Thou hast what thou needest?"

"There are very few shells for this *máquina,* so I will keep it," Robert Jordan said. "Thou canst not get more. For that other and the one of Pablo, yes."

"I cleaned out the barrel," Agustín said. "Where thou plugged it in the dirt with the fall."

"What became of the pack-horse?"

"The gypsy caught it."

Agustín was on the horse now but he did not want to go. He leaned far over toward the tree where Robert Jordan lay.

"Go on, *viejo,*" Robert Jordan said to him. "In war there are many things like this."

"*Qué puta es la guerra,*" Agustín said. "War is a bitchery."

"Yes man, yes. But get on with thee."

"*Salud, Inglés,*" Agustín said, clenching his right fist.

"*Salud,*" Robert Jordan said. "But get along, man."

Agustín wheeled his horse and brought his right fist down as though he cursed again with the motion of it and rode up the draw. All the others had been out of sight long before. He looked back where the draw turned in the timber and waved his fist. Robert Jordan waved and then Agustín, too, was out of sight. . . . Robert Jordan looked down the green slope of the hillside to the road and the bridge. I'm as well this way as any, he thought. It wouldn't be worth risking getting over on my belly yet, not as close as that thing was to the surface, and I can see better this way.

He felt empty and drained and exhausted from all of it and from them going and his mouth tasted of bile. Now, finally and at last, there was no problem. However all of it had been and however all of it would ever be now, for him, no longer was there any problem.

They were all gone now and he was alone with his back against a tree. He looked down across the green slope, seeing the gray horse where Agustín had shot him, and on down the slope to the road with the timber-covered country behind it. Then he looked at the bridge and across the bridge and watched the activity on the bridge and the road. He could see the trucks now, all down the lower road. The gray of the trucks showed through the trees. Then he looked back up the road to where it came down over the hill. They will be coming soon now, he thought.

Pilar will take care of her as well as any one can. You know that. Pablo must have a sound plan or he would not have tried it. You do not have to worry about Pablo. It does no good to think about Maria. Try to believe what you told her. That is the best. And who says it is not true? Not you. You don't say it, any more than you would say the things did not happen that happened. Stay with what you believe now. Don't get cynical. The time is too short and you have just sent her away. Each one does what he can. You can do nothing for yourself but perhaps you can do something for another. Well, we had all our luck in four days. Not four days. It was afternoon when I first got there and it will not be noon today. That makes not quite three days and three nights. Keep it accurate, he said. Quite accurate.

I think you better get down now, he thought. You better get fixed around some way where you will be useful instead of leaning against this tree like a tramp. You have had much luck. There are many worse things than this. Every one has to do this, one day or another. You are not afraid of it once you know you have to do it, are you? No, he said, truly. It was lucky the nerve was crushed, though. I cannot even feel that there is anything below the break. He touched the lower part of his leg and it was as though it were not part of his body.

He looked down the hill slope again and he thought. I hate to leave it, is all. I hate to leave it very much and I hope I have done some good in it. I have tried to with what talent I had. *Have, you mean. All right, have.*

I have fought for what I believed in for a year now. If we win here we will win everywhere. The world is a fine place and worth the fighting for and I hate very much to leave it. And you had a lot of luck, he told himself, to have had such a good life. You've had just as good a life as grandfather's though not as long. You've had as good a life as any one because of these last days. You do not want to complain when you have been so lucky. I wish there was some way to pass on what I've learned, though. Christ, I was learning fast there at the end. I'd like to talk to Karkov. That is in Madrid. Just over the hills there, and down across the plain. Down out of the gray rocks and the pines, the heather and the gorse, across the yellow high plateau you see it rising white and beautiful. That part is just as true as Pilar's old women drinking the blood down at the slaughterhouse. There's no *one* thing that's true. It's all true. The way the planes are beautiful whether they are ours or theirs. The hell they are, he thought.

You take it easy, now, he said. Get turned over now while you still have time. Listen, one thing. Do you remember? Pilar and the hand? Do you believe that crap? No, he said. Not with everything that's happened? No, I don't believe it. She was nice about it early this morn-ing before the show started. She was afraid maybe I believed it. I don't though. But she does. They see something. Or they feel something. Like a bird dog. What about extra-sensory perception? What about obscenity? he said. She wouldn't say good-by, he thought, because she knew if she did Maria would never go. That Pilar. Get yourself turned over, Jordan. But he was reluctant to try it.

Then he remembered that he had the small flask in his hip pocket and he thought, I'll take a good spot of the giant killer and then I'll try it. But the flask was not there when he felt for it. Then he felt that much more alone because he knew there was not going to be even that. I guess I'd counted on that, he said.

Do you suppose Pablo took it? Don't be silly. You must have lost it at the bridge. "Come on now, Jordan," he said. "Over you go."

Then he took hold of his left leg with both hands and pulled on it hard, pulling toward the foot while he lay down beside the tree he had been resting his back against. Then lying flat and pulling hard on the leg, so the broken end of the bone would not come up and cut through the thigh, he turned slowly around on his rump until the back of his head was facing downhill. Then with his broken leg, held by both hands, uphill, he put the sole of his right foot against the instep of his left foot and pressed hard while he rolled, sweating, over onto his face and chest. He got onto his elbows, stretched the left leg well behind him with both hands and a far, sweating, push with the right foot and there he was. He felt with his fingers on the left thigh and it was all right. The bone end had not punctured the skin and the broken end was well into the muscle now.

The big nerve must have been truly smashed when that damned horse rolled on it, he thought. It truly doesn't hurt at all. Except now in certain changes of positions. That's when the bone pinches something else. You see? he said. You see what luck is? You didn't need the giant killer at all.

He reached over for the submachine gun, took the clip out that was in the magazine, felt in his pocket for clips, opened the action and looked through the barrel, put the clip back into the groove of the magazine until it clicked, and then looked down the hill slope. Maybe half an hour, he thought. Now take it easy.

Then he looked at the hillside and he looked at the pines and he tried not to think at all.

He looked at the stream and he remembered how it had been under the bridge in the cool of the shadow. I wish they would come, he thought. I do not want to get in any sort of mixed-up state before they come.

Who do you suppose has it easier? Ones with religion or just taking it straight? It comforts them very much but we know there is no thing to fear. It is only missing it that's bad. Dying is only bad when it takes a long time and hurts so much that it humiliates you. That is where you have all the luck, see? You don't have any of that.

It's wonderful they've got away. I don't mind this at all now they are away. It is sort of the way I said. It is really very much that way. Look how different it would be if they were all scattered out across that hill where that gray horse is. Or if we were all cooped up here waiting for it. No. They're gone. They're away. Now if the attack were only a success. What do you want? Everything. I want everything and I will take whatever I get. If this attack is no good another one will be. I never noticed when the planes came back. *God, that was lucky I could make her go.*

I'd like to tell grandfather about this one. I'll bet he never had to go over and find his people and do a show like this. How do you know? He may have done fifty. No, he said. Be accurate. Nobody did any fifty like this one. Nobody did five. Nobody did one maybe not just like this. Sure. They must have.

I wish they would come now, he said. I wish they would come right now because the leg is starting to hurt now. It must be the swelling.

We were going awfully good when that thing hit us, he thought. But it was only luck it didn't come while I was under the bridge. When a thing is wrong something's bound to happen. You were bitched when they gave Golz those orders. That was what you knew and it was probably that which Pilar felt. But later on we will have these things much better organized. We ought to have portable short wave transmitters. *Yes, there's a lot of things we ought to have.* I ought to carry a spare leg, too.

He grinned at that sweatily because the leg, where the big nerve had been bruised by the fall, was hurting badly now. Oh, let them come, he said. I don't want to do that business that my father did. I will do it all right but I'd much prefer not to have to. I'm against that. Don't think about that. Don't think at all. I wish the bastards would come, he said. I wish so very much they'd come.

His leg was hurting very badly now. The pain had started suddenly with the swelling after he had moved and he said, Maybe I'll just do it now. I guess I'm not awfully good at pain. Listen, if I do that now you wouldn't misunderstand, would you? Who are you talking to? Nobody, he said. Grandfather, I guess. No. Nobody. Oh bloody it, I wish that they would come.

Listen, I may have to do that because if I pass out or anything like that I am no good at all and if they bring me to they will ask me a lot of questions and do things and all and that is no good. It's much best not to have them do those things. So why wouldn't it be all right to just do it now and then the whole thing would be over with? Because oh, listen, yes, listen, *let them come now.*

You're not so good at this, Jordan, he said. Not so good at this. And who is so good at this? I don't know and I don't really care right now. But you are not. That's right. You're not at all, at all. Oh not at all, at all. I think it would be all right to do it now? Don't you?

No, it isn't. Because there is something you can do yet. As long as you know what it is you have to do it. As long as you remember what it is you have to wait for that. *Come on. Let them come. Let them come. Let them come!*

Think about them being away, he said. Think about them going through the timber. Think about them crossing a creek. Think about them riding through the heather. Think about them going up the slope. Think about them O. K. tonight. Think about them traveling, all night. Think about them hiding up tomorrow. Think about them. God damn it, think about them. *That's just as far as I can think about them,* he said.

Think about Montana. *I can't.* Think about Madrid. *I can't.* Think about a cool drink of water. *All right.* That's what it will be like. Like a cool drink of water. *You're a liar.* It will just be nothing. That's all it will be. Just nothing. Then do it. *Do it.* Do it now. It's all right to do it now. Go on and do it now. *No, you have to wait.* What for? You know all right. *Then wait.*

I can't wait any longer now, he said. If I wait any longer I'll pass out. I know because I've felt it starting to go three times now and I've held it. I held it all right. But I don't know about any more. What I think is you've got an internal hemorrhage there from where that thigh bone's cut around inside. Especially on that turning business. That makes the swelling and that's what weakens you and makes you start to pass. It would be all right to do it now. Really, I'm telling you that it would be all right.

And if you wait and hold them up even a little while or just get the officer that may make all the difference. One thing well done can make—

All right, he said. And he lay very quietly and tried to hold on to himself that he felt slipping away from himself as you feel snow starting to slip sometimes on a mountain slope, and he said, now quietly, then let me last until they come.

Robert Jordan's luck held very good because he saw, just then, the cavalry ride out of the timber and across the road. He watched them coming riding up the slope. He saw the trooper who stopped by the gray horse and shouted to the officer who rode over to him. He watched them both looking down at the gray horse. They recognized him of course. He and his rider had been missing since the early morning of the day before.

Robert Jordan saw them there on the slope, close to him now, and below he saw the road and the bridge and the long lines of vehicles below it. He was completely integrated now and he took a good long look at everything. Then he looked up at the sky. There were big white clouds in it. He touched the palm of his hand against the pine needles where he lay and he touched the bark of the pine trunk that he lay behind.

Then he rested as easily as he could with his two elbows in the pine needles and the muzzle of the submachine gun resting against the trunk of the pine tree.

As the officer came trotting now on the trail of the horses of the band he would pass twenty yards below where Robert Jordan lay. At that distance there would be no problem. The officer was Lieutenant Berrendo. He had come up from La Granja when they had been ordered up after the first report of the attack on the lower post. They had ridden hard and had then had to swing back, because the bridge had been blown, to cross the gorge high above and come around through the timber. Their horses were wet and blown and they had to be urged into the trot.

Lieutenant Berrendo, watching the trail, came riding up, his thin face serious and grave. His submachine gun lay across his saddle in the crook of his left arm. Robert Jordan lay behind the tree, holding onto himself very carefully and delicately to keep his hands steady. He was waiting until the officer reached the sunlit place where the first trees of the pine forest joined the green slope of the meadow. He could feel his heart beating against the pine needle floor of the forest.

GUIDE QUESTIONS

1. How does the structure, and with it the pace, of the sentences change in the description of Robert Jordan crossing the road? Why?
2. What impression do you get of the previous relations between Robert Jordan and Maria in the scene of their parting? What is the mood of the scene?
3. What impression do you get of the previous relations between Robert Jordan and Agustín in the scene of their parting? What is the mood of the scene?
4. After all the others have gone, Hemingway says that for Robert Jordan, "now, finally and at last, there was no problem." What does he mean?

5. How do you interpret the passage in which Robert Jordan reviews his part in the Spanish Civil War?
6. How do you interpret the paragraph beginning: "Who do you suppose has it easier?"
7. What is the purpose of the italics which are used fairly frequently toward the end?
8. What is it that Robert Jordan is strongly moved to do, and debates with himself, but does not do? Why doesn't he do it?
9. What is the final impression produced, for you, by "The End of Robert Jordan"?
10. Is Robert Jordan an older version of Nick in "Indian Camp"? Explain why he is or is not.
11. Compare Robert Jordan's outlook on life and death with that of the old waiter in "A Clean, Well-Lighted Place."

VOCABULARY

Give the derivations and definitions of the following words:

duffle, taut, trajectory, hackamore, foreshortening, acrid, crupper, gorse, integrated.

Edmund Wilson

HEMINGWAY: GAUGE OF MORALE

ERNEST HEMINGWAY's *In Our Time* was an odd and original book. It had the appearance of a miscellany of stories and fragments; but actually the parts hung together and produced a definite effect. There were two distinct series of pieces which alternated with one another: one a set of brief and brutal sketches of police shootings, bullfight crises, hangings of criminals, and incidents of the war; and the other a set of short stories dealing in its principal sequence with the growing-up of an American boy against a landscape of idyllic Michigan, but interspersed also with glimpses of American soldiers returning home.

From *The Wound and the Bow* by Edmund Wilson. Published by Oxford University Press. Copyright 1947 by Edmund Wilson. Reprinted by permission of the author.

It seems to have been Hemingway's intention—*'In Our Time'*—that the war should set the key for the whole. The cold-bloodedness of the battles and executions strikes a discord with the sensitiveness and candor of the boy at home in the States; and presently the boy turns up in Europe in one of the intermediate vignettes as a soldier in the Italian Army, hit in the spine by machine-gun fire and trying to talk to a dying Italian: *'Senta,* Rinaldi. *Senta,'* he says, 'you and me, we've made a separate peace.'

But there is a more fundamental relationship between the pieces of the two series. The shooting of Nick in the war does not really connect two different worlds: has he not found in the butchery abroad the same world that he knew back in Michigan? Was not life in the Michigan woods equally destructive and cruel? He had gone once with his father, the doctor, when he had performed a Caesarean operation on an Indian squaw with a jacknife and no anaesthetic and had sewed her up with fishing leaders, while the Indian hadn't been able to bear it and had cut his throat in his bunk. Another time, when the doctor had saved the life of a squaw, her Indian had picked a quarrel with him rather than pay him in work. And Nick himself had sent his girl about her business when he had found out how terrible her mother was. Even fishing in Big Two-Hearted River—away and free in the woods—he had been conscious in a curious way of the cruelty inflicted on the fish, even of the silent agonies endured by the live bait, the grasshoppers kicking on the hook.

Not that life isn't enjoyable. Talking and drinking with one's friends is great fun; fishing in Big Two-Hearted River is a tranquil exhilaration. But the brutality of life is always there, and it is somehow bound up with the enjoyment. Bullfights are especially enjoyable. It is even exhilarating to build a simply priceless barricade and pot the enemy as they are trying to get over it. The condition of life is pain; and the joys of the most innocent surface are somehow tied to its stifled pangs.

The resolution of this dissonance in art made the beauty of Hemingway's stories. He had in the process tuned a marvelous prose. Out of the colloquial American speech, with its simple declarative sentences and its strings of Nordic monosyllables, he got effects of the utmost subtlety. F. M. Ford has found the perfect simile for the impression produced by this writing: 'Hemingway's words strike you, each one, as if they were pebbles fetched fresh from a brook. They live and shine, each in its place. So one of his pages has the effect of a brook-bottom into which you look down through the flowing water. The words form a tessellation, each in order beside the other.'

Looking back, we can see how this style was already being refined and developed at a time—fifty years before—when it was regarded in most literary quarters as hopelessly non-literary and vulgar. Had there not been the nineteenth chapter of *Huckleberry Finn?*—'Two or three nights went by; I reckon I might say they swum by; they slid along so quick and smooth and lovely. Here is the way we put in the time. It was a monstrous big river down there—sometimes a mile and a half wide,' and so forth. These pages, when we happen to meet them in Carl Van Doren's anthology of world literature, stand up in a striking way beside a passage of description from Turgenev; and the pages which Hemingway was later to write about American wood and water are equivalents to the transcriptions by Turgenev—the *Sportsman's Notebook* is much admired by Hemingway—of Russian forests and fields. Each has brought to an immense and wild country the freshness of a new speech and a sensibility not yet conventionalized by literary associations. Yet it *is* the European sensibility which has come to Big Two-Hearted River, where the Indians are now obsolescent; in those solitudes it feels for the first time the cold current, the hot morning sun, sees the pine stumps, smells the sweet fern. And along with the mottled trout, with its 'clear water-over-gravel color,' the boy from the American Middle West fishes up a nice little masterpiece. In the meantime there had been also Ring Lardner, Sherwood Anderson, Gertrude Stein, using this American language for irony, lyric poetry or psychological insight. Hemingway seems to have learned from them all. But he is now able to charge this naïve accent with a new complexity of emotion, a new shade of emotion: a malaise. The wholesale shattering of human beings in which he has taken part has given the boy a touch of panic. . . .

We suffer and we make suffer, and everybody loses out in the long run; but in the meantime we can lose with honor. This code still markedly figures, still supplies a dependable moral backbone, in Hemingway's next book of short stories, *Men Without Women*. Here Hemingway has mastered his method of economy in apparent casualness and relevance in apparent indirection, and has turned his sense of what happens and the way in which it happens into something as hard and clear as a crystal but as disturbing as a great lyric. Yet it is usually some principle of courage, of honor, of pity—that is, some principle of sportsmanship in its largest human sense —upon which the drama hinges. The old bullfighter in *The Undefeated* is defeated in everything except the spirit which will not accept defeat. You get the bull or he gets you: if you die, you can die game; there are certain things you cannot do. The burlesque show manager in *A Pursuit Race* refrains from waking his advance publicity agent when he overtakes him and realizes that the man has just lost a long struggle against whatever anguish it is that has driven him to drink and dope. 'They got a cure for that,' the manager had said to him before he went to sleep; ' "No," William Campbell said, "they haven't got a cure for anything." ' The burned major in *A Simple Enquiry*—that strange picture of the bedrock stoicism compatible with the abasement of war —has the decency not to dismiss the orderly who has rejected his proposition. The brutalized Alpine peasant who has been in the habit of hanging a lantern in the jaws of the stiffened corpse of his wife, stood in the corner of the woodshed till the spring will make it possible to bury her, is ashamed to drink with the sexton after the latter has found out what he has done. And there is a little sketch of Roman soldiers just after the Crucifixion: 'You see me slip the old spear into him?— You'll get into trouble doing that some day.—It was the least I could do for him. I'll tell you he looked pretty good to me in there today.'

This Hemingway of the middle twenties—*The Sun Also Rises* came out in '26—expressed the romantic disillusion and set the favorite pose for the period. It was the moment of gallantry in heartbreak, grim and nonchalant banter, and heroic dissipation. The great watchword was 'Have a drink'; and in the bars of New York and Paris the young people were getting to talk like Hemingway. . . . We are compelled to recognize that, as soon as Hemingway drops the burning-glass of the disciplined and objective art with which he has learned to concentrate in a story the light of the emotions that flood in on him, he straightway becomes befuddled, slops over.

This befuddlement is later to go further [than it did in *Death in the Afternoon*], but in the meantime he publishes another volume of stories—*Winner Take Nothing*—which is almost up to its predecessor. In this collection he deals much more effectively than in *Death in the Afternoon* with that theme of contemporary decadence which is implied in his panegyric of the bullfighter. The first of these stories, *After the Storm,* is another of his variations—and one of the finest—

on the theme of keeping up a code of decency among the hazards and pains of life. A fisherman goes out to plunder a wreck: he dives down to break in through a porthole, but inside he sees a woman with rings on her hands and her hair floating loose in the water, and he thinks about the passengers and crew being suddenly plunged to their deaths (he has almost been killed himself in a drunken fight the night before). He sees the cloud of sea birds screaming around, and he finds that he is unable to break the glass with his wrench and that he loses the anchor grapple with which he next tries to attack it. So he finally goes away and leaves the job to the Greeks, who blow the boat open and clean her out.

But in general the emotions of insecurity here obtrude themselves and dominate the book. Two of the stories deal with the hysteria of soldiers falling off the brink of their nerves under the strain of the experiences of the war, which here no longer presents an idyllic aspect; another deals with a group of patients in a hospital, at the same time crippled and hopeless; still another (a five-page masterpiece) with a waiter, who, both on his own and on his customers' account, is reluctant to go home at night, because he feels the importance of a "clean well-lighted café" as a refuge from the "nothing" that people fear. *God Rest You Merry Gentlemen* repeats the theme of castration of *The Sun Also Rises;* and four of the stories are concerned more or less with male or female homosexuality. In the last story, *Fathers and Sons,* Hemingway reverts to the Michigan forest, as if to take the curse off the rest: young Nick had once enjoyed a nice Indian girl with plump legs and hard little breasts on the needles of the hemlock woods.

These stories and the interludes in *Death in the Afternoon* must have been written during the years that followed the stockmarket crash. They are full of the apprehension of losing control of oneself which is aroused by the getting out of hand of a social-economic system, as well as of the fear of impotence which seems to accompany the loss of social mastery. And there is in such a story as *A Clean Well-Lighted Place* the feeling of having got to the end of everything, of having given up heroic attitudes and wanting only the illusion of peace.

GUIDE QUESTIONS

1. How does "Indian Camp," the story from *In Our Time* which you have read, fit into the pattern of the book as described by Wilson?

2. According to Wilson, what are the sources of Hemingway's style? What are its characteristics? Show how this description of it fits what you have read.
3. What is the "code" that Wilson says "supplies a dependable moral backbone" in Hemingway's work in the middle 1920's? Where is it illustrated in what you have read?
4. Tell why you agree or disagree with Wilson's evaluation of "A Clean, Well-Lighted Place."
5. What is the general impression of Hemingway's short stories produced by Wilson's appraisal of them?

VOCABULARY

Give the derivations and definitions of the following words:

idyllic, vignette, tranquil, dissonance, obsolescent, naïve, malaise, stoicism, disillusion, panegyric, revert, illusion.

Max Eastman

BULL IN THE AFTERNOON

THERE ARE GORGEOUS PAGES in Ernest Hemingway's book about bullfights —big humor and reckless straight talk of what things are, genuinely heavy ferocity against prattle of what they are not. Hemingway is a full-sized man hewing his way with flying strokes of the poet's broad axe which I greatly admire. Nevertheless, there is an unconscionable quantity of bull—to put it as decorously as possible—poured and plastered all over what he writes about bullfights. By bull I mean juvenile romantic gushing and sentimentalizing of simple facts.

For example, it is well known and fairly obvious that bulls do not run and gallop about the pasture; they stand solid "dominating the landscape with their confidence" as Hemingway brilliantly says. Therefore when they have dashed about the ring some minutes, tossed a few horses, repeatedly charged and attempted to gore a man and thrown their heads off because he turned out to be a rag, they soon get winded

From *Art and the Life of Action.* Copyright 1934 by Max Eastman. Reprinted by permission of the author.

and their tongues hang out and they pant. Certain bulls, however, for reasons more or less accidental, go through the ordeal in a small area without much running and therefore get tired in the muscles before they get winded. These bulls do not hang their tongues out and pant. This plain fact, which would be obvious to anybody without smoke in his eyes, is romanticized by Hemingway to mean that some bulls are so "brave" that they will never let their tongues out, but hold their mouths "tight shut to keep the blood in" even after they are stabbed to death and until they drop. This is not juvenile romanticism, it is child's fairy-story writing. And yet Hemingway asks us to believe that what drew him to bullfights was the desire to learn to put down "what really happened in action; what the actual things were which produced the emotion that you experienced."

In pursuit of this rigorous aim he informs us that bullfights are "so well ordered and so strongly disciplined by ritual that a person feeling the whole tragedy cannot separate the minor comic-tragedy of the horse so as to feel it emotionally." And he generalizes: "The *aficionado,* or lover of the bullfight, may be said, broadly, then, to be one who has this sense of the tragedy and ritual of the fight so that the minor aspects are not important except as they relate to the whole." Which is just the kind of sentimental poppycock most habitually dished out by those art nannies and pale-eyed professors of poetry whom Hemingway above all men despises. Hemingway himself makes plain all through his book that the performance itself is not an artistic tragedy as often as one time out of a hundred. When it is, there is about one man out of a thousand in the grandstand who would know what you were talking about if you started in on "the whole tragedy" as opposed to the "minor comic-tragedy of the horse." The *aficionado,* or bullfight fan, is the Spanish equivalent of the American baseball fan. He reacts the same way to the same kind of things. If you could get the authorization to put on a bullfight in the Yankee Stadium, you would see approximately the same crowd there that you do now, and they would behave, after a little instruction from our star reporters and radio announcers, just about the way the Spanish crowd behaves. And they would not be— "broadly"—the kind of people, if there are such people, who can see an infuriated bull charge across a bull ring, ram his horns into the private end of a horse's belly and rip him clear up to the ribs, lifting and tossing his rider bodily in the air and over against the fence with the same motion, and keep their attention so occupied with the "whole tragedy" that they cannot "separate" this enough to "feel it emotion-ally." Bullfights are not wholly bad, but sentimentalizing over them in the name of art-form and ritual is.

GUIDE QUESTIONS

1. Why does Eastman think *Death in the Afternoon* is a bad book?
2. Why does Eastman think this book is "untypical" of Hemingway?
3. On the basis of the selection from the book which you have read, tell why you agree or disagree with Eastman's judgment.

VOCABULARY

Give the derivations and definitions of the following words:
unconscionable, decorously.

W. M. Frohock

HEMINGWAY'S DISCIPLINE

WE [American writers of the 20's and 30's] imitated almost everything Hemingway did: the famous dialogue which sounds so much like tran-scribed talk precisely because it leaves out all the things we say but never hear ourselves say; the deceptive simplicity of description; the understatement, or seeming understatement, of the emotions; the delight in such elementary pastimes as fighting, fishing and sexual intercourse; the fascination with pain and violent death; the fine, irresponsible, free-associative spoofing. But in general we missed the fact that these things, new and shining as they were to us (with the added and somewhat false luster they also had through contrast with the great complexity of Joyce, Lawrence and Proust) were only ancil-lary.

From *The Novel of Violence in America,* by W. M. Frohock. Copyright 1946 by University Press in Dallas, copyright 1950 by W. M. Frohock. Used by permission of Southern Methodist University Press.

It is a mystery now to us how we contrived to miss the existence, in the center of these things which we imitated, of a discipline which Hemingway had worked out for himself and which made the difference between him and his imitators. He loved and admired Flaubert, and he wanted to achieve an accuracy of statement like Flaubert's —the difference between them being that whereas Flaubert had aimed especially at accuracy of statement regarding the exterior world, trying to nail an object with the one word that fitted it, for Hemingway the great necessity was to be accurate in the statement of emotions. Critics have rarely said much about this, although Edmund Wilson, whose chapter on Hemingway in *The Wound and the Bow* I admire, mentions it in passing. Yet Hemingway's varying career can be summed up in reference to this discipline. He adheres to it in the early short stories and the first two novels, and they are admirable. In the nineteen thirties either he runs away from the discipline or it runs away with him; he preaches it, rather raucously, but has such great trouble with the practice that it is hard to admire much that he writes. And then, in a third stage, he returns to it again—not with complete success, because the job that he tackles is bigger than any of the earlier ones; but with enough success so that it is once more possible to regard him as a major novelist.

From the beginning the thing that stirred him most was violence, and the emotions of which he wrote were those stimulated by pain and killing—war, and bull-fighting, and big game-hunting, and fishing to kill rather than for sport, and love conceived as something in itself very akin to violence. Purposely he chose a material which was stronger stuff than that of Frank Norris, and wrote about it as Sherwood Anderson might have written, if Anderson, who was a great story-teller but a lazy artist, had not sloughed the job whenever a specific emotion was involved. The places where Anderson dodged, saying "that's another thing" or "but let that pass," are the ones in which by instinct Hemingway saw his major goal.

The discipline is present and fullgrown in *The Sun Also Rises*, and becomes explicitly visible when the Paris episode is over and the characters have got into Spain. Jake and Bill are now on top of the bus from Pamplona to Burguete:

The bus climbed steadily up the road. The country was barren and rocks stuck up through the clay. There was no grass beside the road. Looking

back we could see the country spread out below. Far back the fields were
squares of green and brown on the hillsides. Making the horizon were the
brown mountains. They were strangely shaped. As we climbed higher the
horizon kept changing. As the bus ground slowly up the road we could see
other mountains coming up in the south. Then the road came over the
crest, flattened out, and went into a forest. It was a forest of cork oaks,
and the sun came through the trees in patches, and there were cattle
grazing back in the trees. We went through the forest and the road came
out and turned along a rise of land, and out ahead of us was a rolling
green plain, with dark mountains beyond it. These were not like the
brown, heat-baked mountains we had left behind. These were wooded and
there were clouds coming down from them. The green plain stretched
off. It was cut by fences and the white of the road showed through the
trunks of a double line of trees that crossed the plain toward the north.
As we came to the edge of the rise we saw the red roofs and white houses
of Burguete ahead strung out on the plain, and away off on the shoulder
of the first dark mountain was the gray metal-sheathed roof of the monastery of Roncesvalles.

This comes extremely close to being a classic example of getting a
maximum of effect from the least expenditure of materials. Twelve of
the eighteen adjectives are color references, and remarkably unspecific;
of the rest four are relatively empty—"barren, heat-baked, rolling,
spread out"—and of the other two, one tells you only that the shape
of the mountains on the horizon was strange. This leaves only the
metal-sheathed roof, and even here again, except in relation to the
others, there is nothing arresting. The adverbs—"slowly, steadily,
higher"—contribute no more. This is also true of the verbs: "was-were"
turn up thirteen times; most of the others are simple statements about
the movement of the bus and changes in the countryside resulting
from it. Only one, "ground," makes much of a sense impression, taken
by itself, and the sense impression is one which we are too used to. Out
of the others I find that I can get images as follows—rocks sticking up
out of the ground, a flattened road, cows grazing, sunlight through
trees, a road stretching away, fields cut by lines of trees. And there is
nothing in all of this, except the mention of cork oaks and the monastery at the very end, to identify the scene as specifically Spanish. You
can find most of the rest of it, even the red roofs, in the American West.

At first glance the sentence structure presents the same simplicity.
But attempt complicating it and you see what Hemingway is doing:
change the three sentences from "Making the horizon . . ." as far as

". . . the horizon kept changing," into "the brown, strangely shaped
mountains that made the horizon kept changing as we climbed higher,"
and you discover that in doing it you have interfered with a procession
which has a characteristic orderliness and pace of its own. Up to the
moment when the bus comes over the crest, Hemingway has been
setting out straight statements each containing one sense impression,
with a full pause after each, as the eye wanders farther from the grass-
less shoulder of the road to the mountainous horizon; but slowly, with
recognizable purposelessness. But presently the impressions become
somewhat more specific. This forest above the crest is identifiable as
cork oak; there are patterns of light and shadow; those are cows you
see through the trees. And as he does this, the sentences become relatively more complicated, there is less pause between the impressions,
and they are coming thick and fast when you at last see the monastery
roof and know that it is Roncesvalles and wake up to being in Spain.

In other words, the procession and pace here are essentially emotional. We now remember how the ride started. The two men are on
the bus with a number of Basque country people, among whom Jake
feels especially at home. We get the feeling that to Hemingway, un-
spoiled people of this sort are always good. (See his treatment of the
African tribe in *Green Hills of Africa* for the type of primitive he likes
particularly.) Wineskins have passed around. Jake and Bill are happy
and full of good fellowship, completely relaxed and certainly mellowed
by the wine. They are watching the view without paying any special
attention to it until the bus nears its destination, where they have the
right to expect a great deal of pleasure which they have come a long
distance to get. Taken this way, the description makes particularly good
sense; and a substitute job, full of color and precise detail and sharp,
striking imagery, would be phoney. Jake and Bill are in no mood for
distinguishing between colors, or for looking closely at particular parts
of the landscape, and their minds are too comfortable for them to be
making any particularly acute associations which might produce metaphor. From this point of view, anything but what Hemingway has
produced would be emotionally faked, unnatural, a sort of impurity.
Certainly there would be nothing hard or clean about it. This constant checking of the writing against the emotion involved is what I
mean by discipline. It should be the central element in any discussion
of Hemingway.

GUIDE QUESTIONS

1. If you have read anything by American writers of the period 1925-1950 that showed the influence of Hemingway, which Frohock says was pervasive, tell who they were and how the influence showed itself.
2. Apply the method of analysis which Frohock uses to any selected passage of what you have read by Hemingway. Is it true as a general rule that Hemingway gets "a maximum of effect from the least expenditure of materials"? Explain.
3. What is the "discipline" which Frohock says is Hemingway's distinguishing mark? Where is this "discipline" evident in what you have read?
4. Compare what Frohock says about Hemingway's style with what Wilson says about it. Are the two critics in essential agreement?

VOCABULARY

Give the derivations and definitions of the following words:

understatement, ancillary, raucously, slough, acute, metaphor.

James Gray

TENDERLY TOLLS THE BELL

IT IS NO LONGER POSSIBLE to make a guessing game of Hemingway's place in American literature. Now at forty-odd he has produced a novel of unquestionable importance. *For Whom the Bell Tolls* is not merely Hemingway's best book; it is one of the finest books written by an American in our time.

The scene is Spain; the theme is war. But to say so gives little idea of the universality of the book's interest or of the high quality of the interpretive gift that it reveals. Hemingway has chosen a moment of

From "Tenderly Tolls the Bell for Three Soldiers," in *On Second Thought*, by James Gray. Copyright 1946 by the University of Minnesota. Used by permission of the University of Minnesota Press and the *St. Paul Pioneer Press and Dispatch*.

tension when the spirit of man becomes quickened by a challenging crisis to an intensification of itself. Aware of the significance of its struggle, our human nature declares its character with dramatic emphasis. The contradictions are still there: the cruelty matched by tenderness, the cowardice by courage, the treachery by loyalty. But each is brilliantly defined in the light of a flaming disaster.

This long novel covers only four days in actual time. It begins with the appearance in the mountains of a young American intellectual who has gone to Spain to fight with the Loyalists. He is on a mission to blow up a bridge, which will be the signal for the attack on Segovia. There behind the Fascist lines he must seek the help of the guerrillas of the mountains . . . peasants, gypsies, women refugees from other battles . . . and among them he finds a microcosm of the Loyalist world in which all its attitudes, its loyalties, its fears are vividly dramatized.

Each figure is strikingly individualized. Pablo, once the dominating leader of the guerrillas, has become their potential enemy because his peasant shrewdness predicts the collapse of the cause and his impulse is to take to safety. But there is still his admiration of personal courage to control his wavering faith. In the end it saves him from treachery. Pilar, woman of the earth, lover of its pleasures, helps to bully her man, Pablo, back into loyalty with her mystical awareness of the unimportance of personal failure. Anselmo, the gentle old man who cannot kill animals, kills men unwaveringly because it is necessary. Maria, pitiful victim of Fascist violence, finds herself healed of all the scars left upon her mind by the act of rape when the enveloping generosity of an honest love is offered by the young American. Robert Jordan himself, warm in blood but cool in head, becomes for the reader the interpreter of the struggle as he feels growing within him the "deep, sound, and selfless pride" of complete identification with these people and with the impulse that makes them fight.

The scope of the book, deliberately compressed in time for purposes of drama, is widened again by several retrospective glimpses of other scenes. Robert Jordan's reflections call into being the strange Russian intellectuals who direct the war from Madrid; Pilar remembers the slaughter of the Fascists when Loyalists take an embattled town; Maria describes the cruel perversity of the revenge when the Fascists have their turn at violence.

Hemingway, evidently determined to be innocent of any special

pleading for the Loyalists, scrupulously reveals in the peasant temperament a curious, contradictory, and fascinating combination of elements.
A droll formality in speech is balanced by a rugged gift for obscenity;
a gift for idealistic self-sacrifice goes hand in hand with an inclination
toward primitive savagery. Yet through the whole character of each
there blows a gusty, invigorating love of life. The relations of such
people toward one another and toward their cause produce that finest
kind of drama in which sensibility, thought, and humor reveal themselves against the background of man's tragic plight.

All the Hemingway themes are restated here: the courage of which
human nature is capable when it has managed to identify itself with
a moral issue; the humor that is ever present in the story of the appe-
tites; the tenderness that declares itself in honest passion. But of none
of these things has he ever written so well as he does now. With a new
maturity of insight and a new subtlety of emphasis, he communicates
his admiration for the simple profundity of faith that moved and
occasionally inspired the Loyalists.

GUIDE QUESTIONS

1. Gray speaks of the "contradictions" in *For Whom the Bell Tolls:* "the
   cruelty matched by tenderness, the cowardice by courage, the treachery
   by loyalty." Show where you have observed these "contradictions" in
   other things that you have read by Hemingway.
2. How much of the love theme to which Gray refers is in "The End of
   Robert Jordan"? How many of the characters he mentions? How much
   of the "peasant temperament"?
3. Gray says that "all the Hemingway themes are restated" in *For Whom
   the Bell Tolls.* How many of the themes mentioned have you observed
   in the selections you have read? Discuss.
4. Compare Gray's estimate of Hemingway with Wilson's. With Eastman's. Which of these estimates is closest to your own?

VOCABULARY

Give the derivations and definitions of the following words:

*guerrilla, microcosm, retrospective, perversity, scrupulously, droll, plight,
profundity.*

Leo Gurko

HEMINGWAY IN SPAIN

AS BEFITS A PERIOD that lifted foreign correspondence into a form of literary art, the war in Spain attracted creative writers from nearly every country, some of whom, like André Malraux, came to fight with the International Brigade, while others went simply as reporters whose personal sympathies were more or less on the side of the besieged government. Among those in this second classification was one of America's most distinguished and influential novelists, a writer who had always been attracted by the smell of death, the stronger and more dramatic the better, to whose imagination the bloodshed in Spain was a high and passionate stimulant. Ernest Hemingway came to Spain on assignment as a reporter; he left with plans for a play, *The Fifth Column,* and a novel, *For Whom the Bell Tolls.* The civil war might have been made to order for him; it embodied most of the salient features of the script Hemingway had been working with for fifteen years: two sides fighting with unbridled ferocity, every known variety of cowardice and heroism, characters who were aficionado and characters who were not, and a backdrop of great events against which the fortunes of selected individuals could be projected in dimensions somewhat larger than life.

It was the act of dying that bound these several elements together, and made them centrally attractive to Hemingway. He had already studied men dying in every kind of situation he could lay hands on: the Swede lying in bed waiting for the gunmen in "The Killers" to get him; Jake, in *The Sun Also Rises,* consigned to a living death by his sexual impotence, drinking himself into an actual one, while Lady Brett follows the same course along the road of sexual dissipation; Catherine Barkley in *A Farewell to Arms* dying in childbirth for no particular reason at all, against the canvas of the retreat at Caporetto in which thousands of Italian soldiers were slaughtered; Manuel, the bullfighter in *The Undefeated,* being killed by the bull; Morgan, the smuggler in *To Have and Have Not,* living a hard jungle existence in the dangerous waters off the Florida Keys, and dying bloodily in the pursuit of his profession. When Hemingway ran out of human death, he fell back on animals, took to big game hunting, and described in *The Green Hills of Africa* the supreme thrill of drawing his rifle sights on a buck and despatching it with an accuracy and released tension beautiful to behold.

In Spain, however, he found men dying in a slightly different context, no longer out of mere resignation or boredom, or for purely occupational reasons or purely accidental ones. They were now dying for a political cause, for an idealism greater than their own egos. It was a new kind of dying for Hemingway, and it drew him; it inflamed his creative ardor, and inspired the longest and most grandiose of his novels. *For Whom the Bell Tolls* has little of the tight, clipped, under-accented style which made Hemingway famous. For him, indeed, it sprawls and rambles, goes off on frequent digressions, and even pries the author out of his traditional impersonality. He begins it in what appears to be a new vein. After all the cynical disillusioned heroes, Robert Jordan is a refreshing type. He has gone to fight with the Loyalists partly because his grandfather had fought for freedom in the Civil War and he wants to do the same in his time. But Hemingway whittles away at his idealism until pretty soon it begins to look a little threadbare. First, there are André Marty and the Communists who, according to Hemingway, seek to organize the Loyalists' cause for their own purposes, and come in for some savage blasting outside the framework of the plot. Then the Loyalists themselves turn out to be pretty brutal, and the one massacre described at length in the novel is a massacre of the fascists by the government forces. There are even stinging comments on the Spaniards as a people. They are characterized as treacherous.

"Of course they turned on you. They turned on you often but they always turned on every one. They turned on themselves, too. If you had three together, two would unite against one, and then the two would start to betray each other. Not always, but often enough for you to take enough cases and start to draw it as a conclusion."

And as callous, too:

"He (Lister, a Loyalist leader) was a true fanatic and he had the complete Spanish lack of respect for life. . . .

"But they (the Spanish) did that on purpose and deliberately. Those who did that are the last flowering of what their education has produced. Those are the flowers of Spanish chivalry. What a people they have been. What sons of bitches from Cortez, Pizarro, Menendez de Avila all down through Enrique Lister to Pablo. And what wonderful people. There is no finer and no worse people in the world. No kinder people and no crueler."

After a few hundred pages of this, Jordan and his idealism are a pretty sickly looking pair. He clings to it to the end, however, and gives up his life to save his comrades, but by that time our feeling is, "What a damn fool! What an admirable damn fool!"

Having battered away at the one redeeming motive that has ever animated his heroes, Hemingway succeeded in preserving the continuity of his nihilism. Death as a form of art has been his abiding theme, and made him one of the inevitable writers of the era of global wars. He encompassed the postwar 20's even more than the 30's, and now, in the atomic age, he seems more than ever destined to be nourished with a fresh supply of variations on his major theme, and to articulate in fiction the destructive forces of the century.

GUIDE QUESTIONS

1. According to Gray, "the Hemingway themes . . . restated" in *For Whom the Bell Tolls* are courage, humor, and tenderness. What, according to Gurko, is the major Hemingway theme of the book?
2. Does Robert Jordan, in Gurko's view, really differ from Hemingway' earlier heroes? Explain.
3. Is your opinion of Robert Jordan, after reading "The End of Robert Jordan," that he is "an admirable damn fool"? Discuss.
4. Compare Gurko's estimate of *For Whom the Bell Tolls* with Gray's.
5. Compare Gurko's general estimate of Hemingway with Wilson's. With Eastman's.

VOCABULARY

Give the derivations and definitions of the following words:

salient, unbridled, context, grandiose, callous, nihilism, articulate.

WRITING AND STUDY AIDS

PATTERN OF ORGANIZATION SUGGESTED BY THE GENERAL TOPIC:

The method of comparison and contrast is frequently used, both incidentally and integrally, in all kinds of writing to make a subject clear and emphatic. Sometimes comparison-contrast is merely a device; sometimes it is a pattern of organization. Here you are asked to consider and use it in the latter way.

The selections from Ernest Hemingway's writings have likenesses and differences of their own. You have compared and contrasted them as you studied them. Hemingway's critics, too, have likenesses and differences— of method, viewpoint, emphasis, and evaluation. In reading them you have made further comparisons and contrasts. A third set of likenesses and differences is also present here. Hemingway makes a certain impression on you, and he makes a certain impression on a critic. The extent to which you agree or disagree with the critic opens the way for this third kind of comparison and contrast.

In this assignment your method of organization should be one which tries to show, as clearly as possible, the resemblances and differences between various parts of Hemingway's work, between what the different critics have said about Hemingway, or between what you think of Hemingway and what one of the critics thinks about him. The comparisons and contrasts you wish to make should be adequately developed in your composition.

ASSIGNMENTS:

Short themes:

1. Nick and Robert Jordan
2. Basic elements of Hemingway's style
3. The old waiter and the young waiter
4. The early and the recent Hemingway
5. A comparison of any other Hemingway story with one of those here
6. "Indian Camp" and "A Clean, Well-Lighted Place"
7. Hemingway and bullfighting
8. Two critics—two views
9. A point of agreement/disagreement with Wilson/Eastman/Frohock/ Gray/Gurko
10. Why Hemingway is a major writer

Long themes:

1. Violent action and blank despair in Hemingway
2. Progressive disillusionment—key to Hemingway?
3. Hemingway as interpreter of life
4. Hemingway and his critics
5. Contradictions in Hemingway's work
6. My theory about Hemingway
7. A comparison of Hemingway and ⸺⸺⸺

READINGS FOR FURTHER STUDY:

The following books by Ernest Hemingway, published by Charles Scribner's Sons, New York:

In Our Time. 1925.
The Sun Also Rises. 1926.
Men Without Women. 1927.
A Farewell to Arms. 1929.
Death in the Afternoon. 1932.
Winner Take Nothing. 1933.
To Have and Have Not. 1937.
The Fifth Column and the First Forty-Nine Stories. 1938.
For Whom the Bell Tolls. 1940.
Across the River and into the Trees. 1950.
The Old Man and the Sea. 1952.

McCaffery, John K. M., ed., *Ernest Hemingway: The Man and His Work.* Cleveland: World Publishing Company, 1950. An anthology of critical essays.

Ross, Lillian. "How Do You Like It Now, Gentlemen?" *The New Yorker,* Vol. 26, No. 12 (May 13, 1950), 36-38, 40-46, 48-52, 55-62.

VII. EXAMPLES AND ILLUSTRATIONS

✎ Some Difficulties of Communication

ONE OF THE GREAT AND CONTINUING PROBLEMS OF THE HUMAN RACE IS THAT of how to say what one means. It is easy enough, perhaps, to express certain ideas to one's own satisfaction, but, if the listener or reader is taken into consideration, difficulties arise. And, the more complex the idea or the more strange or alien one's audience, the greater the difficulty.

Learned and profound men particularly, but all men to some degree, are at times intensely aware of this persistent struggle to make others know what they mean. The problem oppresses them. They think and write about it as one of the great obstacles which nature places in the way of intelligent action.

The readings included in this section are examples of writing of this kind. William James, a great American psychologist and philosopher, thinks of the problem as a species of blindness. Helen Keller, from a more literal blindness, welcomes the discovery of language as her great triumph over isolation and frustration. Hayakawa approaches language somewhat more analytically, and discovers some of the tendencies of language to create new difficulties of its own. In the same vein, Lippmann describes the vulnerability of men to "stereotypes," to the acceptance of words without relation to things.

Emerson was not as learned a student of language as some of the others represented here, but he states a belief which in one form or another many men have accepted. And Joseph Conrad, consummate master of the English language despite the fact that it was not his native tongue, undertakes to describe how he, an artist, could hope to make men understand, not only bare ideas, but ideas in their subtlest intonations and shadings.

Careful reading of these essays will define and focus ideas which have occurred to you already, and by joining to them your own observations on the peculiarities of words, you may find yourself deeply involved in material both interesting and provocative.

William James

ON A CERTAIN BLINDNESS

NOW THE BLINDNESS IN HUMAN BEINGS of which this discourse will treat is the blindness with which we all are afflicted in regard to the feelings of creatures and people different from ourselves.

We are practical beings, each of us with limited functions and duties to perform. Each is bound to feel intensely the importance of his own duties and the significance of the situations that call these forth. But this feeling is in each of us a vital secret, for sympathy with which we vainly look to others. The others are too much absorbed in their own vital secrets to take an interest in ours. Hence the stupidity and injustice of our opinions so far as they deal with the significance of alien lives. Hence the falsity of our judgments so far as they presume to decide in an absolute way on the value of other persons' conditions or ideals.

Take our dogs and ourselves, connected as we are by a tie more intimate than most ties in this world; and yet, outside of that tie of friendly fondness, how insensible, each of us, to all that makes life significant for the other!—we to the rapture of bones under hedges, or smells of trees and lamp-posts, they to the delights of literature and art. As you sit reading the most moving romance you ever fell upon, what sort of a judge is your fox-terrier of your behavior? With all his good will toward you, the nature of your conduct is absolutely excluded from his comprehension. To sit there like a senseless statue, when you might be taking him to walk and throwing sticks for him to catch! What queer disease is this that comes over you every day, of holding things and staring at them like that for hours together, paralyzed of motion and vacant of all conscious life?

The African savages came nearer the truth; but they, too, missed it when they gathered wonderingly round one of our American travellers who, in the interior, had just come into possession of a stray copy of the New York *Commercial Advertiser,* and was devouring it column by column. When he got through, they offered him a high price for the mysterious object; and, being asked for what they wanted it, they said: "For an eye medicine,"—that being the only reason they could conceive of for the protracted bath which he had given his eyes upon its surface.

The spectator's judgment is sure to miss the root of the matter, and to possess no truth. The subject judged knows a part of the world of reality which the judging spectator fails to see, knows more while the spectator knows less; and, wherever there is conflict of opinion and difference of vision, we are bound to believe that the truer side is the side that feels the more, and not the side that feels the less.

GUIDE QUESTIONS

1. What is the particular blindness in human beings with which James is concerned?
2. By what means does he develop the idea outlined in the first two paragraphs?
3. How is the example of the relationship between a man and his dog particularly well adapted to serve James's purpose? The example of the savages and the *Commercial Advertiser?*
4. By what details does James introduce a note of humor into the passage?
5. If you had written the sentence beginning "The African savages came nearer the truth . . . ," how would you have punctuated it? And the sentence following it?
6. If you were condensing this passage and wished to omit one or the other of the two examples, which one would you choose to omit? Why?

VOCABULARY

Give the derivations and definitions of the following words:

treat, feelings, functions, significance, situations, vital, sympathy, vainly, alien, absolute, fondness, rapture, comprehension, mysterious, protracted.

Helen Keller

EVERYTHING HAS A NAME

THE MOST IMPORTANT DAY I REMEMBER in all my life is the one on which my teacher, Anne Mansfield Sullivan, came to me. I am filled with wonder when I consider the immeasurable contrast between the two lives which it connects. It was the third of March, 1887, three months before I was seven years old.

On the afternoon of that eventful day, I stood on the porch, dumb, expectant. I guessed vaguely from my mother's signs and from the hurrying to and fro in the house that something unusual was about to happen, so I went to the door and waited on the steps. The afternoon sun penetrated the mass of honeysuckle that covered the porch, and fell on my upturned face. My fingers lingered almost unconsciously on the familiar leaves and blossoms which had just come forth to greet the sweet southern spring. I did not know what the future held of marvel or surprise for me. Anger and bitterness had preyed upon me continually for weeks and a deep languor had succeeded this passionate struggle.

The morning after my teacher came she led me into her room and gave me a doll. The little blind children at the Perkins Institution had sent it and Laura Bridgman had dressed it; but I did not know this until afterward. When I had played with it a little while, Miss Sullivan slowly spelled into my hand the word "d-o-l-l." I was at once interested in this finger play and tried to imitate it. When I finally succeeded in making the letters correctly I was flushed with childish pleasure and pride. Running downstairs to my mother I held up my hands and made the letters for doll. I did not know that I was spelling a word or even that words existed; I was simply making my fingers go in monkey-like imitation. In the days that followed I learned to spell in this uncomprehending way a great many words, among them pin, hat, cup and a few verbs like sit, stand and walk. But my teacher had been with me several weeks before I understood that everything has a name.

One day, while I was playing with my new doll, Miss Sullivan put my big rag doll into my lap also, spelled "d-o-l-l" and tried to make me understand that "d-o-l-l" applied to both. Earlier in the day we had had a tussle over the words "m-u-g" and "w-a-t-e-r." Miss Sullivan had tried to impress it upon me that "m-u-g" is *mug* and "w-a-t-e-r" is *water,* but I persisted in confounding the two. In despair she had dropped the subject for the time only to renew it at the first opportunity. I became impatient at her repeated attempts and, seizing the new doll, I dashed it upon the floor. . . .

We walked down the path to the well-house, attracted by the fragrance of the honeysuckle with which it was covered. Some one was drawing water and my teacher placed my hand under the spout. As the cool stream gushed over one hand she spelled into the other the word water, first slowly, then rapidly. I stood still, my whole attention fixed upon the motions of her fingers. Suddenly I felt a misty consciousness as of something forgotten—a thrill of returning thought; and somehow the mystery of language was revealed to me. I knew then that "w-a-t-e-r" meant the wonderful cool something that was flowing over my hand. That living word awakened my soul, gave it light, hope, joy, set it free! There were barriers still, it is true, but barriers that could in time be swept away.

I left the well-house eager to learn. Everything had a name, and each name gave birth to a new thought. As we returned to the house every object which I touched seemed to quiver with life. That was because I saw everything with the strange, new sight that had come to me. On entering the door I remembered the doll I had broken. I felt my way to the hearth and picked up the pieces. I tried vainly to put them together. Then my eyes filled with tears; for I realized what I had done, and for the first time I felt repentance and sorrow.

I learned a great many new words that day. I do not remember what they all were; but I do know that mother, father, sister, teacher were among them—words that were to make the world blossom for me, "like Aaron's rod, with flowers." It would have been difficult to find a happier child than I was as I lay in my crib at the close of that eventful day and lived over the joys it had brought me, and for the first time longed for a new day to come. . . .

I had now the key to all language, and I was eager to learn to use it. Children who hear acquire language without any particular effort; the words that fall from others' lips they catch on the wing, as it were, delightedly, while the little deaf child must trap them by a slow and often painful process. But whatever the process, the result is wonderful. Gradually from naming an object we advance step by step until we have traversed the vast distance between our first stammered syllable and the sweep of thought in a line of Shakespeare.

At first, when my teacher told me about a new thing I asked very few questions. My ideas were vague, and my vocabulary was inadequate; but as my knowledge of things grew, and I learned more and more words, my field of inquiry broadened, and I would return again and again to the same subject, eager for further information. Sometimes a new word revived an image that some earlier experience had engraved on my brain.

I remember the morning that I first asked the meaning of the word, "love." This was before I knew many words. I had found a few early violets in the garden and brought them to my teacher. She tried to kiss me; but at that time I did not like to have any one kiss me except my mother. Miss Sullivan put her arm gently around me and spelled into my hand, "I love Helen."

"What is love?" I asked.

She drew me closer to her and said, "It is here," pointing to my heart, whose beats I was conscious of for the first time. Her words puzzled me very much because I did not then understand anything unless I touched it.

I smelt the violets in her hands and asked, half in words, half in signs, a question which meant, "Is love the sweetness of flowers?"

"No," said my teacher.

Again I thought. The warm sun was shining on us.

"Is this not love?" I asked, pointing in the direction from which the heat came, "Is this not love?"

It seemed to me that there could be nothing more beautiful than the sun, whose warmth makes all things grow. But Miss Sullivan shook her head, and I was greatly puzzled and disappointed. I thought it strange that my teacher could not show me love.

A day or two afterward I was stringing beads of different sizes in symmetrical groups—two large beads, three small ones, and so on. I had made many mistakes, and Miss Sullivan had pointed them out again and again with gentle patience. Finally I noticed a very obvious error in the sequence and for an instant I concentrated my attention on the lesson and tried to think how I should have arranged the beads. Miss Sullivan touched my forehead and spelled with decided emphasis, "Think."

In a flash I knew that the word was the name of the process that was going on in my head. This was my first conscious perception of an abstract idea.

GUIDE QUESTIONS

1. What is the great discovery which Helen Keller made when she was a child and which she describes in this passage?
2. Why was the word "love" difficult for her?
3. What was the occasion of her "first conscious perception of an abstract idea"?
4. How might one translate Miss Keller's narrative into a point-by-point exposition on the process of learning language, using her particular experiences as illustrative material? Would the result of this translation be necessarily inferior to the form that Miss Keller has used?

VOCABULARY

Give the derivations and definitions of the following words:

languor, uncomprehending, vainly, traversed, vague, inadequate, symmetrical, sequence, abstract.

S. I. Hayakawa

MAPS AND TERRITORIES

THERE IS A SENSE IN WHICH WE ALL LIVE in two worlds. First, we live in the world of happenings about us which we know at first hand. But this is an extremely small world, consisting only of that continuum of the things that we have actually seen, felt, or heard—the flow of events constantly passing before our senses. So far as this world of personal experience is concerned, Africa, South America, Asia, Washington, New York, or Los Angeles do not exist if we have never been to these places. Chiang Kai-shek is only a name if we have never seen him. When we ask ourselves how much we know at first hand, we discover that we know very little indeed.

Most of our knowledge, acquired from parents, friends, schools, newspapers, books, conversation, speeches, and radio, is received *verbally*. All our knowledge of history, for example, comes to us only in words. The only proof we have that the Battle of Waterloo ever took place is that we have had reports to that effect. These reports are not given us by people who saw it happen, but are based on other reports: reports of reports of reports, which go back ultimately to the first-hand reports given by people who did see it happening. It is through reports, then, and through reports of reports, that we receive most knowledge: about government, about what is happening in China, about what picture is showing at the downtown theater—in fact, about anything which we do not know through direct experience.

Let us call this world that comes to us through words the *verbal world,* as opposed to the world we know or are capable of knowing through our own experience, which we shall call the *extensional world.* . . . The human being, like any other creature, begins to make his acquaintance with the extensional world from infancy. Unlike other creatures, however, he begins to receive, as soon as he can learn to understand, reports, reports of reports, reports of reports of reports. In addition he receives inferences made from reports, inferences made from other inferences, and so on. By the time a child is a few years old, has gone to school and to Sunday school, and has made a few friends, he has accumulated a considerable amount of second- and third-hand information about morals, geography, history, nature, people, games—all of which information together constitutes his verbal world.

Now this verbal world ought to stand in relation to the extensional world as a *map* does to the *territory* it is supposed to represent. If a child grows to adulthood with a verbal world in his head which corresponds fairly closely to the extensional world that he finds around him in his widening experience, he is in relatively small danger of being shocked or hurt by what he finds, because his verbal world has told him what, more or less, to expect. He is prepared for life. If, however, he grows up with a false map in his head—that is, with a head crammed with false knowledge and superstition—he will constantly be running into trouble, wasting his efforts, and acting like a fool. He will not be adjusted to the world as it is; he may, if the lack of adjustment is serious, end up in a mental hospital.

Some of the follies we commit because of false maps in our heads are so commonplace that we do not even think of them as remarkable. There are those who protect themselves from accidents by carrying a rabbit's foot in the pocket. Some refuse to sleep on the thirteenth floor of hotels—this is so common that most big hotels, even in the capitals of our scientific culture, skip "13" in numbering their floors. Some plan their lives on the basis of astrological predictions. Some play fifty-to-one shots on the basis of dream books. Some hope to make their teeth whiter by changing their brand of tooth paste. All such people are living in verbal worlds that bear little, if any, resemblance to the extensional world.

Now, no matter how beautiful a map may be, it is useless to a traveler unless it accurately shows the relationship of places to each other, the structure of the territory. If we draw, for example, a big dent in the outline of a lake for, let us say, artistic reasons, the map is worthless. But if we are just drawing maps for fun without paying any attention to the structure of the region, there is nothing in the world to prevent us from putting in all the extra curlicues and twists we want in the lakes, rivers, and roads. No harm will be done *unless someone tries to plan a trip by such a map.*

Similarly, by means of imaginary or false reports, or by false inferences from good reports, or by mere rhetorical exercises, we can manufacture at will, with language, "maps" which have no reference to the extensional world. Here again no harm will be done unless someone makes the mistake of regarding such "maps" as representing real territories.

We all inherit a great deal of useless knowledge, and a great deal of misinformation and error (maps that were formerly thought to be accurate), so that there is always a portion of what we have been told that must be discarded. But the cultural heritage of our civilization that is transmitted to us—our socially pooled knowledge, both scientific and humane—has been valued principally because we have believed that it gives us accurate maps of experience. The analogy of verbal worlds to maps is an important one. . . . It should be noticed that there are two ways of getting false maps of the world into our heads: first, by having them given to us; second, by making them up for ourselves by misreading the true maps given to us.

GUIDE QUESTIONS

1. How does Hayakawa define the "verbal world"? The "extensional world"?
2. List five items which might be added to Hayakawa's examples, in his second paragraph, of things belonging exclusively to the verbal world.
3. List five items which belong to the extensional world of every human being. Every American citizen. Every American citizen less than sixteen years old.
4. Try to supply another figure of speech in place of Hayakawa's figure of "maps and territories." Test it by using it consistently from the fourth paragraph to the end of the passage. For example, try the terms "reports and events."
5. What are the reasons for the existence of "false maps"?
6. How does Hayakawa's explanation of the verbal and extensional worlds modify your understanding of Helen Keller's discovery?

VOCABULARY

Give the derivations and definitions of the following words:

extensional, adjustment, astrological, predictions, curlicues, inferences, heritage, transmitted, analogy.

Walter Lippmann

STEREOTYPES

EACH OF US LIVES AND WORKS on a small part of the earth's surface, moves in a small circle, and of these acquaintances knows only a few intimately. Of any public event that has wide effects we see at best only a phase and an aspect. This is as true of the eminent insiders who draft treaties, make laws, and issue orders, as it is of those who have treaties framed for them, laws promulgated to them, orders given at them. Inevitably our opinions cover a bigger space, a longer reach of time, a greater number of things, than we can directly observe. They have, therefore, to be pieced together out of what others have reported and what we can imagine.

Yet even the eyewitness does not bring back a naïve picture of the scene.[1] For experience seems to show that he himself brings something to the scene which later he takes away from it, that oftener than not what he imagines to be the account of an event is really a transfiguration of it. Few facts in consciousness seem to be merely given. Most facts in consciousness seem to be partly made. A report is the joint product of the knower and known, in which the rôle of the observer is always selective and usually creative. The facts we see depend on where we are placed, and the habits of our eyes.

An unfamiliar scene is like the baby's world, "one great, blooming, buzzing confusion."[2] This is the way, says Mr. John Dewey,[3] that any new thing strikes an adult, so far as the thing is really new and strange. "Foreign languages that we do not understand always seem jibberings, babblings, in which it is impossible to fix a definite, clearcut, individualized group of sounds. The countryman in the crowded street, the landlubber at sea, the ignoramus in sport at a contest between experts in a complicated game, are further instances. Put an inexperienced man in a factory, and at first the work seems to him a meaningless medley. All strangers of another race proverbially look alike to the visiting stranger. Only gross differences of size or color are perceived by an outsider in a flock of sheep, each of which is perfectly individualized to the shepherd. A diffusive blur and an indiscriminately shifting suction characterize what we do not understand. The problem of the acquisition of meaning by things, or (stated in another way) of forming habits of simple apprehension, is thus the problem of introducing (1) *definiteness* and *distinction* and (2) *consistency* or *stability* of meaning into what is otherwise vague and wavering."

But the kind of definiteness and consistency introduced depends

---

[1] *E.g., cf.,* Edmond Locard, *L'Enquête Criminelle et les Méthodes Scientifiques* . . .
[2] William James, *Principles of Psychology*, Vol. I, p. 488.
[3] *How We Think*, p. 121.

upon who introduces them. In a later passage[4] Dewey gives an example of how differently an experienced layman and a chemist might define the word metal. "Smoothness, hardness, glossiness, and brilliancy, heavy weight for its size . . . the serviceable properties of capacity for being hammered and pulled without breaking, of being softened by heat and hardened by cold, or retaining the shape and form given, or resistance to pressure and decay," would probably be included in the layman's definition. But the chemist would likely as not ignore these esthetic and utilitarian qualities, and define a metal as "any chemical element that enters into combination with oxygen so as to form a base."

For the most part we do not first see, and then define, we define first and then see. In the great blooming, buzzing confusion of the outer world we pick out what our culture has already defined for us, and we tend to perceive that which we have picked out in the form stereotyped for us by our culture. . . .

GUIDE QUESTIONS

1. What is a stereotype? Does it differ in any important respects from the "maps" of Hayakawa's figure of speech? If so, how does it differ?
2. What is meant by the phrase "habits of simple apprehension"?
3. How would Lippmann's essay have been affected if he had chosen to use his own examples, invented for the purpose, instead of the examples quoted from John Dewey?
4. To what extent is this passage from Lippmann's essay a pertinent commentary on James's observations concerning a "certain blindness in human beings"? Would the analogy of the man and his dog fit well in the context which Lippmann provides?

VOCABULARY

Give the derivations and definitions of the following words:

acquaintance, eminent, promulgated, inevitably, naïve, transfiguration, individualized, ignoramus, medley, proverbially, gross, diffusive, indiscriminately, acquisition, consistency, stability, esthetic, utilitarian, base, culture.

[4] *Ibid.*, p. 133.

Ralph Waldo Emerson

LANGUAGE

LANGUAGE IS A THIRD USE which Nature subserves to man. Nature is the vehicle of thought, and in a simple, double, and threefold degree.

1. Words are signs of natural facts.
2. Particular natural facts are symbols of particular spiritual facts.
3. Nature is the symbol of spirit.

1. Words are signs of natural facts. The use of natural history is to give us aid in supernatural history; the use of the outer creation, to give us language for the beings and changes of the inward creation. Every word which is used to express a moral or intellectual fact, if traced to its root, is found to be borrowed from some material appearance. *Right* means *straight; wrong* means *twisted. Spirit* primarily means *wind; transgression,* the crossing of a *line; supercilious,* the *raising of the eyebrow.* We say the *heart* to express emotion, the *head* to denote thought; and *thought* and *emotion* are words borrowed from sensible things, and now appropriated to spiritual nature. Most of the process by which this transformation is made, is hidden from us in the remote time when language was framed; but the same tendency may be daily observed in children. Children and savages use only nouns or names of things, which they convert into verbs, and apply to analogous mental acts.

2. But this origin of all words that convey a spiritual import,—so conspicuous a fact in the history of language,—is our least debt to nature. It is not words only that are emblematic; it is things which are emblematic. Every natural fact is a symbol of some spiritual fact. Every appearance in nature corresponds to some state of the mind, and that state of the mind can only be described by presenting that natural appearance as its picture. An enraged man is a lion, a cunning man is a fox, a firm man is a rock, a learned man is a torch. A lamb is innocence; a snake is subtle spite; flowers express to us the delicate affections. Light and darkness are our familiar expression for

From *Nature.*

knowledge and ignorance; and heat for love. Visible distance behind and before us, is respectively our image of memory and hope.

Who looks upon a river in a meditative hour and is not reminded of the flux of all things? Throw a stone into the stream, and the circles that propagate themselves are the beautiful type of all influence. Man is conscious of a universal soul within or behind his individual life, wherein, as in a firmament, the natures of Justice, Truth, Love, Freedom, arise and shine. This universal soul he calls Reason: it is not mine, or thine, or his, but we are its; we are its property and men. And the blue sky in which the private earth is buried, the sky with its eternal calm, and full of everlasting orbs, is the type of Reason. That which intellectually considered we call Reason, considered in relation to nature, we call Spirit. Spirit is the Creator. Spirit hath life in itself. And man in all ages and countries embodies it in his language as the FATHER.

It is easily seen that there is nothing lucky or capricious in these analogies, but that they are constant, and pervade nature. These are not the dreams of a few poets, here and there, but man is an analogist, and studies relations in all objects. He is placed in the centre of beings, and a ray of relation passes from every other being to him. And neither can man be understood without these objects, nor these objects without man. All the facts in natural history taken by themselves, have no value, but are barren, like a single sex. But marry it to human history, and it is full of life. Whole floras, all Linnæus' and Buffon's volumes, are dry catalogues of facts; but the most trivial of these facts, the habit of a plant, the organs, or work, or noise of an insect, applied to the illustration of a fact in intellectual philosophy, or in any way associated to human nature, affects us in the most lively and agreeable manner. The seed of a plant,—to what affecting analogies in the nature of man is that little fruit made use of, in all discourse, up to the voice of Paul, who calls the human corpse a seed,—"It is sown a natural body; it is raised a spiritual body." The motion of the earth round its axis and round the sun, makes the day and the year. These are certain amounts of brute light and heat. But is there no intent of an analogy between man's life and the seasons? And do the seasons gain no grandeur or pathos from that analogy? The instincts of the ant are very unimportant considered as the ant's; but the moment a ray of relation is seen to extend from it to man, and the little drudge is seen to be a monitor, a little body with a mighty heart, then all its habits, even that said to be recently observed, that it never sleeps, become sublime.

Because of this radical correspondence between visible things and human thoughts, savages, who have only what is necessary, converse in figures. As we go back in history, language becomes more picturesque, until its infancy, when it is all poetry; or all spiritual facts are represented by natural symbols. The same symbols are found to make the original elements of all languages. It has moreover been observed, that the idioms of all languages approach each other in passages of the greatest eloquence and power. And as this is the first language, so is it the last. This immediate dependence of language upon nature, this conversion of an outward phenomenon into a type of somewhat in human life, never loses its power to affect us. It is this which gives that piquancy to the conversation of a strong-natured farmer or backwoodsman, which all men relish.

A man's power to connect his thought with its proper symbol, and so to utter it, depends on the simplicity of his character, that is, upon his love of truth and his desire to communicate it without loss. The corruption of man is followed by the corruption of language. When simplicity of character and the sovereignty of ideas is broken up by the prevalence of secondary desires,—the desire of riches, of pleasure, of power, and of praise,—and duplicity and falsehood take the place of simplicity and truth, the power over nature as an interpreter of the will is in a degree lost; new imagery ceases to be created, and old words are perverted to stand for things which are not; a paper currency is employed, when there is no bullion in the vaults. In due time the fraud is manifest, and words lose all power to stimulate the understanding or the affections. Hundreds of writers may be found in every long-civilized nation who for a short time believe and make others believe that they see and utter truths, who do not of themselves clothe one thought in its natural garment, but who feed unconsciously on the language created by the primary writers of the country, those, namely, who hold primarily on nature.

But wise men pierce this rotten diction and fasten words again to visible things; so that picturesque language is at once a commanding certificate that he who employs it is a man in alliance with truth and God. The moment our discourse rises above the ground line of familiar facts and is inflamed with passion or exalted by thought, it clothes itself in images. A man conversing in earnest, if he watch his intellectual processes, will find that a material image more or less luminous arises in his mind, contemporaneous with every thought, which furnishes the vestment of the thought. Hence, good writing and brilliant discourse are perpetual allegories. This imagery is spontaneous. It is the blending of experience with the present action of the mind. It is proper creation. It is the working of the Original Cause through the instruments he has already made.

These facts may suggest the advantage which the country-life possesses, for a powerful mind, over the artificial and curtailed life of cities. We know more from nature than we can at will communicate. Its light flows into the mind evermore, and we forget its presence. The poet, the orator, bred in the woods, whose senses have been nourished by their fair and appeasing changes, year after year, without design and without heed,—shall not lose their lesson altogether, in the roar of cities or the broil of politics. Long hereafter, amidst agitation and terror in national councils,—in the hour of revolution,—these solemn images shall reappear in their morning lustre, as fit symbols and words of the thoughts which the passing events shall awaken. At the call of a noble sentiment, again the woods wave, the pines murmur, the river rolls and shines, and the cattle low upon the mountains, as he saw and heard them in his infancy. And with these forms, the spells of persuasion, the keys of power are put into his hands.

3. We are thus assisted by natural objects in the expression of particular meanings. But how great a language to convey such peppercorn informations! Did it need such noble races of creatures, this profusion of forms, this host of orbs in heaven, to furnish man with the dictionary and grammar of his municipal speech? Whilst we use this grand cipher to expedite the affairs of our pot and kettle, we feel that we have not yet put it to its use, neither are able. We are like travellers using the cinders of a volcano to roast their eggs. Whilst we see that it always stands ready to clothe what we would say, we cannot avoid the question whether the characters are not significant of themselves. Have mountains, and waves, and skies, no significance but what we consciously give them when we employ them as emblems of our thoughts? The world is emblematic. Parts of speech are metaphors, because the whole of nature is a metaphor of the human mind. The laws of moral nature answer to those of matter as face to face in a glass. "The visible world and the relation of its parts, is the dial plate of the invisible." The axioms of physics translate the laws of ethics.

Thus, "the whole is greater than its part;" "reaction is equal to action;" "the smallest weight may be made to lift the greatest, the difference of weight being compensated by time;" and many the like propositions, which have an ethical as well as physical sense. These propositions have a much more extensive and universal sense when applied to human life, than when confined to technical use.

In like manner, the memorable words of history and the proverbs of nations consist usually of a natural fact, selected as a picture or parable of a moral truth. Thus; A rolling stone gathers no moss; A bird in the hand is worth two in the bush; A cripple in the right way will beat a racer in the wrong; Make hay while the sun shines; 'Tis hard to carry a full cup even; Vinegar is the son of wine; The last ounce broke the camel's back; Long-lived trees make roots first;—and the like. In their primary sense these are trivial facts, but we repeat them for the value of their analogical import. What is true of proverbs, is true of all fables, parables, and allegories.

This relation between the mind and matter is not fancied by some poet, but stands in the will of God, and so is free to be known by all men. It appears to men, or it does not appear. When in fortunate hours we ponder this miracle, the wise man doubts if at all other times he is not blind and deaf;

> "Can such things be,
> And overcome us like a summer's cloud,
> Without our special wonder?"

for the universe becomes transparent, and the light of higher laws than its own shines through it. It is the standing problem which has exercised the wonder and the study of every fine genius since the world began; from the era of the Egyptians and the Brahmins to that of Pythagoras, of Plato, of Bacon, of Leibnitz, of Swedenborg. There sits the Sphinx at the roadside, and from age to age, as each prophet comes by, he tries his fortune at reading her riddle. There seems to be a necessity in spirit to manifest itself in material forms; and day and night, river and storm, beast and bird, acid and alkali, preëxist in necessary Ideas in the mind of God, and are what they are by virtue of preceding affections in the world of spirit. A Fact is the end or last issue of spirit. The visible creation is the terminus or the circumference of the invisible world. "Material objects," said a French philosopher, "are necessarily kinds of *scoriæ* of the substantial thoughts of the Creator, which must always preserve an exact relation to their first origin; in other words, visible nature must have a spiritual and moral side."

This doctrine is abstruse, and though the images of "garment," "scoriæ," "mirror," etc., may stimulate the fancy, we must summon the aid of subtler and more vital expositors to make it plain. "Every scripture is to be interpreted by the same spirit which gave it forth," —is the fundamental law of criticism. A life in harmony with Nature, the love of truth and of virtue, will purge the eyes to understand her text. By degrees we may come to know the primitive sense of the permanent objects of nature, so that the world shall be to us an open book, and every form significant of its hidden life and final cause.

A new interest surprises us, whilst, under the view now suggested, we contemplate the fearful extent and multitude of objects; since "every object rightly seen, unlocks a new faculty of the soul." That which was unconscious truth, becomes, when interpreted and defined in an object, a part of the domain of knowledge,—a new weapon in the magazine of power.

GUIDE QUESTIONS

1. What question or questions does Emerson appear to be discussing in this essay?
2. Does Emerson fully realize the difficulties pointed out by Hayakawa and Lippmann?
3. What is Emerson's theory of the function of nature in language?
4. In what sense does Emerson use the word *spirit?* The word *emotion?*
5. In the third section of his essay Emerson lists "axioms of physics" which seem to him to suggest corresponding "laws of ethics." How many "axioms of physics" can you cite which seem to you barren of all ethical overtones?
6. What general propositions other than the three which Emerson lists at the outset seem to you to be implicit in his essay?
7. In what ways does Emerson contradict James? Hayakawa? Lippmann? In what ways does he agree with them?

VOCABULARY

Give the derivations and definitions of the following words:

subserves, sign, symbol, right, wrong, spirit, transgression, supercilious, analogous, import, conspicuous, emblematic, subtle, firmament, orbs, capricious, axis, pathos, monitor, radical, phenomenon, piquancy, duplicity, bullion, exalted, spontaneous, curtailed, agitation, cipher, expedite, parable, allegory, terminus, abstruse, scoriae.

Joseph Conrad

Preface to NIGGER OF THE NARCISSUS

A WORK THAT ASPIRES, HOWEVER HUMBLY, to the condition of art should carry its justification in every line. And art itself may be defined as a single-minded attempt to render the highest kind of justice to the visible universe, by bringing to light the truth, manifold and one, underlying its every aspect. It is an attempt to find in its forms, in its colors, in its light, in its shadows, in the aspects of matter and in the facts of life what of each is fundamental, what is enduring and essential—their one illuminating and convincing quality—the very truth of their existence. The artist, then, like the thinker or the scientist, seeks the truth and makes his appeal. Impressed by the aspect of the world the thinker plunges into ideas, the scientist into facts—whence, presently, emerging they make their appeal to those qualities of our being that fit us best for the hazardous enterprise of living. They speak authoritatively to our common-sense, to our intelligence, to our desire of peace or to our desire of unrest; not seldom to our prejudices, sometimes to our fears, often to our egoism—but always to our credulity. And their words are heard with reverence, for their concern is with weighty matters: with the cultivation of our minds and the proper care of our bodies, with the attainment of our ambitions, with the perfection of the means and the glorification of our precious aims.

It is otherwise with the artist.

From *Nigger of the Narcissus* by Joseph Conrad. Reprinted by permission of J. M. Dent and Sons, Ltd., publishers.

Confronted by the same enigmatical spectacle the artist descends within himself, and in that lonely region of stress and strife, if he be deserving and fortunate, he finds the terms of his appeal. His appeal is made to our less obvious capacities: to that part of our nature which, because of the warlike conditions of existence, is necessarily kept out of sight within the more resisting and hard qualities—like the vulnerable body within a steel armor. His appeal is less loud, more profound, less distinct, more stirring—and sooner forgotten. Yet its effect endures forever. The changing wisdom of successive generations discards ideas, questions facts, demolishes theories. But the artist appeals to that part of our being which is not dependent on wisdom; to that in us which is a gift and not an acquisition—and, therefore, more permanently enduring. He speaks to our capacity for delight and wonder, to the sense of mystery surrounding our lives; to our sense of pity, and beauty, and pain; to the latent feeling of fellowship with all creation—and to the subtle but invincible conviction of solidarity that knits together the loneliness of innumerable hearts, to the solidarity in dreams, in joy, in sorrow, in aspirations, in illusions, in hope, in fear, which binds men to each other, which binds together all humanity—the dead to the living and the living to the unborn.

It is only some such train of thought, or rather of feeling, that can in a measure explain the aim of the attempt, made in the tale which follows, to present an unrestful episode in the obscure lives of a few individuals out of all the disregarded multitude of the bewildered, the simple and the voiceless. For, if any part of truth dwells in the belief confessed above, it becomes evident that there is not a place of splendor or a dark corner of the earth that does not deserve, if only a passing glance of wonder and pity. The motive then, may be held to justify the matter of the work; but this preface, which is simply an avowal of endeavor, cannot end here—for the avowal is not yet complete.

Fiction—if it at all aspires to be art—appeals to temperament. And in truth it must be, like painting, like music, like all art, the appeal of one temperament to all the other innumerable temperaments whose subtle and resistless power endows passing events with their true meaning, and creates the moral, the emotional atmosphere of the place and time. Such an appeal to be effective must be an impression conveyed through the senses; and, in fact, it cannot be made in any other way, because temperament, whether individual or collective, is not amenable to persuasion. All art, therefore, appeals primarily to the senses, and the artistic aim when expressing itself in written words must also make its appeal through the senses, if its high desire is to reach the secret spring of responsive emotions. It must strenuously aspire to the plasticity of sculpture, to the color of painting, and to the magic suggestiveness of music—which is the art of arts. And it is only through complete, unswerving devotion to the perfect blending of form and substance; it is only through an unremitting never-discouraged care for the shape and ring of sentences that an approach can be made to plasticity, to color, and that the light of magic suggestiveness may be brought to play for an evanescent instant over the commonplace surface of words: of the old, old words, worn thin, defaced by ages of careless usage.

The sincere endeavor to accomplish that creative task, to go as far on that road as his strength will carry him, to go undeterred by faltering, weariness or reproach, is the only valid justification for the worker in prose. And if his conscience is clear, his answer to those who in the fullness of a wisdom which looks for immediate profit, demand specifically to be edified, consoled, amused; who demand to be promptly improved, or encouraged, or frightened, or shocked, or charmed, must run thus:—My task which I am trying to achieve is, by the power of the written word to make you hear, to make you feel —it is, before all, to make you *see*. That—and no more, and it is everything. If I succeed, you shall find there according to your deserts: encouragement, consolation, fear, charm—all you demand—and, perhaps, also that glimpse of truth for which you have forgotten to ask.

To snatch in a moment of courage, from the remorseless rush of time, a passing phase of life, is only the beginning of the task. The task approached in tenderness and faith is to hold up unquestioningly, without choice and without fear, the rescued fragment before all eyes in the light of a sincere mood. It is to show its vibration, its color, its form; and through its movement, its form, and its color, reveal the substance of its truth—disclose its inspiring secret: the stress and passion within the core of each convincing moment. In a single-minded attempt of that kind, if one be deserving and fortunate, one may perchance attain to such clearness of sincerity that at last the presented vision of regret or pity, of terror or birth, shall awaken in the hearts of the beholders that feeling of unavoidable solidarity; of the solidarity in mysterious origin, in toil, in joy, in hope, in uncertain fate, which binds men to each other and all mankind to the visible world.

It is evident that he who, rightly or wrongly, holds by the convictions expressed above cannot be faithful to any one of the temporary formulas of his craft. The enduring part of them—the truth which each only imperfectly veils—should abide with him as the most precious of his possessions, but they all: Realism, Romanticism, Naturalism, even the unofficial sentimentalism (which like the poor, is exceedingly difficult to get rid of), all these gods must, after a short period of fellowship, abandon him—even on the very threshold of the temple—to the stammerings of his conscience and to the outspoken consciousness of the difficulties of his work. In that uneasy solitude the supreme cry of Art for Art itself, loses the exciting ring of its apparent immorality. It sounds far off. It has ceased to be a cry, and is heard only as a whisper, often incomprehensible, but at times and faintly encouraging.

Sometimes, stretched at ease in the shade of a roadside tree, we watch the motions of a laborer in a distant field, and after a time, begin to wonder languidly as to what the fellow may be at. We watch the movements of his body, the waving of his arms, we see him bend down, stand up, hesitate, begin again. It may add to the charm of an idle hour to be told the purpose of his exertions. If we know he is trying to lift a stone, to dig a ditch, to uproot a stump, we look with a more real interest at his efforts; we are disposed to condone the jar of his agitation upon the restfulness of the landscape; and even, if in a brotherly frame of mind, we may bring ourselves to forgive his failure. We understood his object, and, after all, the fellow has tried, and perhaps he had not the strength—and perhaps he had not the knowledge. We forgive, go on our way—and forget.

And so it is with the workman of art. Art is long and life is short, and success is very far off. And thus, doubtful of strength to travel so far, we talk a little about the aim—the aim of art, which, like life itself, is inspiring, difficult—obscured by mists. It is not in the clear logic of a triumphant conclusion; it is not in the unveiling of one of those heartless secrets which are called the Laws of Nature. It is not less great, but only more difficult.

To arrest, for the space of a breath, the hands busy about the work of the earth, and compel men entranced by the sight of distant goals to glance for a moment at the surrounding vision of form and color, of sunshine and shadows; to make them pause for a look, for a sigh, for a smile—such is the aim, difficult and evanescent, and reserved only for a few to achieve. But sometimes, by the deserving and the fortunate, even that task is accomplished. And when it is accomplished— behold!—all the truth of life is there: a moment of vision, a sigh, a smile—and the return to an eternal rest.

GUIDE QUESTIONS

1. In his first three paragraphs, Conrad distinguishes the artist from the "thinker" and the "scientist." To what particular points of difference does he call attention?
2. What do you think Conrad means by the phrase "terms of appeal"?
3. What do you think he means by: "The motive then, may be held to justify the matter of the work . . ."?
4. What is the "unavoidable solidarity" of which Conrad speaks? And why is it "mysterious"?
5. What function is served by the paragraph in which the author describes the experience of watching the motions of a laborer in a distant field?
6. What kinds of ideas, according to Conrad, are most difficult for one person to convey to another? What reasons does he give for believing that communication of ideas of this kind is not altogether beyond hope?
7. What does Conrad mean by describing the words of the language as "worn thin, defaced by ages of careless usage"? How does he propose, as a writer, to overcome this handicap?
8. Describe the grammatical characteristics of the sentences in the paragraph beginning "To snatch in a moment of courage. . . ."
9. Whether or not you have read it, describe the novel which you would expect to follow this preface.

VOCABULARY

Give the derivations and definitions of the following words:

manifold, hazardous, egoism, credulity, precious, enigmatical, vulnerable, appeal, latent, subtle, invincible, temperament, amenable, responsive, plasticity, evanescent, motive, persuasion, edified, consoled, amused, core, aspire, inspire.

WRITING AND STUDY AIDS

PATTERN OF ORGANIZATION SUGGESTED BY THE GENERAL TOPIC:

An *example* or *illustration* is a specific, familiar fact, event, observation, or anecdote which supports or clarifies a general statement. By clear, well-proportioned examples, an author may make even difficult ideas appear easy and distinct. Essays on the subject of writing or of communication are often rich in examples, for language lends itself to copious citation. The readings for this assignment are no exceptions.

The central problem of this assignment is to arrive at a few generalizations concerning the problems of communication and to write about them in such a way as to make use of many examples. Your own experience with language is extensive. Draw upon the things you know about words.

ASSIGNMENTS:

Short themes:

1. People never know what I mean
2. City talk in the country
3. "Every name has a thing"
4. A dog's eye view of the classroom
5. Two maps of the campus: verbal and extensional
6. Emerson's use of language
7. Professor's language
8. "Terms of appeal"

Long themes:

1. Why people can't say what they mean
2. How people can say what they mean

~~ The Troubled Career of Walter Mitty

IN THE NEW YORKER, ON MARCH 18, 1939, THERE APPEARED A SHORT STORY, "The Secret Life of Walter Mitty," by James Thurber, a cartoonist, writer, and humorist already famous for his contributions to the same magazine. Admirers of Thurber at once recognized that the story was a fine example of his work. It was reprinted many times in anthologies, collections, and texts. People who had never heard of Thurber's work were interested by it. Within a few years it was firmly established as one of the best and most memorable of American short stories.

Under such circumstances it was inevitable that Walter Mitty should sooner or later appear in a motion picture. Rights to the story were purchased by Samuel Goldwyn Productions, Incorporated, and in 1945 work on the screenplay began.

Unlike an author, who addresses his audience directly, a motion picture producer addresses his audience through the medium of actors. Among the actors available to Samuel Goldwyn for this particular picture was Danny Kaye, whose name alone is enough to beckon thousands of customers to the box office. His style of comedy is very well known. It is characterized by set routines and "scat" songs delivered with great energy.

Again unlike an author, a motion picture producer is intensely aware of his audience. He has to invest large quantities of money to make even one motion picture. His tendency is therefore to film the kind of thing that experience has taught him to think people will pay to see. In the work of turning "The Secret Life of Walter Mitty" into a screenplay, Samuel Goldwyn quite naturally exerted the influence that he thought was needed in order to make the picture a box-office success.

When the picture appeared, it was reviewed in *Life* on August 4, 1947, as "the picture of the week." Crowds of movie-goers all over the country were already laughing at the antics of Danny Kaye in "The Secret Life of Walter Mitty," and in the ensuing weeks and months several million people saw the picture. Clearly, Samuel Goldwyn had produced another hit. But James Thurber, the author, was angered and dismayed by what had been done to his short story.

The relationship between the author of a story and the producer of a film based on that story is an interesting and complex one. Two artistic media are involved; often enough, two artistic standards are involved. As a consequence of these complex differences, James Thurber and Samuel Goldwyn found themselves in disagreement over the transference of Thurber's fine story to the screen.

Some of the questions at issue are these: Can a motion picture be judged by literary standards? If not, by what standards can a motion picture be judged? When should a producer attempt to preserve the original values of a story on which he bases a screenplay, and when is he free to substitute new values? Who is the character more worth filming, Walter Mitty or Danny Kaye? Is "The Secret Life of Walter Mitty" a "good" motion picture?

"The Secret Life of Walter Mitty" may be studied as a short story, the form in which it was originally written, in the first reading for this assignment. It is followed by the scenario for the motion picture based on it. The adaptation of the story to the screen may thus be observed at first hand in the two versions. The difference of opinion between Thurber and Goldwyn concerning the result may be observed in their letters to *Life*.

James Thurber

THE SECRET LIFE OF WALTER MITTY

"WE'RE GOING THROUGH!" The Commander's voice was like thin ice breaking. He wore his full-dress uniform, with the heavily braided white cap pulled down rakishly over one cold gray eye. "We can't make it, sir. It's spoiling for a hurricane, if you ask me." "I'm not asking you, Lieutenant Berg," said the Commander. "Throw on the

Reprinted by special permission of the author.

power lights! Rev her up to 8,500! We're going through!" The pounding of the cylinders increased: ta-pocketa-pocketa-pocketa-*pocketa-*
pocketa. The Commander stared at the ice forming on the pilot
window. He walked over and twisted a row of complicated dials.
"Switch on No. 8 auxiliary!" he shouted. "Switch on No. 8 auxiliary!"
repeated Lieutenant Berg. "Full strength in No. 3 turret!" shouted the
Commander. "Full strength in No. 3 turret!" The crew, bending to
their various tasks in the huge, hurtling eight-engined Navy hydro-
plane, looked at each other and grinned. "The Old Man'll get us
through," they said to one another. "The Old Man ain't afraid of
Hell!" ...

"Not so fast! You're driving too fast!" said Mrs. Mitty. "What are
you driving so fast for?"

"Hmm?" said Walter Mitty. He looked at his wife, in the seat
beside him, with shocked astonishment. She seemed grossly unfamiliar,
like a strange woman who had yelled at him in a crowd. "You were
up to fifty-five," she said. "You know I don't like to go more than
forty. You were up to fifty-five." Walter Mitty drove on toward Waterbury in silence, the roaring of the SN202 through the worst storm
in twenty years of Navy flying fading in the remote, intimate airways
of his mind. "You're tensed up again," said Mrs. Mitty. "It's one of
your days. I wish you'd let Dr. Renshaw look you over."

Walter Mitty stopped the car in front of the building where his
wife went to have her hair done. "Remember to get those overshoes
while I'm having my hair done," she said. "I don't need overshoes,"
said Mitty. She put her mirror back into her bag. "We've been all
through that," she said, getting out of the car. "You're not a young
man any longer." He raced the engine a little. "Why don't you wear
your gloves? Have you lost your gloves?" Walter Mitty reached in a
pocket and brought out the gloves. He put them on, but after she
had turned and gone into the building and he had driven on to a red
light, he took them off again. "Pick it up, brother!" snapped a cop as
the light changed, and Mitty hastily pulled on his gloves and lurched
ahead. He drove around the streets aimlessly for a time, and then
he drove past the hospital on his way to the parking lot.

... "It's the millionaire banker, Wellington McMillan," said the
pretty nurse. "Yes?" said Walter Mitty, removing his gloves slowly.
"Who has the case?" "Dr. Renshaw and Dr. Benbow, but there are
two specialists here, Dr. Remington from New York and Mr. Prit-

chard-Mitford from London. He flew over." A door opened down a long, cool corridor and Dr. Renshaw came out. He looked distraught and haggard. "Hello, Mitty," he said. "We're having the devil's own time with McMillan, the millionaire banker and close personal friend of Roosevelt. Obstreosis of the ductal tract. Tertiary. Wish you'd take a look at him." "Glad to," said Mitty.

In the operating room there were whispered introductions: Dr. Remington, Dr. Mitty. Mr. Pritchard-Mitford, Dr. Mitty." "I've read your book on streptothricosis," said Pritchard-Mitford, shaking hands, "A brilliant performance, sir." "Thank you," said Walter Mitty. "Didn't know you were in the States, Mitty," grumbled Remington. "Coals to Newcastle, bringing Mitford and me here for a tertiary." "You are very kind," said Mitty. A huge, complicated machine, connected to the operating table, with many tubes and wires, began at this moment to go pocketa-pocketa-pocketa. "The new anesthetizer is giving way!" shouted an interne. "There is no one in the East who knows how to fix it!" "Quiet man!" said Mitty, in a low, cool voice. He sprang to the machine, which was now going pocketa-pocketa-queep-pocketa-queep. He began fingering delicately a row of glistening dials. "Give me a fountain pen!" he snapped. Someone handed him a fountain pen. He pulled a faulty piston out of the machine and inserted the pen in its place. "That will hold for ten minutes," he said. "Get on with the operation." A nurse hurried over and whispered to Renshaw, and Mitty saw the man turn pale. "Coreopsis has set in," said Renshaw nervously. "If you would take over, Mitty?" Mitty looked at him and at the craven figure of Benbow, who drank, and at the grave, uncertain faces of the two great specialists. "If you wish," he said. They slipped a white gown on him; he adjusted a mask and drew on thin gloves nurses handed him shining...

"Back it up, Mac! Look out for that Buick!" Walter Mitty jammed on the brakes. "Wrong lane, Mac," said the parking-lot attendant looking at Mitty closely. "Gee. Yeh," muttered Mitty. He began cautiously to back out of the lane marked "Exit Only." "Leave her sit there," said the attendant. "I'll put her away." Mitty got out of the car. "Hey, better leave the key." "Oh," said Mitty, handing the man the ignition key. The attendant vaulted into the car, backed it up with insolent skill, and put it where it belonged.

They're so damn cocky, thought Walter Mitty, walking along Main Street; they think they know everything. Once he had tried to take his chains off, outside New Milford, and he had got them wound around the axles. A man had had to come out in a wrecking car and unwind them, a young, grinning garageman. Since then Mrs. Mitty always made him drive to a garage to have the chains taken off. The next time, he thought, I'll wear my right arm in a sling; they won't grin at me then. I'll have my right arm in a sling and they'll see I couldn't possibly take the chains off myself. He kicked at the slush on the sidewalk. "Overshoes," he said to himself, and he began looking for a shoe store.

When he came out into the street again, with the overshoes in a box under his arm, Walter Mitty began to wonder what the other thing was his wife had told him to get. She had told him twice, before they set out from their house for Waterbury. In a way he hated these weekly trips to town—he was always getting something wrong. Kleenex, he thought, Squibb's, razor blades? No. Toothpaste, tooth-brush, bicarbonate, carborundum, initiative and referendum? He gave it up. But she would remember it. "Where's the what's-its-name?" she would ask. "Don't tell me you forgot the what's-its-name." A newsboy went by shouting something about the Waterbury trial.

. . . "Perhaps this will refresh your memory." The District Attorney suddenly thrust a heavy automatic at the quiet figure on the witness stand. "Have you ever seen this before?" Walter Mitty took the gun and examined it expertly. "This is my Webley-Vickers 50.80," he said calmly. An excited buzz ran around the courtroom. The judge rapped for order. "You are a crack shot with any sort of firearms, I believe?" said the District Attorney, insinuatingly. "Objection!" shouted Mitty's attorney. "We have shown that the defendant could not have fired the shot. We have shown that he wore his right arm in a sling on the night of the fourteenth of July." Walter Mitty raised his hand briefly and the bickering attorneys were stilled. "With any known make of gun," he said evenly, "I could have killed Gregory Fitzhurst at three hundred feet *with my left hand*." Pandemonium broke loose in the courtroom. A woman's scream rose above the bedlam and sud-denly a lovely, dark-haired girl was in Walter Mitty's arms. The Dis-trict Attorney struck at her savagely. Without rising from his chair, Mitty let the man have it on the point of the chin. "You miserable cur!" . . .

"Puppy biscuit," said Walter Mitty. He stopped walking and the buildings of Waterbury rose up out of the misty courtroom and surrounded him again. A woman who was passing laughed. "He said 'Puppy biscuit,' " she said to her companion. "That man said 'Puppy biscuit' to himself." Walter Mitty hurried on. He went into an A. & P., not the first one he came to but a smaller one farther up the street. "I want some biscuit for small, young dogs," he said to the clerk. "Any special brand, sir?" The greatest pistol shot in the world thought a moment. "It says 'Puppies Bark for It' on the box," said Walter Mitty.

His wife would be through at the hairdresser's in fifteen minutes, Mitty saw in looking at his watch, unless they had trouble drying it; sometimes they had trouble drying it. She didn't like to get to the hotel first; she would want him to be there waiting for her as usual. He found a big leather chair in the lobby, facing a window, and he put the overshoes and the puppy biscuit on the floor beside it. He picked up an old copy of *Liberty* and sank down into the chair. "Can Germany Conquer the World Through the Air?" Walter Mitty looked at the pictures of bombing planes and of ruined streets.

. . . "The cannonading has got the wind up in young Raleigh, sir," said the sergeant. Captain Mitty looked up at him through tousled hair. "Get him to bed," he said wearily. "With the others. I'll fly alone." "But you can't, sir," said the sergeant anxiously. "It takes two men to handle that bomber and the Archies are pounding hell out of the air. Von Richtman's circus is between here and Saulier." "Somebody's got to get that ammunition dump," said Mitty. "I'm going over. Spot of brandy?" He poured a drink for the sergeant and one for himself. War thundered and whined around the dugout and battered at the door. There was a rending of wood and splinters flew through the room. "A bit of a near thing," said Captain Mitty carelessly. "The box barrage is closing in," said the sergeant. "We only live once, Sergeant," said Mitty, with his faint, fleeting smile. "Or do we?" He poured another brandy and tossed it off. "I never see a man could hold his brandy like you, sir," said the sergeant. "Begging your pardon, sir." Captain Mitty stood up and strapped on his huge Webley-Vickers automatic. "It's forty kilometers through hell, sir," said the sergeant. Mitty finished one last brandy. "After all," he said softly, "what isn't?" The pounding of the cannon increased; there was the rat-tat-tatting of machine guns, and from somewhere came the menacing pocketa-pocketa-pocketa of the new flame-throwers. Walter Mitty

walked to the door of the dugout humming "Auprés de Ma Blonde."
He turned and waved to the sergeant. "Cheerio!" he said....

Something struck his shoulder. "I've been looking all over this hotel
for you," said Mrs. Mitty. "Why do you have to hide in this old chair?
How did you expect me to find you?" "Things close in," said Walter
Mitty vaguely. "What?" Mrs. Mitty said. "Did you get the what's-its-
name? The puppy biscuit? What's in that box?" "Overshoes," said
Mitty. "Couldn't you have put them on in the store?" "I was thinking,"
said Walter Mitty. "Does it ever occur to you that I am sometimes
thinking?" She looked at him. "I'm going to take your temperature
when I get you home," she said.

They went out through the revolving doors that made a faintly
derisive whistling sound when you pushed them. It was two blocks
to the parking lot. At the drugstore on the corner she said, "Wait
here for me. I forgot something. I won't be a minute." She was more
than a minute. Walter Mitty lighted a cigarette. It began to rain, rain
with sleet in it. He stood up against the wall of the drugstore, smoking.... He put his shoulders back and his heels together. "To hell with
the handkerchief," said Walter Mitty scornfully. He took one last drag
on his cigarette and snapped it away. Then, with that faint, fleeting
smile playing about his lips, he faced the firing squad; erect and
motionless, proud and disdainful, Walter Mitty the Undefeated, inscrutable to the last.

GUIDE QUESTIONS

1. What proportion of the story is given over to Walter Mitty's daydreams?
2. How do the various dreams get started? What kind of thing suggests them?
3. What overlapping of dream and reality is there in Mitty's daydreams?
4. What evidence is there that the real Walter Mitty is characterized by cowardice? Timidity? Sensitiveness? Absent-mindedness?
5. What evidence is there in the story to suggest that Mitty, the worm, may turn?
6. Does the containing framework of the shopping trip in Waterbury have any narrative structure? Would it be possible to dramatize the story as a whole without giving structure to the shopping trip?
7. In what sense does the story hinge upon an essential conflict? At what point is the conflict resolved or confirmed?

VOCABULARY

Give the derivations and definitions of the following words:

rakishly, distraught, craven, insinuatingly, bickering, pandemonium, bed-lam, derisive, inscrutable.

Samuel Goldwyn Productions, Inc.

THE SECRET LIFE OF WALTER MITTY

1x FADE IN—A STORM AT SEA. A small sailing ship pitches and tosses on the crest of mountainous waves. The scene is one of indescribable violence.

> NARRATOR'S VOICE: Somewhere off the South China coast, in the worst typhoon of forty years, the little schooner India Queen ploughed through an ocean gone mad...

2x DECK OF INDIA QUEEN—FULL SHOT. The gale is ripping and clawing at the rigging. Seamen stagger around trying to reef the sails and secure the deck cargo.

3x SHOT BELOW DECK. Showing pumping auxiliary engines.

> NARRATOR'S VOICE: Straining engines went "ta-pocketa-pocketa-pocketa," driving the tortured vessel forward. Up on deck Captain Walter Mitty stood astride his bridge, barking orders...

4x MED. SHOT ON BRIDGE—CAPTAIN WALTER MITTY (Danny Kaye). In sou'wester and oilskins, shouting through megaphone.

> MITTY: Reef the mizzen! Close haul the spinnaker. Batten the hatches! (*he calls to helmsman struggling with wheel*) Hard a-lee! Hard a-lee!
>
> HELMSMAN: Aye, aye, sir.

Before he can obey, a huge wave washes him right off the deck and knocks MITTY against the mast. He struggles to his feet and

---

A condensed version of the scenario is printed here by special permission of Samuel Goldwyn Productions, Inc.

grabs the wildly spinning wheel, holding the ship to course with one hand, his other arm dangling. A GIRL fights her way to his side, her beautiful blonde hair tossing in the gale, her soaked dress clinging to the lissome lines of her figure.

MITTY (*gruffly to* GIRL): What are you doing up here? Get below.

GIRL: Can't I do something to help? You haven't had your clothes off in three days.

MITTY: Somebody's got to get the India Queen through. There's a half million dollars worth of rare spices aboard and I promised your father—

GIRL (*suddenly noticing his arm*): Captain Mitty—you're hurt!

MITTY: It's nothing. Just a broken arm. *A second mate runs in agitatedly.*

SECOND MATE: Captain, the bulkheads are going! We ought to send up distress flares if you ask me—

MITTY: I'm not asking you, Mr. Berg. (*he shouts off*) Man the pumps, lads—lively! We'll ride this twister out and be in Bombay for breakfast.

The men cheer and bend to with new heart. The GIRL looks at MITTY through moist sapphire eyes.

GIRL: May I say, Captain Mitty, you're the bravest man I've ever met.

MITTY: Thank you, Miss Lee. May I say something to *you?*

GIRL: Anything.

MITTY: If we reach Liverpool safely, will you be Mrs. Mitty?

GIRL: I'd be honored.

5x   TWO SHOT—YOUNG SEAMAN AND OLD MARINER. The younger man is cowering, terrified.

YOUNG SEAMAN: We're done for—we'll never make it.

OLD MARINER: Easy, son. The Old Man'll get us through. The Old Man ain't afraid of Hell!

6x   DECK OF SHIP—FULL SHOT. As the mainmast splits and starts to fall to the deck.

6x-1 CLOSE SHOT—GIRL. Staring upward in horror. She opens her mouth to scream

MRS. MITTY'S VOICE: Watch out!

The girl's face DISSOLVES INTO:

7x INT. ˙FORD COUPE—TRANSPARENCY—DAY—CLOSE SHOT—WALTER MITTY AND MRS. MITTY. At the wheel is WALTER MITTY, our hero. He is thirty, pleasant faced, gentle, anything but forceful looking. Beside him sits his mother, MRS. EUNICE MITTY. She is a firm-jawed woman who runs her home and WALTER with an iron hand. There is a dreamy expression on WALTER's face and his mother is regarding him with alarm.

MRS. MITTY: Not so fast! You're driving too fast! What are you driving so fast for?

WALTER comes out of the enchanted world of his daydreams with a start.

WALTER: Hm?

MRS. MITTY: You were up to thirty-five. You know I don't like to go more than thirty. You were up to thirty-five. Walter, you're always doing something else and having your mind on something else. Red light, Walter.

WALTER stops the car at an intersection.

WALTER: I'm sorry, mother.

MRS. MITTY (*irritably*): Besides, you haven't been listening to a single word I've said.

WALTER (*eyes straight ahead*): Yes I have, mother.

MRS. MITTY: What did I say?

WALTER: You said I was up to thirty-five and you don't like to go more than thirty.

MRS. MITTY: Not that! I said we're not going to have it in a church. Green light, Walter.

WALTER (*sticking his hand out for a left turn*): Have what, Mother?

MRS. MITTY: The wedding! You see, you *weren't* listening. Stop, Walter!

WALTER slams on the brakes.

8 EXT. PERTH AMBOY RAILROAD STATION—MED. SHOT—PARKING ZONE WITH WAITING TRAIN VISI-BLE IN BACKGROUND. WALTER has almost run into another

car pulling out. He swerves wildly and parks none too deftly. WALTER and his mother alight. He is burdened with a fat briefcase and a sprinkling can wrapped in paper.

MRS. MITTY: Now did you write down all the things I told you to write down?

CAMERA TRUCKING on platform, as they hurry toward the waiting commuters' train.

WALTER: Oh—I'll remember them, mother.

MRS. MITTY: Oh—no you won't—you just make a list of everything in your book.

With difficulty, WALTER extracts a little black book from his pocket —and scribbles in it as she talks; his briefcase under one arm, the sprinkling can under the other.

MRS. MITTY: Number two thread—snapdragon seeds—sock stretchers—a can of Gleamo Floorwax—(*peering into book*) What's that S. S.?

WALTER: Sock stretchers.

MRS. MITTY: Well write it out—and then the cheese grater, and don't forget to return the sprinkling can. I tried it this morning. The holes are too small. You tell them I have better things to do than stand all day and wait for the water to come out.

They have reached the train.

WALTER: All right, mother. Goodbye, mother.

She gives him a hurried peck on the cheek and he joins the crowd of commuters and climbs into the vestibule. Just in time, for the train starts to pull out.

MRS. MITTY (*shouting*): Oh—and don't forget the cake!

10   DISSOLVE TO: EXT. PIERCE BUILDING—NEW YORK CITY—MED. FULL SHOT. The words PIERCE BUILDING are chiseled in impressive granite. We see WALTER hurry in with the morning crowd of employees.

11   INT. LOBBY—MED. SHOT—AT ELEVATORS. WALTER is the last one to get into a very crowded elevator. He greets two lady employees he's sandwiched between.

WALTER: Morning, Miss Peevy—Miss Rumplemeyer.

In spite of his burdens, he tries to tip his hat but the elevator starter interrupts the action.

ELEVATOR STARTER: Back in the car, please. (*He pushes the extended spout of Walter's sprinkling can flat against* WALTER *so that the door can close*) Keep that thing in, Bud.

As the elevator doors close...

12   DISSOLVE TO: FOYER. Double glass doors read "Pierce Publishing Company—Editorial Offices." WALTER and other employees enter from the elevator.

13   INT. MAIN EDITORIAL ROOM—MED. SHOT—SHOOTING TOWARDS ENTRANCE DOORS. Employees are entering the vast room—others are already at their desks. The walls are lined with lurid posters and magazine cover blowups from recent issues of the company's string of pulp magazines. The posters are a motley pictorial assortment of murder, rape, arson and derring-do. We see first the two posters on each side of the doors. One reads: "RACY DETECTIVE STORIES—A PIERCE PUBLICATION," and it shows a beautiful terrified girl, bound and gagged in a chair, her dress strap torn to expose a bare white shoulder. Over her hovers a fiendish-looking individual with a long hypodermic needle. The other reads: "FRONTIER STORIES—A PIERCE PUBLICATION." It shows a clean-cut-looking cowboy and a savage-looking villain shooting each other in the stomach. In the background is a beautiful girl bound and gagged in a chair.

WALTER appears and CAMERA TRUCKS him across the room towards his office—affording us an opportunity to read other posters arranged on pillars at intervals along the aisle. A poster reads: "TERROR STORIES—A PIERCE PUBLICATION." It shows a terrifying black-hooded figure reaching for the throat of a beautiful girl chained to a wall and clad only in a torn slip. Another poster shows a girl with an infant in her arms, holding out her hand pleadingly toward a handsome cad in a monogrammed dressing gown who has turned away from her to light a cigarette. The legend reads: COULD SHE REMOVE THAT SIN? Read the heart-tugging story of Ella Schwartzkopf in "WILD CONFESSIONS"—plus another gripping installment of "I MARRIED MY UNCLE." Another reads: "ASTOUNDING ADVENTURE STORIES—A PIERCE PUBLICATION." I* shows a number of small green men with antennae growing out of their heads gathered around a beautiful terrified girl cowering on the ground. Her dress strap is torn, exposing a bare white shoulder.

WALTER passes a row of artists starting work at their drawing boards, before them covers in various stages of completion. A little elderly artist has just finished a particularly gory one showing a half-naked young lady frantically defending herself with a bloody ax against several hairy sex-crazed assailants. WALTER stops to look, admiringly.

WALTER: Oh—that's pretty, Mr. Grimsby.

ARTIST (*critically*): Feels a bit mild. I think I'll tear the dress off her other shoulder.

WALTER (*appraisingly*): Yes, and you could put a little more blood on the ax.

The artist grunts in approval as WALTER continues on, CAMERA TRUCKING, and we sight other magazine covers such as AIR ACES, EXOTIC LOVE STORIES and SENSATIONAL MURDER STORIES, and a final poster at WALTER's office door reads:

PIERCE PUBLICATIONS

Good Taste and Good Reading
for Thirty Years.

WALTER enters his office.

14 INT. WALTER'S OFFICE—FULL SHOT. It is a small, rather dingy cubicle. Here, too, cover blowups decorate the walls. Most prominent is a poster captioned "SPICY SEA STORIES," showing a schooner on a storm tossed ocean. WALTER's desk is piled high with manuscripts, galley proofs and art, in addition to items like paste pot, shears and reading glasses. Also on the desk is a bottle of milk.

WALTER enters, hangs up his coat and hat and dons a gray office coat that has various colored pencils in the breast pocket. He sits down at his desk, puts on his glasses, extracts a batch of proofs from his briefcase and starts to work studying them. He hears the cooing of pigeons, turns, glances towards the window and smiles to see a cluster of pigeons on the window ledge looking in at him expectantly. He removes his glasses, rises, goes to his coat, takes out a little brown paper bag full of toast, opens the window and kneels on the floor to feed the pigeons on the ledge.

15   CLOSE SHOT—AT WINDOW—WALTER AND PIGEONS. It is obvious that this is a morning ritual.

> WALTER: Well, good morning, good morning, everybody—think I'd forgotten you? I smuggled in some cookies today while my mother wasn't looking...Hello, Emily. Don't be so greedy, Elmer, you're fat enough already.

16   WIDER ANGLE—TO INCLUDE DOOR. It is flung open by the OFFICE BOY, who reacts at the sight of WALTER on his knees with the pigeons.

> OFFICE BOY: Hey—dream boy!

Two passing stenographers glance in and snicker as they go by. WALTER gets to his feet.

> WALTER: Hmm?

> OFFICE BOY: The old man is screaming for you—

> WALTER: Oh, oh—the conference!

He glances at his watch, and swiftly rummages though the file boxes on his desk, mumbling to himself.

> WALTER: Air Aces...Spicy Sea Stories...No, Terror Stories— Here it is...

He scoops up a stack of galley proofs, starts to rush off, then rushes back and swallows a sip of milk. He hurries out past the OFFICE BOY who watches him, shaking his head.

17   INT. MAIN EDITORIAL ROOM. CAMERA TRUCKS with WALTER as he comes out of his office and starts hurrying across the room, passing a couple of open office doors.

18   MED. LONG SHOT—SHOOTING THROUGH DOOR. A beautiful girl in a torn, shredded dress, is cowering against the wall, her eyes distended in horror as a creature with the body of a man and the head of a wolf reaches for her with long talons. A white-smocked photographer lifts a flash bulb.

> PHOTOGRAPHER: Hold it!

The flash bulb goes off and the two models relax.

WALTER (*as he passes*): H'lo, Fred.

WOLF MAN (*waving back*): How's it goin', Walter?

19   FULL SHOT IN CORRIDOR. As WALTER hurries through a door which reads: BRUCE W. PIERCE.

21   INT. PIERCE'S OFFICE—FULL SHOT. As WALTER enters. We find ourselves in a large, well-appointed sanctum. Four men and a woman are draped around the room. The woman, an illustrator, wears a smock and holds a few large drawings. The others are the Business Manager, the Advertising Manager, the Circulation Manager and the Composing Room Foreman. MR. PIERCE is behind a tremendous walnut desk. He frowns as WALTER closes the door behind him.

PIERCE (*coldly*): *Well*—Mitty! I see you finally chose to honor us with your presence.

WALTER: Yes sir, I—

PIERCE (*brusquely*): Where are the proofs to "Air Aces"?

WALTER: Right here, Mr. Pierce. All checked and ready to go.

He sets them on the desk. Without even glancing at them, PIERCE transfers them to the compositor.

PIERCE: Put it to bed.

The make-up man nods and hurries out. PIERCE lifts a freshly printed copy of "Terror Stories" from his desk and fixes WALTER with an icy regard.

PIERCE: And what's the meaning of this, Mitty?

WALTER (*nervously*): The meaning of what, Mr. Pierce?

PIERCE: You let the Vampire Man be killed off in the first installment of "The Lady and the Vampire"—and there are thirty-three issues to go.

WALTER: I—er—I beg to differ, Mr. Pierce. He isn't really dead.

PIERCE: What do you mean, he isn't dead? The villagers drove a stake through his heart, didn't they? Anybody knows *that* kills a vampire.

WALTER: Yes sir, but if you'll read further on, you'll find that the stake only went through his left lung. (*cheerfully*) You don't have to worry, Mr. Pierce. He'll be back sucking blood in the next issue.

PIERCE coughs and changes the subject.

PIERCE: Well, sit down, Mitty. If you'd been on time, you'd know why I called this meeting.

WALTER sits down as PIERCE stands up and faces the group dramatically.

PIERCE: To repeat, ladies and gentlemen. I have called this meeting to inform you that Pierce Publications is forging a new link in its chain. Ours is a great and proud list of magazines— Racy Detective Stories, Astounding Adventure Stories, Terror Stories, Wild Confessions, Air Aces, Frontier Stories—er—er—

WALTER: Exotic Love Stories.

PIERCE: Exotic Love Stories.

WALTER: And Sensational Murders.

PIERCE: And Sensational Murders. (*he frowns at* WALTER) Mitty, when I need your help, I'll ask for it.

WALTER (*meekly*): Yes, sir.

PIERCE: But a new and virgin field of fiction has come to my attention—a rich and as yet untapped vein, embracing thousands of undiscovered readers. Gentlemen, and Miss Worth, starting the first of next month, we go to press with a new baby— (*leaning forward reverently*) Hospital Love Stories!

His announcement is the signal for gasps of admiration. The others crowd around the desk, shaking his hand and ad libbing: "Brilliant, Chief"..."It's a dilly, B. W."..."You've done it again, Mr. Pierce."

PIERCE (*modestly*): Thank you...Thank you, gentlemen (*he notices* WALTER *sitting quietly and frowns*) Well, what do *you* think, Mitty?

WALTER: Oh, I've always liked it, Mr. Pierce. Don't you remember, I suggested the idea in a memorandum last month—

PIERCE: Oh, *that!* (*he snorts*) I had this idea two years ago. (*briskly*) Now the type of stories we want—you may take notes, gentlemen— (*everyone complies,* WALTER *producing his memorandum book*) Well, now, let's see—Hospital Love Stories—what have we got to sell? Romance in the operating room! Handsome young internes—I don't want any doctors over thirty—beautiful blonde nurses—you can't get too many nurses—

24 CLOSE SHOT—WALTER. His pencil strays. A beatific half-smile comes over his face. He looks up at MR. PIERCE.

25 MED. SHOT—PIERCE—FROM WALTER'S ANGLE. His mouth is opening and closing, but no sound comes out.

26 CLOSE SHOT—WALTER. His expression becomes even more beatific, as we

28 DISSOLVE TO: INT. OPERATING ROOM—FULL SHOT. Three white-clad surgeons are bent over an operating table. Two nurses attend. An anesthetist is busy at a huge complicated machine near the head of the table which is making the rhythmic hum of ta-pocketa-pocketa-pocketa. As BENBOW and MITTY join the tense group:

> NARRATOR'S VOICE (*fading in*): —and Mitty, the surgical genius, entered the breathless hush of the operating room, the tense silence broken only by the sound of the huge anesthetizing machine going ta-pocketa-pocketa-pocketa.... There were whispered introductions—

> BENBOW: Dr. Remington, Dr. Renshaw, and this is Dr. Pritchard-Mitford of St. John's Hospital, London...Dr. Walter Mitty.

They exchange nods and keep working.

> REMINGTON: Read your book on Streptothricosis. A brilliant performance, sir.

> MITTY: Thank you.

> PRITCHARD-MITFORD: Didn't know you were in the States, Mitty. Coals to Newcastle, bringing me up here for a Tertiary.

> MITTY: You are very kind.

Suddenly the huge machine begins to whir, and the sound becomes pocketa-pocketa-*queep*-pocketa-*queep*.

> INTERNE: The new anesthetizer is giving way! There is no one in the East who knows how to fix it!

> MITTY (*cooly*): Quiet, man. (*he quickly fingers the dials of the machine*) Give me a fountain pen.

The INTERNE hands him a pen. MITTY swiftly pulls a faulty piston out of the machine and inserts the fountain pen in its place. The sound returns to normal.

MITTY: That will hold for ten minutes. Get on with the operation.

The BLONDE NURSE murmurs in awe to the interne:

BLONDE NURSE: He is not only the greatest surgeon in the world, but he is also a mechanical genius!

RENSHAW: Good Heavens!

BENBOW: What is it?

RENSHAW: Coreopsis has set in!

PRITCHARD-MITFORD: Poor devil! If you would take over, Mitty?

MITTY: If you wish.

MITTY stretches out his hands. The BLONDE NURSE and another nurse immediately start slipping rubber gloves on him.

BENBOW (*stepping back*): It's hopeless.

Through following, the BLONDE NURSE ties on MITTY's mask and slips a large surgeon's reflector on his head.

MITTY: There's one chance—the Vienna Trepan.

PRITCHARD-MITFORD (*aghast*): The operation Heinzleman performed on a rabbit?

MITTY (*stepping to the table*): Precisely. (*to* NURSE) Blood pressure, please.

BLONDE NURSE (*appearing at his side*): Thirty over eighty.

MITTY (*holding out hand*): Scalpel! (*she hands him a scalpel, he uses it and hands it back*) Sock stretcher! (*she hands him a sock stretcher. The routine is the same*) Sprinkling can! (*she hands him a sprinkling can, he sprinkles lightly and hands it back*) Cheese grater! (*she hands him the grater—he uses it vigorously*) Number Two thread! (*he takes a quick stitch*) Floor wax! (*she hands him the can of wax*)

He starts to peel off his gloves. The BLONDE NURSE looks up at him through moist, sapphire eyes.

BLONDE NURSE: Doctor, do you—will he—

MITTY (*nods*): Your brother will play the violin again. I grafted new fingers on him.

29 HEAD CLOSEUP—BEAUTIFUL BLONDE NURSE AND
WALTER. She is looking at him worshipfully, her eyes shining.

BLONDE NURSE: You're wonderful, wonderful...

30 TRICK REVOLVING WIPE TO: INT. PIERCE'S OFFICE—
HEAD CLOSEUP—WALTER MITTY. His chin cupped in
his palm, and a dreamy, faraway look in his eyes.

31 FULL SHOT—IN OFFICE. WALTER is the center of attention
as PIERCE scowls at him.

PIERCE: Mitty! I asked you a question. I'd like an answer.

WALTER (*dreamily*): Ta-pocketa-pocketa-pocketa—

PIERCE: What's that?

WALTER (*coming to with a start*): Oh, I—er—I was just thinking, we could put out a *pocket-size* edition—

PIERCE: Pocket-size edition!

WALTER (*with a gulp*): For midgets.

PIERCE (*glares at him*): You weren't *thinking* at all—you were
daydreaming again.

WALTER: No, sir. I was really thinking—I was thinking about
hospitals—for Hospital Stories—

PIERCE (*pounding his desk*): I *finished* talking about Hospital
Stories ten minutes ago. The subject, for your information, is
the next issue of Racy Detective.

WALTER: Oh.

PIERCE: I disapprove of the lead story—the one you made me
buy. I don't believe that a blind jockey could dope a horse in
full view of twenty thousand people.

WALTER: It's all explained on page twenty, Mr. Pierce. He had
the poisoned needle strapped to his riding boot.

PIERCE: Oh, I see. (*clears his throat and takes a pile of manuscript from his desk*) Well, never mind then. Get busy on
these proofs. I want them read and corrected by tomorrow
morning.

WALTER: Yes, sir.

He takes the pile of pages and goes out. PIERCE looks after him,
tapping his fingers.

PIERCE (*half to himself*): Pocket-size edition. Not a bad idea....

32 DISSOLVE TO: EXT. SUBURBAN STATION—LATE AFTERNOON—MED. SHOT—STATION SIGN—"PERTH AMBOY, NEW JERSEY."

33 FULL SHOT—STATION. Commuters are getting off the 6:45 to be greeted by their women folk, waiting in lined-up cars. WALTER alights, his arms loaded with packages which include his proof-laden *briefcase* and a large *garden rake.* He looks around, sees someone OFFSCENE and CAMERA TRUCKS him to—

34 MED. SHOT—THE MITTY COUPE. MRS. MITTY is waiting at the wheel. She allows her cheek to be kissed, then starts peering through the packages in WALTER's arms.

MRS. MITTY: You didn't bring it. You forgot to bring the cake.

WALTER: What cake?

MRS. MITTY: Gertrude and her mother are coming to dinner. I told you to stop at Edling's and bring home a cake— (*she breaks off*) What's that thing?

WALTER (*sheepishly*): I thought you said *rake!*

MRS. MITTY sighs as WALTER enters the car.

MRS. MITTY: Walter, you're getting more absent-minded every day. It's all that daydreaming you do—

WALTER: I got everything else, Mother. (*pointing to various bundles*) The Number Two thread, the floor wax, the sock stretchers, and—and—

MRS. MITTY: Did you get the snapdragon seeds?

WALTER: Well, they didn't have snapdragons, but the man in the store said petunias were just as pretty.

MRS. MITTY: Oh, he did! (*severely*) Tell me, Walter, who has to look at the flowers, the man in the store or you and me?

WALTER: Well, I guess you and me, Mother.

MRS. MITTY: Exactly.

She is about to go on, when horns begin to honk impatiently behind them. She glances around, glares, then quickly drives off.

35 WIPE TO: EXT. MITTY HOME. A two-story frame house that has been in the family for many years—chiefly because no-

body else would want to buy it. Walter and his mother are mounting the front steps.

MRS. MITTY: —So remember that, Walter, when I say snapdragon seeds, I mean snapdragon seeds.

WALTER: Yes, Mother.

They go inside.

36   INT. HALL—FULL SHOT. A staircase leads up to the second floor. Doors lead off to living room, dining room and kitchen. MRS. MITTY grabs some of the packages and starts off toward the kitchen, calling back to WALTER.

MRS. MITTY: Hurry and clean up now. They'll be here any minute.

WALTER: All right, Mother.

She hurries off to the kitchen. WALTER hangs his hat on a hall-tree and starts up the staircase.

37   MED. SHOT—AT SECOND FLOOR LANDING. As WALTER enters his bedroom, removing his coat.

38   INT. BEDROOM. The room contains an assortment of schoolday mementoes, including a baseball bat, fishing tackle, a framed diploma and a pennant reading: PERTH AMBOY HIGH. WALTER hangs his coat on the back of a chair, sets the briefcase on a battered desk and starts into the bathroom, removing his shirt.

39   INT. BATHROOM. Another door leads off to his mother's bedroom. WALTER closes both doors and proceeds to wash. He is just groping for a towel, when there is a KNOCK AT DOOR.

MRS. MITTY'S VOICE (*o. s.*): Walter, don't touch the guest towels. I just put them up.

WALTER jumps at her voice, his hands an inch away from the guest towels. Soap in his eyes, he gropes blindly around the room till his fingers come in contact with a shirt hanging on a hanger. He buries his face in it.

MRS. MITTY'S VOICE: And put on that clean shirt I hung out for you.

WALTER opens his eyes and is startled to discover he's used the clean shirt as a towel.

WALTER (*gulps*): Yes, Mother.

He tries to rub out the soapy finger smudges with a handkerchief. Failing in this, he thrusts the *clean* shirt into a laundry hamper and puts on his *old* shirt.

41   INT. LOWER HALLWAY. MRS. MITTY is greeting WALTER's future bride and her mother. MRS. GRISWOLD, *the mother,* is an opinionated power-house, addicted to odd hats. GERTRUDE, *her daughter,* is one of Perth Amboy's prettiest products, but not one of its brightest. She is carrying a small dog in her arms and continually talks baby talk to it.

MRS. MITTY (*effusively*): Irmagarde!

MRS. GRISWOLD: Eunice! How *are* you, dear?

The two women exchange kisses, their bosoms making the transaction somewhat difficult.

MRS. MITTY: My, what a *sweet* hat! And Gertrude looks too cute for words!

GERTRUDE (*too cute for words*): I hope you don't mind my bringing Queenie, Mrs. Mitty. She doesn't like to be alone— (*to the dog*) Do you, Queenie—in that great big house?

MRS. MITTY: Not at all, darling. (*calls upstairs*) Wal-ter! (*coyly*) Someone's down here to see you.

42   ANOTHER ANGLE. As WALTER hurries down the steps, buttoning his coat.

WALTER: Hello, Mrs. Griswold ... Hello, Gertrude.

He kisses her. The dog growls jealously.

GERTRUDE (*chiding dog*): Now, now, Queenie. Say hello to your future daddy, Waltie Mittens.

She waves the little dog's paw at WALTER. WALTER stares in open dislike.

MRS. MITTY: Well, don't stand there like a stick, Walter. Wave back.

WALTER does so, feeling a bit foolish. The dog promptly snaps at his hand, biting his finger.

44   DISSOLVE TO: MED. SHOT—DINNER TABLE. WALTER sits beside GERTRUDE, who has the dog on her lap. The two mothers are dominating the conversation.

MRS. GRISWOLD (*flatly*): Frankly, I don't approve of honeymoons. All that packing and unpacking—

MRS. MITTY: But Walter's always had his heart set on seeing Yellowstone Park.

MRS. GRISWOLD (*to* WALTER, *aggressively*): Why?

WALTER: Well, I thought—

GERTRUDE: Do they let dogs in?

WALTER: Honey, you're not going to take Queenie along?

The dog gives a vicious bark at WALTER as though it understands.

WALTER (*nervously, to dog*): I was only asking.

GERTRUDE: I wouldn't dream of leaving little Queenie. (*fondles the dog*)

WALTER: But Gertrude, all we've got is an upper berth—

MRS. GRISWOLD: Well, let's face it. They just don't trust each other. That's why they don't get along.

WALTER (*indicating dog, pouting*): Well, she always starts it.

WALTER starts to reach for the bread platter in front of GERTRUDE. QUEENIE emits a low growl. WALTER draws his hand back quickly.

WALTER: You see!

GERTRUDE: Queenie! You old cross-patch! (*explanatively*) She hasn't been feeling well.

MRS. MITTY: It's probably her stomach, poor thing. Why don't you try those new Vitamin Puppy Biscuits? Walter would be happy to pick some up for you in town.

GERTRUDE: Oh, wonderful.

MRS. MITTY: Make a note of that, won't you, Walter dear? Get the ten-pound economy size.

WALTER takes the small black memorandum book from his pocket and makes a penciled notation.

MRS. MITTY: Walter, you haven't *touched* your nice milk toast —and you *know* the doctor said it's good for your nervous stomach. (*to* MRS. GRISWOLD) That's why the Air Force turned him down.

WALTER returns the memorandum book to his pocket and picks up his spoon glumly.

GERTRUDE: It's cold in here. Queenie is shivering.

MRS. MITTY (*sweetly*): Walter—

WALTER (*anticipating her*): Yes, Mother—the furnace. (*he puts down his spoon and rises*) Excuse me.

As he goes, MRS. GRISWOLD turns to MRS. MITTY.

MRS. GRISWOLD: Walter's a *very* lucky man. You know Tubby Wadsworth proposed half a dozen times.

GERTRUDE (*snickering, pleased*): He's still doing it, Mother.

MRS. GRISWOLD (*archly*): Well, you've got to hand it to Tubby. When he gets his teeth into something he doesn't let go. I wish Walter had his gumption.

45   INT. CELLAR. WALTER is picking up some old newspapers to start a new fire. He rises and moves to the furnace but walks right into a clothesline which catches him under the chin. He retreats, ducks under it, gets to the furnace and starts to crumple one of the papers. A picture on a page catches his eye.

46   INSERT—PICTURE. It shows a grinning British pilot sitting in the cockpit of his plane. The caption reads: BRITISH ACE BAGS NINETEENTH.

47   CLOSE SHOT—WALTER. Looking at the picture. He sighs and holds a match to it, and stuffs it into the furnace with the poker. OVERSCENE, we begin to hear the drone of an airplane in a dive. As the fire consumes the page—

48   DISSOLVE THROUGH THE MOUNTING FLAMES TO: MACHINE GUNS OF BRITISH SPITFIRE. Firing directly into CAMERA.

49   LONG SHOT—DOG FIGHT IN CLOUDS. And OVER-SCENE, dramatically, the Narrator's voice:

NARRATOR'S VOICE: The Spitfire dived through the clouds, its machine guns belching lead....

50   COCKPIT OF SPITFIRE—CLOSE SHOT—WALTER MITTY. In the uniform of the RAF, firing his machine guns.

NARRATOR'S VOICE: Oblivious of the ominous ta-pocketa-ta-pocketa of his failing engines, Wing Commander Walter Mitty, the most feared man in the entire RAF Desert Patrol, clung to the tail of the Messerschmitt.

51 EXTREME LONG SHOT IN THE SKY—(MINIATURE).
The skillful German pilot is outmaneuvered by the still more
skillful WALTER MITTY, who uses every trick an airman has up his
sleeve—and some that he hasn't.

52 COCKPIT OF MESSERSCHMITT—CLOSE SHOT—GER-
MAN PILOT.

GERMAN PILOT (*fearfully*): Gott im Himmel, it's Walter Mitty—
I'm a lost man!

53 FULL SHOT—DOG FIGHT IN CLOUDS. MITTY's tracer bullets are blasting his target.

54 COCKPIT OF SPITFIRE—CLOSE SHOT—MITTY.

NARRATOR'S VOICE: Mitty's jaw was a grim, straight line as he
gave the Jerry three more lethal bursts and watched him go
down in flames!

MITTY looks over the side, then licks a swastika sticker and pastes
it beside a triple line of stickers on the outside of the plane.

55 WIPE TO: INT. FRENCH-ARAB CAFE IN ABD-EL-FEZ.
It is the typical atmosphere-laden desert cafe, with French Legion-
naires, British pilots, fezzed Moroccans, burnoosed Arabs, and a
number of beautiful native girls are circulating as barmaids. A
brown-skinned, delectable French-Arab girl, COSETTE (Virginia
Mayo) is seen in background serving beer to officers at a tiny
table. A group of young RAF flyers are grouped around a piano,
singing lustily.

Wing Commander MITTY enters, his uniform rumpled and torn,
a white silk muffler knotted carelessly at his throat. As he crosses
toward bar, the young officers around the piano break off and
greet him boisterously.

BRITISH PILOTS (*ad lib*): I say, there's Wing Commander Mitty,
fellows!...He made it!...Good old Mitty!...How many
this time, old chap? ...

MITTY casually holds up five fingers. The pilots cheer as he passes
them and joins an RAF Colonel at the bar.

56 MED. CLOSE—MITTY AND COLONEL.

COLONEL: Well done, Mitty!

MITTY: Thank you, sir.

COLONEL: That makes seventy-three, doesn't it?

MITTY: Seventy-one, sir. Two were only probables.

COLONEL (*indicating bottle on counter*): Spot of brandy?

MITTY: Quite.

He pours himself a drink rather awkwardly, his arm appearing to be stiff and sore. The COLONEL notices his torn sleeve.

COLONEL (*anxiously*): I say, old man, you're wounded.

MITTY (*pouring another drink*): Just a scratch. I set the bone myself.

COLONEL: Good chap. Wish there were more like you.

57X MED. SHOT—GROUP OF AIRMEN AT THE TABLE.

LIEUTENANT (*lowering his voice*): Mitty looks a bit done in, fellows.

CAPTAIN: He's got the courage of a lion, though. Never gives up.

2ND LIEUTENANT: Delightful chap. I studied music with him at the Royal Academy. Never forget his imitation of old Professor Gruenwald. Remember, Captain?

CAPTAIN (*laughing at the reminiscence*): Rather! Drove the old Professor balmy! Wish he'd do it now.

They all react as the voice of Professor Gruenwald is heard.

MITTY'S VOICE (*imitating the Professor*): Silence! What is all the chatterboxing?

58X CLOSE SHOT—MITTY. He glowers at the group, in the manner of the old Professor.

59X FULL SHOT—GROUP OF AIRMEN AND MITTY. They laugh uproariously as MITTY approaches them. On the way he borrows a pair of pince-nez glasses, takes a waiter's alpaca coat and grabs a handful of papers.

MITTY (*in dialect*): The class will please come to order.

60X CLOSE SHOT—MITTY. As he arranges his papers and goes into the number.

61X NUMBER (*Kaye sings scat imitation of a symphony*). At the conclusion of the number the men applaud. MITTY is back in his uniform and the COLONEL is slapping him on the back.

COLONEL: Good show, Mitty.

As the COLONEL tucks his swagger stick under his arm and exits scene, COSETTE appears with a tray of drinks and gives MITTY a flirtatious look. The blouse she wears exposes one bare white shoulder.

> COSETTE (*purring sexily*): Oh—you are so brave—so strong—so handsome.... (*archly*) You like Cosette, non?

> MITTY (*with a laugh*): Ra-ther.

As she holds up her mouth coquettishly for a kiss,

64 DISSOLVE TO: INT. WALTER'S BASEMENT—FULL SHOT. Walter, still facing the open furnace door, the poker in his hand, is slowly coming out of the daydream. Coming onto the landing above is MRS. MITTY.

> MRS. MITTY: Walter! (*failing to win his attention*) Walter!! (*he regards her vacantly*) Will you please come up here! Your milk toast is getting soggy!

WALTER, still in the mood of the dream, uses the hot poker like a British officer's swagger stick and slips it under his armpit saying:

> WALTER: Righto.

The poker burns him and he drops it and hollers. MRS. MITTY stares, a strange look on her face.

65 FADE OUT. FADE IN—EXT. PERTH AMBOY STATION —DAY—MED. SHOT—WALTER AND HIS MOTHER. She is rushing WALTER to the train which is about to pull out. CAMERA TRUCKS WITH THEM as they hurry across platform. WALTER, his briefcase under one arm, the garden rake and a bundle under the other, is trying desperately to scribble last-minute reminders in his little black memorandum book as his mother fires them at him.

> MRS. MITTY: ...Puppy biscuit, shoe polish, paper doilies and—and—what else?

> WALTER (*busy scribbling*): Snapdragon seeds.

He drops the rake and, as he bends to pick it up, drops the bundle. His mother retrieves them.

> MRS. MITTY: If you'd gotten up on time, you'd have *made* the 7:15. (*shoving bundle under his arm*) There was no reason for you to oversleep—

WALTER: I had to stay up and read those proofs for Mr. Pierce.

MRS. MITTY (*pushing him toward train*): Take a cab from the station. (*as he boards*) Never mind the expense. I'll take it out of your allowance.

67 INT. MOVING TRAIN—CLOSE SHOT—WALTER. Seated, staring out the window, the bundles on the seat beside him. There is a relaxed expression on his face.

68 MED. SHOT—AT END OF CAR. A girl enters from the adjoining coach, glances back over her shoulder nervously, then proceeds down the aisle, searching for an empty seat. The girl, ROSALIND VAN HOORN (Virginia Mayo), is strikingly beautiful, with sapphire eyes and golden blonde hair. She is wearing a dress of emerald green that enhances rather than conceals the lissome lines of her figure.

She stops at the empty seat beside WALTER and looks down inquiringly at the bundles.

WALTER: Oh—pardon me.

He quickly switches the items to his lap and the girl sits down beside him.

69 CLOSE SHOT—ROSALIND. She again glances back over her shoulder nervously and starts at something she sees.

70 MED. SHOT—END OF CAR. A squat, unattractive man with pale grey eyes has just entered from the coach behind. Seeing no seat available, he opens his newspaper and stands reading.

71 MED. CLOSE—WALTER AND ROSALIND. ROSALIND quickly turns her eyes straight ahead. WALTER gets his first good look at her. He stares, open-mouthed. The girl, in some strange manner, *bears a general resemblance to all the girls in his daydreams!* She flushes under his intent regard. WALTER realizes he is staring impolitely, turns toward the window, but slowly his eyes wander back to her face.

72 CLOSE SHOT—THE PALE-EYED MAN. Ever so slightly, we see his glance lift from the newspaper and go to the girl down the aisle. The train slows and we hear the conductor's voice OVERSCENE.

CONDUCTOR'S VOICE: Manhattan Transfer!

73 WIDER ANGLE. As the conductor passes the man and proceeds down the aisle.

CONDUCTOR (*calling*): Manhattan Transfer!

Several passengers rise as the train grinds to a stop.

74 MED. SHOT—ROSALIND AND WALTER. As the conductor passes, calling the station. ROSALIND seems to make an impulsive decision. She rises swiftly, glances over her shoulder once more to see if the pale-eyed man is watching, then, for his benefit, turns a beaming smile on WALTER, *bends over and kisses him full on the mouth!*

ROSALIND (*loudly to* WALTER): Goodbye, darling. Have a nice day at the office.

WALTER is too stunned to speak. All he can do is gape.

ROSALIND (*patting his cheek*): See you at Mother's tonight.

With a wave, she heads down the aisle and disappears. WALTER stares after her, open-mouthed. He touches his lips unbelievingly.

75 CLOSE SHOT—THE PALE-EYED MAN. He hesitates a moment, folds his newspaper and slides casually down the aisle after the girl in green.

76 DISSOLVE TO: EXT. MANHATTAN RAILROAD TERMINAL—CAB STAND. Commuters are hurrying through scene. Among them is WALTER, glancing nervously at his watch. Laden with briefcase, rake and packages, he starts for an unoccupied cab down the line, but stops as he comes abreast of one of the taxis. The girl in green is seated inside, looking anxiously out of the window, as WALTER comes face to face with her.

WALTER (*startled*): Hello.

ROSALIND (*seeing him*): Oh—hello.

WALTER: I thought you got off at—

ROSALIND (*quickly*): Just pretended to. I was trying to avoid a masher.

WALTER (*flushing*): I'm terribly sorry if I gave the wrong impression—I mean I—

ROSALIND: Oh, it wasn't you. (*brushing him off with a prop smile*) But I appreciate your coming to my assistance. Thank you.

WALTER: You're welcome. (*he takes the small gloved hand she proffers*) Well—goodbye.

ROSALIND scarcely hears him. She looks over his shoulder and suddenly stiffens.

77   LONG SHOT—FROM HER ANGLE. The pale-eyed man has just sauntered onto the taxi ramp and is looking about.

78   MED. CLOSE—ROSALIND AND WALTER. WALTER releases her hand and is about to turn away, when she *suddenly grabs his lapels and kisses him again.*

ROSALIND: Oh, darling, you shouldn't have done it.

WALTER: Huh?

ROSALIND (*gushing*): It's the loveliest bracelet in the world. Come on, we'll go to the dressmaker's together.

She opens the door and practically yanks the bewildered WALTER into the taxicab.

78A CLOSE SHOT—THE PALE-EYED MAN. He sights ROSALIND and WALTER and starts moving towards them, then stops in frustration.

79   INT. MOVING TAXICAB (PROCESS). It has pulled away, and WALTER has landed beside ROSALIND, still clutching the rake and his other burdens.

WALTER (*bewildered*): Another masher?

ROSALIND doesn't answer. She is looking through the rear window. She turns and addresses the driver.

ROSALIND: Pier 47, North River, driver!

CAB DRIVER: Pier 47, yes ma'am.

WALTER: Excuse me, but I've gotta get to work. I'm late. (*glancing at watch*) It's a quarter to nine!

ROSALIND: I'll drop you off. Where do you go?

WALTER: Pierce Building. Forty-third and Madison.

ROSALIND (*to driver*): The Pierce Building first, driver.

As the driver nods WALTER notices that ROSALIND is staring at him intently.

WALTER: What's the matter?

ROSALIND: You've got a good face.

WALTER (*drawing back a little*): Well—er—you've got one too.

ROSALIND (*with a smile*): Don't be alarmed, I'm not going to kiss you again.

WALTER: Oh, I wasn't thinking of that.

ROSALIND: I think I can trust you, Mr.—er—

WALTER: Mitty. Walter Mitty.

ROSALIND: My name is Rosalind Van Hoorn.

WALTER: That's a nice name.

ROSALIND: Mr. Mitty, I need your assistance. Will you help me?

WALTER: Me? How?

ROSALIND: I'm on my way to meet the Gripsholm. I'm being followed and I'm frightened. Please come with me.

WALTER: You're—frightened?

ROSALIND: Yes.

WALTER: And you—you want *me* to help you?

ROSALIND: Yes.

WALTER (*overcome*): Gosh.

ROSALIND: I'm sure I wouldn't have to worry if you were along.

WALTER (*expanding*): Well, I guess I can handle myself in a pinch. I do a little boxing at the "Y" and, believe me, I'd like to see any masher try to—

ROSALIND: You're very kind, Mr. Mitty. (*peremptorily to driver*) Never mind the Pierce Building, driver. Go right to the Gripsholm.

WALTER (*carried away*): Yes, never mind the Pierce Building— (*he breaks off abruptly as reality floods back*) What am I saying! I can't, I'm late for work! Stop! Stop, driver! There's my office now! (*as the cab slows down, he flings the door open and rushes out, carrying the rake and bundles*)

WALTER (*over his shoulder*): Goodbye!

87 EXT. STREET—OUTSIDE PIERCE BUILDING. WALTER dashes toward the entrance, then stops and runs back to the taxicab. He opens the door and thrusts a bill at ROSALIND.

WALTER: Here's my share of the cab ride. I hope you get there all right

He closes the door and watches the cab pull away. There is a wistful expression on his face, as though he might have liked to follow this strange encounter to its conclusion. He sighs, looks at his watch again and starts into the building making a motion to put his briefcase under his arm—then reacts in consternation. The briefcase is gone! The elevator starter, smoking a cigarette on the sidewalk, watches Walter's agitation.

ELEVATOR STARTER: What's the matter, Walter?

WALTER (*panicky*): My briefcase—I left it in that taxicab! It had all the proofs to Air Aces. Mr. Pierce'll kill me!

He thrusts the rake and bundles into the elevator starter's arms and motions to a waiting cab.

WALTER: Taxi, taxi! (*to driver as cab pulls up*) Pier 47, North River—the Gripsholm!

88   DISSOLVE TO: EXT. STREET—AT ENTRANCE TO PIER 47. WALTER's cab pulls up and he alights. He quickly pays the driver and rushes up to a uniformed taxi starter.

WALTER (*breathlessly*): Excuse me—did you see a girl in a green dress? She came here in a cab to meet the Gripsholm and it had my briefcase in it. I didn't see the driver's face, but the back of his head was sort of oblong. (*he illustrates with his hands*)

STARTER: Give me that again.

WALTER: Listen, I'm in an awful hurry. Which cab was she in?

STARTER: I don't know, but you're welcome to look. (*he points off*)

89   LONG SHOT—LINE OF WAITING TAXICABS. Hundreds of them, all alike.

90   MED. SHOT—WALTER AND STARTER. WALTER's face falls. Desperately, he turns and hurries toward pier entrance.

91   WIPE TO: IMMIGRATION OFFICIAL'S DESK—CLOSE SHOT—PASSPORT WALLET HELD IN OFFICIAL'S HANDS. The picture is that of a middle-aged Dutchman. The name reads: Carl Maasdam.

MAASDAM'S VOICE (*with an accent*): Carl Maasdam, Rotterdam.

91A MED. SHOT—OFFICIAL—ROSALIND AND CARL MAAS-
DAM. ROSALIND's companion walks with a little difficulty, indi-
cating a convalescence of some sort. He wears a voluminous ulster,
a knitted scarf and tinted glasses. She is holding him by the arm.
OFFICIAL (*taking declaration coupon from wallet*): Okay, Mr.
Maasdam.

CAMERA TRUCKING, ROSALIND and MAASDAM leave the roped-
off area, a porter wheeling luggage behind them. As they reach
the street, MAASDAM takes a monogrammed silver cigar case from
his pocket and extracts a cigar. His fingers tremble slightly as he
tries to light it. ROSALIND takes the matches from him and holds
one to his cigar.

> MAASDAM: Thank you, my dear. (*he takes a satisfied puff and
> glances around*) So this is the United States of America.

> ROSALIND (*smiling*): There's plenty more of it outside (*taking
> his arm*) Come on, Carl. Uncle will be so glad to see you.

> MAASDAM: No more delighted than I'll be to see *him*. (*shakes
> his head*) It's incredible. I can't believe he's living. When they
> bombed Rotterdam, everybody thought he was—he was—

> ROSALIND: You'll find Uncle Peter very much alive.

They exit through door to street.

92 EXT. STREET AT PIER ENTRANCE. As ROSALIND and MAAS-
DAM emerge. MAASDAM glances around rather apprehensively.

> MAASDAM: You're quite sure you came here unobserved?

> ROSALIND (*reassuringly*): Now, Carl, you mustn't trouble your-
> self any more. You're in safe hands now.

She motions off and the same taxicab she took to the pier pulls
into SCENE. The driver hops out and holds the door as ROSALIND
helps MAASDAM inside. Suddenly there is a shout from OFF-
SCENE.

> WALTER'S VOICE: Hey—wait!

ROSALIND turns, startled, as WALTER enters breathlessly.

> WALTER (*panting*): My briefcase—I left it in your cab. I followed
> you all the way down here—

> ROSALIND (*relieved*): Oh, I'm sorry I put you to all that trouble.
> (*as* MAASDAM *looks on questioningly*) Mr. Maasdam, this is
> Mr. Mitty.

MAASDAM (*holding up briefcase from inside cab*): Is this what you're looking for, young man?

WALTER: Yes, thanks.

He starts inside eagerly, but ROSALIND has his arm.

ROSALIND: Please, we're in a dreadful hurry. Would you mind helping the driver with the luggage?

WALTER: But I—I'm— (*he glances at his watch dubiously*)

ROSALIND: We can drop you off.

WALTER: Okay, sure.

He picks up a couple of suitcases, ROSALIND a small handbag, and they proceed to rear of cab where the driver and the porter are busy shoving a large steamer trunk into the baggage compartment.

93   CLOSER SHOT—AT REAR OF CAB. The porter goes out of scene, leaving WALTER and the driver to stow the final pieces of luggage. As they are thus engaged, with their heads thrust into the compartment, a strange sound is heard, a sort of "Click!"

WALTER: What was that?

DRIVER: What?

WALTER: That click.

DRIVER: I didn't hear nothin'.

WALTER shrugs and passes it off.

94   INT. CAB—CLOSEUP—MAASDAM'S HAND. The hand slips a little black book into WALTER's briefcase.

94A EXT. TAXICAB—ANOTHER ANGLE. ROSALIND tips the porter, who exits. WALTER joins her as they enter the cab, the driver taking the wheel. As the cab pulls away

95   WIPE TO: INT. MOVING CAB (PROCESS). MAASDAM is seated between ROSALIND and WALTER. ROSALIND is still rather tense and keeps glancing out of the window. WALTER is looking at his watch nervously. MAASDAM seems to be tired and dozing, his chin sunk into his chest.

WALTER: Sorry to keep rushing you like this, but our whole next issue is in here. (*indicating briefcase*) I'm in the publishing business. (*getting no answer*) We put out thirty magazines.

He still gets no answer. MAASDAM's head droops onto his shoulder.

WALTER embarrassedly moves over.

WALTER (*to* ROSALIND): He must be pretty tired.

ROSALIND (*busy glancing out window*): Yes, he's had quite a trip.

MAASDAM's head still rests on WALTER's shoulder. WALTER squeezes further into his corner.

WALTER (*politely to* MAASDAM): Am I crowding you? (*to* ROSALIND) Guess he fell asleep.

MAASDAM's heavy wool muffler is tickling WALTER's nose. He tries to push the man's head away, but it falls back onto his shoulder. WALTER is very embarrassed and, since there is no further space for him to squeeze into, he tries to straighten the man up. As he does, MAASDAM *slumps to the floor and lies inert*. A stifled scream from ROSALIND accompanies WALTER's bewildered stare.

ROSALIND: Carl!

WALTER's eyes half pop out of his head. A slowly widening crimson stain is spreading over the white shirt front of the man on the floor! ROSALIND bends over the man, feeling his pulse. She looks up at WALTER, whitefaced.

WALTER (*paralyzed*): Is he—is he—

ROSALIND (*nodding dumbly*): Stabbed.

The little black book that MAASDAM dropped into MITTY's briefcase contains a list of hiding places in which art objects from the Royal Netherlands Museum in Rotterdam were placed for safekeeping before the war. Friends of the Royal Netherlands Museum and of its curator, PETER VAN HOORN, ROSALIND's uncle, are trying to keep the list from falling into the hands of an unscrupulous villain named WILHELM KRUG, better known as "The Boot."

Partly by accident and partly by his inability to resist ROSALIND's "sapphire" eyes, MITTY becomes a central figure in the plot of the hidden museum pieces. KRUG's two sinister helpers, HENDRIK and DR. HOLLINGSHEAD (Boris Karloff) pursue him methodically throughout the rest of the story.

MITTY discovers that he has the book while he is trying to buy some puppy biscuit in the pet shop of a department store. At the same time he discovers that he is being pursued by HENDRIK, the killer. In his flight MITTY passes through (1) a ladies' fitting room, and the lingerie department, where he hides the book in a black corset lying on the counter and marked for delivery to a MRS. FOLLINSBEE, (2) a meeting of the board of directors of the Pierce Publishing Company, where with one of his pigeon friends he makes a disastrous diversion, (3) his own office, where he escapes DR. HOLLINGSHEAD only by climbing around on the ledge outside of the building.

After these adventures MITTY goes home to a party which includes not only his fiancee, GERTRUDE, and her mother, but TUBBY WADSWORTH as well. TUBBY is MITTY's rival for GERTRUDE's affections, a practical joker and clown. He makes MITTY a present of a book which when opened shoots flour all over the place. While playing bridge with TUBBY, who always wins games, MITTY drifts off into a dream of himself as Gaylord Mitty, fearless gambler and habitué of the Mississippi River packets. He gambles for Colonel Tubby Wadsworth's fiancée (Rosalind), and when Colonel Tubby attempts to draw a pistol, Mitty nonchalantly takes it away from him with a flick of his gold-headed cane. He then releases Rosalind from Colonel Tubby's bargain and gives her back the title to her plantation, announcing that Fort Sumter has been fired on and his regiment leaves at dawn.

On the following day MITTY again encounters the real ROSALIND. As a friendly gesture she gives him two little golden Dutch shoes that were on the chain with her car keys. When she learns what he has done with the book she leads him on a search for MRS. FOLLINSBEE, who turns out to be the manageress of a style salon. ROSALIND has to pose as a model and wear the black corset in order to get the book. MITTY, caught in a flurry of women, fades off into a dream in which he appears as Anatole Mitty, famous *couturier,* and snaps back to consciousness only when ROSALIND slips the black book in his hand and darts back stage again.

Because of rain, GERTRUDE and her mother spend that night as guests of MITTY's mother. ROSALIND secretly enters the house and calls MITTY downstairs by playing "Beautiful Dreamer" on the piano. ROSALIND removes her dress in order to dry it by the fire and sits in the kitchen in her slip. There ensues a series of awkward encounters in halls and on stairways. WALTER gets ROSALIND away undetected, however. They go to deliver the book to ROSALIND's uncle, PETER VAN HOORN, but ROSALIND discovers at the last moment that Uncle Peter is an imposter; in fact, he is himself The Boot. She hides the book in a desk drawer. The Boot drugs MITTY with a glass of brandy and makes a prisoner of ROSALIND.

When MITTY awakens he is turned over to his mother and MR. PIERCE. The Boot (alias VAN HOORN) tells them that MITTY's story is an illusion, one of MITTY's daydreams, and recommends that he be taken to a psychiatrist. The psychiatrist to whom he is taken is DR. HOLLINGSHEAD.]

267x-1   INT. HOLLINGSHEAD'S OFFICE. DR. HOLLINGSHEAD leads the apprehensive WALTER toward a couch. On a nearby wall, clearly visible, is a large portrait of Whistler's Mother.

HOLLINGSHEAD (*indicating couch*): Now just lie down here and make yourself comfortable. (WALTER *hesitates*) Go ahead.

WALTER (*nervously*): Can't you examine me standing up?

HOLLINGSHEAD: It's necessary for you to be completely relaxed. (*indicating couch*) Please.

WALTER lies down but remains suspiciously rigid.

HOLLINGSHEAD: Now, my boy, close your eyes—(WALTER *closes one eye*) The left one too. (WALTER *closes his left eye but opens the right one*) Now tell me just what is troubling you.

CLOSE SHOT—WALTER. He hesitates, then sighs and speaks haltingly.

WALTER: Well—the day before yesterday I met a girl. She looked like all the girls I've ever dreamed about...

268x-1   INT. HOLLINGSHEAD'S OFFICE—CLOSE SHOT—HOLLINGSHEAD. Looking down at WALTER.

WALTER'S VOICE:...And when I woke up, he said he had no niece. She was gone.

HOLLINGSHEAD: What about the black book?

268x-2   MED. SHOT—THE TWO.

WALTER: That was gone too.

HOLLINGSHEAD: Was it in your possession when you came to the house?

WALTER: Well, I thought I gave it to Mr. Van Hoorn's niece —but he says he has no niece. (*he opens his eyes suspiciously*) Why are you asking me these things?

HOLLINGSHEAD: Because, as a psychiatrist, I must know your innermost mental processes. (*he crosses to his desk as* WALTER *sits up*) Tell me, Mr. Mitty, what business are you in?

WALTER: I'm a proofreader—at the Pierce Publishing Company.

HOLLINGSHEAD: I see. Well, I think I can diagnose your trouble. You're suffering from a romantic delusion, aggravated by overwork and incessant daydreaming.

WALTER (*slowly*): You mean—I dreamed the whole thing?

HOLLINGSHEAD (*nodding*): Don't you see, Mr. Mitty? You've obviously been affected by all those pulp magazines you're continually proofreading.

WALTER: I have?

HOLLINGSHEAD: You've been frustrated all your life, so you live in your daydreams. You imagine yourself the hero about to rescue the heroine from the villain. Just like those lurid covers, you get fantastic ideas. The heroine is always in danger. She is tied to a chair, bound and gagged—

WALTER (*wistfully*): But she was so—so real. She had the prettiest mouth and—when she touched me I—I got hot and cold—

He suddenly breaks off as the door to an adjoining room swings ajar.

268x-3   WALTER'S ANGLE—SHOOTING INTO ADJOINING ROOM. ROSALIND is tied to a chair, bound and gagged! She is struggling to free herself.

268x-4   CLOSE SHOT—WALTER. His jaw sags.

WALTER: Rosalind!

268x-5   MED. SHOT. The door to the other room swings closed. WALTER rushes to the door, flings it open and stares into the other room.

268x-6 INT. ADJOINING ROOM—WALTER AT DOOR. It is empty. There is no trace of ROSALIND or the chair she sat in.

268x-7 MED. CLOSE—WALTER. He is stunned. HOLLINGSHEAD joins him at the door.

HOLLINGSHEAD (*kindly*): What's the matter?

WALTER: I—I just saw her. She was—sitting over there. (*almost sheepishly*) She was bound and gagged.

HOLLINGSHEAD shakes his head and sighs, leading him back to:

268x-8 INT. OFFICE.

HOLLINGSHEAD: I'm afraid, my boy, you're in love with a girl who doesn't exist.

He gives WALTER's shoulder a consoling pat. WALTER stands looking back pathetically at the spot where ROSALIND was.

WALTER (*almost inaudibly*): They were right. I daydream too much.

HOLLINGSHEAD: Exactly, my boy. And this can lead to all sorts of serious complications. Why I had a patient in here last week suffering from the same type of romantic delusion.

WALTER: You did?

HOLLINGSHEAD: The poor man was in bad shape. No matter how a woman was dressed, he fancied he saw her in a bathing suit. Scopophilia—an extreme case, of course.

WALTER (*nervously*): Of course.

They have crossed back to desk by this time. HOLLINGSHEAD presses a buzzer. A beautiful nurse enters, clad only in a scanty bathing suit. WALTER stares wide-eyed as the nurse goes to the desk. HOLLINGSHEAD doesn't react at all.

HOLLINGSHEAD: Miss Appleby, bring me those Wilcox charts, will you please.

NURSE: Certainly, Doctor.

As she starts to leave, HOLLINGSHEAD regards her sternly.

HOLLINGSHEAD: Oh, Miss Appleby, there's a spot on your uniform.

NURSE: Sorry, Doctor. I'll change immediately. (*she goes out.*

WALTER *is staring*)

WALTER (*uncertainly*): Doctor, did—did she really have a spot on her uniform?

HOLLINGSHEAD: You saw it, didn't you?

WALTER: Well, I—er—(*laughs nervously*) Sure I saw it. An ink spot.

HOLLINGSHEAD: Mercurochrome.

WALTER: Oh, yes, mercurochrome. Looked like red ink. (*fumbling*) I—er—it was hardly noticeable—

HOLLINGSHEAD (*leaning forward tensely*): *You didn't see any uniform!*

WALTER breaks down completely and blubbers.

WALTER: You're right. I saw her in a bathing suit. Oh Doctor, Doctor, I've got Scopophilia! What shall I do?

HOLLINGSHEAD: My boy, what you need is a good long rest.

WALTER: Well—I'm getting married tomorrow.

HOLLINGSHEAD: Capital! Go home and marry your Gertrude and forget everything. I'm sure you'll be a changed man.

WALTER: I—I feel better already.

As HOLLINGSHEAD leads him to the door, he looks up at the portrait of Whistler's Mother and reacts with great shock.

268x-9 CLOSE SHOT—PORTRAIT. The grey-haired old woman seated in the rocking chair is clad in a scanty bathing suit.

[Himself convinced that his mind is playing him tricks, MITTY returns to his suburban nonentity. WALTER and GERTRUDE meet at the altar, but in his mind there is the image of ROSALIND. At the correct moment he gropes in his pocket for the ring, but finds instead the little Dutch shoes that ROSALIND gave him. He dashes out of the chapel, commandeers a flower truck, and starts for VAN HOORN's house.

While waiting for a traffic light to change, he sees a cowboy riding along the street wearing a sign advertising a rodeo. He immediately fades into a dream of Slim Mitty, the Perth Amboy Kid, sworn enemy of Toledo Tubby. He saves a damsel from Toledo Tubby, shoots a gun out of his hand, and is engaged in giving him a spectacular beating when the honking of cars starts the chase to save the real ROSALIND going again.

The villains in The Boot's house see him approaching, but decide to let him find ROSALIND in the hope that when she sees him she may become excited and tell them where she has hidden the black book.

MITTY climbs into a window of the house and a chase begins. He finds ROSALIND and they run into and out of one trap after another. Finally caught, MITTY is saved by the arrival of two policemen looking for the man who stole the flower truck. MITTY and ROSALIND manage to persuade the policemen to arrest the real criminals. MR. PIERCE arrives to add to the general uproar.

They are leaving the house when TUBBY, MRS. MITTY, MRS. GRISWOLD, and GERTRUDE, with a coat over her bridal gown, burst in through the door.]

II (Cont.)

WALTER (*to group*): Oh, I'm glad you came. (*indicating* ROSALIND *excitedly*) You see, Gertrude, she *does* exist. Now do you understand why I ran out on the wedding?

GERTRUDE stares horrified.

TUBBY (*stepping forward belligerently*): I understand, you two-timer! You see, ladies, I was right all along.

He jabs an accusing finger at ROSALIND, who reacts in surprise.

MRS. MITTY (*terribly upset*): Oh, Walter, how could you?

WALTER (*going to* MRS. MITTY): Wait a minute, Mother. Rosalind can explain everything—she was with me every minute—

MRS. GRISWOLD: So! All the time you've been making advances to my daughter and carrying on with this—this Jezebel!

ROSALIND (*angrily*): Jezebel! Walter, what is this all about?

WALTER (*trying to pacify* MRS. GRISWOLD): Mrs. Griswold, you don't understand. It was entirely innocent. Remember the time I was out all night?—And you thought I was crazy... (*triumphantly*) Well, I was with *her*—(*he indicates* ROSALIND)

All react in horror at WALTER's ill-advised explanation.

MRS. MITTY (*starting to sob*): Oh, Walter, to think that we should hear these things on your wedding day!

WALTER (*going to* MRS. MITTY): Mother, you've got it all wrong...

ROSALIND (*to* MRS. MITTY): Mrs. Mitty, this is all very embar
rassing. Walter never even told me he was being married.

GERTRUDE (*furiously, to* WALTER): Oh, you didn't! Walte
Mitty, you're nothing but a two-faced, sneaking—thing!

PIERCE (*holding up his hands for silence*): Quiet! It's all ver
simple. Fortunately this has been harmless. The girl has bee
living here with a gang of crooks—

MRS. GRISWOLD: A gun moll!

ROSALIND: But I didn't realize it—

PIERCE: Tut, tut— (*continuing*) Walter was being used whil
the girl was in trouble, and I'm sure she has no further design
on him.

TUBBY (*putting his arm around* GERTRUDE): Why don't yo
let him do his own alibiing?

ROSALIND (*furiously*): How dare you! All of you!

Mortified, she runs out the front door.

WALTER: Rosalind, wait!

He starts after her, PIERCE takes his arm.

PIERCE (*aside*): Let her go. You're well rid of her.

MRS. GRISWOLD (*to* WALTER): Go on, run after her, you—yo
milk drinking Casanova!

TUBBY: Milk? I'd like to see what he drinks when he's out wit
that blonde.

GERTRUDE: She's a bleached blonde! (*to* WALTER) You filth
drunkard!

MRS. MITTY: Oh, why did you do it, Walter? I've always trie
to bring you up well—I've always tried...

MRS. GRISWOLD (*snorting*): You can't make a lily out of a ra
weed.

Suddenly WALTER squares his shoulders. He turns toward his to
mentors with jaw thrust forward.

WALTER: SHUT UP—ALL OF YOU!

A shocked silence falls over the group.

MRS. GRISWOLD: Well!...I never thought I'd be insulted on n
daughter's wedding day! Oh, I could hide my face in sham

WALTER: If I had your face, I'd hide it too! And while you're at it, do the same thing with those hats.

They all gasp. MRS. MITTY looks stunned.

MRS. MITTY: Walter!... I'm absolutely speechless!

WALTER: Congratulations, Mother—

TUBBY (*advancing on* WALTER *belligerently*): I ought to punch you right in the nose!

WALTER (*disdainfully*): Oh, pipe down, Lardface.

And WALTER, with an open hand, shoves TUBBY in the face and sends him sprawling to the couch where he lands, astonished and cowed. GERTRUDE lets out a scream and rushes to TUBBY to protect him.

WALTER (*quietly—confidently*): Now you're all going to listen to me. For years I've been listening to you, and you almost had me in a straitjacket. Your small minds are all muscle-bound with suspicion. That's because the only exercise you get is jumping to conclusions. You ought to be ashamed of yourselves— every one of you!

PIERCE: Now, hold on, Mitty! I don't think—

WALTER: You never think, brother.

PIERCE (*roaring*): What!

WALTER (*his nose right under* PIERCE's): The only good idea you ever had was to hire me to do your thinking for you!

As all eyes look in astonishment at the new WALTER.

312x DISSOLVE TO: INT. PIERCE PUBLISHING COMPANY— CLOSE SHOT—GLASS PANELED DOOR. A workman is lettering on the door the words: "WALTER MITTY—ASSO- CIATE EDITOR." He is adding the last "R."

WALTER'S VOICE: Associate Editor.

313x MED. SHOT—DOOR TO WALTER'S NEW OFFICE. MR. PIERCE is displaying it to the proud and happy gaze of WALTER. On WALTER's arm is ROSALIND, obviously Mrs. Mitty. He opens the door with a grand gesture, allowing WALTER to enter ahead of him.

PIERCE: Go ahead, take a look at it, Walt.

314x INT. WALTER'S NEW OFFICE. It contains an impressive
mahogany desk, etc. WALTER beams.

> PIERCE: Well, "Cowboy Stories" has to meet its deadline..
> (*smiling, he indicates the galley proofs on desk*) Let's get on
> the ball, Walt, old man.
> WALTER (*briskly*): Right you are—er—Bruce.

GUIDE QUESTIONS

1. Are Mitty's daydreams essential to the screenplay? In what way are
   the daydreams made to function in the plot?
2. In what ways is the character of Walter Mitty in the screenplay dif
   ferent from the character of Walter Mitty in Thurber's story?
3. What is gained by the carry-over of Mitty's dreams into reality? For
   example, his using the hot poker as a swagger stick?
4. What other formula than that of the worm that turns could have been
   used in the containing action?
5. What indicates that Mitty is so completely reformed in the screenplay
   that he will never daydream again?
6. By what criteria were the dream sequences in the movie selected from
   all the possible dream sequences that might have been used? What
   evidence is there that the choice of them was influenced to some extent
   by the fact that the picture was to be filmed in color?
7. By what criteria could you determine whether the conflict of the story
   as a whole is physical or psychological?
8. How does the real Rosalind differ from her dream-world counterpart?
9. Summarize Thurber's story and Goldwyn's scenario, allowing one para
   graph for each. Try to indicate in the two summaries the essential dif
   ferences of value and treatment.

VOCABULARY

Give the derivations and definitions of the following words:

*mizzen, spinnaker, batten, lissome, bulkheads, cowering, deftly, motley
derring-do, cubicle, ritual, rummage, talons, sanctum, brusquely, beatific
opinionated, addicted, effusively, glumly, gumption, drone, lethal, burnoose
delectable, alpaca, retrieve, gape, sidle, frustration, consternation, panicky
apprehensively, dubiously. inert.*

Samuel Goldwyn

LETTER TO *LIFE*

SIRS.

I am delighted that you chose my production of *The Secret Life of Walter Mitty* as the "Movie of the Week" in your Aug. 4 issue and that you consider Mitty's dream life to be "highly entertaining" since this is a picture which is designed for entertainment. I was, however, somewhat startled at your statement that Jim Thurber "grows almost profane when he thinks of how his story has been corrupted." Either Mr. Thurber has been misquoted or has in the past year done as complete a switch as ever Walter Mitty did from real life to dream world.

As I need not tell you, the original story, "The Secret Life of Walter Mitty," is a pure gem, which added great luster to the little magazine in which it was first published. However, in order to convert such a gem into a feature length motion picture it is necessary first to elaborate it into a screenplay.

I must confess that in the preparation of the screenplay I departed quite completely from traditional Hollywood policy by constantly consulting the author of the story itself. Ken Englund, one of the co-authors of the screenplay, made a special trip to New York to get from Mr. Thurber his ideas as to how the screenplay should be handled. I, of course, was only too happy to get Mr. Thurber's ideas and to pay him for them. After they had finished, Mr. Thurber wrote me a long letter in which he detailed his delight at the way the story was handled. Let me quote:

"It was a great pleasure to work with a man as intelligent and skillful as Ken Englund and I want to thank you for giving me the opportunity to do so. It isn't often that I meet a man whose ideas and whose sense of story so beautifully coincide with my own."

From *Life*, August 18, 1947. Reprinted by special permission of Samuel Goldwyn.

That hardly leads me to believe that Jim Thurber thinks that hi story in being translated to the screen has been corrupted.

And when it appears from your review that Mitty's real life ad ventures are so exciting as to bring about a result in which "the delicat point of Thurber's story is lost," all I can say is that Jim Thurber saic in that same letter:

"The melodrama still remains the spine of our structure, but I fee and so does Ken Englund, that it no longer sticks out, but that it ha been ingeniously interlaced with the dreams and the private life o our hero."

At that time, at least, Jim Thurber knew that there was a lot t learn in translating a story to the screen, for he concluded that lette by saying:

"I feel that I have learned a great deal in a short time about som of the problems that face a motion picture producer and a motion pic ture writer. Let me thank you again for selecting Ken Englund t work with me on this story and let me say once more that I am en thusiastic about this picture."

This account would not be complete, however, if I were not to ad that on March 15, 1946, just before we were to start shooting, we sen Mr. Thurber a copy of the shooting script, telling him "we would b delighted and grateful to have any suggestion or idea you may hav on the script." On March 25th we received the following telegran "WRITING AIR MAIL LETTER CONTAINING A FEW MINOR SUGGESTIONS BU NO MAJOR OPERATION AS SCRIPT SEEMS IN EXCELLENT SHAPE. THURBER."

And finally, on April 10th, Mr. Thurber wrote us, "Don't think tha I fail to realize how difficult it is going to be to follow Walter Mitt with something as good."

James Thurber is much too fine a man to be saddled with anythin but his own words. That is why I have quoted so extensively froi what he, himself, has actually said about the way we handled his story

And now—like Mitty, The Undefeated—with a faint, fleeting smi playing about my lips, I face the firing squad of your reporters an researchers; erect and motionless, proud and disdainful, inscrutabl to the last.

SAMUEL GOLDWYN

HOLLYWOOD, CALIF.

James Thurber

LETTER TO *LIFE*

SIRS:

I wonder why Samuel Goldwyn, Inc., erect, motionless, jaw thrust out, guard down, assumes it is the reporters and researchers of *Life* who have him backed against the wall. The challenge is for me, and I gleefully accept it, in spite of my opponent's choice of that obsolete weapon of controversy, the excerpt-lifter.

On or about Nov. 25, 1945, Mr. Goldwyn brought to New York a completed 160-page script of "Mitty" by Everett Freeman and Ken Englund. Creative work had begun Jan. 2, 1945, and in the ensuing ten months several story treatments and a screen play were rejected by Mr. Goldwyn. Mr. Freeman alone for a few weeks, then with Miss Czensi Ormonde for a week or so, and from then on with Mr. Englund, developed the story line. During this vital period my counsel, criticism, and collaboration were never once sought.

I was confronted by a set story line appallingly melodramatic for poor Walter. An absolutely new and different story line was called for, but the shooting schedule, the budget, and the few days allotted to me would not permit of this. The miracle expectancy of Mr. Goldwyn is as famous as his inability to comprehend the problems of writing. He told me the first sixty pages were all right and asked me not to read the last 100 pages, which he said were too "blood and thirsty." I read the entire script, of course, and I was horror and struck. Mr. Goldwyn expected me to remove the blood and thirst without reading it but somehow to preserve the melodrama. It was a task for wizards, stated in the wondrous dialectic of Oz.

Beginning Dec. 3, 1945, Ken Englund and I worked six hours a day for ten days on an impossible assignment. We could not take out the melodrama but we could attempt to cover it up with additional dream

From *Life*, August 18, 1947. Reprinted by special permission of James Thurber.

scenes and other devices. The letter from which Mr. Goldwyn quotes about the "spine" was several pages long. I wrote that a courtroom dream and a firing squad dream like those in my original story, together with a dozen other suggestions I made, might obscure or at least dilute the melodrama.

Mr. Englund took the fruits of our collaboration back to Mr. Goldwyn, who sent me a telegram dated Dec. 26: "HAVE JUST SPENT ENTIRE DAY WITH ENGLUND LISTENING TO YOUR IDEAS AND SUGGESTIONS WHICH I THINK ARE BRILLIANT.... YOUR SINCERITY AND INTEREST IN THIS STORY ARE VERY GRATIFYING TO ME FOR AS I TOLD YOU IN NEW YORK I WANT THIS STORY TO HAVE THE REAL THURBER FLAVOR. I THINK YOUR SUGGESTION FOR THE COURTROOM SCENE IS BRILLIANT AND CAN DEVELOP INTO A GREAT COMEDY ROUTINE...."

On Jan. 7 I wrote Mr. Goldwyn: "I have great confidence that Ken Englund can do that scene well because ... he seemed to have understood thoroughly both the courtroom scene and the firing squad scene." Between Jan. 7 and the middle of March, when I received the completed screen play as of that date, I had expressed in letters to Mr. Englund my fears that the new dream scenes so important to Walter and Ken and me would somehow not be used, and that my efforts to eliminate the lamentable psychiatrist scene which I had carefully rewritten would go for naught. I had also heard that Mr. Kaye's wife, Sylvia Fine, was opposed to the new dream scenes, especially the firing squad scene, on the ground that "they slowed up the story." On April 1 I wrote Mr. Goldwyn's Pat Duggan as follows: "To say that dreams slow up the story is to say the locomotive slows up the cow.... I will personally undertake to thrash anyone who mangles the dreams. They are wonderful."

On April 4 Mr. Duggan wrote me: "We do appreciate your suggestions and we are doing our best to correct the elements in the script that disturbed you." Between March 20 and April 10 I sent in numerous ideas, each accompanied by wistful and futile praise of the Englund-Thurber arrangements, designed to save what I could out of the looming wreckage. On April 10 I wrote a letter to Mr. Duggan about 1,200 words long and it is from this that Sam Goldwyn, Inc. quotes merely: "Don't think that I fail to realize how difficult it is going to be to follow 'Walter Mitty' with something as good." In reply to this letter Mr. Duggan wrote me on April 19: "Thanks ever so much for your letter of the 10th with the added scenes—we're shooting them."

Next to the worry about our new dream scenes, the greatest fear of Mr. Englund and myself was the possibility that this movie might be spoiled by one or more of Mr. Kaye's and Miss Fine's famous, but to me, deplorable scat or git-gat-gittle songs. Mr. Englund and Mr. Freeman and myself had strongly suggested that Mr. Kaye's song in the RAF scene be *Molly Malone*. Our hopes and prayers were doomed to be shattered. Mr. Goldwyn lifted the song and substituted what is to me an utterly horrifying, shockingly out-of-taste-and-mood piece of scat. Another dream scene was written and shot, in which Mr. Kaye did sing *Molly Malone*. Members of Goldwyn, Inc. have told me it was a charming and effective dream. In audience tests it did not produce the shock or embarrassment laughs which Goldwyn, Inc. loves but does not understand and the scene was cut out, along with the courtroom dream and the firing squad dream. My defeat was complete.

In fairness to Mr. Goldwyn, I am happy to say that he insisted on every one of the Englund-Thurber ideas being incorporated in what turned out to be the next-to-last script. Ken wrote me: "He is sincerely anxious to put Thurber on the screen. He is absolutely sincere, of that I am convinced." This next-to-last script ran to nearly 180 pages. It was out of the final shooting script and the movie made from it, however, that almost everything I had written, suggested and fought for was dropped. On Nov. 13, 1946, I wrote Ken Englund: "I heard Danny Kaye and his wife on *We, The People* some weeks ago and she said, 'It is based on a story by James Thurber,' and then she added in a low voice, 'was.' Since so much that you and I put in was taken out and so much that we took out was put back in, I was pleased when I heard that the picture was to be called by another name, any other name. . . ." My beloved new dream scenes had been dropped, the operation dream had been hammed up, the RAF scene had been ruined by scat, the psychiatric scene had not only been restored, but it finally contained a bathing girl incident which will haunt me all the days of my life.

I salute again the gifted, overwhelmed Ken Englund, the skillful Everett Freeman, long since in the doghouse for a brave, face-to-face appraisal of the Goldwyn sense of humor, and the sensitive but frustrated director, Norman McLeod. The incredible Sam Goldwyn and the talented but obedient Danny Kaye prove in the first thirty minutes of *The Secret Life of Walter Mitty* that they could have made a movie both financially and artistically successful. Lord have mercy on them. Sorry, Walter, sorry for everything.

JAMES THURBER

WEST CORNWALL, CONN.

P.S. This letter was written by Jamie Thurber, aged 52, without help of his parents or teacher. "The little magazine," so much bigger than Goldwyn, Inc., except in physical size, needs no other defense than the revealing slur itself.

GUIDE QUESTIONS

1. What is the real point on which Goldwyn and Thurber differ?
2. What was Goldwyn's opinion of Thurber's story? What is the effect of the last paragraph of his letter?
3. What does Goldwyn seek to prove in his letter?
4. What does Thurber seek to prove in his letter?
5. What is the device of the "excerpt-lifter"?
6. What explanation can you offer for Thurber's desire to eliminate the psychiatrist scene?
7. What difference of opinion between Thurber and Goldwyn is revealed by Thurber's discussion of the "git-gat-gittle" number in the RAF scene?
8. What is Thurber's general opinion of the melodrama of the containing story?
9. What does Thurber mean by a "story line"? Does he oppose the elaboration of a story line in the screenplay?
10. What does Thurber mean by his comment on Sylvia Fine's opposition to additional dream scenes? What other means might he have used to refute her?

VOCABULARY

Give the derivations and definitions of the following words:

luster, fleeting, disdainful, gleefully, collaboration, confronted, appallingly, melodramatic, allotted, thrash, wistful, deplorable, appraisal, slur.

WRITING AND STUDY AIDS

PATTERN OF ORGANIZATION SUGGESTED BY THE GENERAL TOPIC:

This assignment calls for the elaboration of consequences after a stated cause. Differences between the two versions of the story, or differences of opinion between Goldwyn and Thurber, may be regarded as the complex effects of a simple cause.

The cause of these differences should be defined first. It may be defined as the influence of highly publicized, type-cast actors, as the essentially commercial nature of the motion picture industry, as the character of motion picture audiences, as the sensitivity of an author for the integrity of his work, as the comic inventiveness of Goldwyn and his writing staff, or as the basic differences between the media of words and pictures.

Development of an essay in terms of antecedents and consequences is a mode of rhetorical "proof." In effect, the essay will be an argument designed to establish your explanation of the differences of opinion between Thurber and Goldwyn. Why did they disagree? Give the reasons that seem to you most fundamental. These reasons should lead naturally to a detailed account of their apparent causes and effects as shown in the story and the scenario.

ASSIGNMENTS:

Short themes:

1. A dramatization of the courtroom dream
2. The character of Walter Mitty
3. Another story line for Walter Mitty
4. The formula of the turning worm
5. The movie audience—ideal and actual
6. Movie stars and actors
7. The dream scenes
8. Another daydream for Walter Mitty

Long themes:

1. Author *versus* producer
2. Thurber *versus* Goldwyn
3. The Hollywood theory of comedy
4. The media of words and pictures

✒ The Case against the Comics

NO ONE DENIES THAT THE COMICS, FOR BETTER OR WORSE, HAVE BECOME firmly entrenched in American life. Both young and old read them. The question is whether they are for better or worse, especially in the case of the young. A lively debate is in progress as to whether the comic strip and comic book diet of American youth is a harmless diversion or a corrupting influence. The participants in this debate are educators, psychologists, municipal authorities, criminologists, radio commentators, publishers, cartoonists, parents, and other assorted experts and amateurs. Although a considerable and growing body of writing has been produced on the problem, both pro and con, no verdict is in sight. Meanwhile the comics continue to flourish.

In order to understand a controversy it is necessary to know what the people on both sides take as a starting point. If we know that, we can anticipate where they will arrive, and we should even be able to predict, in a general way, the route they will follow in getting there. The reason for this is that the starting point of a discussion depends on the assumptions that are made to begin with, and the assumptions that are made to begin with set limits to the course of the discussion and determine where it will lead. An assumption, then, is the point at which argument begins; it is an unproved principle or theory adopted as a basis for discussion. Whatever the assumption is, once it has been adopted it commits the person adopting it to a definite view which he then maintains, if anyone disputes his assumption, with all the resources of argument at his command.

The four readings for this assignment illustrate the fundamental part played by assumptions in argument, specifically, in the debate over the comics. In all of them you will observe that what is assumed to be the truth about the influence of the comics becomes a guiding principle which the writer uses as the groundwork of his developed discussion. All of them attack the comics, but at the same time they make clear the main lines of argument on both sides of this controversy. And the assumptions on which the attacks are based differ in important ways that must be noted. Lawrence Kessel's study of "Some Assumptions in Newspaper Comics" rests on a number of implied assumptions of its own. So you will see here a double set of assumptions at work, those in the comics and those of an educational psychologist studying them. John Mason Brown is a dramatic critic, writer, and lecturer; he is also a perturbed parent, and it is chiefly in this role that he writes in "I Hate the Comics." Marya Mannes, in "I Hate the Comics, Too," makes two points: comics are a waste of time, and ugly. Frederic Wertham's essay, "The Comics—Very Funny!" gives the view of a clinical psychologist who sees a causal connection between comic books and juvenile delinquency. Does he prove his case? Are his assumptions plausibly and carefully developed? These are questions to ask and answer as you read each of the essays. The basic assumptions in any piece of controversial writing should be watched, for it is upon them that the structure of the argument is grounded. When a writer's initial assumptions are fully understood, the relevance of what he is saying—of what he is obliged to say—becomes apparent. As you read each of these selections, try to formulate and keep clearly in mind the primary assumption from which the argument, in each case, proceeds.

Lawrence Kessel

SOME ASSUMPTIONS IN NEWSPAPER COMICS

A NUMBER OF CONCLUSIONS almost force themselves upon the investigator of newspaper comics. It seems clear that the ideas, values, and attitudes expressed in the comics mirror our time and reflect opinions held by large numbers of people. They are, perhaps, a kind of social history and a definite part of our culture. In keeping with this theory is the statement of "Aunt Het," a cartoon character. Aunt Het criticized one of her neighbors, a teacher, thus:

From *Childhood Education,* April, 1943. Copyright, 1943, by Association for Childhood Education. Reprinted by permission of the author and the publisher.

Bill is a highbrow, with a lot of college degrees, and I reckon he's smart in some ways; but his being too snooty to read the comic strips is just plain silly. How can he teach history like it was important if he feels above the history we're making? Folks that dig up our civilization are going to learn more about us from our comic strips than by looking at ruins.

The purpose of this study was to determine specifically what were the assumptions in newspaper comics. Assumptions were defined as those attitudes, values, or beliefs which are represented as being commonly accepted but which, if critically considered, might be questioned. No attempt has been made to say whether the assumptions are bad or good, sound or specious; frequently they are a little of both. The important thing is that they are assumptions accepted uncritically by children.

The assumptions were found in (1) soliloquies by characters, (2) conversations between or among characters, (3) general intimations that were not verbally expressed but were implicit in attitudes underlying action or were expressed in the drawing.

The daily comics of four Chicago newspapers were examined from June 24, 1941, to October 30, 1941—a period of seventeen weeks. This was the summer preceding the entrance of the United States into World War II, and the comics clearly reflected a feeling of impending crisis. The investigation was concluded at this time because relatively few new assumptions were appearing but those previously noted were beginning to reappear. The newspapers in which the comics appeared were the Chicago *Tribune, Daily News, Herald-American,* and *Daily Times.* After two months' study of the comics it was noticed that the basic assumptions could be grouped into convenient categories, five of which are discussed here: race and nationality, morality and ethics, government and politics, education, and socio-economics. Assumptions grouped under the headings of love and marriage, masculinity and femininity, and manners were also found but space does not permit their presentation here.

RACE AND NATIONALITY. Very definite attitudes were expressed in the newspaper comics concerning race or nationality. Although Americans were regarded as the greatest people in the world, the English were also looked upon with respect. The white race was regarded as superior, although American Indians were also given certain admirable qualities. The following assumptions are those concerning race and nationality:

That strange and foreign customs of other peoples are necessarily inferior to our own. That American ways are better than foreign ways. The chief evidence of narrow patriotism and hatred and distrust of foreign people was found in the general attitudes of "Don Winslow," "The Phantom," "Buck Rogers," "Tim Tyler's Luck," and "Scorchy Smith."

That Orientals are an especially sinister and sadistic race. In "Chief Wahoo" an Oriental "moon-faced fiend," who was also referred to as a "slant-eyed ape," tortured the hero. In "Terry and the Pirates" an Oriental hung Burma from the ceiling by her arms. He refused her anything to drink and offered her only crackers to eat.

That the English are the most honorable of European peoples. The only foreigners looked upon with any admiration were the English. Cleo, the beautiful and very intelligent niece of Mr. and Mrs. Nebb, came to the United States as a refugee from England. Her beauty, charm, and refinement were frequently mentioned.

In "Abbie an' Slats" Mr. Groggins invented a very powerful explosive which was offered to the British government, but the humanitarian attitude of the British was seen in the statement by a delegate from the British high command who said, "Gentlemen!!! We have examined your formula!! It is certainly the most devastating explosive known to man! If our country used it in the war, it might become known, in turn, to the enemy and used by him. Therefore, in the interests of humanity—the formula must be destroyed!!! We will pay you $100,000 for it!!"

That America is the greatest country in the world. Spunkie, the little refugee boy, wrote in his letter, "Over here, 'old glory'—'the red, white and blue'—'the stars and stripes'—they *all* names of the American flag—but believe me, no matter which one you say, you talking about the greatest flag of the greatest country in the world—America!"

That Indians are people superior in dependability and courage. Indians were held in great admiration in the newspaper comics. An especially clear example occurred when the Oriental character in "Chief Wahoo" tried using physical force to obtain information from the little Indian chief but found his efforts in vain. He said, "So stupid of me! Had forgotten red man's ability to endure pain! But white man has less will-power!" Again, Tonto, in "The Lone Ranger," was a brave and dependable character and the Indian princess, Minnie-ha-cha, was a beautiful and brave girl.

That Negroes are inferior. All Negroes were stock stereotypes of ignorant, superstitious colored people. Much more was implied in the way they were drawn than by what was said. Never did they appear as social equals to white men, and never did they appear in any of the skilled trades, professions, or more respected positions. They appeared only as porters, garbage collectors, washwomen, and clean-up men.

MORALITY AND ETHICS. Rather simple and naive attitudes toward good and evil appeared in the newspaper comics. They are, however, attitudes which are fairly common in the minds of people in general. Here are some of them:

That it is right and natural for those who have been wronged to seek revenge. Many of the plots centered about the quest of some wronged person for revenge. It was apparently believed that there should be some kind of balancing, or evening, of pain for pain. It was never satisfactory to let a wrongdoer go unpunished.

That criminals can be recognized by characteristic physical stigmata. That character can be judged by physical appearance. Persons who were corrupt, who represented the underworld, or who were in any other way undesirable were usually ugly and deformed. Women spies were the only exceptions to this rule.

That we should obey laws because if we don't we shall be punished. The comics assumed that rigorous measures must be taken to keep society under control. They seemed to indicate that this control must be derived from some dominant power, since it is entirely the law at present that keeps men from misbehavior. The apparent assumption was that people conform to laws and certain social patterns because they fear the consequences of violating them.

That all people are either good or bad. All of the characters were either admirable or evil. Those that were evil had no redeeming virtues, and those that were good never erred.

GOVERNMENT AND POLITICS. *That such terms as "democracy," "liberty," "American way," "Americanism," and "un-American" have definite meanings that are self-evident.* These terms were used very frequently and very loosely. Apparently it was assumed that they had a specific meaning for all people. In many cases their use seemed forced, the main purpose being to get them into the lines regardless of the context. The terms "refugee," "tourists," and "alien" were abused in many of the comics by their close relationship in use with "saboteur," "fifth columnist," and "spy."

That America is a land of equal opportunity for all people. An example of this illusion appeared in "Ramblin' Bill" when the hero started off to look for work and said, "Now to find a job. This is a land of equal opportunity and that's all I need."

That American government is today unqualifiedly and completely democratic. Qualifications or limitations of the term "democracy" were never made. Democracy in the United States was frequently mentioned, but it was regarded as a completely existing state rather than an ideal or limited condition.

That in our society today the law provides the best method of settling disputes. In "Mary Worth's Family" Tom Kane pleaded with the Boomville workingmen who had been unjustly treated by Mayor Gribble: "But this is a *democracy* we live in and there are *legal* ways of handling men like Gribble! Now keep your shirts on and I'll tell you how we can cook his goose without fire!" In general, the newspaper comics held a simple faith in the power of the law as the maintainer of harmony and good in the world.

That World War II was caused by the ambitions of a few power-mad dictators. In "Joe Palooka" there appeared this example: "To think that a few power-mad dictators can upset the normal lives of all decent people." Again in "Buck Rogers" a rather allegorical expression of this idea appeared. It was, of course, set in terms of the twenty-fifth century, A.D. "Madwolf Hetlah, dictator of Mars! It seems impossible that one lunatic could cause so much misery!"

EDUCATION. In general it can be said that the newspaper comics took a so-called "practical" point of view on matters of education and the arts. Some of the assumptions were:

That higher education outside of professional training is interesting but useless. It is interesting to note that in "Gasoline Alley" Skeezix did not go to college but learned from the school of experience. Nina went to business college for about six months after graduating from high school and from there to a job in a doctor's office.

In "Abbie an' Slats" Sir Bertram Bedlam of Alexandria, Egypt, sent his old friend, Mr. Groggins of Crabtree Corners, an Egyptian mummy as a token of their long friendship. When Groggins received it he did not know what to do with it, but was advised to "Put it in a cool place and forget about it. It's useless but educational."

That culture is a personal quality which can be acquired through certain activities. A rather superficial definition of culture was implied in the comics. It was assumed to be a kind of veneer which can be acquired for oneself by attending lectures or going to college. It was regarded as having a certain feminine quality and as being an endeavor followed primarily by women. In "The Nebbs" Mr. Nebb was proud of his niece, Cleo, who had just arrived from England, where she had graduated from Lady Margaret's Hall. Speaking of her, Mr. Nebb said, "She's a nice girl—the manner with which she meets folks is so graceful and assured. . . . She has education, culture, and poise."

That serious literature and the great books are dull reading material. In "Terry and the Pirates" Burma was horrified when she found that the only reading material available consisted of such things as Gibbon's *Decline and Fall of the Roman Empire,* a *Complete Shakespeare,* and poems by Keats.

That works of art are an expensive, impractical extravagance. In "Chief Wahoo" a good example of this common belief was found. It occurred in a strip in which the little Indian chief, Wahoo, and Steve Roper were forced to take shelter in an art gallery to escape a sudden cloudburst. As they looked over the pictures Steve remarked, "Well! Some nice work in here, Wahoo. 'Cows Grazing, price $200'!" To this remark the always sagacious little Indian replied, "Paleface fulla prunes! For that much wampum, can buy cows that give milk!" And upon seeing a statue of a Greek god he remarked, "Ugh! Could make lotta arrow-heads outa all that stone!"

That scientists are sinister. Scientists and science were regarded as something mysterious, esoteric, and all-powerful. People engaged in science were usually evil and abnormal persons, often physically imperfect. References were made frequently to "criminal scientist," "scientists of sudden death," and "sinister scientist."

SOCIO-ECONOMICS. The social and economic ideas expressed in the comics reflect bourgeois ideals of ambition, independence, and respectability. However, the fact that cartoonists are a well-paid group and that newspapers are a "big business" should be kept in mind.

That if one does his work faithfully and well, he is sure to be successful. That ability is what makes for success. This belief was seen in Skeezix's remark, "As poor as my chances look here, I'm going to follow through. If I can't make a place for myself that will be worth something, it will be my own fault." And Uncle Walt assured him, "If you go ahead with your work the best you know how, there is nothing to worry about." In "Mary Worth's Family" Mary Worth encouraged Connie Barclay, saying, "You're an intelligent girl. I'm sure you can find some sort of work!"

That if a man really wants to work he can find a job. In "Tillie the Toiler" this remark was found: "His name is Whay and he's a lug who managed to stay on relief three years."

That it is a shameful thing to accept charity. In "Harold Teen" Veronica explained to Timothy, "Poor Mother couldn't accept charity. She's so proud. She must never know you are willing to help us."

That if a man has money he is worth considering in matrimony. In "The Nebbs" a woman remarked about young, rich Stuyvie Swagger, "He's a good catch for some girl. I understand they have a lot of money." Again in "Winnie Winkle" Mr. Winkle charged his married daughter with the scandalous act of having lunch with another man. But when Winnie explained, "Dan Manley is president of the national bank," he replied, "President of the bank? Say, why don't you ask him over for dinner?"

That social and economic status is fixed and one should not step out of his class. In the strip called "Little Annie Rooney" Annie's old sailor friend, Captain Ezra, explained, "There's nothing wrong about working but if folks saw a doctor digging a sewer or a judge driving a coal wagon, they'd be shocked, not because they were working, but because they weren't working at their own jobs. When you get a mite older you'll learn that unless you stay in your own little rut or groove, folks will think you're a crackpot. An ant can work and be respected, but if a butterfly ever worked, his family would disown him!"

That we should live simply, regardless of the luxury we can afford. That the simple things in life are best, and that happiness is independent of material comforts. Mrs. Gump made the trite but beautiful-sounding remark, "Money never buys happiness and the lack of it never chases real joy from the hearts of true lovers." Annie Rooney would gladly have given up her luxurious home with Captain Jim if she could have had apple dumplings, chocolate cake, and cookies in the simple home of Captain Ezra and his wife. Interestingly enough, it later turned out that the simple-living Captain Ezra "could buy and sell most of the folks in this town."

That the industrial leaders of the nation are altruistic in their war efforts. In "Little Orphan Annie" Bill Slagg took the place of Warbucks while the latter was ill. While looking over the financial reports of the Warbucks corporation, he remarked: "Gad! Millions! More millions! But every penny accounted for. Receipts—costs—where's the profit? There must be a cut for the manufacturer. Ah, here it is— chicken feed—and what's this? Even *this* little profit is all turned back into the plant. Then it's true. Warbucks claimed he wasn't making a dime out of all this. I didn't believe him. Few others did either, I'm sure. His *personal contribution* for preparedness, he said." Capitalism was taken for granted in the newspaper comics. The kind and generous Daddy Warbucks has, of course, symbolic value as the self-made, gruff, but big-hearted business man.

That financial independence develops along with chronological maturity. The assumption that at a certain age a young man or woman becomes independent and from that time does not need and should not accept further financial support from parents was seen especially in "Gasoline Alley," where Skeezix and Nina were examples of such independent and self-reliant people.

That rich people are snobbish, lazy, and have bad habits and manners. "Little Annie Rooney" presented this notion most persistently, although "The Nebbs" and "Winnie Winkle" also expressed this idea. Besides snobbishness and idleness, the rich were associated with marital difficulties and drinking in excess.

That the employer has no responsibility toward his employee's security. Mr. Casper's employer sold his firm and made these farewell remarks to his former employees, "The new boss will take charge today. I hope he'll keep all of you on here but, of course, I can't vouch for that."

To eliminate the worst of the newspaper comics would probably be impossible now, and if it were possible, it would still be no solution. The problem is deeper and more basic. If there is violence, restlessness, immorality, and narrow-mindedness in the comics, radio programs, books and magazines, one should look for the causes in society today. Attempts to promote "nice" comics are only screens that may hide temporarily the real problems but do not solve them. A real cure can only come through basic social changes in the areas that cause immorality, war, crime, violence, and ignorance. It is here that education can play its part. It can help children to learn to think and to think critically. It must teach them to be, above all, intellectually honest and alert. Assumptions may not in themselves be bad; everyone makes assumptions, but it is important that we help children to recognize assumptions when they are made and to think about them critically. It is hoped that this study may be a tool for steps in that direction.

GUIDE QUESTIONS

1. What is the advantage of the classification and presentation of the material under the five headings used?
2. Find the dictionary definition of *assumption* which is closest to Kessel's definition of the term. How do the two differ?
3. Kessel's basic assumption is that "the comics mirror our time and reflect opinions held by large numbers of people." Tell why you agree or disagree.
4. Another assumption made by Kessel is that the assumptions in newspaper comics are "accepted uncritically by children." Attack or defend this idea.
5. "No attempt has been made to say whether the assumptions [in newspaper comics] are bad or good . . . frequently they are a little of both." Mark the assumptions that are listed with a B, G, or LOB depending on whether you consider them bad, good, or "a little of both."
6. What additional assumptions can you detect in Kessel's final paragraph?
7. Discuss the essay as a piece of social research work: aims, procedures, conclusions.
8. Examine the comic strips in one or more of today's newspapers, or over a period of several days. What assumptions in the five categories discussed in this essay can you clearly identify? What other assumptions do you observe?

VOCABULARY

Give the derivations and definitions of the following words:

specious, soliloquy, intimation, implicit, impending, sinister, sadistic, humanitarian, stereotype, stigmata, context, allegorical, superficial, sagacious, esoteric, bourgeois, altruistic.

John Mason Brown

I HATE THE COMICS

THE COMICS, ALAS, like death and taxes, are very much with us. And, to my way of thinking, they are equally unfunny. Why they are called comics, when people who read them—young and old—almost always look like undertakers, eludes me. But we'll let that pass, just as most of us as parents have had to let comics pass into our homes—against our wills, against our wishes, against our better judgment.

I love comedians, the highest and the lowest. I love cartoons, too. My allergy to comics, however, is complete, utter, absolute. I know there are bad comics, and I presume there are good comics. I have read a few of both—under protest. But I regret them both. I deplore them. And, to continue the understatement, I abhor them. So far as I am concerned, they might just as well be written in a foreign language for which no dictionary has ever been published. I wish they had been.

Let me quickly admit that I am low enough, and sometimes defeated enough, as a parent, to make use of comics. I mean in desperate moments when, of a rainy Sunday morning or afternoon, I want peace in the home. Or when I am traveling with my two sons on a train and need to subdue them. Then—yes, I'll confess it—then I do resort to comics. Without shame, without conscience. On such occasions I don't so much *distribute* comics as I *administer* them to my sons. Much as a barkeep would pour out a Mickey Finn, or a doctor employ a hypodermic. As knockout drops for unruly children, as sedatives, as Maxim silencers comics do have their undeniable uses. This much I'll concede gratefully.

I'll also grant that so long as other people's children read comics we have scant hope, and perhaps less right, to keep our own from doing so. It would be unfair for us to deny to our children what is now a group experience and, when they have grown up, will have become a group memory of their generation.

From *The Saturday Review of Literature*, March 20, 1948. Reprinted by permission of the publishers.

If I hate the comics, I have my reasons. I know that, as part of a healthy diet, everyone needs a certain amount of trash. Each generation has always found its own trash. I doubt if our grandfathers were harmed by the dime novels about Kit Carson, Jesse James, etc., on which they fed. I doubt, too, if Little Nemo, Mutt and Jeff, Foxy Grandpa, Buster Brown, or the Katzenjammer Kids did serious damage to those of my vintage when we read them once a week.

Give me Henty, *The Rover Boys, The Motor Boys,* or *Tom Swift on the Mississippi,* or any books written in words for those who can read, any day in preference to the comic books. The comic books, however, as they are nowadays perpetually on tap, seem to me to be, not only trash, but the lowest, most despicable, and most harmful form of trash. As a rule, their word selection is as wretched as their drawing, or the paper on which they are printed. They are designed for readers who are too lazy to read, and increase both their unwillingness and inability to do so.

I won't and can't deny that comic books fascinate the young as, in terms of pigs, rabbits, rodents, morons, hillbillies, and supermen, they tell their illustrated stories. But, as a writer, I resent the way in which they get along with the poorest kind of writing. I hate their lack of both style and ethics. I hate their appeal to illiteracy and their bad grammar. I loathe their tiresome toughness, their cheap thrills, their imbecilic laughter.

I despise them for making only the story count and not the *how* of its telling. I detest them, in spite of their alleged thrills and gags, because they have no subtlety and certainly no beauty. Their power of seduction, I believe, lies in the fact that they make everything too easy. They substitute bad drawing for good description. They reduce the wonders of the language to crude monosyllables, and narratives to no more than printed motion pictures.

What riles me when I see my children absorbed by the comics is my awareness of what they are not reading, and could be reading; in other words, my awareness of the more genuine and deeper pleasures they could be having. To compare Bugs Bunny or Donald Duck with *The Jungle Book* or even *The Travels of Babar;* to set Wanda, the Wonder Woman against *Alice in Wonderland,* or Batman and Robin, Dick Tracy, and Gene Autry against *Treasure Island,* Li'l Abner against *Huck Finn* or *Tom Sawyer,* or Superman and Captain Marvel against Jules Verne or *Gulliver's Travels,* is to realize that, between the modern cave-drawing (which a comic book is) and a real book, a good book, there is—to put it mildly—a difference. A tragic difference, which is hard on the young and may be harder on the future.

Anatole France once described even the best books as being "the opium of the Occident." Well, most comics, as I see them, are the marijuana of the nursery; the bane of the bassinet; the horror of the house; the curse of the kids; and a threat to the future. They offer final and melancholy proof that, even among the young, the mind is the most unused muscle in the United States.

I don't care how popular comics are with the young or, worse still, with the old. They seem to me to be sad proofs of arrested under-development. Time in the modern world is no longer something to be wasted. The moment has overtaken us, whether we like it or not, and most of us do not, when as a people we must grow up. In order to grow up, we must put behind us that fear of the best and that passion for the mediocre which most Americans cultivate.

GUIDE QUESTIONS

1. The first two paragraphs state Brown's position very forcefully. Do they give any explicit reasons for his position?
2. In the third and fourth paragraphs, what two concessions are made to defenders of the comics? Why are these concessions of no comfort to the opposition?
3. Why does Brown defend "trash"? What difference does he see between harmless trash and harmful trash? Is the difference valid?
4. What is Brown's main reason for attacking the comics? What method of organization is used in developing this reason? What assumptions underlie it?
5. Show that although the essay is humorous its purpose is serious.

VOCABULARY

Give the derivations and definitions of the following words:

sedative, vintage, despicable, rile, bane, bassinet, mediocre.

Marya Mannes

I HATE THE COMICS, TOO

I'M ALL IN FAVOR of adults looking at comic strips in the newspapers
—it keeps them from *reading* the editorials. And since, by some curious
coincidence, the most popular strips are neighbors of the most irresponsible press, this is an excellent thing. The strips save people from contamination and also from thought—a maturing process which is
definitely un-American.

My fight is against the power of comic books over children, because
I consider them first and foremost a colossal waste of time—the infinitely precious time of growth. A child grows by learning, by playing, and by dreaming. Comics supply none of these needs. They do not
teach, unless you consider education a series of facts coated with the
laxative of fiction. They're not play, because the child is passively
reading them. And they kill dreams.

They kill dreams by presenting the child with ready-made images
and ready-made ideas that leave him nothing to create by himself.
They do not stimulate imagination; they substitute for it.

Comics replace fantasy, which is the soul of a child, with contrived
formulas of an adult mind which knows a good business when it
sees one—the business of selling 40,000,000 comic books a month to
children who cannot discriminate.

Comic books are not only a waste of time, but a waste of eyesight.
With few exceptions, comics are very ugly—bad in drawing, bad in
color, bad in print. The human beings in them are ugly even when
they're meant to be handsome. Stalwart young men with coat-hanger
shoulders and nutcracker jaws are travesties of the male. The bosomy,
over-painted and abysmally vulgar women are travesties of the female.
The so-called funny characters are merely repulsive.

The crime and horror comics are not only ugly in appearance, but
ugly in thought. Oh, yes, they make it clear that crime doesn't pay.

From America's Town Meeting of the Air, March 2, 1948, on the ABC network.
Used by permission of The Town Hall, Inc.

They are full of righteous conclusions and sentiments, where right triumphs and wrong is punished, but right triumphs by force and violence; right triumphs by the fist and the gun. The impact of the fist on the jaw is the comic's law. It is an ugly law.

Comics language is, in the main, ugly. It perverts the English language with slang, with sloppy contractions, with bad grammar. It is the speech of the vulgar and the illiterate; or, at the other extreme, so stilted in an effort towards correctness that it becomes laughable. I'm all for laughing, but I choose my comedy.

There are, of course, exceptions. It would be dishonest to deny the harmlessness of some—the Disney comics, a few westerns, some teen-age strips, or the charm and humor of a strip like "Happy, the Humbug." It would be dishonest to deny the efforts of some others, like *True Comics,* to supply the child with truth instead of horror. It would be dishonest to deny the homespun comedy of Li'l Abner or the gentle satire of a strip like "Mr. and Mrs." In measured doses, these can supply the relaxation and entertainment to which a child has every right.

But the doses are not measured. Comic books are the addiction of three out of four American homes. In one out of three American homes they are virtually the only reading matter. Repeat, the *only* reading matter. Forty million children are growing up with this kind of nourishment. The comics are not food; they are a drug.

They are killers—killers of time. What an indictment of our time that it has to be killed! What an indictment of a way of life that a child has nothing better to do than read comics!

I know by heart the arguments of the defense. Comics, they say, supply a universal human need for adventure, for excitement. They are merely today's version of yesterday's dime novels or the fairy tales of the past. Nonsense, even the cheapest dime novels our fathers read as boys demanded the ability to read and to imagine. As for fairy tales and legends, they are the accretions of human experience. They are not the commercial stencils of businessmen in syndicates.

The defense will say comics give an outlet to the aggressive needs of children. Nonsense, the aggressive needs of children can be satisfied far more naturally by a game of prisoner's base. Comics are not an outlet; they are a sublimation.

The final triumphant argument for the defense is that comics give people what they want, therefore they are all right. Fine; children want to go to the movies every day, listen to the radio all night, and never go to school. Is that all right?

I say it is not.

I say with Mr. Brown that the comic book is the greatest opiate on the market. I say that, with few exceptions, it is a killer of time and a killer of the imagination.

I believe it keeps a child from the joy of reading, the excitement of thought, and the happiness of play.

I believe that a steady, uncontrolled and indiscriminate diet of comic books can stunt a child's mental and spiritual growth just as much as a steady malnutrition can stunt his physical growth.

Those who make comics may not be in the business for their health, but they should be in it for our children's health. Until they are, they stand guilty of more than taking candy from a baby; they are taking imagination from the child—and that's a crime.

GUIDE QUESTIONS

1. What assumptions concerning the education of children underlie the main criticism made here?
2. How do Miss Mannes's concessions differ from Brown's?
3. What assumptions underlie "the arguments for the defense," as given here?
4. What is the effect of the statements beginning "I know," "I say," "I believe"? What evidence is given in support of what Miss Mannes "knows," "says," and "believes"?

VOCABULARY

Give the derivations and definitions of the following words:

coincidence, contamination, fantasy, discriminate, travesty, abysmal, addiction, indictment, sublimation, opiate.

Frederic Wertham, M.D.

THE COMICS . . . VERY FUNNY!

AN ANXIOUS MOTHER consulted me some time ago. Her four-year-old daughter is the only little girl in the apartment house where they live. The boys in the building, from about three to nine years old, hit her, beat her with guns, tie her up with rope whenever they get a chance. They hit her with whips which they buy at the circus. They push her off her bicycle and take her toys away. They handcuff her with handcuffs bought with coupons from comic books. They take her to a vacant lot and use her as a target for bow and arrow. They make a spearhead and scare her. Once, surrounding her in this way, they pulled off her panties to torture her (as they put it). Now her mother has fastened the child's panties with a string around her neck so the boys can't pull them down.

What is the common denominator of all this? Is this the "natural aggression" of little boys? Is it the manifestation of the sex instinct? Is it the release of natural tendencies or the imitation of unnatural ones? The common denominator is comic books.

I examine in the clinic a boy of eleven, referred to me because he fights in school and is inattentive. He says:

I buy comic books every week. They kill animals, sometimes they kill people. One of the girls is the best fighter. Sometimes they tie her up and sometimes they put her in a snake cave so that the snakes would kill her.

I examine a boy of fourteen referred to the clinic for stealing. I ask him: "Do you think your stealing had anything to do with the comic books?" He answers: "Oh, no. In the comic books it is mostly murder."

A boy of seventeen is referred to me by the Juvenile Aid Bureau because in an argument he stabbed a boy of thirteen in the right arm "with full intent." He says: "I don't read many comic books—only

bout ten a week. I like crime comics. Sometimes they kill the girl.
n one of the books the girl wanted more money so they stabbed her
a the back." Was it "full intent," or was it perhaps imitation that
notivated him in his own actions?

A boy of thirteen is a problem at home and at school. He is a
eal comic-book addict. He says: "They have some kind of guns that
noot out a ray and kill a lot of people." Is that a natural fantasy?
s that a penis symbol? Or is it a kind of reality that a lot of adults
read now and which these kids will have to face sooner or later?

A boy of fifteen took a boy of twelve up a fire escape and threatened
o push him down if he didn't give him a quarter. He says: "I read
wo comic books a day." A thirteen-year-old boy is referred to me by
ne State Charities Aid Association. He was caught stealing five dollars.
When asked why he took it he confided to me that the older boys in
chool got up a gang and threatened him. If he did not get them the
noney they would beat him up. So he stole the money and gave it to
nem.

The experts of the comic-book industry tell us that what the children
ead in comic books is pure fantasy. But when I examine these many
nildren and adolescents who tell me what they read in comic books, I
sk myself with Bernardo in *Hamlet:* "Is not this something more than
ntasy?"

Think of the many recent violent crimes committed by young boys
nd girls. A twelve-year-old boy who kills his younger sister; a twelve-
ear-old boy who kills his older sister; a thirteen-year-old burglar who
perates with a shotgun; a seventeen-year-old boy who kills a thirteen-
ear-old boy and leaves a note signed "The Devil"; a public school in
ew York City where two police officers circulate on the grounds and
the corridors to prevent violence; a mathematics teacher who has
give examinations with a policeman present in the classroom; a
irteen-year-old who shot a nurse and was sent to a reformatory
where, incidentally, he will read more comic books); a gang of
dolescent bandits led by a fifteen-year-old girl; two twelve-year-old
oys and one of eleven stopping a man on the street and shooting
m with a semi-automatic; a fifteen-year-old boy third-degreed as a
spect in a murder case; three sixteen-year-old boys killing a fourteen-
ar-old "for revenge"; a New York City school where the older
upils threaten the younger ones with violence and with maiming
em, robbing them of their money, watches, and fountain pens. The

young victims don't dare tell the names of their tormentors. When two
of them were asked by a teacher, they refused to answer, saying: "W
don't want our eyes cut out." Actually one sixteen-year-old boy in thi
school was beaten with a broken bottle and cut so severely that sever
stitches had to be taken around his eyes. Adults are horrified at thi
attack. They don't know that this is old stuff for comic-book readers
In one of the "good" comic books, *Classics Illustrated,* in a rendering
of the novel by Eugene Sue, *The Mysteries of Paris,* there is a pictur
of a man tied down in a chair—a man whose eyes have been gouge
out and whose blood runs down from beneath the bandage.

A twenty-year-old youth in New York City has just killed a police
man. Is that so astonishing when he can see anywhere a typical comic
book cover showing a man and a woman shooting it out with the polic
to the accompaniment of these words: "We'll give those flatfeet
bellyful of lead"? A nineteen-year-old youth has just been sentence
to the electric chair for the murder of a girl of fifteen, despite th
jury's recommendation of clemency, by a judge who had previousl
disregarded a recommendation of mercy in the case of a sixteen-yea
old participant in a holdup with a fatal shooting. There are recer
cases where young men branded girls' breasts with burning cigarette
and carved initials into their flesh with a knife. A thirteen-year-old bo
in Chicago has just murdered a young playmate. He told his lawye
that he reads all the crime comic books he can get hold of. He ha
evidently not kept up with the theories that comic-book readers neve
imitate what they read. He has just been sentenced to twenty-two yea
in jail; while the comic-book publishers who filled his mind wit
thoughts and methods of murder, and their experts who say his readin
was good for him, continue as before.

All these manifestations of brutality, cruelty, and violence and th
manner in which they are committed—that is the folklore of the com
books.

Comic books are the greatest book publishing success in history an
the greatest mass influence on children. If I make the most conserv
tive estimate from my own researches, one billion times a year a chil
sits down and reads a comic book. Crime does not pay, but crim
comics do.

Recently while walking in one of the crowded sections of New Yor
City I saw a sign: "Saturday Morning [which is the Saturday matine
for children] Comic Books Will Be Given Out Free to the First 5(

tending." I looked to see what was playing in that movie theater that
orning. There were two horror films: "The Son of Frankenstein"
d "The Bride of Frankenstein." The posters calling attention to the
ovie showed girls in various stages of being overpowered. As I stood
ere I was reminded of the story of the little boy who was asked
1at he wanted to be when he grew up and replied enthusiastically:
want to be a sex maniac!"

There are two opinions about comic books. The one says they are
ry harmful to children; the other says they are good for the little
ddies. John Mason Brown has called comic books the "marijuana of
e nursery." The question can be put this way: Are comic books the
arijuana of the nursery or the penicillin of a happy childhood? The
ference of opinion is reflected also in the conflict in the child's mind.
iefly summarized, it is a conflict between super-ego and sub-machine
n.

What is the case *for* the comic books? Seventeen points are adduced
favor of them. It is said:

(1) That the children have their "own choice" in selecting this
rature. (Go to any candystore or newsstand, and see what other
oks you can get for ten cents. The children are bombarded with at
st sixty million comic books a month. That is seven hundred and
enty million of them a year.)

(2) That they reflect the children's minds and if there is something
ong with them, it must be the child's fault, and the child must have
en neurotic or disturbed or unstable in the first place. (That reminds
of the owner of the dog that had killed a rabbit, who claimed in
urt that the rabbit had started the fight.)

(3) That it is good for children to find release for their aggressive
ires. (Is there one sentence in Freud to indicate that it is advisable
children to see over and over again pictures of violence and
ture?)

(4) That they are educational. (Let's look at one of the much-
unted "good" comic books used as window-dressing for the whole
dustry. It would seem that no better choice could be made than the
mic-book version of the novel by Charles Dickens, *Great Expecta-
ns*. The first nine pictures of this "educational" book show a grue-
1e, evil-looking man threatening a little boy with a big knife, and
one picture the little boy is crying out: "Oh, don't cut my throat,
" Is this Charles Dickens speaking, or is it the circulation manager

of a comic-book publishing firm? As for the claim that comic boo
lead children to read the classics, many children whose confidence
have gained have told me that when they have to make a book repc
in school, they use the comic-book version for their report so that th
won't have to read the book.)

(5) That there are good comic books. (That reminds me of t
story of the polite clergyman who was asked about a bad egg whi
he had just started to eat: "Isn't it good?" "Madam," he answere
"parts of it are excellent.")

(6) That the children identify themselves with the good figures
the comic books. (That is like saying that the spectators in the Gra
Guignol who watch the rape, murder, and violence identify themselv
with the gendarme who breaks into the room a few seconds before t
curtain falls. There are comic books in which girls are bound a
burned, sold as slaves, thrown to the animals, and rescued only at t
last moment by a good and faithful elephant. Do the experts of t
comic-book industry claim that the children identify themselves wi
the elephant?)

(7) That the children don't imitate these stories. (But the incre
of violence in juvenile delinquency has gone hand in hand with t
increase in the distribution of comic books.)

(8) That comic books prevent crime and delinquency. (As a matt
of fact, we are getting to the roots of one of the contributing cau
of juvenile delinquency when we study the influence of comic boo
You cannot understand present-day juvenile delinquency if you
not take into account the pathogenic and pathoplastic influence of t
comic books, that is, the way in which they cause trouble or determi
the form that trouble takes.)

(9) That in comic books children are never threatened, killed,
tortured. (But that happens in even "good" comic books. In one con
book a little boy is stuffed into a sack with the following dialogi
"Stop struggling, in you go." And the little boy: "No . . . No . .
want my mother!")

(10) That they are good for reading. (But the emphasis is on pictu
and not on printed matter, and good teachers know that they have
get rid of comic books to make their children read real books.)

(11) That comic books make a lot of money. (They do!)

(12) That when dealing with crime the comic books show the v
tory of law and order. (But what they really show is what Marga

sborn, in her novel *The Ring and the Dream,* called "the trapped
struction of some human prey.")

(13) That comic books must be all right because they are so wide-
read. (That is like saying that infantile paralysis is all right because
many children have it.)

(14) That comic books should be left as they are, because curbing
em would mean interference with free speech. (As if censoring what
ults read has anything to do with planning for children the kind of
ding matter that will not harm them.)

(15) That the "experts" have approved of comic books, so they must
all right. (But experts are not needed, only common sense.)

(16) That comic books are socially harmless. (On the contrary, they
munize a whole generation against pity and against recognition of
elty and violence.)

(17) That comic books are a healthy outlet. (On the contrary, they
mulate unhealthy sexual attitudes: sadism, masochism, frigidity.)

It is pretty well established that seventy-five per cent of parents are
ainst comic books. (The other twenty-five per cent are either in-
ferent or misled by propaganda and "research.") Since the comic-
ok industry enjoys second-class mailing privileges, the parents, as
payers, are paying for what they do not want. The apologists of
nic books, who function under the auspices of the comic-book
siness (although the public is not let in on that secret), are sociolo-
ts, educators, psychiatrists, lawyers, and psychologists. They all agree
at this enormous over-stimulation of fantasy with scenes of sex and
lence is completely harmless. They all rely on arguments derived
m misunderstood Freud and bandy around such words as "aggres-
n," "release," "vicarious," "fantasy world." They use free associations
bolster up free enterprise.

My own clinical studies and those of my associates of the Lafargue
nic, the first carried out independently from the comic-book indus-
, and the first leading to their condemnation, have convinced me
t comic books represent systematic poisoning of the well of child-
d spontaneity. Many children themselves feel guilty about reading
m.

The worst sector of comic books is increasing and the best, if there
a best, is getting smaller. The comic-book publishers seduce the
ldren and mislead the parents. Their mass production is a serious
ger to the production of good inexpensive children's books. The

publishers of these good children's books, instead of fighting the ex
perts of the comic-book industry and decoding their "codes," lie o
psychoanalytic couches themselves, and delve into their own dream
instead of providing decent fare for the dreams of childhood.

When I recently conducted a symposium on the psychopathology o
comic books, I was blamed for not allotting more time to a represent
tive of the comic-book business who was there. I am even more guilt
than that: I once conducted a symposium on alcoholism and didn
invite a single distiller.

GUIDE QUESTIONS

1. What is the primary assumption on which Wertham bases his obje
   tions to comic books?
2. Tell why you think the examples of juvenile delinquency cited l
   Wertham do or do not constitute proof of his primary assumption.
3. Various assumptions underlie the seventeen points listed as comprisin
   "the case *for* the comic books." Analyze these assumptions.
4. Analyze Wertham's comments on the seventeen points in favor of com
   books. In which of these comments is he (a) giving evidence to refu
   a point in his opponents' argument, (b) telling jokes, (c) answerin
   one assumption with another, (d) restating his own primary assum
   tion, (e) arguing by analogy, (f) agreeing with his opponents? Noti
   that in some of his comments he may be doing more than one of the
   things. Which of these comments do you consider most effective
   argument? Least effective as argument?
5. Why does Wertham think the self-defense of the comic-book indust
   should not be admitted in this discussion? Tell why you agree or d
   agree with this point of view.
6. Comment on the effectiveness of the organization or method of prese
   tation used in the essay.
7. On the basis of your own experience with comic books, now or at
   earlier age, do you think the line of argument taken in the essay is fa
   or unfair, logical or illogical, well supported or poorly supported, prov
   or unproved? Notice that when you make these decisions it would
   possible for your opinion to involve both favorable and unfavorab
   judgments.

VOCABULARY

Give the derivations and definitions of the following words:
motivate, fantasy, clemency, folklore, super-ego, adduce, sadism, masochism, andy, vicarious, spontaneity, symposium, psychopathology.

WRITING AND STUDY AIDS

PATTERN OF ORGANIZATION SUGGESTED BY THE GENERAL TOPIC:

An *assumption,* as you have seen, is an idea or principle on which an xpository or argumentative structure may be based. It may be called the working hypothesis with which any investigation, scientific or otherwise, usually begins—a postulate or theory which must be tested by seeing where t leads. It need not depend on a visible argument. It is something to be aken for granted, *assumed.* Assumptions are indispensable; without them discussion would never get started. And they are neither good nor bad until ested by logical development to see whether they lead to defensible con- lusions. The basic assumptions on which an essay rests, and from which t proceeds, are not always expressly stated in the essay. Even if they are not expressed, however, they must be clearly understood by the author, for n assumption, by its nature, is the principle to which all the ideas and rguments in the essay should conform.

The problem of this assignment is to illustrate the effect of a single, firmly understood assumption on the development of a unified composition. You have seen how some of the assumptions made in newspaper comics were pointed out in Kessel's study, and what his own assumptions were; you have een how, in the essays by Brown, Mannes, and Wertham, basic assump- ions necessarily control and direct the course of an argument. You do not have to agree with these critics. It does not matter what assumptions made n the comics seem to you questionable, or what assumption concerning the comics as a social force seems to you the true one. What matters is that n your discussion you adopt one clear assumption, recognize its implica- ions and limits while following it through to a conclusion, and admit nothing to your discussion that is not consistent with it.

ASSIGNMENTS:

Short themes:

1. My favorite comic strip/comic book
2. A good comic/A bad comic
3. Little brother's/sister's opinion of the comics
4. Sunday at my house and the funnies
5. " 'Taint funny, McGee"/"That's a joke, son"
6. The comics and I before I could read
7. My parents' opinion of the comics
8. My first reaction to Brown/Mannes/Wertham

Long themes:

1. Some assumptions made by Kessel
2. A reply to Brown/Mannes/Wertham
3. A study of some assumptions in comic strips/comic books
4. Psychologists *versus* the comics
5. Qualified cartoonists and crackpot critics/Crackpot cartoonists and qualified critics
6. The case against the comics/The case for the comics
7. "I naturally assume that . . ."/"You illogically imagine that . . ."

READINGS FOR FURTHER STUDY.

Bender, Lauretta. "The Psychology of Children's Reading and the Comics," *Journal of Educational Psychology,* Vol. 18, No. 4 (Dec., 1944), 223-231.

Bender, Lauretta, and Reginald S. Laurie, "The Effect of Comic Books on the Ideology of Children," *American Journal of Orthopsychiatry,* Vol. 11, No. 3 (July, 1941), 540-550.

Crist, J. "Horror in the Nursery," *Collier's,* Vol. 121 (Mar. 27, 1948), 22-23 ff.

Frank, Josette. "What's in the Comics?" *Journal of Educational Psychology,* Vol. 18, No. 4 (Dec., 1944), 214-222.

Leaf, Munro. "Lollipops or Dynamite?" *Christian Science Monitor Magazine,* Nov. 13, 1948, p. 4.

Murrell, J. L. "How Good are the Comic Books?" *Parents,* Vol. 26 (Nov., 1951), 32-33.

Rhyne, Charles S. *Comic Books—Municipal Control of Sale and Distribution.* Washington, D. C.: National Institute of Municipal Law Officers, Report No. 124, 1948.

Waugh, Coulton. *The Comics*. New York: The Macmillan Company, 1947. Reviewed by William Laas, "A Half-Century of Comic Art," *Saturday Review of Literature,* Vol. 31, No. 12 (Mar. 20, 1948), 30, 39-41.

Wigransky, David Pace. "Cain before Comics," *Saturday Review of Literature,* Vol. 31, No. 30 (July 24, 1948), 19-20. Letter from a young boy answering Dr. Fredric Wertham's article.

Choosing a Vocation

A CHILD MAY ANNOUNCE TO INDULGENT PARENTS AN AMBITION TO GROW UP and be a jet pilot, a tramp, or a bareback rider in the circus. Later, after the fantasy period of occupational choices has passed, first awareness of the world of work leads the adolescent to form a tentative self-image in relation to it: doctors live in nice houses, newspaper men get to meet so many new people, engineers build great bridges, teachers enjoy some prestige in the community, Daddy and Daddy's friends are lawyers, Uncle Harry seems happy in the insurance business. At the age of twelve or fourteen young person may see himself in any of these vocations for any of these reasons. But his thinking about his career during these years—and until he finishes high school—is only tentative; he has not really decided what he wants to do. He needs competent guidance; he needs to examine his interests critically; he needs to evaluate objectively his mental ability, his aptitudes, and his personality traits. Analysis of these factors will help him to estimate his fitness for whatever field of work he is interested in, and, he is fortunate, his high school counselors will see that the analysis made. On starting college at seventeen or eighteen, he enters the period of realistic occupational choices. At first his college courses will probably enable him to explore rather widely in the liberal arts, social studies, and science. These explorations may help him to crystallize his choice by showing him what he would *not* like to make his life work, or by opening up new areas that he may want to consider. Meanwhile, lingering uncertainty contends with both external and internal pressures that tend to force crystallization of his choice of an occupation. Finally comes specification; he decides that he will go into medicine, journalism, engineering, teaching, law business, or something else. The details still have to be worked out, but the all-important decision has been made, and he is now ready to specialize in preparation for his chosen career. These, then, are the steps and the stages in a typical process of choosing a vocation.

What factors should be taken into consideration in choosing a vocation? What are the stages most people go through during the period of realistic choices in college? What can be said about premature specialization after a choice has been made? These questions are analyzed in the readings for this assignment. The factors everyone should consider in choosing a vocation, such as his physical characteristics, intelligence, interests, school grades, aptitude, and personality, are discussed by Samuel Spiegler in "People and Jobs." Most of what he has to say is a matter of common sense, but it is surprising how many young people fail to pay attention to such matters in their vocational planning. In "The Period of Realistic Choices," Eli Ginzberg studies some actual case histories in making his analysis of the three stages of occupational choice that most college students pass through between the time they are freshmen and seniors; he labels these three stages "exploration," "crystallization," and "specification." Ask yourself, as you read this revealing study, how your own "case history" compares with those Ginzberg is analyzing, and what stage you find yourself in at present. In the last of the readings, "Letter to a Seventeen-Year-Old Son," another aspect of the problem of choosing a vocation is discussed. Here is a young man facing two decisions, one of them immediate and the other long-range. Should he enlist now, or wait to be drafted; and if he goes to college and waits to be called into military service, should he begin to specialize at once in the physical sciences, the field he is almost sure to enter eventually, or should he first study the "word sciences" of language, politics, economics, and history? The thoughtful consideration of these alternatives is perhaps more urgent for young Americans today than it was in the last year of World War II, when one father whose name is unknown, for the letter is anonymous, tried to help his son by analyzing the choices open to him. In these three readings the method of analysis is applied to various aspects of the subject of vocational choice, a subject of universal concern. Perhaps these analyses, if you study them closely, will be able to throw some light on your own thinking in the matter.

Samuel Spiegler

PEOPLE AND JOBS

JOB MAKES THE MAN. Occupation determines, in a large degree, what kind of friends a man has, what part of town he lives in, his hobbies, his leisure, so many of the individually small but cumulatively tremendous influences that fix the pattern of his existence. If he is a doctor, he must be prepared to go to the aid of a patient at any hour; and it is, therefore, wise for him not to promise to make a fourth at bridge unless a fifth is available to replace him if he has to leave suddenly. If he is a plumber, he must make the best of broken nails and calloused fingers. If he is a night watchman, he must sleep while most of the world wakes, and rise with the moon rather than the sun. If he is an apartment-house superintendent, he must live in the building for whose care he is responsible, though he may yearn for a cottage in the country. In such ways and in innumerable others, the job determines the way of life.

All this is pretty obvious. Yet most vocational choices are made without the slightest evidence of consideration for even such obvious matters. How many young men and women would decide against a medical career, for example, if they could really be made to appreciate while still in high school, or even in the earlier years of college, what demands the profession would make upon their time, their energies, and their spirits? Perhaps a large proportion. Many find the pace too hard while yet in medical school, and are forced to drop out. How many young people actually know their own abilities, their own capacities, their own temperaments well enough to appraise intelligently their chances for happiness in some vocation on which they have set their hearts? All too few. And even more, unfortunately, blunder into any occupation that chances to offer itself at a propitious moment, and spend their lives wondering if they might not have been happier doing something else.

From *Your Life's Work* by Samuel Spiegler. By permission of the publishers, The Riverdale Press.

Even the apparently successful person may find his true purposes frustrated. There was the author who was going to write a "great" play, but who instead found himself earning large sums by writing short stories for popular magazines. According to ordinary standards . . . he was a great success; yet before he died he wrote a touching letter to a friend in which he confessed that he looked upon his life as wasted. Probably he had never been altogether happy because he had never really done the thing he wanted to do. "Man does not live by bread alone." Many different factors contribute to satisfactory living, and personal feelings of satisfaction are highly important to its achievement; success is much more a matter of inner conviction than of the opinion of others . . . Each must find [this inner conviction] for himself; to the extent to which he fails, some part of his work has been in vain.

With so much at stake, the choice of an occupation deserves all the care which it is possible to give to it. It is not an easy choice for most people. It was easy enough for young Mozart; he was composing music almost as soon as he could talk. There was no question in his mind about his vocation. It had, as it were, chosen him. Genius of this sort occurs occasionally. For the ordinary run of mortal beings the choice is not made so easy by an early and unquestionable compulsion to do some one thing and the obvious capacity for doing it surpassingly well. The choice must be made the hard way, on the basis of methodical and painstaking thought. . . .

The only way in which anyone can intelligently go about the important business of deciding what kind of occupation to enter or prepare for is by considering two sets of facts. One of these sets of facts has to do with the person; the other with the occupations being considered. [Here] we shall discuss what information about the individual and about the world of work it is necessary to have when the choice of an occupation is being made.

THERE IS NO SUCH THING AS THE ONE RIGHT JOB FOR EVERYBODY. Modern psychology has shown us that no two persons are any more alike than any two sets of finger-prints. Every person is unique. There is nobody else in the world exactly like him. It is all too easy to conclude from this fact that since everybody is different from everybody else, and particular jobs have their particular requirements, there must be *one right job* for everybody. This is a totally wrong conclusion.

The facts are that (1) job requirements are not unique but overlap to a great extent, and (2) that the uniqueness of people is due to individual differences which range all the way from the difference between a genius and an idiot to the difference between an idiot and his idiotic twin. In other words, there are many similarities among jobs as well as many differences; and there are also similarities, as well as differences, among people. As a matter of fact, so-called "families" of occupations are being worked out by various investigators who are studying job requirements. These "families" include jobs that have so many things in common that a person who can do one can very easily learn to do any of the others. As for people, we all know that for practical purposes it is possible to classify them, too, within limits. Some people are bright, and some are dull; some are aggressive, while others are shy; and so on. . . .

A given person's particular characteristics would seem to qualify him for a level of work or a *general type* of work, rather than for some specific occupation. This is especially true of manual occupations and of many clerical occupations. There is no particular evidence that machinists, for example, who work with metals, have different personal qualifications from pattern-makers, who work with wood. . . . The personal requirements for typist and comptometer operator are quite similar. On the professional level, it is easier to find differences. . . . But even here it is strongly probable that most successful doctors might have been equally successful lawyers or engineers if they had expended their energies in those fields rather than in the field of medicine.

This is not intended as a denial of highly specific talents in occasional instances. It would be silly to maintain that Jascha Heifetz would have succeeded equally well as a college professor (or even as a pianist) or that Albert Einstein could have achieved distinction as a portrait painter equal to that which he has reached as a physicist. The infrequent occurrence of genius, as has been noted before, is a fact.

No one single characteristic alone, no matter how highly developed, should be taken as an indication of vocational aptitude. Take mechanical ability, for example. Mechanical ability is equally important for architects, aviators, bookbinders, bricklayers, industrial chemists, dentists, industrial designers, engineers, jewelers, lithographers, sculptors, and surgeons—to take a few examples at random.

In planning a career each person should seek to select a vocational goal which is, first on a *level* of skill or competence at which he can learn to perform efficiently; second, in a *field of work* in which he is interested. . . .

Those personal characteristics which have to do with [these two] points will be discussed in this chapter. The discussion will be organized under the following headings: Physical Characteristics, Intelligence, Interest, Educational Achievement, Aptitude, Personality. . . .

PHYSICAL CHARACTERISTICS

HEALTH. Good health is a desirable thing in every occupation. Other things being equal, the person of robust constitution, who never knows a day's illness, has a tremendous advantage over his sickly co-worker. This is true of "pick-and-shovel" laborers as well as of manicurists. Not to the same degree, of course. A manicurist in poor health may do poorer work, please fewer customers, tire more easily, and earn less money than the girl who is full of healthful energy; but the ditch-digger in ill health may soon find himself no longer a ditch-digger—or anything else, occupationally speaking. Nevertheless, there are many occupations which, while not demanding great physical exertion, make great demands on nervous energy. Accounting is such an occupation, especially at certain seasons of the year; window display work is another. Any doctor will tell you that his daily work often leaves him weary and exhausted. The only easy jobs are those made easy by the lazy, unambitious people who hold them.

Now this does not mean that those whose health is not of the best cannot compete successfully in the working world with their more fortunate fellows. . . . General health conditions may limit the range of choice open to any one person, but they do not in any sense destroy opportunity. Indeed, the theory has been advanced that poor health has contributed to the success of many persons who have been engaged in intellectual occupations. Many artists, writers, and other brain workers who have achieved distinction are known to have suffered from painful and incurable diseases. Possibly, it is argued, because these people found it impossible to engage in normal physical activities, all their energies became concentrated in their mental efforts.

But it is not necessary to take such an extreme position. Health varies among individuals as do other human characteristics. Of course, it is better to enjoy perfect health than to suffer illness or discomfort. It is also better to possess superior intelligence than to be a little less than normally bright. Could we choose, we doubtlessly would be a world of vigorous, brilliant people, none of whom ever requires the services of a physician or a psychologist. Since we cannot choose, we must make the best adjustments we can. . . .

PHYSIQUE. "A strong back and a weak mind," it has been said, are the requirements for many kinds of unskilled manual labor. This is true only within very wide limits. To be sure, any really heavy labor requires the use of the large muscles of the body and makes demands on physical strength and endurance. But there is no evidence that a weak mind is equally requisite. On the contrary, men employed at so-called common labor have been found in some cases to be more intelligent than clerical and other white-collar workers in the same plants. It is well also to remember that more than a few company officials began their working careers as manual laborers.

What is more to the point, there are very few occupations which can properly be called unskilled. Trundling a loaded wheelbarrow, swinging a heavy sledge hammer, wielding a thick iron crowbar, or even mopping a floor requires some skill. It is not only because his muscles are soft that the high school or college boy who gets a summer job with a construction gang finds that he cannot handle the heavy tools with which he must work. He finds that he has many things to learn from experienced laborers—where to grip the sledge handle, how to raise it aloft, how to bring it down on the proper spot with a maximum of force and a minimum of effort.

Nevertheless, more than ordinary physical strength is needed for such occupations. However skillful he may be in the handling of his sledge hammer, the owner of a weak back or a tender palm will find himself in a short while exhausted and perhaps seriously injured. Within limits, muscles and palms can be hardened—but only within limits. For many persons, occupations which involve really hard physical exertion must be ruled out.

STATURE. At the very extremes, such personal characteristics as height and weight may be important qualifications for employment: the circus side-show has no use for men and women of normal build; but giants and midgets, fat ladies and human skeletons may get on the pay-roll. These are rather uncommon occupations. But there are quite a number of jobs for which bodily dimensions within a certain range are absolute requirements, and there are a greater number for which tall people or lean people or short people or plump people are preferred.

There are some fairly obvious examples. Take ushers in motion-picture theaters, for example. Have you ever seen one who was of less than medium height? Most are taller than average; and the gaudily uniformed chap who stands outside the theater is likely to be tallest of all. Policemen, firemen, army and navy personnel, and many other members of uniformed services must meet rigid specifications as to height and weight. Racing jockeys must be small and light; they diet more carefully than any debutante.

Sometimes necessary height and weight requirements are not always clear to those outside the occupation. Many machines used in factories have such dimensions that very short persons cannot operate them. Women of less than certain minimum height cannot become efficient telephone switchboard operators because their arms are too short to reach the panel to manipulate the plugs. Fat men do not make good boilermakers because boilermakers sometimes must crawl inside the boilers through openings which are designed to admit men of ordinary girth. . . .

GENERAL APPEARANCE. In the white-collar occupations, good general personal appearance is a prime requisite. There have been too many books written on the importance of personal appearance, on the necessity of being shaved and of having clean fingernails, on dresses being businesslike and lipstick being discreet, to make it necessary to spend time on such matters here.

Just one point: blemishes, deformities, and other unfortunate physical disfigurements may be real handicaps. Some of these can be overcome or concealed. Some can be removed or corrected by treatment. The manager of a public employment service in a large city likes to relate the experience of a young woman who was trying to get a job as a stenographer. She was an excellent stenographer; but she couldn't get a job. . . . At length, somebody in the placement office sent the girl to a free dental clinic to have her protruding teeth straightened. After that operation was completed, she had no trouble in finding a good job. Not all deformities are so readily repaired as buck teeth. Some, unfortunately, are beyond correction. In other cases, the costs of surgery are prohibitive. There is no very satisfactory way of advising those with really objectionable and irremediable deformities. Many will have to find employment in occupations which involve a minimum of contacts with the public.

THE FIVE SENSES. All normal human beings have five senses: the senses of seeing, hearing, smelling, feeling, and tasting. But each of us has them in varying degrees, and each does not necessarily have all five senses equally developed. . . .

All the senses can be trained, within limits. What we call good eyesight, in a jeweler, for example, is often only ordinary eyesight which has been trained to see certain things which only a jeweler would notice. The "good eyesight," in other words, is eyesight which has been specially "educated." The same can be done with other senses. One can be trained to distinguish qualities and even origins of cocoa beans by crushing them and snuffing the aroma which they give off; or to tell the difference between blends of tea by tasting the brews; or to detect minute flaws in glass or china from the tinkle made when it is struck lightly with a piece of wood; or to know the quality of woolen cloth by feeling it with the fingers.

On the other hand, some persons are really deficient in one or more of the five senses. There is such a thing as defective eyesight. To a certain extent, it can be corrected by glasses and by treatment. But generally, excessive use of poor eyes tends to make them weaker. It is, therefore, wise for those with subnormal vision to choose occupations which do not require close work. Similarly, defective hearing may disqualify one for certain kinds of work, as in the case of a would-be piano tuner. A doctor, to take another example, must have a delicate sense of touch, for many diagnoses must be made by the physician on the basis of what his fingers tell him. Again, there may be cooks who never eat their own cooking, but certainly they must be able to detect the slightest suggestion of a rancid odor in the butter and to sample the flavor of a sauce by trying a drop of it on the tongue. Before deciding upon an occupation, it is well to consider whether it makes any special demands on one or more of the five senses.

INTELLIGENCE

We come now to the questions perhaps most frequently raised when vocational decisions are about to be made: how intelligent must one be to have a reasonable chance of success in such and such an occupation?

The answer is not nearly as easy as it seems. To begin with, there are several different kinds of "intelligence." A boy may be very "smart" in arithmetic and very dull when it comes to composition. He may have a real flair for getting along with people, and no ability at all in making diagrams. He may learn foreign languages with hardly a furrow in his youthful brow, and struggle without success to make sense out of the history of ancient Rome.

Intelligence has been defined as the ability to solve new problems. But there are so many different kinds of problems. In life, some kinds of problems are fairly common to everybody, while others are rather specialized. The specialized problems are likely to have some vocational connections, and the kinds of intelligence needed to solve them are the kinds that have vocational significance. The special problems of engineers are certainly different from those of clergymen. . . . The engineer needs a highly developed ability to solve problems involving relationships between shapes and sizes, and mathematical procedures; whereas the clergyman must be able to solve problems regarding people, their relationships to each other, their thoughts and their emotions. The engineer, in other words, needs mechanical and mathematical intelligence primarily, while the clergyman needs social intelligence.

But there is a kind of "general intelligence" upon which most other special kinds of intelligence more or less depend. This general intelligence is largely the ability to understand and to use words—the English language. The psychologists call this ability "verbal facility," and they usually concede that this is what is measured by "intelligence tests." It is perfectly obvious, if one gives it a little thought, that this is very much what has passed for intelligence all the while, anyhow. The smart boys and girls are those who get good marks in school. . . . And the boys and girls who get good marks in school are the boys and girls who understand most quickly what the teacher is trying to explain to them, and who read books most rapidly and get the most meaning out of them in the shortest time. They are the boys and girls with the greatest "verbal facility."

By and large, this is the kind of intelligence that enables students to get through school and into college, and through college and into professional schools. It is also the kind of intelligence which is practically essential for any reasonable expectation of success in various occupations. We shall, therefore, give some attention to the matter.

OCCUPATIONS AND INTELLIGENCE. . . . It is possible for a person of moderate intelligence to succeed in an occupation for which high intelligence is usually considered necessary, but it is not likely for him to enjoy more than a mediocre success in it. . . . It apparently is [also] possible . . . to fail to use all one's mental resources in a vocational field. The first of these conclusions is shown to be true by the fact that some men of rather low intelligence are engaged in "intellectual" pursuits; the second is justified by the fact that a few men of very high intelligence are working at jobs requiring almost exclusively the use of brawn rather than brain.

Of course, a certain minimum amount of intelligence is needed for certain occupations. It is quite impossible for a feeble-minded person to acquire a professional knowledge of medicine, to master the theories of statistics, or to learn how to compute the stresses on a steel bridge.

Theoretically, perhaps, intelligence should make for greater efficiency on any job. It does, as a practical matter, up to a certain point; beyond that point it makes for inefficiency and sometimes worse. It is known that too much intelligence may disqualify one for certain kinds of work almost as surely as too little intelligence. In factories in which most of the work is done by automatic machinery, personnel directors may reject applicants for jobs on the ground that they are too intelligent. This is because under working conditions which require little exercise of skill or ingenuity, the intelligent worker tends to rebel against the monotony of his job, and thus becomes a danger to the morale of the other workers and may even undermine the efficiency of the shop. A large department store in New York City has found that young women of average intelligence make the most efficient and most contented cashiers. Both the more intelligent and the less intelligent make a larger number of errors, and either quit or are discharged more frequently than those of average intelligence. The brighter girls quit because they are dissatisfied; the duller ones are fired because of inefficiency.

It would seem, then, that there is a certain level of intelligence for each kind of occupation. . . . Psychologists call it "optimum" intelligence. This does not mean, of course, that the optimum for bookkeeping, let us say, can be set at 105; and that, therefore, only those persons with intelligence quotients of exactly 105 should become bookkeepers. All it means is that, other things being equal (which they never are) the person with 105 intelligence will have a better chance of becoming a successful and happy bookkeeper than another person whose intelligence is much higher or much lower; and the greater the difference the greater the danger that the choice of occupation will prove unwise. In fact, even this is too dogmatic. The psychologist is more likely to say that the optimum range of intelligence for book-keeping is between 95 and 120 . . . and that anyone with higher intel-ligence and a desire to engage in bookkeeping should perhaps consider higher forms of accounting, while anyone with lower intelligence might be happier and more efficient as a bookkeeping machine opera-tor. At the same time no psychologist or vocational adviser would dogmatically order either choice, for he knows that personal charac-teristics can overcome handicaps of intelligence.

It does not follow, either, from the concept of optimum intelligence, that one should under all circumstances avoid occupations with re-quirements well below his intelligence level. One of the simpler jobs in modern factory processes is punch press operation. What the suc-cessful punch press operator really needs is a combination of a [moderate] amount of intelligence—particularly mechanical—and a con-siderable amount of manual ability. It is of the utmost importance that the distinction between mechanical intelligence and manual ability be recognized. A punch press operator certainly needs a large degree of manual dexterity, because that is the quality that enables him to make quick accurate movements with his hands. He also needs well-de-veloped "hand-foot coordination," which means that he must be able to move his hands and feet at just precisely the correct moments in order that there shall be neither lost motion nor lost time in the operation of the machine. He does not require a high degree of me-chanical intelligence, which is the ability to think in mechanical terms.

Does this mean that intelligent young men should shun jobs operat-ing punch presses—and the thousands of other machines in modern industry which make similar demands on their operators—under all circumstances? Not at all. Such a job might make an excellent begin-ning for a career as a skilled machinist, a tool and die maker, or an engineer. It is not necessary that a prospective tool maker should be-come proficient on all the machines and tools in a modern factory, but it is essential that he understand thoroughly their operation. . . .

The skilled trades—such as machinist, pattern-maker, auto mechanic, airplane mechanic, coppersmith, and a multitude of others—do require a considerable degree of general intelligence. . . . A not uncommon error among educators has been that of recommending trade training to pupils who fail in commercial and academic subjects in high school. Apparently this practice has been based on the erroneous assumption that less intelligence is required for the mastery of trade subjects. The trade schools have, in fact, been forced to set their standards in accordance with the capacities of their pupils. A considerable proportion of these being retarded and backward pupils, the general level of pupil capacity is naturally not high. . . . In recent years there has been a revolt by the trade schools and a new awareness of the real requirements of the skilled trades, so that a practice that never made sense is being corrected. Lack of intelligence never qualified anybody for a skilled manual occupation. Those occasional "poor pupils" who did well after transfer to a trade school probably did so because they at last found school subjects in which they were interested. It is to this question of interest that we next turn our attention.

INTEREST

Very much like the familiar argument as to the priority of the hen or the egg is the problem of which is cause and which is effect as between interest and ability. It seems perfectly reasonable that if some one is interested in some activity or some kind of information, he will enjoy participating in the activity or searching out and acquiring the information. Since he enjoys it, it is easy for him. Therefore, what one is interested in, he finds easy.

But the reverse is equally reasonable. Many people have special abilities. Because of these special abilities, they find it easy to do certain kinds of things, to solve certain kinds of problems, or to master certain kinds of facts. Finding these things easy to do, they naturally do them as often as possible in preference to doing things which they find difficult. People are interested in the things they do best and most easily.

For practical purposes, it does not matter which of the foregoing lines of reasoning is the more nearly correct. In point of fact, both probably are true. So far as the problems of vocational choice are concerned, the only important fact is the existence of interests, whether they are the cause or the effect of special ability.

. . . In the process of choosing a vocation, careful thought should be given to the interests of the person. Lack of interest can destroy desire, sap ambition, and undermine the will. Anybody who has tried to force the study of a musical instrument upon an uninterested child will know that this is so. On the other hand, a dominant interest will sometimes make up for limitations of physical strength or mental capacity, literally in spite of obstacles. Wherever such interest exists, it is folly not to exploit it in the cause of vocational success.

Generally speaking, however, there rarely is such a thing as a specific occupational interest. A boy is interested in electricity or a girl in fashion design, let us say. The boy's interest may be capitalized upon vocationally in any one of a large number of specialized occupations, ranging from that of installing wiring systems for lights in buildings to that of experimentation with giant machines to make artificial lighting. Or, to take a different kind of example, it may find expression in the field of electrical refrigeration or in the field of X-ray therapy. Similarly, the girl interested in fashion design may find satisfying work as a general dressmaker or as a designer for a large wholesale manufacturer of dresses; she may express her interest in drawing sketches for magazines or in selling women's clothing. Interests, that is to say, do not by themselves always throw light on the levels of performance or the exact kinds of activities which one is likely to find most satisfactory.

Besides, it is unusual for a person to have a single truly dominating interest. . . . Rather than one overwhelming interest that clearly stands out from all other interests, most people have a number of moderate interests. Thus a boy may be interested in stamp collecting and in aviation and in radio all at once—and without losing his interest in baseball. Or a girl may be interested in cookery and in medical technology and in being an air hostess, also all at once—and without necessarily losing interest in dancing. Any one of these interests, even baseball or dancing, may have vocational significance. Which, if any of them, really suggests a reasonable vocational choice will depend upon many other factors, such as are being discussed here.

Very often, a person is not aware of his interests as such. Ask a dozen people to tell you in what they are interested. If they are adults, with jobs or businesses, the chances are that most of them will mention some activity closely connected with the way in which they make their livings. If they are young people who have not yet made relatively final vocational choices, they are likely to say anything that pops into their heads or confess that they don't know—or, perhaps, answer with considerable assurance that they are interested in medicine, law, journalism, or some other professional or occupational field. All too frequently, these latter young people know less about their true interests than the others.

This is so because opinions about their interests are totally unformed. Does the young man declare an interest in medicine because he has seen a motion picture about the career of a great doctor; or because he has enjoyed and been sincerely interested in his courses in biology and physics and chemistry, in learning the names of all the bones in the human body, and in studying physiological specimens under the microscope in the school laboratory? It is interest in such matters that makes for success in medicine. And the young woman who says she is interested in journalism: has she been dazzled, perchance, by the exploits of some outstandingly successful women journalists? Or has she been really interested in learning how to set down on paper the facts about what she had seen and heard in simple, straightforward language, in checking up meticulously on every detail of everything she writes? These are some of the interests that make for success in newspaper work.

It is not possible to be interested, in a sense that has significance for vocational planning, in an activity of which one is ignorant. For that reason, records of past performance are more revealing of true interests than are expressions of opinion. The boy who has stayed up nights mixing vari-colored chemicals in test tubes in his room probably is interested in chemistry—provided he was not merely fascinated by the colors. The girl who went to the library to do research work on the dress that was part of her sewing course probably is interested in costume designing. Successful participation in extracurricular activities —in clubs, on school papers, etc.—is also probably indicative of real interests. This kind of evidence is much more to be trusted than a vague feeling that "I'd like to be an engineer."

But what of the boy or girl who has no consciousness of a special interest, and whose school and personal history reveals no particular leaning? Can it be assumed that this boy or girl has no interests worth taking into account for vocational guidance purposes? Not necessarily, say the psychologists. For it has been found that people with different sorts of general interests succeed in different kinds of occupations. Successful salesmen, for instance, are more interested in politics than are successful research chemists. There are many other ways, too, in which the interests of successful people in various walks of vocational life differ. There are tests with which a trained counselor or psychologist can find out how closely a person's interests resemble those of most people in a number of occupations. It may be assumed that success is more likely in an occupation in which successful people have interests like one's own, than in an occupation whose successful followers have quite different interests.

EDUCATIONAL ACHIEVEMENT

Educational achievement is merely an impressive phrase signifying how well one has done in school—how rapidly he progressed and what marks he got. There is a close relationship between intelligence and educational achievement. Naturally, the brighter students learn more and faster and get better marks than the dull ones. [But it] happens sometimes that bright pupils get poor marks. Of course, this is not because they are bright, but because some other personal characteristic or some circumstance in their lives interferes with their doing the best work of which they are capable. Children who do unsatisfactory work in school have been found to be suffering from poor vision; when they are provided with glasses their school achievement improves markedly. In other cases, unsatisfactory home conditions, insufficient sleep, malnutrition, real or imaginary troubles prevent most efficient application of mental powers, and so result in poor school records. Such cases, however, are the exception rather than the rule. In general, school achievement is a fairly good measure of intelligence, just as intelligence is a fairly good measure of ability to do school work.

Do the best students become the most successful men and women in their vocational lives? The common sense reply is yes; but such evidence as is available on the point does not altogether bear out common sense. A number of comparisons have been made, for instance, between the marks made by college students and the success attained by the same students some years after graduation. Many of the successful students were found to have become successful business or professional [people]. . . . But a good many poor students also achieved success, and more than a few very good students turned out to be comparatively unsuccessful competitors in the working world. Success in these comparisons was measured in terms of income, rating by superiors, and inclusion in *Who's Who*. These are fairly good standards of measures according to contemporary standards. It is interesting that in two of the highest level professions, engineering and medicine, the students who received high marks in college did not achieve any greater success—as defined—than the students who received lower marks.

In part, this lack of close relationship between scholastic records and vocational success appears to be due to a certain lack of relationship between subjects studied in college and information needed for success in an occupation. It has been shown that pupils who make high marks in chemistry, for example, subsequently earn higher incomes as chemists than do their classmates who made poor marks in chemistry. The same probably is true of other strictly vocational subjects.

APTITUDE

The fourth of our personal characteristics that play important parts in determining fitness for particular vocations is aptitude. . . . Aptitude is a combination of ability to learn and desire to learn. The boy with an aptitude for mechanics usually demonstrates it by tinkering with mechanical contrivances and successfully coping with mechanical problems. What is more he usually seeks out mechanical contrivances to tinker with, [perhaps as a hobby]. Theoretically, the aptitude may exist without either ability or desire having shown itself; but as a practical matter, one will have been drawn to the activities for which he has aptitude and will have acquired some competence in their performance by the time he is ready to consider his aptitudes in connection with the selection of an occupation. Neither desire alone nor capacity alone is aptitude. One may have an intense desire to become an actor and possess no talents for the stage. Conversely, one may find that he can learn to solve the most intricate mathematical problems with ridiculous ease and yet set his heart upon composing poetry. Aptitude for an activity implies not only the capacity to perform the activity with efficiency, but also to derive satisfaction from its performance. [Many vocational aptitude tests are available which can be used to determine a person's natural leanings toward one field of work or another.]

PERSONALITY

Nobody "has" personality. Everybody *is* a personality. . . . All the other factors we have been talking about are parts of personality—

physical attributes, intelligence, interests, aptitudes. . . . . [Personality] means temperament, character, likes and dislikes, deportment, alertness or the lack of it, all these and other intangible aspects of a person put together. It is difference in "personality" that makes it possible for one person to tell you an unpleasant truth about yourself without offending you in the slightest degree, and for another person to arouse your antagonism by paying you a compliment.

What about the connection between this complicated and indefinable something and the business of choosing a vocation? Is there any connection? Very definitely there is, but it is not a cut-and-dried connection. . . . In the first place, there are as many "kinds of personalities" as there are people. In the second place, personality is more important in relation to people than it is in relation to things; that is to say, whether a particular personality is desirable for a particular job may depend more on the temperament of the boss than on the precise nature of the work. For example, it is quite commonly said that aggressiveness . . . is not wanted in clerical workers. But who can say that this is invariably true? In a large number of offices, perhaps in a majority, aggressiveness in clerks is looked upon as a nuisance. But some employers like aggressiveness in general, and when they find a clerk who has it, together with other desirable traits, they promote him to the sales department, or even make him a junior executive. Generalization about such matters is dangerous.

Especially, it is dangerous to generalize about occupational classifications which embrace great numbers of specific occupations, each different from the other. Sometimes there may be greater differences in personal requirements between two occupations within one of these categories than between two occupations in totally different categories. To take clerical workers again: a bookkeeping machine operator in a bank probably has need of personality characteristics quite different from those that would be most useful to a rate clerk in a railroad freight office. Yet both are clerical workers. A doctor who does not treat patients, but confines his professional activities to the research laboratory certainly has more in common with a research chemist, so far as his probable personality is concerned, than he has with his medical colleagues who spend their days looking at tongues and feeling pulses. It is the specialty within an occupation that often determines the kind of personality that will make for success.

Of course, there are some pretty safe generalizations, too. It would be hard to imagine that the fellow who works his way through the crowd at a baseball game with a basket over his arm, selling peanuts and frankfurters, is a "shrinking violet" type of personality. Some occupations require certain ways of acting and thinking. It would be quite absurd to imagine, . . . let us say, . . . an auctioneer with a strong sense of self-consciousness.

For a long time, some psychologists believed they could classify people into a few types according to personality traits. Two of the largest classifications were those of the "introverts" and the "extraverts." . . . The introverts are the people who are concerned chiefly with what goes on in their own minds and hearts. They are the thinkers, the philosophers, the dreamers of dreams, and the creators of ideas. The extraverts, on the other hand, are the people who are concerned chiefly with what is going on about them. They want to do something, rather than to think about it. They like to be with people rather than alone with their thoughts or with a book. They are the doers—the successful businessmen, politicians, and generals. Fortunately, both extreme introversion and extreme extraversion are rare. The extreme introvert, turning his mind always in upon himself, often becomes a brooding recluse; while the extreme extravert, ever ready to act upon impulse, may make a painful nuisance of himself. At the same time, it must not be overlooked that genius sometimes wears the outward appearance of an unbalanced personality; a brooding recluse may produce great poetry; and an energetic talker may become a leader of men, for good or for ill.

It is clear that personality, considered in this light, plays a role of the greatest importance in vocational planning. A strongly extraverted person desires to be in the public eye, craves the open plaudits of admirers, thrives upon being the center of attention. He wants to join lodges and be elected to office, to be the grand marshal of the parade. Could such a person be happy in a job which kept him confined to study or laboratory, working anonymously, withdrawn largely from the world of clamor and competition? Scarcely so. Yet the person of strong introvert tendencies would find just such a job ideally suited to him; while he might suffer genuine panic if he were suddenly thrust into the limelight. It is well that choices of vocational aims be made with full awareness of such personal idiosyncrasies.

GUIDE QUESTIONS

1. "How many young people actually know their own abilities, their own capacities, their own temperaments well enough to appraise intelligently their chances for happiness in some vocation on which they have set their hearts?" Answer this question for yourself and for other young people that you know.

2. The idea that "there must be *one right job* for everybody" has been called by another writer on vocational guidance "the fallacy of the perfect niche." Tell why you agree or disagree with this idea.

3. Discuss what is said on the subject of "Physical Characteristics" in the light of the fact that more and more physically handicapped persons are now being gainfully employed.

4. Which of the physical characteristics discussed—health, physique, stature, general appearance, and the five senses—is most important in the vocation for which you are preparing?

5. Why is "verbal facility" the same thing as "general intelligence"? Does your experience in school bear out what Spiegler says on this point?

6. Most schools give intelligence tests, but very few schools tell a student what his I.Q. (intelligence quotient) is. Why do you think they do not? Tell why you think this a good or a bad policy.

7. Analyze the relation between your own interests and abilities. Do you consider your interests the cause or the effect of your special abilities?

8. Does what is said about high grades in school and success in later life confirm or conflict with your personal opinion on this point?

9. Explain the theoretical connection between hobbies and vocational aptitudes.

10. You have probably taken some kind of vocational aptitude test. Explain how the results did or did not surprise you.

11. In your opinion, would an introvert or an extravert be more successful in your chosen vocation?

12. How might high schools and colleges help students to select vocations? Tell what vocational guidance you have had or would like to have.

13. What makes the organization of the essay clear? Do the six main headings seem to be an adequate break-down of the subject? Would you suggest different or additional main headings? Explain the purpose of the sub-headings where these occur.

VOCABULARY

Give the derivations and definitions of the following words:

*cumulatively, propitious, requisite, manipulate, girth, irremediable, flair
facility, concede, mediocre, dexterity, priority, perchance, meticulously, intangible, recluse, plaudit, idiosyncrasy.*

Eli Ginzberg

THE PERIOD OF REALISTIC CHOICES

AS A FIRST APPROXIMATION, we distinguished three major periods in the
process of formulating occupational decisions: the fantasy period,
which usually comes to an end at about eleven; the period of tentative
choices, which includes the ages of eleven to seventeen; and the period
of realistic choices, which starts with college and includes the period of
graduate instruction and early employment. . . .

The period of realistic choices can be divided into three distinct
stages. The first can be characterized as "exploration." This is the stage
during which the new college student tries to acquire the experience
which he needs to resolve his occupational choice. He hopes to gain
this experience by exploring various subjects of study; by engaging in
discussions with informed persons—teachers and advisors; by attending conferences and otherwise obtaining information about various
fields of knowledge and the vocations.

The stage of exploration is followed by one of "crystallization,"
which covers the time when the individual is able to assess the multitude of factors influencing the occupational choice which he has had
under consideration, and is finally able to commit himself.

In the last stage of this period the young adult is concerned with
what we have termed "specification." For example, in the crystallization stage he may have decided to become a physicist. But he was not

sure which branch of physics to enter, or whether to seek a livelihood in the academic life, in private industry, or in government. During the stage of specification these alternatives are reviewed in respect to a field of specialization and to particular career objectives. But, although a decision may have been made by the end of his college education, he does not necessarily adhere to it throughout his adult life. Under the impact of new emotional or reality influences, those who have not made a firm choice, and even some who have, may shift. Nevertheless, once having crystallized his choice, the individual hesitates to reopen the question unless the situation warrants jeopardizing a part, if not the whole, of his investment in preparation.

THE EXPLORATION STAGE

Most freshmen have acquired some clarification of occupational choice, particularly with respect to the relationship between themselves and reality. By the time they enter college they are no longer speculating about an indefinite range of vocations. Their focus has narrowed. However, they hesitate to shape their college program in terms of a firm occupational objective.

The college freshman conveys the impression that he has a need to review, perhaps more critically than heretofore, his experiences of the period of tentative choices and his reactions to them. This is one part of his task—to get a deeper insight into his major needs and desires. But to do so, he must test himself through new experiences. Most freshmen appreciate the fact that they are under a series of conflicting pressures. On the one hand, they must come to a decision about their choice in the near future. But they also recognize that to commit themselves prematurely would be a mistake. They want to discover as much as possible about themselves and about the outside world so that their eventual choice will not entail work which would prove frustrating.

They must build a bridge between the present and the future; but at best they have only a vague idea of what a desirable future would be. But more and more the decision-making is in their own hands. They are no longer circumscribed by the rigid curriculum of high school, but they have a new problem: to select among the wide range of courses in college. Many educators contend that college students should base their selections on the contribution that various courses can make to their cultural development, but it is questionable whether in our society, with its emphasis on monetary success, the freshman has an adequate incentive to do so.

Most of the college freshmen we interviewed were in search of new exposures and experiences to broaden and deepen their understanding of reality. Further, they were interested in testing themselves. They realized that it was no longer sensible to view their occupational choice uncritically in terms of general interests, capacities, and values. These factors must now be carefully assessed. Some of the group consider these elements actively; others are more passive; but no one is really oblivious to them. Francis is typical. He tells us that he has not decided what course to pursue because his ideas keep changing. "I thought of writing, psychology, one of the sciences; I still haven't settled down." He expects to do a lot of reading and acquire information about various fields from his courses, and then to decide upon a field of concentration "by the end of my sophomore year at the latest." Henry is a little closer to a decision, although he says, "I'm still looking, but it will be in science. . . . I think I've taken a program that will allow me a certain amount of flexibility." He plans to settle on a choice during the summer: "I'll talk with my father, my advisors, and people." Jeffrey picked Columbia because "I hadn't decided on a vocation; I wanted a good liberal arts college where you would have a chance to decide for yourself. The other colleges make you decide what you want to major in immediately, while Columbia gives you a couple of years."

Now that the decision cannot be much longer postponed, the individual adopts a more cautious attitude, for he realizes the seriousness of a permanent commitment. The fact that college freshmen are much more aware of the many relevant factors than are juniors or even seniors in high school increases their difficulty in crystallizing their choice. For instance, Henry tells us that "Einstein's theory fascinates me. Math I hate; I'm not good at it. But I like its applications." His choice is made difficult because, in spite of his interest in physics, he does not like theoretical mathematics, although he "likes its applications." Gerald, who is undecided between English and social studies, finds that part of his difficulty is in assessing his grades in these two fields. Although he used to do superior work in the social sciences in high school, he received only a grade of "B" in his college course while in English he secured an "A." In high school he had never

hought of himself as outstanding in English, but was considered an
honor student in the social sciences. Here is another example of the
overevaluation of a particular grade.

The freshman group have at least this advantage—an increasing
recognition of the fields which do not interest them and which they
definitely plan to eschew. Jeffrey is sure that he would never want to
be a doctor: "There is too much responsibility there, for instance, if
you are a surgeon. I don't think I'd do too well in law—I don't have
too much initiative, and I wouldn't like trial work. I don't have much
feeling about teaching one way or the other. . . . I suppose I'll major
in business since I've eliminated science, and I have no inclination for
law or teaching. So there's only business left." Leonard, on the other
hand, is sure that "I wouldn't particularly care to be in business. . . .
I don't think I would like the office work too much in a big corporation. I've thought of government work. . . . I feel I'd be doing more
for society." Robert is certain that among the types of work that he
would never want to do are "engineering, medicine, anything mathematical; and I would never be a professional soldier, or bus driver, or
bartender. It's a strange array. Professional soldiering is such a limited
life and boils down to nothingness. They are getting no place. They
never arrive anywhere particularly in their lives. . . . Bartending just
popped into my head as a joke. It might be a bit more attractive than
other things; in fact, I might very well like to be a bartender—talk to
all kinds of people." Robert, who comes from a family with an income in the higher brackets, recognizes that a person with his background might seriously consider engineering or a military career but
not bartending.

There are many factors that contribute to uncertainty about occupational choice. Oscar is caught in the predicament of having two widely
different yet strong interests—music and medicine. He points out that
his interest in music "was created early in life. It always held an attraction for me." His interest in medicine started later, but is quite real.
However, he says, "One thing bothers me. Whereas chemistry should
be the main thing, the main drive that would make me want to go
into medicine, I cannot exactly connect the two together." The rather
tenuous and indirect relations between important subjects in the curriculum and major fields of adult endeavor make it difficult for Oscar,
as for many others, to clarify his choice.

Sometimes the indecision is grounded in reality considerations rather than in the subjective problem of interest and its translation into a suitable vocation. Henry realizes that if he concentrates on the sciences, one possible career would be teaching. But he is aware that fluent speech is a prerequisite for teaching and feels that he does not have this competence and wonders whether he would ever acquire it.

The deliberateness and concern with which the college freshman group are exploring the various aspects of their choice arises out of several facts. Many are still undecided between strong interests; others have real doubts whether they possess the capacities to succeed in the field of their special interest; and almost all are conscious of their limited knowledge of the world—the actual work entailed in an occupation; the hurdles in preparing for it; and the probable rewards from it. The exploratory process would probably be less confusing were it not that these freshmen desire to find a field that will yield substantial work satisfaction.

The extent to which they look forward to finding a gratifying vocation is illustrated by the following comments. Leonard hopes to find an interesting job: "I think that is the most important; it would give me the most satisfaction." Miles, who is looking forward to a career as a script writer in Hollywood, and who "can't stand much regulation—day after day the same," is desirous of getting satisfaction out of his work: "I would like to know I am doing something creative or progressive—not just a cog in a very insignificant wheel. I'm not too satisfied with settling along normal trends of life and being swallowed." Henry thinks "there is a great deal of satisfaction in the sciences—just stuff in your mind"; but he goes on to add that it is also pleasurable "to see your ideas in operation. Every man likes to control his endeavors and go along as he wishes." Gerald approaches the question of work satisfaction from the viewpoint of being able to solve problems: "I enjoy it first of all if it doesn't present such a problem that it weighs me down. I enjoy it if it presents a problem and is interesting. And I enjoy it if I am successful, if I feel I am beating it." Francis feels sure that it is very important to get work that will interest him because he will be doing it for the rest of his life. He is sure that he would "hate to do anything repetitious, not creative, or that did not have a thoughtful element to it." Robert wants to get personal satisfaction out of his work and feels that financial return is a matter of lesser moment.

The run of the evidence is clear. These freshmen look forward to accomplishment; in fact, they hope to find a field which will present

m with challenging problems. They are eager for variety and hope
avoid routine tasks. Several emphasize that they hope to be able to
ermine the actual focus and method of their work—they are look-
; for an opportunity for independence in their work.

n addition to Robert, one other freshman had passed beyond the
;e of exploration, even beyond crystallization. Eric had already
cified his choice. He had been playing the piano since the age of
:. At eleven he had recognized that he was very fond of music. At
irteen he began to play the organ in church. "I'm pretty determined
)ut majoring in music, at least I've never thought about majoring
anything else." There are two reasons that Eric was able to reach
stage of specification at a relatively early age. He realized as early
eleven that he had real interest and some real talent for music. He
l his first job at eleven and has had regular paid employment since
een. Thus he has had plenty of opportunity to explore the extent of
interest and to react to specific work situations.

Ve can now summarize the major characteristics of the decision-
king of the freshman group. Despite the marked shift toward
lism which distinguishes the entire period of decision-making in
lege and graduate school, these freshmen are still subjectively ori-
ed, although their subjectivity has a different quality from that of
high school group. Several facts help to explain this: some of the
shmen must decide between two or more strong interests; almost all
them are looking for a type of work which will yield direct satisfac-
ns; they still do not know how to absorb and deal with the relevant
ernal forces. Moreover, this is probably their last chance to deter-
ne their real desires. And to do this, they must remain introspective.
e further consideration that at most they can receive rather limited
p from others intensifies the introspective approach.

Although these freshmen have difficulty in acquiring a clear percep-
n of reality factors, their efforts in this direction are many and
ied. We have noted their attempt to evaluate their capacities through
iewing their grades in school. Most freshmen still have fanciful
ions about the economic facts of life: Peter believes that "a really
cessful commercial artist makes about $100 to $150 a week and if
s very successful, upwards of $200 a week. A physician makes be-
een $50 and $80 a week. I imagine that would be about the average."
rald reaches the conclusion that a major in English would offer
)re occupational opportunities than a major in the social sciences.

An indication that their approach to resolving their choice has alter
significantly since high school is the increasing pressure that they f
to come to a decision. Several students look forward to making a
cision during the summer after the freshman year; few think of po
poning it beyond the end of the sophomore year. The pressure exert
by time is definitely present.

Further indication of the importance they attach to the pressu
exerted by time is their concern with the length of preparation. So
question whether they will be financially able to attend gradu
school; others will be able and plan to go to graduate school; s
others, who have no worry about finances, nevertheless contempl
terminating their formal education at the end of college. Few, howev
had reached the degree of specificity in considering the future su
gested by Oscar, who replied to the question of whether he thoug
he might get married, "Yes, June 6th—around right after I get c
of medical school, 1955 or 1956." It should be added that he went
to say, "It's always fun to make plans."

Although most freshmen sensed that they were in an explorato
stage, few had developed specific stratagems to help resolve their u
certainties about their occupational choice. A few looked forward
reviewing their plans with competent advisors. Others expected
take some type of vocational test. But it was the exception for a fre
man to plan deliberately to accumulate evidence, internal and extern
that might be of use. In part, he did not know what evidence w
most relevant. In part, he hoped that his choice might be spontai
ously resolved after he had had the benefit of additional experien
The lack of an effective stratagem is illustrated by Peter, who claim
that he was immensely interested in medicine but who knew that I
chances of being admitted to medical school had been jeopardized
his failure in chemistry. Yet Peter was unable to consider a feasil
alternative. He continued to hope that medicine was still possible f
him. Francis did not know how to begin to find a career that wou
provide an outlet for his interest in people. These examples are ill
trative of the difficulties that individuals face in the exploratory stag

Before concluding this discussion of the exploratory stage, it is
order to point up some of the particular difficulties that account f
the failure to develop effective stratagems. The manifold new exp
riences in college are initially confusing, never clarifying. All freshm
require time to order their new life with its broadened horizons. N

ly does the freshman have to assimilate many new ideas and ex-
iences, he must also reassess many assumptions that he has taken
granted. In fact, most teaching in the freshman year is deliberately
ected to developing among the students a critical point of view.
Then, the experience which they acquire is not quite what they had
ected. They wanted to learn more about the external world, and,
tead of acquiring an insight into the reality of the market place,
y are immersed in academic subjects which are related tenuously,
it all, to specific vocations. So the freshman discovers that college,
tead of answering his questions, has added to them. He needs time
absorb the new and to reevaluate the old. Small wonder that he
ks forward to a spontaneous resolution of his choice problem.

THE CRYSTALLIZATION STAGE

Crystallization depends on all of the individual's previous experi-
e and development, but it is most directly related to the exploratory
ge. In that stage, individuals were aware that there were many
es of work which they would not consider except under unusual
umstances. They were more hesitant about making a positive choice
ause of the fear that a premature commitment would preclude their
ling a truly satisfying occupation. Finally, they had reached a degree
ntellectual and emotional maturity which permitted them to recog-
e a possible conflict between their capacities, interests, and values,
I the objective conditions presented by the real world.

s a result of these exploratory considerations, most college students
finally able to move toward a positive solution. They become in-
asingly conscious of the attraction of a certain type of work; find
mselves able to spend many hours at it; and are not discouraged
minor obstacles which at an earlier time might have led them to
ct it. Raymond put it in these words: "Well, the more I work with
the more interested I become, and the more I learn, the more I
lize there is to learn; it stimulates my interest. I think I'll get my
ree in power engineering." A graduate student of physics pointed
that he gets lots of fun out of the work, even "out of the boring
t. Certain phases are less interesting than others, so you devote as
ch time as possible to the interesting ones. And if you have to work
h the boring ones, you get it over with." Persons who are less
ure fail to realize that no work is ever completely satisfying. Hence,

they are alarmed when they find themselves bored, even if it is o
occasionally, and continue to search for the impossible—a type of w
that is completely satisfying all of the time.

Students move toward crystallization when they become aware
their propensities. Raymond pointed out that his brother's profess
was law, and added, "I wouldn't like that; it seems somewhat
stract. . . . From the beginning I realized I liked to use my hanc
Vincent, who decided, on the basis of a strong interest in mathemat
to take up engineering, remembers that he considered physics, "bu
seemed too specific at the time, I don't know why." William room
with a student who was going to be an industrial engineer. At
time he was thinking of concentrating in physics, but suddenly fou
that he, too, was interested in industrial engineering, because "it wa:
too theoretical, and it appealed to me."

The true explanation of these gross distinctions between the "th
retical" and the "practical," between "abstract" and "concrete," betwe
"intellectual" and "realistic" is obscure. But we can be relatively c
tain that individuals take a step toward crystallizing their choice
becoming aware of their propensities and thereby recognizing the ty
of work that they want to avoid. One further step is required:
propensity must be translated into an occupation. Many students, e
graduate students, are unable to make this translation. Frequently th
are good students and are content with their educational progress. I
them time seems to be standing still; they act as if they are unc
cerned about the problem of earning a living.

Although some remain for a long time in this pre-crystallizati
stage, the pressures on most students are so great that they impe
choice. As students enter the junior or senior year, they know t
they must think about what they will do upon graduation. The edu
tional structure itself exerts pressure; different professions require c
ferent preparation; a student who is undecided between a post-gradu.
course in chemistry and medical school cannot postpone his decisi
indefinitely. Some find it easier to resolve the remaining uncertaint
about their future work after they have clarified important life valu
Robert put it in these terms: "Two weeks ago I wouldn't have h
this so crystallized. For one thing I have been undergoing a lot
emotional strain since February first. I became involved amorous
It's a great flood tide of emotions, and it stirred everything up. Eve
thing was moving, and I suddenly felt that everything was well

fined. . . . Finally I realized there's one type of thing I'm attracted to and capable of being successful in and want to be part of. Of necessity, finally, I had the strength to realize what I want and what I can have."

Crystallization is the process whereby the individual is finally able to synthesize the many forces, internal and external, that have relevance for his decision. The actual process cannot be observed save in retrospect; this is true not only for the observer, but for the individual. It is a commitment, and the individual recognizes this by his willingness to bring his explorations to a close and by his ability to make definite plans for the future, subject to change in details. For instance, Robert, who dates the exact point of crystallization as two weeks prior to the interview, is convinced that he is going ahead with "history," although he has not determined whether he will aim at college teaching or will eventually seek a position in government. In short, further decisions will be required, but these are of less importance.

One criterion of crystallization of choice is an unswerving attitude. Alvin, who is determined to pursue a career in international business, stated, "I can't see any possible change in my *likes*. Of course, there might be such a thing as a fine offer of a job. Everybody is interested in a certain sense in security, and if I thought I might get it that way, well." Actually, he is saying that, as far as he can judge, there is no possibility of his changing his choice; the only outside contingency that he is willing to consider would be an unusual job opportunity. Brian, who is about to embark upon a journalistic career, could not conceive of changing his plans unless "I found my whole feeling had been changed and I didn't want what I had wanted before." All of these expressions reflect an internal stabilization which, unless it is disturbed, presages that the individual will not alter his present plans fundamentally.

This firmness of commitment differentiates an actual crystallization from the apparent one of the fifteen- and sixteen-year-olds. The high school junior has seldom had an opportunity to test the strategic elements in his tentative choice and has therefore been unable to weigh its appeal for him. Moreover, he has not yet confronted the wide range of alternatives that will probably open in college. Of course, his tentative choice may remain the final one, but he cannot determine this without considerable exploration.

Many college seniors and graduate students appear to have crystal-

lized, in some cases even specified, their choice, but a careful stud
reveals a pseudo-crystallization. These young adults have much i
common with the high school junior, for like him, they have no
analyzed the essential elements and have not fully accepted the com
mitments entailed. Clement points out that he has followed courses i
international relations for quite a while: "I suppose in imitation o
my father and the fact that most of his friends and my friends wer
in this general area. I knew languages and liked the people. . . .
didn't think too much about the whole problem. I just plugged along
I never really gave any other job possibility a chance." It was no
until his senior year in college that Clement began to question where
he was headed.

Sometimes the individual requires a still longer time to recognize
that his decision was falsely based. Duncan, who returned to Columbia
as a graduate student of physics after being employed in industry
remarked that it was "strange that I went through five years o
chemical engineering and decided I didn't want it." He recalls that
he had seriously thought of shifting to chemistry at the end of his
second year in college, but when he talked with his father "he had
some doubts. I wasn't quite sure I wanted to end up in chemical engineering and his attitude was that he knew many people who had
gone through with it who had eventually ended up in all sorts of
other things. In any case, engineering background was excellent training for anything. Engineering is the best sort of college training is
his idea." Duncan continued to study chemical engineering. In his
graduate work he shifted to electrical engineering, but it was only
after he was employed in industry, primarily in the field of electrical
engineering, that he realized that he really wanted to study physics.
He had wanted to change at the beginning of his junior year in
college—at least, he wanted to shift away from chemical engineering—
just at the time when crystallization is most likely to occur. But he
was not strong enough to resist his father, who persuaded him against
shifting.

In the cases of Clement and Duncan we note the role of key persons—in both instances, the father. Clement continued to identify
himself with his father and actually failed to consider the question of
an occupational choice. Duncan became aware that he was dissatisfied
with his father's choice for him, but when he sought to shift, his
father persuaded him to remain in engineering.

The role played by key persons in the decision-making of individuals who emerge with pseudo-crystallized choices involves an interplay between the emotional needs of two persons—the individual making the choice and the individual who influences him. Pseudo-crystallization is also abetted by the fears of juniors and seniors about delaying choice. Forced to select a field of concentration, they translate it into an occupation—but without full emotional acceptance, and frequently the choice will not hold up under future pressures.

Some students complete their formal schooling without having been able to crystallize a choice or after having made only a pseudo-crystallization. Yet they may eventually find satisfactory work. Our modern industrial society offers a tremendous range of jobs and many will probably be able to work out a reasonable adjustment for themselves commensurate with their educational background and their current goals and values. But probably—in fact, almost certainly—they will have failed to develop their own resources to a maximum and to make the best use of the available educational resources.

In any event, even crystallized choices are not always final, since they may be subject to reconsideration in the light of new experiences or the reevaluation of old ones. But the greater opportunity an individual has had to test himself and reality, and the more time and energy he has invested in acquiring a specific preparation, the less likely he is to become dissatisfied with his chosen field or to become positively attracted to a new field. A tentative generalization can be formulated in these terms: An individual who has crystallized his choice is unlikely to reopen the question unless after further experience he discovers that he is dissatisfied with his work. The only likelihood would arise from unusual external circumstances compelling him to work in an entirely new field, which, he discovers, satisfies certain interests, capacities, and values of which he had previously been unaware.

Most of the seniors had already crystallized their choice. But there were several in a stage of pre-crystallization or pseudo-crystallization, as well as a few who had almost reached the stage of specification. Samuel was on the verge of crystallization. For many years he had been preparing for a career in science, possibly in engineering, but then his interests began to shift from "materials" to "people." He received good grades in all his courses, so he gained little help in the occupational problem by a review of his performance in school. He was

currently considering law, but pointed out: "I've heard a lot of dis
couraging things about lawyers. It's impossible to tell just what it'
like from how it looks. Awful hard. Good solid opinions from peopl
who know would shift my mind. You can't make a foundation on wha
you just hear people say. Just lately I thought of business, and I can'
tell why. . . . I'd like being able to run things the way I want, bein;
able to organize things." It could be assumed that within a shor
time immediately before or after graduation, Samuel would make ;
decision either to enter law school or start in business.

Raymond was to receive a degree in mechanical engineering withir
a few months. He stated that he had never had any other choice
"From the beginning I realized that I liked to use my hands. It wa
impressed upon me. By whom? My brother who is a lawyer, but whc
had thought he wanted to be an engineer." Raymond stated that he
was consistently good in mathematics, science, and chemistry, anc
went on to say, "My interest lay in those subjects where my marks
were good." He was quite unconcerned about his future but was aware
that the question of specialization was still open. Only recently he
had begun to realize that he might like to teach, in which case he
would have to go to graduate school. However, he was not certain
about it, knowing that the job market for engineers was better now
than it might be later. He would soon have to make important decisions as to the next step in his career, but he had no doubt that the
decisions would be in the field of his choice. Other seniors, such as
Brian, the journalist, and Gilbert, who was completing his course in
mining engineering, had worked out in detail the succeeding steps in
their career planning. But for most seniors, specification was still in the
future.

THE STAGE OF SPECIFICATION

This stage represents a process of closure, the selection of the spe-
cifics of an occupational choice after a generalized choice has been
made. It is the period of final commitment. Robert, the senior who
knew that he was going on with history, was uncertain whether he
would eventually teach or enter government service. Raymond re-
affirmed in college his earlier decision to pursue an engineering career
and shortly before graduation realized that he would have to decide
between continuing with graduate work in order to teach or obtain-

ing a job in industry while employment opportunities were favorable. Alvin had reached a decision in his junior year to go into international business, but he was undecided, even in the second half of his senior year, about his next move: "I plan to go to the Columbia School of International Affairs or to the Harvard Graduate Business School if I can specialize in International Affairs."

It is difficult for a student to plan in advance the various stages in his career or even to determine definitely his field of specialization. He must first acquire considerable experience in the field of his choice. It is usually impossible to acquire this within the formal school structure, particularly without going to graduate school. Even those who pursue several years of graduate studies find it difficult to acquire the requisite knowledge, skill, and experience to make the subtle distinction required for specification. And even if the individual confidently plans the details of his career objectives and commits himself to a field of specialization while still in school, it is possible that he may change his mind after he has had actual work experience.

Brian was one of the few who were able to plan in detail while still a senior in college. First he would "try to get into the Journalism School and start out in some small town paper and travel around the country a bit. . . . As a newspaper man I would like to begin for about five years working for small town papers, doing reporting work, and then I would like to get a position either with one of the big news agencies, A.P., U.P., or do editing news copy that comes through or working on the City Desk in some major paper in a major city; and then I would like to operate by myself or with some people I know starting a paper of my own." A major reason for this early specification was that Brian had held a journalistic post throughout his school years and had therefore already accumulated the experience which usually comes only after college.

Herbert, who is nearing the end of his preparation for a Ph.D. degree in physics, illustrates another facet of specialization. In response to the question about his choice of field, he replied, "Right now I have a choice between two: either nuclear physics or atomic." Before his choice could be thus narrowed, Herbert had to pass through several stages. First, he had to decide that he wanted to become a physicist, which in his case meant discarding his undergraduate specialization, engineering. Then, within the field of physics, he had to decide between experimental and theoretical work, though the two are not mutually exclusive. And only after his decision to concentrate on theoretical physics was he confronted with the alternative of specializing in nuclear or atomic physics.

Two principal criteria can be employed to test whether an individual is in the stage of specification. One is his willingness to specialize. To be willing to confine oneself to a relatively narrow field one must have a strong conviction based at least upon initial experience that this will prove satisfying and meaningful. As long as one remains uncertain as to which field offers the greatest challenge and, equally important, the best opportunity for making use of one's skills, no intelligent commitment can be made.

The second test of specification is resistance to deflection from one's chosen course. Of course, when confronted by a very attractive alternative which is more or less consistent with the individual's major values and interests, he will not bluntly ignore or reject it. He may well accept it. This criterion emphasizes resistance to deflection rather than the impossibility of yielding to it.

Many individuals, particularly those engaged in college teaching, appear to have reached a specific choice because they are willing to make the sizable investment of time and money required to obtain a Ph.D. degree. At first, it might seem that if one were willing to specialize to the extent required for this degree, he must be convinced that he would derive great satisfaction from such concentrated work; and further, that he is committed to his specialty for the duration of his working life. More careful scrutiny shows, however, that many students are under substantial external pressure to obtain a Ph.D. degree. This is particularly true if they plan to remain in college teaching. In most instances promotion is blocked for instructors who do not have their doctorate. Many candidates for a doctorate reveal that their interest in their specialty is definitely secondary to their career objectives. They are willing to specialize—but as a means to an end. They have a minor interest in their work per se, and are actually looking for major gratifications elsewhere. They are, therefore, relatively easy to deflect.

Joel illustrates this. When he entered the Navy he had developed an interest in economics and accounting and had thought about going into business. He said, "I didn't want to make an occupational decision until my senior year, and by that time I was in the Navy." He thought about staying in the Navy, but decided against it because he disliked its rigid, rank-conscious structure. When he left the Navy he looked for a job in a small business, but failed to find one. "I continued looking for a job and didn't find exactly what I wanted, and became more and more interested in teaching and realized that I could go on. . . . As I think about it now I will stay in teaching and establish a good reputation; as soon as I feel I do have a reputation, I can let up a little bit and start looking around for outside part-time consulting work." Joel went on to relate in detail the kind of life which he hopes to build for his family; his plan includes a job that "doesn't take all of my waking hours." Joel is not determined upon economics and accounting as fields of specialization; he has not even decided upon teaching, although he enjoys, as he says, "making difficult things easy." At twenty-seven he has worked out a pattern of the type of life which he would like to lead, including "breaking 85 in my golf game." His current specialization was more or less inflicted on him; he would be easy to deflect. In short, it is his life plan which is specified, and his occupation was chosen to fit this.

Just as there is pseudo-crystallization, so there is pseudo-specification. The case of Lewis falls in this category. A senior in college, he plans to enter a book publishing firm. He explains that he first became interested in it at about thirteen, because "I knew some people in that business and they always seemed to like it. I always liked those people." Lewis continues, "I like books for one thing, good ones. . . . It's a responsible kind of business. You are an outlet for information to the public. In that way it is important. The good jobs in it are *very* interesting." He states that he would hate "a job that depends on whom you know. I don't think that is true so much in the book publishing field." Lewis had pursued a wide range of cultural courses, including such specialized subjects as Dante and Medieval Culture, the Ancient Epic, and Advanced Latin Composition. His evaluation of his college program is interesting: "It's pretty senseless—no rhyme or reason to it but adding up points." He could afford to be haphazard because he felt sure that he would enter the publishing business, and the courses which he did take had at least a tangential relation to work in a literary field. However, Lewis's assumption that there is little "backslapping" in publishing, that it is important work because it helps to mold the public mind, and other evaluations, all point to his immaturity and naivete. He does not have a true picture of the field and it will probably fail to yield him the satisfactions which he seeks. Future disappointment is also foreshadowed by his statement that "I wouldn't like to go into any firm where in a year I couldn't look forward to something good coming up. I want no bad beginning in the publishing line." Lewis says that unless his very stringent conditions in this field are met, "I might look into newspaper, radio—because of my literary background; they are all allied fields and you get ahead more quickly." Here we have the final evidence that his specification which seemed so definite is really spurious.

This discussion of specification can be concluded by emphasizing that not all individuals can realize their major goals and values through a specific type of work, but the ones who do so give the best clues to the nature of specification. Gilbert had been looking forward to a career as a mining engineer from the age of ten or eleven; throughout the period of his formal education he tested and retested his interests and returned each time, with heightened assurance, to his choice. It would be difficult for Gilbert to find satisfaction in any work other than that of a mining engineer. Although every individual is concerned with the choice of an occupation which will yield him a high level of satisfaction, the majority are primarily responsive to the impact of external conditions—including the income and prestige that attach to the work —while a minority seem to be propelled primarily by internal forces which must find expression.

Let us now summarize the three stages in the period of realistic choices. In the exploration stage the young adult is striving to link his decision-making to reality. This is in contrast to the preceding period when his preoccupation was largely with subjective elements. But our case materials suggest that even though his behavior during the exploration stage is increasingly "reality-oriented," the individual now makes a final attempt to link his choice effectively with his basic interests and values. The emphasis which college educators place on exposing freshmen and sophomores to various courses and fields of endeavor, and the eagerness with which many students look forward to this opportunity, reflects their intense desire, almost their need, to test their interests and values.

An essential characteristic of the next stage, crystallization, is the quality of acceptance, which stands in contrast to the confused or vague activity, almost hyperactivity, of the exploration stage. Most individuals have now committed themselves to a vocational objective, at least to the extent of being able to direct their efforts henceforth to further their choice, even though they remain uncertain about the details.

The final stage in the realistic period is specification, which involves specialization and planning within the area of choice. Our study included a few persons who were sufficiently advanced in formal education or who had had enough experience in the Army or in industry to be specific even in the details of their choice. This does not mean that an individual must delay specification until he has acquired considerable training or experience, but simply that he is likely to do so. We also noted that some individuals became so dissatisfied with work in their chosen field that they found it necessary to return to school and seek a new field. It appeared, however, that the choices of these particular individuals had never been really crystallized. Hence, it required a relatively small amount of external pressure to upset the prior decision. However, some persons respond to work experience by reopening what had been a truly crystallized choice. This problem offers a challenge for future research.

GUIDE QUESTIONS

1. Why do you suppose the "fantasy period" and the "period of tentative choices," analyses of which precede this discussion, are so called? Review your own thinking about a vocation during childhood and in high school.

2. Which of these causes of uncertainty during the exploration stage of choosing a vocation do you consider most important: (a) lack of knowledge about the outside world, (b) desire for broader experiences in order to test one's interests and capacities, (c) fear of making a premature commitment, (d) difficulty in assessing one's grades in different subjects, (e) need to narrow the possibilities by a process of elimination, (f) equally strong attraction toward two or more fields, (g) doubt as to whether one has the talents necessary to succeed in the field of his special interest, (h) determination to find a career that is personally gratifying, (i) confusion brought on by the many new experiences in college? Explain how several of these causes of uncertainty might operate together to delay a final decision.

3. What internal and external influences tend to make students crystallize their choice of a vocation?

4. What is meant by "pseudo-crystallization"? What other "key persons"

besides one's parents might influence a pseudo-crystallized choice of vocation?

5. Why is it "difficult for a student to plan in advance the various stages in his career or even to determine definitely his field of specialization"?

6. How can the stage of "specification" be recognized?

7. As a rule, when an occupation becomes specified in one's mind, the thought of a life plan for one's family is still secondary or only dimly realized. In the case of Joel, however, this order was reversed. To what extent do you believe a person's life plan should be thought out before he chooses a specific vocation?

8. Discuss the case of Lewis as an example of pseudo-specification. Explain why you do or do not think this case is intended to show that Lewis, or anyone who has already chosen a specific vocation, should stop thinking about other possible alternatives.

9. Which of the three stages in the period of realistic vocational choices—exploration, crystallization, or specification—do you consider most difficult for a student? In which stage do you find yourself?

10. Tell why you agree or disagree with the majority who put external conditions, such as income and prestige, ahead of personal satisfaction in choosing a vocation.

11. How were the case histories for this study obtained? Why is the study of case histories a good method to use in investigating the problems of vocational choice?

12. How well does Ginzberg relate his running analysis of the evidence to the evidence itself? Does his interpretation of the evidence seem at all points carefully reasoned and convincing? Discuss.

13. Only one student, Robert, is mentioned in connection with all three stages in the period of realistic choices. Why? Which other students are mentioned in connection with more than one stage? Analyze their statements.

14. Try to get statements from students you know that will illustrate each of the three stages discussed by Ginzberg. Analyze the evidence you obtain in this way and relate it to Ginzberg's conclusions.

VOCABULARY

Give the derivations and definitions of the following words:

fantasy, tentative, alternative, entail, circumscribed, assess, oblivious, commitment, relevant, eschew, gratifying, subjective, introspective, stratagem, feasible, immerse, tenuously, preclude, propensity, impel, synthesize, ret-

rospect, criterion, presage, commensurate, facet, deflection, scrutiny, spurious, propel, hyperactivity.

Anonymous

LETTER TO A SEVENTEEN-YEAR-OLD SON

DEAR GREG:

IN ONE SENSE I have been planning to write this letter for several years in order to pull together for what they may be worth some notions on your choice of an occupation and how to train yourself for it. In another sense the letter is occasioned by the recent news story about Pearlstein, the Brooklyn College basket-baller, who carried a couple of books but never went to class. In still another sense the reason for the letter is the too-brief talk we had the other day when you showed me a pamphlet about an Army plan for training seventeen-year-olds in colleges as members of the Enlisted Reserve. In still another sense this is an answer to ideas you have put forward from time to time about enlisting next month. So you see you're in for a large dose of the Old Man's ideas on Life, Education, War, and What-not—especially What-not.

In a novel by Bulwer-Lytton, whose books you would not like (which is just as well), a character says: "What a terrible and unfair advantage merely living longer gives a man!" It is both a wise and sad remark, one that can serve as a warning to members of different generations when dealing with each other. The older always know that they know more; the young always know that the old don't know enough to keep from messing up the world. Both, of course, are quite right.

What follows in this letter is just an attempt to apply the advantage I have, because I have lived longer, to you, because I know you better than a teacher does, or a college catalogue, or a newspaper, or a recruiting poster. . . . I'm not sure I know many answers, and anyhow I couldn't expect you to accept the ones I think I know. But now that you are up against decisions that involve very general questions of what kind of a world it is and how to act in it, it would be wrong and lazy of me, I think, if I didn't try to pass on my ideas.

Your problem of Navy enlistment next month, or of entering the Army Enlisted Reserve, is all bound up, it seems to me, with what you're going to do later, and that's why I'll try to handle them all together. We might start with the more specific problems and work toward the more general ones.

There are three kinds of soldiers: professionals, citizens, and bums. (All this applies to Navy people as well.) Professional soldiering isn't a bad life if you have that kind of temperament. It requires a high sense of honor and duty, a low degree of curiosity, ambition, and independence. The pay is poor but the security is practically perfect. A professional soldier *can* learn almost anything. Almost none of them learn any more than they have to. General Beukema of West Point is perhaps the only one of the hundreds of professionals I have met in the past three years who really struck me as an outstanding all-round man. I have an impression General Marshall is another, but I doubt if the same could be said of many other top officers. Soldiering is a respectable but deadening sort of profession. I know lots of young men to whom I would recommend it. You are not one of them, although I can think of a lot of people who would be more unhappy as professional soldiers than you would be. If you want to be one, the thing to do is to go to West Point (or Annapolis or V.M.I.) and learn the profession from the ground up and do it right. . . .

The citizen soldier is a very different animal. He goes into the Army because his country decides that it needs a few years of his life. (Sometimes it takes his life, but it tries not to. People get killed in other occupations, too. The element of war risk will be left out of this discussion and the Army will be treated just like coal mining or driving a racing automobile, both of which are highly dangerous.) The citizen soldier goes into an army on the terms laid down by his country. If he has good sense and normal patriotism, he goes willingly and tries like hell to make the best of it. But the young man's duty to go into the Army is like the citizen's duty to pay taxes. It is not exalted, or poetic, or heroic. In a democracy, the decision to go in or stay out (as a citizen soldier, not as a professional) ought not to be left to the individual. Leaving it to him is bad for him and bad for the country. We have learned since the last war that "recruiting" is a bad business. We have adopted a sane, responsible attitude toward how to get the huge armies we seem to need. Ninety-five per cent of the men now in uniform would say today that they would not enlist. The other five per cent (except the professionals) are by no means the best soldiers. They are mostly the ones I've classified above as bums. That may be a harsh term. What I mean is young men who have an especially hard time adjusting to life, who get in trouble with the police, who haven't any purpose or sense of responsibility, and who, by and large, are having a rotten time. In peace, police magistrates give a lot of these guys a choice between the house of correction and the services. Many of them pick the services. Sometimes, but not usually, they get straightened out. In wartime this group tends to expand greatly. Perfectly decent kids can't see beyond the war, can't sit down and think their way through to a purpose. The pressures and distorted values of wartime play tricks like that on all of us, but especially on the youngsters. But a kid who joins the army before he has to in wartime, is (to put it brutally) being motivated in part by the same sort of thing that gets the young bums in peacetime. . . .

Anyway, unless you change in a most unlikely way or unless my ideas change on this point, I would be against your going in. Since the law delegates to your mother and me part of the responsibility for deciding whether you ought to go in at 17, we have a duty to consider the case as citizens, not just as parents. On this point we are agents of the government, in a way, and we have tried to think about it as agents of the government. We think it is best not only for you but for the country that you stay out until the country takes you.

If you agree, that brings you to the decision of what you do with the intervening year. That's a tough one. I think I can understand how futile it would seem to take a year of college or do a year of work at this point, knowing that the Army and the war lie ahead. The temptation to say "Oh hell, why don't I get it over with" must be very strong. To give in to that, however, is the easy way. What you are really up against is the tough decision that every youngster has to make of what he's going to do with himself. Most of us try to duck it. Your generation is simply faced with the old problem in a more complicated, less attractive, and more immediate form.

You can't and you don't have to decide in the next year what profession you want to adopt. But you have to work on that choice as hard as you can from here on out. You can't ignore it, Army or no Army, war or no war. You've got to find out as much about yourself as you

can, but above all you've got to find out an awful lot about the world
so as to know where you fit best. Those two jobs are the real subject
matter of education, in and out of schools. . . .

II

On the broader question of education and postwar occupation, and
not with particular reference to the Army, I go wholeheartedly along
with you in judging that your general bent and aptitude are along the
line of the physical sciences. That's true of most American boys. Amer
icans as a people have outstanding mechanical aptitude and a tre
mendous number of them want to work with things rather than with
words and ideas. For every American boy who wants to be a lawyer
there must be a hundred who want to be aviation and automotive
engineers. As a result, most male students in American schools learn
the physical sciences a lot better than they learn the word sciences. You
are an example of this. The word subjects like history, English, and
other languages seem irrelevant nuisances that you'll never use. Partly
for this reason and partly because schools and parents do an incredibly
bad job of explaining the purpose of the word subjects to boys, Amer
ican education is sadly off base in terms of future citizenship and in
terms of what people need to lead happy, useful lives.

Men a lot better than I am have tried to make the points I'm going
to make now, but instead of referring you to their writings I'm going
to try my own version. People like Hutchins of Chicago go to ridicu
lous lengths in making claims for the kind of education that stresses
the word subjects. They give the impression that just reading Virgil
and Homer and studying dead civilizations unlocks the understanding
of life. They reduce the "utilitarian subjects" to the level of cooking.
But the other extreme is just as bad, and has made a lot more headway
in forming the actual attitude of American youth toward education.

To listen to the utilitarians you would think that human progress
began with the development of the scientific method about three hun
dred years ago and that the outstanding achievements of man have
been the invention of radio, the harnessing of electricity, and the
development of modern medicine. As a matter of fact, the greatest in
vention of the human race is language (and thought—thinking is just
talking to yourself, not out loud. You think with words, and you can't
think without words.)

To realize the relative importance of language suppose first of all
at all the doctors in Washington suddenly died. The death rate would
) up, maybe epidemics would result, work would be performed less
ficiently. Within a month you would probably notice some difference
your daily life. But now suppose everybody in Washington suddenly
•rgot language. Work, all work, would stop. Transit would stop. All
od distribution would stop. People unable to organize their food
ipply would kill each other to get at what food was available. Within
week most of the population would be dead and the rest would be in
ock Creek Park grubbing for roots to eat. It's a far-fetched example,
it you need one like that to point out the obvious.

It's a bad thing that there should be people like me around who
on't know a volt from a velocity; bad for me and bad for the society
: which I'm a part. My education was one-sided, I must admit. But
's a thousand times worse that the world is full of people who can't
iake a clear statement of a thought, which is another way of saying
iey can't think straight. Talking (either to yourself or somebody else)
a technique like building dynamos or growing turnips or removing
insils. Centuries upon centuries went into developing the technique
f talking. The finest men who ever lived gave their lives to it—and
ieir contribution is, even in a strictly utilitarian sense, the most im-
ortant. The radio is useful only because of the words and music that
ime over it. Radio is a marvel, of course, but compared to a symphony
r a poem or a news broadcast it's just a mechanical gadget, a detail
iat helps us get the all-important sounds faster and more conveniently.

Not everybody has to work in words (although there are calcula-
ons indicating that in a really advanced civilization like ours about
) per cent of the people work in, or in support of, the word occupa-
ons, as distinguished from the thing occupations). But everybody has
) know a lot about words and how to use them. I can get by without
eing able to build a dynamo; but the dynamo builder can't get by
ithout words.

The next most important human developments are the sciences of
olitics and economics. They are particular branches of the word
ciences. They are the techniques by which people organize their rela-
ons with one another. A herd of sheep follows a set of rules that are
ifferent from the behavior of an individual sheep and which can't be
gured out even if you know all about an individual sheep. Sheep pick
eaders, make herd decisions as to where they will graze, whether they

will run or walk, and so on. Those rules and decisions, which nobo
understands, are sheep politics.

Even with the tenderest care by shepherds and dogs, sheep could
survive without their politics. Men are their own shepherds and do
They don't get any help in working out their politics of how to orga
ize themselves to survive and progress. They have to figure out eve
hard decision in the light of factors whose interrelation is as mu
more complex than radar as radar is more complex than a simple lev
Fortunately, each generation doesn't have to start from scratch. T
record of politics, economics, and sociology—and of technological
velopment, for that matter—is contained in history and in art. (A
including music, is really a highly intensified kind of history. You m
not believe this; sometime if you're interested I'll try to prove it to yc
Give me a month's notice to get the evidence together.)

Sheep have a herd instinct that tells them to get under a shelteri
bank when they smell a blizzard coming. Men have no political instir
to protect them. Instead, we have history, which takes the place
instinct. A people which doesn't know history is like a sheep whi
can't smell a wolf in the wind. In a democracy a citizen cannot entire
delegate to experts his duty of thinking (language) and his share
exercising the herd instinct for self-preservation (history).

Not all history (as I indicated in that crack about art) is contain
in history books. Some of the best history is in novels: Lord Wave
who is a damned good soldier, as Marshal Rommel found out, tc
the graduating class at Sandhurst, the British West Point, to lea
something about history and humanity and to do it by reading go
historical and other novels. One of the most important questions
our day, for instance, is what the Russian people are like. If anybo
ever wrote a decent history of Russia, I haven't been able to find
But there was a crop of magnificent Russian novelists and story-tellc
who told the Russians and the rest of the world about the Russi
character. Almost all that the world really knows of Russian tempe
ment, personality, and development comes from Tolstoy (try *War a
Peace*), Dostoievski (too gloomy for you), Chekhov (you might li
him since you liked Saroyan: Saroyan is phony Chekhov).

Whether our chances of getting on with the Russians are good
bad, they are a lot better than they would be if there had been
Russian novelists, who made Russians into real, understandable pc
ple. Russian temperament has undoubtedly been changing since t

Russian revolution; there have been no great writers handling the post-revolutionary period. Russian development and foreign relations in the next fifty years will be partly determined by whether novelists and playwrights arise in Russia who can explain the Russians to themselves and the rest of the world.

The ultra-materialists and the utilitarians tend to interpret all history in terms of things. They will explain the British Empire, for instance, by talking about the British coal and iron deposits. Undoubtedly, the British Empire would have been unlikely without the coal and iron. But the Chinese had more coal and iron than the British, yet they went downhill during all the period in which coal and iron were most important. If you look for reasons for the difference, one thing worth noticing is that the English language kept getting better and better, more flexible, clearer, better able to express complicated things, during all the period of Britain's growth, while the Chinese language ceased to grow, tended to break up into dialects and to be a less and less useful instrument. A good case can be made for saying that Shakespeare (responsible for the greatest single advance in the English language) had more to do with the growth of the British Empire than his contemporary, Queen Elizabeth (who was a first-rate practitioner of politics), and that either of them was considerably more important than all the scientists and inventors put together.

III

I want to repeat for emphasis that this is *not* said to pooh-pooh the physical scientists or to try to talk you out of a field of work where I agree you belong. It is said to redress a balance in present-day American thinking, especially among people of your age. Ultra-materialism, which concentrates on things, bears a large part of the responsibility for the war and for the mess the peace is quite likely to be. On every side people say the Germans are the way they are because their standard of living was so low. The Germans themselves believe they went to war in order to better a subnormal and unjust living standard imposed on them. Actually their living standard was one of the highest in the world. What ailed them was bad thinking, bad understanding of human nature, including their own, and an inability to present such case as they had in language that would induce other people to listen to them.

The German and American educational systems seem to be more alike than a lot of Americans realize. It's one of the things that worry me most about this country. Both our educational systems turn out enormous quantities of people sufficiently educated to be intelligent soldiers, skilled laborers, foremen, engineers, and third-rate lawyers and journalists. But as *people,* as human beings, it is doubtful if these expensively educated Germans and Americans are as wise, as happy, as mentally healthy as a French peasant or a German peasant or an American pioneer of a century ago. Obviously, the answer isn't to go back to illiterate peasantry. An industrialized world requires more education, not less. But—and this is the important thing—it requires an education that gives to a man of our time the simple human understanding that the peasant and the pioneer used to get naturally out of the lives they led and the surroundings in which they grew up.

Medicine, for instance, is a pretty good profession, especially for one of your temperament which contains a better-than-average knack of getting along with people and a mechanical and scientific bent. But too many of our American physicians, though expensively trained and full of medical information, are dull fellows and unenlightened citizens because their knowledge of people is limited to their specialty. This fact shouldn't discourage you from being a doctor; it should simply discourage you from being the kind of doctor who thinks human beings are just digestive machines with pocketbooks, or that the circulation of the blood is more important than the Constitution of the United States.

That goes for all the other fields open to you. Take farming: in your time that is going to be a far better profession than it has been for three generations. Why? Partly because of scientific advances; but these were making considerable headway in the seventy-five years ending about 1930, during which farming as a way of life kept getting more and more unattractive and insecure. The main reason is because around 1930 some smart people dealing with words and ideas (including a lot of smart dirt farmers) began to figure out what was wrong with farming and began to make some headway in doing something about it. The things that were wrong weren't on the farm itself, they weren't physical things; they were ideas embodied in tariff laws; they were complicated matters like the relation of interest rates to farm prices and the relation of the price of what the farmer sold and what he bought. Farming is a physical science, but it was politics, economics, and the language which finally expressed clearly and effectively what was wrong, that saved the American farmer, and that promise to make farming a decent life again. This doesn't mean that you must be an agricultural economist or a farm lobbyist. It means that a farmer has to know enough politics, economics, history, languages, and human nature to be a good farmer-citizen. You can apply this to engineering or anything else.

The world is full of wonderful technicians making $60 a week and eating their hearts out because the profits of their work and the direction of their work are in the hands of lawyers, bankers, politicians, and other word-artists and organizers. The world, say the technicians, ought not to be like that. So it oughtn't, but the reason why it is lies in the technicians and the way they were trained. Organization—which is done with thoughts, with words—will always be more important, more difficult than any technique in the physical field. The organizers will always get the power because they perform the hardest job. The technicians will always be slaves to the word-artists until the technicians learn how to handle people, how to think logically outside their own narrow fields, how to talk, and how to live.

It's worth noticing that in this highly scientific war almost every important leader has been conspicuously a non-scientist. Roosevelt organized the greatest industrial war effort ever seen, yet there are few Americans who know as little about the technical side of industry as F.D.R. did. Churchill is strictly a poet. He looks very deeply into his country's history, into its soul, and puts what he sees in words that make people act. His speech "we will fight in the streets . . . on the hills" is worth more in purely military terms than all the secret weapons that ever came out of German laboratories. Churchill got that way from reading Shakespeare.

IV

What does this add up to in terms of the decisions that you must soon make? In the first place, it is an argument against over-specialization at an early age in engineering or any other physical science. It is a plea that in choosing a college, picking courses, and above all in your general reading and interests, you try to develop that side of you which needs most development—namely, what the colleges call liberal arts or the humanities. These are the really practically important achievements of the human race; the ones which determine whether we go ahead or back. An engineer or a farmer, as well as a lawyer or a journalist, who doesn't know a little of them is likely to be frustrated as a person and not very useful as a citizen.

You have a year before General Hershey starts breathing down your neck. Why not use it on music and history and art and language? Such studies have a most important bearing on the period of soldiering which you will apparently have to go through. The Army, except for basic training and combat (which takes up a minority of time of a minority of soldiers), is an idle life. Those stand it best who have resources inside themselves, who have the habit of reading and remembering books, of listening to and recalling music. Again, the "liberal arts" are the distilled history of civilization, and the preservation of civilization is the only thing that justifies the war: it cannot possibly be justified in terms of living standards or sheer brute survival. To justify the war one must speak of human freedom, and freedom must be more than a sound; it must be an idea that has the deepest association in one's character. To fight for freedom one must understand what it is, how it grew, who expressed it, who worked out this, that or the other advance, what endangers it and why.

It sickened me when I was in Italy to see so many of our guys going up to battle without much idea why. They were fighting over some of the most important ground in the history of human development. Italy is really one of the greatest laboratories in the science of human language and organization. A lot of what they were fighting for came out of the very ruins through which they crawled. But they didn't know and nobody bothered to tell them clearly what it was all about. Even the silly Jap, dying in the belief that his wall-eyed emperor is a God, is better off than a soldier whose education is so defective he doesn't have any idea what he's fighting for.

What college you go to is important but not as important as the attitude with which you go. I assume you read the Pearlstein story. We all got a laugh at this guy walking around a campus and never attending a class or cracking a book. Probably his Polish ancestors would have given their eye-teeth for his chance to get into a college. Yet in one generation, so bad is our system of explaining education to the young, the Pearlsteins produce an offspring without enough curiosity to sit through a lecture. I think about half our high school and college students are Pearlsteins. Let me say again that it is not the fault of the Pearlsteins but of the schools that the Pearlstein attitude develops. But every individual Pearlstein must accept the responsibility for not learning. Bad as they are, the schools have the stuff on tap. You can get it if you look for it.

It may take you quite a while to digest this. Don't try to accept or reject it right away. Let it rattle around a little and jot down some comments or points on which you might like further examples or argument. Above all don't worry about yourself. You're doing fine. If you weren't I wouldn't bother to write such a long letter to you.

Love,
C.B.

GUIDE QUESTIONS

1. Why does the writer say that he is going to "start with the more specific problems and work toward the more general ones"? Why not the other way around?

2. The first section of the letter, which deals with specific problems, is an analysis of the question: "To enlist, or not to enlist?" For what reasons does the writer disapprove of a military career?

3. After disposing of the enlistment problem, the writer next considers the question: "To specialize or not to specialize in the physical sciences from the start?" Why does he consider the word sciences more important than the physical ones?

4. What is the fundamental connection between the argument against premature enlistment and the argument against premature specialization in the physical sciences?

5. Discuss the statement that language, politics, and economics are the three most important developments in the history of human progress.

6. Interpret the view that art is "a highly intensified kind of history," and the view that "not all history . . . is contained in history books."

7. Why does the writer believe that history cannot be explained in terms of physical things such as natural resources?

8. According to the writer's analysis, what changes in the educational system will have to be made before scientists and technicians will cease to be controlled by word-artists and organizers?

9. How many different occupational fields does this father consider open to his son? In what field does he think his son will eventually find a place? What kind of foundation does he advocate for successful work in this field? Tell why you agree or disagree.

10. The overall method of organization used is the analysis of alternatives or choices. Summarize in a single sentence the argument in each of the numbered sections, showing that each part of the argument deals with the son's immediate and long-range problems of choice in preparing himself for his life work.

11. What impression do you get from the general style of the letter? Are its language and tone appropriate to its purpose?

VOCABULARY

Give the derivations and definitions of the following words:

exalted, intervening, irrelevant, utilitarian, technological, practitioner, redress, materialism, induce, unenlightened, embodied, tariff, lobbyist.

WRITING AND STUDY AIDS

PATTERN OF ORGANIZATION SUGGESTED BY THE GENERAL TOPIC:

Spiegler's "People and Jobs" is an example of analysis by partition. His topic is the things which should be considered in choosing a vocation, and he divides it into six distinct parts, presented separately. His purpose is to examine the general factors that influence the problem of vocational choice, and he partitions them in order to clarify their individual relations to the total problem. The same method is used by Ginzberg in "The Period of Realistic Choices" when he sorts the evidence illustrating the three stages which he wishes to discuss. Furthermore, as you observed, the analysis here rests on the use of examples, case histories. In "Letter to a Seventeen-Year-Old Son" the method is analysis of alternatives, that is, rejection of certain possible choices in favor of other possible choices, these concerning both immediate and long-range decisions in planning an education and a life work.

Your aim in this assignment is the development of an idea by *analysis.* Your general topic is the problem of choosing a vocation, which can be divided into distinct parts, or stages, or alternatives. These are the methods of analysis illustrated in the readings. Two of the readings are objective and one is subjective; your analysis may be either impersonal or personal. Select the method of analysis best adapted to the development of your topic and make it the purpose of what you write to give a thoughtful, well-balanced discussion of a subject that concerns you vitally.

ASSIGNMENTS:

ort themes:

. Brain *versus* brawn
. Geniuses are like that
. How smart do we need to be?
. Fortitude or aptitude?
. The meaning of grades
. The importance of vacation jobs
. An occupation that chose me
. My opinion of factory work/farm work/office work/professional work/government work
. "Doctor, lawyer, merchant, chief . . ."
. There have to be Indians as well as chiefs
. Personality traits desirable in my chosen vocation
. Why I consider ———— a necessary study for everybody
. My decision and how I made it
. Why I prefer a life of leisure
. If money were no object, I would ————

ng themes:

. Square pegs in round holes
. Vocational guidance
. Principles of choosing a vocation
. The case history of an occupational choice
. What I expect to get out of college
. An analysis of why I decided to become a lawyer/doctor/business man/engineer/housewife/career girl
. Early explorations in search of a vocation
. Crystallization of occupational choice among my friends
. To specialize or not to specialize?
. Why so many Americans want to be ————

READINGS FOR FURTHER STUDY:

*mbs, Arthur W. "Non-Directive Techniques and Vocational Counseling," *Occupations,* Vol. 25 (Feb., 1947), 261-67.

*eg, Maethel E., and Donald G. Paterson, "Changes in Social Status of Occupations," *Occupations,* Vol. 25 (Jan., 1947), 205-8.

*nahue, Wilma T., Clyde H. Coombs, and Robert M. W. Travers, editors. *The Measurement of Student Adjustment and Achievement.* Ann Arbor, Mich.: University of Michigan Press, 1949.

Dyer, Dorothy T. "The Relation between Vocational Interests of Men i
College and Their Subsequent Occupational Histories for Ten Years
Journal of Applied Psychology, Vol. 23 (Apr., 1939), 280-88.

Ginzberg, Eli, *et al. Occupational Choice.* New York: Columbia Universit
Press, 1951.

Gregory, Wilbur S. "From High School to College," *Occupations,* Vol. 1
(Dec., 1939), 190-98.

Harris, Seymour E. *The Market for College Graduates.* Cambridge, Mass
Harvard University Press, 1949.

Hollingsworth, H. L. *Vocational Psychology and Character Analysis.* Ne
York: D. Appleton and Company, 1929.

Kirchheimer, Barbara A., and Robert B. Headley. "A Demonstration (
Vocational Counseling," *Occupations,* Vol. 27 (Feb., 1949), 317-21.

Neuberg, Maurice J. *Principles and Methods of Vocational Choice.* Ne
York: Prentice-Hall, Inc., 1934.

Smith, George Baxter. "Intelligence and the Extra-Curriculum Activiti
Selected in High School and College," *School Review,* Vol. 44 (Nov
1936), 681-88.

Strong, Edward K., Jr. *Vocational Interests of Men and Women.* Stanfor
University, Cal.: Stanford University Press, 1943.

Super, Donald E. *The Dynamics of Vocational Adjustment.* New Yorl
Harper & Brothers, 1942.

Super, Donald E. "Experience, Emotion, and Vocational Choice," *Occupe
tions,* Vol. 27 (Oct., 1948), 23-27.

⚡ The Idea of Progress

THE IDEA OF HUMAN PROGRESS INVOLVES AN ESTIMATE OF THE PAST, AN
interpretation of the present, and a prophecy of the future. As J. B. Bury
says, in *The Idea of Progress,* "It is based on an interpretation of history
which regards men as slowly advancing in a definite and desirable direction, and infers that this progress will continue indefinitely."

It may seem surprising that an idea so simple and obvious to us as the
idea of progress was unknown in classical antiquity and the ensuing ages.
Yet the Greeks, for all their brilliance of speculation, scarcely got beyond
the sterile notion of world-cycles, in which

> Worlds on worlds are rolling ever,
> From creation to decay.

The Romans, for the most part, shared this conception of history as endlessly and monotonously repeating itself, with no possibility of any new
thing under the sun. And the men of the Middle Ages, preoccupied in
their efforts to achieve a better world after death, had little time to interest
themselves in the further development of this world during life. Nor did
the boldest minds of the Renaissance do more than dimly foreshadow the
modern faith in an unlimited future for mankind.

Long in germination, at last the idea of progress appeared in positive
form when the Abbé de Saint-Pierre published in 1737 his work entitled
Observations on the Continuous Progress of Universal Reason. "Here,"
says Bury, "we have for the first time, expressed in definite terms, the
vista of an immensely long progressive life in front of humanity." Once
enunciated, this new philosophy gained swift influence over the precursors

373

of the French Revolution. It also spread to the New World, where the acceptance of it by leading thinkers such as Franklin and Paine assured the idea of progress a place in the doctrines underlying American culture. Franklin was of the opinion that in a thousand years the power of man over matter would reach unimagined heights, with incalculably beneficial results; but he wished that "moral science" were as likely to show such gains, in order that "men would cease to be wolves to one another." Thomas Paine, in his *Common Sense* and his *Rights of Man,* sketched a political philosophy which looked forward confidently to the abolition of the ills of society along with the monarchical system of government. Still later, especially after the announcement of Darwin's theory of evolution through natural selection, the idea of progress continued to exert a powerful influence on the opinions of the world.

In the last century progress was so much taken for granted that an imaginary "law of progress" became almost a part of man's creed, a law which it was felt had regulated the advance from savagery to civilization, and which would make inevitable the continued improvement of life. Some optimistic philosophers, impressed by the evidence of technological gains and social evolution, deduced the infinite perfectibility of the human species. Now, on the other hand, some thinkers of a more skeptical turn of mind admit the reality of the great changes that have occurred in the course of human events, but consider progress to be an illusion; they find no demonstrable improvement in the ethics and morals of human beings. More typical of our modern popular attitude is the bright and often unthinking affirmation of a belief in "progress" without knowing what it means.

Is the human race going backward, is it standing still, or is it really progressing? Before one may intelligently take sides in this question, it is necessary to understand some of the profound implications of the problem. The readings for this topic give answers which differ interestingly from one another because of the breadth of the subject, because of the various classifications or subdivisions of it which different approaches make possible, and because of the personal philosophies of its interpreters. The Christian pessimism of Dean Inge, the sturdy optimism of Will Durant, and the scientific moderation of Wilson D. Wallis represent different interpretations of human progress; yet all of them try to see the problem clearly and to see it whole by a careful classification or analysis of their ideas on it. As you study these various interpretations, note the importance of classification as an expository method.

William Ralph Inge

THE IDEA OF PROGRESS

THE BELIEF IN PROGRESS, not as an ideal but as an indisputable fact, not as a task for humanity but as a law of Nature, has been the working faith of the West for about a hundred and fifty years. Some would have us believe that it is a long neglected part of the Christian revelation, others that it is a modern discovery. The ancient Pagans, we are told, put their Golden Age in the past; we put ours in the future. The Greeks prided themselves on being the degenerate descendants of gods, we on being the very creditable descendants of monkeys. The Romans endeavored to preserve the wisdom and virtue of the past, we to anticipate the wisdom and virtue of the future. This, however, is an exaggeration. The theory of progress and the theory of decadence are equally natural, and have in fact been held concurrently wherever men have speculated about their origin, their present condition, and their future prospects. Among the Jews the theory of decadence derived an inspired authority from Genesis, but the story of the Fall had very little influence upon the thought of that tenaciously optimistic race. Among the Greeks, who had the melancholy as well as the buoyancy of youth, it was authorized by Hesiod, whose scheme of retrogression from the age of gold to the age of iron was never forgotten in antiquity. Sophocles, in a well-known chorus imitated by Bacon, holds that the best fate for men is "not to be born, or being born to die." Aratus develops the pessimistic mythology of Hesiod. In the Golden Age Dike or Astraea wandered about the earth freely; in the Silver Age her visits became fewer, and in the Brazen Age she set out for heaven and became the constellation Virgo. Perhaps Horace had read the lament of the goddess: "What a race the golden sires have left— worse than their fathers; and your offspring will be baser still." In the

Adapted from "The Idea of Progress," in *Outspoken Essays: Second Series,* by William Ralph Inge. Reprinted by permission of Longmans, Green & Co., Inc.

third century after Christ, when civilization was really crumbling Pagans and Christians join in a chorus of woe.

On the other side, the Introduction to the First Book of Thucydides sketches the past history of Greece in the spirit of the nineteenth century. Lucretius has delighted our anthropologists by his brilliant and by no means idealized description of savage life, and it is to him that we owe the blessed word Progress in its modern sense.

> Usus et impigrae simul experientia mentis
> Paulatim docuit pedetemtim *progredientes.*
> Sic unum quicquid paulatim protrahit aetas
> In medium, ratioque in luminis erigit oras.

Pliny believes that each age is better than the last. Seneca, in a treatise, parts of which were read in the Middle Ages, reminds us that "not a thousand years have passed since Greece counted and named the stars, and it is only recently that we have learned why the moon is eclipsed. Posterity will be amazed that we did not know some things that will be obvious to them." "The world," he adds, "is a poor affair if it does not contain matter for investigation for men in every age. We imagine that we are initiated into the mysteries of Nature; but we are still hanging about her outer courts." These last are memorable utterances, even if Seneca confines his optimism to the pleasure of exploring Nature's secrets.

But the deepest thought of antiquity was neither optimistic nor pessimistic. It was that progress and retrogression are only the incoming and outgoing tide in an unchanging sea. The pulse of the universe beats in an alternate expansion and contraction. The result is a series of cycles, in which history repeats itself. Plato contemplates a world-cycle of 36,000 solar years, during which the Creator guides the course of events; after which he relaxes his hold of the machine, and a period of the same length follows during which the world gradually degenerates. When this process is complete the Creator restores again the original conditions, and a new cycle begins. Aristotle thinks that all the arts and sciences have been discovered and lost "an infinite number of times." Virgil in the Fourth Eclog tries to please Augustus by predicting the near approach of a new Golden Age, which, he says, is now due. This doctrine of recurrence is not popular to-day; but whether we like it or not, no other view of the macrocosm is even tenable. Even if those physicists are right who hold that the universe

unning down like a clock, that belief postulates a moment in past
e when the clock was wound up; and whatever power wound it up
e may presumably wind it up again. Still, I must admit that on the
ole the ancients did tend to regard time as the enemy: *damnosa
d non imminuit dies?* They would have thought the modern notion
1uman perfectibility at once absurd and impious.

"he Dark Ages knew that they were dark, and we hear little talk
ut progress during those seven centuries which, as far as we can
might have been cut out of history without any great loss to pos-
ty. The Middle Ages (which we ought never to confuse with the
rk Ages), though they developed an interesting type of civilization,
their hopes mainly on another world. The Church has never enraged the belief that this world is steadily improving; the Middle
es, like the early Christians, would have been quite content to see
earthly career of the race closed in their own time. Even Roger
on, who is claimed as the precursor of modern science, says that all
e men believe that we are not far from the time of Antichrist, which
s to be the herald of the end. The Renaissance was a conscious re-
ery from the longest and dreariest set-back that humanity has ever
erienced within the historical period—a veritable glacial age of the
it. At this time men were too full of admiration and reverence for
newly recovered treasures of antiquity to look forward to the
are. In the seventeenth century a doctrine of progress was already
he air, and a long literary battle was waged between the Ancients
the Moderns.

ut it was only in the eighteenth century that Western Europe be-
to dream of an approaching millennium without miracle, to be
dually ushered in under the auspices of a faculty which was called
son. Unlike some of their successors, these optimists believed that
ection was to be attained by the self-determination of the human
l; they were not fatalists. In France, the chief home of this heady
trine, the psychical temperature soon began to rise under its in-
nce, till it culminated in the delirium of the Terror. The Goddess
Reason hardly survived Robespierre and his guillotine; but the
ef in progress, which might otherwise have subsided when the
nch resumed their traditional pursuits—*rem militarem et argute
ui*—was reinforced by the industrial revolution, which was to run a
y different course from that indicated by the theatrical disturbances
'aris between 1789 and 1794, the importance of which has perhaps

been exaggerated. In England above all, the home of the new indus
progress was regarded as that kind of improvement which can
measured by statistics. This was quite seriously the view of the
century generally, and there has never been, nor will there ever
again, such an opportunity for gloating over this kind of improveme
The mechanical inventions of Watt, Arkwright, Crompton, Steph
son, and others led to an unparalleled increase of population. Expe
and imports also progressed, in a favorite phrase of the time, by le
and bounds. Those who, like Malthus, sounded a note of warni
showing that population increases, unlike the supply of food, by g
metrical progression, were answered that compound interest follc
the same admirable law. It was obvious to many of our grandpare
that a nation which travels sixty miles an hour must be five times
civilized as one which travels only twelve, and that, as Glanvill l
already declared in the reign of Charles II, we owe more gratitude
the inventor of the mariner's compass "than to a thousand Alexand
and Cæsars, or to ten times the number of Aristotles." The histori
of the time could not contain their glee in recording these triump
Only the language of religion seemed appropriate in contemplating
magnificent a spectacle. If they had read Herder, they would h
quoted with approval his prediction that "the flower of human
captive still in its germ, will blossom out one day into the true fo
of a man like unto God, in a state of which no man on earth
imagine the greatness and the majesty." Determinism was much
vogue by this time; but why should determinism be a depress
creed? The law which we cannot escape is the blessed law of progres
"that kind of improvement that can be measured by statistics." We l
only to thank our stars for placing us in such an environment, and
carry out energetically the course of development which Nature
prescribed for us, and to resist which would be at once impious
futile.

Thus the superstition of progress was firmly established. To becc
a popular religion, it is only necessary for a superstition to enslav
philosophy. The superstition of progress had the singular good fortu
to enslave at least three philosophies—those of Hegel, of Comte, and
Darwin. The strange thing is that none of these philosophies is re
favourable to the belief which it was supposed to support. Leaving
the present the German and the French thinkers, we observe w
astonishment that many leading men in Queen Victoria's reign fou

ossible to use the great biological discovery of Darwin to tyrannize
the minds of their contemporaries, and to give their blessing to
economic and social movements of their time. Scientific optimism
no doubt rampant before Darwin. But Herbert Spencer asserts
perfectibility of man with an assurance which makes us gasp.
ogress is not an accident but a necessity. What we call evil and
morality must disappear. It is certain that man must become perfect."
e ultimate development of the ideal man is certain—as certain as
conclusion in which we place the most implicit faith; for instance,
all men will die." "Always towards perfection is the mighty move-
t—towards a complete development and a more unmixed good."

has been pointed out by Mr. Bradley that these apocalyptic prophe-
have nothing whatever to do with Darwinism. If we take the so-
d doctrine of evolution in Nature as a metaphysics of existence,
ch Darwin never intended it to be, "there is in the world nothing
value, or good, or evil. Anything implying evolution, in the or-
ry sense of development or progress, is wholly rejected." The sur-
l of the fittest does not mean that the most virtuous, or the most
ul, or the most beautiful, or even the most complex survive: there
o moral or æsthetic judgment pronounced on the process or any
of it.

rwinism (Mr. Bradley goes on to say) often recommends itself because
confused with a doctrine of evolution which is radically different.
anity is taken in that doctrine as a real being, or even as the one real
g; and humanity (it is said) advances continuously. Its history is de-
oment and progress toward a goal, because the type and character in
h its reality consists is gradually brought more and more into fact.
which is strongest on the whole must therefore be good, and the ideas
h come to prevail must therefore be true. This doctrine, though I
inly cannot accept it, for good or evil more or less dominates or sways
minds to an extent of which most of us perhaps are dangerously un-
e. Any such view of course conflicts radically with Darwinism, which
teaches that the true idea is the idea which prevails, and this leaves
the end with no criterion at all.

lthough the main facts of cosmic evolution, and the main course of
an history from pithecanthropus downwards, are well known, it
be worth while to recall in bald and colourless language what
ice really tells us about the nature and destiny of our species. It is
ifferent from the gay colours of the rhapsodists whom I have just

quoted, that we must be amazed that such doctrines should ever
passed for scientific. Astronomy gives us a picture of a wildernes
space, probably boundless, sparsely sown with aggregations of
mental particles in all stages of heat and cold. These heavenly be
are in some cases growing hotter, in other cases growing colder;
the fate of every globe must be, sooner or later, to become cold
dead, like the moon. Our sun, from which we derive the warmth w
makes our life possible, is, I believe, an elderly star, which has
outlived the turbulent heats of youth, and is on its way to join
most senile class of luminiferous bodies, in which the star 19 Pis
is placed. When a star has once become cold, it must apparentl
main dead until some chance collision sets the whole cycle going a
From time to time a great conflagration in the heavens, which
curred perhaps in the seventeenth century, becomes visible from
earth; and we may imagine, if we will, that two great solar sys
have been reduced in a moment to incandescent gas. But space is
ably so empty that the most pugnacious of astral knights-errant m
wander for millions of years without meeting an opponent worth
its bulk. If time as well as space is infinite, worlds must be born
die innumerable times, however few and far between their perio
activity may be. Of progress, in such a system taken as a whole,
cannot be a trace. Nor can there be any doubt about the fate of
own planet. Man and all his achievements will one day be oblite
like a child's sand-castle when the next tide comes in.

The racial life of the species to which we happen to belong is a
episode even in the brief life of the planet. And what we call civ
tion or culture, though much older than we used to suppose, is a
episode in the life of our race. For tens of thousands of years
changes in our habits must have been very slight, and chiefly
which were forced upon our rude ancestors by changes of clin
Then in certain districts man began, as Samuel Butler says, to
to live beyond his income. This was the beginning of the vast s
of inventions which have made our life so complex. And, we use
be told, the "law of all progress is the same, the evolution of the si
into the complex by successive differentiations." This is the g
according to Herbert Spencer. As a universal law of nature it is
crously untrue. Some species have survived by becoming more
plex, others, like the whole tribe of parasites, by becoming more sir
On the whole, perhaps the parasites have had the best of it.

progressive species have in many cases flourished for a while and then paid the supreme penalty. The living dreadnoughts of the Saurian age have left us their bones, but no progeny. But the microbes, one of which had the honour of killing Alexander the Great at the age of thirty-two, and so changing the course of history, survive and flourish. Our own species, being rather poorly provided by nature for offence and defence, had to live by its wits, and so came to the top. It developed many new needs, and set itself many insoluble problems. Physiologists like Metchnikoff have shown how very ill-adapted our bodies are to the tasks which we impose upon them; and in spite of the Spencerian identification of complexity with progress, our surgeons try to simplify our structure by forcibly removing various organs which they assure us that we do not need. If we turn to history for a confirmation of the Spencerian doctrine, we find, on the contrary, that civilization is a disease which is almost invariably fatal, unless its course is checked in time. The Hindus and Chinese, after advancing to a certain point, were content to mark time; and they survive. But the Greeks and Romans are gone; and aristocracies everywhere die out. Do we not see to-day the complex organization of the ecclesiastic and college don succumbing before the simple squeezing and sucking apparatus of the profiteer and trade-unionist? If so-called civilized nations show any protracted vitality, it is because they are only civilized at the top. Ancient civilizations were destroyed by imported barbarians; we breed our own.

It is also an unproved assumption that the domination of the planet by our own species is a desirable thing, which must give satisfaction to its Creator. We have devastated the loveliness of the world; we have exterminated several species more beautiful and less vicious than ourselves; we have enslaved the rest of the animal creation, and have treated our distant cousins in fur and feathers so badly that beyond doubt, if they were able to formulate a religion, they would depict the Devil in human form. It is a pity that our biologists, instead of singing pæans to Progress and thereby stultifying their own researches, have not preached us sermons on the sin of racial self-idolatry, a topic which really does arise out of their studies. *L'anthropolatrie, voilà l'ennemi*, is the real ethical motto of biological science, and a valuable contribution to morals.

It was impossible that such shallow optimism as that of Herbert Spencer should not arouse protests from other scientific thinkers. We

are not likely to forget the second Romanes Lecture, when Professor
Huxley astonished his friends and opponents alike by throwing down
the gauntlet in the face of Nature, and bidding mankind to find sal
vation by accepting for itself the position which the early Christian
writer Hippolytus gives as a definition of the Devil—"he who resists
the cosmic process." The revolt was not in reality so sudden as some
of Huxley's hearers supposed. He had already realized that "so far
from gradual progress forming any necessary part of the Darwinian
creed, it appears to us that it is perfectly consistent with indefinite
persistence in one state, or with a gradual retrogression. Suppose, *e.g.*
a return of the glacial period or a spread of polar climatical condition
over the whole globe." The alliance between determinism and op
timism was thus dissolved; and as time went on, Huxley began to
see in the cosmic process something like a power of evil. The natural
process, he told us, has no tendency to bring about the good of man
kind. Cosmic nature is no school of virtue, but the headquarters of
the enemy of ethical nature. Nature is the realm of tiger-rights; it has
no morals and no ought-to-be; its only rights are brutal powers.
Morality exists only in the "artificial" moral world: man is a glorious
rebel, a Prometheus defying Zeus. This strange rebound into Maniche
ism sounded like a blasphemy against all the gods whom the lecture
was believed to worship, and half-scandalized even the clerics in his
audience. It was bound to raise the question whether this titanic revolt
against the cosmic process had any chance of success. One recent
thinker, who accepts Huxley's view that the nature of things is cruel
and immoral, is willing to face the probability that we cannot resist it
with any prospect of victory. Mr. Bertrand Russell, in his arresting es
say, "A Free Man's Worship," shows us Prometheus again, but Pro
metheus chained to the rock and still hurling defiance against God. He
proclaims the moral bankruptcy of naturalism, which he yet holds to
be forced upon us.

That man is the product of causes which had no prevision of the end
they were achieving; that his origin, his growth, his hopes and fears, his
loves, and his beliefs, are but the outcome of accidental collocations of
atoms; that no fire, no heroism, no intensity of thought and feeling, can
preserve an individual beyond the grave; that all the labours of the age,
all the devotion, all the inspiration, all the noonday brightness of human
genius, are destined to extinction in the vast death of the solar system, and
that the whole temple of man's achievement must inevitably be buried

beneath the débris of a universe in ruins—all these things, if not quite beyond dispute, are yet so nearly certain, that no philosophy which rejects them can hope to stand. Only within the scaffolding of these truths, only on the firm foundation of unyielding despair, can the soul's habitation henceforth be safely built.

Man belongs to "an alien and inhuman world," alone amid "hostile forces." What is man to do? The God who exists is evil; the God whom we can worship is the creation of our own conscience, and has no existence outside it.

If I wished to criticize this defiant pronouncement, which is not without a touch of bravado, I should say that so complete a separation of the real from the ideal is impossible, and that the choice which the writer offers us, of worshiping a Devil who exists or a God who does not, is no real choice, since we cannot worship either. But my object in quoting from this essay is to show how completely naturalism has severed its alliance with optimism and belief in progress. Professor Huxley and Mr. Russell have sung their palinode and smashed the old gods of their creed. No more proof is needed, I think, that the alleged law of progress has no scientific basis whatever.

But the superstition has also invaded and vitiated our history, our political science, our philosophy, and our religion.

The historian is a natural snob; he sides with the gods against Cato, and approves the winning side. He lectures the vanquished for their wilfulness and want of foresight. The nineteenth-century historian was so loath to admit retrogression that he liked to fancy the river of progress flowing underground all through the Dark Ages, and endowed the German barbarians who overthrew Mediterranean civilization with all the manly virtues. If a nation, or a religion, or a school of art dies, the historian explains why it was not worthy to live.

In political science the corruption of the scientific spirit by the superstition of progress has been flagrant. It enables the disputant to overbear questions of right and wrong by confident prediction, a method which has the double advantage of being peculiarly irritating and incapable of refutation. On the theory of progress, what is "coming" must be right. Forms of government and modes of thought which for the time being are not in favor are assumed to have been permanently left behind. A student of history who believed in cyclical changes and long swings of the pendulum would take a very different and probably much sounder view of contemporary affairs. The votaries of progress mistake the flowing tide for the river of eternity, and when the tide turns they are likely to be left stranded like the corks and scraps of seaweed which mark the high-water line. This has already happened, though few realize it. The praises of Liberty are mainly left to Conservatives, who couple it with Property as something to be defended, and to conscientious objectors, who dissociate it from their country, which is not to be defended. Democracy—the magic ballot-box—has few worshipers any longer except in America, where men will still shout for about two hours—and indeed much longer—that she is "great." But our pundits will be slow to surrender the useful words "progressive" and "reactionary." The classification is, however, a little awkward. If a reactionary is anyone who will not float with the stream, and a progressive anyone who has the flowing tide with him, we must classify the Christian Fathers and the French Encyclopedists as belonging to the same type, the progressive; while the Roman Stoics under the Empire and the Russian bureaucrats under Nicholas II will be placed together under the opposite title, as reactionaries. Or is the progressive not the supporter of the winning cause for the time being, but the man who thinks that "any leap in the dark is better than standing still"; and is the reactionary the man whose constitutional timidity would deter him from performing this act of faith when caught by a mist on the Matterhorn? Machiavelli recognizes fixed types of human character, such as the cautious Fabius and the impetuous Julius II, and observes that these qualities lead sometimes to success and sometimes to failure. If a reactionary only means an adherent of political opinions which we happen to dislike, there is no reason why a bureaucrat should not call a republican a reactionary, as Maecenas may have applied the name to Brutus and Cassius. Such examples of evolution as that which turned the Roman Republic into a principate and then into an empire of the Asiatic type, are inconvenient for those who say, "It is coming," and think that they have vindicated the superiority of their own theories of government.

We have next to consider the influence of the superstition of progress on the philosophy of the last century. Hegel and Comte are often held to have been the chief advocates of the doctrine of progress among philosophers. Both of them give definitions of the word—a very necessary thing to do, and I have not yet attempted to do it. Hegel defines progress as spiritual freedom; Comte as true or positive social philosophy. The definitions are peculiar; and neither theory can be made to it past history, though that of Comte, at any rate, falls to the ground if it does not fit past history. Hegel is perhaps more independent of facts; his predecessor Fichte professes to be entirely indifferent to them. "The philosopher," he says, "follows the *a priori* thread of the world-plan which is clear to him without any history; and if he makes use of history, it is not to prove anything, since his theses are already proved independently of all history." Certainly, Hegel's dialectical process cannot easily be recognized in the course of European events; and, what is more fatal to the believers in a law of progress who appeal to him, he does not seem to have contemplated any further marked improvements upon the political system of Prussia in his own time, which he admired so much that his critics have accused him of teaching that the Absolute first attained full self-consciousness at Berlin in the nineteenth century. He undoubtedly believed that there has been progress in the past; but he does not, it appears, look forward to further changes; as a politician, at any rate, he gives us something like a closed system. Comte can only bring his famous "three stages" into history by arguing that the Catholic monotheism of the Middle Ages was an advance upon Pagan antiquity. A Catholic might defend such a thesis with success; but for Comte the chief advantage seems to be that the change left the Olympians with only one neck for Positive Philosophy to cut off. But Comte himself is what his system requires us to call a reactionary; he is back in the "theological stage"; he would like a theocracy, if he could have one without a God. The State is to be subordinate to the Positive Church, and he will allow "no unlimited freedom of thought." The connexion of this philosophy with the doctrine of progress seems very slender. It is not so easy to answer the question in the case of Hegel, because his contentment with the Prussian government may be set down to idiosyncrasy or to prudence; but it is significant that some of his ablest disciples have discarded the belief. To say that "the world is as it ought to be" does not imply that it goes on getting better, though some would think it was not good if it was not getting better. It is hard to believe that a great thinker really supposed that the universe as a whole is progressing, a notion which Mr. Bradley has stigmatized as "nonsense, unmeaning or blasphemous." Be that as it may, popularized Hegelianism has laid hold of the idea of a self-improving universe, of perpetual and universal progress, in a strictly temporal sense. The notion of an evolving and progressing cosmos, with a Creator who is either improving himself (though we do not put it quite so crudely) or who is gradually coming into his own, has taken strong hold of the popular imagination.

To show how the belief in a law of progress has prejudicially affected the religious beliefs of our time, I need only recall the discussions whether the perfect man could have lived in the first, and not in the nineteenth or twentieth century—although one would have thought that the ancient Greeks, to take one nation only, have produced many examples of hitherto unsurpassed genius; the secularization of religion by throwing its ideals into the near future—a new apocalyptism which is doing mischief enough in politics without the help of the clergy; and the unauthorized belief in future probation, which rests on the queer assumption that, if a man is given time enough, he must necessarily become perfect. In fact, the superstition has distorted Christianity almost beyond recognition. Only one great Church, old in worldly wisdom, knows that human nature does not change, and acts on the knowledge. Accordingly, the papal syllabus of 1864 declares: "*Si quis dixerit:* Romanus pontifex potest ac debet cum progressu, cum liberalismo, et cum recenti civilitate sese reconciliare et componere, *anathema sit.*"

Our optimists have not made it clear to themselves or others what they mean by progress, and we may suspect that the vagueness of the idea is one of its attractions. There has been no physical progress in our species for many thousands of years. The Cro-Magnon race, which lived perhaps twenty thousand years ago, was at least equal to any modern people in size and strength; the ancient Greeks were, I suppose, handsomer and better formed than we are; and some unprogressive races, such as the Zulus, Samoans, and Tahitians, are envied for either strength or beauty. Although it seems not to be true that the sight and hearing of civilized peoples are inferior to those of savages, we have certainly lost our natural weapons, which from one point of view is a mark of degeneracy. Mentally, we are now told that the men of the Old Stone Age, ugly as most of them must have been, had as large brains as ours; and he would be a bold man who should claim that we are intellectually equal to the Athenians or superior to the Romans. The question of moral improvement is much more difficult. Until the Great War few would have disputed that civilized man had become much more humane, much more sensitive to the sufferings of others, and so more just, more self-controlled, and less brutal in his pleasures and in his resentments. It was often forgotten that, if progress means the improvement of human nature itself, the question to be asked is whether the modern civilized man behaves better in the same circumstances than his ancestor would have done. Absence of temptation may produce an appearance of improvement; but this is hardly what we mean by progress, and there is an old saying that the Devil has a clever trick of pretending to be dead. It seems to me very doubtful whether when we are exposed to the same temptations we are more humane or more sympathetic or juster or less brutal than the ancients. During the Great War, even if some atrocities were magnified with the amiable object of rousing a good-natured people to violent hatred, it was the well-considered opinion of Lord Bryce's commission that no such cruelties had been committed for three hundred years as those which the Germans practised in Belgium and France. It was startling to observe how easily the blood-lust was excited in young men straight from the fields, the factory, and the counter, many of whom had never before killed anything larger than a wasp, and that in self-defence. As for the Turks, we must go back to Genghis Khan to find any parallel to their massacres in Armenia; and the Russian terrorists have reintroduced torture into Europe, with the help of Chinese experts in the art. With these examples before our eyes, it is difficult to feel any confidence that either the lapse of time or civilization has made the *bête humaine* less ferocious. On biological grounds there is no reason to expect it. No selection in favour of superior types is now going on; on the contrary, civilization tends now, as always, to an *Ausrottung der Besten*—a weeding-out of the best; and the new practice of subsidizing the unsuccessful by taxes extorted from the industrious is erected into a principle. The best hope of stopping this progressive degeneration is in the science of eugenics. But this science is still too tentative to be made the basis of legislation, and we are not yet agreed what we should breed for. The two ideals, that of the perfect man and that of the perfectly organized State, would lead to very different principles of selection. Do we want a nation of beautiful and moderately efficient Greek gods, or do we want human mastiffs for policemen, human greyhounds for postmen, and so on? However, the opposition which eugenics has now to face is based on less respectable grounds, such as pure hedonism ("would the superman be any happier?"); indifference to the future welfare of the race ("posterity has done nothing for me; why should I do anything for posterity?"); and, in politics, the reflection that the unborn have no votes.

We have, then, been driven to the conclusion that neither science nor history gives us any warrant for believing that humanity has advanced, except by accumulating knowledge and experience and the instruments of living. The value of these accumulations is not beyond dispute. Attacks upon civilization have been frequent, from Crates, Pherecrates, Antisthenes, and Lucretius in antiquity to Rousseau, Walt Whitman, Thoreau, Ruskin, Morris, and Edward Carpenter in modern times. I cannot myself agree with these extremists. I believe that the accumulated experience of mankind, and his wonderful discoveries are of great value. I only point out that they do not constitute real progress in human nature itself, and that in the absence of any real progress these gains are external, precarious, and liable to be turned to our own destruction, as new discoveries in chemistry may easily be

GUIDE QUESTIONS

1. Interpret: "The Greeks prided themselves on being the degenerate descendants of gods, we on being the very creditable descendants of monkeys."
2. What was the cyclical theory of Plato?
3. Summarize in a topic sentence the thought of Dean Inge's first paragraph.
4. Why does the fourth paragraph give a greater sense of movement than any of the first three paragraphs?
5. What were the grounds for Herbert Spencer's assertion of "the perfectibility of man with an assurance which makes us gasp"?
6. What does Dean Inge consider the proper interpretation of Darwinism?
7. Comment on the appropriateness of the author's style to his subject in the passage in which he describes the universe pictured by astronomy.
8. Interpret: ". . . civilization is a disease which is almost invariably fatal, unless its course is checked in time." What evidence is given for this statement?
9. In the author's opinion, what should biologists have been doing instead of "singing paeans to Progress"?
10. What did Thomas Henry Huxley mean by advocating resistance to the "cosmic process"? What did he favor in place of the "cosmic process"?

11. How does Dean Inge indicate that he intends to classify or subdivide his ideas in discussing the four fields which "the superstition" of progress "has also invaded"? What are these fields?
12. State in one topic sentence the thought of each of the four paragraphs devoted to these fields.
13. What evidence does the author present against the idea of physical progress? Against the idea that man is more humane today than formerly?

VOCABULARY

Give the derivations and definitions of the following words:

decadence, macrocosm, postulates, millennium, determinism, apocalyptic, luminiferous, incandescent, astral, sonorous, sporadic, transient, stultify, titanic, prevision, vitiated, votaries, pundit, reactionary, principate, positivism, dialectical, monotheism, theocracy, stigmatize, cosmos, secularization, humane, eugenics, tentative, hedonism.

Will Durant

IS PROGRESS A DELUSION?

"IF YOU WISH TO CONVERSE WITH ME," said Voltaire, "define your terms." What shall we mean by "progress"? Subjective definitions will not do; we must not conceive progress in terms of one nation, or one religion, or one code of morals; an increase of kindness, for example, would alarm our young Nietzscheans. Nor may we define progress in terms of happiness; for idiots are happier than geniuses, and those whom we most respect seek not happiness but greatness. Is it possible to find an objective definition for our term?—one that will hold for any individual, any group, even for any species? Let us provisionally define progress as increasing control of the environment by life; and let us mean by environment all the circumstances that condition the coordination and realization of desire. Progress is the domination of chaos by mind and purpose, of matter by form and will.

It need not be continuous in order to be real. There may be "plateaus" in it, Dark Ages and disheartening retrogressions; but if the last stage is the highest of all we shall say that man makes progress. And in assessing epochs and nations we must guard against loose thinking. We must not compare nations in their youth with nations in the mellowness of their cultural maturity; and we must not compare the worst or the best of one age with the selected best or worst of all the collected past. If we find that the type of genius prevalent in young countries like America and Australia tends to the executive, explorative, and scientific kind rather than to the painter of pictures or poems, the carver of statues or words, we shall understand that each age and place calls for and needs certain brands of genius rather than others, and that the cultural sort can only come when its practical predecessors have cleared the forest and prepared the way. If we find that civilizations come and go, and mortality is upon all the works of man, we shall confess the irrefutability of death, and be consoled if, during the day of our lives and our nations, we move slowly upward, and become a little better than we were. If we find that philosophers are of slighter stature now than in the days of broad-backed Plato and the substantial Socrates, that our sculptors are lesser men than Donatello or Angelo, our painters inferior to Velasquez, our poets and composers unnameable with Shelley and Bach, we shall not despair; these stars did not all shine on the same night. Our problem is whether the total and average level of human ability has increased, and stands at its peak today.

When we take a total view, and compare our modern existence, precarious and chaotic as it is, with the ignorance, superstition, brutality, cannibalism and diseases of primitive peoples, we are a little comforted: the lowest strata of our race may still differ only slightly from such men, but above those strata thousands and millions have reached to mental and moral heights inconceivable, presumably, to the early mind. Under the complex strain of city life we sometimes take imaginative refuge in the quiet simplicity of savage days; but in our less romantic moments we know that this is a flight-reaction from our actual tasks, that this idolatry of barbarism, like so many of our young opinions, is merely an impatient expression of adolescent maladaptation, part of the suffering involved in the contemporary retardation of individual maturity. A study of such savage tribes as survive shows their high rate of infantile mortality, their short tenure of life, their inferior speed, their inferior stamina, their inferior will, and their superior plagues. The friendly and flowing savage is like Nature—delightful but for the insects and the dirt.

The savage, however, might turn the argument around, and inquire how we enjoy our politics and our wars, and whether we think ourselves happier than the tribes whose weird names resound in the textbooks of anthropology. The believer in progress will have to admit that we have made too many advances in the art of war, and that our politicians, with startling exceptions, would have adorned the Roman Forum in the days of Milo and Clodius,—though Mr. Coolidge was an appreciable improvement upon Nero. As to happiness, no man can say; it is an elusive angel, destroyed by detection and seldom amenable to measurement. Presumably it depends first upon health, secondly upon love, and thirdly upon wealth. As to wealth, we make such progress that it lies on the conscience of our intellectuals; as to love, we try to atone for our lack of depth by unprecedented inventiveness and variety. Our thousand fads of diet and drugs predispose us to the belief that we must be ridden with disease as compared with simpler men in simpler days; but this is a delusion. We think that where there are so many doctors there must be more sickness than before. But in truth we have not more ailments than in the past, but only more money; our wealth allows us to treat and cherish and master illnesses from which primitive men died without even knowing their Greek names.

There is one test of health—and therefore in part of happiness—which is objective and reliable: we find it in the mortality statistics of insurance companies, where inaccuracy is more expensive than in philosophy. In some cases these figures extend over three centuries. In Geneva, for example, they show an average length of life of twenty years in 1600, and of forty years in 1900. In the United States in 1920 the tenure of life of white people averaged fifty-three; and in 1926 it was fifty-six. This is incredible if true. Nevertheless, similar reports come to us from Germany: the Federal Statistical Bureau of Berlin tabulates the average length of life in Germany as twenty in 1520, thirty in 1750, forty in 1870, fifty in 1910, and sixty in 1920. Taking the figures for granted, we may conclude, with the permission of the pessimist, that if life is a boon at all, we are making great strides in the quantity of it which we manage to maintain. Recently the morticians (*nés* undertakers) discussed in annual convention the dangers that threatened their profession from the increasing tardiness of men in keeping their appointments with death. But if undertakers are miserable, progress is real.

Having made these admissions and modifications, let us try to see the problem of progress in a total view. It is unnecessary to refute the pessimist; it is only necessary to enclose his truth, if we can, in ours. When we look at history in the large we see it as a graph of rising and falling states—nations and cultures disappearing as on some gigantic film. But in that irregular movement of countries and that chaos of men, certain great moments stand out as the peaks and essence of human history, certain advances which, once made, were never lost. Step by step man has climbed from the savage to the scientist; and these are the stages of his growth.

First, *speech*. Think of it not as a sudden achievement, nor as a gift from the gods, but as the slow development of articulate expression, through centuries of effort, from the mate-calls of animals to the lyric flights of poetry. Without words, or common nouns, that might give to particular images the ability to represent a class, generalization would have stopped in its beginnings, and reason would have stayed where we find it in the brute. Without words, philosophy and poetry, history and prose, would have been impossible, and thought could never have reached the subtlety of Einstein or Anatole France. Without words man could not have become man, nor woman woman.

Second, *fire*. For fire made man independent of climate, gave him a greater compass on the earth, tempered his tools to hardness and durability, and offered him as food a thousand things inedible before. Not least of all it made him master of the night, and shed an animating brilliance over the hours of evening and dawn. Picture the dark before man conquered it; even now the terrors of that primitive abyss survive in our traditions and perhaps in our blood. Once every twilight was a tragedy, and man crept into his cave at sunset trembling with fear. Now we do not creep into our caves until sunrise; and though it is folly to miss the sun, how good it is to be liberated from our ancient fears! This overspreading of the night with a billion man-made stars has brightened the human spirit, and made for a vivacious jollity in modern life. We shall never be grateful enough for light.

Third, *the conquest of the animals*. Our memories are too forgetful, and our imagination too unimaginative, to let us realize the boon we have in our security from the larger and sub-human beasts of prey. Animals are now our playthings and our helpless food; but there was time when man was hunted as well as hunter, when every step from cave or hut was an adventure, and the possession of the earth was still at stake. This war to make the planet human was surely the most vital in human history; by its side all other wars were but family quarrels, achieving nothing. That struggle between strength of body and power of mind was waged through long and unrecorded years; and when at last it was won, the fruit of man's triumph—his safety on the earth—was transmitted across a thousand generations, with a hundred other gifts from the past, to be part of our heritage at birth. What are all our temporary retrogressions against the background of such a conflict and such a victory?

Fourth, *agriculture*. Civilization was impossible in the hunting age; it called for a permanent habitat, a settled way of life. It came with the home and the school; and these could not be till the products of the field replaced the animals of the forest or the herd as the food of man. The hunter found his quarry with increasing difficulty, while the woman whom he left at home tended an ever more fruitful soil. This patient husbandry by the wife threatened to make her independent of the male; and for his own lordship's sake he forced himself at last to the prose of tillage. No doubt it took centuries to make this greatest of all transitions in human history; but when at last it was made, civilization began. Meredith said that woman will be the last creature to be civilized by man. He was as wrong as it is possible to be in the limits of one sentence. For civilization came through two things chiefly: the home, which developed those social dispositions that form the psychological cement of society; and agriculture, which took man from his wandering life as hunter, herder and killer, and settled him long enough in one place to let him build homes, schools, churches, colleges, universities, civilization. But it was woman who gave man agriculture and the home; she domesticated man as she domesticated the sheep and the pig. Man is woman's last domestic animal; and perhaps he is the last creature that will be civilized by woman. The task is just begun: one look at our menus reveals us as still in the hunting stage.

Fifth, *social organization*. Here are two men disputing: one knocks the other down, kills him, and then concludes that he who is alive must have been right, and that he who is dead must have been wrong

—a mode of demonstration still accepted in international disputes
Here are two other men disputing: one says to the other, "Let us
not fight—we may both be killed; let us take our difference to some
elder of the tribe, and submit to his decision." It was a crucial moment
in human history! For if the answer was No, barbarism continued;
if it was Yes, civilization planted another root in the memory of man
the replacement of chaos with order, of brutality with judgment, of
violence with law. Here, too, is a gift unfelt, because we are born
within the charmed circle of its protection, and never know its value
till we wander into the disordered or solitary regions of the earth
God knows that our congresses and our parliaments are dubious in
ventions, the distilled mediocrity of the land; but despite them we
manage to enjoy a security of life and property which we shall
appreciate more warmly when civil war or revolution reduces us to
primitive conditions. Compare the safety of travel today with the
robber-infested highways of medieval Europe. Never before in history
was there such order and liberty as exist in England today,—and may
some day exist in America, when a way is found of opening municipal
office to capable and honorable men. However, we must not excite
ourselves too much about political corruption or democratic misman
agement; politics is not life, but only a graft upon life; under its
vulgar melodrama the traditional order of society quietly persists, in
the family, in the school, in the thousand devious influences that
change our native lawlessness into some measure of cooperation and
goodwill. Without consciousness of it, we partake in a luxurious patri
mony of social order built up for us by a hundred generations of trial
and error, accumulated knowledge, and transmitted wealth.

Sixth, *morality*. Here we touch the very heart of our problem—
are men morally better than they were? So far as intelligence is an
element in morals, we have improved: the average of intelligence is
higher, and there has been a great increase in the number of what we
may vaguely call developed minds. So far as character is concerned
we have probably retrogressed; subtlety of thought has grown at the
expense of stability of soul; in the presence of our fathers we intellec
tuals feel uncomfortably that though we surpass them in the number
of ideas that we have crowded into our heads, and though we have
liberated ourselves from delightful superstitions which still bring them
aid and comfort, we are inferior to them in uncomplaining courage
fidelity to our tasks and purposes, and simple strength of personality

But if morality implies the virtues exalted in the code of Christ, we have made some halting progress despite our mines and slums, our democratic corruption, and our urban addiction to lechery. We are a slightly gentler species than we were: capable of greater kindness, and of generosity even to alien or recently hostile peoples whom we have never seen. In one year (1928) the contributions of our country to private charity and philanthropy exceed two billions of dollars—one half of all the money circulating in America. We still kill murderers if, as occasionally happens, we catch them and convict them; but we are a little uneasy about this ancient retributive justice of a life for a life, and the number of crimes for which we mete out the ultimate punishment has rapidly decreased. Two hundred years ago, in Merrie England, men might be hanged by law for stealing a shilling; and people are still severely punished if they do not steal a great deal. One hundred and forty years ago miners were hereditary serfs in Scotland, criminals were legally and publicly tortured to death in France, debtors were imprisoned for life in England, and respectable people raided the African coast for slaves. Fifty years ago our jails were dens of filth and horror, colleges for the graduation of minor criminals into major criminals; now our prisons are vacation resorts for tired murderers. We still exploit the lower strata of our working classes, but we soothe our consciences with "welfare work." Eugenics struggles to balance with artificial selection the interference of human kindliness and benevolence with that merciless elimination of the weak and the infirm which was once the mainspring of natural selection.

We think there is more violence in the world than before, but in truth there are only more newspapers; vast and powerful organizations scour the planet for crimes and scandals that will console their readers for stenography and monogamy; and all the villainy and politics of five continents are gathered upon one page for the encouragement of our breakfasts. We conclude that half the world is killing the other half, and that a large proportion of the remainder are committing suicide. But in the streets, in our homes, in public assemblies, in a thousand vehicles of transportation, we are astonished to find no murderers and no suicides, but rather a blunt democratic courtesy, and an unpretentious chivalry a hundred times more real than when men mouthed chivalric phrases, enslaved their women, and ensured the fidelity of their wives with irons while they fought for Christ in the Holy Land.

Our prevailing mode of marriage, chaotic and deliquescent as it i
represents a pleasant refinement on marriage by capture or purchas
and *le droit de seigneur*. There is less brutality between men an
women, between parents and children, between teachers and pupil
than in any recorded generation of the past. The emancipation
woman, and her ascendancy over man, indicate an unprecedente
gentility in the once murderous male. Love, which was unknown t
primitive men, or was only a hunger of the flesh, has flowered into
magnificent garden of song and sentiment, in which the passion of
man for a maid, though vigorously rooted in physical need, rises lik
incense into the realm of living poetry. And youth, whose sins so di
turb its tired elders, atones for its little vices with such intellectu
eagerness and moral courage as may be invaluable when educatic
resolves at last to come out into the open and cleanse our public lif

Seventh, *tools*. In the face of the romantics, the machine-wrecke
of the intelligentsia, the pleaders for a return to the primitive (dir
chores, snakes, cobwebs, bugs), we sing the song of the tools, tl
engines, the machines, that have enslaved and are liberating man. W
need not be ashamed of our prosperity: it is good that comforts ar
opportunities once confined to barons and earls have been made l
enterprise the prerogatives of all; it was necessary to spread leisure
even though at first misused—before a wide culture could come. The
multiplying inventions are the new organs with which we control o
environment; we do not need to grow them on our bodies, as anima
must; we make them and use them, and lay them aside till we nec
them again. We grow gigantic arms that build in a month the pyr
mids that once consumed a million men; we make for ourselves gre
eyes that search out the invisible stars of the sky, and little eyes th
peer into the invisible cells of life; we speak, if we wish, with qui
voices that reach across continents and seas; we move over the lar
and the air with the freedom of timeless gods. Granted that me
speed is worthless: it is as a symbol of human courage and persiste
will that the airplane has its highest meaning for us; long chaine
like Prometheus, to the earth, we have freed ourselves at last, ar
now we may look the eagle in the face.

No, these tools will not conquer us. Our present defeat by tl
machinery around us is a transient thing, a halt in our visible progre
to a slaveless world. The menial labor that degraded both master ar
man is lifted from human shoulders and harnessed to the tirelc

muscles of iron and steel; soon every waterfall and every wind will pour its beneficent energy into factories and homes, and man will be freed for the tasks of the mind. It is not revolution but invention that will liberate the slave.

Eighth, *science*. In a large degree Buckle was right: we progress only in knowledge, and these other gifts are rooted in the slow enlightenment of the mind. Here in the untitled nobility of research, and the silent battles of the laboratory, is a story fit to balance the chicanery of politics and the futile barbarism of war. Here man is at his best, and through darkness and persecution mounts steadily towards the light. Behold him standing on a little planet, measuring, weighing, analyzing constellations that he cannot see; predicting the vicissitudes of earth and sun and moon; and witnessing the birth and death of worlds. Or here is a seemingly unpractical mathematician tracking new formulas through laborious labyrinths, clearing the way for an endless chain of inventions that will multiply the power of his race. Here is a bridge: a hundred thousand tons of iron suspended from four ropes of steel flung bravely from shore to shore, and bearing the passage of countless men; this is poetry as eloquent as Shakespeare ever wrote. Or consider this city-like building that mounts boldly into the sky, guarded against every strain by the courage of our calculations, and shining like diamond-studded granite in the night. Here in physics are new dimensions, new elements, new atoms, and new powers. Here in the rocks is the autobiography of life. Here in the laboratories biology prepares to transform the organic world as physics transformed matter. Everywhere you come upon them studying, these unpretentious, unrewarded men; you hardly understand where their devotion finds its source and nourishment; they will die before the trees they plant will bear fruit for mankind. But they go on.

Yes, it is true that this victory of man over matter has not yet been matched with any kindred victory of man over himself. The argument for progress falters here again. Psychology has hardly begun to comprehend, much less to control, human conduct and desire; it is mingled with mysticism and metaphysics, with psychoanalysis, behaviorism, glandular mythology, and other diseases of adolescence. Careful and modified statements are made only by psychologists of whom no one ever hears; in our country the democratic passion for extreme statements turns every science into a fad. But psychology will outlive these ills and storms; it will be matured, like older sciences, by the respon-

sibilities which it undertakes. If another Bacon should come to map
out its territory, clarify the proper methods and objectives of its attack, and point out the "fruits and powers" to be won,—which of us,
knowing the surprises of history and the pertinacity of men, would
dare set limits to the achievements that may come from our growing
knowledge of the mind? Already in our day man is turning round
from his remade environment, and beginning to remake himself.

Ninth, *education*. More and more completely we pass on to the
next generation the gathered experience of the past. It is almost a
contemporary innovation, this tremendous expenditure of wealth and
labor in the equipment of schools and the provision of instruction for
all; perhaps it is the most significant feature of our time. Once colleges were luxuries, designed for the male half of the leisure class;
today universities are so numerous that he who runs may become a
Ph. D. We have not excelled the selected geniuses of antiquity, but
we have raised the level and average of human knowledge far beyond
any age in history. Think now not of Plato and Aristotle, but of the
stupid, bigoted and brutal Athenian Assembly, of the unfranchised
mob and its Orphic rites, of the secluded and enslaved women who
could acquire education only by becoming courtesans.

None but a child would complain that the world has not yet been
totally remade by these spreading schools, these teeming bisexual universities; in the perspective of history the great experiment of education is just begun. It has not had time to prove itself; it cannot in a
generation undo the ignorance and superstition of ten thousand years;
indeed, there is no telling but the high birth rate of ignorance, and
the determination of dogma by plebiscite, may triumph over education
in the end; this step in progress is not one of which we may yet say
that it is a permanent achievement of mankind. But already beneficent
results appear. Why is it that tolerance and freedom of the mind
flourish more easily in the northern states than in the South, if not
because the South has not yet won wealth enough to build sufficient
schools? Who knows how much of our preference for mediocrity in
office, and narrowness in leadership, is the result of a generation recruited from regions too oppressed with economic need and political
exploitation to spare time for the ploughing and sowing of the mind?
What will the full fruitage of education be when every one of us is
schooled till twenty, and finds equal access to the intellectual treasures
of the race? Consider again the instinct of parental love, the profound

impulse of every normal parent to raise his children beyond himself: here is the biological leverage of human progress, a force more to be trusted than any legislation or any moral exhortation, because it is rooted in the very nature of man. Adolescence lengthens: we begin more helplessly, and we grow more completely towards that higher man who struggles to be born out of our darkened souls. We are the raw material of civilization.

We dislike education, because it was not presented to us in our youth for what it is. Consider it not as the painful accumulation of facts and dates, but as an ennobling intimacy with great men. Consider it not as the preparation of the individual to "make a living," but as the development of every potential capacity in him for the comprehension, control, and *appreciation* of his world. Above all, consider it, in its fullest definition, as the technique of transmitting as completely as possible, to as many as possible, that technological, intellectual, moral, and artistic heritage through which the race forms the growing individual and makes him human. Education is the reason why we behave like human beings. We are hardly born human; we are born ridiculous and malodorous animals; we *become* human, we have humanity thrust upon us through the hundred channels whereby the past pours down into the present that mental and cultural inheritance whose preservation, accumulation and transmission place mankind today, with all its defectives and illiterates, on a higher plane than any generation has ever reached before.

Tenth and last, *writing and print.* Again our imagination is too weak-winged to lift us to a full perspective; we cannot vision or recall the long ages of ignorance, impotence and fear that preceded the coming of letters. Through those unrecorded centuries men could transmit their hard-won lore only by word of mouth from parent to child; if one generation forgot or misunderstood, the weary ladder of knowledge had to be climbed anew. Writing gave a new permanence to the achievements of the mind; it preserved for thousands of years, and through a millennium of poverty and superstition, the wisdom found by philosophy and the beauty carved out in drama and poetry. It bound the generations together with a common heritage; it created that Country of the Mind in which, because of writing, genius need not die.

And now, as writing united the generations, print, despite the thousand prostitutions of it, can bind the civilizations. It is not necessary any more that civilization should disappear before our planet passes away. It will change its habitat; doubtless the land in every nation will refuse at last to yield its fruit to improvident tillage and careless tenancy; inevitably new regions will lure with virgin soil the lustier strains of every race. But a civilization is not a material thing, inseparably bound, like an ancient serf, to a given spot of the earth; it is an accumulation of technical knowledge and cultural creation; if these can be passed on to the new seat of economic power the civilization does not die, it merely makes for itself another home. Nothing but beauty and wisdom deserve immortality. To a philosopher it is not indispensable that his native city should endure forever; he will be content if its achievements are handed down, to form some part of the possessions of mankind.

We need not fret then, about the future. We are weary with too much war, and in our lassitude of mind we listen readily to a Spengler announcing the downfall of the Western world. But this learned arrangement of the birth and death of civilizations in even cycles is a trifle too precise; we may be sure that the future will play wild pranks with this mathematical despair. There have been wars before, and wars far worse than our "Great" one. Man and civilization survived them; within fifteen years after Waterloo, defeated France was producing so many geniuses that every attic in Paris was occupied. Never was our heritage of civilization and culture so secure, and never was it half so rich. We may do our little share to augment it and transmit it, confident that time will wear away chiefly the dross of it, and that what is finally fair and worthy in it will be preserved, to illuminate many generations.

GUIDE QUESTIONS

1. According to Durant, why cannot progress be defined in terms of happiness?
2. Analyze and comment on Durant's definition of progress.
3. Argue for or against the superior condition of the savage, being careful to state the facts on which you base your view.
4. In what ways is man's war for the conquest of the animals still being carried on?
5. Comment on the argument for agricultural progress. Is it convincing?
6. What progress have we made in "social organization"?

7. Interpret the statement that in the test of morality "we touch the heart of the problem." Under what headings are the arguments here classified?

8. It is accepted by Durant that man's tools and machines have at least temporarily defeated him. Explain this in more detail.

9. Comment on the view that the achievements of modern science show man at his best. Is this view consistent with Durant's statement: "Yes, it is true that this victory of man over matter has not yet been matched with any kindred victory of man over himself"?

10. What should psychology contribute to the progress of mankind? What should education contribute?

11. Comment on Durant's arrangement or order of the ten steps by which "man has climbed from the savage to the scientist." Can you devise a better arrangement? Can you think of other stages of man's growth?

VOCABULARY

Give the derivations and definitions of the following words:

retrogression, prevalent, tenure, articulate, subtlety, dubious, patrimony, fidelity, retributive, monogamy, deliquescent, chicanery, fruitage, ennobling, improvident, lassitude, precise, augment.

Wilson D. Wallis

THE NATURE OF PROGRESS

PROGRESS CONSISTS IN performing a function with greater ease or with greater proficiency or efficiency, and in doing something desirable. The test of desirability is more difficult to apply than that of efficiency, for that which is desired may not be desirable, and that which is wanted may satisfy no actual need. The desirability of a thing depends, moreover, upon contingencies which ramify indefinitely. That which is desirable, all things considered, is the final test of progress. But all things cannot be considered. No one, therefore, can know what is really

By permission from *Culture and Progress*, by Wilson D. Wallis. Copyright, 1930, by McGraw-Hill Book Co., Inc.

most desirable. Yet it may be possible, although an element of error intrudes, to discover the more desirable.

It is only by treating the matter in its whole length and breadth, and by developing in their natural order all the principles involved, that we can determine what is the best; for it is always with the *best* that we must concern ourselves in theory. To neglect this research, under the pretext that the best is not practicable in existing circumstances, is attempting to solve two questions at one operation; it is to miss the advantage of placing the questions in the simplicity that can alone render them susceptible of demonstration; it is to throw ourselves without a clue into an inextricable labyrinth, or rather it is to shut our eyes wilfully to the light, by placing ourselves in the impossibility of finding it.[1]

Where the issue is uncertain, the more desirable can be ascertained, at least provisionally, by including more relevant data, and thus men can make progress in understanding progress. Progress, however, is not synonymous with evolution. Whether a series of changes which illustrates evolution illustrates progress also can be ascertained only by reference to a larger system and by considering the effect of these changes upon human life and purposes. By way of illustration let us recur to the story of the development of weapons. Men begin with a stick or a stone, and the arm is the only instrument of propulsion. The spear thrower sends the implement farther, but its range is outdistanced by the bow-shot arrow. Thus, in the evolution of weapons, the bow-using American Indians had advanced beyond the spear-throwing Australians. The Romans devised siege engines and vessels with banks of oars; no implements or craft of primitive man could cope with these contrivances. Then came liquid fire, and mechanical devices for throwing it; finally, cannon and explosives, which vanquished all other weapons. But the development of weapons is not the whole story. Superior strategy and better defense offset the initial benefit of the bowman's greater range; the more penetrable arrow encounters a less penetrable material, for shields of wood, skin, or metal make it difficult for the wielder of the bow and arrow to reap the initial advantage. Explosives shatter defensive walls, but earthworks, sandbags, and steel ramparts make it more difficult for the marksman to do more than score useless hits. The first use of poison gas is terrifying and efficacious;

[1] Turgot, *Sur les impositions*, 1764; transl. in Stephens, W. Walker, *The Life and Writings of Turgot*, p. 309, London, 1895.

ut masks afford protection to the wary, and possibly some new gas will neutralize the most deadly vapors. Throughout human history each improvement in destructive devices has been followed by improvement in defensive devices which to some extent offset the advantages of the innovator, so that no one profits, and perhaps all lose. If, therefore, the evolution of weapons is viewed in its larger setting and not merely as improvement in the technique of taking or of defending lives or property, the problem of progress takes on new complexion. Men have not necessarily made progress because they can shoot at one another with high explosives at a distance of 20 miles rather than throw stones at one another at a distance of 100 paces as, perhaps, did Stone-age men. When the improved fire-arms are possessed by the enemy also, the resulting advantage is not obvious; and

. . in war it is rare that all the learning is on one side. Samuel Champlain with his French fire-arms gave the Hurons their most complete victory over the Iroquois. The Iroquois realized at once the value of the gun, and for a century and a half French Canada had cause to regret that Champlain had ever used his fire-arms in Indian wars, for Dutch and English could supply similar weapons to savages who never forgave the first wrong.[2]

Man has developed more effective techniques for fighting, but each new device with which he can kill is also a new device with which he can be killed. If being blown to atoms is preferable to having one's skull smashed, perhaps the evolution of weapons betokens progress. If being able to kill and be killed by scores and hundreds is preferable to killing and being killed one at a time, then, too, men may have gained. But to ascertain whether a so-called "improvement" is progress, one must inquire beyond the process itself and learn whether it serves human purposes better under the new conditions than did the old device under the old conditions. More efficient weapons may be merely weapons with which to fight more dangerous foes, and they may be relatively no more efficient under the new conditions than were the old under more primitive conditions. The real need is not more efficient weapons, but a culture in which weapons are superfluous; and abolition of the presumed need for them would be a further step in progress than any new type of weapon has brought or can bring.

By his ability to control a fluctuating environment, by improved

[2] Glover, T. R., *Democracy in the Ancient World,* p. 107, New York, 1927.

tools, weapons, and mechanical devices, man acquires greater powe
He learns to control and even to create a sustaining environment. Th
cultivation of plants and the domestication of animals are followed b
industrialism and applied science. These later stages are superimpose
upon the earlier and supplement rather than supplant them. So far a
power is concerned, Western civilization is the highest attainment c
culture, and the key to power is knowledge. Man increases the amoun
and range of knowledge, organizes it, and makes transfer from on
field to another feasible and fruitful. When cooperation supplement
knowledge there is greater efficiency. Increase in power, however, doe
not always connote progress, although progress implies increase i
power. The increased ferocity of the tiger may enhance its immediat
power to destroy, but it also stimulates in men additional incentives t
destroy it. The nitroglycerine which can destroy enemies is, in thei
hands, a weapon of comparable destructive power, and it is "a singula
fact, that, when man is a brute, he is the most sensual and loathsom
of all brutes." [3] Often the device which man uses to increase his powe
proves to be a boomerang. Slaves may be an immediate advantage t
the master, but in the long run enslavement of others is also enslave
ment of self. Again, the power which man develops may redound t
the good of some but not of all. The Industrial Revolution bring
increments of power, but the benefits are for the few, and the many
pay heavily for them. Civilization is an interdependent whole, yet the
accretion of power which affects the various elements of the culture
differently may bring progress to only a portion of the culture.

Nowhere is it truer than in science that one generation shall labor and
another shall enter into the fruits of its labors. In the middle eighties of
the last century, a chemist prepared dichloroethylsulfide. In 1918 every
one called it by a simpler name—"mustard gas." What an unfortunate
example! And yet how few are the examples of the achievements of science
which are wholly without unfortunate aspects if we look at the full possibilities. The industry which grasps the nitrogen from the air and with its
fertilizers multiplies the yield of our vast acreage may tomorrow send
forth the munitions which will strew those same fields with human wreckage. The radio may fill the night with music or it may turn back the page
of science and teach the multitudes that the earth is flat. The telegraph
may one day spread joy with the news that the income tax has been reduced
half of one per centum, and next day sorrow at the news that families

[3] Hawthorne, Nathaniel, *Passages from the American Note-Books*, p. 34, Boston, 1883.

will be split asunder in each petty nation in order that their individual coinage may be made safe for their monied classes. The same reproducing device which may lift our souls to the heights of a grand symphony may also cause us to respond once more to the pulse of primitive strains. The food which science has given us is better and more varied than that of kings of yesteryear, but this very blessing has given us many a sleepless night, and 'twould be a happy bargain if we could trade our teeth for theirs. The automobile may be a pleasure and a business necessity, but little permanent value can it offer to the group or the individual if its acquirement by easy-payment plans obligates the future to decreasing currency values and forced increased production. The mortgaging of homes to satisfy the cravings of a world on pleasure bent may reduce us to a new form of wandering tribes, the very wealthy migrating from one palatial residence to another, the poor journeying in worn-out vehicles from one place of short employment to another. The morning paper gives us news from all corners of the earth of war, pestilence, and famine; the murders, suicides, and robberies; the sorrows and intrigues of the world are laid before us at breakfast and the evening paper adds the daring daylight hold-ups. And so on, examples showing the pleasant results and likewise the equally unpleasant consequences and dangers of applied science could be added without end.[4]

Science is a good old barn-door fowl; build her a hen-roost, and she will lay you eggs, and golden eggs. Give your money to science, for there is an evil side to every other kind of almsgiving ... It is science that will redeem man's hope of Paradise.[5]

But more precisely it is science which enables man to attain a finer paradise or to create a fiercer hell than was possible in a prescientific age. Science, it is true, may create Paradise; but it was in Paradise that man fell. Indeed, practically every power which is capable of increasing the good is capable also of increasing the evil, for nothing automatically effects a good purpose. The sun which returns with the dawn and provides the conditions under which life can bestir anew provides also the conditions under which evil designs can be carried out. The light which assists the hunter brings greater danger to the hunted. If achievement in one phase of culture necessarily brought improvement in other phases the issues would be simple. But progress along one line sometimes leads to maladjustments elsewhere; a step forward at one point

---

[4] Lucasse, Walter W., "Progress and the Sciences," in *Sci. Monthly*, 25: 214-215, 1927; reprinted in Wallis, Wilson D., and Willey, Malcolm M., *Readings in Sociology*, New York, 1930.

[5] Moore, George, *Modern Painting*, Carra ed., 19: 113-114, 1923.

may shift the center of gravity and necessitate readjustments in other phases of the culture. The development of the automobile, for example, works hardship upon the horse-trader, and the mechanic supplants the smith. It makes new demands upon the department of highways and even upon highwaymen. It affects social life in many ways. The neighborhood church becomes a different institution, the rural community is expanded, the bounds of municipal influence are extended. The possibilities of crime are increased and crimes as well, while new situations are introduced into the lives of the young. In short, every phase of the culture is affected by the presence of the automobile.

The culture may become more diverse, but the parts remain interdependent; and if gains in one phase of the culture are not to be offset by losses in another, then with every new device, idea, or knowledge, there must be a new integration, a new evaluation, and a new orientation of the culture. Where perfection prevails there can, of course, be no progress; yet one of the threats inherent in progress is the fact that the higher man climbs the further he can fall. As Sir Thomas More said when assuming his duties as Lord Chancellor, "the higher the post of honor the greater the fall," [6] and *facilis est descensus Averni*—the road to hell is easy. For now, at last, "man has a greater power for evil against his fellow-man than the devils have." [7] The fall of a highly developed culture is, therefore, a greater calamity than the fall of a crude one. But the fact that degeneration has been a common characteristic of culture, if not a universal one, does not imply that there has been no progress. As the death of individuals paves the way to progress within the culture, so, it may be, the death of cultures paves the way to progress in human civilization. There is some justification for the philosophy implicit in a Greenland Eskimo account of the creation, which says that the first woman, who had been created out of the thumb of the first man, Kallak, brought death into the world and justified it thus: "Let us die to make room for our successors." [8] As a matter of fact, however, human culture, like the human race, does not die. The early historical civilizations disintegrate, but they are succeeded by others which pass on the torch. Babylonia falls, but Assyria,

[6] Quoted in Kautsky, Karl, *Thomas More and His "Utopia," with a Historical Introduction*, p. 155, London, 1927.

[7] Gott, Samuel, *Nova Solyma*, bk. II, chap. VI.

[8] Crantz, *Histoire von Grönland*, vol. I, p. 262, Leipzig, 1770.

Persia, Greece come upon the world stage. As a nation and a world power the Hebrews fail, but their contributions to religion and ethics are a heritage of later civilizations. Greece falls a prey to internal strife and barbarian invasions, but Hellenistic civilization becomes widespread, and other cultures are benefited, Western Europe, finally, most of all. Chaldea influences Assyria, Ionian Greece contributes culture traits to Persia, Athenian civilization transforms the Dorian.

Athens mounts to the peak of history at the hour when the moors of Brittany were being covered with their dull flowers of stone; Rome comes to reap them; Rome goes down in the flood that rolls from the North; then the rhythm quickens—great peoples grow up on the cadavers of great peoples.[9]

Something has been lost, but much has been gained. With cultures as with individuals there is not only decay and death but also birth and new life. Yet whether the new total is a gain over the old is not easily determined, for civilization acquires new evils as well as new goods.

Cultures are humanity's diverse experiments, and out of them, possibly, will come a civilization superior to all predecessors. Throughout them all runs a thread of something fundamentally human—

> Our deeds still travel with us from afar,
> And what we have been makes us what we are

The present can utilize the past, and with increase in the number of culture traits there is a more rapid and a more fructifying oscillation of interacting culture influences. The traits of the culture develop in interrelation, and each is responsive to change in any part of the culture. When permanent abode supplants nomadism there is usually a strengthening and a localization of the family circle. The house becomes the "castle" only when it is a place of permanent abode. Mrs. Benedict says,

It is ... an ultimate fact of human nature that man builds up his culture out of disparate elements, combining and recombining them; and until we have abandoned the superstition that the result is an organism functionally interrelated, we shall be unable to see our cultural life objectively, or to control its manifestations.[10]

[9] Faure, Élie, *History of Art,* vol. I; Turgot (*Universal History*) uses almost the same phraseology.

[10] Benedict, Ruth F., "The Concept of the Guardian Spirit in North America," *Memoirs Amer. Anthrop. Assoc.,* No. 29, pp. 84-85, 1923.

The result may not be an organism, and certainly is not such if biological analogy is meant; but assuredly the culture traits are functionally interrelated, or their continued existence in the culture would be most precarious. In this functional interrelation lies the significance of new traits, for the culture is soon busily "combining and recombining them." Each new trait is a stimulus or a challenge to others. Hence, "for no idea of historical importance can a clear and unique line of descent be established. Suggestions and influences always cross one another and mix." [11] Trade routes are means of intercommunication as well as channels for the exchange of articles. New agricultural appliances suggest new mechanical devices in other phases of culture, and these, in turn, react upon agriculture. Performances in war challenge the ability of the story-teller, and mythology and folklore are enriched. The greater the number of radiating influences, the richer the culture content. Specialization brings a new focusing of attention and the development of keener instruments of control. Knowledge gained in one sphere is transferred to others and becomes a stimulus in many lines of thought.

Enlargement of the culture horizon, therefore, increases the possibilities of progress. For primitive man, limited to the territory of the tribe for means of subsistence, inspiration, and effort, the world is small. When, through trade or other contact, tribal barriers break down, the culture world is enlarged. When the geographical horizon expands the mental horizon enlarges. With the growth of the mathematical and the astronomical sciences the sky is no longer a covering vault, but a step into infinite stellar spaces. The center of interest shifts from the individual or the tribe to the larger universe of which man is now aware. It no longer is obvious that all things were made for man, but the world is now merely one of several planets in a solar system which is one of many solar systems, and man is but one of the many animals on the earth. Inspired by Nicholas of Cusa, and by the timidly enunciated hypothesis of Copernicus, the imagination of Bruno "outsoared the solar system and the sphere of the fixed stars, and went flying through an infinite universe of endless worlds." [12] Previously, man has seen everything from his own point of view, self-centered; now he views himself and his culture from many objective points of view. A new in-

[11] Reichwein, Adolf, *China and Europe: Intellectual and Artistic Contacts in the Eighteenth Century,* p. 102, New York, 1925.

[12] Taylor, Henry O. *Freedom of the Mind in History,* p. 152, London, 1923.

ectual orientation reveals a new world with new meaning, and life correspondingly enriched—sometimes through the discovery of its erty. Yet "the further we go, the more distant the goal," for the ation of a problem poses new problems; and complete realization of ry purpose would bring a state of satiety of which the oyster is a , if pale, representative. The reward is in the race that is run, not in prize. Progress consists in harmonizing rather than in achieving aplete harmony; those who have finished a task have undertaken no at one. Value lies in the achievement of harmony, but no final end attained if the end is worthy of supreme effort. Value, in short, involves the possibility of a conflict of purposes, and achieving rather than npleting ends is its characteristic. In the realm of mind the same test olies. Intellectual progress involves the ability to break down old its and systems of thought, and with loss of ability to do this degention sets in. A closed system in philosophy, education, or any other d cripples development. The value of a possession, then, is measured its contribution to the realization of a purpose. Completion of a rpose, unless it is part of an unrealized purpose, results in the inertss of petrifaction. Only things of eternal value are worthy of effort; d upon human potentiality no limit can be placed. Perhaps men will vays sail a troubled sea; but were there no breeze to make it such ere would be none to move their barques onward.

Professor Cheney finds that during the period of recorded history lture has developed as if "some inexorable necessity" were controlling he progress of human affairs." Historical development, he says, is t the result of the voluntary action of individuals or of groups of dividuals, it is not due to chance, but it is guided by law. Men play e parts assigned to them and they do not write the play. He specifies e following six phases of this alleged law of development:

1. *Continuity.*—All developments arise from preceding conditions.
2. *Impermanence of cultures.*—Cultures languish and die because they not accommodate themselves to the changing demands of the times. onservatism, therefore, tends to effect its own destruction and the death d disappearance of the culture which it obstinately upholds.
3. *Interdependence of individuals, classes, tribes, and nations.*—Among its which are interdependent one does not progress or retrograde without affecting the others. No portion of mankind has progressed at the pense of another, but all have fallen or risen together.

4. *A tendency toward the development of democracy.*—Considered
its entirety, democracy has justified itself as the best form of governm
yet devised.

5. *The necessity of free consent.*—Individuals and groups can be o
temporarily, not permanently, compelled.

6. *Progress in the moral sphere.*—Moral influences have grown and h
become more widely diffused than material influences.

Cheney does not conceive these changes as merely a summary
what has taken place, but as "natural laws, which we must acc
whether we want to or not, whose workings we cannot obviate, hc
ever much we may thwart them to our own failure or disadvanta
laws to be accepted and reckoned with as much as the laws of grav
tion, or of chemical affinity, or of organic evolution, or of hun
psychology."[13] Waiving the question of the correctness of this su
mary of the changes which have characterized the period of recorc
history, the conclusion is based on a misconception of the nature
law. The culture changes in Western civilization, or in all histori
civilizations taken in their totality, constitute a unique event in
unique culture world. The thing which has been has never been befc
and there is no basis for the induction that it will be again, or tha
will persist.

The whole civilization of each particular race, whether of the Her
of South-West Africa, the Hottentots, or the different Bantu tribes, ou
to be regarded as a single and unique occurrence in the course of histor
events and in the intellectual happenings of society.[14]

Physics and chemistry discover laws only when they consider th
respective data distributively, not when they consider them collective
neither the universe as a whole, nor the solar system as a unique c
course of matter, furnishes laws for physics or for chemistry, or even
astronomy. To the extent that a thing or an event is unique, there
be no inference that it will occur again, and none that its occurre
was inevitable, unless one define inevitable as that which has happen
rather than as that which could not have been otherwise. Men
always make progress, but there can be no guarantee that they
always do so.

[13] Cheney, Edward F., "Law in History," in *Amer. Hist. Rev.*, 29: 231-248, 19
and *Law in History,* chap. I, New York, 1927.
[14] Thurnwald, Richard, "The Social Problems of Africa," in *Africa*, 2: 134, 1929.

.s our expectations of limitless progress for the race cannot depend
.n the blind operation of the laws of heredity, so neither can they
end upon the deliberate action of national governments. Such ex-
ination as we can make of the changes which have taken place
ing the relatively minute fraction of history with respect to which
have fairly full information, shows that they have been caused by
ultitude of variations, often extremely small, made in their sur-
ndings by individuals whose objects, though not necessarily selfish,
e often had no intentional reference to the advancement of the
munity at large. But we have no scientific ground for suspecting
t the stimulus to these individual efforts must necessarily continue;
know of no law by which, if they do continue, they must needs
coordinated for a common purpose or pressed into the service of
common good. We cannot estimate their remoter consequences;
her can we tell how they will act and react upon one another, nor
w they will in the long run affect morality, religion, and other funda-
ntal elements of human society. The future of the race is thus en-
passed with darkness; no faculty of calculation that we possess,
instrument that we are likely to invent, will enable us to map out
course, or penetrate the secret of its destiny. It is easy, no doubt,
ind in the clouds which obscure our path what shapes we please: to
in them the promise of some millennial paradise, or the threat of
less and unmeaning travel through waste and perilous places. But
such visions the wise man will put but little confidence: content, in
ober and cautious spirit, with a full consciousness of his feeble
vers of foresight, and the narrow limits of his activity, to deal as
y arise with the problems of his own generation.

JIDE QUESTIONS

Analyze Wallis' definition of "progress."
Comment on the development of weapons as an explanation of the
distinction between progress and evolution.
Interpret: "The real need is not for more efficient weapons, but a culture in which weapons are superfluous." Does this seem unattainable
at present?
Argue for or against the view that science is a mixed blessing which
often carries the possibility of both good and evil.
Is it convincingly demonstrated that "every phase of the culture is

affected by the presence of the automobile"? Have any other in tions had so widespread an influence?

6. Explain the statement that the fall of great civilizations in the "does not imply that there has been no progress."
7. Interpret: "The reward is in the race that is run, not in the pr Apply this philosophy to the question of progress.
8. What is Wallis' criticism of Cheney's "laws" of history?
9. Does the author's refusal to admit that there is any guarantee for continual advance of civilization show that he is a pessimist? W Why not?

VOCABULARY

Give the derivations and definitions of the following words:

ramify, intrude, ascertain, provisional, relevant, synonymous, propul. cope, vanquish, efficacious, betoken, fluctuating, feasible, connote, enhe incentive, inherent, disintegrate, diverse, predecessor, fructify, oscilla nomadism, subsistence, enunciate, satiety, inert, petrifaction, inexorable viate, thwart, waive.

WRITING AND STUDY AIDS

PATTERN OF ORGANIZATION SUGGESTED BY THE GENERAL TOPIC:

In dealing with a subject as large and many-sided as the progres civilization, it may be wise to break down the general idea into sub sions. One can often clarify the problem as a whole by classifying component parts. Such a method sets up useful limitations and prev biting off more than can be comfortably chewed.

A careful classification of the points they propose to deal with in trea the idea of progress serves to clarify the writing of Dean Inge, Will Dur and Wilson D. Wallis. Dean Inge uses at least two distinct method classification or subdivision: he examines the idea of progress in to of historical periods, and he divides it into categories in order to discuss effects in various fields of knowledge. Will Durant groups his points u ten major headings. In a similar way, Wallis' organization is largely erned by his wish to consider both the "good" and "bad" aspects of

culture change. Grouping, separating, limiting, dividing—all of these illustrate various methods of classification for the purpose of clear exposition.

In your own writing on this topic, try to classify or group your ideas as an
aid to effective composition.

ASSIGNMENTS:

Short themes:

1. A definition of progress
2. My personal progress in college
3. If I had been born a hundred years ago
4. I advance in retreat
5. Widening my culture horizon

Long themes:

1. Progress in the fine arts
2. War and progress
3. The pioneer and progress
4. Of man's inhumanity to man
5. The necessity of ethical improvement
6. The treatment of criminals—then and now
7. The poor are always with us
8. Politics and progress
9. Are we so modern, after all?

READINGS FOR FURTHER STUDY:

Beard, Charles A., editor. *A Century of Progress*. New York: Harper
and Brothers, 1932.

Becker, Carl. "Progress," *Encyclopedia of the Social Sciences*. New York:
The Macmillan Company, 1930-1935. Vol. 12, 495-99.

Bury, J. B. *The Idea of Progress*. New York: The Macmillan Company,
1932.

Capek, Karel. *R.U.R.* Garden City, N. Y.: Doubleday, Page and Company,
1923.

Emerson, Ralph Waldo. "Civilization." Frequently reprinted.

Huxley, Aldous. *Brave New World*. Garden City, N. Y.: Doubleday, Doran
and Company, 1932.

Lewisohn, Ludwig. "The Fallacy of Progress," *Harper's Magazine,* Vol.
167 (June, 1933), 103-12.

Randall, John Herman. "The World Conceived as a Process of Growth
and Evolution," *The Making of the Modern Mind*. Rev. ed. Boston:
Houghton Mifflin Company, 1940. Pages 454-82.

Russell, Bertrand. "Currents of Thought in the Nineteenth Century," *A History of Western Philosophy*. New York: Simon and Schuster, 1945.

Teggert, Frederick J. "The Idea of Progress," *Theory of History*. New Haven: Yale University Press, 1925. Pages 76-93.

Thoreau, Henry David. *Walden*. Frequently reprinted.

Toynbee, Arnold J. *A Study of History*. Abridgment of Vols. 1-6 by D. C. Somervell. New York: Oxford University Press, 1947. Introduction, pp. 12-47; "Challenge and Response," pp. 60-79; "The Rhythm of Disintegration," pp. 548-58.

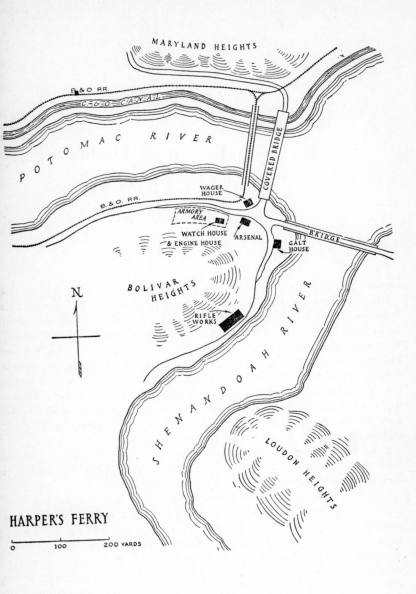

MARYLAND HEIGHTS

B & O RR.

C. & O. CANAL

P O T O M A C   R I V E R

B. & O. RR.

WAGER HOUSE

COVERED BRIDGE

ARMORY AREA

WATCH HOUSE & ENGINE HOUSE

ARSENAL

BRIDGE

GALT HOUSE

N

BOLIVAR HEIGHTS

RIFLE WORKS

S H E N A N D O A H   R I V E R

LOUDON HEIGHTS

HARPER'S FERRY

0   100   200 YARDS

⚓ John Brown at Harper's Ferry

LATE IN THE EVENING ON OCTOBER 16, 1859, JOHN BROWN WITH A FEW MEN captured the government ordnance works at Harper's Ferry, Virginia. His intention, apparently, was to free the slaves. On the following day, after some lively fighting in which a number of men were killed, "Captain Brown and about half his band were trapped and surrounded in the "Engine House." At dawn on October 18, Colonel Robert E. Lee, commanding detachment of U. S. Marines which had arrived during the night, sent last demand to John Brown that he surrender. John Brown refused. Twelve marines at once stormed the Engine House and overpowered its defenders John Brown was tried and convicted of treason at Charlestown, Virginia and on the second day of December he was hanged.

Long before his execution he had become the stuff of legend. So intense were the sectional and political differences which he epitomized that it even now hard for Americans to consider his story calmly.

Many accounts of the raid at Harper's Ferry have been written, but since most of them are colored in one way or another by the leanings of the authors, it is quite difficult to arrive at the facts of the story. In this assign ment several of the original, eye-witness accounts are reprinted. The accounts, of course, may also be colored by the preference of the eye witnesses for one side or the other. An eye-witness of an event has no special right to be believed unless he demonstrates his objective veracity Remember also that he can only be in one place at one time, a fact which should, if he is absolutely truthful, limit the scope of his testimony. On the basis of these accounts, you will be able to make a fairly complete recon struction of events, but only if you weigh with utmost care the statement of each witness. Assume the role of a historian as you read and try to discover, without violation of the evidence available to you, precisely what happened at Harper's Ferry.

from Appendix to

THE MASON REPORT

Colonel Lee to the Adjutant General

HEADQUARTERS HARPER'S FERRY,
October 19, 1859.

COLONEL:

I have the honor to report, for the information of the Secretary of War, that on arriving here on the night of the 17th instant, in obedience to Special Orders No. 194 of that date from your office, I learn that a party of insurgents, about 11 P. M. on the 16th, had seized the watchmen stationed at the armory, arsenal, rifle factory, and bridge across the Potomac, and taken possession of those points. They then dispatched six men, under one of their party, called Captain Aaron C. Stevens, to arrest the principal citizens in the neighborhood and incite the negroes to join in the insurrection. The party took Colonel L. W. Washington from his bed about 1½ A. M. on the 17th, and brought him, with four of his servants, to this place. Mr. J. H. Allstadt and six of his servants were in the same manner seized about 3 A. M., and arms placed in the hands of the negroes. Upon their return here, John E. Cook, one of the party sent to Mr. Washington's, was dispatched to Maryland, with Mr. Washington's wagon, two of his servants, and three of Mr. Allstadt's, for arms and ammunition, &c. As day advanced, and the citizens of Harper's Ferry commenced their usual avocations, they were separately captured, to the number of forty, as well as I could learn, and confined in one room of the fire-engine house of the armory, which seems early to have been selected as a point of defense. About 11 A. M. the volunteer companies from Virginia began to arrive, and the Jefferson Guards and volunteers from Charlestown, under Captain J. W. Rowen, I understood, were first on the ground. The Hamtramck Guards, Captain V. M. Butler; the

From Appendix to *The Mason Report*, U. S. Congress; Senate, Select Committee on the Harper's Ferry Invasion, Rep. Com. No. 278, June 15, 1860, pp. 40-45.

Shepherdstown troop, Captain Jacob Rienahart; and Captain Alburtis's company from Martinsburg arrived in the afternoon. These companies, under the direction of Colonels R. W. Baylor and John T. Gibson, forced the insurgents to abandon their positions at the bridge and in the village, and to withdraw within the armory inclosure, where they fortified themselves in the fire-engine house, and carried ten of their prisoners for the purpose of insuring their safety and facilitating their escape, whom they termed hostages, and whose names are Colonel L. W. Washington, of Jefferson county, Virginia; Mr. J. H. Allstadt, of Jefferson county, Virginia; Mr. Israel Russell, justice of the peace, Harper's Ferry; Mr. John Donahue, clerk of Baltimore and Ohio railroad; Mr. Terence Byrne, of Maryland; Mr. George D. Shope, of Frederick, Maryland; Mr. Benjamin Mills, master armorer, Harper's Ferry arsenal; Mr. A. M. Ball, master machinist, Harper's Ferry arsenal; Mr. J. E. P. Dangerfield, paymaster's clerk, Harper's Ferry arsenal; Mr. J. Burd, armorer, Harper's Ferry arsenal. After sunset more troops arrived. Captain B. B. Washington's company from Winchester, and three companies from Fredericktown, Maryland, under Colonel Shriver. Later in the evening the companies from Baltimore, under General Charles C. Edgerton, second light brigade, and a detachment of marines, commanded by Lieutenant J. Green accompanied by Major Russell, of that corps, reached Sandy Hook, about one and a half mile east of Harper's Ferry. At this point I came up with these last-named troops, and leaving General Edgerton and his command on the Maryland side of the river for the night, caused the marines to proceed to Harper's Ferry, and placed them within the armory grounds to prevent the possibility of the escape of the insurgents Having taken measures to halt, in Baltimore, the artillery companies ordered from Fort Monroe, I made preparations to attack the insurgents at daylight. But for the fear of sacrificing the lives of some of the gentlemen held by them as prisoners in a midnight assault, I should have ordered the attack at once.

Their safety was the subject of painful consideration, and to prevent, if possible, jeopardizing their lives, I determined to summon the insurgents to surrender. As soon after daylight as the arrangements were made Lieutenant J. E. B. Stewart, 1st cavalry, who had accompanied me from Washington as staff officer, was dispatched, under a flag, with a written summons, (a copy of which is hereto annexed, marked A.) Knowing the character of the leader of the insurgents, I did not expect it would be accepted. I had therefore directed that the volunteer troops, under their respective commanders, should be paraded on the lines assigned them outside the armory, and had prepared a storming party of twelve marines, under their commander, Lieutenant Green, and had placed them close to the engine-house, and secure from its fire. Three marines were furnished with sledge-hammers to break in the doors, and the men were instructed how to distinguish our citizens from the insurgents; to attack with the bayonet, and not to injure the blacks detained in custody unless they resisted. Lieutenant Stewart was also directed not to receive from the insurgents any counter propositions. If they accepted the terms offered, they must immediately deliver up their arms and release their prisoners. If they did not, he must, on leaving the engine-house, give me the signal. My object was, with a view of saving our citizens, to have as short an interval as possible between the summons and attack. The summons, as I had anticipated, was rejected. At the concerted signal the storming party moved quickly to the door and commenced the attack. The fire-engines within the house had been placed by the besieged close to the doors. The doors were fastened by ropes, the spring of which prevented their being broken by the blows of the hammers. The men were therefore ordered to drop the hammers, and, with a portion of the reserve, to use as a battering-ram a heavy ladder, with which they dashed in a part of the door and gave admittance to the storming party. The fire of the insurgents up to this time had been harmless. At the threshold one marine fell mortally wounded. The rest, led by Lieutenant Green and Major Russell, quickly ended the contest. The insurgents that resisted were bayoneted. Their leader, John Brown, was cut down by the sword of Lieutenant Green, and our citizens were protected by both officers and men. The whole was over in a few minutes.

After our citizens were liberated and the wounded cared for, Lieutenant Colonel S. S. Mills, of the 53d Maryland regiment, with the Baltimore Independent Greys, Lieutenant B. F. Simpson commanding, was sent on the Maryland side of the river to search for John E. Cook, and to bring in the arms, &c., belonging to the insurgent party, which were said to be deposited in a school-house two and a half miles distant. Subsequently, Lieutenant J. E. B. Stewart, with a party of marines, was dispatched to the Kennedy farm, situated in Maryland, about four and a half miles from Harper's Ferry, which had been rented by John Brown, and used as the depot for his men and munitions. Colonel Mills saw nothing of Cook, but found the boxes of arms, (Sharp's carbines and belt revolvers,) and recovered Mr. Washington's wagon and horses. Lieutenant Stewart found also at the Kennedy farm a number of sword pikes, blankets, shoes, tents, and all the necessaries for a campaign. These articles have been deposited in the government storehouse at the armory.

From the information derived from the papers found upon the persons and among the baggage of the insurgents, and the statement of those now in custody, it appears that the party consisted of nineteen men—fourteen white and five black. That they were headed by John Brown, of some notoriety in Kansas, who in June last located himself in Maryland, at the Kennedy farm, where he has been engaged in preparing to capture the United States works at Harper's Ferry. He avows that his object was the liberation of the slaves of Virginia, and of the whole South; and acknowledges that he has been disappointed in his expectations of aid from the black as well as white population, both in the Southern and Northern States. The blacks whom he forced from their homes in this neighborhood, as far as I could learn, gave him no voluntary assistance. The servants of Messrs. Washington and Allstadt, retained at the armory, took no part in the conflict, and those carried to Maryland returned to their homes as soon as released. The result proves that the plan was the attempt of a fanatic or madman, which could only end in failure; and its temporary success was owing to the panic and confusion he succeeded in creating by magnifying his numbers. I append a list of the insurgents, (marked B.) Cook is the only man known to have escaped. The other survivors of the expedition, viz.: John Brown, A. C. Stevens, Edwin Coppic, and Green Shields, (*alias* S. Emperor,) I have delivered into the hands of the marshal of the western district of Virginia and the sheriff of Jefferson county. They were escorted to Charlestown by a detachment of marines, under Lieutenant Green. About nine o'clock this evening I received a report from Mr. Moore, from Pleasant Valley, Maryland, that a body of men had, about sunset, descended from the mountains, attacked the house of Mr. Gennett, and from the cries of murder and the screams of the women and children, he believed the residents of the valley were being massacred. The alarm and excitement in the village of Harper's Ferry was increased by the arrival of families from Sandy Hook, fleeing for safety. The report was, however, so improbable that I could give no credence to it, yet I thought it possible that some atrocity might have been committed, and I started with twenty-five marines, under Lieutenant Green, accompanied by Lieutenant Stewart, for the scene of the alleged outrage, about four and a half miles distant. I was happy to find it a false alarm. The inhabitants of Pleasant Valley were quiet and unharmed, and Mr. Gennett and his family safe and asleep.

I will now, in obedience to your dispatch of this date, direct the detachment of marines to the navy-yard at Washington in the train that passes here at 1¼ A. M. to-night, and will myself take advantage of the same train to report to you in person at the War Department. I must also ask to express my thanks to Lieutenant Stewart, Major Russell, and Lieutenant Green, for the aid they afforded me, and my entire commendation of the conduct of the detachment of marines, who were at all times ready and prompt in the execution of any duty.

The promptness with which the volunteer troops repaired to the scene of disturbance, and the alacrity they displayed to suppress the gross outrage against law and order, I know will elicit your hearty approbation. Equal zeal was shown by the president and officers of the Baltimore and Ohio Railroad Company in their transportation of the troops, and in their readiness to furnish the facilities of their well-ordered road.

A list of the killed and wounded, as far as came to my knowledge, is herewith annexed, (marked C;) and I inclose a copy of the "Provisional Constitution and ordinances for the people of the United States," of which there were a large number prepared for issue by the insurgents.

I am, very respectfully, your obedient servant,

R. E. LEE, *Colonel Commanding.*

Colonel S. Cooper,
Adjutant General U. S. Army, Washington City, D. C.

A

HEADQUARTERS HARPER'S FERRY,
October 18, 1859.

Colonel Lee, United States army, commanding the troops sent by the President of the United States to suppress the insurrection at this place, demands the surrender of the persons in the armory buildings.

If they will peaceably surrender themselves and restore the pillaged property, they shall be kept in safety to await the orders of the President. Colonel Lee represents to them, in all frankness, that it is impossible for them to escape; that the armory is surrounded on all sides by troops; and that if he is compelled to take them by force he cannot answer for their safety.

R. E. LEE,
Colonel Commanding United States Troops.

B

List of Insurgents—14

John Brown, of New York, commander-in-chief, badly wounded; prisoner.

Aaron C. Stevens, Connecticut, captain, badly wounded; prisoner.

Edwin Coppic, Iowa, Lieutenant, unhurt; prisoner.

Oliver Brown, New York, captain; killed.

Watson Brown, New York, captain; killed.

Albert Hazlett, Pennsylvania, lieutenant; killed.

William Leeman, Maine, lieutenant; killed.

Stuart Taylor, Canada, private; killed.

Charles P. Tidd, Maine, private; killed.

William Thompson, New York, private; killed

Adolph Thompson, New York, private; killed.

John Kagi, Ohio, private; killed.

Jeremiah Anderson, Indiana, private; killed.

John E. Cook, Connecticut, captain; escaped.

Negroes—5

Dangerfield Newby, Ohio; killed.

Louis Leary, Oberlin, Ohio; killed.

Green Shields, (alias Emperor,) New York, unhurt; prisoner.

Copeland, Oberlin, Ohio; prisoner.

O. P. Anderson, Pennsylvania, unaccounted for.

C

List of the killed and wounded by the insurgents—14

Fontaine Beckham, railroad agent and mayor of Harper's Ferry; killed.

G. W. Turner, Jefferson county, Virginia; killed.

Thomas Boerly, Harper's Ferry; killed.
Heywood Shepherd, negro, railroad porter; killed.
Private Quinn, marine corps; killed.
Mr. Murphy; wounded.
Mr. Young; wounded.
Mr. Richardson; wounded.
Mr. Hammond; wounded.
Mr. McCabe; wounded.
Mr. Dorsey; wounded.
Mr. Hooper; wounded.
Mr. Woollet; wounded.
Private Rupert, marine corps; wounded.

Colonel Lee to the Secretary of War

HARPER'S FERRY ARSENAL,
October 18, 1859.

SIR:

Upon a more deliberate examination of the wounds of O. Brown, they are believed not to be mortal. He has three wounds, but they are not considered by the surgeon as bad as first reported. Please direct me what to do with him and the other white prisoners.

I am, very respectfully, your obedient servant,

R. E. LEE,
Colonel Commanding.

Hon. Secretary of War,
Washington, D. C.

GUIDE QUESTIONS

1. During what hours was Colonel Lee an eye-witness of the raid on Harper's Ferry?
2. Who were the members of John Brown's party?
3. What casualties were suffered on both sides?
4. In what general state of mind did Colonel Lee find the inhabitants of Harper's Ferry?
5. In what ways does Colonel Lee's report indicate his intention to avoid making a biased statement?
6. What pattern of organization does Colonel Lee use in his report?

VOCABULARY

Give the derivations and definitions of the following words:

insurgent, avocation, threshold, notoriety, fanatic, credence, alacrity, approbation.

Osborne P. Anderson

A VOICE FROM HARPER'S FERRY

Chapter VIII

COUNCIL MEETINGS : ORDERS GIVEN : THE CHARGE : ETC.

On Sunday morning, October 16th, Captain Brown arose earlier than usual, and called his men down to worship. He read a chapter from the Bible, applicable to the condition of the slaves, and our duty as their brethren, and then offered up a fervent prayer to God to assist in the liberation of the bondmen in that slaveholding land. . . .

After breakfast had been despatched, . . . we listened to preparatory remarks to a council meeting to be held that day. At 10 o'clock, the council was assembled. I was appointed to the Chair, when matters of importance were considered at length. After the council adjourned, the Constitution was read for the benefit of the few who had not before heard it, and the necessary oaths taken. . . .

In the afternoon, the eleven orders presented in the next chapter were given by the Captain, and were afterwards carried out in every particular by the officers and men.

In the evening, before setting out to the Ferry, he gave his final charge, in which he said, among other things: "And now, gentlemen, let me impress this one thing upon your minds. You all know how dear life is to you, and how dear your life is to your friends. And in remembering that, consider that the lives of others are as dear to them as yours are to you. Do not, therefore, take the life of anyone, if you can possibly

From *A Voice from Harper's Ferry* (Boston: Printed for the Author, 1861). Chaps. 8-15, pp. 28-51.

avoid it; but if it is necessary to take life in order to save your own, then make sure work of it."

Chapter IX

The orders given by Captain Brown, before departing from the Farm for the Ferry, were:

1. Captain Owen Brown, F. J. Merriam, and Barclay Coppic to remain at the old house as sentinels, to guard the arms and effects till morning, when they would be joined by some of the men from the Ferry with teams to move all arms and other things to the old school-house before referred to, located about three-quarters of a mile from Harper's Ferry—a place selected a day or two beforehand by the Captain.
2. All hands to make as little noise as possible going to the Ferry, so as not to attract attention till we could get to the bridge; and to keep all arms secreted, so as not to be detected if met by anyone.
3. The men were to walk in couples, at some distance apart and should anyone overtake us, stop him and detain him until the rest of our comrades were out of the road. The same course to be pursued if we were met by anyone.
4. That Captains Charles P. Tidd and John E. Cook walk ahead of the wagon in which Captain Brown rode to the Ferry, to tear down the telegraph wires on the Maryland side along the railroad; and to do the same on the Virginia side, after the town should be captured.
5. Captains John H. Kagi and A. D. Stevens were to take the watchman at the Ferry bridge prisoner when the party got there, and to detain him there until the engine house upon the Government grounds should be taken.
6. Captain Watson Brown and Stewart Taylor were to take positions the Potomac bridge, and hold it till morning. They were to stand on opposite sides, a rod apart, and if anyone entered the bridge, they were to let him get in between them. In that case, pikes were to be used, not Sharp's rifles, unless they offered much resistance, and refused to surrender.

7. Captains Oliver Brown and William Thompson were to execute a similar order at the Shenandoah bridge, until morning.

8. Lieutenant Jeremiah Anderson and Adolphus Thompson were to occupy the engine house at first, with the prisoner watchman from the bridge and the watchman belonging to the engine-house yard, until the one on the opposite side of the street and the rifle factory were taken, after which they would be reinforced, to hold that place with the prisoners.

9. Lieutenant Albert Hazlett and Private Edwin Coppic were to hold the Armory opposite the engine house after it had been taken, through the night and until morning, when arrangements would be different.

10. That John H. Kagi, Adjutant General, and John A. Copeland, (colored) take positions at the rifle factory through the night, and hold it until further orders.

11. That Colonel A. D. Stevens (the same Captain Stevens who held military position next to Captain Brown) proceed to the country with his men, and after taking certain parties prisoners bring them to the Ferry. In the case of Colonel Lewis Washington, who had arms in his hands, he must, before being secured as a prisoner, deliver them into the hands of Osborne P. Anderson. Anderson being a colored man, and colored men being only *things* in the South, it is proper that the South be taught a lesson upon this point.

John H. Kagi being Adjutant General, was the near adviser of Captain John Brown, and second in position; and had the old gentleman been slain at the Ferry, and Kagi been spared, the command would have devolved upon the latter. But Col. Stevens holding the active military position in the organization second to Captain Brown, when order eleven was given him, had the privilege of choosing his own men to execute it. The selection was made after the capture of the Ferry, and then my duty to receive Colonel Washington's famous arms was assigned me by Captain Brown. The men selected by Col. Stevens to act under his orders during the night were Charles P. Tidd, Osborne P. Anderson, Shields Green, John E. Cook and Sherrard Lewis Leary. We were to take prisoners, and any slaves who would come, and bring them to the Ferry.

A few days before, Capt. Cook had travelled along the Charlestown turnpike, and collected statistics of the population of slaves and the nasters' names. Among the masters whose acquaintance Cook had made, Colonel Washington had received him politely, and had shown him a sword formerly owned by Frederic the Great of Prussia, and presented by him to Genl. Washington, and a pair of horse pistols, formerly owned by General Lafayette, and bequeathed by the old General to Lewis Washington. These were the arms specially referred to in the charge.

At eight o'clock on Sunday evening, Captain Brown said: "Men, get on your arms; we will proceed to the ferry." His horse and wagon were brought out before the door, and some pikes, a sledge-hammer and crowbar were placed in it. The Captain then put on his old Kansas cap, and said: "Come, boys!" when we marched out of the camp behind him, into the lane leading down the hill to the main road. As we formed the procession line, Owen Brown, Barclay Coppic, and Francis J. Merriam, sentinels left behind to protect the place as before stated, came forward and took leave of us; after which, agreeably to previous orders, and as they were better acquainted with the topography of the Ferry, and to effect the tearing down of the telegraph wires, C. P. Tidd and John E. Cook led the procession. While going to the Ferry, the company marched along as solemnly as a funeral procession, till we got to the bridge. When we entered, we halted, and carried out an order to fasten our cartridge boxes outside of our clothes, when everything was ready for taking the town.

Chapter X

THE CAPTURE OF HARPER'S FERRY : COL. A. D. STEVENS AND PARTY SALLY OUT
TO THE PLANTATIONS : WHAT WE SAW, HEARD, DID, ETC.

As John H. Kagi and A. D. Stevens entered the bridge, as ordered in the fifth charge, the watchman, being at the other end, came toward them with a lantern in his hand. When up to them, they told him he was their prisoner, and detained him a few minutes, when he asked them to spare his life. They replied, they did not intend to harm him; the object was to free the slaves, and he would have to submit to them for a time, in order that the purpose might be carried out.

Captain Brown now entered the bridge in his wagon, followed by the rest of us, until we reached that part where Kagi and Stevens held their prisoner, when he ordered Watson Brown and Stewart Taylor

to take the positions assigned them in order sixth, and the rest of u
to proceed to the engine house. We started for the engine-house, takin₃
the prisoner along with us. When we neared the gates of the engine
house yard, we found them locked, and the watchman on the inside
He was told to open the gates, but refused, and commenced to cry
The men were then ordered by Captain Brown to open the gates forci
bly, which was done, and the watchman taken prisoner. The tw₄
prisoners were left in the custody of Jerry Anderson and Adolphu
Thompson, and A. D. Stevens arranged the men to take possession o
the Armory and rifle factory. About this time, there was apparentl
much excitement. People were passing back and forth in the town, an₄
before we could do much, we had to take several prisoners. After th
prisoners were secured, we passed to the opposite side of the street an₄
took the Armory, and Albert Hazlett and Edwin Coppic were ordere₄
to hold it for the time being.

The capture of the rifle factory was the next work to be done. Wher
we went there, we told the watchman who was outside of the buildin₃
our business, and asked him to go along with us, as we had come t₄
take possession of the town, and make use of the Armory in carryin₃
out our object. He obeyed the command without hesitation. John H
Kagi and John Copeland were placed in the Armory, and the prisoner
taken to the engine-house. Following the capture of the Armory, Olive
Brown and William Thompson were ordered to take possession of th
bridge leading out of town, across the Shenandoah river, which the
immediately did. These places were all taken, and the prisoners se
cured, without the snap of a gun, or any violence whatever.

The town being taken, Brown, Stevens, and the men who had n₄
post in charge, returned to the engine house, where council was held
after which Captain Stevens, Tidd, Cook, Shields Green, Leary an₄
myself went to the country. On the road, we met some colored men, t₄
whom we made known our purpose, when they immediately agree₄
to join us. They said they had been long waiting for an opportunity o
the kind. Stevens then asked them to go around among the colore₄
people and circulate the news, when each started off in a different direc
tion. The result was that many colored men gathered to the scene o
action. The first prisoner taken by us was Colonel Lewis Washingtor
When we neared his house, Capt. Stevens placed Leary and Shield
Green to guard the approaches to the house, the one at the side, th
other in front. We then knocked, but no one answering, although f₄

males were looking from upper windows, we entered the building and commenced a search for the proprietor. Col. Washington opened his room door, and begged us not to kill him. Capt. Stevens replied, "You are our prisoner," when he stood as if speechless or petrified. Stevens further told him to get ready to go to the Ferry; that he had come to abolish slavery, not to take life but in self-defense, but that he *must* go along. The Colonel replied: "You can have my slaves, if you will let me remain." "No," said the Captain, "you must go along too; so get ready." After saying this, Stevens left the house for a time, and with Green, Leary and Tidd, proceeded to the "Quarters," giving the prisoner in charge of Cook and myself. The male slaves were gathered together in a short time, when horses were tackled to the Colonel's two-horse carriage and four-horse wagon, and both vehicles brought to the front of the house.

During this time, Washington was walking the floor, apparently much excited. When the Captain came in, he went to the sideboard, took out his whiskey, and offered us something to drink, but he was refused. His fire-arms were next demanded, when he brought forth one double-barrelled gun, one small rifle, two horse-pistols and a sword. Nothing else was asked of him. The Colonel cried heartily when he found he must submit, and appeared taken aback when, on delivering up the famous sword formerly presented by Frederic to his illustrious kinsman, George Washington, Capt. Stevens told me to step forward and take it. Washington was secured and placed in his wagon, the women of the family making great outcries, when the party drove forward to Mr. John Allstadt's. After making known our business to him, he went into as great a fever of excitement as Washington had done. We could have his slaves, also, if we would only leave him. This, of course, was contrary to our plans and instructions. He hesitated, puttered around, fumbled and meditated for a long time. At last, seeing no alternative, he got ready, when the slaves were gathered up from about the quarters by their own consent, and all placed in Washington's big wagon and returned to the Ferry.

. . . While we were absent from the Ferry, the train of cars for Baltimore arrived, and was detained. A colored man named Haywood, employed upon it, went from the Wager House up to the entrance to the bridge, where the train stood, to assist with the baggage. He was ordered to stop by the sentinels stationed by the bridge, which he refused to do, but turned to go in an opposite direction, when he was fired upon, and received a mortal wound. Had he stood when ordered, he would not have been harmed. No one knew whether he was white or colored, but his movements were such as to justify the sentinels in shooting him, as he would not stop when commanded. The first firing happened at that time, and the only firing, until after daylight on Monday morning.

Chapter XI

THE EVENTS OF MONDAY, OCT. 17 : ARMING THE SLAVES : TERROR IN THE SLAVEHOLDING CAMP : IMPORTANT LOSSES TO OUR PARTY : THE FATE OF KAGI : PRISONERS ACCUMULATE : WORKMEN AT THE KENNEDY FARM : ETC.

Monday, the 17th of October, was a time of stirring and exciting events. In consequence of the movements of the night before, we were prepared for commotion and tumult, but certainly not for more than we beheld around us. Gray dawn and yet brighter daylight revealed great confusion, and as the sun arose, the panic spread like wild-fire. Men, women and children could be seen leaving their homes in every direction; some seeking refuge among residents, and in quarters further away, others climbing up the hillsides, and hurrying off in various directions, evidently impelled by a sudden fear, which was plainly visible in their countenances or in their movements.

Capt. Brown was all activity, though I could not help thinking that at times he appeared somewhat puzzled. He ordered Sherrard Lewis Leary, and four slaves, and a free man belonging in the neighborhood, to join John Henry Kagi and John Copeland at the rifle factory, which they immediately did. Kagi, and all except Copeland, were subsequently killed, but not before having communicated with Capt. Brown, as will be set forth further along.

As fast as the workmen came to the building, or persons appeared in the street near the engine house, they were taken prisoners, and directly after sunrise, the detained train was permitted to start for the eastward. After the departure of the train, quietness prevailed for a short time; a number of prisoners were already in the engine house, and of the many colored men living in the neighborhood, who had assembled in the town, a number were armed for the work.

Capt. Brown ordered Capts. Charles P. Tidd, Wm. H. Leeman, John E. Cook, and some fourteen slaves, to take Washington's four-horse wagon, and to join the company under Capt. Owen Brown, consisting of F. J. Merriam and Barclay Coppic, who had been left at the Farm the night previous, to guard the place and the arms. The company, thus reinforced, proceeded, under Owen Brown, to move the arms and goods from the Farm down to the school-house in the mountains, three-fourths of a mile from the Ferry.

Capt. Brown next ordered me to take the pikes out of the wagon in which he rode to the Ferry, and to place them in the hands of the colored men who had come with us from the plantations, and others who had come forward without having had communication with any of our party. It was out of the circumstances connected with the fulfilment of this order, that the false charge against Anderson as "leader," or "ringleader," of the negroes, grew.

The spectators, about this time, became apparently wild with fright and excitement. The number of prisoners was magnified to hundreds, and the judgment-day could not have presented more terrors, in its awful and certain prospective punishment to the justly condemned for the wicked deeds of the life time, the chief of which would no doubt be slaveholding, than did Capt. Brown's operations.

The prisoners were also terror-stricken. Some wanted to go home to see their families, as if for the last time. The privilege was granted them, under escort, and they were brought back again. Edwin Coppic, one of the sentinels at the Armory gate, was fired at by one of the citizens, but the ball did not reach him, when one of the insurgents close by put up his rifle, and made the enemy bite the dust.

Among the arms taken from Col. Washington was one double-barrel gun. This weapon was loaded by Leeman with buckshot, and placed in the hands of an elderly slave man, early in the morning. After the cowardly charge upon Coppic, this old man was ordered by Capt. Stevens to arrest a citizen. The old man ordered him to halt, which he refused to do, when instantly the terrible load was discharged into him, and he fell, and expired without a struggle.

After these incidents, time passed away till the arrival of the United States troops, without any further attack upon us. The cowardly Virginians submitted like sheep, without resistance, from that time until the marines came down. Meanwhile, Capt. Brown, who was considering a proposition for release from his prisoners, passed back and forth from the Armory to the bridge, speaking words of comfort and encouragement to his men. "Hold on a little longer, boys," said he, "until I get matters arranged with the prisoners." This tardiness on the part of our brave leader was sensibly felt to be an omen of evil by some of us, and was eventually the cause of our defeat. It was not part of the original plan to hold on to the Ferry, or to parley with prisoners; but by so doing, time was afforded to carry the news of its capture to several points, and forces were thrown into the place, which surrounded us.

At eleven o'clock, Capt. Brown despatched William Thompson from the Ferry up to Kennedy Farm, with the news that we had peaceful possession of the town, and with directions to the men to continue on moving the things. He went; but before he could get back, troops had begun to pour in, and the general encounter commenced.

Chapter XII

RECEPTION TO THE TROOPS : THEY RETREAT TO THE BRIDGE : A PRISONER :
DEATH OF DANGERFIELD NEWBY : WILLIAM THOMPSON : THE MOUNTAINS
ALIVE : FLAG OF TRUCE : THE ENGINE HOUSE TAKEN

It was about twelve o'clock in the day when we were first attacked by the troops. Prior to that, Capt. Brown, in anticipation of further trouble, had girded to his side the famous sword taken from Col. Lewis Washington the night before, and with that memorable weapon, he commanded his men against General Washington's own State.

When the Captain received the news that the troops had entered the bridge from the Maryland side, he, with some of his men, went into the street, and sent a message to the Arsenal for us to come forth also. We hastened to the street as ordered, when he said—"The troops are on the bridge, coming into town; we will give them a warm reception." He then walked around amongst us, giving us words of encouragement, in this wise:—"Men! be cool! Don't waste your powder and shot! Take aim, and make every shot count!" "The troops will look for us to retreat on their first appearance; be careful to shoot first." Our men were well supplied with firearms, but Capt. Brown had no rifle at that time; his only weapon was the sword before mentioned.

The troops soon came out of the bridge, and up the street facing us, we occupying an irregular position. When they got within sixty or seventy yards, Capt. Brown said, "Let go upon them!" which we did, when several of them fell. Again and again the dose was repeated.

There was now consternation among the troops. From marching in solid martial columns, they became scattered. Some hastened to seize upon and bear up the wounded and dying—several lay dead upon the ground. They seemed not to realize, at first, that we would fire upon them, but evidently expected we would be driven out by them without firing. Capt. Brown seemed fully to understand the matter, and hence, very properly and in our defense, undertook to forestall their movements. The consequence of their unexpected reception was, after leaving several of their dead on the field, they beat a confused retreat into the bridge, and there stayed under cover until reinforcements came to the Ferry.

On the retreat of the troops, we were ordered back to our former post. While going, Dangerfield Newby, one of our colored men, was shot through the head by a person who took aim at him from a brick store window, on the opposite side of the street, and who was there for the purpose of firing upon us. Newby was a brave fellow. He was one of my comrades at the Arsenal. He fell at my side, and his death was promptly avenged by Shields Green, the Zouave of the band, who afterwards met his fate calmly on the gallows, with John Copeland. Newby was shot twice; at the first fire, he fell on his side and returned it; as he lay, a second shot was fired, and the ball entered his head. Green raised his rifle in an instant, and brought down the cowardly murderer, before the latter could get his gun back through the sash.

There was comparative quiet for a time, except that the citizens seemed to be wild with terror. Men, women and children forsook the place in great haste, climbing up hillsides and scaling the mountains. . . . During this time, Wm. Thompson, who was returning from his errand to the Kennedy Farm, was surrounded on the bridge by the railroad men, who next came up, taken a prisoner to the Wager House, tied hand and foot, and, at a late hour of the afternoon, cruelly murdered by being riddled with balls, and thrown headlong on the rocks.

Late in the morning, some of his prisoners told Capt. Brown that they would like to have breakfast, when he sent word forthwith to the Wager House to that effect, and they were supplied. He did not order breakfast for himself and men, as was currently but falsely stated at the time, as he suspected foul play; on the contrary, when solicited to have breakfast so provided for him, he refused.

Between two and three o'clock in the afternoon, armed men could be seen coming from every direction; soldiers were marching and counter-marching; and on the mountains, a host of bloodthirsty ruffians swarmed, waiting for their opportunity to pounce upon the little band. The fighting commenced in earnest after the arrival of fresh troops. Volley upon volley was discharged, and the echoes from the hills, the shrieks of the townspeople, and the groans of their wounded and dying, all of which filled the air, were truly frightful. The Virginians may well conceal their losses, and Southern chivalry may hide its brazen head, for their boasted bravery was well tested that day, and in no way to their advantage. It is remarkable, that except that one fool-hardy colored man was reported buried, no other funeral is mentioned, although the Mayor and other citizens are known to have fallen. Had they reported the true number, their disgrace would have been more apparent; so they wisely (?) concluded to be silent.

The fight at Harper's Ferry also disproved the current idea that slaveholders will lay down their lives for their property. Col. Washington, the representative of the old hero, stood "blubbering" like a great calf at supposed danger; while the laboring white classes and non-slaveholders, with the marines, (mostly gentlemen from "furrin" parts) were the men who faced the bullets of John Brown and his men. Hardly the skin of a slaveholder could be scratched in open fight; the cowards kept out of the way until danger was passed, sending the poor whites into the pitfalls, while they were reserved for the bragging, and to do the safe but cowardly judicial murdering afterwards.

As strangers poured in, the enemy took positions round about, so as to prevent any escape, within shooting distance of the engine house and Arsenal. Capt. Brown, seeing their manoeuvres, said: "We will hold on to our three positions, if they are unwilling to come to terms, and die like men."

All this time, the fight was progressing; no powder and ball were wasted. We shot from under cover, and took deadly aim. For an hour before the flag of truce was sent out, the firing was uninterrupted, and one and another of the enemy were constantly dropping to the earth.

One of the Captain's plans was to keep up communication between his three points. In carrying out this idea, Jerry Anderson went to the rifle factory, to see Kagi and his men. Kagi, fearing that we would be overpowered by numbers if the Captain delayed leaving, sent word by Anderson to advise him to leave the town at once. This word Anderson communicated to the Captain, and told us also at the Arsenal. The message sent back to Kagi was, to hold out for a few minutes longer, when we would all evacuate the place. Those few minutes proved disastrous, for then it was that the troops before spoken of came pouring in, increased by crowds of men from the surrounding country. After an hour's hard fighting, and when the enemy were blocking up the avenues of escape, Capt. Brown sent out his son Watson with a flag of truce, but no respect was paid to it; he was fired upon and wounded severely. He returned to the engine house, and fought bravely after that for fully an hour and a half, when he received a mortal wound, which he struggled under until the next day. The contemptible and savage manner in which the flag of truce had been received, induced severe measures in our defense, in the hour and a half before the next one was sent out. The effect of our work was, that the troops ceased to fire at the buildings, as we clearly had the advantage of position.

Capt. A. D. Stevens was next sent out with a flag, with what success I will presently show. Meantime, Jeremiah Anderson, who had brought the message from Kagi previously, was sent by Capt. Brown with another message to John Henrie, but before he got far on the street, he was fired upon and wounded. He returned at once to the engine house, where he survived but a short time. . . .

Capt. Stevens was fired upon several times while carrying his flag of truce, and received severe wounds, as I was informed that day, not being myself in a position to see him after. He was captured, and taken to the Wager House, where he was kept until the close of the struggle in the evening, when he was placed with the rest of our party who had been captured.

After the capture of Stevens, desperate fighting was done by both sides. The marines forced their way inside the engine-house yard, and commanded Capt. Brown to surrender, which he refused to do, but said in reply, that he was willing to fight them, if they would allow him first to withdraw his men to the second lock on the Maryland side. As might be expected, the cowardly hordes refused to entertain such a proposition, but continued their assault, to cut off communication between our several parties. The men at the Kennedy Farm having received such a favorable message in the early part of the day, through Thompson, were ignorant of the disastrous state of affairs later in the day. Could they have known the truth, and come down in time, the result would have been very different; we should not have been captured that day. A handful of determined men, as they were, by taking a position on the Maryland side, when the troops made their attack and retreated to the bridge for shelter, would have placed the enemy between two fires. Thompson's news prevented them from hurrying down, as they otherwise would have done, and thus deprived us of able assistance from Owen Brown, a host in himself, and Tidd, Merriam and Coppic, the brave fellows composing that band.

The climax of murderous assaults on that memorable day was the final capture of the engine house, with the old Captain and his handful of associates. This outrageous burlesque upon civilized warfare must have a special chapter to itself, as it concentrates more of Southern littleness and cowardice than is often believed to be true.

Chapter XIII

THE CAPTURE OF CAPTAIN JOHN BROWN AT THE ENGINE HOUSE

One great difference between savages and civilized nations is, the improved mode of warfare adopted by the latter. Flags of truce are always entitled to consideration, and an attacking party would make a wide departure from military usage, were they not to give opportunity for the besieged to capitulate, or to surrender at discretion. Looking at the Harper's Ferry combat in the light of civilized usage even where one side might be regarded as insurrectionary, the brutal treatment of Captain Brown and his men in the charge by the marines on the engine house is deserving of severest condemnation, and is one of those blood-thirsty occurrences, dark enough in depravity to disgrace a century.

Captain Hazlett and myself being in the Arsenal opposite, saw the charge upon the engine house with the ladder, which resulted in opening the doors to the marines, and finally in Brown's capture. The old hero and his men were hacked and wounded with indecent rage and at last brought out of the house and laid prostrate upon the ground, mangled and bleeding as they were. A formal surrender was required of Captain Brown, which he refused, knowing how little favor he would receive, if unarmed, at the hands of that infuriated mob. All of our party who went from the Farm, save the Captain, Shields Green, Edwin Coppic and Watson Brown (who had received a mortal wound some time before), the men at the Farm, and Hazlett and I, were either dead or captured before this time; the particular of whose fate we learned still later in the day, as I shall presently show. Of the four prisoners taken at the engine house, Shields Green, the most inexorable of all our party, a very Turco in his hatred against the stealers of men, was under Captain Hazlett, and consequently of our little band at the Arsenal; but when we were ordered by Captain Brown to return to our positions, after having driven the troops into the bridge, he mistook the order, and went to the engine house instead of with his own party. Had he remained with us, he might have eluded the vigilant Virginians. As it was, he was doomed, as is well-known, and became a free-will offering for freedom, with his comrade, John Copeland. Wiser and better men no doubt there were, but a braver man never lived than Shields Green.

Chapter XIV

SETTING FORTH REASONS WHY O. P. ANDERSON AND A. HAZLETT ESCAPED FROM THE ARSENAL, INSTEAD OF REMAINING, WHEN THEY HAD NOTHING TO DO : TOOK A PRISONER, AND WHAT RESULTED TO THEM, AND THIS NARRATIVE, THEREFROM : A PURSUIT, WHEN SOMEBODY GOT KILLED, AND OTHER BODIES WOUNDED

Of the six men assigned a position in the arsenal by Captain Brown, four were either slain or captured; and Hazlett and myself, the only ones remaining, never left our position until we saw, with feelings of intense sadness, that we could be of no further avail to our commander, he being a prisoner in the hands of the Virginians. We therefore, upon consultation, concluded it was better to retreat while it was possible, as our work for the day was clearly finished, and gain a position where in the future we could work with better success, than to recklessly invite capture and brutality at the hands of our enemies. The charge of deserting our brave old leader and of fleeing from danger has been circulated to our detriment, but I have the consolation of knowing that, reckless as were the half-civilized hordes against whom we contended the entire day, and much as they might wish to disparage his men, they would never have thus charged us. They know better. John Brown's men at Harper's Ferry were and are a unit in their devotion to John Brown and the cause he espoused. To have deserted him would have been to belie every manly characteristic for which Albert Hazlett, at least, was known by the party to be distinguished, at the same time that it would have endangered the future safety of such deserter or deserters. John Brown gave orders; those orders must be obeyed, so long as Captain Brown was in position to enforce them; once unable to command, from death, being a prisoner, or otherwise, the command devolved upon John Henry Kagi. Before Captain Brown was made prisoner, Captain Kagi had ceased to live, though had he been living, all communication between our post and him had been long cut off. We could not aid Captain Brown by remaining. We might, by joining the men at the Farm, devise plans for his succor; or our experience might become available on some future occasion.

The charge of running away from danger could only find form in the mind of some one unwilling to encounter the difficulties of a Harper's Ferry campaign, as no one acquainted with the out-of-door and in-door encounters of that day will charge anyone with wishing to escape danger, merely. It is well enough for men out of danger, and who could not be induced to run the risk of a scratching, to talk flippantly about cowardice, and to sit in judgment upon the men who went with John Brown, and who did not fall into the hands of the Virginians; but to have been there, fought there, and to understand what *did* transpire there, are quite different. As Capt. Brown had all the prisoners with him, the whole force of the enemy was concentrated there, for a time, after the capture of the rifle factory. Having captured our commander, we knew that it was but little two of us could do against so many, and that our turn to be taken must come; so Hazlett and I went out at the back part of the building, climbed up the wall, and went upon the railway. Behind us, in the Arsenal, were thousands of dollars, we knew full well, but that wealth had no charms for us, and we hastened to communicate with the men sent to the Kennedy Farm. We traveled up the Shenandoah along the railroad, and overtook one of the citizens. He was armed, and had been in the fight in the afternoon. We took him prisoner, in order to facilitate our escape. He submitted without resistance, and quietly gave up his gun. From him, we learned substantially of the final struggle at the rifle factory, where the noble Kagi commanded. The number of citizens killed was, according to his opinion, much larger than either Hazlett or I had supposed, although we knew there were a great many killed and wounded together. He said there must be at least seventy killed, besides wounded.

Hazlett had said there must be fifty, taking into account the defense of the three strong positions. I do not know positively, but would not put the figure below thirty killed, seeing many fall as I did, and knowing the "dead aim" principle upon which we defended ourselves. One of the Southern published accounts, it will be remembered, said twenty citizens were killed, another said fifteen. At last it got narrowed down to five, which was simply absurd, after so long an engagement. We had forty rounds apiece when we went to the Ferry, and when Hazlett and I left, we had not more than twenty rounds between us. The rest of the party were as free with their ammunition as we were, if not more so. We had further evidence that the number of dead was larger than published, from the many that we saw lying dead around.

When we had gone as far as the foot of the mountains, our prisoner begged us not to take his life, but to let him go at liberty. He said we might keep his gun; he would not inform on us. Feeling compassion for him, and trusting to his honor, we suffered him to go, when he went directly into town, and finding everything there in the hands of our enemies, he informed on us, and we were pursued. After he had left us, we crawled or climbed up among the rocks in the mountains, some hundred yards or more from the spot where we left him, and hid ourselves, as we feared treachery, on second thought. A few minutes before dark, the troops came in search of us. They came to the foot of the mountains, marched and counter-marched, but never attempted to search the mountains; we supposed from their movements that they feared a host of armed enemies in concealment. Their air was so defiant, and their errand so distasteful to us, that we concluded to apply a little ammunition to their case, and having a few cartridges on hand, we poured from our excellent position in the rocky wilds, some well-directed shots. It was not so dark but that we could see one bite the dust now and then, when others would run to aid them instantly, particularly the wounded. Some lay where they fell, undisturbed, which satisfied us that they were dead. The troops returned our fire, but it was random shooting, as we were concealed from their sight by the rocks and bushes. Interchanging of shots continued for some minutes, with much spirit, when it became quite dark, and they went down into the town. After their return to the Ferry, we could hear the drum beating for a long time; an indication of their triumph, we supposed. Hazlett and I remained in our position three hours, before we dared venture down.

Chapter XV

THE ENCOUNTER AT THE RIFLE FACTORY

As stated in a previous chapter, the command of the rifle factory was given to Captain Kagi. Under him were John Copeland, Sherrard Lewis Leary, and three colored men from the neighborhood. At an early hour, Kagi saw from his position the danger in remaining, with our small company, until assistance could come to the inhabitants. Hence his suggestion to Captain Brown, through Jeremiah Anderson, to leave. His position being more isolated than the others, was the first to invite an organized attack with success; the Virginians first investing the factory with their hordes, before the final success at the engine house. From the prisoner taken by us who had participated in the assault upon Kagi's position, we received the sad details of the slaughter of our brave companions. Seven different times during the day they were fired upon, while they occupied the interior part of the building, the insurgents defending themselves with great courage, killing and wounding with fatal precision. At last, overwhelming numbers, as many as five hundred, our informant told us, blocked up the front of the building, battered the doors down, and forced their way into the interior. The insurgents were then forced to retreat the back way, fighting, however, all the time. They were pursued, when they took to the river, and it being so shallow, they waded out to a rock, mid-way, and there made a stand, being completely hemmed in, front and rear. Some four or five hundred shots, said our prisoner, were fired at them before they were conquered. They would not surrender into the hands of the enemy, but kept on fighting until everyone was killed, except John Copeland. Seeing he could do no more, and that all his associates were murdered, he suffered himself to be captured. . . . John Copeland was taken to the guard-house, where the other prisoners afterwards were, and thence to Charlestown jail. His subsequent mockery of a trial, sentence and execution, with his companion Shields Green, on the 16th of December—are they not part of the dark deeds of this era, which will assign their perpetrators to infamy, and cause after generations to blush at the remembrance?

IDE QUESTIONS

During what hours was Anderson an eye-witness of the raid on Harper's Ferry?

What were his movements and stations in the town?

What casualties, according to him, were suffered on both sides?

Who were the members of John Brown's party?

udging from the eleven orders issued by John Brown to his men, what do you think was his immediate purpose? His ultimate purpose?

udging from the nature of Anderson's account and the date of its publication, what do you think was his purpose in writing it?

From what point of view does he describe the storming of the Engine House?

By what devices does Anderson seek to develop characterizations of the persons in his story?

What was Anderson's attitude toward his leader, John Brown?

CABULARY

the derivations and definitions of the following words:

ade, invest, sentinel, pike, topography, custody, alternative, impel, pective, consternation, forestall, ensue, insurrectionary, depravity, inable, detriment, disparage, espouse, succor, transpire, perpetrator, ny.

testimony from

THE MASON REPORT

JANUARY 6, 1860.

RENCE BYRNE *sworn and examined:*

BY THE CHAIRMAN:

Q. WILL YOU PLEASE to state your age, and where you reside, and what your occupation is?

I am forty-two years of age. I reside in Washington county, Mary-

om *The Mason Report*, U. S. Congress; Senate, Select Committee on the Harper's Invasion, Rep. Com. No. 278, June 15, 1860, pp. 13-45.

land, about three miles northwest of Harper's Ferry. I am enga
in farming.

Q. Are you a landholder and slaveholder?

A. I am a landholder jointly with my brother Joseph. I am a sl
holder.

Q. Will you state whether you formed the acquaintance of J
Brown, recently executed in Jefferson county, Virginia, and
what name he passed when you formed his acquaintance, and w
you formed it?

A. I was not personally acquainted with him.

Q. Do you know the place he lived at—the Kennedy farm?

A. Very well, sir.

Q. How far is your residence from that?

A. My place is not quite a mile and a half south of the Kennedy fa

Q. Did you know there was such a man in the neighborhood, altho
you had not seen him personally?

A. I knew there was a man who had rented the Kennedy farm.

Q. By what name did he pass?

A. By the name of Smith. I had seen him frequently and passed
on the road. I knew him by sight, but not personally.

Q. Will you state whether you were taken into custody by any p
of men, and who they were, and at what time, and where?

A. I would rather state it in my own way. On the morning of
17th of October I left home on horseback early, between 5 an
o'clock, and I had progressed about a mile and a quarter whe
passed a wagon on the road, driven by a colored man. Almos
the same time that I passed the tail-end of the wagon—I goin;
the direction of Harper's Ferry and the wagon towards the K
nedy farm—I heard a voice call out, "Mr. Byrnes, stop." I rei
up my horse and looked back, and recognized John E. Cook
the ground. I had known Cook before in that neighborhood.
approached me on the right side of my horse, and remarked to
"I am very sorry to inform you that you are my prisoner," or so
thing like that. I do not remember the exact words. I had left hc
with a view of riding a distance of about six miles. I looked at I
and smiled, and said, "You are certainly joking." He said, "I
not." I looked down, and under his coat I saw a barrel of a
protruding, and he kept moving it and jerking it. I thought
wanted to attract my attention, from his actions, to his be

armed; and almost a moment afterwards a second man approached me, whom I have learned since was C. P. Tidd, but at that time he was unknown to me. He presented his gun to me and said, "No parley here, or I will put a ball in you," or "through you;" "You must go with us to your place; we want your negroes," or something like that. I told him if that was the case I would go back rather than that he should put a ball through me.

Well, you went back where?

To my house.

What did they do after you got there?

I passed my brother on the porch just before entering the door, and I whispered to him, "civil war," or something like that; perhaps I said "servile war." I walked in. I do not know whether Cook preceded me or not, but I know we all got into the room about the same time. Cook, Leeman, and Tidd seated themselves uninvited. I walked up and down the floor, and Cook commenced making a kind of speech, sitting down, what we term a higher-law speech. My mind was busy with the future, and I paid very little attention to what he said.

What was the subject?

The subject of slavery. He said that all men were created equal. That was a quotation. I remember that distinctly. Just about the time he commenced, I asked my sister, who I saw was very much alarmed, where a cousin of mine was, who was then on a visit to my house. She answered that she was up stairs, and I told her to call her down and be witness to every thing that was said and done, as she was a lady of considerable nerve. I was too much excited to pay much attention to the speech. The first word my cousin said when she came down was, "Cowhide those scoundrels out of the house; why do you suffer them to talk to you?" I did not heed her, either. I do not recollect all her remarks.

There were three men then, Cook, Tidd, and Leeman; were they all armed?

All armed.

With what?

Sharp's rifles and revolvers.

What requirements or demands did they make of you?

I am a little too fast. Just after my arrest on the road, on turning back, they made a proposition to me to this effect, that I had better

be quiet and give up my slaves; or, if I would give up my sla
voluntarily, they would enter into an article of agreement with 1
They said they would first take me before their captain, and th
were certain that if I would give up my slaves voluntarily their c
tain would enter into an article of agreement with me to protect
person and property. I told them that was something I would
do, that I looked to the State government, or, if that failed, to
federal government to protect me in my person and property. Th
remarked they would have them any how.

Q. What demands did they make of you in the house, and how w
they made?

A. They addressed my brother, in the house, and said: "Mr. Byrne,
want your slaves." My brother's reply was, "Captain Cook, y
must do as I do when I want them—hunt for them." They w
too early in the morning. My brother's servant and my own, t
men, had left home the Saturday evening preceding, and had
returned yet, Monday morning. They did not get them. They
not want the negro women or children at that time.

Q. Did they become satisfied that the negro men were not at hor

A. Yes, sir.

Q. What did they do then?

A. They kept my brother and myself prisoners there. Two of th
remained with us, and Tidd started with some five or six or se
negroes to the Kennedy farm, in Colonel Washington's wag
I did not know whose wagon it was at the time, but Cook told
afterwards that it was Colonel Washington's wagon.

Q. They left two of the men at your house, holding you and y
brother in their custody?

A. Yes, sir; Cook and Leeman remained.

Q. How long did they remain?

A. I do not know; I had no idea of the time. I did not notice
clock, though it was on the mantel.

Q. What time in the morning was it when they first arrested y

A. I do not know exactly, but it was between five and six o'cloc
little after daylight.

Q. Can you give an idea of the time they remained, as near as you
come; whether they went away before noon?

A. Yes, sir. They left shortly after, say, a late breakfast.

Q. Then they were not there more than three or four hours, if so
   much?

A. Not so much.

Q. Did they give you any reasons for their going away, when they
   did go away?

A. They said I would have to go to Harper's Ferry, that their orders
   were to take me to Harper's Ferry before their captain.

Q. Did they do so?

A. They took me to Harper's Ferry and placed me in the watch-house.
   It was between 9 and 10 o'clock on Monday morning when I got
   into the watch-house.

Q. Who took you?

A. I was detained at my place until the wagon went to the Kennedy
   farm and returned back. Tidd, who had charge of the wagon and
   the negroes, came to Cook and remarked that they were ready to
   proceed. I was escorted by them. We went first to the school-house,
   where the arms were deposited. We had to pass by it on the road.

Q. What was in the wagon?

A. There were boxes. They seemed to be well filled with something.
   I did not know at the time what was in them.

Q. Was the wagon heavily loaded?

A. It seemed to pull pretty heavily, but it was a damp morning.

Q. How many horses?

A. Four horses. It was a heavy farm wagon.

Q. Did you know any of the negroes who were with them?

A. I did not.

Q. What was done at the school-house? Was there anybody in the
   school-house when you got there?

A. Yes, sir; Mr. Currie, the teacher, and his pupils. The school was in
   session.

Q. What passed when they arrived at the school-house?

A. I do not know that I heard all that passed. I do not think I did.

Q. I do not mean so much in conversation as what was done.

A. Some of the party went in; I shall not be positive who, but one
   of the three, or perhaps two, went in and asked him to suspend
   school for a while, and then he could go on; they wanted to occupy
   one corner of the house, saying they wanted to deposit some boxes
   there, but I shall not be positive about that; but I know Mr. Currie

came out, and I whispered across the fence to him—I did not g
in—that I was a prisoner, and remarked to him, "You have nothin
to fear, you are not a slaveholder." I did not know at the tim
whether he owned slaves or not. My object was to put him on hi
guard, and he whispered in my ear, "I am."

Q. What was done there? What did these men do?

A. The wagon was unloaded there, and the boxes placed in the schoo.
house. As soon as the wagon was unloaded, Cook or Tidd tol
Leeman to accompany me down to Harper's Ferry.

Q. Did you leave the rest with the wagon at the school-house, whe
you went away?

A. Tidd, Cook, and the negroes were left behind with the wagon a
the school-house. I proceeded with Leeman about one hundred o
one hundred and fifty yards south of the school-house, and I wa
met by one of the Brown party, whom I had known by the nam
of Thompson. He came up smiling. He was armed, and, I think
had a blanket over his shoulders. He extended his hand and said
"How are you, Byrne?" I said, "Good morning, Mr. Thompson
I am well; how are you?" I was then disposed to put on a cheerfu
face, and I asked him what was the news at Harper's Ferry. He said
the people were more frightened than hurt, and he passed on. It
commenced raining about the same time, and Leeman suggested
that we get under a tree until the shower passed. We sat down on
the side of the road. I had an umbrella, and proposed to him to sit
up close to me, and my umbrella would be some protection to him.
He did so. He remarked to me, "Our captain is no longer John
Smith," or I. Smith, or J. Smith, or something like that, but was
"John Brown, of Kansas notoriety," I think he said, but I shall
not be positive about that, for I was disposed to assume a character
that I did not have at the time, that of cheerfulness. My mind was
busy with the future. I was fearful of a bloody civil war. I was
under the impression that, unless they were there in great numbers,
they would not be foolish enough to make an attack on the borders
of two slaveholding States.

Q. Did you have any further conversation with Leeman at that time,
as to Brown's objects or purposes in coming there?

A. I did not feel disposed to question him at all; but he appeared to
be very serious, had very little to say while at the house, and I am

inclined to think he was meditating his escape from them, judging from his manner.

Q. Did you proceed to the Ferry afterwards?

A. We sat under this tree, Leeman and myself, until the shower had almost ceased, and we started. Whether Thompson overhauled us at that point, or at a point further down near Harper's Ferry, I do not recollect; but I know that Thompson and Leeman were with me almost all the distance from the school-house to the Virginia side of the bridge. There Thompson stopped, and Leeman passed through the town as far as the watch-house with me.

Q. Did you meet any armed men after you got on the Virginia side of the bridge, and before you got to the watch-house?

A. I passed two armed men on the bridge—a white man and a colored man. I think the white man was a son of Brown, or Smith, as he was called.

Q. Did you pass any after you left the bridge?

A. Not that I recollect.

Q. Did they speak to you in any way?

A. This white man had a mit on, and as soon as he saw me he took it off and shook hands with me.

Q. Had you seen him before?

A. I think I had.

Q. Did he call you by name?

A. I do not recollect that he did.

Q. What time did you get to the Ferry?

A. I do not recollect exactly, but I think it was between nine and ten o'clock in the morning.

Q. The watch-house is in the inside of the armory yard, adjoining the engine-house?

A. Yes, sir; under the same roof. They are adjoining rooms. The watch-house is on the west end of the building. . . .

Q. When did you see Brown first at the watch-house?

A. Almost immediately after my arrival. I saw him moving about in front of the engine-house.

Q. Did he come and speak to you?

A. He did not, and I did not ask to be taken to him.

Q. He did not speak to you on your coming?

A. No, sir.

Q. Did he at any time while you remained there?

A. Not until after I first addressed him. He put his hand on me and said, "I want you, sir." He went around to different ones, and I think he selected five hostages in the first place out of the watch-house. I was one of the second batch that was taken out. He just walked around and put his hand on or pointed to us; I think he put his hand on me and said, "I want you, sir."

Q. What did he want with you?

A. We were taken in the engine-house and pointed to the back part of the room, and told to stand there.

Q. Then Brown came into the watch-house some time after you got there, and selected five men, you among them?

A. Ten altogether, five the first time, and five the second time. I was one of the second five. . . .

Q. What time were you put in the engine-house?

A. I think it was after the middle of the day on Monday, but I could not say positively.

Q. How long did you remain in the engine-house?

A. Until sometime Tuesday morning, until we were rescued by the marines.

Q. Did you have any conversation with Brown while you were in the engine-house, or did you hear him conversing with any of the rest of the party on the subject of what brought him there, or what he expected or intended to do?

A. Yes, sir; at different times there was a great deal said. I cannot recollect one fifth part.

Q. Can you recollect anything that would disclose what his object was in coming to the Ferry; what his purpose was; what he was after; what his object was in taking the prisoners and keeping them there; what his general object was?

A. At one time I heard him remark: "Gentlemen, if you knew my past history, you would not blame me for being here," or something to that effect. He then went on to state that he had gone to Kansas a peaceable man, and was hunted down like a wolf by the pro-slavery men from Virginia and Kentucky, and he lost some members of his family; I think he said a son; "and now," said he, "I am here." At that time he did not say for what purpose. One son of his was laying on my right who had been wounded on Monday about the middle of the day on the street. He seemed to suffer intensely, and complained very much. He asked to be dispatched, or killed, or put out of his misery, or something of that kind, I think, and Brown remarked to him, "No, my son, have patience; I think you will get well; if you die, you die in a glorious cause, fighting for liberty," or "freedom," or something like that.

Q. Can you recollect anything that passed tending to show what his object was in coming to Harper's Ferry with a body of armed men?

A. I do not recollect that I heard him say, but I know his men said they were there for the purpose of giving freedom to the slaves.

Q. Did I understand you to say that Brown's son, who was wounded, had been shot in the street and came into the engine-house wounded, or was he shot while in the engine-house?

A. He was wounded in the street and came into the watch-house, and afterwards went into the engine-house before I was in there. I first saw him in the watch-house after he was wounded. There was some firing before I was taken into the engine-house, and he asked for his rifle, and moved in himself from the watch-house to the engine-house; but when I went in the engine-house he was laying down on the floor, and I heard his father remark that he had exerted himself too much.

Q. Did he die before your rescue?

A. No, sir; I think he was brought out alive. He was speechless, though.

Q. Was there much firing by the party in the engine-house; much shooting at persons outside?

A. There was a good deal of firing on Monday evening.

Q. Can you tell in what way the party inside fired out—through the doors, or through windows, or through loop-holes, or how?

A. Some through the doors, and some through port holes, or loop-holes.

Q. Were those loop-holes made after you got there, or before?

A. I know that some of them were made after I was taken in.

Q. Was anybody of Brown's party killed in the engine-house while you were there?

A. They were killed about the door. When the firing was going on, I kept as close to the floor as I could. I got down, and did not see much until there was a cessation of the firing; but there were two of Brown's party killed on Monday evening. I do not think they died until some time during the night. They were shot about the door of the engine-house in which they were.

Q. Can you tell us how many of Brown's party were in there?

A. I do not think I can; not when I was first taken in; but I can tell you how many there were on Tuesday morning.

Q. How many of Brown's party, dead and alive together, were in there when you were rescued by the marines?

A. There were two dead, one in a dying condition, (Brown's son,) and five or six active men, including a negro, at the time the attack was made by the marines.

Q. How many negroes were there in Brown's party in the engine-house, that Brown brought with him, not negroes of the neighborhood?

A. But one.

Q. What was his name?

A. Shields Green, I understood.

Q. At what time were you rescued, and when, and how?

A. I do not know what time it was. I had no time-piece, and did not inquire after I got out.

Q. I do not speak accurately as to hours of course, but was it in the morning, or the middle of the day, or at night?

A. It was Tuesday morning.

Q. How was the rescue made?

A. By the marines; but I cannot tell how it was done, because we were inside, and they were outside. We first heard a hammering at the door, and then the Brown party commenced firing at the door. The door was closed, and an engine run against it at that time. They barricaded it as well as they could. There was a cessation for a moment or two, and during this time one of Brown's men turned round to him and said, "Captain, I believe I will surrender." His answer was, "Sir, you can do as you please." This man was then down on his knees, and he got upon his feet, and turned round to me and said, "Hallo 'surrender' for me." I hallooed at the top of my voice, and Mr. Daingerfield hallooed at the same time, "One man surrenders;" but we could not make ourselves heard on the outside. Coppic was further over to the left, and partly sheltered by an engine. A portion of his body was sheltered. He said to this man, "Get down on your knees, sir, or your head will be shot off."

But he did not heed them until they commenced hitting on the door, and then he got down.

Q. Were any propositions made to you, or to any of the other prisoners in the engine-house, by Brown, as to your being redeemed by putting a slave in your place, or anything of that sort?

A. No sir. I heard of that afterwards. No such proposition was made to me. I did not hear it there. . . .

TERENCE BYRNE.

DANIEL WHELAN *sworn and examined*

BY THE CHAIRMAN:

Q. STATE YOUR AGE and where you live?

A. I live at Harper's Ferry; I am about thirty-nine years of age.

Q. What was your business at the Ferry at the time of the invasion by John Brown?

A. I was a watchman at the armory gate on Sunday night.

Q. In whose service were you?

A. In the United States service.

Q. State when you first saw or heard or knew anything of Brown's party; what occurred when they came there?

A. The first time I ever saw them I heard the noise of their wagon coming down the street from the depot, and then I advanced about three yards out from the watch-house door, and observed the wagon standing facing the armory gate.

Q. Was the gate locked?

A. Yes, sir; I went and I advanced a little closer; I thought it was Mr. Mason, the head watchman; there were two men at the padlock striving to open it; I told them to "hold on;" I went to the gate, and when I observed it was not Mr. Mason, I drew aside at the gate and looked until I observed them, and saw they were strangers; when they all came into the yard I think there was about twenty-five men; they asked me to open the gate; I told them I could not open the gate by any means; "Open the gate," said they; I said, "I could not if I was stuck," and one of them jumped up on the pier of the gate over my head, and another fellow ran and put his hand on me and caught me by the coat and held me; I was inside and they were outside, and the fellow standing over my head upon the pier, and then when I would not open the gate for them, five or six ran in from the wagon, clapped their guns against my breast, and told me I should deliver up the key; I told them I could not; and another fellow made answer and said they had not time now to be waiting for a key, but to go to the wagon and bring out the crowbar and large hammer, and they would soon get in; they went to the little wagon and brought a large crowbar out of it; there is a large chain around the two sides of the wagon-gate going in; they twisted the crowbar in the chain and they opened it, and in they ran and got in the wagon; one fellow took me; they all gathered about me and looked in my face; I was nearly scared to death with so many guns about me; I did not know the minute or the hour I should drop; they told me to be very quiet and still and make no noise or else they would put me to eternity; one of them ordered the wagon to be marched in, and all were in the wagon except four who had me; they took the wagon down the yard and passed the horses' heads to the gate where Colonel Barbour's office is; after that, the head man of them, Brown, ordered all the men to dispatch out of the yard, but he left a man at each side of the big gate along with himself; he himself still had me and Bill Williams, the watchman whom he brought down off the Potomac bridge; those other two men were at the gate, and then he said, "I came here from Kansas, and this is a slave State; I want to free all the negroes in this State; I have possession now of the United States armory, and if the citizens interfere with me, I must only burn the town and have blood."

Q. Were you the only watchman in the armory yard?

A. There was another above in the upper end, but they did not go near him until about 1 o'clock.

Q. How far was the upper end from the gate?

A. About 300 yards, I guess.

Q. You saw nothing of him until about 1 o'clock in the morning?

A. Not until the train came down, and he was coming down to see where I was, and Brown met him and marched him into the watch-house.

Q. What time in the night was it when Brown's party appeared there at the gate?

A. To the best of my knowledge it was a quarter before eleven o'clock on Sunday night, the 16th of October.

Q. What did they do with you after they took you?

A. They kept me in the yard and began to question me about all the officers. I told them as well as I could, and the leader said he would have all those gentlemen in the morning; and with that, before he took me into the watch-house, they had old Mr. Williams down from the rifle-works. He was the other watchman up at the rifle-works. They also brought in two or three young fellows off the street. The men scattered out of the armory yard and brought them in. I had a sword in my hand, and when they all came to view me Cook took that out of my hand. I knew Cook well. There were two old muskets in the watch-house, and they took them and put them into the wagon, and I could get no person to tell me anything about them since.

Q. There were no watchmen in the armory yard except you at the gate, and one man at the far end, about 300 yards off?

A. That was all.

Q. Was the gate kept locked always at night?

A. Always. I had the key on Monday night when Mr. Daingerfield was marched out, and he asked who was the watchman last night, I said, "I was the watchman." He said, "Why don't you open this gate?" "I could not open it," said I. "Have you the key?" "Yes," said I, "I have the key." "Well," said Daingerfield, on Monday, about 8 or 9 o'clock, when he was taken prisoner, "you had better open the gate." I was going to open the little gate by the word of Mr. Daingerfield, and Mr. Brown struck up, took the two keys, and said he was the man who could open it, and kept the keys. They were picking them up, and brought in Mr. Allstadt and Mr. Washington there, and their negroes, their wagons and horses.

Q. Did they keep you confined in the watch-house, or leave you go about the yard?

A. They kept me until I was taken out of it by the force of Martinsburg or the Charlestown company, I do not know which.

Q. What time of day was that?

A. About three o'clock on Monday.

his
DANIEL ✕ WHELAN.
mark

JOHN D. STARRY, *sworn and examined*

BY THE CHAIRMAN:

Q. WILL YOU STATE what is your age, where you reside, and what your profession is?

A. I am thirty-five years of age. I reside at Harper's Ferry. I am a practising physician.

Q. Will you state at what time you first heard of the presence of an armed party at Harper's Ferry; where you heard it; and what occurred when you first became aware of it?

A. On Sunday night, the 16th of October, about half past one o'clock, I heard a shot fired in the direction of the Baltimore and Ohio railroad bridge, the iron span of the bridge, and immediately afterwards a cry of distress, as if somebody had been hurt. At the same time I heard considerable confusion about the Baltimore and Ohio railroad train—the starting point just opposite the hotel. I jumped out of my bed. My room is nearly opposite the railroad bridge. I went to the window and saw two armed men passing from the bridge towards the armory gate. These men were low fellows. While I was standing there, a tall man came from the direction of the armory gate, and met them near the Winchester railroad. Some noise about the hotel attracted his attention, and he turned and went towards the armory gate again. About that time some of the passengers came out from between the hotel and the railroad station, and the tall man said to them, "The first man that fires at me I will shoot," or, "the first man who interrupts me," or some such expression as that. In a very short time I was in the street, and there was some firing going on between the railroad party or citizens and that man. I did not know who fired first. There were several shots passed between them. I was then going across the street towards the railroad office. When I got there I found the negro porter, Hayward, shot, the ball entering from behind, through the body, nearly on a line with the base of the heart, a little below it. He told me that he had been out on the railroad bridge looking for a watchman who was missing, and he had been ordered to halt by some men who were there, and, instead of doing that, he turned to go back to the office, and as he turned they shot him in the back. I understood from him that he walked from there to the office, and when I found him he was lying on a plank upon two chairs in the office.

Q. Will you state in whose employment that negro was?

A. He was in the employment of the Baltimore and Ohio Railroad Company, and it was his duty to be up whenever the train arrived to attend to baggage, and receive whatever baggage was put off for the station, and attend to everything about the office during the absence of Mr. Beckham, the agent. He was a free negro, and had permission of the county court to remain in Jefferson county. I believe he did not belong to the county.

Q. How long did he live?

A. I saw him about daylight; he was still living. I understood he died between twelve and one o'clock on Monday, the next day. Soon after that, which was probably about two o'clock in the morning, I stood at the corner of the railroad station and saw three men, who, I supposed, were the three I had first seen, coming from the armory gate, and I stood at the corner of the depot until they got within five or six feet of me. I then passed back the angle of the station until I got to the office-door and went in, and said to the passengers, and others who were there, "Here go these three men now whom I saw go into the armory yard, and I will go down to the armory and see what is going on."

Q. Could you see whether those men were armed?

A. Yes, sir; I knew they were armed. I stood until they were very close to me. I went then to the armory gate, and before I got to the gate I called for the watchman. I was ordered to halt. I did so, and inquired of the men who halted me, what had become of the watchmen. I wanted to inquire why they allowed persons to go in and out of that gate, when they knew they were shooting down those whom they met in the street. I did not understand it, and I asked for Medler and Murphy, the watchmen. The fellow told me that there were no watchmen there; that he did not know Medler or Murphy, but, said he, "There are a few of us here." I did not say anything more to him, but turned and went up the street, and came off on the Winchester railroad, and down to the railroad office again. Soon after that, I was on the platform, and some of that party from the bridge hailed me to know if that train was coming over—the train which they had stopped. I told them I thought it was very doubtful; I did not think it would come over until after daylight; we did not understand their movements, and should like to know what they were doing. He said to me, "Never mind, you will find out in a day or two." I asked him if he expected to stay there a day or two. He made no reply to that. I passed on around the railroad office or post office, I do not remember which. That was about three o'clock, I suppose. I watched them from that time until daylight, sometimes very close to them, and sometimes further off. About four o'clock I heard a wagon coming down the street. I did not know what that meant, and I watched them as closely as I could. About five minutes after five o'clock, I saw a four-horse team driving over the Baltimore and Ohio railroad bridge. I did not know whose it was. In that wagon there were three men standing up in the front part, with spears in their hands, white men, and two were walking alongside, armed with rifles. I did not see any negroes. I saw but these men. I understood afterwards there were negroes with them, but I did not see them. About daylight, as these strangers seemed to have possession of the public works there, I determined to get on my horse and go and notify Mr. Kitzmiller, acting superintendent of the armory, of the condition of things there, but before I did that I went to the island of Virginius, and roused up Mr. Welch and others there. I knew there were a good many men about the mill and cooper-shop there. I told them the condition of things as well as I could. I met no one on the way. I then got my horse and came out into Shenandoah street, and had to go perhaps fifty yards before I made the turn of the street leading to the hill. About the time I was making that turn, I saw three of these men coming across from the armory gate towards the arsenal. They had just made a few steps from the gate into the street. I did not know whether their intention was to stop me or not. They made a sort of half turn, and I was out of their sight in a moment. I went to Mr. Kitzmiller and informed him that the armory was in possession of an armed band. I then passed up to Bolivar, and roused up some of the people, and went from there to Hall's Works, and found three of these men there armed. I rode up to the fence, which was probably twenty-five or thirty steps from where they were. They stepped out in front of one of the buildings, and marched down inside of the fence fifty or sixty yards, and out into the public street, and down towards the armory. I went back to the hillside then, and tried to get the citizens together, to see what we could do to get rid of these fellows. They seemed to be very troublesome. When I got on the hill I learned that they had shot Boerley. That was probably about 7 o'clock. Boerley was an Irishman, living there, a citizen of the town. He died very soon afterwards.

Q. Tell us about that incident; did you see Boerley?

A. I did not see him.

Q. Did you see him after he was dead?

A. No, sir. Dr. Claggett, who is here, saw him after he was dead, and was with him when he died.

Q. Do you know anything of the killing of Mr. Turner?

A. No, sir; I will go on with what I was stating; I had ordered the Lutheran church bell to be rung to get the citizens together to see what sort of arms they had; I found one or two squirrel rifles and a few shot guns; I had sent a messenger to Charlestown in the meantime for Captain Rowan, commander of a volunteer company there: I also sent messengers to the Baltimore and Ohio railroad to stop the trains coming east, and not let them approach the Ferry, and also a messenger to Shepherdstown. When I could find no guns fit for use, and learned from the operatives and foremen at the armory that all the guns that they knew of were in the arsenal and in possession of these men, I thought I had better go to Charlestown myself, perhaps; I did so, and hurried Captain Rowan off. When I returned to the Ferry, I found that the citizens had gotten some guns out of one of the workshops—guns which had been placed there to keep them out of the high water—and were pretty well armed. I assisted, from that time until some time in the night, in various ways, organizing the citizens and getting them to the best place of attack, and sometimes acting professionally.

Q. State the position of the armory and armory yard in reference to the rivers.

A. It is just at the confluence of the two rivers. After passing across the bridge, these men had about 60 yards to go to get to the armory gate, down the street, in front of the hotel. They would go up the Potomac river. The arsenal is rather up the Shenandoah river from there. It is probably about 60 yards from the armory gate to the arsenal gate on the Shenandoah side.

Q. Where are Hall's rifle works?

A. About half a mile up the Shenandoah river.

Q. These armed parties were in possession of those three points?

A. Yes, sir; and the Baltimore and Ohio railroad bridge also.

Q. Were you aware of the killing of any other person than this free negro you have mentioned?

A. No, sir; I did not see the others; I saw Mr. Turner after he was dead, and also Mr. Beckham; I did not know that Mr. Turner was shot until after he was dead. . . .

Q. Will you state where your chamber was, in what part of the town?

A. Nearly opposite the mouth of the Baltimore and Ohio railroad bridge, within 50 steps of the mouth of the Baltimore and Ohio railroad bridge, in a building across from the hotel; I was awake at the time the shot was fired and the cry of distress heard. My first idea was that some one had been shot at the train.

Q. When you first went out was the train there?

A. Yes, sir; it had attempted to cross the bridge before Hayward was shot, and was ordered back again by the conductor.

Q. Did you see any of Brown's party killed?

A. I saw a man shot in the Potomac river on Monday, I suppose about one o'clock. He was shot from near the small bridge, at the upper end of the trestle work, or from the hill side. He was attempting to cross the Potomac river from the Virginia to the Maryland side.

Q. Have you any means of knowing how many of them were killed except those in the engine-house?

A. I saw part of the fight at Hall's works; I went to put on some dry clothes at half past three o'clock, and that fight was then over. A yellow fellow was brought down on the bank of the river and citizens were tying their handkerchiefs together to hang him; I put my horse between the armory wall and the fence and held him there until I allowed the officer to get off some 25 or 30 steps with the prisoner; I said to them that two or three of Brown's men were in Hall's works, and if they wanted to show their bravery they could go there. They did so. They were the citizens and neighbors of the Ferry. I organized a party about half past two or three o'clock, and sent them over there, with directions to commence the fight as soon as they got near enough; that party was under the command of a young man named Irwin. He went over, and at the first fire Kagi, and the others who were with him in Hall's works, went out the back way towards the Winchester railroad, climbed out on the railroad and into the Shenandoah river. They were met on the opposite side by a party who were there and driven back again, and two of them were shot; Kagi was killed, and a yellow fellow, Leary, was wounded and died that night; and the yellow fellow Copeland was taken unhurt.

Q. How many of the Brown party did you see dead, including those who were in the engine-house?

A. Four dead and Stevens wounded, and the yellow fellow Leary wounded. I saw ten of Brown's party dead altogether, including those in the engine-house.

Q. How many of those ten were negroes?

A. I only give you the names of the negroes as given to me by Stevens—Leary and Anderson and Dangerfield Newby were the negroes killed. Anderson was of very light color, but was given to me by Stevens, one of the party, as a colored man.

Q. Do you know the number of citizens who were killed?

A. Four; three white men and the negro Hayward. Hayward first, Boerley, Mr. Turner, and Mr. Beckham. Beckham was the last shot, about four o'clock in the evening.

Q. Were there any of the citizens wounded?

A. Edward McCabe was wounded. There were some of the Berkeley men wounded, who were acting as military. I do not know any other citizen of Harper's Ferry who was wounded but McCabe.

JOHN D. STARRY.

§

LEWIS W. WASHINGTON *sworn and examined*

BY THE CHAIRMAN:

Q. WILL YOU PLEASE to state your age, and where you reside, and what your occupation is?

A. I am about forty-six years of age. I reside in Jefferson county, Virginia. I am a farmer.

Q. Are you a landholder and slaveowner?

A. Yes, sir.

Q. How far is your residence from Harper's Ferry?

A. It is about five miles.

Q. Will you state whether you saw an armed party at your house, who they were, what their business was, and what brought them there, on the night of Sunday, the 16th of October last?

A. There was a body at my house, five of whom I saw, and the other I did not see. They appeared at my chamber door about half past one o'clock in the morning. My name was called in an under tone, and supposing it to be by some friend who had possibly arrived late, and being familiar with the house, had been admitted in the rear by the servants, I opened the door in my nightshirt and slippers. I was in bed and asleep. As I opened the door there were four armed men with their guns drawn upon me just around me. Three had rifles, and one a large revolver. The man having a revolver held in his left hand a large flambeau, which was burning. The person in command turned out to be Stevens. He asked me my name, and then referred to a man of the name of Cook, who had been at my house before, to know whether I was Colonel Washington. On being told that I was, he said, "You are our prisoner." I looked around, and the only thing that astonished me particularly was the presence of this man Cook, who had been at my house some three or four weeks before that. I met him in the street at Harper's Ferry as I was passing along. He came out and addressed me by name, and said, "I believe you have a great many interesting relics at your house; could I have permission to see them if I should walk out some day?" I said, "Yes." At that time I supposed he was an armorer, engaged in the public works at Harper's Ferry, almost all of whom know me, though I do not know them; but I am familiar with the faces of most of them. I had not seen this man before, or I should have recognized him. He came out to my house about four weeks before this attack. While there he was looking at a pistol that General Lafayette had presented to General Washington about the period of the revolution. He asked me if I had ever shot it. I told him I had. He asked, "Does it shoot well?" I told him I had not shot it for six or eight or ten years, that I had merely tried it, and cleaned it, and put it in the cabinet, and, I remarked, it would never be shot again. He was very curious about arms. He finally told me that he belonged to a Kansas hunting party, and found it very profitable to hunt buffaloes for their hides. He unbuttoned his coat and showed me two revolvers, and said, he was in the habit of carrying them in his occupation, that he had been attacked with chills and fevers some time ago, and was wearing them to accustom his hips to their weight. He asked if I was fond of shooting. I said I formerly was; and then he said, "You would possibly like to try these?" We went in front of my house, and under a tree we stuck up a target, and fired some twenty-four shots. He then told me that he had a rifle, a twenty-two shooter, that he would like me to look at, as he saw I had some fondness for fire-arms. He said to me, "When you come down to the Ferry, if you will call, I should like you to see it and try it." I was at the Ferry, it so happened, ten or fifteen days from that period, and inquired for him. I happened to know his name in this way: he did not introduce himself when he came, but in taking up his large revolver, (the size used in the army,) I found "John E. Cook" engraved on the breech of it on a brass plate, and he said, "I engraved that myself; I borrowed the tools from a silver-smith, a bungler, and thinking I could do it better myself, I did it." Then, said I, "I presume that is your name?" and he said, "Yes." When I asked for him at the Ferry, they told me he had left, and I supposed, in all probability, he had gone to Kansas, as he told me he intended to go in a few days. Believing that he had gone to Kansas, I was surprised to find him among the number at my house.

Q. You say that he had before asked permission to go to your house and see certain relics, and that he did go there; did you show him those arms?

A. Yes; he saw and handled them.

Q. What did they consist of?

A. The sword presented by Frederick the Great to General Washington, which he used as his dress sword, and one of the pistols presented to him by Lafayette.

Q. How did they come into your possession?

A. They descended to my father, and from him to me. My grandfather had the first choice of five swords left by the general.

Q. Shortly after midnight of the 16th of October, you were in bed and heard your name called at your chamber door, and opened it, and found an armed party with their arms presented towards you?

A. Yes, sir. I looked around at every gun to see if it was cocked, and found that they were all cocked.

Q. Who composed that party?

A. I only knew Cook's name at the time. I afterwards learned the
others. The party consisted of Stevens, Cook, Tidd, Taylor, and
the negro man Shields Green. There was a sixth man whom I did
not see; but Cook afterwards told me his name was Meriam. He
was engaged in hitching up the horses, as I understood.

Q. How did they get in your house?

A. They broke in the rear door of the house, and in that way reached
the back entry that enters my dining room. They attacked it with
the end of a fence rail used as a battering ram.

Q. You did not hear them?

A. No, sir; that is about fifty feet from my chamber, with about five
feet of walls interposing.

Q. Where is your chamber?

A. On the front of the house on the first floor.

Q. Was there any other white person in the house besides yourself?

A. No, sir; they asked me directly for my overseer. I told them he
was not there; that his family did not reside on my place, and he
went to his own house every night.

Q. What did your family consist of?

A. My daughter had left the morning before for Baltimore; she had
been spending the summer with me. Mr. William Turner and his
two daughters were with me the night preceding. I was then alone.

Q. Was your daughter the only member of your family?

A. I have two daughters, one of whom has never resided with me,
and the other was with me temporarily only, spending a few
months in summer. She resides with her grandmother. She is a
young lady grown. She had gone off the morning before, Saturday,
with Mr. Turner and his daughters to Baltimore. This attack was
on Sunday night or Monday morning, at the change of hours. After
looking around I observed that each man had two revolvers sticking in his belt in front besides the rifle. I remarked to them, "You
are a very bold looking set of fellows, but I should doubt your
courage; you have too many arms to take one man." I said to one
of them, "I believe with a pop-gun I could take either of you in
your shirt tail." At that time the fire began falling from the flambeau, and I asked them to come in my room and light my candles,
so as to prevent my house from being burnt. After going in, and
while dressing myself, I said, "Possibly you will have the courtesy
to tell me what this means; it is really a myth to me." Stevens

spoke up and said, "We have come here for the purpose of liberating all the slaves of the South, and we are able (or prepared) to do it," or words to that effect. I went on deliberately and dressed myself, and went into the dining room, thinking that possibly there was a better fire there; the fire in my chamber had gone out. I went into the dining room, and when I first got in, Stevens said to me, "You have some fire-arms, have you not?" I replied, "Yes, but all unloaded." He said, "I want them," and Cook made a signal to him that he had seen a very handsome gun in my closet. It was a gun which I had imported from England, and thinking he was a workman in the armory, I showed it to him, to get his opinion. I opened my closet in the dining room, and they took out the guns.

Q. What guns were they?

A. A shot gun and a rifle, and an old pistol of Harper's Ferry make of 1806, which was merely kept as a curiosity. They took them. Then Stevens said to me, "Have you a watch, sir?" I replied, "I have." Said he, "Where is it?" I said, "It is on my person." Said he, "I want it, sir." Said I, "You shall not have it." Said he, "Take care, sir." He then asked, "Have you money?" I remarked, "It is very comfortable to have a good deal of it these times; money is rather scarce." Then he made the same remark to me that he did before, "Take care, sir." I then said to him, "I am going to speak very plainly; you told me your purpose was philanthropic, but you did not mention at the same time that it was robbery and rascality. I do not choose to surrender my watch." He yielded the point; did not insist on it. I told him there were four there with arms, and they could take it, but I would not surrender it. Then he said to me, "I presume you have heard of Ossawatomie Brown?" I said, "No, I have not." "Then," said he, "you have paid very little attention to Kansas matters." I remarked to him that I had become so much disgusted with Kansas, and everything connected with it, that whenever I saw a paper with "Kansas" at the head of it I turned it over and did not read it. "Well," said he, "you will see him this morning," speaking apparently with great glorification. After some little time they announced to me that my carriage was ready at the door.

Q. Did they inquire about plate?

A. Yes; they saw in my cabinet a camp-service that belonged to General Arista in the Mexican war; I had taken it out of the case where it belonged and placed it in the cabinet; it is of very rare and beautiful workmanship; Stevens said, "I do not know but we shall want that," but afterwards he said he did not know but that it was plated-ware, instead of silver. After some little time, one came and announced that the carriage was at the door. I went out, and found the fellow, Shields Green; they called him "Emperor;" it was the first time I had seen him; he drove the carriage to the door, and as soon as I went out I found my large farm wagon with four horses hitched behind the carriage. I said to the men, "These horses" (referring to the carriage horses) "will not drive in that way; they are high-spirited horses; they are on the wrong side;" Tidd, I think, went up and said, "This horse is reined too short." One horse is slightly shorter than the other, and they had got the small harness on the large horse; we got on some little distance when the horses refused to work; by the by, this Emperor, as they termed him, Shields Green, was ordered off the seat when the carriage was about leaving the house, and my house servant, one of my slaves, was put in his place; Cook was on the back seat with me, and Tidd by the side of the driver; the other men were in the wagon behind; I only saw the wagon indistinctly, and did not know who was being placed in it.

Q. Did they tell you anything about taking your negroes?

A. They said, "We ordered your wagon to take your servants;" and I supposed they were going to take women and all, but it seems they did not want women. I did not know until I got in my field who was in the wagon. When the carriage horses refused to pull, I said, "These horses must be shifted;" I got down and put my foot on the wheel, and one of my servants came to help shift the horses, the servant whom they afterwards had in Maryland and who returned; the carriage horses were shifted in the field, and they went very well until they reached some point on the road; in the hurry of putting the harness on, the hames came loose near the top of the hill near Mr. Allstadt's house.

Q. What direction did they take on leaving your house?

A. The direction of Harper's Ferry by the usual road that led to the Ferry.

Q. Where was your first stopping place?

A. At the house of Mrs. Henderson, widow of Richard Henderson; they stopped the carriage just in front of the house; there were four or five daughters in the house who had recently lost their father, and I remarked to the party in front of me, "There is no one here but ladies, and it would be an infamous shame to wake them up at this hour of the night." Tidd jumped out, went to the wagon, and made some remark, and they went on; they went on to Allstadt's; I heard them take a fence rail from opposite the house; we stopped on the main road in front of the house; I did not hear any directions given there; a portion of the party was left with me in my carriage; Allstadt's inclosure bordering on the pike has a post and rail fence around it; the road on the opposite side of the pike has one of our Virginia worm fences, and from this fence I heard rails moving; being familiar with the sound, I knew what they were taking; they then went towards Allstadt's house, and I heard the jar of the rail against the door, and in a few moments there was a shout of murder and general commotion in the house; I thought first it was his servants hallowing murder, but he told me afterwards it was his daughters; finding this commotion going on, they put their heads out of the window and hallooed murder; one of these fellows drew his rifle on them and ordered them to go in and shut the window; I supposed of course what their purpose was; they took a number of negroes from him, I do not know exactly how many, and Allstadt was placed in the wagon with the negroes and taken to Harper's Ferry; they mentioned to him, as he afterwards informed me, that I was in my carriage; we then proceeded on to Harper's Ferry. Up to that time I supposed it was merely a robbing party who possibly had some room at the Ferry; I did not look on the thing as very serious at all until we drove to the armory gate, and the party on the front seat of the carriage said, "All's well," and the reply came from the sentinel at the gate, "All's well;" then the gates were opened and I was driven in and was received by old Brown; the carriage drove into the armory yard nearly opposite the engine-house.

Q. What did Brown say? How did he know who you were?

A. I presume he knew who had been sent for, and he at once assumed who I was.

Q. Did he address you by name?

A. He did not at that moment, but as "sir." He said, "You will find a fire in here, sir; it is rather cool this morning." Afterwards he came and said, "I presume you are Mr. Washington." He then remarked to me, "It is too dark to see to write at this time, but when it shall have cleared off a little and become lighter, if you have not pen and ink, I will furnish them to you, and I shall require you to write to some of your friends to send a stout, able-bodied negro; I think after a while, possibly, I shall be enabled to release you, but only on the condition of getting your friends to send in a negro man as a ransom." Then he said, "I shall be very attentive to you, sir, for I may get the worst of it in my first encounter, and if so, your life is worth as much as mine. I shall be very particular to pay attention to you. My particular reason for taking you first was that, as the aid to the governor of Virginia, I knew you would endeavor to perform your duty, and perhaps you would have been a troublesome customer to me; and, apart from that, I wanted you particularly for the moral effect it would give our cause, having one of your name as a prisoner."

Q. Did he tell you what his purpose was; what "cause" he was in?

A. He spoke generally of it. He said, perhaps, "This thing must be put a stop to," or something of that sort. He used general terms.

Q. "This thing," alluding to what?

A. Alluding to slavery.

Q. Did you see your negroes after they were brought there?

A. Yes, sir.

Q. What was done with them?

A. They were brought in to the fire. The engine-house and the watch-house are divided by a wall. I should suppose the engine-house to be, perhaps, twenty-two or twenty-four feet square. The engine-house being partitioned off, is of course about twenty-two or twenty-four feet, as the other may be, the one way, by about ten the other. The stove was in the small watch-house. The engine-house and watch-house are divided. They are under the same roof—a wall between them. There is no communication between them through that wall. The servants were all taken into the engine-house, and we into the watch-house, but they came in repeatedly to warm themselves, each negro having a pike in his hand.

Q. How many of your negroes did they take, including your house servants?

A. My servants were almost all away, that being Sunday night. They took two of mine, and one, the husband of one of my servants.

Q. Did they take but three negro men of yours, altogether?

A. Only three there. One other heard something was wrong, and got in the wagon at Allstadt's. I understood that was the point where he overtook them. That man who joined them at Allstadt's did not belong to me, but to Dr. Fuller. He was hired at my house.

Q. Do you know what use was made of your negroes afterwards, by the party at the Ferry?

A. In a short time after they first appeared with these pikes in their hands, I saw my house-servant walking about without one. My other servant was taken, with my team, over to Maryland, as I afterwards understood, to remove the arms from the Kennedy farm to the school-house.

Q. Did any of the servants remain with you in the engine-house or watch-house?

A. Yes, sir; my house-servant was in the engine-house with me all the time.

Q. Did they put him to any use at all?

A. Not at all. They made a servant of Allstadt's drill some port-holes.

Q. How many servants did they bring from Allstadt's?

A. I do not know; five or six perhaps.

Q. How many of yours and Allstadt's together were with you in the engine-house?

A. There was one of mine and one of Allstadt's that I know, and a servant I have known for some time, one of Mr. Daniel Moore's, who resides near Allstadt. He was arrested on the bridge or in the Ferry. He had a wife there, possibly. I do not recollect exactly the number of Mr. Allstadt's servants there.

Q. Did they put any of the slaves they had captured to any work in the engine-house?

A. None, except one servant of Mr. Allstadt, named Phil. Old Brown said to him, "You are a pretty stout looking fellow; can't you knock a hole through there for me?" There were some mason's tools with which he effected it. The holes were loop-holes to shoot through.

Q. Did they make more than one loop-hole?

A. Yes, sir; four I think.

Q. How long were you detained in the engine-house?

A. I went in there about twelve o'clock on Monday, noon, and I was in there until Tuesday at seven. I was taken into the watch-house first, but he took us out as hostages about eleven or twelve o'clock on Monday.

Q. What time did you arrive at the watch-house?

A. I suppose about half past three; some time before daylight on Monday morning.

Q. After being in there until about midday on Monday, they took you out and carried you into the engine-house. Did they take any others with you?

A. Nine others.

Q. Did he say for what reason you were taken out and carried to the engine-house?

A. He did not specify it at that time, but I understood it very well from the remarks he had made early in the morning. He just came and said, "I want you to walk with me;" and we went from one room to the other.

Q. What was the largest number of persons that he had as prisoners at any time in the watch-house?

A. I should say, at a rough estimate, perhaps thirty-odd; between thirty and forty.

Q. Who were they?

A. They were principally the armorers, the workmen of the armory, and officers of the armory; for instance, Mr. Kitzmiller, who was acting as superintendent at the time in the absence of Mr. Barbour, Mr. Daingerfield, who was the paymaster's clerk, and Mr. Mills, the master armorer, and several others, operatives, and some who were not. One was the watchman on the bridge, I believe, and one was an old man who rang the bell.

Q. They were all citizens of the Ferry and workmen there?

A. Yes, sir.

Q. Were any of those men armed?

A. None.

Q. Did you find any of them there when you first went there?

A. Yes, sir; perhaps four or five.

Q. Were they brought in in a body or brought in singly?

A. Generally one or two at a time. As they made their appearance they were arrested, as I understood.

Q. Will you state whether you heard any conversation of Brown's during the night in the engine-house, in which he disclosed his purpose in coming there?

A. I think two or three different times, possibly, he made remarks to the effect that he came for the purpose of freeing the slaves, and that he meant to carry it out. I heard a remark made by Stevens pretty early. He was talking to a young man, and asked him what his view in reference to slavery was, and this young man said, "Of course, being born south, my views are with the south on that subject." Stevens asked him if he was a slaveholder. He said he was not. "Well," said Stevens, "you would be the first fellow I would hang, for you defend a cause not to protect your own interest in doing so," and he used an oath at the time.

Q. Did you hear anything from Brown from which you could learn whether he expected assistance, and where it was to come from?

A. I do not know that I heard any such expressions. I supposed at that time he was very strong. I supposed from his actions the force was a large one. Some one asked him the number of his force, and he made an evasive answer. Said he, "I cannot exactly say. I have four companies—one stationed" at such a place, and so on. He used the term "companies."

Q. What points did he designate?

A. The arsenal was one, Hall's works was another, and some other point in the yard.

Q. Can you tell how many of Brown's party you found in the engine-house when you went there?

A. Up to a certain period they were in and out until the firing became very severe in the street. There were eight, I think, of his party in the engine-house.

Q. I mean from the time they were beleaguered so that they could not get out?

A. Then I think there were eight.

Q. How many of them were negroes?

A. One, I think.

Q. Was there not more than one negro?

A. Yes, but not with us. There was only one negro of his party in the engine-house. There were several slaves, but only one of his party.

Q. Do you know what his name was?

A. Shields Green.

Q. What was his color?

A. Black.

Q. Will you state whether that negro, Shields Green, was armed?

A. Yes, sir, like the rest, with a rifle and revolver, and a butcher knife in his sheath.

Q. Did he use his arms; did he fire?

A. Yes, sir, very rapidly and diligently. I do not know with what effect.

Q. What was his deportment?

A. It was rather impudent in the morning. I saw him order some gentlemen to shut a window, with a rifle raised at them. He said, "Shut that window, damn you; shut it instantly." He did it in a very impudent manner. But when the attack came on, he had thrown off his hat and all his equipments, and was endeavoring to represent himself as one of the slaves.

Q. Will you state at what time you were delivered from their custody?

A. I suppose it was about half-past seven o'clock on Tuesday morning.

Q. Did Brown give any reasons for keeping you gentlemen confined there?

A. Yes. He alluded to the fact that through us he expected to gain his terms. He was very anxious towards the last. He was very solicitous to have some capitulation by which he could gain his terms, and was very obstinate in reference to his terms.

Q. Did you hear what his terms were?

A. Yes, sir, there were several. One was that he was to be permitted to leave the Ferry, and take all his prisoners to a point about half a mile or three-quarters of a mile above the Ferry, on the Maryland side, unmolested; and at this point he promised to release the prisoners.

Q. Was that refused?

A. Yes, sir.

Q. Now will you state in what manner you were ultimately rescued?

A. By the marines.

Q. How did they do it?

A. They broke in the door, and entered with a charge. In the excitement of the moment there was a gun or two fired, I believe, in the act of breaking in the door.

Q. A gun or two fired, by whom?

A. By both parties.

Q. While you were confined there during Monday, was there much firing from the engine-house?

A. A good deal.

Q. Did you know of anybody being killed?

A. I did not know at the time. I knew the parties who were killed, but I did not know the fact at the time.

Q. Did you see any of the citizens who were killed at the Ferry?

A. I think not.

Q. Were you acquainted with George W. Turner?

A. Intimately.

Q. Was he killed there?

A. He was killed there, I believe. He was killed in the street; not near us.

Q. Were you at his funeral?

A. He was merely entombed for a short time, and was buried recently at Charlestown. I was at that funeral.

Q. Will you state where he lived?

A. He lived at a place called Wheatland, about five miles from Charlestown, and about eight miles or eight miles and a half from my house.

Q. Were you on terms of intimate relations?

A. Yes, sir.

Q. What was his character as a citizen and a gentleman?

A. Very fine. None better. He was a graduate of West Point, and a distinguished officer of the army.

Q. Was he a man of fortune?

A. Yes, sir.

Q. A landholder and slaveholder?

A. Yes, sir.

Q. Did you know Mr. Beckham, who was killed?

A. Yes, sir; for many years.

Q. What was his character as a citizen?

A. Very good indeed. He was an estimable man. He was mayor of the town, and had been for many years employed by the Baltimore and Ohio Railroad Company as their agent.

Q. Did you know Boerley, who was killed?

A. I knew him slightly. I had known him some years merely to speak to him.

Q. Do you know what his business was?

A. I think he kept a small grocery store.

Q. Did you know the negro, Hayward, who was killed?

A. Yes, sir.

Q. Did you know whether he was free or slave?

A. I understood he was free.

Q. What was his position in life?

A. He was the porter of the railroad station, and attended to the baggage. He was always remarkably civil.

Q. Was he esteemed and considered a man of respectability in his position?

A. Very much so. He was very trustworthy.

Q. Did you get back all your slaves?

A. Yes, sir; except the servant that was drowned at Hall's works. The others made their escape from those men who armed them in Maryland, and came down to the river, and were put across by a white woman in a boat, and were at home when I got there. They must have gone back on Tuesday night, I imagine. I did not go back until Wednesday evening. I remained at the Ferry with the governor two days.

Q. Did you find your negroes at home when you went back?

A. Yes, sir.

Q. Did you get back your wagon and horses?

A. After a while. The wagon was used afterwards in bringing over arms to the Ferry. On Thursday one of my horses was running up the mountain, and I went over and got him, and took the negro boy who showed me where he had hidden my gun that they had given him to arm himself when he escaped. This was a double-barreled shot gun.

Q. You lost none of your negroes?

A. No, sir.

Q. But a man whom you had hired from Dr. Fuller was drowned in the canal?

A. Yes, sir.

Q. Did it excite any spirit of insubordination amongst your negroes?

A. Not the slightest. If anything, they were much more tractable than before.

Q. Had you any reason to believe that there was any alarm amongst them when they were carried off; had you any knowledge of that?

A. No; I could not see what transpired when they were taken; it was out of my sight. . . .

Q. I understood you to say that they carried off a pistol and sword belonging to your family relics; did you recover them?

A. I recovered the sword; Brown carried that in his hand all day

Monday, and when the attacking party came on he laid it on a fire engine, and after the rescue I got it.

Ω. By whom did you say that sword had been given to General Washington?

Λ. By Frederick the Great.

LEWIS W. WASHINGTON.

GUIDE QUESTIONS

1. What is the precise relationship of each of the witnesses to the events at Harper's Ferry in time? In place?
2. What was the state of the weather during the raid?
3. How would you characterize John Brown's treatment of his prisoners?
4. How would you characterize the witnesses themselves?
5. How would you describe the behavior of the liberated slaves?
6. What elements of local militia became involved prior to the arrival of the U. S. Marines?
7. Define exactly the period during which Dr. Starry was absent from Harper's Ferry.
8. How do you account for the fact that Daniel Whelan was freed "about three o'clock on Monday," much earlier than Colonel Washington, John Allstadt, and others?
9. Which one of the witnesses gives the most coherent account of events? Which one gives the most incoherent account?
10. Which one of these accounts is most helpful in establishing: (a) the events of Sunday night, October 16; (b) reactions of the townspeople; (c) occurrences outside the town of Harper's Ferry; (d) the events of Monday, October 17; (e) casualties; (f) the situation inside the Engine House; (g) the capture of John Brown; (h) the various times when events took place; (i) a general impression of the raid?
11. If you could turn back time and confront these witnesses, what questions would you ask them that the Mason Commission failed to ask them?

VOCABULARY

Give the derivations and definitions of the following words:

parley, servile, hostage, cessation, musket, confluence, flambeau, bungler, philanthropic, hame, evasive, beleaguer, diligent, deportment, solicitous, capitulation, insubordination, tractable, transpire, impropriety, turnpike, hostile.

WRITING AND STUDY AIDS

PATTERN OF ORGANIZATION SUGGESTED BY THE GENERAL TOPIC:

The problem of a paper based on the reading materials for this assign
ment is one of chronological narrative. The structure must be a structur
of *time,* with events succeeding one another in order from the arrival o
John Brown at the Potomac bridge on the night of October 16 until th
attack by the Marines on the Engine House a little over thirty hours later
The story should be limited to the events which took place within the towr
of Harper's Ferry. The only comments necessary will be in explanation o
the geography of the place, or of inadequacies or inconsistencies in the
evidence available to you. It is enough to *get the story right.*

ASSIGNMENTS:

Short themes:

1. The value of Osborne P. Anderson as a witness
2. The character of Lewis Washington
3. A description of the town of Harper's Ferry
4. The behavior of "liberated" slaves at Harper's Ferry
5. J. H. Kagi at Harper's Ferry
6. A. D. Stevens at Harper's Ferry
7. The role of John D. Starry

Long themes:

1. John Brown at Harper's Ferry
2. The raid on Harper's Ferry

READINGS FOR FURTHER STUDY:

Benét, Stephen Vincent. *John Brown's Body.* New York: Doubleday, Doran
and Co., 1928.

Ehrlich, Leonard. *God's Angry Man.* New York: The Press of the Readers
Club, 1941.

Thoreau, Henry David. "A Plea for Captain John Brown," an address
delivered before the citizens of Concord, Mass., on October 30, 1859.
Frequently reprinted.

Villard, Oswald Garrison. *John Brown, A Biography Fifty Years After.*
Boston: Houghton Mifflin Co., 1910.

Warren, R. P. *John Brown, The Making of a Martyr.* London: Payson and
Clark, Ltd., 1929.

☞ Three Humorous Essays

WHEN A MAN IN FORMAL DRESS, COMPLETE WITH TOP HAT, FALLS DOWN, he is funny. When a man of dignified bearing, but without the top hat, falls down, he is funny too, but not as funny as he would have been if he had worn the hat. When an ordinary, casually dressed man takes a tumble, he may cause a smile, but there is nothing especially hilarious about it.

One of the explanations which men have given for this odd disparity is based on the word "incongruity." Incongruous things are thought of as being funny; congruous things are not.

So it is in the humor of English prose. Congruous expressions are not in themselves funny, although they may be used to tell of very funny and incongruous things. Incongruous expressions are funny, even though their content may be solemn.

Everyone is familiar with the incongruities of expression which arise from distortions of grammar, diction, and pronunciation. These are the sources of humor in the speech of small children, the sources of humor in the "boners" which teachers like to collect from student themes—"How can I write about Keats when I don't even know what they are?" for example.

Another source of humorous expression is the distortion of expository pattern. Analysis, for example, is a well-defined manner of behavior in the statement of ideas. It has its general rules and normal procedures. A writer who uses it announces implicitly his intention to conform with these rules and procedures. Analysis becomes, for the moment, his formal dress.

One of the sources of humor in prose is the incongruity which sometimes occurs, either deliberately or inadvertently, in the organization of ideas. Grossly disproportionate analyses, warped comparisons, and whim-

sical definitions are funny in themselves, containing both the tumble an
the top hat.

The readings of this section are examples of this kind of humor. Forster'
meticulous account of his bit of woodland is a deliberate use of formalit
for comic effect. Riesman's report on the "Nylon War" has a corresponc
ence with reality which the war itself patently lacks. Potter's advice o:
"Gamesmanship" is a model of excessive clarity.

In reading these essays, you will discover two kinds of things: (1) yo
will recognize the devices and patterns of expression which the author
pretend to use seriously, and (2) you will recognize the tricks and distor
tions by which they make clear their real intentions.

E. M. Forste

MY WOOD

A FEW YEARS AGO I wrote a book which dealt in part with the difficulties
of the English in India. Feeling that they would have had no difficulties
in India themselves, the Americans read the book freely. The more
they read it the better it made them feel, and a cheque to the author
was the result. I bought a wood with the cheque. It is not a large
wood—it contains scarcely any trees, and it is intersected, blast it, by
a public footpath. Still, it is the first property that I have owned, so it
is right that other people should participate in my shame, and should
ask themselves, in accents that will vary in horror, this very important
question: What is the effect of property upon the character? Don't let's
touch economics; the effect of private ownership upon the community
as a whole is another question—a more important question, perhaps,
but another one. Let's keep to psychology. If you own things, what's
their effect on you? What's the effect on me of my wood?

In the first place, it makes me feel heavy. Property does have this
effect. Property produces men of weight, and it was a man of weight
who failed to get into the Kingdom of Heaven. He was not wicked,
that unfortunate millionaire in the parable, he was only stout; he stuck
out in front, not to mention behind, and as he wedged himself this

From *Abinger Harvest* (London: Edward Arnold, 1936), pp. 23-26. By permission of
Harcourt, Brace and Co., Inc.

way and that in the crystalline entrance and bruised his well-fed flanks, he saw beneath him a comparatively slim camel passing through the eye of a needle and being woven into the robe of God. The Gospels all through couple stoutness and slowness. They point out what is perfectly obvious, yet seldom realized: that if you have a lot of things you cannot move about a lot, that furniture requires dusting, dusters require servants, servants require insurance stamps, and the whole tangle of them makes you think twice before you accept an invitation to dinner or go for a bathe in the Jordan. Sometimes the Gospels proceed further and say with Tolstoy that property is sinful; they approach the difficult ground of asceticism here, where I cannot follow them. But as to the immediate effects of property on people, they just show straightforward logic. It produces men of weight. Men of weight cannot, by definition, move like the lightning from the East unto the West, and the ascent of a fourteen-stone bishop into a pulpit is thus the exact antithesis of the coming of the Son of Man. My wood makes me feel heavy.

In the second place, it makes me feel it ought to be larger.

The other day I heard a twig snap in it. I was annoyed at first, for I thought that someone was blackberrying, and depreciating the value of the undergrowth. On coming nearer, I saw it was not a man who had trodden on the twig and snapped it, but a bird, and I felt pleased. My bird. The bird was not equally pleased. Ignoring the relation between us, it took fright as soon as it saw the shape of my face, and flew straight over the boundary hedge into a field, the property of Mrs. Henessy, where it sat down with a loud squawk. It had become Mrs. Henessy's bird. Something seemed grossly amiss here, something that would not have occurred had the wood been larger. I could not afford to buy Mrs. Henessy out, I dared not murder her, and limitations of this sort beset me on every side. Ahab did not want that vineyard—he only needed it to round off his property, preparatory to plotting a new curve—and all the land around my wood has become necessary to me in order to round off the wood. A boundary protects. But—poor little thing—the boundary ought in its turn to be protected. Noises on the edge of it. Children throw stones. A little more, and then a little more, until we reach the sea. Happy Canute! Happier Alexander! And after all, why should even the world be the limit of possession? A rocket containing a Union Jack, will, it is hoped, be shortly fired at the moon. Mars. Sirius. Beyond which . . . But these

immensities ended by saddening me. I could not suppose that my wood
was the destined nucleus of universal dominion—it is so very small
and contains no mineral wealth beyond the blackberries. Nor was I
comforted when Mrs. Henessy's bird took alarm for the second time
and flew clean away from us all, under the belief that it belonged
to itself.

In the third place, property makes its owner feel that he ought to
do something to it. Yet he isn't sure what. A restlessness comes over
him, a vague sense that he has a personality to express—the same sense
which, without any vagueness, leads the artist to an act of creation.
Sometimes I think I will cut down such trees as remain in the wood,
at other times I want to fill up the gaps between them with new trees.
Both impulses are pretentious and empty. They are not honest movements towards money-making or beauty. They spring from a foolish
desire to express myself and from an inability to enjoy what I have
got. Creation, property, enjoyment form a sinister trinity in the human
mind. Creation and enjoyment are both very very good, yet they are
often unattainable without a material basis, and at such moments
property pushes itself in as a substitute, saying, 'Accept me instead—
I'm good enough for all three.' It is not enough. It is, as Shakespeare
said of lust, 'The expense of spirit in a waste of shame': it is 'Before,
a joy proposed; behind, a dream.' Yet we don't know how to shun it.
It is forced on us by our economic system as the alternative to starvation. It is also forced on us by an internal defect in the soul, by the
feeling that in property may lie the germs of self-development and
of exquisite or heroic deeds. Our life on earth is, and ought to be,
material and carnal. But we have not yet learned to manage our
materialism and carnality properly; they are still entangled with the
desire for ownership, where (in the words of Dante) 'Possession is
one with loss.'

And this brings us to our fourth and final point: the blackberries.

Blackberries are not plentiful in this meagre grove, but they are
easily seen from the public footpath which traverses it, and all too
easily gathered. Foxgloves, too—people will pull up the foxgloves, and
ladies of an educational tendency even grub for toadstools to show them
on the Monday in class. Other ladies, less educated, roll down the
bracken in the arms of their gentlemen friends. There is paper, there
are tins. Pray, does my wood belong to me or doesn't it? And, if it
does, should I not own it best by allowing no one else to walk there?

There is a wood near Lyme Regis, also cursed by a public footpath, where the owner has not hesitated on this point. He has built high stone walls each side of the path, and has spanned it by bridges, so that the public circulate like termites while he gorges on the blackberries unseen. He really does own his wood, this able chap. Dives in Hell did pretty well, but the gulf dividing him from Lazarus could be traversed by vision, and nothing traverses it here. And perhaps I shall come to this in time. I shall wall in and fence out until I really taste the sweets of property. Enormously stout, endlessly avaricious, pseudo-creative, intensely selfish, I shall weave upon my forehead the quadruple crown of possession until those nasty Bolshies come and take it off again and thrust me aside into the outer darkness.

GUIDE QUESTIONS

1. Why does Forster spell the word "cheque" as he does?
2. What are the effects on Forster of his possessing a wood?
3. What is the "quadruple crown" mentioned in the last paragraph?
4. How might Forster have phrased the fourth item in his analysis of effects if he had wished to conform strictly to the ordinary methods of analysis?
5. What details of language do you find in the essay which suggest that Forster intended to achieve a generally humorous tone?
6. How do you account for the presence in this essay of an unusual number of allusions to Biblical stories?

VOCABULARY

Give the derivations and definitions of the following words:

intersect, participate, crystalline, asceticism, antithesis, depreciating, Ahab, Canute, Alexander, nucleus, destined, dominion, alternative, carnal, Dives, Lazarus, avaricious, quadruple.

David Riesman

THE NYLON WAR

TODAY—AUGUST 1, 1956—the Nylon War enters upon the third month since the United States began all-out bombing of the Soviet Union with consumers' goods, and it seems time to take a retrospective look. Behind the initial raid of June 1 were years of secret and complex preparations, and an idea of disarming simplicity: that if allowed to sample the riches of America, the Russian people would not long tolerate masters who gave them tanks and spies instead of vacuum cleaners and beauty parlors. The Russian rulers would thereupon be forced to turn out consumers' goods, or face mass discontent on an increasing scale.

The Nylon War was conceived by an army colonel—we shall call him "Y"—whose name cannot yet be revealed. Working with secret funds which the Central Intelligence Agency had found itself unable to spend, Y organized shortly after World War II the so-called "Bar Harbor Project," the nucleus of what, some seven years later, became "Operation Abundance," or, as the press soon dubbed it, the "Nylon War." After experiments with rockets and balloons, it was concluded that only cargo planes—navigating, it was hoped, above the range of Russian radar—could successfully deliver the many billion dollars worth of consumer goods it was planned to send. Nevertheless, when Y and his group first broached their plans to a few selected Congressional leaders in the winter of 1948 they were dismissed as hopelessly academic. America had neither the goods nor the planes nor the politics to begin such an undertaking. But in the fall of 1953, with the country bogged down in a seemingly endless small-scale war in Korea, Y's hopes revived. For one thing, the cargo planes needed for the job were beginning to become available. Moreover, a certain amount of over-ordering by the Armed Services, panicky over Korea, had created a

From *Common Cause,* a Journal of One World, Vol. 4, No. 7, February, 1951. Reprinted by permission of the author. The editors have changed some of the names of public officials.

stockpile of consumer goods. More important, the Administration, having locked up all known and many suspected Communists in one of the old camps for Japanese aliens, had still not convinced the country that it was sufficiently anti-Soviet, though at the same time many Americans wanted peace but did not dare admit it. A plan which, in fact and in presentation, took attention away from alleged Far-Eastern bungling, and which was both violently anti-Soviet and pro-peace, appeared to offer the possibility of restoring the Administration's tottering position in the country.

This is not the place to recount the political maneuverings that preceded Eisenhower's success in securing a two billion dollar initial appropriation from Congress, nor the Potomac maneuverings that led to the recruitment of top-flight production and merchandising talent from civilian life. Our story begins with Eisenhower going before Congress to secure authority to "bring the benefits of American technology to less fortunate nations" by round-the-clock bombing, the day after the news of the first raids hit the American public.

The planners of the Bar Harbor Project had staked American prestige, their professional futures, and the lives of six thousand airmen on the belief that the Soviets would not know of these first flights nor meet them with armed resistance. When the opening missions were accomplished without incident, permitting Eisenhower to make his appeal, Washington was immensely relieved; but when the second wave of planes met with no resistance either, Washington was baffled. It was at first assumed that the Soviet radar network had again simply failed to spot the high-flying planes—cruising at 48,000 feet and self-protected from radar by some still presumably secret device. We now know that what actually happened was a division of opinion in the Kremlin—we can piece the story together from intelligence reports and from clues in *Pravda*. A faction, led by foreign trade chief Mikoyan, maintained that the scheme was a huge hoax, designed to stampede Russia into a crusade against a fairy-tale—and so to make her the laughing stock of the world. He counselled, wait and see. And, indeed, it *was* a fairy-tale for secret police boss Beria, who argued that the raids had never taken place, but that reports of them had been faked by some Social Democratic East Germans who had somehow gotten access to the communications networks. When this idea was exploded, Beria counselled shooting the planes down, on the ground that they were simply a screen spying out plants for an atomic attack.

Malenkov himself believed with repentant economist Varga that American capitalism had reached so critical a point that only through forcible gifts overseas could the Wall Street ruling clique hope to maintain its profits and dominance. Coupled with these divisions of opinion, which stalemated action, was the fear in some quarters that America might welcome attacks on its errand-of-mercy planes as a pretext for the war of extermination openly preached by some only mildly rebuked American leaders.

At any rate, the confusion in the Politburo was more than mirrored by the confusion in the target cities caused by the baptismal raids. Over 600 C-86s streamed high over Rostov, and another 200 over Vladivostok, dropped their cargoes, and headed back to their bases in the Middle East and Japan. By today's standard these initial forays were small-scale—200,000 pairs of nylon hose, 4,000,000 packs of cigarettes, 35,000 Toni-wave kits, 20,000 yo-yos, 10,000 wrist watches, and a number of odds and ends from P-X overstock. Yet this was more than enough to provoke frenzied rioting as the inhabitants scrambled for a share. Within a few hours after the first parcels had fallen, the roads into the target cities were jammed. Road blocks had to be thrown up around the cities, and communications with the outside were severed. The fast-spreading rumors of largesse from above were branded "criminally insane," and their source traced to machinations of the recently purged "homeless cosmopolitan, Simeon Osnavitch (Rosenblum)."

But the propaganda of the deed proved stronger than the propaganda of the word. As Odessa, Yakutsk, Smolensk, and other cities became targets of aggressive generosity, as Soviet housewives saw with their own eyes American stoves, refrigerators, clothing, and toys, the Kremlin was forced to change its line and, ignoring earlier denials, to give the raids full but negative publicity. David Zaslavsky's article in the June 10 *Izvestia* heralded the new approach. Entitled "The Mad Dogs of Imperialism Foam at the Mouth," he saw the airlift as harbinger of America's economic collapse. "Unable because of the valiant resistance of the peace-loving democracies to conquer foreign markets, America's Fascist plutocracy is now reduced to giving away goods. . . ." Taking another line, *Red Star* argued that to accept American consumer goods would make stalwart Russians as decadent as rich New Yorkers.

However, the Russian people who could get access, either directly or through the black market that soon arose, to American goods seemed not to fear decadence. Again, there was a change of line. Falling back on a trick learned during Lend-Lease, it was claimed that the goods were Russian-made, and *Pravda* on June 14 stated that the Toni-wave kit had been invented by Pavlov before World War I. However, Colonel Y's staff had anticipated this altogether routine reaction. On June 17, the target cities of that day—Kiev, Stalingrad, Magnitogorsk—received their wares wrapped in large cartoons of Malenkov bending over, in a somewhat undignified pose, to pick up a dropped Ansco camera. This forced still another switch of line. On June 20 Beria went on the air to announce that the Americans were sending over goods poisoned by atomic radiation, and all papers and broadcasts carried scare stories about people who had died from using Revlon or Schick shavers. And indeed booby traps (planted by MVD) succeeded in killing a number of overeager citizens. For a while, this permitted specially-recruited Party members to gather up the goods and take them to headquarters for alleged de-radiation.

But here something unexpected occurred. We know from a few people who managed to escape to the West that a number of Party elements themselves became disaffected. Asked to turn in all American goods, they held on to some possessions secretly—there was a brisk underground trade in Russian labels. Sometimes wives, having gotten used to the comforts of Kleenex and other disappearing items, would hide them from their more ascetic husbands; children of Party members cached pogo sticks and even tricycles. Thus it came about that when Party members were ordered to join "decontamination" squads the depots were re-entered at night and portable items taken. By the beginning of July, all attempts to deceive the people had only made matters worse; things were getting out of hand.

Faring badly in the "War," the Kremlin turned to diplomacy. On July 5 in the U. N. General Assembly, Zarubin described the airlift as "an outrage remindful of Hitlerite aggression" and, invoking Art. 39 of the U. N. Charter, he called on the Security Council to halt the "shameful depredations of the American warmongers." Lodge replied that "these gifts are no more or less than a new-fashioned application of ancient principles," and the Russian resolution was defeated, 9-2. The next step occurred in Washington, when Ambassador Zorin handed Secretary Dulles a sharply worded note warning that "should these present outrages continue, the U.S.S.R. will have no recourse but to reply in kind."

Seattle was the first American city to learn the meaning of the Soviet warning as on July 15 a hundred Russian heavy bombers (presumably from bases in the Kuriles) left behind them 15,000 tins of caviar, 500 fur coats, and 80,000 copies of Stalin's speeches on the minorities question. When the Russian planes came, followed in by American jets, many were apprehensive, but as the counter-attack had been anticipated it proved possible to prevent incidents in the air and panic on the ground. Since then, Butte, Minneapolis, Buffalo, and Moscow, Idaho, have been added to the list of America's front-line cities. But in quantity and quality the counter-offensive has been unimpressive. Searing vodka, badly styled mink coats (the only really selling item), undependable cigarette lighters—these betray a sad lack of know-how in production and merchandising. In an editorial, "Worse than Lend-Lease," the N. Y. *Daily News* has charged that the Nylon War gives the Soviets free lessons in the secrets of America's success, but truly conservative papers like the *Herald Tribune* see the comparative showing of Americans and Russians as a world demonstration of the superiority of free enterprise.

It is clear, at any rate, that free enterprise has not suffered much of a jolt—nor, indeed, has the mounting inflation been much reduced—by the Russian campaign. To be sure, the massive air-borne shipments of caviar have made luxury grocers fear inventory losses and Portugal, heavily dependent on the American anchovy market, has been worried. But these pin-pricks are nothing to what is now becoming evident on the Russian side—namely the imminent collapse of the economy. For the homeland of centralized economic planning is experiencing its own form of want in the midst of plenty. Soviet consumers, given a free choice between shoddy domestic merchandise and airlift items, want nothing to do with the former and in a score of fields Russian goods go unwanted as the potential buyer dreams of soon owning an American version. Soviet housewives, eager to keep up with American-supplied "Joneses," pester their local stores, often to the point of creating local shortages—indeed, the American refrigerators have created demands, not only for electricity, but also for many foods which can now be stored (and hoarded).

Much of this disruption is the result of careful planning by the Bar

Harbor Project's Division of Economic Dislocation. The Division, for example, early began studies of Russian power distribution, and saw to the landing of 60-cycle radios, shavers, toasters, milking machines, in 60-cycle areas; 25-cycle appliances in 25-cycle areas, and so on, especially with an eye to areas of power-shortage or competition with critical industries. In cooperation with G.E., methods were worked out by which the Russian donees could plug their appliances, with appropriate transformers, directly into high-voltage or street power lines; thus simply shutting off house current could not save the Russian utilities from overload. Similarly, drawing on the American monopolistic practice of tie-in sales, goods were dropped whose use demanded other items in short supply—oil ranges, for instance, were dropped throughout the Baku fields. Of course, mistakes were made and in one or two cases bottlenecks in the Russian economy were relieved, as when some containers were salvaged to repair a tin shortage of which the planners had not been advised.

But it is not only on the production end that the raids have been disruptive. Last Friday's raid on Moscow—when 22,000 tons of goods were dropped—may be taken as an illustration. For the first time General Norstad's airmen tackled—and successfully solved—the knotty engineering problem of dropping jeeps (complete with 150 gallons of gasoline and directions in simple Russian). So skillfully was the job done that half the three hundred vehicles parachuted down landed directly on the Kremlin's doorstep—in the center of Red Square. The raid was given wide advance publicity through the Voice and leaflets and when the great day came Moscow's factories were deserted as people fought for rooftop perches; in addition, an estimated 250,000 collective farmers swarmed into the city. In fact, as people drift from place to place hoping that their ship may fly in, the phase "rootless cosmopolite" at last assumes real meaning. Economists, talking learnedly of "multipliers," calculate that Russian output is dropping 3 per cent a month.

The Kremlin has reacted in the only way it knows, by a series of purges. Sergei Churnik, erstwhile head of the cigarette trust, is on trial for "deliberate wrecking and economic treason." Bureaucrats live in terror lest their region or their industry be next disrupted by the American bombardment, and they waver between inactivity and frantic Stakhanovite shows of activity. These human tragedies testify to the growing fear in the Politburo concerning the long-run consequences of the American offensive. The tangible proofs of American prosperity, ingenuity, and generosity can no longer be gainsaid; and the new official line that Wall Street is bleeding America white in order to create scarcity and raise prices at home, while "believed," has little impact against the ever-mounting volume, and fascinating variety, of goods and rumors of goods. Can the capitalistic gluttons of privilege be such bad fellows if we, the Russians, are aided by them to enjoy luxuries previously reserved for the dachas of novelists and plant managers? In an article in the *New Statesman and Nation,* Geoffrey Gorer has recently contended that the airlift serves to revive primitive Russian "orality," and that the image of America can no longer be that of a leering Uncle Sam or top-hatted banker but must soon become amiably matronly. It is thoughts along this line that most worry the Politburo although, of course, the MVD sees to it that only a tiny fraction of the mounting skepticism expresses itself openly or even in whispered jokes. But what is the MVD to do about a resolution of the All-Workers Congress of Tiflis that "Marxist-Leninist-Stalinist democracy demands that party cadres install officials who can cope with the mounting crisis"?

Translated into plain talk, this means that the Russian people, without saying so in as many words, are now putting a price on their collaboration with the regime. The price—"goods instead of guns." For Russia's industrial plant, harassed by the rapidly growing impact of Operation Abundance, cannot supply both, let alone carry on the counter-offensive against America. Intelligence reports speak of scheduled production cutbacks varying from 25 per cent on tanks to 75 per cent on artillery; it is symptomatic that washing machines, designed to compete with the American Bendixes which are being dropped in ever-increasing numbers, will soon start rolling off the assembly lines of the great Red October Tank Works—after its former manager had been shot for asserting that conversion to peacetime production could not be achieved in less than two years.

Meanwhile, diplomatic moves are under way—so, at least, the Alsop brothers report—to liquidate the Nylon War. It is obvious why the Russian leaders are prepared to make very considerable concessions in the satellite countries, in China, and in Indo-China in order to regain the strategic initiative in their domestic affairs. But on the American side the willingness of many to listen to Russian overtures is based on the success, rather than the failure, of the campaign. One sees a repetition of 1940 as the Washington *Times-Herald* and the *Daily Compass* join hands in attacking Operation Abundance, the former calling it "an international WPA," the latter arguing "you can't fight ideas with goods." Addressing the Stanford Alumni Club of Los Angeles, Herbert Hoover spoke for millions in observing that the monthly cost of the airlift has already exceeded the entire Federal budget for the year 1839. Still another tack has been taken by Senators who want the airlift to continue, but with different targets; some, insisting that charity begins at home, have wanted free goods landed on their districts; others have supported the claims of Japan, the Philippines, or Franco. Still others fear that many of the airlift items could be reconverted in some way for use by the Russian war machine; they are especially opposed to the jeep-delivery program, despite reports it is wreaking havoc with the Russian road system as well as with the gasoline supply. And the House Un-American Affairs Committee has charged that trade secrets are being delivered to Russia by Red spies disguised as plane pilots.

These are the obvious enemies, and against them stand some obvious friends of the Nylon War. Both AFL and CIO, now in their eighth round of wage increases, vigorously support the program, though it is rumored that the Railroad Brotherhoods have done so only in return for a fact-finding board's support of a 14-hour week. Farmers have become reconciled by the promise that bulk agricultural products will soon move over the aerial transmission belt—in part to encourage the wanderings of Russian farmers. The business community is divided, with the CED, Juan Trippe, and Baruch leading the supporters of the airlift.[1] But it would be a mistake to assume that support of Operation Abundance springs only from hopes of material gain. The renewed fight against oppression and want, the excitement of following the raids in maps and betting pools, the ridiculousness of the Russian response—all these things have made many millions of Americans less anxious than they have been since the days in October 1952 when it seemed as if the Korean War would be quickly concluded.

Indeed, it is just this loss of tension which has given rise to much of the covert opposition to the Nylon War, as distinguished from the

---

[1] It goes without saying that there are many fights within pressure groups as to *what* the airlift shall carry—and ideological considerations are not confined to the Soviet side. Thus, the Committee Against Juvenile Delinquency has registered strong protests against sending comic books. . . .

overt opposition already discussed. On the one hand, certain leaders are frightened that the Russian dictatorship may indeed be overthrown —as Colonel Y in his more optimistic moments had ventured to hope. This is thought to raise the possibility of all sorts of chaotic movements developing in Central and Eastern Europe, and even further west—Franco, for instance, feels threatened at the loss of his "enemy," and has offered to act as mediator in the Nylon War. On the other hand, it has become increasingly difficult for American politicians to frighten the American public about Russia: the once-feared monolith now appears as almost a joke, with its crude poster-and-caviar reprisals, its riots over stockings, soap, Ronsons, and other gadgets which Americans regard in matter-of-fact fashion. The sharp drop in war sentiment in the United States has resulted in psychological and even actual unemployment for a number of people.

What do the coming months hold? It is significant that this depends almost entirely on the outcome of the American domestic struggle: the Nylon War has altered the whole power-complex which, as the Korean War dragged on, still heavily favored Russia. It is now Russia, not America, whose resources are overcommitted, whose alliances are over-strained. In fact, Mao's visit to Moscow at the end of July seems to have been attended with apprehension lest he ask America to cut Red China in on Operation Abundance—at a price, of course. The possibility that this may redound to the credit of the Eisenhower Administration in the 1956 campaign is not the least of the nightmares haunting many Americans, and at this writing it is impossible to predict whether the opponents of the program will win out.

Meanwhile, Operation Abundance marches on, solving technical problems of incredible complexity. The latest move is the perfection of an ordering system whereby Russians can "vote" for the commodities they most want, according to a point system, by the use of radio-sending equipment, battery-run, with which we have provided them. The commodities available will be described over the Voice of America—now for the first time having something to "sell"—by Sears Roebuck-type catalogues, and by dropped samples in the case of soft goods. The method making it impossible for the Russian government effectively to jam this two-way communication of distributor and consumer is still the great secret of the Nylon War.

GUIDE QUESTIONS

1. When are the events described in the essay supposed to have taken place? When was the essay first published?
2. What is the effect of Riesman's frequent use of verbs in the passive voice?
3. What indications are there that Riesman wishes to avoid both explicit recommendation and explicit condemnation of the "Nylon War"?
4. Is the narrative strictly chronological?
5. To what extent does Riesman explore the causes of the various events which he describes?
6. In what passages is the vocabulary designed to imitate recognizable "special" vocabularies?
7. Apart from the discrepancy of dates, what indications are there in the essay that Riesman is treating his subject in a playful manner?

VOCABULARY

Give the derivations and definitions of the following words:

dubbed, broached, recount, maneuverings, initial, technology, presumably, clique, stalemate, frenzied, largesse, harbinger, decadent, disaffected, depredations, apprehensive, searing, disruption, donees, monopolistic, leering, harassed, symptomatic, liquidate, strategic, covert, overt, monolith.

Stephen Potter

GAMESMANSHIP

or THE ART OF WINNING GAMES WITHOUT ACTUALLY CHEATING

I. WHAT IS IT?

Oᴿɪɢɪɴs.

What is gamesmanship? Most difficult of questions to answer briefly. "The Art of Winning Games Without Actually Cheating"—

From *The Theory and Practice of Gamesmanship,* by Stephen Potter. Reproduced by permission of Henry Holt and Company, Inc.

that is my personal "working definition." What is its object? There have been five hundred books written on the subject of games. Five hundred books on play and the tactics of play. Not one on the art of winning.

I well remember the gritty floor and the damp roller-towels of the changing-room where the idea . . . came to me. Yet my approach to the thing had been gradual.

There had been much that had puzzled me—I am speaking now of 1928—in the tension of our games of ping-pong at the Meynells'. Before that there had been the ardours and endurances of friendly lawn tennis at the Farjeons' house near Forest Hill, where Farjeon had wrought such havoc among so many visitors, by his careful construction of a "home court," by the use he made of the net with the unilateral sag, or with a back line at the hawthorn end so nearly, yet not exactly, six inches wider than the back line at the sticky end. There had been a great deal of hard thinking on both sides during the wavering tide of battle, ending slightly in my favour, of the prolonged series of golf games between E. Lansbury and myself.

8TH JUNE 1931.

But it was in that changing-room after a certain game of lawn tennis in 1931 that the curtain was lifted, and I began to see. In those days I used to play lawn tennis for a small but progressive London College —Birkbeck, where I lectured. It happened that my partner at that time was C. Joad, the celebrated gamesman, who in his own sphere is known as metaphysician and educationist. Our opponents were usually young men from the larger colleges, competing against us not only with the advantage of age but also with a decisive advantage in style. They would throw the service ball very high in the modern manner: the back-hands, instead of being played from the navel, were played, in fact, on the back-hand, weight on right foot, in the exaggerated copy-book style of the time—a method of play which tends to reduce all games, as I believe, to a barrack-square drill by numbers; but, nevertheless, of acknowledged effectiveness.

In one match we found ourselves opposite a couple of particularly tall and athletic young men of this type from University College. We will call them Smith and Brown. The knock-up showed that, so far as play was concerned, Joad and I, playing for Birkbeck, had no chance.

U. C. won the toss. It was Smith's service, and he cracked down a cannonball to Joad which moved so fast that Joad, while making some effort to suggest by his attitude that he had thought the ball was going to be a fault, nevertheless was unable to get near with his racket, which he did not even attempt to move. Score: fifteen-love. Service to me. I had had time to gauge the speed of this serve, and the next one did, in fact, graze the edge of my racket-frame. Thirty-love. Now Smith was serving again to Joad—who this time, as the ball came straight

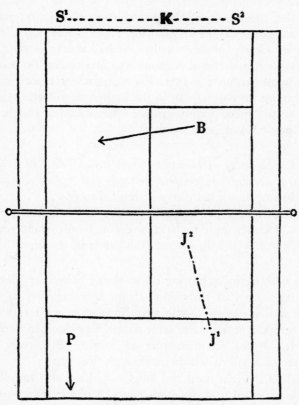

FIG. 1. *Key:* P = Potter, J = Joad, S = Smith, B = Brown. The dotted line represents Smith's path from S¹ to S². K represents the point he has reached on the cross-over when Joad has moved along the line (dot and dash) J¹ (where he had tried to return Smith's service) to J². Smith having arrived at, but not further than, the point K on the line S¹–S², J (Joad) speaks.

towards him, was able, by grasping the racket firmly with both hands, to receive the ball on the strings, whereupon the ball shot back to the other side and volleyed into the stop-netting near the ground behind Brown's feet.

Now here comes the moment on which not only this match, but so much of the future of British sport was to turn. Score: forty-love. Smith at S1 (see Fig. 1) is about to cross over to serve to me (at P). When Smith gets to a point (K) *not less than one foot and not more than two feet* beyond the centre of the court (I know now what I only felt then—that timing is everything in this gambit), Joad (standing at J²) called across the net, in an even tone:

"Kindly say clearly, please, whether the ball was in or out."

Crude to our ears, perhaps. A Stone-Age implement. But beautifully accurate gamesmanship for 1931. For the student must realise that these two young men were both in the highest degree charming, well-mannered young men, perfect in their sportsmanship and behaviour. Smith (at point K) stopped dead.

SMITH: I'm so sorry—I *thought* it was out. (*The ball had hit the back netting twelve feet behind him before touching the ground.*) But what did you think, Brown?
BROWN: I *thought* it was out—but do let's have it again.
JOAD: No, I don't want to have it again. I only want you to say clearly, if you will, whether the ball is in or out.

There is nothing more putting off to young university players than a slight suggestion that their etiquette or sportsmanship is in question. How well we know this fact, yet how often we forget to make use of it. Smith sent a double fault to me, and another double fault to Joad. He did not get in another ace service till halfway through the third set of a match which incidentally we won.

That night I thought hard and long. Could not this simple gambit of Joad's be extended to include other aspects of the game—to include all games? For me, it was the birth of gamesmanship. . . .

II. THE PRE-GAME

. . . Let us start with a few simple exercises for beginners: and let us begin with the pre-game, for much of the most important gamesmanship play takes place before the game has started. Yet if mistakes are made, there is plenty of time to recover.

The great second axiom of gamesmanship is now worded as follows: THE FIRST MUSCLE STIFFENED (in his opponent by the Gamesman) IS THE FIRST POINT GAINED. Let us consider some of the processes of Defeat by Tension.

The standard method is known as the "flurry."

The "flurry" is for use when changing in the locker-room before a rackets match, perhaps, or leaving home in your opponent's car for, say, a game of lawn tennis. The object is to create a state of anxiety, to build up an atmosphere of muddled fluster.

Supposing, for instance, that your opponent has a small car. He kindly comes along to pick you up before the game. Your procedure should be as follows (1) Be late in answering the bell. (2) Don't have your things ready. Appearing at last, (3) call *in an anxious or "rattled" voice* to wife (who need not, of course, be there at all) some taut last-minute questions about dinner. Walk down path and (4) realise you have forgotten shoes. Return with shoes; then just before getting into car pause (5) *a certain length of time* (see any threepenny edition of Bohn's *Tables*) and wonder (i) whether racket is at the club or (ii) whether you have left it "in the bath-room at top of the house."

Like the first hint of paralysis, a scarcely observable fixing of your opponent's expression should now be visible. Now is the time to re-double the attack. Map-play can be brought to bear. On the journey let it be known that you "think you know a better way," *which should turn out, when followed, to be incorrect and should if possible lead to a blind alley.* (See Fig. 2.)

Meanwhile, time is getting on. Opponent's tension should have in-creased. Psychological tendency, if not temporal necessity, will cause him to drive faster, and—behold! now the gamesman can widen his field and bring in carmanship by suggesting, with the minutest stiffen-ing of the legs at corners, an unconscious tendency to put on the brakes, indicating an unexpressed desire to tell his opponent that he is driving not very well, and cornering rather too fast.

NOTE I.—The "flurry" is best used before still-ball games, especially golf, croquet or snooker. Anxious car-driving may actually improve opponent's execution in fast games, such as rackets or ping-pong.

NOTE II.—Beginners must not rush things. The smooth working of a "flurry" sequence depends on practice. The motions of pausing on the doorstep ("Have I got my gym shoes?"), hesitating on the running-board, etc., are exercises which I give my own students; but I always recommend that they practise the motions for at least six weeks, *positions only,* before trying it out with the car, suitcase and shoes.

FIG. 2. Sketch plan to show specimen Wrong Route from Maida Vale to Dulwich Covered Courts.

CLOTHESMANSHIP.

The "flurry" is a simple example. Simpler still, but leading to the most important subdivision of our subject, is the question of clothesmanship, or the "Togman," as he used to be called.

The keen observer of the tennis-court incident described above would have noticed a marked disparity in clothes. The trousers of the young undergraduate players were well creased and clean, with flannel of correct colour, etc., etc. C. Joad, on the other hand, wore a shirt of deep yellow, an orange scarf to hold up his crumpled trousers, and— standing out very strongly, as I remember, in the hot June sunlight— socks of deep black.

Instinctively, Joad had demonstrated in action what was to become the famous "Second Rule" of gamesmanship, now formulated as follows:

IF THE OPPONENT WEARS, OR ATTEMPTS TO WEAR, CLOTHES CORRECT AND SUITABLE FOR THE GAME, BY AS MUCH AS HIS CLOTHES SUCCEED IN THIS FUNCTION, BY SO MUCH SHOULD THE GAMESMAN'S CLOTHES FAIL.

Corollary: Conversely, if the opponent wears the wrong clothes, the gamesman should wear the right.

"If you can't volley, wear velvet socks," we Old Gamesmen used to say. The good-looking young athlete, perfectly dressed, is made to feel a fool if his bad shot is returned by a man who looks as if he has never been on a tennis-court before. His good clothes become a handicap by virtue of their very suitability.

It is true that against the new golf-club member, inclined to be modest and nervous, a professional turn-out can be effective. A well-worn but well-cut golf jacket and a good pair of mackintosh trousers can, in this situation, be of real value. (My own tip here is to take an ordinary left-hand glove, cut the thumb off, make a diamond-shaped hole on the back, and say, "Henry Cotton made this for me—he never plays with any other.")

COUNTER-GAMESMANSHIP.

But the average gamesman must beware, at this point, of counter-gamesmanship. He may find himself up against an experienced hand, such as J. K. C. Dalziel, who, when going out to golf, used to keep two changes in the dickey of his car—one correct and the other incorrect. One golf-bag covered in zipps and with five woods, twelve irons and a left-handed cleek; a second bag containing only three irons and one wood, each with an appearance of string-ends tied round their necks. I always remember Jimmy Dalziel's "bent pin" outfit, as he used to call it. ("The little boy with the bent pin always catches more than the professional angler.") Many is the time I have scoured London with him to find a pair of odd shoe-laces. His plan was simple. If he found, at the club-house, that his opponent was rather

FIG. 3. Clothesmanship: **wrong clothes** in which Miss E. Watson beat Mrs. de Greim in the Finals of the Waterloo Cup Croquet Tourney, 18th August 1902.

humbly dressed, he would wear the smart outfit. If the conditions were reversed, out would come the frayed pin-stripe trousers, the stringy clubs and the fair-isle sweater.

"And I don't want a caddie," he would say.

Of course, in his correct clothes, he would automatically order a caddie, calling for "Bob," and mumbling something about "Must have Bob. He knows my game. Caddied for me in the Northern Amateur."

III. THE GAME ITSELF

SOME BASIC PLAYS

"How to Win Games Without Being Able to Play Them." Reduced to the simplest terms, that is the formula, and the student must not at first try flights too far away from this basic thought.

To begin with, let him, say, carry on the "flurry" motive. Let him aim at tension. Let him, for instance, invent some "train which he would rather like to catch if the game was over by then," but "doesn't want to hurry."

SPORTSMANSHIP PLAY.

Remember the slogan: "THE GOOD GAMESMAN IS THE GOOD SPORTSMAN." The use of sportsmanship is, of course, most important. In general, with the athletic but stupid player, ex-rowing or ex-boxing, perhaps, who is going to take it out of you, by God, if he suspects you of being unsporting, extreme sportingness is the thing, and the instant waiving of any rule which works in your favour is the procedure.

On the other hand, playing against the introvert crusty cynical type, remember that sportingness will be wasted on him. There must be no unsportingness on your part, of course; but a keen knowledge of little-known rules and penalties will cause him to feel he is being beaten at his own game. (See under "Croquet, rulesmanship in.")

When questioned about the etiquette of gamesmanship—so important for the young player—I talk about Fidgets. If your adversary is nervy, and put off by the mannerisms of his opponent, it is unsporting, and therefore not gamesmanship, to go in, e.g., for a loud noseblow, say, at billiards, or to chalk your cue squeakingly, when he is either making or considering a shot.

On the other hand, a basic play, in perfect order, can be achieved by, say, whistling fidgetingly *while playing yourself*. And I once converted two down into two up when playing golf against P. Beard, known also as the leader of an orchestra, by constantly whistling a phrase from the Dorabella Variation with one note—always the same note—wrong.[1]

A good general attack can be made by talking to your opponent about his own job, in the character of the kind of man who always tries to know more about your own profession than you know yourself.

PLAYING-FOR-FUN PLAY.

The good gamesman, like the good sportsman, never plays for large sums of money. But something can usually be made out of the situation if your opponent expresses a wish to play for the "usual half-crown," or a wish not to do so. It is obviously easy for the gamesman to make his opponent feel awkward by countering his suggestion that they should play for stakes with a frank "Come, let's play for the fun of the game." Alternatively, if your opponent refuses your offer to play for half a crown here is a neat counter:

LAYMAN: Half a crown on it? No, I'm not particularly anxious to play for money. What *is* the point? If one starts worrying about the pennies . . .
GAMESMAN: Exactly. If money is important to you, much better not.
LAYMAN: But I meant——
GAMESMAN: (*Friendly.*) Of course.

NICE CHAPMANSHIP.

A bigger subject which may be introduced here revolves round the huge question of nice chapmanship and its uses. (I refuse to use the hideous neologism "nicemanship" which I see much in evidence lately.)

Here is the general principle: that Being a Nice Chap *in certain circumstances* is valuable when playing against extremely young, public schooly players who are genuinely nice. A train of thought can be

[1]

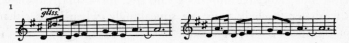

started in their minds to the effect that "it would be rather a rotten trick to beat old G. by too much." Thereby that fatal "letting up" is inaugurated which can be the undoing of so many fine players. R. Lodge, at sixty-five, always said that he had never been beaten, in a key match, by any decently brought up boy under twenty-five, and that he could always "feel 'em out by their phizzes."

AUDIENCE PLAY.

Nice chapmanship is, of course, closely associated with sportsmanship, especially in its relation to the question of playing or not playing to the audience. There is obviously some value in a good hearty "Have it again" early in the game (of darts, for instance), or the lawn tennis ball slammed into the net after the doubtful decision, especially if this is done so that your opponent can see through the ploy[2] but the onlookers cannot.

But the experienced gamesman knows that if he is playing to a small audience he must make up his mind whether he is going to play *to* the audience, or whether he is going to retire behind an impersonal mask of modesty.

In general, the rule holds—LET YOUR ATTITUDE BE THE ANTITHESIS OF YOUR OPPONENT'S; and let your manner of emphasising this different attitude put him in the wrong.

For example, if your opponent is a great showman, assume (e.g., at snooker) an air of modest anonymity; be appreciative, even, of his antics; then quietly play your shot, so that the audience begins to say, "I prefer G.'s game. He gets on with it, anyhow."

Per contra, when in play against a dour opponent, who studiously avoids all reaction to the audience, implying that "this is a match"—*then,* by all means be the "chap who doesn't care a damn" . . . though "Of course—sh!—old L. is taking this devilish seriously so I must keep a straight face."

(There is some danger of counter-gamesmanship here. The layman, if he is wise, will pursue his poker-faced policy and you may find your assumption of ill-suppressed gaiety wearing thin. I have myself experienced a partial paralysis in this situation.)

---

[2] Sub-plays, or individual manoeuvres of a gambit, are usually referred to as "ploys." It is not known why this is.

So much for some of the principal general ploys. Now for some common technical phrases.

RUGGERSHIP AND RUGGERSHIP COUNTER-PLAY.

Under the heading of "Ruggership" comes all that great interplay of suggestion summarised in the phrase "Of course, this isn't my game," with the implication that "this game is rather an amusing game, but not grand, dangerous and classical like my game. . . ." If "my game" is rugger or polo or tennis (see under "Tennis players, how to press home advantage of, over lawn tennis players"), then very good work can be done with this gambit.

But it has severe weaknesses, and a promising gamesman in his second year may be able to counter with some such simple enquiry as this:

COUNTER-GAMESMAN (*with interest*): When did you *last play* rugger?
GAMESMAN: Oh! How long since actually playing? I wonder. . . . I was talking to Leggers the other day——
COUNTER-GAMESMAN: Yes, but how long is it since you played yourself? I mean what date, roughly, was it when you last held a ball in your hand?
GAMESMAN (*hard-pressed*): 1913.
COUNTER-GAMESMAN: A bit of a time. But that, I imagine, is one of the grand things about rugger. If you've ever kicked a rugger ball, at a prep school or home club, you feel that you're a rugger player for the rest of your life.

Much exaggerated praise has been churned out in honour of gamesmanship and its part in the building of the British character. Still, if we study the records, they do reveal not a little of courage in the overcoming of apparently hopeless odds. I am thinking, of course, of G. Tearle—not the actor, but the croquet-player. And, indeed, some of the prettiest effects of gamesmanship are to be seen when an expert in, say, croquet, plays golf, it may be, off the same handicap, against a real expert in, say, rugger—a man who really has played rugger, twice capped for England. The rugger man certainly starts with a tremendous advantage. His name is a legend, his game is glorious. Croquet is considered, by the lay world, to be piddling. The two meet on the common ground of golf; and even golf, to the rugger man, is considered fairly piddling. Yet I have seen Tearle not only break down this view *but reverse it,* so that in the end the Rugger international would sometimes even be heard claiming that he came from croquet people, but that his character "was not suited to the game."

Tearle by long practice actually made capital out of croquet. And let me add that Tearle's triumph demonstrates once again that it is in these long-drawn-out reversal tactics that training and the proper diet stand you in such good stead.

COUNTERPOINT.

This phrase, now used exclusively in music, originally stood for Number Three of the general Principles of Gamesmanship. "PLAY AGAINST YOUR OPPONENT'S TEMPO." This is one of the oldest of gambits and is now almost entirely used in the form "My Slow to your Fast." E.g., at billiards, or snooker, or golf especially, against a player who makes a great deal of "wanting to get on with the game," the technique is (1) to agree (Jeffreys always adds here "as long as we don't hurry on the shot"); (2) to hold things up by fifteen to twenty disguised pauses. Peg-top tees for golf were introduced by Samuel in '33 for this use. The technique is to tee the ball, frame up for the shot, and then at the last moment stop, pretend to push the peg a little further in or pull it a little further out, and then start all over again.

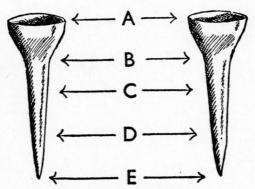

FIG. 4. Samuel's "Championship" (2d.) and "Golden Perfecto" (4/6) golf tees. A = "Cup," B = "Neck," C = "Upper Shaft," D = "Lower Shaft," E = Point or "Plungebill."

At the next hole vary this with Samuel's "Golden Perfecto" peg tee, made in such a way that the ball, after sitting still in the cup for two to three seconds, rolls off. (Fig. 4.)

Through the green, the usual procedure is to frame up for the shot and then decide on another club at the last moment.

NOTE.—*Do not attempt to irritate partner by spending too long looking for your lost ball.* This is unsporting. But good gamesmanship which is also very good sportsmanship can be practised if the gamesman makes a great and irritatingly prolonged parade of spending extra time looking for his *opponent's* ball.

At billiards, the custom of arranging to be summoned to the telephone on fake calls, so as to break your opponent's concentration, is out of date now and interesting only as a reminder of the days when "couriers" were paid to gallop up to the old billiard halls for the same purpose. In snooker, the usual practice is to walk quickly up to the table, squat half down on the haunches to look at sight-lines, move to the other end of the table to look at sight-lines of balls which may come in to play later on in the break which you are supposed to be planning. Decide on the shot. Frame up for it, and then at the last moment see some obvious red shot which you had "missed," and which your opponent and everybody else will have noticed before you moved to the table, and which they know is the shot you are going to play in the end anyhow.

"MY TO-MORROW'S MATCH."

In a Key Friendly, or any individual match which you are particularly anxious to win, the best general approach (Rule IV) is the expression of *anxiety to play to-day, because of the match tomorrow.* Construct a story that you are playing A. J. du C. Masterman.[3] Or perhaps the name should be A. C. Swinburne (your opponent will feel he has vaguely heard of this name). Go on to say (if the game is golf)—"Do you mind if I practise using my Number One iron to-day?"—(no need to use it or even have one)—"as I want to know whether to take it to-morrow." Take one practice shot after having picked up your ball, at a lost hole. Seek the advice of opponent. Ask

---

[3] "Names impress according to the square of their initials."

him "What *he* would do if he found himself playing against a *really* long driver, like A. C. Swinburne."

GAME LEG (also known as "Crocked Ankle Play," or "Gamesman's Leg").[4]

"Limpmanship," as it used to be called, or the exact use of minor injury, not only for the purpose of getting out of, but for actually winning difficult contests, is certainly as old as the mediaeval tourneys, the knightly combats, of ancient chivalry. Yet, nowadays, no device is more clumsily used, no gambit more often muffed. "I hope I shall be able to give you a game," says the middle-aged golfer to his young opponent, turning his head from side to side and hunching up his shoulders. "My back was a bit seized up yesterday . . . this wind." How wretchedly weak. "O.K. My youth *versus* your age," says the young counter-gamesman to himself, and rubs this thought in with a variety of subsequent slanting references: "You ought to take it easy for a week or two," etc. No, if use the hackneyed ankle gambit you must, let the injury be the result of a campaign in one of the wars, or a quixotic attempt to stop a runaway horse, at least.

But, here as so often, it is the *reply,* the counter, wherein the ploy of the gamesman can be used to best effect. Indeed, there is nothing prettier than the right use of an opponent's injury. There is the refusal to be put off even if the injury is genuine. There is the adoption of a game which, though apparently ignoring and indeed even favouring your opponent's disability, will yet benefit you in the end. In their own different ways, the "Two F's," Frier and Frith-Morteroy, were the greatest masters of the art of "Countering the Crock." No one who heard them will ever forget their apologies for sending a short one to the man with the twisted ankle, their excuses for the accidental lob in the sun against an opponent with sensitive eyes. But the Frith-Morteroy counter, though not for beginners, has more of grace, and needs more of explanation. Let it be lawn tennis—Frith's game. Frith against "Novice Gamesman," we will call him.

Novice Gamesman is limping slightly. "Hopes he can give F.-M. a game, but his rugger knee has just been prodded back into place by old Coutts of Welbeck Street." Right. F.-M. is full of sympathy. F.-M. sends not a single short one. In fact he does nothing whatever. His supporters become anxious—and then—during, say, the *first* game of

[4] Usually shortened now into "Game Leg."

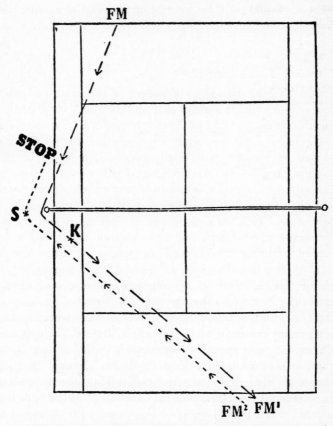

FM

STOP

S

K

FM² FM¹

FIG. 5. Diagram of tennis court to show Frith-Morteroy's path of changing, and the position S from which he makes his "echo" attack, in Morteroy Counter Game Leg play. Point K on the line FM–FM¹ is the position from which the demi-cry is made (see text). At point S, on the line FM², the full cry is made (see text). "STOP" marks the usual position for the actual verbal interchange or "parlette."

the *second* set, while they are changing sides Frith is heard to say (on arriving at point K—see Fig. 5) "Ooo!" sharply.

NOVICE GAMESMAN: What's that?
FRITH-MORTEROY: Nothing. Nothing. I thought——
N. G. (*further away*): What did you say?
F.-M.: Nothing.

The game continues. But at that next cross over, Frith says "Ow!" (point S, Fig. 5). He pauses a minute, and stands as if lost in thought.

N. G.: What's up?
F.-M.: Nothing. Half a moment.
N. G.: Something wrong?
F.-M. (*rubs his chest with his knuckles*): No. No. It's only the old pump.
N. G.: Pump?
F.-M.: Yes. The ancient ticker.
N. G.: What—heart?
F.-M.: I'm supposed not to be using it full out at the moment. Only a temporary thing.
N. G.: Good Lord.
F.-M.: It's all right now!
N. G.: Good.
F.-M.: Couple of crocks!
N. G.: Well. Shall we get on?

"*Couple* of crocks." Observe the triple thrust against the Novice Gamesman. (1) Frith establishes the fact that he, also, labours under handicap, (2) the atmosphere which Novice Gamesman has built up with so much restraint, but so much labour—the suggestion of silent suffering—is the precise climate in which Frith is now going to prosper, and (3)—most important of all—Frith has won the gamesmanship part of the contest already, set and match, by sportingly waiting, say twenty-five minutes, before revealing his own somewhat worse disability. Novice Gamesman having mentioned his rugger knee—a stale type of affliction anyhow—is made to look a fool and a fusser. More, he is made to look unsporting.

I believe it is true to say that once Frith-Morteroy had achieved his position, he was never known to lose a game. He made a special study of it—and I believe much of his spare time was spent reading the medical books on the subject of minor cardiac weaknesses.

JACK RIVERS OPENING.

After this most successful of basic plays, may I dare to end this chapter with a very simple but favourite gambit of my own?

I call it the Jack Rivers Opening. I have written elsewhere of the sporting-unsporting approach, always to be revered as the parent of modern gamesman play. But if sporting-unsporting is vaguely regarded as a thing of the past, the gamesman knows that it is a habit of thought still rooted in many British players.

Perhaps the most difficult type for the gamesman to beat is the man who indulges in pure play. He gets down to it, he gets on with it, he plays each shot according to its merits, and his own powers, without a trace of exhibitionism, and no by-play whatever. In golf, croquet or ping-pong—golf especially—he is liable to wear you down by playing the "old aunty" type of game.

My only counter to this, which some have praised, is to invent, early in the game or before it has started, an imaginary character called "Jack Rivers." I speak of his charm, his good looks, his fine war record and his talent for games—and, "by the way, he is a first-class pianist as well." Then, a little later: "I like Jack Rivers's game," I say. "He doesn't care a damn whether he wins or loses so long as he has a good match."

Some such rubbish as this, although at first it may not be effective, often wears down the most successfully cautious opponent, *if the method is given time to soak in.* Allow your opponent to achieve a small lead, perhaps, by his stone-walling methods; and the chances are that—even if he has only been hearing about Jack Rivers for thirty minutes—he will begin to think: "Well, perhaps I am being a bit of a stick-in-the-mud." He feels an irrational desire to play up to what appears to be your ideal of a good fellow. After all, he remembers hadn't he been once chaffed for breaking a window with a cricket ball when he was on holiday at Whitby? He himself was a bit mad once. Soon he is throwing away point after point by adopting a happy-go-lucky, hit-or-miss method which doesn't suit his game in the least.

Meanwhile *you* begin to play with pawky steadiness, and screen this fact by redoubling your references to Jack Rivers. You talk of the way in which Jack, too, loved to open his shoulders for a mighty smite landing him in trouble as often as not; but the glorious thing about him was that he didn't care two hoots for that . . . and so long as he had a good smack, and a good game . . . , etc.

So much for the Principal Plays, in gamesmanship. Now for the other gambits which must be brought into play as the game progresses

IV. WINMANSHIP

. . . The assiduous student of gamesmanship has little time for the *minutiae* of the game itself—little opportunity for learning how to play the shots, for instance. His skill in stroke-making may indeed be almost non-existent. So that the gamesman who finds himself winning in the early stages of the match is sometimes at a loss. Therefore, this seems to me the place to set down a few words of help and friendly advice to the winning gamesman, to help him keep his lead; to assist him to maintain his advantage, and rub his opponent's face in the dirt.

A NOTE ON CONCENTRATION.

Very often the opponent will show signs, just as he is beginning to lose, of being irritated by distractions. At golf, "somebody has moved." At billiards, "somebody talked." Take this opportunity of making him feel that he is not really a player at all by talking on these lines:

Somebody yelling, did you say? Do you know, I didn't notice it. I'm a fool at games. Don't seem to be able to be aware of anything outside them, when I'm playing the shot. I remember, once, Joyce Wethered was putting. 18th green—semi-final. An express train went by within fifteen feet of her nose.
"How did you manage to sink that putt—with that train . . . ?"
"What train?" she said.

Always tell the same story to the same man, for your example. (See under "Story, constant repetition of, to the same person.")

WHEN TO GIVE ADVICE.

In my own view (but compare Motherwell) there is only one correct time when the gamesman can give advice: and that is when the gamesman has achieved a *useful* though not necessarily a *winning* lead. Say three up and nine to play at golf, or, in billiards, sixty-five to his opponent's thirty. Most of the accepted methods are effective. E.g., in billiards, the old phrase serves. It runs like this:

GAMESMAN: Look . . . may I say something?
LAYMAN: What?
GAMESMAN: *Take it easy.*
LAYMAN: What do you mean?
GAMESMAN: I mean—you know how to make the strokes, but you're stretching yourself on the rack all the time. Look. Walk up to the ball. Look at the line. And make your stroke. Comfortable. Easy. It's as simple as that.

In other words, the advice *must be vague,* to make certain it is not helpful. But, in general, if properly managed, the mere giving of advice is sufficient to place the gamesman in a practically invincible position.

NOTE.—According to some authorities the advice should be quite genuine and perfectly practical.

WHEN TO BE LUCKY.

The uses of the last of the three basic plays for winmanship are, I think, no less obvious, though I believe this gambit is less used than the other, no doubt because a certain real skill in play is involved, making it a little out of place in the gamesman world. I have worded the rule as follows. LET THE GAMESMAN'S ADVANTAGE OVER AN OPPONENT APPEAR TO BE THE RESULT OF LUCK, NEVER OF PLAY. Always sporting, the good gamesman will say:

I'm afraid I was a bit lucky there . . . the balls are running my way. It's extraordinary, isn't it, how once they start running one way, they go on running one way, all through an entire game. I know it's impossible according to the law of averages . . .

and so on, till your opponent is forced to break in with a reply. Unless he sees through the gambit and counter-games, he is likely to feel an ebbing of confidence if he can be made to believe that it is not your play (which he knows is liable to collapse) but Fate, which is against him.

Yet in spite of the ease with which most games-players can be persuaded that they are unlucky, I know the difficulties of this gambit: and as I have had many complaining letters from all parts of the country from gamesmen saying: "They can't do it," "What's the point?," "No good," etc., I will end this with a few notes:

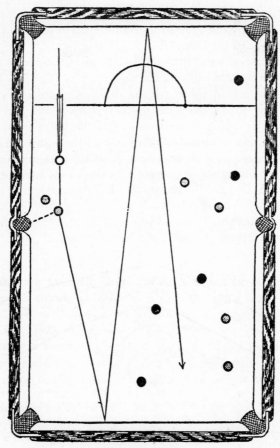

Fig. 6. Diagram of billiards table to show Disguised
Fluke play. Key: Black balls = red balls; shaded balls
= coloured balls; white ball = white ball; end of cue
= end of cue. Player has framed up as if to hit blue
(on extreme right) but actually pots black (ball on extreme right but one). Straight line = path of white
ball after impact (leaving an easy red). Dotted line =
path of black into middle pocket.

NOTE I.—The best shot to practise with cue and ivories is undoubtedly the Imitation Fluke. E.g., in billiards, play for an in-off the
red top left of a kind which will give colour to your apology that you
meant to pot the red top right. A. Boult (the snooker player, not the

conductor) demonstrates a shot, suitable for volunteer only, in which he pots the black while apparently framing up to hit a ball of inferior scoring value (e.g., the blue). (See Fig. 6.)

A good tip, says Boult, is to chalk the end of the cue ostentatiously, while apologising after making the shot.

NOTE II.—In my pamphlet for the British Council I listed eighteen ways of saying "Bad luck." I do not believe there are more.

NOTE III (For advanced students only).—Different from fluke play, though sometimes confused with it, is the demonstration of another kind of advantage over an opponent in which the gamesman tries to prove that he is favoured not by good luck but by *a fortunate choice of instruments.* To get away from text-book formulae, let me explain this by example.

In golf, for instance. You find yourself two up at the fifth hole. You wish to make certain of your advantage.

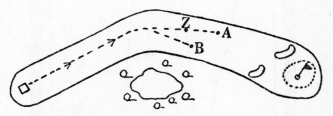

FIG. 7. Diagram of golf hole. A = point reached by Games-man's drive. B = opponent's drive. Z = point on arrival at which Gamesman commences Gamesplay or "Parlette."

Supposing, for whatever reason, you hit your drive; and supposing you hit it five or preferably ten yards farther than your opponent. Procedure: walk off the tee *with* opponent, in the normal method of the two-up walk-off, conversing, and listening rather charmingly to what he says, etc. (See Number Twelve in my *Twenty-five Methods of Tee-leaving:* Scribners, August 1935.) As you approach the balls on the fairway, but before parting company (see Fig. 7) say, "Much of a muchness." Opponent will then say over his shoulder:

"You're ten yards farther at least."

"So I am," you say.

Nearing the green you start thinking aloud in his presence.

"Funny. I thought those drives were level. It's that ball of mine."

"What are you using? Ordinary two-dot, isn't it?"

"Oh, no—no—that's how it's been repainted. Underneath it's a Madfly."

"Madfly?"

"Madfly. Pre-war only. It goes like sin. Really does put ten yards on to your shot. I'll see if I can get you one. Honestly, I hardly feel it's fair of me to play with it."

With proper management the gamesman can wreak far more havoc by suggesting that he has the advantage of a better ball, than by demonstrating that he has a better swing.

Tennis rackets strung with a special gut giving out a particularly high "ping," suggesting a tigerish resilience, are made by dealers who cater for this sort of thing. G. Odoreida, on his first appearance at St. Ives, brought with him a racket in which a stretch of piano wire, tuned to high G, was substituted for one of the ordinary strings. When "testing his racket" before play, he plucked the piano wire, adding smilingly: "I like something you can hit with."

A propos of this, an amusing correspondence followed with "Wagger"—W.A.G.A. the West Australian Gamesman's Association—which august body considered this action ungamesmanlike.

GUIDE QUESTIONS

1. What use does Potter make of the various "figures" in the essay?
2. What general divisions of his material does Potter use?
3. In your opinion, how did Potter arrive at the word "gamesmanship" as the title for his book?
4. What is the importance of the variations in size of type in the printing of the essay?
5. What advantage is gained by the use of names, as though of real persons, in the essay?
6. What indications does the essay contain that Potter does not seriously mean what he says?

VOCABULARY

Give the derivations and definitions of the following words:

gambit, introvert, crusty, cynical, fidgets, adversary, neologism, anonymity, hackneyed.

WRITING AND STUDY AIDS

PATTERN OF ORGANIZATION SUGGESTED BY THE GENERAL TOPIC:

No single mode of organization is suggested by this topic. It invites instead a review and appraisal of the idea that the arrangement and interrelation of parts within an essay are practical, important elements in any writing problem. Structure, like grammar, punctuation, and spelling, is a fact. The writer either knows something about structure or he doesn't, and what he doesn't know will have a great deal to do with what ideas he can express in an understandable fashion.

The range of possibilities for theme topics in this section is practically unlimited. In general, however, it will be most useful to write critical descriptions of the readings provided and of others like them, or to attempt imitations of them, devising some "gambit" of your own in which the organization of your theme is the more appropriate for not being appropriate at all.

ASSIGNMENTS:

Short themes:

1. An instance of gamesmanship
2. A report on the recent policies of the coffee shop
3. The effects of too small an allowance
4. Forster as analyst
5. Riesman as historian
6. Coach Potter

Long themes:

1. Five types of stupidity
2. Ideas of humor
3. Varieties of English essays
4. The signs of clear writing
5. The ethics of exposition
6. How not to write an essay
7. Prosemanship